THE BILL JAMES
PLAYER RATINGS BOOK 1993

Also by Bill James

The Baseball Abstract (1977–1988)
The Historical Baseball Abstract (1986)
The Baseball Book (1990–1992)
This Time Let's Not Eat the Bones (1989)

THE BILL JAMES PLAYER RATINGS BOOK 1993

Collier Books
Macmillan Publishing Company
New York

Maxwell Macmillan Canada
Toronto

Maxwell Macmillan International
New York Oxford Singapore Sydney

Collier Books
Macmillan Publishing Company
866 Third Avenue
New York, NY 10022

Maxwell Macmillan Canada, Inc.
1200 Eglinton Avenue East
Suite 200
Don Mills, Ontario M3C 3N1

Macmillan Publishing Company is part of the Maxwell Communication Group of Companies.

ISBN 0-02-041563-X

Macmillan books are available at special discounts for bulk purchases for sales promotions, premiums, fund-raising, or educational use. For details, contact:

Special Sales Director
Macmillan Publishing Company
866 Third Avenue
New York, NY 10022

First Collier Books Edition 1993

10 9 8 7 6 5 4 3 2 1

Printed in the United States of America

This book is for Bruce Dickson, whose genuine enjoyment of everything in baseball has been a compass for me when the nattering nabobs of night baseball (thank you, Spiro) could find only things to harp about.

ACKNOWLEDGMENTS

Rob Neyer has worked as hard on this book as I have, and since I get to divide up the workload, you can imagine who gets the good assignments. Rob has helped me through four years and I-don't-know-how-many books now, but is leaving on . . . well, by the time you read this he will have left. He will remain a friend, but I will miss him all the same, and I want to thank him for his good and great service over the years.

John Dewan has provided unmeasurable support in a variety of ways, for which I am grateful. I would also like to thank a few of the other people who make up STATS, Inc.—Sue Dewan, Dick Cramer, Steve Moyer, Bob Mecca, Art Ashley, Ross Schaufelberger, Jim Musso, Matt Greenberger, Alissa Hudson, Dave Pinto. It's a wonderful company to work with, and I'm sure I'm missing a few people that I should name.

Three other friends (Craig Wright, Eddie Epstein, and Pete DeCoursey) were kind enough to read drafts of the manuscript and call my attention to places where my judgment faltered or my research was inadequate, and this service is greatly appreciated. Mike Kopf is in the office and does similar things for me from time to time, and that also, I would hope, makes this a better book.

Liz Darhansoff and Chuck Verrill represent my interests in the publishing world, and no one has yet suggested that I was under-represented. Bill Rosen is my new editor, which means that Melissa Thau, who is Bill's assistant, has a daily list of phone calls to make and manuscripts to manipulate toward the task of getting this book done. Her patience and good humor are much appreciated.

It would be possible to write a baseball book without a wife, but it wouldn't be much fun. It wouldn't be possible to write a baseball book *and* have a family without a wife who was willing to shoulder the redhead's share of the child raisin' for a period of several long weeks. Thanks, Susie.

I am indebted to the media relations representatives of all 26 teams except the Minnesota Twins, as well as those of a good many minor league teams, whose names I probably should have kept in a list in my pocket, but unfortunately didn't. I appreciate the time and cordiality of every professional baseball man who has spared a few minutes to tell me what he knew, or not, but if I listed them all you wouldn't know whether I was bragging or complaining. My thanks go out to Jim Carothers, Peter Gethers, Dan Okrent, Randy Hendricks, Alan Hendricks, Joe Sambito, Tom Reich, Sam Reich, Don Zminda, Jack Etkin, Heather Campbell, Mike Sowell, Allen Barra, Kent Earl, and my wonderful children, Rachel and Isaac. Thanks.

Bill James

CONTENTS

Acknowledgments   vii

Introduction   xi

Stop the Presses   xxi

Players   1

Pitchers   159

Highest-Valued Players by Position   283

INTRODUCTION

Hello, and welcome to the *Player Ratings Book*. I'm Bill James. I've been writing baseball books for years—in fact, not to be immodest, I kind of invented this market. I'm guessing that most of you have read some of my books before, and if you have, you have my permission to skip this article entirely (it's pretty boring, really). If you don't know me, we might have fewer misunderstandings if you'll stick around.

This is a different kind of baseball book than I have written before. In essence, this is one section of *The Baseball Abstract* or *The Baseball Book* expanded to book length. There are comments here about every player who played in the majors last year, unless somehow we missed somebody, or who has a reasonably good chance to play in '93.

The players are evaluated on a dollar scale. The best player in baseball (Barry Bonds) is worth $100, so what are you worth? Barry Bonds is worth $100, so what is Ken Griffey, Jr., worth? $94. What is Henry Cotto worth? $16. What is Eddie Taubensee worth? $17. What is Lance Painter worth? $7, who the hell is Lance Painter? He's a left-handed pitcher in the San Diego system; what is Jevon Crudup worth? He's not in the book; he's a Big Eight basketball player. He's worth a lot in the Big Eight.

There is no formula for these dollar values. They represent purely subjective judgments about the players, although there is a logic behind them which will be explained later. Three points about the values:

1) The values look *forward*, not backward. Chipper Jones is worth more than Darryl Strawberry, which, based on what they have done in the past, may seem a little strange—but Chipper Jones (don't you hate that name already) is ten years younger than Darryl Strawberry, those being, specifically, the ten best years of a ballplayer's career. It's not only *likely* that Jones will do more in the rest of his career than Strawberry will, it is virtually *certain*. Jones is valued at $40; Strawberry at $34. It is extremely likely that Jones's future accomplishments will outdistance those of Strawberry by a much wider margin than that.

2) The values look to a degree at the rest of a player's career, but are heavily weighted toward what I would expect of the player in 1993. That's why Strawberry is worth almost as much as Jones: because Strawberry will play this summer, probably, while Jones won't, probably. An old player who is still good, like Ozzie Smith or Dave Winfield, is still valuable. A Grade C prospect who is a year away from the majors and blocked behind a star might be valued at $3 or $5, while a Grade C prospect who has a job in hand might be worth as much as $20, in an unusual case. I'll deal in a moment with what, specifically, is meant by the term "Grade C prospect".

3) The values do not imitate any specific game except baseball.

There are many "shadow games" which are based on baseball, but which adapt and shape it to their own purposes. Rotisserie, Strat-O-Matic, APBA, Fantasy Games, Earl Weaver Baseball; they're all based on baseball, but they're all different.

It's my assumption that many or most of you play those games, and bought this book to help you evaluate the players for your game. The problem is that each of those games focuses on baseball through its own peculiar lens, and each one distorts the game in one way or another. What makes a player valuable in one game might be of no particular use in another. What game should I evaluate? Should I give a player extra value because he's a base stealer, and rotisserie gives weight to that? Should I treat relief closers as precious because some table games will punish you if you don't have one—or should I assume, as some other table games do, that a reliever who pitches 70 innings with an ERA of 1.88 is of exactly the same value whether he has zero saves or 41?

There is only one sensible answer to this: evaluate players based on their on-field value in the real game. It has to be done this way, for this reason: that *the sum of all other images of the game of baseball must be the original game.* Suppose that you were trying to build a three-dimensional image of Sigmund Freud, based on a collection of two-dimensional pictures of him, taken one at a time. It is obvious, is it not, that the best composite of those other pictures, with their individual distortions, would be Freud himself?

This won't always work perfectly for you. Let us take, for example, the fact that in my book, Tony Phillips ($70) has a higher value than Cecil Fielder ($66). You may not agree with me—we'll get to that in a minute, too—but in my opinion, that's their real value; Tony Phillips *is* a better player than Cecil Fielder. But in a lot of other games, shadow games, he isn't. Many of those games will basically ignore defense, minimize baserunning, and heavily emphasize home runs and RBI, which will make Fielder seem much more valuable than he really is.

In playing *your* game, you may have to adjust for that. You just have to put it under the heading of "things I know that Bill James doesn't."

The hardest thing about writing a baseball book is guessing what the audience already knows. There are dangers on either side of this. If you repeat for the audience that which they already know the book becomes boring and pointless, because the reader doesn't learn anything—but on the other hand, if you wander too far afield, you wind up spitting out a lot of trivial stuff that nobody cares about, just because it's different. The information which we find most interesting is that which is adjacent to what we already know.

So it's a road you can drive off of on either side, and further, it is impossible for me to guess accurately what you know. It is impossible because there are so many of you. Some of you might know anything. Taken all together, you might know almost as much as I do. No; I'm just joking; all taken together, you'd know vastly more than I do. I've got to write a comment about some guy who played in the Eastern League last year, who, not spilling any trade secrets, three months ago I never heard of. One of you guys reading this book is his next door neighbor and has known him since he was a baby. There's no way that I'm going to have a more accurate picture of that player than you do, if you are that neighbor.

Not that I'm apologizing for my research; I'm not. As you'll see when you get to the comments, my research is pretty formidable. It's not my research mostly, it's Rob Neyer's, but Rob does it at my direction, and frankly, we are as thorough as is humanly possible. But as careful as we are, there are 1100 players in this book more or less, and it is simply not possible for two people to find out everything there is to know about all 1100. If you have season's tickets, you may have seen your players play fifty times last year, plus television. It is not possible for me to have seen *everybody* play fifty times in a year.

The point I'm making is: trust your own knowledge if you really know something. If you're a Seattle Mariners fan, it's a good guess that you will know more about Edgar Martinez than I do. You don't need to get emotional about this. I'm not underrating Bret Boone and Omar Vizquel on purpose. I just don't know as much about them as you do. But if you're *not* a Seattle Mariners fan, then it's a good guess that I've looked at their players more carefully than you have.

The next question you would probably want to ask is, on what basis do I evaluate players? What's my basis for saying that Mickey Morandini is worth $3 more than Sid Bream? What's my reason for saying that Kirt Manwaring is worth $1 more than Mike Scioscia? And what's this nonsense about Tony Phillips?

I can't really answer those questions in a thorough way here, for this reason. I've written many books about baseball, and one of the main things those books are about is why baseball teams win. In other words, I have explained how I evaluate players at great length—book length. Multiple book length. I can't repeat that all here. Let me summarize a few major principles:

1) The number of runs a team scores is essentially a function of two things: the number of men on base, and the team slugging percentage. Nothing else really changes the number of runs a team will score. Baserunning, base stealing, bunting, hitting behind the runner, making contact . . . it's all worth keeping track of, but none of it really matters a whole lot.

2) The batting average is important, but it's not the whole game. It is not uncommon for a .250 hitter to contribute more runs to his team than a .300 hitter.

3) A shortstop who puts 80 runs on the scoreboard is worth more than a first baseman who puts up 100. A player's offensive contribution can only be evaluated in the context of his defensive contribution, and vice versa.

4) Contrary to popular belief, a player's minor league hitting statistics (if you know how to read them) will predict his major league hitting ability in virtually every case.

5) A player's hitting or pitching statistics are very heavily colored by the park in which he plays.

6) The best predictor of future performance by a pitcher is his strikeout to walk ratio.

7) Power pitchers in baseball are vastly more durable and more consistent than finesse pitchers.

8) Career length for batters is essentially a function of ability. Career length for a pitcher is primarily a function of two things: his ability to stay healthy, and how many strikeouts he gets.

9) An individual player may reach his peak at any age between 21 and 37, but any group of players will reach their peak value, as a group, at age 27.

The only exceptions to this are a) knuckleballers, b) Tommy John–type pitchers, and c) those who are specifically selected because they happened to peak at another age.

10) In evaluating a prospect, the first thing you want to know is his age. A 23-year-old who is 10 percent better than his league is a better gamble than a 24-year-old who is 20 percent better than his league. A 21-year-old rookie who hits .260 will normally have a better career than a 25-year-old rookie who hits .300.

It's not that *all* young players improve; they don't. Many players level off about age 23. The key is that *some young players improve dramatically*. A 25-year-old player (non-pitcher) will never improve dramatically; a 22-year-old often will. The vast majority of players will be near their peak ability at age 25, and will retain that level for about five years.

11) A pitcher's won-lost record in an individual season doesn't mean much of anything.

I'm not just saying these things. As those of you who have read my books over the years know, there is extensive research which will support every one of those statements. I wanted to explain these things because you will find, when you read comments about young players, that I very often will mention their age as a significant factor. You will find, in discussing a pitcher, that I often discuss his strikeout/walk ratio, or his strikeout rate by itself. I don't do this because it's a habit, or because I need to have something to say. I cite these things because that's what's most important. But having said that, I don't have time here to repeat all the research. If you want to thoroughly understand why I evaluate players the way I do, you'll just have to go to the library.

There are a lot of other things that I know as a consequence of my research or someone else's, more minor things which may come into play in this comment or that one, but which aren't systematically important. I know, for example, that you need to be skeptical of what a player hits in his second year at Double-A. I know that in the long run virtually every player, if not *actually* every player, will hit better with the platoon advantage than without it. I know that the vast majority of fluke seasons occur between the ages of 26 and 28. I know that a young player who strikes out a lot will always strike out a lot, although he will probably trim the totals in his prime seasons. I know that hitting ability changes astonishingly little after the age of 25, so that a player may *seem* to have totally lost his ability to hit, like Kal Daniels now, only to re-discover it after several years. I know that it is not particularly unusual for a pitcher to have a better record in the majors than he did in the minors. I know that a player who has speed as a central skill will tend to age somewhat better than a player who doesn't. All of these things, and a hundred more like them, will become relevant at some point in the book.

This is not to say, however, that research is the only thing that counts in evaluating a player. If you ask me how I evaluate players, I'm not going to tell you I evaluate them by research. I'm going to tell you that everything counts. In evaluating a player's defense, for example . . . the world has tended to divide into those who believe that defensive statistics tell the whole truth, and those who believe in evaluating defense by visual observation. I believe that everything counts. If a player has good defensive statistics, or bad defensive statistics, I want to know that. I want to know why. But if his defensive reputation is good or bad, I also want to know that, and I want to know why.

Most of the time, they're going to agree. If a player has bad defensive stats, most of the time he's going to have a bad defensive reputation as well. When they *don't* agree, as in the case of Roberto Alomar or Carney Lansford, then you need to look skeptically at *both*, the stats and the visual reports, to figure out why.

These are the primary sources we use to compile a summary of each player's abilities:

1) *STATS Inc.* STATS Inc., a Chicago company of which I am a director, is the nation's largest and finest resource for statistical information about baseball. I can download from STATS a statistical profile which contains almost every data split you can imagine—what the player has hit at home and on the road, what he has hit against left-handed and right-handed pitchers, what he has hit on grass fields or turf, in each month or against each team, what he has hit when he has hit the first pitch or when behind in the count. That's just the beginning, actually, and then you can check all of the same information over a period of years. Through an arrangement with Howe Sportsdata International, STATS has career batting records for minor league players. Through STATS I can check a day-by-day performance log for any player.

Almost every stat in this book comes, in one way or another, from STATS, Inc.

2) *Baseball America*. I don't work with *Baseball America*, but I admire the publication. BA is the best source of information about minor league players. Rob Neyer reads and indexes all of their articles, so that when we need to find out something about some guy who played in the Cleveland system, we can find the article.

3) *Personal observation*. I go to games, I watch them on TV, and I make notes. I visit minor league ballparks, I talk to minor league managers and media people. I don't claim to be Tracy Ringolsby, but I do make an effort to get out in the field and do some of my own research.

4) *Friends*. I know a lot of other people who live and die baseball, and I talk to them. It is not an exaggeration, I think, to say that I have at least one good

friend who roots for every major league team. Some of them are agents, some of them are consultants, some of them work for the teams, some of them are just fans—but the things that they know are invaluable.

5) *Media guides*. We collect the media guides from all 26 teams, and these, too, are invaluable for finding information about obscure players.

6) *Other media*. We collect all significant baseball or baseball-related publications—*The Sporting News*, *USA Today*, *The Baseball Weekly*, *Baseball Digest*; you name it, we got it. *The Baseball Weekly*, from *USA Today*, is very useful for tracking down injuries. One other book which was especially valuable in putting this one together is *The Scouting Report*, which is an irreplaceable (and extremely accurate) source for information like what pitches a pitcher throws, what small things a player does well or doesn't, and why and how his role on the team has evolved.

You probably don't care about a lot of this stuff, but it comes under the heading of "giving credit where credit is due." Rob Neyer has worked for me for years. It is Rob's job to put all of this information together, and it is my job to make sense of it.

In any case, what I was saying is, it all counts. I don't believe in taking any information and throwing it away. I believe in trying to use as much of it as I can.

I've got 61 to 69 words to say what I have to say about each player. This means two things. First, the syntax is strange, and sometimes bothersome. A comment may be originally written like this: "Greg played last year with the Durham Bulls in the Carolina League (A Ball), and played very well. He hit .319 with some power, and his defense improved as the season went on." Then I'll add some other stuff and start chopping, and by the time you read it that will have been reduced to "Played A Ball (Durham), hit .319, defense improving." I'm sorry if it's not graceful, but in this form, grace is optional. Brevity is required.

Second, you will find sometimes that my evaluations are blunt to the point of being rude. In part, this is because of the brevity. I simply don't have *time* to dance around the question of whether a player can play.

More than that, I feel that I owe it to you to tell you what I think. I understand this, and you should, too: that sometimes I'm going to be wrong. I have a responsibility, as I see it, to risk being wrong. I feel it is my obligation to those of you who purchased this book to tell you honestly what I think of a player, rather than hedging my bets with ambiguous remarks. I hope you understand this, because sometimes those things I say are going to be thrown back in my face. Somewhere in this book, there is probably some young player who is going to hit .318 after I have said flatly that he's never going to be a major league hitter. I'll catch hell for having written that—but I still think it is my responsibility to risk it.

But I also have a responsibility, a competing responsibility, not to pretend to know things that I don't. Many times I simply don't know whether a young player is going to be any good. Most of the time I can't tell you *exactly* how good a young player might be. As it would be inappropriate, I think, to wuss off the issue by not giving a clear answer when there is clear evidence, it would also be inappropriate to pretend that the evidence was clear when it was not. That's how my reputation survives: because I am *not* going to be wrong very often on a definitive statement. If my comment says that this player is never going to hit, 99 times in a hundred he's not going to hit, because I wouldn't write that if I didn't have a good reason. I don't like to look stupid, any more than you do.

The normal situation is mixed evidence. When the evidence about a young player is clear and convincing, then you have one of two answers: This is a Grade A prospect, or this guy is no prospect. Throughout this book, I have used the terms "Grade A prospect," "Grade B prospect," etc. These terms have a very specific meaning, such that someone else, doing their own research but grading players on the same scale, should be able to classify the prospects the same way that I have classified them in most cases.

Grade A prospect. The term Grade A prospect means that all of the information about a young player is positive, or that the positive information about the player is overwhelmingly greater than the negative information. Grade A prospects normally do carry small negatives. Carlos Delgado isn't a great catcher, and some people think Chipper Jones won't make it as a shortstop. But the positive information about them is so positive that these concerns are essentially swamped.

What the term Grade A prospect does not mean is that the guy is going to be a star, and especially what it does not mean is that he is going to be a superstar. Many Grade A prospects will go on to become major league stars, but many will not. What we're saying with the term is that there is no apparent reason that this player cannot become a star.

Grade B prospect. The term Grade B prospect is a term of praise, not of reservation. The term Grade B prospect means that the information available about the player is essentially positive, but with some significant limitation. A Grade B prospect is an exciting young player who strikes out too much, or a player who has hit extremely well in the minors, but started a year late.

There are Grade B prospects who will go on to become major league stars. Again, the term is *not* meant at all to say that the player *won't* be a major league star—only that there is something here to worry about.

Grade C prospect. The term Grade C prospect means that there is a more or less even mix of information which makes you think that the player *will* be a good major league player, and information which makes you think that he won't.

Remember, age and ability. A Grade A prospect is a player who tears up the Texas League when he is 22. A Grade B prospect is a player who tears up the Texas League when he is 23. A Grade C prospect is a player who tears up the Texas League when he is 24. You look at the record and say, "Gee, he looks great . . . but if he's really that good, why is he in the Texas League at age 24? Shouldn't he be in the majors by now?"

A Grade A prospect is a player who hits .300 in the Eastern League at age 22. A Grade B prospect is a player who hits .275 in the Eastern League at age 22. A Grade C prospect is a player who hits .250 in the Eastern League at age 22.

These are over-simplifications, of course. It's a balancing act. If a player hits .340 in the Southern League, you might consider that four points in his favor; if he's 24 years old, that's four points against him.

If he's at Double-A at age 20, that's five points in his favor, none against.

If he's there at 21, that's four in his favor, one against him.

If he's there at 22, that's three in his favor, two against him.

If he's there at 23, that two in his favor, three against him.

If he's there at 24, that's one in his favor, four against him.

If he's there at 25, that's against him.

But normally, of course, you have *multiple* seasons to evaluate, so then you get into "this year's good, for a player at that level at that age, but that one's not so good." If you graded out a Grade C prospect, he'd grade out like Frank Tanana's won-lost record—10 and 9, or 11 and 14, or 13 and 10, or something like that.

This is all done informally. I will get out a piece of paper and total up the pluses and minuses if I have trouble categorizing a player—but normally I don't have trouble. It's usually pretty obvious.

Can a Grade C prospect go on to become a major league star? Sure, it happens. It doesn't happen a lot, but it happens. For every one who becomes a star, there's going to be 30 or 50 or 100 who fall by the wayside quickly.

Grade D prospect. And the term Grade D prospect means, of course, that the information about the player is *predominantly*, but not *overwhelmingly*, negative. The term Grade D prospect means that there is *something* here that you have to like. Three years in four he hasn't pitched well, but that other year, that makes you wonder.

If I could identify young players who had a 100 percent chance to be major league stars, that would be great. I can't, and nobody else can. My guess is that a young player who is identified here as a Grade A prospect, like Wilfredo Cordero or Melvin Nieves, has probably a 40 percent chance to be a major league star,

a 65 percent chance to be a good, solid regular (or better), and an 85 percent chance to be a major league regular of some stripe, at least for a few years. That's for position players only, and the percentages are just a guess; for pitchers, the picture is entirely different.

A Grade B prospect would have, in my opinion, probably a 10 to 15 percent chance of being a major league star, a 40 to 50 percent chance of being a good major league player, and a 70 percent chance of being at least a marginal regular. Virtually all Grade A and Grade B prospects will at least play in the major leagues.

A Grade C prospect would have only a very slight chance of being a major league star, and perhaps a 50-50 chance of even playing regularly for a couple of years.

For a Grade D prospect to turn things around and become a major league star has probably happened, but it would be extremely rare. Most Grade D prospects will never play regularly in the major leagues for more than a couple of months, but a few will.

The comments above apply only to non-pitchers; for pitchers, everything is different. For a pitcher who is identified as a Grade A prospect, the probability that he will be a major league star, or superstar, or even a rotation starter, is dramatically lower. The reason for this is primarily injuries. *Whereas there are only a few young position players who look tremendous, and almost all of those will go on to have good careers, there are many young pitchers who look tremendous, but most of whom will hurt their arms before they finish their second major league season.*

But on the other end, the Grade D prospects, the percentages for a pitcher are much *higher*. For a guy who can't hit to learn to hit is rare if the guy is 22, but it will happen. After age 25 it never happens. A *position player's level of ability very rarely takes a leap forward after the age of 25.*

But for a *pitcher* to make a great leap forward—that will happen. A pitcher can learn a new pitch, or *stop* throwing a pitch, and become dramatically more successful. Sometimes a pitcher will struggle with his control for ten years, finally overcome that, and suddenly leap to another level of ability, which he might hold for 10 years.

Look how many front-line major league pitchers there are who have been, at some point in their professional career, considered to be of very little value: Dave Stewart, Jeff Montgomery, Bob Tewksbury, Charlie Leibrandt, Tim Belcher, Doug Jones, Tom Candiotti, Dennis Martinez, Ken Hill, Sid Fernandez. Just look at one team, the Blue Jays. Two years ago, Jack Morris was thought to be washed up. Tom Henke was considered expendable in 1984, when he posted a 6.35 ERA in 25 games with the Rangers. Juan Guzman's career was going nowhere just two years ago; at that time you could have gotten Guzman and Morris both for not much.

So a pitcher who is a Grade D prospect has more value than a position player who is a Grade D prospect, just on the theory that you never know about a pitcher.

Another thing that I ought to explain here is how the two scales tie together, the dollar scale and the prospect scale. A Grade A prospect is worth, in general, $20 to $40, depending on three things:

1) Whether he is a pitcher or a position player. A shortstop who is a Grade A prospect is worth more than a pitcher with an equally impressive record.

2) Subtle gradations of quality within the range described by the class.

3) Whether the player is ready to come to the major leagues now, or whether he is a year or two away.

A Grade B prospect is worth, in general, $10 to $25, depending on the same variables. A Grade C prospect is generally valued at anywhere up to $15, although on occasion I would go higher. A Grade D prospect is generally valued at $5 or less.

A scale translating the dollar values into labels might look like this:

$70–$100	The best players in baseball
$50–$70	All-Stars
$40–$50	Very good players, marginal stars
$30–$40	Quality regulars
$20–$30	Run-of-the-mill regulars, good platoon players
$10–$20	Role players

About 45 percent of the players in the book are valued below $10. These are guys who might play or might not. They might be in the majors; they might be in the minors. Most of them will be up and down during the summer, or will be released, or have been released, or something.

If you put these two scales together, you'll see that a Grade A prospect is worth more than a role player, which makes sense. A Grade B prospect is in the same range of value as a role player, which you will be able to confirm in mid-summer. When a team gets caught in a tough place because of an injury, they'll trade a Grade B prospect to acquire a role player to fill in during the injury. But you won't trade a Grade A prospect to acquire a role player.

Another thing I should discuss briefly is relative values. Let's see: Barry Bonds is worth $100, while Steve Reed, John Jaha, Bill Gullickson, Junior Felix, and Mike Fetters are all worth about $20 apiece. Does that mean that you should trade Barry Bonds for Steve Reed, John Jaha, Bill Gullickson, Junior Felix, and Mike Fetters?

No, it doesn't mean that, for this reason. A roster spot has a value of about $10 to $20, the value of a role player. If you trade for five guys like Steve Reed and Mike Fetters, you don't gain much of anything, because you have to cut five other guys who are almost as good. If your talent is real deep, like that of the Atlanta Braves, then the value of a roster spot might be as high as $18 or $20, while if your talent is thin, like that of Seattle or Kansas City, then the value of the roster spot might be only $10 to $12.

So let's say the value of the roster spot is $15. If you give up Barry Bonds, the incremental cost is $85—while if you acquire five guys who are worth $20 each, the incremental gain is only $25. You'd never make that trade. In fact, the value of the roster spot increases by about $1 per player as more players are included; if the first roster spot is worth $15, the second one is probably worth $16, the third one $17, etc. So it is literally true that *there is no number of $20 players who would be worth as much as one Barry Bonds or Frank Thomas*, because after about five such players, you're cutting other guys who are just as good to make room for the ones you are acquiring.

Now, you *can* make the math work; you can add up a package of players who are worth as much as Barry Bonds. But you have to use good players. You can get value for Barry Bonds: Tony Fernandez and Larry Walker. That works. On the one side you've got $50 for Fernandez, $65 for Walker, and on the other side you've got $100 for Bonds, $15 for the roster spot. You can get value for Barry Bonds: Gregg Olson and Roberto Kelly. If you're losing games in the bullpen, that's a good trade.

I ought to explain the meaning of a few terms. **Secondary Average** is a shorthand way of consolidating the *other* things that a player does, than hit for average, which tend to create runs for his team. The formula is Extra Bases on Hits, plus Walks, plus Stolen Bases, divided by At Bats. The normal secondary average is about the same as the normal batting average, about .260. If a comment says that a player has hit .237 but with a secondary average of .409, this is just a somewhat more precise way of saying that even if he hits .237, this guy will help his team score runs. Conversely, if a player hits .280 but has a secondary average of .153, then he's *not* going to help his team score a lot of runs, despite having a pretty good batting average.

I think the only unusual abbreviation that I have used here is **MLE**, which stands for Major League Equivalent. If a player hits .321 for Hagerstown, what is the equivalent major league batting average?

If you're not familiar with this concept, then you're probably not going to believe that I can actually do that, that I can actually look at what a guy has hit in Double-A ball and figure out what he would probably hit in the majors. There's probably nothing I can say here that will change your mind, so I'm not going to try. The only thing I'll ask is, give it two years. Pick this book up two years from now and compare the MLEs shown now to the major league stats which will be available then for the same players, and you'll find that in almost every case, *if the player has had a good number of major league at bats*, he has in fact hit the way I said he would. There are no MLEs for pitchers.

I think those may be the only terms of my own invention that I used in this book; at any rate I can't think of any others. There's not a lot of jargon here. Occasionally I'll say something like "this player has an estimated 19 percent chance to get 3000 hits," which is based on a method I've explained a dozen times before, and won't explain here because it's not important.

For some players, I will show the player's **projected 1993 batting stats**. I'll give you a short history of these things. About ten years ago, in one of the *Baseball Abstracts*, I introduced a method to project a player's batting stats for the rest of his career. It was just a toy, just something I liked to play around with, and I introduced it making absolutely no claims about its accuracy—in fact, I emphasized that it *wouldn't* work.

Well, I continued to play around with it after that, and a year or two later I dumped that system entirely and developed a different one, learning from the mistakes of the first one and incorporating some additional information, like MLEs. I would refer to this occasionally in my books, but never took it seriously.

In 1990 STATS Inc. and I began publishing a little handbook, a simple reference book. John Dewan, who runs STATS Inc., was looking for some "fun features" to include in the book, and he asked about running projections for everybody, and including those.

I said no.

He said why not?

I said because we don't know if they work or not.

He said OK, we won't *claim* they work. We'll just say here are these projections, we don't know whether they're right or wrong, it's just for the hell of it.

So we did. That was 1990, and we've been doing it ever since, and by now we have a pretty good sense of how accurate the system is. We've also improved and refined the system in some small ways, with John's input.

I don't know how to summarize its accuracy for you in a way that would be meaningful. I'll tell you this: in the majors somewhere is a player like Gary Sheffield or Darren Daulton of 1992, who is going to have a season which is way out of line with what he has done before. There is absolutely no way that we're going to have an accurate projection for that player.

Somewhere in the majors, also, there is a player like Kelly Gruber or Eric Davis of last year, who is going to hit 50 points less than what he has hit before. Once more, there is absolutely no way that we're going to predict this. *We are not claiming to be clairvoyant.* We are only trying to predict the predictable.

The projection system does obvious things. It projects that a player will hit next year the same way he has hit over a period of years. If he's young, it projects

that he will improve a little bit; if he's old, it projects that he will decline. If he has played well, it projects that his playing time will increase; if he has played poorly, it projects that his playing time will decrease. This is not brain surgery. With the exceptions of the odd cases . . . well, we're not afraid of the results. A few players, we'll be way off; in most cases, we'll be pretty close.

There are projections given here for probably 200 or 300 players, which means that there are no projections for about 800 or 900.

First, there are no projections for pitchers, because we don't have a tested method to project the records of pitchers. Pitchers are unpredictable by nature. That eliminates about 400 players.

Second, there are no projections for players who probably will play all season or a significant portion of the season in the minor leagues. I don't have a system for projecting what a player will hit in Las Vegas, and I don't think you'd want to know, anyway. That eliminates several hundred more players.

Third, there are no projections for players who have retired, or who have played so poorly that they may be forced to retire.

Fourth, there are a few cases where I didn't run the projection simply because I didn't trust it. Computers are the ultimate idiots. They only know what you tell them. In many cases, I'm going to know something about the player that the computer doesn't know. If that causes me to believe that the projection may be misleading, then it doesn't make sense for me to run the projection anyway.

When I have a projection, when that projection seems reasonable to me, then I'll run it. This leads into a more general question, which is **how did I decide what information to run about each player**?

How I decided what information to run about each player.

What I tried to do was choose the best available information about each player. For some players, we might have as many as nine lines of data to choose from for each player. Those would include:

1990 Minor League Performance
1990 Major League Performance
1991 Minor League Performance
The 1991 MLE (Major League Equivalent)
1991 Major League Performance
1992 Minor League Performance
The 1992 MLE (Major League Equivalent)
1992 Major League Performance
Projected 1993 Major League Performance

Actually, it's worse than that, because sometimes a player plays with two or three minor league teams in one season. Suppose that a player plays for both Jacksonville and Calgary. In that case, what shows above as one option is actually three: 1992 Jacksonville, 1992 Calgary, and 1992 combined minor league performance.

Suppose a player plays for **three** minor league teams in a season, which is not at all uncommon, or four. The options multiply.

I used the following principles to sort among these problems.

1) This is not a reference book. If you want a complete statistical record for any player, there are books which provide that—*The Baseball Register*, from *The Sporting News*, the annual update to the Macmillan *Baseball Encyclopedia*, *Who's Who in Baseball*, and the *Major League Handbook* from STATS Inc. There are others. This isn't that kind of a book. I *can't* provide a complete statistical picture of any player in three lines, so the idea of comprehensiveness doesn't enter in.

2) Major league performance is always preferred to minor league performance. If a guy has played 90 games at Canton and 20 at Cleveland and I only have space for one or the other, I figure that most of you would rather know what a player has done in the major leagues.

3) I don't like to run data in samples so small that it doesn't mean anything. If a guy has gone 2-for-11 last year, even in the major leagues, that really doesn't do anything to describe his skills or establish his level of ability. I don't *have* to run it, because this isn't a reference book, and in most cases I'm not *going* to run it.

4) I don't normally add together performance at A Ball and Double-A. I'll add together Double-A and Triple-A because there really isn't much difference in the quality of competition, but A Ball is a whole different thing.

I generally used a "10 game rule" for 1992 major league performance. If a player had 10 games or more, 25 or more at bats, I figured it was hard to throw that out the window. With that exception, I tried to choose those three lines of data which would give the best picture of the player's skills at this time.

Well, I think that's about it. Hey, I got a couple of other things I've got to throw in here, to save myself a frustration buildup. For fifteen years I've had a forum in which I could say anything I wanted to say about baseball, or for that matter about anything else as long as I didn't go on too long about it. This year, as a consequence of my own decisions, I no longer have that.

Now, in a lot of ways this is a relief. For one thing I no longer have to make a prediction about who is going to win what next year. I don't actually *know* very much about how to predict future performance of base-

ball teams, and what little I do know I have already told the American public several times. It's a relief not to have to do that. It is a relief not to *have* to say anything about the Montreal Expos if I don't want to.

But I did have just a couple of things I wanted to say here. They're related, a larger point drawing off a trivial point. I am puzzled about these things, genuinely puzzled, and I thought I would ask my audience to think about them.

Whenever one slugger is acquired to bat behind another one, sportswriters will say that this will make the first slugger a better hitter. It never happens. The idea is based on false assumptions, and if you do any research you'll quickly see that there is no such effect.

Years ago, when Bob Horner batted behind Dale Murphy in the Atlanta lineup, Horner would get hurt and miss about 50 games a year. Whenever Horner injured himself, somebody would surely say that with Horner out this would effect Murphy, too—even though it didn't. I finally looked up what Murphy had hit with Horner in the lineup or out, and there was no difference. There was never a season, a single season, when Murphy hit significantly worse when Horner *wasn't* there than he did when he was.

I did a lot of other things like that, but that's the flagship study. Anyway, I did this research, and I reported it, and sportswriters generally ignored me, and continued to assert that there is some sort of synergistic interaction among power hitters.

Now, I understand that. I understand that because I am inherently skeptical of research in other fields. All those medical studies that tell you that margarine is good for you on Tuesday and Thursdays but bad for you on Wednesdays and after 7:00 PM . . . I take all of those with a grain of salt. The studies of sociologists who tell you that capital punishment has no impact on the crime rate and that excessive TV has no visible impact on a child's values . . . I pay no attention to any of that. I mean, how do I know whether this guy has really studied the issue fairly, or whether he is a political partisan who is trying to weigh in on a political issue with a study so designed that the answer was a foregone conclusion? Besides, I know myself, as a researcher, that the most suspect conclusion is the finding of no effect. If you find no connection between A and B, this means either that A and B are not connected, or that you didn't look in the right place.

So I understand why people ignore research, and I understand why other people ignore *my* research. If I was them, I'd probably do the same thing.

What I **don't** understand is *why people don't learn the same things from experience.*

Every year there are three or four places where one slugger is put behind another one, and sportswriters will always write that this will make slugger A better. Last year, for example, George Bell was traded from the Cubs to the White Sox. When this happened, sportswriters predictably wrote that, as a side benefit, this would reduce Frank Thomas's phenomenal number of walks, get him more pitches to hit, and improve his other numbers. I was on Roy Firestone a year ago, and he asked me about it. I told him it was nonsense, it wasn't going to happen, and then after I was gone he taped an after-segment with some smartass 24-year-old who assured the audience that I didn't know what I was talking about.

The other one of those a year ago was Bobby Bonilla, who moved from Pittsburgh to New York. This, or so it was said, was sure to hurt Barry Bonds, who would have no one to hit behind him in Pittsburgh, and to help Howard Johnson, who would have Bonilla (and Eddie Murray) hitting behind him in New York.

Well, of course it didn't happen. None of it happened, as it never does. George Bell drove in 100 runs, but Frank Thomas's walks *didn't* go down, to any significant extent, and his other numbers didn't go up. The fifth-place hitters for the Pirates, hitting behind Bonds, hit .236 for the season with 11 home runs, in spite of which Bonds had the best season of his life. Howard Johnson derived no apparent benefits from having Eddie Murray and Bobby Bonilla hitting behind him, losing 36 points off his batting average and 80 percent of his home runs.

But this won't stop anybody from writing that such an effect still exists. What they'll do is, they'll say that it didn't happen *there*, but it happened over *here*, Cleveland or San Diego or some damn place. They'll say this in the most improbable places. Sean McDonough said during the World Series that the signing of Dave Winfield had helped Joe Carter tremendously—even though Carter actually didn't have as good a year last year as he had in 1991, when Winfield was in California. Then they'll make up *another* case, 1993, and they'll say that it's going to happen *there*.

The most curious case is George Bell, because this is the second straight season for him. Remember, in 1991 Bell signed with the Chicago *Cubs* as a free agent, and the people who write that sort of thing immediately said, Jah, great, that will make Andre Dawson a better hitter. Well, of course it didn't happen; Bell had a solid year for the Cubs, Dawson's numbers moved neither upward nor down.

And yet, when *the same player* moved to another team one year later, people still anticipated the same effect! Isn't that remarkable? Wouldn't you think that the people who started to say this about George Bell in 1992 would remember, halfway through their sentence, that they had said the same thing about George Bell in 1991? Wouldn't you think that they would pause and say . . . maybe not?

Well, that's a trivial issue. It doesn't really matter very much whether people believe this or not; it's just kind of curious.

But this other issue, this is important.

When the free agent era began, it was common to assert that the acquisition of this big star or that one was going to turn around a certain team. When the Atlanta Braves signed Andy Messersmith in 1976, it was written by many people that this would put the Braves, who were not a very good team, in the pennant race. In subsequent years, the signings of other free agents were each, in turn, proclaimed to have a huge impact on the following pennant race—even, in many cases, to have decided the race in December.

I was a smartass young sportswriter myself then, and I decided to study the issue. What I was asking was: how much impact does an individual player, a star player, actually have on the performance of his team?

The first time I studied that issue, the conclusion was that an individual player, even Babe Ruth in his best years, has shockingly little impact on the performance of his team. I had trouble believing that, so I designed a second study. Same answer. I designed a third study, a fourth, a fifth, a sixth . . . I eventually invented more than a dozen ways to study that issue, all of which insisted that the addition of a star player in his prime (not Babe Ruth) would probably have an impact of no more than three wins on the expected performance of the team in the following season. It's a team game.

So I wrote that. I explained the research, outlined the different approaches, reported the results. There were other factors involved. Almost all free agents have passed their peak years by the time they sign the new contract, so that, in signing a free agent, you are buying into a market that is certain to decline. A lot of free agents who have superb stats in one park might not post comparable stats with another team. My conclusion was, it's a bad risk. A megabuck free agent *isn't* going to help your team very much, and he can plunge your team into a cycle of decline.

That's what I was writing in 1981.

The baseball world ignored me, and I understand that. It's hard to believe that the uncompensated addition of a star player could mean as little as three games to a team.

What I *don't* understand is failing to learn the same thing from experience. Every winter five or six big-name, All-Star–type free agents will sign contracts for a million or two more than they would have gotten last winter, and every winter it will be written that the teams signing them have all but clinched the pennant. Two years ago the Dodgers signed Darryl Strawberry. That gave them the National League West in 1991. Then they signed Eric Davis; that gave them the National League West in 1992.

The truth is that *all* of the teams which have adopted signing whole-scale free agents as a method of a building a team have destroyed themselves. The Braves were the first big spenders. They started out with a mediocre team, and after signing Andy

Messersmith, Gary Matthews, Jeff Burroughs, and a couple of other guys, they were so far out of the pennant race they couldn't even hear it rattle.

Nonetheless, other people imitated them. The Angels did the same thing. The Yankees, who entered the free agent era with an outstanding team, added a couple of free agents to that team and won the World Series—and attributed this not to the outstanding team, but to the free agents. Then they added more free agents, and more, and more, and more, until they had gutted the organization.

Well, that worked so well that the Royals decided to imitate them, and the Royals brought in Mike Boddicker and Mark Davis and Storm Davis and Wally Joyner, and then the Royals stunk. Los Angeles decided to get in the act, and the Dodgers brought in a bunch of free agents, and then they couldn't win, either.

But it never seems to sink in. Sportswriters never seem to realize that the teams they were saying were sure to win last winter because they had added the best free agents (the New York Mets and the Dodgers) didn't win. Instead, what they prefer to do is re-interpret the season so that the free agents really *were* the critical factor. See, Dave Winfield really *did* win Toronto the World Championship. Never mind that the Blue Jays were already a championship quality team, that Dave Winfield at the time was a second-line free agent who was only in the market at all because California didn't want him, and that Winfield signed with Toronto because they already had the best team in the league and he wanted to get back in the World Series.

I could understand failing to learn from the experience of the Mets, the Yankees, the Dodgers, the Royals and the Angels, if the policy of throwing money at free agents were delivering some secondary benefits. It's been ruinous. It's cost the owners millions and millions of dollars; hell, it must be a billion by now.

But instead of saying, OK, we signed Darryl Strawberry (or Mark Davis, or Danny Tartabull, or whoever) and that didn't work, let's not do any more of that, what do they say?

"You've got to keep the fans happy."

The dumbest argument of all, you've got to keep the fans happy. When a team signs a free agent, and the performance of the team goes to hell in a handbasket, what they always say is, "Yeah, but it helped us sell some season tickets." The Royals will tell you that: yeah, we signed Wally Joyner, we had a miserable year, but the week after we signed Wally Joyner, we sold 800 season tickets.

What is wrong with that argument is that it focuses on an extremely minor secondary benefit of signing a free agent—you sell a few hundred season tickets—while ignoring a massive secondary cost. The secondary cost is the salary structure. Let's say that the New York Yankees were to sign Kirby Puckett for $10 million a year, which for all I know may already have happened by the time you read this. Is that the end of the money?

Why, not at all. What that means is, the top salary in baseball has gone up 40 percent. And what that means is, every other salary in baseball, sooner or later, is going to go up 40 percent. If you sign Kirby Puckett for $10 million, everybody else on the team is going to want a raise. And one way or another, through free agency or arbitration, they're going to get it.

Then, on the other hand, does it *really* help attendance? Gee, I don't know, how much is the Dodgers' attendance up? How much has the Royals' attendance gone up, since they started signing free agents and losing games? Nothing could be more obvious than this: that the fans simply want to win. If you win, the fans will be happy; if you don't, they won't. There's no second verse here.

So I simply can't understand it. I am genuinely puzzled. Somebody will sign Kirby, or Joe Carter, or David Cone, or somebody will corral two or three of the available free agents, and the sportswriters will write that they have locked up the pennant, or at least that they have improved themselves tremendously. I *simply cannot understand why teams cannot learn from experience to abandon a policy which almost never works, and which is incidentally ruinous.* Can you understand this? If you can, explain it to me.

STOP THE PRESSES

The deadline for the main part of this book was late October, several weeks before the November 17 expansion draft. Most of this book was set in type before the Rockies and Marlins chose their poison, so to speak. This article, on the other hand, was written *after* the expansion draft (one day after), and is intended to update the comments on those players who have been most affected by the formation of the new teams.

It is a guess that both of the new teams, in Denver and Miami, will play in hitter's parks. In the case of the Colorado Rockies this is well established, since Denver has had a minor league team playing in that park for years, and it has always been a hitter's park. For the Marlins, the effects of the park are more problematic, since the ball usually does not travel well at or near sea level. As I understand it, however—I haven't been there—Joe Robbie Stadium is small for baseball, with outfield fences which cut straight across, like Wrigley, rather than tapering back from the foul pole. The foul territory is also small. In exhibition games which have been played there the ball has seemed to travel well. I don't claim to *know*, but my guess is that the park will favor the hitters, and the possibility exists that it will favor the hitters to a very significant extent.

So then, as a general principle, all *hitters* selected by the expansion teams might tend to perform *better* than I had projected them to perform, while pitchers might tend to perform worse.   Being selected by an expansion team is not a great benefit for a pitcher, for two other reasons. First, while a hitter's record, in general, represents the skills of the individual hitter, a pitcher's record to a substantial extent embodies the abilities of his team. If the team is bad, the pitcher's record will reflect it from bottom to top—not just wins and losses, but also hits allowed, earned run average, and quite possibly everything else. Second, opportunity will come to a pitcher anyway. For a position player, opportunity is precious. If you're a second baseman and you're in the Cubs organization or the Blue Jays or the Indians, you're up a creek without a paddle. But a pitcher, if he pitches well, will always get a chance due to an injury or somebody's ineffectiveness.

So being selected by an expansion team, which can be a great opportunity for a position player, really *isn't* any bargain for a pitcher in general, and particularly isn't any bargain for a pitcher in this expansion draft. It's pretty much like being traded to the Tigers.

I also wanted to say this: don't underestimate the extent to which the addition of two new hitter's parks can alter the statistics of the entire league. Let's say that eight runs a game, on average, are scored in the existing twelve parks, but that the average is ten per game in Denver and eleven in Miami. That would move the *league* average from 8.00 to 8.36, a fairly significant leap. In fact, that's exactly what happened in the first expansion, in the American League in 1961. Many of you will remember that the 1961 expansion was accompanied by a flurry of home-run hitting, as Roger Maris hit 61 home runs and four other American Leaguers hit 45 or more.

This caused an understandable misunderstanding. What sportswriters generally *thought* had happened was that Maris, Mantle, Killebrew, *et al.*, had taken advantage of the expansion pitchers to boost their home-run rates. That wasn't what had really happened, and one way you can tell that that wasn't what happened is to study the ERAs and home run rates of the pitchers who were already in the league in 1960. By the same logic, bringing all of those expansion hitters into the league should have made the established pitchers *better*—but they weren't better. Their ERAs went up, and their home runs allowed jumped. Almost two-thirds of the pitchers who pitched 150 or more innings in the American League in both 1960 and 1961 had higher ERAs in 1961 than in 1960.

What had *really* happened was that the American League had added two home-run parks in one season—old Metropolitan Stadium in Minnesota, where 181 home runs were hit in 80 home games, and Wrigley Field in Los Angeles, where 248 were hit in 82 games. In fact, the American League per game home-run rate actually *dropped* in 1961 *in the eight pre-existing parks*, but so many home runs were hit in Minnesota and Los Angeles that home run rates for the entire league were inflated.

This is worth mentioning, because I suspect that exactly the same thing may happen in 1993: So many home runs will be hit in Denver and Miami that home-run rates for the entire league will be inflated, and sportswriters will write that home runs are being hit because the expansion has diluted the quality of the pitching. You should know that that's probably not what is really happening.

Since World War II most election years have tended to be pitchers' years, and 1992 followed this pattern, producing the lowest league ERAs since 1989. If you chart anything from the stock market to the temperature, it will tend to go up-down-up-down. Most downs are followed by ups, most ups are followed by downs. For this reason, it would be likely anyway that overall hitting would increase in 1993.

So . . . expect a hitting year, and expect the expansion teams to be in the middle of it.

A second general point, before we get to specific player comments. The Colorado Rockies would appear, on the basis of their first-round draft picks, to be run by dumb guys. Jerald Clark, excuse me? Alex Cole? Scott Aldred? Hey, did you guys know that Henry Cotto was available?

The Rockies have put together the best defensive infield that any first-year expansion team has ever had—Galarraga at first, Charlie Hayes at third, Freddie Benavides at short. Those are all Gold Glove types. Throw in Dante Bichette, and the defensive support for the Rockies' pitchers will be very good.

Also, in the interests of fairness, it should be pointed out that the Rockies' draft selections improved dramatically in the second round, as if the drafting had suddenly been turned over to the B team, only to discover that the B team actually knew what they were doing. The Rockies picked up seven or eight players who might help them a lot from the middle of the second round on. There were three rounds.

They're going to lose, anyway. Charlie Hayes and Andres Galarraga may hit 25 homers each in Denver, but they're going to lose games 5–4 in Denver and 5–1 on the road. My guess for the Rockies is that they'll start out playing fairly well, begin to fall apart about June 10, lose 90–95 games—and continue to lose big for five years.

The Marlins, on the other hand, had a terrific draft. This draft, in its design, offered teams an opportunity to pick up youngsters with the potential to grow into quality players or even stars. The Rockies, for the most part, passed by that opportunity, choosing instead to pick up traditional expansion-type players like Andy Ashby and Freddie Benavides. The Marlins saw daylight and hit it.

In the beginning, the Marlins will be a worse team, probably winning no more than 40 percent of their games before August 1, and finishing their first season with a record only a little better than the Rockies'. But their minor league talent will actually be *better* than some NL teams this year, and by the end of their third season, they'll be able to play with anybody in the National League.

From there, I'll take the players affected in alphabetical order:

Scott Aldred, Colorado

His selection by the Rockies does almost nothing to alter his status. He moves from a poor team in a hitter's park to another poor team in another hitter's park. The Tigers were convinced that he was going to be a pitcher despite a serious lack of supporting evidence, and his selection by the Rockies suggests that they have the same conviction. The value I originally put on him ($2) was too low; it should have been in the $5–$8 range.

Jack Armstrong, Florida

The Marlins wouldn't have drafted him if they didn't have a specific reason to think they could turn his career around. At this point we don't know what it is, although there has been speculation that he might move to the bullpen, where he could simply come in and throw hard. I have certainly seen cases like this where the team thought they knew something and did. I have certainly seen more cases where the removal of one problem merely exposed another one. Increase his value from $4 to $10.

Andy Ashby, Colorado

Scott Aldred, second verse. There's no evidence he can pitch, but they think he can. Increase value from $5 to $7.

Brad Ausmus, Colorado

Ausmus was the Yankees' Triple-A catcher; I didn't put him in the book (although I mentioned him in the Matt Nokes comment) because I didn't think there was any way the Yankees would have him in the majors. Now he may be in The Show, backing up Girardi, so we'll set his value at $6.

Bret Barberie, Florida

Probably the two players whose value has been most increased by the expansion draft are Bret Barberie and Chris Donnels, and Barberie more than Donnels. Barberie moves from a situation in which he would have had to fight for playing time at his second-best defensive position (third base) to a situation in which he will have a job at his best position (second). He is moving from a tough park for a hitter (Montreal) to what is thought to be a good hitter's park. He should be expected to play more and hit better than I had projected for him, and I would increase his value from $14 to about $28.

Freddie Benavides, Colorado

I said he would never be a regular, but the Rockies will give him a shot to prove me wrong. In the lineup he's almost indistinguishable from David Howard, who I evaluated at $14, so let's set him there.

Dante Bichette, Colorado

Will have better offensive stats in Denver than he would have had in Milwaukee, which combined with his defense will probably keep him in the lineup. Increase his value from $18 to $22.

Willie Blair, Colorado

My comment on him before was "He's a gamble." He's probably a worse gamble with Colorado than with Houston, due to the park and the team. Reduce his value from $18 to $17.

Doug Bochtler, Colorado

A right-handed pitcher from the Montreal system who was one of the Rockies' good second-round picks. He wasn't in the book because he wouldn't have made the majors this year had he been in the Montreal system, but he's a Grade B prospect, very young. He pitched better last year in Double-A than he had ever pitched in A-Ball, which is a good sign. He struck out 89 men in 13 starts at Harrisburg. Probably won't start the season in the majors; I'd set his value at about $15.

Denis Boucher, Colorado

He pitched very well last year at Colorado Springs, which apparently made him attractive to the Rockies, who drafted him in the third round. The Rockies have many pitchers and he's just one of them; increase his value from $4 to $7.

Ryan Bowen, Florida

If he couldn't get anybody out in Houston, why would we expect him to in Miami? I'd leave his value about $8, based on his outstanding arm.

Glenn Braggs, Cincinnati

Has signed to play in Japan.

Cris Carpenter, Florida

Carpenter was a setup man in St. Louis, and will probably do the same job now for the Marlins. He's a good pitcher, but has been vulnerable to the long ball in St. Louis, which might be made worse by the move to Miami. I'll leave his value at $16.

Chuck Carr, Florida

The seventh player taken by the Marlins, Carr is penciled in as their starting center fielder. The park, with a grass field and short dimensions, probably

doesn't suit his skills as well as Busch Stadium, but he's been given an opportunity which substantially increases his value. $20.

Vinny Castilla, Colorado

The Rockies' other new shortstop, with Freddie Benavides. He's comparable to Benavides except probably slower. Since Benavides is likely to be a disappointment as an everyday shortstop, Castilla may get a chance. I'd compare him to Todd Cruz, if you remember Todd Cruz. Increase value to $10.

Braulio Castillo, Colorado

An outfielder selected by the Rockies. The Rockies selected a strong defensive team, with the notable exception of center field. This suggests that there may be another move coming, the signing of a center fielder. If that doesn't happen the Rockies will start out with Alex Cole, who is not a center fielder, in center. This would lead to Castillo getting a chance at the job. Increase his value to $9.

Norm Charlton, Seattle Mariners

Has rejoined Lou Piniella in Seattle, where he apparently will be the closer. I had him valued so highly anyway ($38) that it would be difficult to justify increasing that.

Scott Chiamparino, Florida

Nothing has really changed for him. His competition for a starting job in Florida is just as thick as the competition in Texas, although there are more jobs open. I had him at $8; improved opportunity increases him to $10.

Jerald Clark, Colorado

He can't play, so the fact that he has been selected by an expansion team doesn't really mean much. The ESPN commentary at the time of his selection focused on the statement that he was a fly-ball hitter moving into a home-run park, but a) he is *not* a fly-ball hitter, and b) Jack Murphy Stadium in San Diego is one of the best home-run parks in the National League. He might hit a little better than he has in the past, but his future is very limited.

Alex Cole, Colorado

A better offensive player than Jerald Clark, but nobody is a good player if you ask him to do the things that he's not good at, and as of now it looks as if the Rockies will be asking Alex to play center field. If the Rockies find a center fielder he could wind up with Clark's job, in left. I valued him at $16; I think that's fair.

Jeff Conine, Florida

Conine is one of the players whose value has unquestionably increased as a consequence of the expansion. He's gone from playing part-time out of position to playing full-time at his best position, which is first base. He'll hit better in Miami than he would have in Kansas City, and could well have a slugging percentage near .500. Increase his value to $34.

Jim Corsi, Florida

His selection probably reduces his value. He's moving out of one of the best pitcher's parks in baseball, and he is leaving two men (LaRussa and Duncan) who are the best in the business at handling pitchers. Cut his value from $18 to $14.

Steve Decker, Florida

The new start means a lot to him. Two years ago I thought he would hit .270 with 15 homers. He gets another shot at it, and he certainly wouldn't be the first player to come through on his second try. Increase his value to $18.

Chris Donnels, Florida

Probably the player most helped by the draft, other than Barberie. Donnels and Gary Scott are the only apparent third base candidates on the team, and while Scott is still a prospect, it's not exactly like competing with Howard Johnson. Donnels can play, and he may now get to show that. Increase value to $20.

Tom Edens, Houston

Edens was traded from Minnesota to Houston as a consequence of the expansion. Art Howe works his relievers harder than anyone else in baseball today, plus of course the Astrodome is an easier place to post a 1.90 ERA than the Metrodome. He could wind up with Xavier Hernandez' stats. Increase his value to $26.

Monty Fariss, Florida

In my opinion, Fariss is likely to latch on to the left field job for the Marlins, at least for one year, while Nigel Wilson works on a few things in Triple-A. He can hit a little, possibly enough to hold the job as a left fielder. Increase his value to $19.

Junior Felix, Florida

Like Steve Decker and Jack Armstrong, he gets a chance to reclaim his promise of two years ago. He's moving to a better hitter's park, probably, and the Angels were too quick to give up on him. Increase his value from $21 to $24.

Scott Frederickson, Colorado

Right-handed reliever, probably (but not certainly) will spend the year in Triple-A. Grade C prospect; his value would be about $4.

Joe Girardi, Colorado

The tenth player chosen by the Rockies, late in their brain-dead phase. His status hasn't changed dra-

matically. He was the Cubs' catcher, competing with Wilkins; now he's the Rockies' catcher, competing with Owens and Ausmus.

Mel Hall, New York Yankees

Has signed to play in Japan. Write him off.

Bryan Harvey, Florida

Leaving aside the speculation about a later trade, what we have really learned about Harvey is that the doctors are convinced that he is healthy. He is probably going to a tougher park, and he is probably going to a team which won't give him a huge number of save opportunities. On balance, his health is the key factor. Increase his value from $35 to $40.

Charlie Hayes, Colorado

Probably will have better stats in Denver than he would have had in New York. Move his value from $27 to $31.

Butch Henry, Colorado

Faces a tougher challenge to stay in the rotation in Denver than he would have in Houston. Reduce his value from $15 to $12.

Greg Hibbard, Chicago Cubs

Drafted from the White Sox and traded to the Cubs. Decrease his value from $18 to $17 because he is moving to a tougher park.

Trevor Hoffman, Florida

Value is increased due to improved opportunity. I'd increase him from $11 to about $20.

Darren Holmes, Colorado

The Rockies' best selection in the first round, other than Nied. He will probably be the Rockies' closer, which will increase his value in rotisserie and many other fantasy games. I had him valued at $26; I'd move him up to $34.

Danny Jackson, Philadelphia Phillies

Danny is very powerful in this sense: that he is either going to win the game or lose it. He pulls his team along. He's about as good a gamble now as he was before.

John Johnstone, Florida

Johnstone was a hot prospect in 1990, had an off year in 1991 (his first year at Double-A) and recovered in 1992. He's a Grade B prospect, and will probably spend 1993 in Triple-A, which puts his value in the range of $6 to $9.

Calvin Jones, Colorado

I didn't think he could pitch before; I don't believe he can pitch now.

Curtis Leskanic, Colorado

A Grade C prospect from the Twins system, probably will spend the year in Triple-A. His value would be about $4–$5.

Richie Lewis, Florida

The Marlins took a fling of pitchers, but Lewis is one of the more experienced (minor league) pitchers, having finished a successful season at Triple-A, and would appear to be likely to be one of the first players to get a shot at a starting job. Increase his value from $9 to $17.

Al Martin, Pittsburgh Pirates

May have a better chance to play in '93 because the Pirates lost Alex Cole.

Jose Martinez, Florida

A starting pitcher, the second player picked by Florida. I didn't have him in the book because I didn't think there was any chance the Mets would call him to the majors in 1993. I love him; I didn't understand before why the Mets weren't obviously excited about him, and I think the Marlins made a fine selection. He probably won't begin the '93 season in the majors, so I'd set his value in the mid twenties—maybe $26.

Rob Maurer, Texas

His opportunity may increase a little bit because of the Rangers' loss of Kevin Reimer and the retirement of Brian Downing. Increase his value to $14.

Jamie McAndrew, Florida

McAndrew was a first-round draft pick in 1989, and was regarded as a top prospect through 1990. His status in the Dodger system apparently slipped after two so-so seasons, as the Dodgers didn't protect him or pull him back through two rounds. He still needs to establish a track record in Double-A and Triple-A, and will probably spend 1993 attempting to do that. $7.

Brett Merriman, Colorado

I should have had Merriman in the book to begin with; my failure to list him after he posted a 1.42 ERA in 22 games at Edmonton was probably an oversight.

Merriman is 26 years old, 27 in mid-summer, and doesn't have a consistent record of success over a period of years. He was a starting pitcher through 1990, not very successful, and has pitched well in relief for two years, but with unimpressive strikeout/walk ratios. This makes him a Grade C prospect, a mixed bag.

I would expect him to be in the major leagues. That would make his value about $11.

Kevin Mitchell, Cincinnati Reds

Was traded from the Mariners on draft day. This doesn't significantly alter the outlook for him.

Tim Naehring, Boston Red Sox

Inherits the Red Sox second base job with the loss of Jody Reed. Increase his value to $19.

Rob Natal, Florida

His status is improved as a result of the draft. The Marlins' two catchers at this writing are Natal and Decker. They're both right-handed hitters, and they're the same age, 27. Decker was far ahead of Natal two years ago, but their careers have converged since then, Natal playing better, Decker worse. Natal is marginally better off after the draft because his position in the organization is less fixed, and also because it may be a better park. Increase his value to $14.

David Nied, Colorado

Nied was the only player identified in this book as a Grade A prospect who was exposed to the draft, and so was the first player taken.

Nied's value does not increase significantly as a consequence of his selection. He does catch a break in getting out from behind the strongest starting rotation in baseball, but he'll be pitching for a bad team in a tough park with a manager who may or may not know how to run a pitching staff. Good luck.

Lance Painter, Colorado

Has a chance to be in the majors earlier, because of the draft, than he would have been had he remained in San Diego. His situation is not *essentially* changed.

Pat Rapp, Florida

Value is increased due to better opportunity, and also is increased because a) he won't have to pitch for Roger Craig, and b) his quick selection is the first sign in his entire career that somebody regards him as something special. Increase value from $9 to $22.

Jody Reed, Los Angeles

Was drafted by Denver and traded to the Dodgers. He will not hit for the Dodgers (in Dodger Stadium) the way he did in Fenway, and his value should be reduced because of this. However, the late reports on his health insist that there is no injury, and by being traded to the Dodgers he recovers his standing as a full-time regular. No net impact on his value.

Steve Reed, Colorado

Will be in the Rockies' bullpen, setting up Holmes and/or Seanez. I might be a little less enthusiastic about him, in that he'll be moving to a hitter's park, but his value is still around $20.

Kevin Reimer, Milwaukee

Was drafted by Colorado and traded to Milwaukee. His value is decreased because he is moving to a tougher park for a hitter, and is not helped by opportunity, since the Brewers already have a full-time DH in Paul Molitor. Cut his value from $31 to $26.

Armando Reynoso, Colorado

Reynoso has earned a chance to pitch in the majors by pitching consistently well in the minors (and the Mexican League) for many years. I'm not especially optimistic about what he's going to do with the chance once he gets it, but I'm happy that we're going to find out. No change in value (I had anticipated that he would probably go to an expansion team).

Kevin Ritz, Colorado

Situation is essentially unchanged after moving from Detroit to Colorado.

Mo Sanford, Colorado

A year ago he was one of the top pitching prospects in baseball. In '92 the Reds didn't protect him, didn't pull him back for two rounds, and he wasn't taken until the middle of the third round. His minor league season wasn't *that* bad, and he's healthy. Why would he slip so far?

There may be something here we don't know. It may also be a simple case of the team (and other teams) losing perspective on the player's skills once they began to see his negatives. Hell, he struck out 157 men in 149 innings last year, and now has 723 Ks in 642 minor league innings. The $20 value still seems fair to me.

Rudy Seanez, Colorado

Is thought to have closer-type ability, which may surface in Colorado. Who knows? I don't know how to place a value on him.

Keith Shepherd, Colorado

No essential change in his situation after moving from Philadelphia to Colorado.

Dave Silvestri, New York Yankees

Silvestri was the Yankees' shortstop at Triple-A. Speculation is that the Yankees, having lost Charlie Hayes, may move Silvestri to third base and call him up. In my opinion, this will happen if a) George Steinbrenner has really changed, or b) there isn't a free agent breathing who can play third base. Anyway, his chances have improved, so lift his value to $15.

Jeff Tabaka, Florida

A year ago Tabaka moved from the Phillies system to the Brewers as a minor league free agent. His season with El Paso was borderline amazing, far better than anything he had ever done in the Philadelphia system. He posted a 2.52 ERA at El Paso, 75 strikeouts in 82 innings. Grade C prospect; value about $8.

Jim Tatum, Colorado

In this case I am *certain* there is something I'm miss-ing, something I don't know. I can't understand why Tatum would slide to the third round after hitting .329 at Denver with 101 RBI. If his defense is adequate and he can find a job (left field?) he could surprise people with his bat. Value remains at $24.

David Weathers, Florida

Will receive a better shot with Florida than he would have in Toronto. Increase value from $4 to $10.

Eric Wedge, Colorado

He had elbow surgery after the season, which we didn't know about when we wrote the original comment. His situation in Colorado is similar to that in Boston. He probably isn't going to be the catcher, and at first base he has competition (Galarraga, Tatum). He can hit.

Nigel Wilson, Florida

The question about Nigel Wilson is still the same as it was: Do his 1992 minor league hitting stats reflect real improvement, or a run of good luck? We may find out a little sooner than we would have otherwise. He may be in the majors this year, whereas he might have been in the minors had he stayed with Toronto. I had his value at $12; because of his selection I would move that to about $23.

This is the difference between the Marlins' selections and the Rockies': If the Rockies get real, real lucky, Charlie Hayes will hit 100 home runs in the rest of his career. If the Marlins get real, real lucky, Nigel Wilson will hit 350 home runs.

Kip Yaughn, Florida

Another smart selection by the Marlins. His minor league numbers last year are superficially unimpressive (7–8, 3.48 ERA), but that was pitching for a bad team in a hitter's park. His strikeout/walk ratio (106–33) and hits allowed rate (88 hits in 116 innings) were both superb. My friend who works for the Orioles told me before the draft that if either of the expansion teams had anybody who had seen him pitch, they were going to lose him if he wasn't protected.

Probably will spend 1993 in Triple-A; I would set his value at about $10.

Eric Young, Colorado

He had a job anyway, but will be more secure in Denver than he would have been in Los Angeles, plus he is moving from one of the worst hitter's parks in baseball to one of the best. Increase his value from $19 to $25.

The other players selected in the expansion draft would appear to me to have little chance to play in the majors in 1993, so I'm not going to list a value for them; this includes Scott Baker, Andres Berumen, Pedro Castellano, Carl Everett, Eric Helfand, Ryan Hawblitzel,

Ramon D. Martinez, Roberto Mejia, Kerwin Moore, Marcus Moore, Jay Owens, Robert Person, Jesus Tavarez, and Darrell Whitmore.

A few days before the expansion draft, the decision was made to keep the San Francisco Giants, at least for now, in Candlehole. This affects the projections for Giants players, sometimes positively, sometimes negatively. The pitchers as a group, and especially Bill Swift, will probably have better Earned Run Averages in San Francisco than they would have had in Tampa Bay, and for that reason you might bump their value up by a dollar or two. Robby Thompson, whose back troubles might have been exacerbated by playing on the turf, is probably also a beneficiary. The rest of the hitters might have benefitted from a possible move, but I didn't really increase anyone's projected value based on the possibility of a move, and no radical adjustments are necessary based on the lack of a move.

Play ball.

PLAYERS

SHAWN ABNER
Chicago White Sox
Right Fielder
$11

He played well for a while last year, but all indications are that his .279 batting average was just a 200-at bat fluke, and doesn't signal real improvement. His strikeout to walk ratio was as bad as ever, he continues to swing at the first pitch and hit behind in the count, and he slumped late in the season. Defense makes him OK sixth outfielder.

YEAR	TEAM/LEVEL	G	AB	R	H	2B	3B	HR	RBI	BB	SB	AVG	OBP	SLG
1991	Two Teams	94	216	27	42	10	2	3	14	11	1	.194	.236	.301
1992	Chicago	97	208	21	58	10	1	1	16	12	1	.279	.323	.351
1993	Projected	94	204	23	48	11	1	2	17	12	2	.235	.278	.328

TROY AFENIR
Cincinnati Reds
Catcher
No Value

Hopeless hitter, will swing at anything that doesn't swing at him first. Defensive skills not good enough to recommend him as backup catcher. He keeps getting trials and was actually hitting cleanup for Nashville when I saw them play, but I don't see anything to like about him. Expansion will give him yet another shot at a major league job, but he won't hold it.

YEAR	TEAM/LEVEL	G	AB	R	H	2B	3B	HR	RBI	BB	SB	AVG	OBP	SLG
1991	Oakland	14	14	0	2	0	0	0	0	0	0	.091	.091	.091
1992	Nashville AAA	42	130	15	33	6	1	6	24	11	5	.254	.310	.454
1992	Cincinnati	16	34	3	6	1	2	0	4	5	0	.176	.282	.324

MANNY ALEXANDER
Baltimore Orioles
Shortstop Prospect
$7

Dominican shortstop. Good defense, very fast, stole 43 bases last year at Hagerstown. He's a leading candidate to replace Ripken if Cal ever leaves shortstop, but Alexander isn't going to drive Ripken off. He doesn't walk or hit for power. He'll be a major league player, will receive a trial as a regular but most probably will settle into a role as an Al Newman type.

YEAR	TEAM/LEVEL	G	AB	R	H	2B	3B	HR	RBI	BB	SB	AVG	OBP	SLG
1991	Frederick A	134	548	81	143	17	3	3	42	44	47	.261	.318	.319
1992	Hagerstown AA	127	499	70	129	23	8	2	41	25	43	.259	.300	.349
1992	MLE	133	503	59	116	19	5	1	35	17	30	.231	.256	.294

LUIS ALICEA
St. Louis Cardinals
Second Baseman
$20

Good player, tough position. He hits well enough and fields well enough to be an everyday second baseman, but has stiff competition from Oquendo and Peña. He could shift to shortstop if Ozzie leaves, but then he'd have to prove himself defensively there, which would be a tough assignment. A better defensive second baseman than Peña, and deserves to play.

YEAR	TEAM/LEVEL	G	AB	R	H	2B	3B	HR	RBI	BB	SB	AVG	OBP	SLG
1991	St. Louis	56	68	5	13	3	0	0	0	8	0	.191	.276	.235
1992	St. Louis	85	265	26	65	9	11	2	32	27	2	.245	.320	.385
1993	Projected	97	261	29	66	13	4	3	24	28	3	.253	.325	.368

ANDY ALLANSON
Milwaukee Brewers
Catcher
$1

Hit .297 in 72 games for Denver after the Brewers sent him down in mid-May. He's a .245 hitter with limited secondary offensive skills, now 31 years old, so there's no question of his being an everyday catcher again. Would be an acceptable backup, but there are a lot of candidates for that role, so things like conduct off the field influence who winds up with that job.

YEAR	TEAM/LEVEL	G	AB	R	H	2B	3B	HR	RBI	BB	SB	AVG	OBP	SLG
1992	Denver AAA	72	266	42	79	16	3	4	31	23	9	.297	.354	.425
1992	MLE	72	252	31	65	13	1	2	22	17	6	.258	.305	.341
1992	Milwaukee	9	25	6	8	1	0	0	0	1	3	.320	.346	.360

ROBERTO ALOMAR
Toronto Blue Jays
Second Baseman
$90

I wrote three years ago, and I still believe, that there are four truly great second basemen in history—Eddie Collins, Rogers Hornsby, Joe Morgan, and Ryne Sandberg. Roberto Alomar is going to be the fifth . . . in 1992, apart from all else, he hit .430 in the late innings of close games . . . has 25 percent chance to get 3000 hits in his career, 1 percent chance for 4000.

YEAR	TEAM/LEVEL	G	AB	R	H	2B	3B	HR	RBI	BB	SB	AVG	OBP	SLG
1991	Toronto	161	637	88	188	41	11	9	69	57	53	.295	.354	.436
1992	Toronto	152	571	105	177	27	8	8	76	87	49	.310	.405	.427
1993	Projected	157	611	94	184	30	6	10	72	69	45	.301	.372	.419

SANDY ALOMAR, JR.
Cleveland Indians
Catcher
$33

I have yet to hear any credible explanation for why he does so well in All-Star voting . . . .250 hitter with limited power, low on-base percentage, injury prone; pluses are above-average throwing arm and good mobility. Not a bad investment in 1993 because 1) he's 27 in June, and 2) he's a better player than he has been able to show the last two years.

YEAR	TEAM/LEVEL	G	AB	R	H	2B	3B	HR	RBI	BB	SB	AVG	OBP	SLG
1991	Cleveland	51	184	10	40	9	0	0	7	8	0	.217	.264	.266
1992	Cleveland	89	299	22	75	16	0	2	26	13	3	.251	.293	.324
1993	Projected	115	392	39	104	20	2	6	45	21	3	.265	.303	.372

MOISES ALOU
Montreal Expos
Left Fielder
$22

Could be a decent Chet Lemon/Keith Moreland/Gary Matthews type player for 4–5 years, but even that's not a sure thing, and there's very little about him that would suggest anything more. He's old for a rookie, never played exceptionally well in the minors, secondary offensive skills OK but not exciting. Hit just .247 after the All-Star break.

YEAR	TEAM/LEVEL	G	AB	R	H	2B	3B	HR	RBI	BB	SB	AVG	OBP	SLG
1990	MLE	126	438	47	105	16	5	5	45	35	6	.240	.296	.333
1992	Montreal	115	341	53	96	28	2	9	56	25	16	.282	.328	.455
1993	Projected	127	388	51	102	19	3	7	48	30	15	.263	.316	.381

RICH AMARAL
Seattle Mariners
Shortstop, Sort Of
$4

Finally got a few major league games in '92 after spending several decades in the minors. His combination of singles and walks (OBP always over .400 in Triple-A) along with 50+ stolen bases a year could make him valuable major league leadoff man, but he isn't a major league shortstop, and nobody seems to be smart enough to figure out a way to use him.

YEAR	TEAM/LEVEL	G	AB	R	H	2B	3B	HR	RBI	BB	SB	AVG	OBP	SLG
1991	Seattle	14	16	2	1	0	0	0	0	1	0	.063	.167	.063
1992	Calgary AAA	106	403	79	128	21	8	0	21	67	53	.318	.414	.409
1992	Seattle	35	100	9	24	3	0	1	7	5	4	.240	.276	.300

RUBEN AMARO
Philadelphia Phillies
Right Fielder
$9

His .219 batting average of 1992 doesn't represent what he is capable of hitting, but he's never going to hit well enough to be a regular outfielder. He was a minor league infielder, but didn't play any at second last year and isn't a good enough glove to be a regular infielder. Should have three-to-six-year career as a utility player.

YEAR	TEAM/LEVEL	G	AB	R	H	2B	3B	HR	RBI	BB	SB	AVG	OBP	SLG
1991	MLE	121	442	68	124	31	2	2	30	43	18	.281	.344	.373
1992	California	10	23	0	5	1	0	0	2	3	0	.217	.308	.261
1992	Philadelphia	126	374	43	82	15	6	7	34	37	11	.219	.303	.348

BRADY ANDERSON
Baltimore Orioles
Left Fielder
$56

The top surprise player of 1992. His offensive explosion was *not* created by Camden Yards. Although he hit 15 of 21 home runs at home, his on-base percentage and slugging percentage were about the same in Baltimore as on the road. . . . Secondary average of .395 was fifth in the league, plus with 749 plate appearances he led the majors by 16. He had a Hall of Famer's season.

YEAR	TEAM/LEVEL	G	AB	R	H	2B	3B	HR	RBI	BB	SB	AVG	OBP	SLG
1991	Baltimore	113	256	40	59	12	3	2	27	38	12	.230	.338	.324
1992	Baltimore	159	623	100	169	28	10	21	80	98	53	.271	.373	.449
1993	Projected	161	611	86	154	18	5	12	64	97	18	.252	.355	.357

DAVE ANDERSON
Los Angeles Dodgers
Utility Infielder
$14

His playing time almost disappeared last summer after the Dodgers were out of the race, but you'd have to assume there will be a role for him somewhere based on his .286 average last year, .280 over the last three years, and ability to play third or short. There is almost no chance that he could ever play regularly or have a big season.

YEAR	TEAM/LEVEL	G	AB	R	H	2B	3B	HR	RBI	BB	SB	AVG	OBP	SLG
1990	San Francisco	60	100	14	35	5	1	1	6	3	1	.350	.369	.450
1991	San Francisco	100	226	24	56	5	2	2	13	12	2	.248	.286	.314
1992	Los Angeles	51	84	10	24	4	0	3	8	4	0	.286	.311	.440

ERIC ANTHONY
Houston Astros

Right Fielder
$32

Is he the best athlete in baseball now? In general, a player who strikes out a lot when he's 22 will strike out a lot when he's 32. Anthony cut his strikeout percentage dramatically last year, but a guy this strong should hit .350 when not striking out. Anthony doesn't; it's more like .280. He hits too many ground balls. He's only 25, and he still has All-Star ability.

YEAR	TEAM/LEVEL	G	AB	R	H	2B	3B	HR	RBI	BB	SB	AVG	OBP	SLG
1991	Houston	39	118	11	18	6	0	1	7	12	1	.153	.227	.229
1992	Houston	137	440	45	105	15	1	19	80	38	5	.239	.298	.407
1993	Projected	142	487	56	119	20	1	18	71	44	10	.244	.307	.400

ALEX ARIAS
Chicago Cubs

Shortstop
$13

I can't understand why the Cubs, desperate for a shortstop, left Arias at Iowa. He's not a star—I'd describe him as Felix Fermin or Alvaro Espinoza with a little more speed—but he's 25 and has almost 700 minor league games, so the Cubs surely didn't feel he needed more time . . . there should be a job for him somewhere even if Dunston is back. Grade C prospect.

YEAR	TEAM/LEVEL	G	AB	R	H	2B	3B	HR	RBI	BB	SB	AVG	OBP	SLG
1992	Iow AAA	106	409	52	114	23	3	5	40	44	14	.279	.357	.386
1992	MLE	106	392	37	97	19	1	4	28	30	8	.247	.301	.332
1992	Chicago	32	99	14	29	6	0	0	7	11	0	.293	.375	.354

BILL ASHLEY
Los Angeles Dodgers

Huge Outfielder
$5

He's Frank Howard's size and tremendously strong, but at this moment he's no threat to Henry Aaron. Has real power, but strikeout/walk ratios worse than Dave Kingman's (110/16 at San Antonio). His strike zone is huge and his swing takes the scenic route, so any major league pitcher is going to carve him up most of the time. Good arm; probably several years away.

YEAR	TEAM/LEVEL	G	AB	R	H	2B	3B	HR	RBI	BB	SB	AVG	OBP	SLG
1992	San Antonio AA	101	380	60	106	23	1	24	66	16	13	.279	.317	.534
1992	MLE	126	446	46	97	20	0	16	50	12	8	.217	.238	.370
1992	Los Angeles	29	95	6	21	5	0	2	6	5	0	.221	.260	.337

OSCAR AZOCAR
San Diego Padres

Pinch Hitter
$11

Pinch hit 56 times last year, among the highest in the National League. Classic pinch hitter image—left-handed contact hitter who swings at everything. Unfortunately he's not really a good enough hitter to help the team much. . . . Good baserunner and OK outfielder, but really would help a team more as defense sub/pinch runner/fifth outfielder than as team's number-one pinch hitter.

YEAR	TEAM/LEVEL	G	AB	R	H	2B	3B	HR	RBI	BB	SB	AVG	OBP	SLG
1991	San Diego	38	57	5	14	2	0	0	9	1	2	.246	.267	.281
1992	San Diego	99	168	15	32	6	0	0	8	9	1	.190	.230	.226
1993	Projected	59	152	14	36	7	1	2	14	4	2	.237	.256	.336

WALLY BACKMAN
Philadelphia Phillies
(Released)
Pinch Hitter
$3

1992 season was ended on August 3 by a broken thumb. It's questionable whether he'll be in the majors this year, but he still deserves a roster spot because he can get on base, which is the most important skill in the game, plus he's an average-plus baserunner and can play two infield positions. No power, can't hit left-handers and is a liability in the field.

YEAR	TEAM/LEVEL	G	AB	R	H	2B	3B	HR	RBI	BB	SB	AVG	OBP	SLG
1991	Philadelphia	94	185	20	45	12	0	0	15	30	3	.243	.344	.308
1992	Philadelphia	42	48	6	13	1	0	0	6	6	1	.271	.352	.292
1993	Projected	108	131	22	34	13	1	1	13	19	2	.260	.353	.397

CARLOS BAERGA
Cleveland Indians
Second Baseman
$78

He may have been the MVP in the American League last year. All of the best young players in baseball are in the American League—Griffey, Thomas, Gonzalez, Alomar. Baerga's in the same class. He hits .300, hits for power, runs the bases well, turns the double play probably better than anybody in the league—and he's 24, and improving every year.

YEAR	TEAM/LEVEL	G	AB	R	H	2B	3B	HR	RBI	BB	SB	AVG	OBP	SLG
1991	Cleveland	158	593	80	171	28	2	11	69	48	3	.288	.346	.398
1992	Cleveland	161	657	92	205	32	1	20	105	35	10	.312	.354	.455
1993	Projected	161	629	89	184	31	1	16	89	42	5	.293	.337	.421

KEVIN BAEZ
New York Mets
No Shortstop
$2

prospect really; he's 26 years old and has nothing going for him as a hitter. As a major leaguer would probably hit under .200 with almost no walks, no stolen bases, and no power. *Nobody* is a good enough fielder to overcome that . . . has also had several serious injuries. Broke a bone by bunting a ball off his face in 1991, broke a finger in 1990.

YEAR	TEAM/LEVEL	G	AB	R	H	2B	3B	HR	RBI	BB	SB	AVG	OBP	SLG
1992	Tidewater AAA	109	352	30	83	16	1	2	33	13	1	.236	.267	.304
1992	MLE	109	340	23	71	13	0	1	25	10	0	.209	.231	.256
1992	New York	6	13	0	2	0	0	0	0	0	0	.154	.154	.154

JEFF BAGWELL
Houston Astros
Apart First Baseman
$70

from the 21-point drop in his batting average, he really had a better year last year than his Rookie of the Year campaign in '91. He struck out less, walked more, hit for more power, stole a few more bases. The Astrodome works against him, but there is little doubt that he'll be back among the league's best hitters in '93.

YEAR	TEAM/LEVEL	G	AB	R	H	2B	3B	HR	RBI	BB	SB	AVG	OBP	SLG
1991	Houston	156	554	79	163	26	4	15	82	75	7	.294	.387	.437
1992	Houston	162	586	84	160	34	6	18	96	84	10	.273	.368	.444
1993	Projected	161	567	80	169	32	5	18	90	78	8	.298	.383	.467

MARK BAILEY
San Francisco Giants
Catcher
No Value

The Astros' starting catcher in the mid-eighties, his career came back to half-life when he hit .301 at Phoenix in '91, .310 last year. Switch hitter, walks a lot and has a little power but couldn't beat a turnip in a 40-yard dash. I don't expect him to be in the majors, but there are worse backup catchers around.

YEAR	TEAM/LEVEL	G	AB	R	H	2B	3B	HR	RBI	BB	SB	AVG	OBP	SLG
1991	Phoenix AAA	63	186	33	56	16	1	6	36	30	1	.301	.397	.495
1992	Phoenix AAA	35	87	15	27	4	0	6	23	20	0	.310	.441	.563
1992	San Francisco	13	26	0	4	1	0	0	1	3	0	.154	.241	.192

HAROLD BAINES
Oakland Athletics
Designated Hitter
$26

Respected veteran, doesn't create a lot of runs but LaRussa loves him, so he'll have a job as long as he doesn't slip below .235. Hit well last year with men on base, .307, and hit well in the playoffs. He's a hot-weather hitter, hits well in mid-summer, and may have been pulled down by the unusually cool summer. Durable, consistent, a plus in the clubhouse.

YEAR	TEAM/LEVEL	G	AB	R	H	2B	3B	HR	RBI	BB	SB	AVG	OBP	SLG
1991	Oakland	141	488	76	144	25	1	20	90	72	0	.295	.383	.473
1992	Oakland	140	478	58	121	18	0	16	76	59	1	.253	.331	.391
1993	Projected	135	420	56	113	24	2	14	70	61	1	.269	.362	.436

STEVE BALBONI
Texas Rangers
First Baseman
$1

He played last summer for Oklahoma City, hoping to catch the eye of an expansion team. He was having a monster season, on target to hit about 45 homers, until stopped by a mid-summer bout with viral meningitis. Spent three weeks in a hospital and lost a lot of weight, but still wound up with good numbers. He's still what he has always been.

YEAR	TEAM/LEVEL	G	AB	R	H	2B	3B	HR	RBI	BB	SB	AVG	OBP	SLG
1991	Oklahoma City AAA	83	301	44	81	15	1	20	63	33	0	.269	.341	.525
1992	Oklahoma City AAA	117	454	75	114	26	2	30	104	55	0	.251	.332	.515
1992	MLE	117	439	59	99	22	1	23	82	42	0	.226	.293	.437

DON BARBARA
California Angels
First Baseman
$4

Left-handed first baseman, hits singles and walks enough to give him a career .414 OBP in the minor leagues. Performance at Midland in '91 was truly impressive; .298 mark at Edmonton last year doesn't show anything. Weighs 215 pounds but has hit only 23 homers in 313 minor league games. He's 24 years old; will have a major league career, but in my opinion mostly as a bench player.

YEAR	TEAM/LEVEL	G	AB	R	H	2B	3B	HR	RBI	BB	SB	AVG	OBP	SLG
1991	Midland AA	63	224	43	81	13	0	10	40	37	0	.362	.450	.554
1992	Edmonton AAA	118	396	70	118	26	1	4	63	78	9	.298	.413	.399
1992	MLE	118	365	41	87	18	0	2	37	45	4	.238	.322	.304

BRET BARBERIE
Montreal Expos
Third Baseman/Second Baseman
$14

A so-so prospect until 1991, he had an exciting year in '91, returned to his previous level in '92. He could be the new Ed Yost, drawing 110 walks a year, but he's got to support that with some other skills, and Sean Berry may make it hard for him to get back in the lineup . . . has had big trouble with left-handed pitching.

YEAR	TEAM/LEVEL	G	AB	R	H	2B	3B	HR	RBI	BB	SB	AVG	OBP	SLG
1991	Montreal	57	136	16	48	12	2	2	18	20	0	.353	.435	.515
1992	Montreal	111	285	26	66	11	0	1	24	47	9	.232	.354	.281
1993	Projected	122	353	44	94	16	2	5	42	57	10	.266	.368	.365

JESSE BARFIELD
New York Yankees
Right Fielder
$4

His 1992 season was lost to injuries suffered in a fight with his sauna, aggravated by attempting to come back too quickly. In my opinion he still has the best outfield arm in baseball, but injuries and fading batting average may give that title to Mark Whiten by default . . . if healthy, he deserves a major league job on the basis of his defense and ability to crunch a left-hander.

YEAR	TEAM/LEVEL	G	AB	R	H	2B	3B	HR	RBI	BB	SB	AVG	OBP	SLG
1990	New York	153	476	69	117	21	2	25	78	82	4	.246	.359	.456
1991	New York	84	284	37	64	12	0	17	48	36	1	.225	.312	.447
1992	New York	30	95	8	13	2	0	2	7	9	1	.137	.210	.221

SKEETER BARNES
Detroit Tigers
Utilityman
$16

Played 1594 minor league games waiting for his chance, finally got it and has played pretty well. Terrific bench player, singles hitter who runs all right and can play five or six positions in the field, will even hit a home run once in a while. Now 36 years old—in fact, he's older than Trammell or Whitaker. Will have short but unique career.

YEAR	TEAM/LEVEL	G	AB	R	H	2B	3B	HR	RBI	BB	SB	AVG	OBP	SLG
1991	Detroit	75	159	28	46	13	2	5	17	9	10	.289	.325	.491
1992	Detroit	95	165	27	45	8	1	3	25	10	3	.273	.318	.388
1993	Projected	84	224	33	59	11	0	4	27	18	11	.263	.318	.366

TOM BARRETT
Boston Red Sox
Second Baseman
No Value

Marty's brother, now 33 years old; a very similar player to his brother. He's not a bad hitter, a .292 hitter through 1168 minor league games, with more speed than Marty and excellent strikeout/walk ratios. He could have had a career if he had gotten the right break at the right time, but second base is the toughest position for a marginal player to catch a break.

YEAR	TEAM/LEVEL	G	AB	R	H	2B	3B	HR	RBI	BB	SB	AVG	OBP	SLG
1991	Pawtucket AAA	102	331	42	89	15	1	0	27	54	8	.269	.365	.320
1992	Pawtucket AAA	91	323	55	82	18	4	1	21	52	13	.254	.361	.344
1992	Boston	4	3	1	0	0	0	0	0	0	0	.000	.000	.000

KEVIN BASS
New York Mets
Outfielder
$18

Played fairly well for Mets after being pushed out of the Giants' outfield. He'll be 34 in May and is a veteran of several knee operations, so his days as a regular are probably behind him, but will last two or three more years as a role player. Switch hitter, has a little power and a little speed, good outfielder and well liked.

YEAR	TEAM/LEVEL	G	AB	R	H	2B	3B	HR	RBI	BB	SB	AVG	OBP	SLG
1991	San Francisco	124	361	43	84	10	4	10	40	36	7	.233	.307	.366
1992	Two Teams	135	402	40	108	23	5	9	39	23	14	.269	.308	.418
1993	Projected	98	290	31	72	15	2	7	32	21	6	.248	.299	.386

KIM BATISTE
Philadelphia Phillies
Started *Shortstop*
$7

the year as the Phillies' shortstop after hitting .292 at Scranton in '91, played himself out of the job with a .224 on-base percentage and 13 errors in just over a month, and didn't receive another look when 17 other people failed as Philadelphia shortstop. Fregosi says he will compete with Juan Bell for the shortstop job in '93.

YEAR	TEAM/LEVEL	G	AB	R	H	2B	3B	HR	RBI	BB	SB	AVG	OBP	SLG
1992	Scranton AAA	71	269	30	70	12	6	2	29	7	6	.260	.282	.372
1992	MLE	71	263	26	64	11	4	1	25	6	4	.243	.260	.327
1992	Philadelphia	44	136	9	28	4	0	1	10	4	0	.206	.224	.257

KEVIN BELCHER
Texas Rangers
A *Outfielder*
$1

prospect three years ago. The Rangers gave up on him and dumped him at Tulsa (Double-A). He decided to relax, quit worrying about his strikeouts, and let the bat fly, and hit 17 homers. He's heavy, has lost his speed, and strikes out too much, but will sign with somebody as six-year free agent, and probably will receive a major league trial this year.

YEAR	TEAM/LEVEL	G	AB	R	H	2B	3B	HR	RBI	BB	SB	AVG	OBP	SLG
1991	Oklahoma City AAA	52	205	23	43	6	2	2	15	26	6	.210	.305	.288
1992	Tulsa AA	121	377	53	91	19	3	17	59	70	6	.241	.365	.443
1992	MLE	124	382	52	89	17	2	16	55	55	4	.233	.330	.414

DEREK BELL
Toronto Blue Jays
A *Outfielder*
$25

top rookie candidate a year ago, but fractured his left wrist April 8 and lost his job, along with the first two months of the season. I still like him. He played very well from June 1 to the end of the season (.298 batting average). I'd rate him among the very best rotisserie or fantasy league investments of 1993. He'll probably go cheaply, but he can play.

YEAR	TEAM/LEVEL	G	AB	R	H	2B	3B	HR	RBI	BB	SB	AVG	OBP	SLG
1991	Syracuse AAA	119	457	89	158	22	12	13	93	57	27	.346	.424	.532
1992	Toronto	61	161	23	39	6	3	2	15	15	7	.242	.324	.354
1993	Projected	110	420	58	112	15	4	10	53	35	18	.267	.323	.393

GEORGE BELL
Chicago White Sox
He *Designated Hitter*
$34

drove in 100 runs for the fourth time in his career, keeping alive the outside chance that he could make the Hall of Fame, but also signaled the possibility of impending decline with career highs in strikeouts and grounding into double plays. Led majors in GIDP, with 29. Batting average also was a career low . . . now 33 years old, retains remarkable consistency.

YEAR	TEAM/LEVEL	G	AB	R	H	2B	3B	HR	RBI	BB	SB	AVG	OBP	SLG
1991	Chicago N	149	558	63	159	27	0	25	86	32	2	.285	.323	.468
1992	Chicago A	155	627	74	160	27	0	25	112	31	5	.255	.294	.418
1993	Projected	151	599	69	158	29	2	23	98	33	4	.264	.302	.434

JAY BELL
Pittsburgh Pirates
Like *Shortstop*
$67

Drabek, he embodies the virtues of the Pirates. He's not brilliant, but he's durable, consistent, and one of the best in the league at his position. Excellent bunter, 51 extra-base hits last year were the most of any NL shortstop, scores 90 runs every year. Limited range, hits left-handers well enough to hit in the middle of the order but never does.

YEAR	TEAM/LEVEL	G	AB	R	H	2B	3B	HR	RBI	BB	SB	AVG	OBP	SLG
1991	Pittsburgh	157	608	96	164	32	8	16	67	52	10	.270	.330	.428
1992	Pittsburgh	159	632	87	167	36	6	9	55	55	7	.264	.326	.383
1993	Projected	159	611	92	160	30	5	12	59	61	10	.262	.329	.386

JUAN BELL
Philadelphia Phillies
A *Shortstop*
$9

switch hitter, fast, excellent range at shortstop; the Phillies are his third organization, not counting a loan to the Rangers in '92, but he's only 25. I think he'll hit near .250 with a low secondary average; the question is whether he'll field .930 or .960. If it's .960 he'll be a major league shortstop because of his range, stolen bases, and decent bat.

YEAR	TEAM/LEVEL	G	AB	R	H	2B	3B	HR	RBI	BB	SB	AVG	OBP	SLG
1991	Baltimore	100	209	26	36	9	2	1	15	8	0	.172	.201	.249
1992	Philadelphia	46	147	12	30	3	1	1	8	18	5	.204	.292	.259
1993	Projected	98	291	37	69	10	2	3	24	23	6	.237	.293	.316

ALBERT BELLE
Cleveland Indians
He's *Designated Hitter/Left Fielder*
$53

a terrific hitter but a little overrated, to be honest. He's a .260 hitter, poor strikeout/walk ratio; he has real power but his slugging percentage is just under .500, not over .500 like Fielder, Canseco, Gonzalez, Tartabull, and Thomas. Factor in that he's not fast and a bad outfielder, and he's not one of the top players in the league.

YEAR	TEAM/LEVEL	G	AB	R	H	2B	3B	HR	RBI	BB	SB	AVG	OBP	SLG
1991	Cleveland	123	461	60	130	31	2	28	95	25	3	.282	.323	.540
1992	Cleveland	153	585	81	152	23	1	34	112	52	8	.260	.320	.477
1993	Projected	156	559	75	156	27	2	32	107	40	6	.279	.327	.506

RAFAEL BELLIARD
Atlanta Braves

Shortstop

$15

Can't they find a helmet that will fit this guy? Maybe the Babe Ruth League would have one . . . good field, no hit. Will hold his job until somebody shows up who can do both, and I don't see anybody on the Atlanta horizon who can for at least a year . . . hits the ball on the ground about 75 percent of the time.

YEAR	TEAM/LEVEL	G	AB	R	H	2B	3B	HR	RBI	BB	SB	AVG	OBP	SLG
1991	Atlanta	149	353	36	88	9	2	0	27	22	3	.249	.296	.286
1992	Atlanta	144	285	20	60	6	1	0	14	14	0	.211	.255	.239
1993	Projected	97	184	16	40	4	1	0	12	11	1	.217	.262	.250

ESTEBAN BELTRE
Chicago White Sox

Shortstop

$1

Got a chance to play after the injuries to Guillen and Grebeck, but his grip on the job only lasted about three weeks, and his performance was such that he may not get another opportunity. I don't see that he has a role on a major league roster. Doesn't hit, run, or field well enough to be a useful utility player.

YEAR	TEAM/LEVEL	G	AB	R	H	2B	3B	HR	RBI	BB	SB	AVG	OBP	SLG
1991	Vancouver AAA	88	347	48	94	11	3	0	30	23	8	.271	.315	.320
1992	Vancouver AAA	40	161	17	43	5	2	0	16	8	4	.267	.304	.323
1992	Chicago	49	110	21	21	2	0	1	10	3	1	.191	.211	.236

FREDDIE BENAVIDES
Cincinnati Reds

Utilityman

$2

A modern Hector Torres. Offensively, he's a match for Esteban Beltre and Kevin Baez, but he fields well enough to hang around a few years as a defensive sub at second and short and occasional pinch runner. He turns 27 in April, so there's probably no development left. Will never be a regular . . . attended Nixon High School in Laredo, Texas.

YEAR	TEAM/LEVEL	G	AB	R	H	2B	3B	HR	RBI	BB	SB	AVG	OBP	SLG
1991	Nashville AAA	94	331	24	80	8	0	0	21	16	7	.242	.277	.266
1991	Cincinnati	24	63	11	18	1	0	0	3	1	1	.286	.303	.302
1992	Cincinnati	74	173	14	40	10	1	1	17	10	0	.231	.277	.318

MIKE BENJAMIN
San Francisco Giants

Shortstop

$1

One of many Giants shortstop candidates, is said to be a heads-up player who plays near the limits of his ability. The limits are severe. He can't really hit or run and doesn't have outstanding defensive tools apart from an above-average arm. He has a long, sweeping swing, easy prey for a major league pitcher. Not a prospect.

YEAR	TEAM/LEVEL	G	AB	R	H	2B	3B	HR	RBI	BB	SB	AVG	OBP	SLG
1990	San Francisco	22	56	7	12	3	1	2	3	3	1	.214	.254	.411
1991	San Francisco	54	106	12	13	3	0	2	8	7	3	.123	.188	.208
1992	San Francisco	40	75	4	13	2	1	1	3	4	1	.173	.215	.267

TODD BENZINGER
Los Angeles Dodgers
First Baseman/Outfielder
$10

A switch hitter and an OK glove man at first base, doesn't hit enough to hold a regular job. The Dodgers had injuries in the outfield and put Benzinger out there to occupy space and eat up at bats, which since Benzinger can't play just made the season worse. Only legitimate reason to have him on a roster would be to back up a bad defensive first baseman.

YEAR	TEAM/LEVEL	G	AB	R	H	2B	3B	HR	RBI	BB	SB	AVG	OBP	SLG
1991	Two Teams	129	416	36	109	18	5	3	51	27	4	.262	.310	.351
1992	Los Angeles	121	293	24	70	16	2	4	31	15	2	.239	.272	.348
1993	Projected	93	265	24	66	14	2	4	32	16	3	.249	.292	.362

DAVE BERGMAN
Detroit Tigers
Pinch Hitter/First Baseman
$1

Has had a 17-year career without ever being a regular, which is not unprecedented but fairly rare. Three or four years ago he had two assets: defense and secondary offensive skills. His secondary average dropped to .149 in '92, meaning that carrying Cecil's glove is about all he has left to do. He was a fine player, and could have been a regular.

YEAR	TEAM/LEVEL	G	AB	R	H	2B	3B	HR	RBI	BB	SB	AVG	OBP	SLG
1990	Detroit	100	205	21	57	10	1	2	26	33	3	.278	.375	.366
1991	Detroit	86	194	23	46	10	1	7	29	35	1	.237	.351	.407
1992	Detroit	87	181	17	42	3	0	1	10	20	1	.232	.305	.265

GERONIMO BERROA
Cincinnati Reds
Left Fielder/Pinch Hitter
$9

A good hitter, trapped in the minors. In the last two years has hit .322 and .328 with excellent power in Triple-A, albeit with poor strikeout/walk ratios. Has bad glove reputation, but when I saw him play last year he made three outstanding plays in one game, plus his defensive stats, poor until 1990, have improved dramatically. I'm anxious to see him in the majors.

YEAR	TEAM/LEVEL	G	AB	R	H	2B	3B	HR	RBI	BB	SB	AVG	OBP	SLG
1991	Colorado Sp AAA	125	478	81	154	31	7	18	91	35	2	.322	.369	.529
1992	Nashville AAA	112	461	73	151	33	2	22	88	32	8	.328	.378	.551
1992	MLE	112	445	58	135	30	1	21	70	27	5	.303	.343	.517

SEAN BERRY
Montreal Expos
Third Baseman
$20

In Royals system he alternated between reputation as good glove/suspect bat and good bat/suspect glove. In the minors he usually took a year to adjust to a new level, which is why he's just reaching the majors at 27. A Grade C prospect, not star material but capable of hitting .260 with 15 homers, and thus capable of winning the Rookie of the Year Award.

YEAR	TEAM/LEVEL	G	AB	R	H	2B	3B	HR	RBI	BB	SB	AVG	OBP	SLG
1991	Omaha AAA	103	368	62	97	21	9	11	54	48	8	.264	.349	.459
1992	Omaha AAA	122	439	61	126	22	2	21	77	39	6	.287	.350	.490
1992	MLE	122	416	44	103	19	1	13	56	28	4	.248	.295	.392

DAMON BERRYHILL
Atlanta Braves
Catcher
$17

Playing in the two best hitting parks in the NL has kept his batting stats respectable. He can't hit much and he can't throw, but he's coming off his best year, and he does have a career record of hitting well with runners in scoring position . . . career batting average in the late innings is almost 50 points below his average through the first six.

YEAR	TEAM/LEVEL	G	AB	R	H	2B	3B	HR	RBI	BB	SB	AVG	OBP	SLG
1991	Two Teams	63	160	13	30	7	0	5	14	11	1	.188	.243	.325
1992	Atlanta	101	307	21	70	16	1	10	43	17	0	.228	.268	.384
1993	Projected	107	314	28	71	16	0	9	38	20	2	.226	.272	.363

DANTE BICHETTE
Milwaukee Brewers
Right Field
$18

In my opinion his .287 batting average definitely does not represent his true ability. First, he's never hit at that level before, either in the majors or the minors. Second, a legitimate .287 hitter does not strike out five times as often as he walks. Third, he hit .247 after the All-Star break. Great arm, good defense, good baserunner—*but don't draft him.*

YEAR	TEAM/LEVEL	G	AB	R	H	2B	3B	HR	RBI	BB	SB	AVG	OBP	SLG
1991	Milwaukee	134	445	53	106	18	3	15	59	22	14	.238	.272	.393
1992	Milwaukee	112	387	37	111	27	2	5	41	16	18	.287	.318	.406
1993	Projected	130	429	45	103	22	2	11	51	21	13	.240	.276	.378

CRAIG BIGGIO
Houston Astros
Second Baseman
$62

I was astonished at how well he adjusted to second base after catching for five years. He must have worked very hard on it in the off-season . . . huge 1992 jumps in walks and stolen bases place him among the best leadoff men in the National League, reflected in secondary average of .323. I'm very impressed with what he has accomplished.

YEAR	TEAM/LEVEL	G	AB	R	H	2B	3B	HR	RBI	BB	SB	AVG	OBP	SLG
1991	Houston	149	546	79	161	23	4	4	46	53	19	.295	.358	.374
1992	Houston	162	613	96	170	32	3	6	39	94	38	.277	.378	.369
1993	Projected	159	590	80	165	27	3	7	48	72	29	.280	.358	.371

DANN BILARDELLO
San Diego Padres
Catcher
$1

Gets 30 at bats a year when somebody is desperate for a catcher and the front office is too busy to check the stats . . . his children are named Trey, Davis, and Kammie, and he was a punter on his college football team, apparently a pretty good one. You should remember this, because in 10 years he will be managing your favorite team's Triple-A affiliate.

YEAR	TEAM/LEVEL	G	AB	R	H	2B	3B	HR	RBI	BB	SB	AVG	OBP	SLG
1990	Pittsburgh	19	37	1	2	0	0	0	3	4	0	.054	.146	.054
1991	San Diego	15	26	4	7	2	1	0	5	3	0	.269	.345	.423
1992	San Diego	17	33	2	4	1	0	0	1	4	0	.121	.216	.152

LANCE BLANKENSHIP
Oakland Athletics
Utilityman
$24

He drew 82 walks last year as a part-time player, which gives him a terrific on-base percentage, which makes him quite valuable. He's a good baserunner, can play the infield or the outfield, can bat ninth or lead off when Rickey's out. As Albert Brooks said in *Broadcast News*, "They told me my price was right and they could plug me in anywhere. Naturally I resigned."

YEAR	TEAM/LEVEL	G	AB	R	H	2B	3B	HR	RBI	BB	SB	AVG	OBP	SLG
1991	Oakland	90	185	33	46	8	0	3	21	23	12	.249	.336	.341
1992	Oakland	123	349	59	84	24	1	3	34	82	21	.241	.393	.341
1993	Projected	125	301	49	68	15	1	3	29	55	16	.226	.346	.312

JEFF BLAUSER
Atlanta Braves
Shortstop
$38

I was writing about him as a potential All-Star for several years, and just as I was about to mark that down as a bad guess he went on a tear after the All-Star break, taking control of a job that seemed to be slipping away from him. He's one of the best-hitting shortstops in the league, but needs to stay healthy and play consistent defense.

YEAR	TEAM/LEVEL	G	AB	R	H	2B	3B	HR	RBI	BB	SB	AVG	OBP	SLG
1991	Atlanta	129	352	49	91	14	3	11	54	54	5	.259	.358	.409
1992	Atlanta	123	343	61	90	19	3	14	46	46	5	.262	.354	.458
1993	Projected	144	437	64	116	24	3	13	56	57	6	.265	.350	.423

MIKE BLOWERS
Seattle Mariners
Third Baseman
$2

Had a good year at Calgary (.370 secondary average), and got a few at bats with Seattle while the batting champ was out. His shot at a regular job, with the Yankees in 1990, was an unmitigated disaster and has cast his career into shadows. He'll never be a regular, but I wouldn't be surprised if he could help a team as a bench player.

YEAR	TEAM/LEVEL	G	AB	R	H	2B	3B	HR	RBI	BB	SB	AVG	OBP	SLG
1992	Calgary AAA	83	300	56	95	28	2	9	67	50	2	.317	.414	.513
1992	MLE	83	279	36	74	23	1	5	43	32	1	.265	.341	.409
1992	Seattle	31	73	7	14	3	0	1	2	6	0	.192	.253	.274

WADE BOGGS
Boston Red Sox
Third Baseman
$54

What you want to know, of course, is whether Boggs is going to bounce back and hit .320 again, or whether he is finished as a star player. I don't know, but I'm inclined to think that he'll be back. He struck out only 31 times last year. He may be so goal-oriented that he was lost at sea when he could no longer reach his normal levels.

YEAR	TEAM/LEVEL	G	AB	R	H	2B	3B	HR	RBI	BB	SB	AVG	OBP	SLG
1991	Boston	144	546	93	181	42	2	8	51	89	1	.332	.421	.460
1992	Boston	143	514	62	133	22	4	7	50	74	1	.259	.353	.358
1993	Projected	137	517	77	163	35	3	7	53	79	1	.315	.406	.435

FRANK BOLICK
Seattle Mariners
Third Baseman
$6

Switch hitter with outstanding peripheral offensive skills, reflected in secondary averages of .406 at Jacksonville and .420 at Calgary (both 1992). He's 26 years old, meaning that he won't get much better, but he's capable of helping a major league team as a backup infielder, or possibly even as a regular. Obviously isn't going to take the job from Edgar Martinez.

YEAR	TEAM/LEVEL	G	AB	R	H	2B	3B	HR	RBI	BB	SB	AVG	OBP	SLG
1992	Jacksonville AA	63	224	32	60	9	0	13	42	42	1	.268	.380	.482
1992	Calgary AAA	78	274	35	79	18	6	14	54	39	4	.288	.374	.551
1992	MLE	141	476	50	117	23	4	21	71	57	2	.246	.326	.443

BARRY BONDS
Pittsburgh Pirates
Left Fielder
$100

Clearly the best player in baseball. The two most important offensive statistics are on-base percentage and slugging percentage, and Bonds led the major leagues in both categories. I don't know where he'll play this year or how he will hit there, but he has always hit better almost everywhere else other than Pittsburgh, so doubt that his stats will suffer in the move.

YEAR	TEAM/LEVEL	G	AB	R	H	2B	3B	HR	RBI	BB	SB	AVG	OBP	SLG
1991	Pittsburgh	153	510	95	149	28	5	25	116	107	43	.292	.410	.514
1992	Pittsburgh	140	473	109	147	36	5	34	103	127	39	.311	.456	.624
1993	Projected	149	502	102	143	33	5	28	103	115	46	.285	.418	.538
		127	436	123	145	44	5	43	90	147	35	.333	.503	.752

BOBBY BONILLA
New York Mets
Right Fielder
$59

Had a .500 slugging percentage in road games, but didn't hit in Shea. Some people thought he was tentative at home; others thought he wasn't picking up the ball well. He may also have been trying to play through an injury in the late season. Whatever, he'll adjust and have better seasons, but he has to hit. He's not earning his pay with defense and baserunning.

YEAR	TEAM/LEVEL	G	AB	R	H	2B	3B	HR	RBI	BB	SB	AVG	OBP	SLG
1991	Pittsburgh	157	577	102	174	44	6	18	100	90	2	.302	.391	.492
1992	New York	128	438	62	109	23	0	19	70	66	4	.249	.348	.432
1993	Projected	144	528	87	144	31	5	20	87	68	4	.273	.356	.464
		99	299	20	44	4	0	20	40	42	6	.147	.246	.361

BRET BOONE
Seattle Mariners
Second Baseman
$24

To be honest, I *don't* see him as a young star, and with his publicity I suspect he will be over-valued in most leagues. He does have some of the markers of a top prospect—he's young, has made steady progress, and has diverse skills. But a .314 average at Calgary isn't really impressive, and that's the best he's done; otherwise his averages are poor. Grade B prospect.

YEAR	TEAM/LEVEL	G	AB	R	H	2B	3B	HR	RBI	BB	SB	AVG	OBP	SLG
1992	Calgary AAA	118	439	73	138	26	5	13	73	60	17	.314	.398	.485
1992	MLE	118	408	47	107	21	3	8	47	38	10	.262	.325	.387
1992	Seattle	33	129	15	25	4	0	4	15	4	1	.194	.224	.318

PAT BORDERS
Toronto Blue Jays
Catcher/World Series MVP
$25

Marginal player, has poor on-base percentage, hit just .196 with runners in scoring position, very slow, and doesn't throw well. With Carlos Delgado, Randy Knorr, and several others in the system he probably won't hold the Toronto starting job for long . . . well, I don't mean to badmouth him. He's not Dave Valle or John Orton. He ranks about eighth among American League catchers.

YEAR	TEAM/LEVEL	G	AB	R	H	2B	3B	HR	RBI	BB	SB	AVG	OBP	SLG
1991	Toronto	105	291	22	71	17	0	5	36	11	0	.244	.271	.354
1992	Toronto	138	480	47	116	26	2	13	53	33	1	.242	.290	.385
1993	Projected	136	409	38	103	22	2	11	49	24	1	.251	.320	.392

MIKE BORDICK
Oakland Athletics
Second Baseman/Shortstop
$28

One of the biggest surprise players of '92; I personally had no hint that he was capable of hitting .300. I wouldn't bet that he'll do it again, but the LaRussa system induces good work habits, and sometimes players will do surprising things within that system. Still, a guy who hits .227 in the Pacific Coast League is not somebody you'd bet on to hit .290 in the majors.

YEAR	TEAM/LEVEL	G	AB	R	H	2B	3B	HR	RBI	BB	SB	AVG	OBP	SLG
1991	Oakland	90	235	21	56	5	1	0	21	14	3	.238	.289	.268
1992	Oakland	154	504	62	151	19	4	3	48	40	12	.300	.358	.371
1993	Projected	155	550	60	132	14	1	3	46	51	8	.240	.304	.285

DARYL BOSTON
New York Mets
Outfielder
$18

He hit just .249 last year but with a secondary average of .349, similar to his secondary average in '91 (.318) and '90 (.294). He's an unusual player, a part-time player who has power and speed and can play a key defensive position (center: he played more in left in '92). He may be the only Mets player who actually earns his paycheck.

YEAR	TEAM/LEVEL	G	AB	R	H	2B	3B	HR	RBI	BB	SB	AVG	OBP	SLG
1991	New York	137	255	40	70	16	4	4	21	30	15	.275	.350	.416
1992	New York	130	289	37	72	14	2	11	35	38	12	.249	.338	.426
1993	Projected	126	301	45	75	16	3	8	33	33	15	.249	.323	.402
		123	323	34	74	12	0	18	49	46	9	.229	.325	.433

RAFAEL (Wild Man from) BOURNIGAL
Los Angeles Dodgers
Shortstop
$3

The ultimate Punch-and-Judy hitter, chokes up almost to the label and never gets much beyond a swinging bunt. He's 26, two and a half years older than Offerman, and probably more of a threat to Dave Anderson's job than Offerman's, but you never know. Bournigal should hit .250 to .270 in the majors, not too many errors. He's a Felix Fermin type.

YEAR	TEAM/LEVEL	G	AB	R	H	2B	3B	HR	RBI	BB	SB	AVG	OBP	SLG
1992	Albuquerque AAA	122	395	47	128	18	1	0	34	22	5	.324	.364	.375
1992	MLE	122	365	28	98	12	0	0	20	13	3	.268	.294	.301
1992	Los Angeles	10	20	1	3	1	0	0	4	1	0	.150	.227	.200

SCOTT BRADLEY
Cincinnati Reds
Catcher
No Value

He played with two teams last year and got six at bats, in all likelihood the last six of his career. Bradley became a part of the politics of firing Jim Lefebvre in Seattle, when the front office cited Lefebvre's failure to use Bradley effectively among the reasons for his dismissal. He wasn't the worst player in the league, but he wasn't a valuable hitter or a valuable glove.

YEAR	TEAM/LEVEL	G	AB	R	H	2B	3B	HR	RBI	BB	SB	AVG	OBP	SLG
1990	Seattle	101	233	11	52	9	0	1	28	15	0	.223	.264	.275
1991	Seattle	83	172	10	35	7	0	0	11	19	0	.203	.280	.244
1992	Two Teams	7	6	1	2	0	0	0	1	2	0	.333	.500	.333

GLENN BRAGGS
Cincinnati Reds (Free Agent)
Left Fielder
$18

I would say about Braggs, as I would about Darryl Boston, that looked at as a regular/potential star he looks awful, but looked at as a role player he looks very good. Doesn't run as well as Boston and can't throw, but all-around offensive skills aren't bad. Tore the cartilage in his knee running out a home run, September 10, and ended the season with knee surgery.

YEAR	TEAM/LEVEL	G	AB	R	H	2B	3B	HR	RBI	BB	SB	AVG	OBP	SLG
1991	Cincinnati	85	250	36	65	10	0	11	39	23	11	.260	.323	.432
1992	Cincinnati	92	266	40	63	16	3	8	38	36	3	.237	.330	.410
1993	Projected	105	299	41	76	15	2	9	41	37	8	.254	.336	.408
		89	282	44	61	22	6	5	37	49	0	.216	.332	.390

JEFF BRANSON
Cincinnati Reds
Second Baseman
$10

Glove man/contact hitter, bats left, gave his career a boost by starting out hot and going 13-for-34 (.382) as a pinch hitter. He's not that good a hitter, but he can also play short, and should have a career as a backup infielder. Was a second round draft pick in 1988, and has an Olympic Gold Medal as a member of the '88 team.

YEAR	TEAM/LEVEL	G	AB	R	H	2B	3B	HR	RBI	BB	SB	AVG	OBP	SLG
1992	Nashville AAA	36	123	18	40	6	3	4	12	9	5	.325	.371	.520
1992	Cincinnati	72	115	12	34	7	1	0	15	5	0	.296	.322	.374
1993	Projected	77	216	19	53	9	1	2	20	13	3	.245	.288	.324

MICKEY BRANTLEY
Cincinnati Reds
Outfielder
$2

Deserves another shot after two solid seasons at Triple-A. Brantley was promoted as a big star, hit .302 as a rookie (1987) and .263 with 15 homers as a soph. The Mariners decided, as they had with Dave Henderson a few years earlier, that if he wasn't a superstar they might as well trash him. Now 31, could help a major league team as a spear carrier.

YEAR	TEAM/LEVEL	G	AB	R	H	2B	3B	HR	RBI	BB	SB	AVG	OBP	SLG
1991	Denver AAA	122	478	78	144	18	5	15	78	38	10	.301	.350	.454
1992	Nashville AAA	62	230	47	73	13	1	7	31	25	1	.317	.384	.474
1992	Tucson AAA	50	156	21	35	8	2	1	23	18	1	.224	.305	.321

SID BREAM
Atlanta Braves
First Baseman
$25

My definition of exactly what you would look for in a platoon player is "Good defense, not enough offense to help you as an everyday player, but good secondary offensive skills." That's Sid Bream to a T. As a regular I wouldn't like him at all, but his defense is excellent, and his secondary average was .293 last year, .303 overall since 1989.

YEAR	TEAM/LEVEL	G	AB	R	H	2B	3B	HR	RBI	BB	SB	AVG	OBP	SLG
1991	Atlanta	91	265	32	67	12	0	11	45	25	0	.253	.313	.423
1992	Atlanta	125	372	46	97	25	1	10	61	46	6	.261	.340	.414
1993	Projected	126	350	33	89	23	1	10	56	41	5	.254	.332	.411
		159	479	60	127	38	2	9	77	67	12	.265	.355	.405

GEORGE BRETT
Kansas City Royals
Designated Hitter
$19

Brett ended the season with 3005 hits, 3034 total runs (runs scored plus RBI), and 3047 secondary bases. Of the 18 players who have 3000 hits, 13 also have 3000 total runs, the exceptions being Lou Brock, Paul Waner, Roberto Clemente, Rod Carew, and Yount. Eleven of the 18 also have 3000 secondary bases, the exceptions being the same five plus Nap Lajoie and Cap Anson.

YEAR	TEAM/LEVEL	G	AB	R	H	2B	3B	HR	RBI	BB	SB	AVG	OBP	SLG
1991	Kansas City	131	505	77	129	40	2	10	61	58	2	.255	.327	.402
1992	Kansas City	152	592	55	169	35	5	7	61	35	8	.285	.330	.397
1993	Projected	109	411	47	111	24	3	8	48	38	4	.270	.332	.401

ROD BREWER
St. Louis Cardinals
First Baseman
$14

Somehow, the Cardinals *should* have a player named "Brewer." Brewer was drafted in 1987 and reached Louisville (Triple-A) quickly, but his career stalled out after two poor seasons at that level. Came back to life last year, hitting .291 with 18 homers, then followed with a strong performance in a callup. Very slow but good first baseman. Grade C prospect but could be a regular.

YEAR	TEAM/LEVEL	G	AB	R	H	2B	3B	HR	RBI	BB	SB	AVG	OBP	SLG
1992	Louisville AAA	120	423	57	122	20	2	18	86	49	0	.288	.368	.473
1992	MLE	120	404	42	103	17	1	13	64	37	0	.255	.317	.399
1992	St. Louis	29	103	11	31	6	0	0	10	8	0	.301	.354	.359

GREG BRILEY
Seattle Mariners
Utilityman
$11

Another would-be star trying to save his career as a utilityman, played second base, third, all three outfield positions last year, and also was used as DH, pinch hitter, and pinch runner. Has developed a reputation for not being able to hit left-handers, although actually his stats don't show that. A useful player, should stay around for years if his salary doesn't get out of line.

YEAR	TEAM/LEVEL	G	AB	R	H	2B	3B	HR	RBI	BB	SB	AVG	OBP	SLG
1991	Seattle	139	381	39	99	17	3	2	26	27	23	.260	.307	.336
1992	Seattle	86	200	18	55	10	0	5	12	4	9	.275	.290	.400
1993	Projected	111	286	32	75	18	2	5	26	22	14	.262	.315	.392

BERNARDO BRITO
Minnesota
First Baseman/Outfielder
$1

A 29-year-old minor league veteran, has hit 22 to 27 home runs in the minor leagues every year since 1987, and had similar numbers even before that, a total of 229 minor league home runs (he'll catch Crash Davis this summer). Right-handed hitter, Andres Galarraga–type hitter, probably as good as Galarraga and more consistent. No prospect, but can play a little if a spot opens.

YEAR	TEAM/LEVEL	G	AB	R	H	2B	3B	HR	RBI	BB	SB	AVG	OBP	SLG
1991	Portland AAA	115	428	65	111	17	2	27	83	28	1	.259	.311	.498
1992	Portland AAA	140	564	80	152	27	7	26	96	32	0	.270	.313	.480
1992	MLE	140	551	63	139	26	6	20	76	25	0	.252	.285	.430

RICO BROGNA
Detroit Tigers
First Baseman
$7

Left-handed-hitting first baseman, a candidate to take Dave Bergman's place as pinch hitter/Cecil Fielder's glove. He was the Tigers' first-round draft pick and has always been considered their top prospect as a position player, for no apparent reason, although he did have a fine year in the Eastern League when he was 20. Too young to write off (23), but a Grade D prospect.

YEAR	TEAM/LEVEL	G	AB	R	H	2B	3B	HR	RBI	BB	SB	AVG	OBP	SLG
1992	Toledo AAA	121	387	45	101	19	4	10	58	31	2	.261	.314	.408
1992	MLE	121	378	41	92	16	2	10	53	28	0	.243	.296	.376
1992	Detroit	9	26	3	5	1	0	1	3	3	0	.192	.276	.346

HUBIE BROOKS
California Angels
Right Fielder
$8

Now 36 years old, has had two poor years since driving in 91 for the Dodgers in '90. Not very good defensively at any position, strikeout/walk ratio terrible, baserunning a negative. Secondary offensive skills have always been poor. He missed the heart of the '92 season (June 15 to early September) with a strained neck, and could have a better season if healthy.

YEAR	TEAM/LEVEL	G	AB	R	H	2B	3B	HR	RBI	BB	SB	AVG	OBP	SLG
1991	New York	103	357	48	85	11	1	16	50	44	3	.238	.324	.409
1992	California	82	306	28	66	13	0	8	36	12	3	.216	.247	.337
1993	Projected	79	265	31	65	13	1	7	37	19	2	.245	.296	.381
		61	255	8	47	14	0	0	29	0	3	.184	.184	.239

SCOTT BROSIUS
Oakland Athletics$4
Utilityman
$4

He had a fine year at Huntsville in 1990, when his MLEs suggested he could be a good major league hitter, Chris Sabo–type. Since then he hasn't done anything. He's 26, his strikeout/walk ratios have degenerated, and he hasn't hit in major league trials. I still think there is some offensive ability there, but he's slipped to a Grade D prospect.

YEAR	TEAM/LEVEL	G	AB	R	H	2B	3B	HR	RBI	BB	SB	AVG	OBP	SLG
1991	Oakland	36	68	9	16	5	0	2	4	3	3	.235	.268	.397
1992	Tacoma AAA	63	236	29	56	13	0	9	31	23	8	.237	.303	.407
1992	Oakland	38	87	13	19	2	0	4	13	3	3	.218	.258	.379

JARVIS BROWN
Minnesota Twins

Pinch Runner
$5

Pinch ran for Twins until June 2, then went to Portland. He can hit a little, so it's not impossible that he will be able to build upon the pinch runner role to have a real career. Not impossible, but not likely; I'm not sure I could name anybody who has ever done that. Outfielder, hits for decent average in the minor leagues and draws 80 walks a year.

YEAR	TEAM/LEVEL	G	AB	R	H	2B	3B	HR	RBI	BB	SB	AVG	OBP	SLG
1991	Minnesota	38	37	2	8	0	0	0	0	2	7	.216	.256	.216
1992	Portland AAA	62	224	25	56	8	2	2	16	20	17	.250	.324	.330
1992	Minnesota	35	15	8	1	0	0	0	0	2	2	.067	.222	.067

JERRY BROWNE
Oakland Athletics

Utilityman
$21

Browne as a hitter is very much like Willie Randolph, but he can't turn the double play, and to the Indians this meant that he was a bad ballplayer. To the A's it meant he needed to be assigned to some other duties . . . hit .465 (20 for 43) in the late innings of close games, the best of any major league player.

YEAR	TEAM/LEVEL	G	AB	R	H	2B	3B	HR	RBI	BB	SB	AVG	OBP	SLG
1991	Cleveland	107	290	28	66	5	2	1	29	27	2	.228	.292	.269
1992	Oakland	111	324	43	93	12	2	3	40	40	3	.287	.366	.364
1993	Projected	123	383	57	103	17	2	4	42	50	6	.269	.353	.360
		115	358	58	120	19	2	5	51	53	4	.335	.421	.441

J. T. BRUETT
Minnesota Twins

Pinch Runner
$6

Took the pinch runner job from Jarvis Brown, I think because the Twins want both Brown and Bruett to get some everyday playing time. He's a similar player to Brown; as a minor league hitter he walks constantly, 60 times in 77 games at Portland last year, 101 times with 437 at bats in '90. May have a future, but will have to battle.

YEAR	TEAM/LEVEL	G	AB	R	H	2B	3B	HR	RBI	BB	SB	AVG	OBP	SLG
1991	Portland AAA	99	345	51	98	6	3	0	35	40	21	.284	.363	.319
1992	Portland AAA	77	280	41	70	10	3	0	17	60	29	.250	.381	.307
1992	Minnesota	56	76	6	19	4	0	0	2	6	6	.250	.313	.303

JACOB BRUMFIELD
Cincinnati Reds

Outfielder
$3

Minor league veteran, was released by the Cubs in 1985. He's an excellent base stealer, but his offense has come along slowly, to say the least; in 1988 and '89 he hit .226 and .228 at Memphis (Double-A). He has begun to hit a little better the last couple of years (in the minors), but will probably be a 25th man if he has a career at all.

YEAR	TEAM/LEVEL	G	AB	R	H	2B	3B	HR	RBI	BB	SB	AVG	OBP	SLG
1992	Nashville AAA	56	208	32	59	10	3	5	19	26	22	.284	.369	.433
1992	MLE	56	200	25	51	9	1	4	15	21	15	.255	.326	.370
1992	Cincinnati	24	30	6	4	0	0	0	2	2	6	.133	.212	.133

MIKE BRUMLEY
Boston Red Sox

Infielder

$1

Veteran minor league glove man; I always confuse him with Doug Strange. He's 30 years old, no power, a little speed, probably wouldn't hit .250 in the majors, but would certainly appreciate the chance to try. He's been in the Cubs system, the Padres, the Tigers, Mariners, the last two years in Pawtucket except for one at bat with the Red Sox. No player, no prospect.

YEAR	TEAM/LEVEL	G	AB	R	H	2B	3B	HR	RBI	BB	SB	AVG	OBP	SLG
1991	Boston	63	118	16	25	5	0	0	5	10	2	.212	.273	.254
1992	Pawtucket AAA	101	365	50	96	15	5	4	41	37	14	.263	.328	.364
1992	MLE	101	354	37	85	16	2	2	30	27	8	.240	.294	.314

TOM BRUNANSKY
Boston Red Sox
(Released)

Right Fielder

$13

One of the rocks upon which Butch Hobson's career is foundering. A July hot streak gave him his best stats in several years, although he hit no better the rest of the year. He's a good outfielder in some parks, doesn't run well enough to play right field on artificial turf. He's only 32, but he also scored only 47 runs last year, and it was a good year.

YEAR	TEAM/LEVEL	G	AB	R	H	2B	3B	HR	RBI	BB	SB	AVG	OBP	SLG
1991	Boston	142	459	54	105	24	1	16	70	49	1	.229	.303	.390
1992	Boston	138	458	47	122	31	3	15	74	66	2	.266	.354	.445
1993	Projected	143	477	52	112	25	2	16	68	61	4	.235	.322	.396
		134	457	40	139	38	5	14	78	83	3	.304	.411	.501

STEVE BUECHELE
Chicago Cubs

Third Baseman

$45

Now 31; his skills are hard to get a handle on because everything seems to fluctuate. He hit 22 homers in '91, only 9 last year—but it wasn't really a bad year. His average was .261, 20 points over his career average, and he drew more walks than usual. Excellent defensive third baseman, very durable. He's one of the better third basemen in the league.

YEAR	TEAM/LEVEL	G	AB	R	H	2B	3B	HR	RBI	BB	SB	AVG	OBP	SLG
1991	Two Teams	152	530	74	139	22	3	22	85	49	0	.262	.331	.440
1992	Two Teams	145	524	52	137	23	4	9	64	52	1	.261	.334	.372
1993	Projected	143	517	57	123	19	2	15	66	51	2	.238	.306	.369
		138	518	30	135	24	5	0	43	55	2	.261	.332	.326

JAY BUHNER
Seattle Mariners

Right Fielder

$57

Excellent defensive outfielder and a hitter with 30–home run power. Career had been a stop-and-go affair until 1992 because he has experimented with injuries. Extremely broad shoulders and no body fat, which may contribute to the injuries. Strikes out enough to keep his average under .250, but walks proportionately. Poor baserunner despite decent speed. A pleasant young man but very intense.

YEAR	TEAM/LEVEL	G	AB	R	H	2B	3B	HR	RBI	BB	SB	AVG	OBP	SLG
1991	Seattle	137	406	64	99	14	4	27	77	53	0	.244	.337	.498
1992	Seattle	152	543	69	132	16	3	25	79	71	0	.243	.333	.422
1993	Projected	151	550	74	135	22	2	27	88	73	2	.245	.334	.440

ERIC BULLOCK
Montreal Expos
Outfielder
No Value

Has been at Triple-A since shortly after Doubleday invented the game, and has .300 batting average in 1119 minor league games. Left-handed contact hitter, pinch-hitter type, had great speed years ago, still has some speed but no power. He's now 33 years old; his play with Montreal in '91 (below) constitutes the better part of his major league experience.

YEAR	TEAM/LEVEL	G	AB	R	H	2B	3B	HR	RBI	BB	SB	AVG	OBP	SLG
1991	Montreal	73	72	6	16	4	0	1	6	9	6	.222	.305	.319
1992	Indianapolis AAA	90	305	50	93	19	3	5	40	34	21	.305	.376	.436
1992	MLE	90	289	36	77	16	1	3	29	24	15	.266	.323	.360

ELLIS BURKS
Boston Red Sox
Center Fielder
$28

1992 season was ended on June 25 by a disc problem in his lower back. His chances of becoming a big star are probably entirely gone. Back trouble almost never goes away, and he's coming off two consecutive sub-par seasons. He was a fine player in 1990, and could be a rotisserie bargain if he is able to get back to 90 percent of that.

YEAR	TEAM/LEVEL	G	AB	R	H	2B	3B	HR	RBI	BB	SB	AVG	OBP	SLG
1991	Boston	130	474	56	119	33	3	14	56	39	6	.251	.314	.422
1992	Boston	66	235	35	60	8	3	8	30	25	5	.255	.327	.417
1993	Projected	122	407	59	112	27	4	14	57	37	7	.275	.336	.464
		2	0	14	1	0	3	2	4	7	4	—	1.000	—

RANDY BUSH
Minnesota Twins (Free Agent)
Designated Hitter/Outfielder
$5

Career may end with the Bush administration. He's a one-dimensional player, a hitter, and can't afford to do things like hit .214 . . . he was batting .234 at the end of last July, when for some unknown reason Kelly decided to increase his playing time. Bush, and the Twins as a team, pitched immediately into a recession, which in baseball we call a slump.

YEAR	TEAM/LEVEL	G	AB	R	H	2B	3B	HR	RBI	BB	SB	AVG	OBP	SLG
1991	Minnesota	93	165	21	50	10	1	6	23	24	0	.303	.401	.485
1992	Minnesota	100	182	14	39	8	1	2	22	11	1	.214	.263	.302
1993	Projected	97	171	17	41	12	1	4	21	19	1	.240	.316	.392
		107	199	7	26	6	1	0	21	0	2	.131	.131	.171

BRETT BUTLER
Los Angeles Dodgers
Center Fielder
$68

He's 35, but I wouldn't be *terribly* concerned about his age. Players of this type historically have aged well. A very slight slowing of the reflexes will kill a power hitter, but since Butler doesn't swing hard, he's not as susceptible to that. He's in great shape. I mean, if he gets 10 pounds overweight his career is over, but I don't imagine he will.

YEAR	TEAM/LEVEL	G	AB	R	H	2B	3B	HR	RBI	BB	SB	AVG	OBP	SLG
1991	Los Angeles	161	615	112	182	13	5	2	38	108	38	.296	.401	.343
1992	Los Angeles	157	553	86	171	14	11	3	39	95	41	.309	.413	.391
1993	Projected	149	556	86	153	19	6	3	35	93	37	.275	.379	.347
		153	481	60	160	15	17	4	40	82	44	.333	.430	.459

FRANCISCO CABRERA
Atlanta Braves
First Baseman/Catcher/NLCS Hero
$15

As I've been writing for several years, this guy is a pretty good major league hitter if they can ever find a place to play him. He's huge, listed at 6-4, 193, and looks bigger; has career total of 13 homers, 51 RBI in 265 at bats. I think he is one of the players most likely to be helped by expansion.

YEAR	TEAM/LEVEL	G	AB	R	H	2B	3B	HR	RBI	BB	SB	AVG	OBP	SLG
1991	Atlanta	44	95	7	23	6	0	4	23	6	0	.242	.284	.432
1992	Atlanta	12	10	2	3	0	0	2	3	1	0	.300	.364	.900
1993	Projected	129	380	38	100	19	1	15	57	18	1	.263	.296	.437

IVAN CALDERON
Montreal Expos
Left Fielder
$17

He had several injuries—a strained rib cage muscle, a shoulder injury that was given several descriptions before arthroscopic surgery uncovered damaged cartilage. My first guess would be that he won't come back to the same level. My second guess would be that he will, but just episodically, just for one year out of three. Not a good enough hitter to be truly valuable at 90 percent.

YEAR	TEAM/LEVEL	G	AB	R	H	2B	3B	HR	RBI	BB	SB	AVG	OBP	SLG
1991	Montreal	134	470	69	141	22	3	19	75	53	31	.300	.368	.481
1992	Montreal	48	170	19	45	14	2	3	24	14	1	.265	.323	.424
1993	Projected	107	381	52	106	24	2	12	53	37	20	.275	.336	.464

KEN CAMINITI
Houston Astros
Third Baseman
$46

He had a marvelous season, about which we can only say *What took you so long?* He's always seemed to have some ability that wasn't coming through. Still, the general principle is that when a player over 26 (Caminiti will be 30 in April) has a year which is way over what he has done before, you need to be very cautious about expecting a repeat.

YEAR	TEAM/LEVEL	G	AB	R	H	2B	3B	HR	RBI	BB	SB	AVG	OBP	SLG
1991	Houston.	152	574	65	145	30	3	13	80	46	4	.253	.312	.383
1992	Houston	135	506	68	149	31	2	13	62	44	10	.294	.350	.441
1993	Projected	146	536	60	139	25	2	9	61	48	8	.259	.320	.364
		118	438	71	153	32	1	13	44	42	16	.349	.406	.516

CASEY CANDAELE
Houston Astros
Utilityman
$6

The failures of Yelding, Cedeno, et al. forced the Astros to use him at shortstop quite a bit. He can't play shortstop, so this put a lot of pressure on his game, and he had a miserable year, posting on-base and slugging percentages lower than his usual batting averages. Nobody is a good player if you ask him to do the things he's not capable of doing.

YEAR	TEAM/LEVEL	G	AB	R	H	2B	3B	HR	RBI	BB	SB	AVG	OBP	SLG
1990	Houston	130	262	30	75	8	6	3	22	31	7	.286	.364	.397
1991	Houston	151	461	44	121	20	7	4	50	40	9	.262	.319	.362
1992	Houston	135	320	19	68	12	1	1	18	24	7	.213	.269	.266
		119	179	0	13	4	0	0	0	8	5	.073	.112	.098

JOHN CANGELOSI
Detroit Tigers
Outfielder
No Value

Signed with Toledo (Tigers system) after being released by the Rangers in late July. The Rangers were using him as a defensive sub in center field, although he's not really a center fielder. He hit just .188 but had more walks (18) than hits (16), so that's a little misleading. I've always liked him, but I don't expect to see him back in the major leagues.

YEAR	TEAM/LEVEL	G	AB	R	H	2B	3B	HR	RBI	BB	SB	AVG	OBP	SLG
1990	Pittsburgh	58	76	13	15	2	0	0	1	11	7	.197	.307	.224
1991	Denver AAA	83	303	69	89	8	3	3	25	59	26	.294	.412	.370
1992	Texas	73	85	12	16	2	0	1	6	18	6	.188	.330	.247

JOSE CANSECO
Texas Rangers
Right Fielder
$64

Everything else being equal, I wouldn't trade Ruben Sierra for two of him. He wasn't *really* fast five years ago, and at 27 is one of the slowest outfielders in the American League. His back trouble is only going to get worse. He will hit a little better in Texas than he would have in Oakland, and he could hit 50-plus home runs in a good season.

YEAR	TEAM/LEVEL	G	AB	R	H	2B	3B	HR	RBI	BB	SB	AVG	OBP	SLG
1991	Oakland	154	572	115	152	32	1	44	122	78	26	.266	.359	.556
1992	Two Teams	119	439	74	107	15	0	26	87	63	6	.244	.344	.456
1993	Projected	139	509	94	132	24	1	33	101	76	18	.259	.356	.505
		84	306	33	62	0	0	8	52	48	0	.203	.311	.261

OZZIE CANSECO
St. Louis Cardinals
Outfielder
$5

His skills and his brother's skills are converging on a common point, about .240 with 30-homer power. At the rate they're going that's where they're both going to be in about three years. In his last two minor league seasons has batted 633 times with 42 homers, 124 RBI, so he does have some ability, and there are rookies around who are older. Grade D prospect.

YEAR	TEAM/LEVEL	G	AB	R	H	2B	3B	HR	RBI	BB	SB	AVG	OBP	SLG
1990	Huntsville AA	97	325	50	73	21	0	20	67	47	2	.225	.333	.474
1992	Louisville AAA	98	308	53	82	19	1	22	57	43	1	.266	.358	.549
1992	MLE	98	295	39	69	16	0	16	42	33	0	.234	.311	.451

CHUCK CARR
St. Louis Cardinals
Outfielder
$11

A speed demon, he stole 71 bases last year (8 at Arkansas, 53 at Louisville, 10 with the Cardinals). He's been in four organizations (Reds, Mariners, Mets, and Cardinals), and until last year was said to be a good center fielder who was never going to hit. He hit .308 at Louisville and looked OK in the callup, which certainly re-opens the debate. He's only 24, has a good arm. Grade C prospect.

YEAR	TEAM/LEVEL	G	AB	R	H	2B	3B	HR	RBI	BB	SB	AVG	OBP	SLG
1992	Louisville AAA	96	377	68	116	11	9	3	28	31	53	.308	.365	.408
1992	MLE	124	468	68	125	13	6	2	26	30	46	.267	.311	.333
1992	St. Louis	22	64	8	14	3	0	0	3	9	10	.219	.315	.266

MARK CARREON
Detroit Tigers
Outfielder
$16

Do you realize if Mike Butcher pitched to Mark Carreon you'd have a dead meat matchup? Carreon, appropriately enough, is a butcher himself, a butcher in the outfield, but hits enough home runs to get by with it, at least as a part-time player . . . 71 percent of his career home runs have been hit before the All-Star break, and 71 percent have been with the bases empty.

YEAR	TEAM/LEVEL	G	AB	R	H	2B	3B	HR	RBI	BB	SB	AVG	OBP	SLG
1991	New York	106	254	18	66	6	0	4	21	12	2	.260	.297	.331
1992	Detroit	101	336	34	78	11	1	10	41	22	3	.232	.278	.360
1993	Projected	90	234	25	58	9	0	7	27	15	2	.248	.293	.376
		96	418	50	90	16	2	16	61	32	4	.215	.271	.378

GARY CARTER
Montreal Expos
Catcher
No Value

Has announced his retirement, leaving Tim Laker, Darrin Fletcher, Bob Natal, and possibly Greg Colbrunn to fight for the Montreal catcher's job. Carter is the best catcher if not the best *player* in the history of the Expos, and is the next-to-last of the exceptional catchers of the late 1970s to pass from the game. There are certainly worse catchers in the Hall of Fame.

YEAR	TEAM/LEVEL	G	AB	R	H	2B	3B	HR	RBI	BB	SB	AVG	OBP	SLG
1990	San Francisco	92	244	24	62	10	0	9	27	25	1	.254	.324	.406
1991	Los Angeles	101	248	22	61	14	0	6	26	22	2	.246	.323	.375
1992	Montreal	95	285	24	62	18	1	5	29	33	0	.218	.299	.340
		89	322	26	63	22	2	4	32	44	0	.196	.287	.314

JOE CARTER
Toronto Blue Jays
Right Fielder
$67

Averaging 110 RBI for seven years, Carter is the game's top RBI man. There are people who exaggerate the value of this. Brett Butler is a more valuable player than Joe Carter. But there are also people who want to give no credit for it, and that's not right, either. There haven't been an awful lot of players in baseball history who could drive in 100 runs every year.

YEAR	TEAM/LEVEL	G	AB	R	H	2B	3B	HR	RBI	BB	SB	AVG	OBP	SLG
1991	Toronto	162	638	89	174	42	3	33	108	49	20	.273	.330	.503
1992	Toronto	158	622	97	164	30	7	34	119	36	12	.264	.309	.498
1993	Projected	155	606	81	152	30	3	26	103	43	17	.251	.300	.439
		154	606	105	154	18	11	35	130	23	4	.254	.281	.493

ADAM CASILLAS
Kansas City Royals
Outfielder/First Baseman
$3

Plays center field and first base, an odd combination. A little guy, chokes up about a foot and pokes at the ball, almost impossible to strike out. Left-handed batter, led the Southern League in hitting a couple of years ago, not fast, no arm, but capable of hitting .280 or better in the majors. Marginal talent but could help some teams, including the Royals, as a pinch hitter.

YEAR	TEAM/LEVEL	G	AB	R	H	2B	3B	HR	RBI	BB	SB	AVG	OBP	SLG
1992	Memphis AA	49	168	25	55	12	2	2	23	32	1	.327	.441	.458
1992	Omaha AAA	89	362	41	111	12	3	0	27	31	3	.307	.359	.356
1992	MLE	138	512	53	148	22	3	1	40	47	2	.289	.349	.350

VINNY CASTILLA
Atlanta Braves
Shortstop
$2

A 25-year-old shortstop from Oaxaca, Mexico, played several years in the Mexican League and was purchased a couple of years ago by the Braves. He earned a major league look with his defense, but there is no indication that he is going to be a major league hitter, and he's not fast enough to pinch run. Probably no future.

YEAR	TEAM/LEVEL	G	AB	R	H	2B	3B	HR	RBI	BB	SB	AVG	OBP	SLG
1992	Richmond AAA	127	449	49	113	29	1	7	44	21	1	.252	.288	.367
1992	MLE	127	439	39	103	26	0	6	35	16	0	.235	.262	.335
1992	Atlanta	9	16	1	4	1	0	0	1	1	0	.250	.333	.313

BRAULIO CASTILLO
Philadelphia Phillies
Center Fielder
$4

Somewhat eccentric talent, has hit .300 in the minors (1991 at San Antonio), hit for some power, and stolen some bases, plus he's a center fielder. Still, he's a Grade D prospect, a long-odds prospect. He strikes out in about 25 percent of his at bats, and his offensive accomplishments, while diverse, are neither impressive nor consistent. A poor man's Glenallen Hill.

YEAR	TEAM/LEVEL	G	AB	R	H	2B	3B	HR	RBI	BB	SB	AVG	OBP	SLG
1992	Scranton AAA	105	386	59	95	21	5	13	47	40	8	.246	.320	.427
1992	MLE	105	379	52	88	20	3	11	42	36	6	.232	.299	.388
1992	Philadelphia	28	76	12	15	3	1	2	7	4	1	.197	.238	.342

ANDUJAR CEDENO
Houston Astros
Shortstop
$17

The new Rafael Ramirez. He strikes out so much that it will be difficult for him to get his average above .240, and a player who strikes out a lot at 22 will normally strike out a lot at 32. In the field his value is largely negated by attempts to do too much, resulting in errors and balls rocketing around the field. Grade C prospect.

YEAR	TEAM/LEVEL	G	AB	R	H	2B	3B	HR	RBI	BB	SB	AVG	OBP	SLG
1991	Houston	67	251	27	61	13	2	9	36	9	4	.243	.270	.418
1992	Houston	71	220	15	38	13	2	2	13	14	2	.173	.232	.277
1993	Projected	81	271	25	64	13	3	6	32	13	4	.236	.271	.373
		75	187	3	15	13	2	0	0	19	0	.079	.163	.169

RICK CERONE
Unemployed
Catcher
No Value

He was released by Montreal on July 16 although he was hitting .270, probably bringing his long major league career to an end. I always thought that his talents were strained as a regular player, which I think is evidenced by the fact that for 16 years he constantly won a regular job and then lost it, but he played good defense and aged unusually well.

YEAR	TEAM/LEVEL	G	AB	R	H	2B	3B	HR	RBI	BB	SB	AVG	OBP	SLG
1990	New York A	49	139	12	42	6	0	2	11	5	0	.302	.324	.388
1991	New York N	90	227	18	62	13	0	2	16	30	1	.273	.360	.357
1992	Montreal	33	63	10	17	4	0	1	7	3	1	.270	.313	.381

WES CHAMBERLAIN
Philadelphia Phillies
Right Fielder
$24

He played better in the field last year, reducing one of his negatives. He hits enough to have a career, but had a .285 on-base percentage last year, which is like a failing grade in your most important subject. He could be a 20/20 man and could drive in 100 runs, and those abilities will earn him a lot of money and make him valuable in rotisserie.

YEAR	TEAM/LEVEL	G	AB	R	H	2B	3B	HR	RBI	BB	SB	AVG	OBP	SLG
1991	Philadelphia	101	383	51	92	16	3	13	50	31	9	.240	.300	.399
1992	Philadelphia	76	275	26	71	18	0	9	41	10	4	.258	.285	.422
1993	Projected	104	355	38	89	19	1	9	46	22	10	.251	.294	.386

(handwritten: 51 167 1 30 20 0 5 32 0 0 .269 .269 .505)

ARCHI CIANFROCCO
Montreal Expos
First/Third Baseman
$10

Had a hot streak in May, and started to look better than he is, but wound up hitting a lot *less* than he is capable of hitting. Could hit .270 with 30 doubles; value will always be limited by lack of power and speed and poor strikeout/walk ratio. Grade C prospect; has a chance to hold a regular job someday, but more likely to be a bench player.

YEAR	TEAM/LEVEL	G	AB	R	H	2B	3B	HR	RBI	BB	SB	AVG	OBP	SLG
1991	Harrisburg AA	124	456	71	144	21	10	9	77	38	11	.316	.378	.465
1992	Indianapolis AAA	15	59	12	18	3	0	4	16	5	1	.305	.373	.559
1992	Montreal	86	232	25	56	5	2	6	16	11	3	.241	.276	.358

DAVE CLARK
Pittsburgh Pirates
Outfielder/Pinch Hitter
$3

Still searching for a home at 30, but a solid major league hitter, capable of hitting .270 to .280 with .400+ slugging percentage in the major leagues, possibly 20–25 homers. Left-handed bat, average speed, no defensive position. Has hit .302 lifetime with slugging percentage over .500 in 760 minor league games; has had trials with Cleveland, the Cubs, Kansas City, and now the Pirates.

YEAR	TEAM/LEVEL	G	AB	R	H	2B	3B	HR	RBI	BB	SB	AVG	OBP	SLG
1992	Buffalo AAA	78	253	43	77	17	6	11	55	34	6	.304	.390	.549
1992	MLE	78	241	33	65	15	4	7	42	26	4	.270	.341	.452
1992	Pittsburgh	23	33	3	7	0	0	2	7	6	0	.212	.325	.394

JACK CLARK
Boston Red Sox
Designated Hitter
$8

The assets are sinking, the deficits are rising. He still has a little power and still has more walks than hits, which is less of an accomplishment now than it was a few years ago. A .323 secondary average will carry a .210 batting average—if you're a shortstop. Oh my God, my career is in trouble, get me another Lamborghini.

YEAR	TEAM/LEVEL	G	AB	R	H	2B	3B	HR	RBI	BB	SB	AVG	OBP	SLG
1991	Boston	140	481	75	120	18	1	28	87	96	0	.249	.374	.466
1992	Boston	81	257	32	54	11	0	5	33	56	1	.210	.350	.311
1993	Projected	77	227	32	49	12	1	9	34	55	1	.216	.369	.369

(handwritten: 22 33 0 0 4 0 0 0 16 2 .000 .571 .121)

JERALD CLARK
San Diego Padres
Left Fielder
$14

He does not hit enough to justify a position as a regular—does not, and never will. He hit .257 after the All-Star break—with 48 strikeouts and 5 walks. He's 29 years old, and a lifetime .237 hitter, with limited secondary offensive skills. He's a fine athlete and he works hard, and people have trouble believing that isn't enough—but it isn't.

YEAR	TEAM/LEVEL	G	AB	R	H	2B	3B	HR	RBI	BB	SB	AVG	OBP	SLG
1991	San Diego	118	369	26	84	16	0	10	47	31	2	.228	.295	.352
1992	San Diego	146	496	45	120	22	6	12	58	22	3	.242	.278	.383
1993	Projected	121	374	34	89	18	2	11	45	21	2	.238	.278	.385

PHIL CLARK
Detroit Tigers
Catcher/Outfielder
$9

Jerald Clark's younger brother, and the Tigers' first-round draft pick in 1986. He's a better hitter than his brother, could hit .275 with a little power, but a knee injury in the minors has eliminated his speed and gradually undermined his status as a prospect. He was originally a catcher, shifted gradually to the outfield over the last three years. Good arm, Grade C prospect.

YEAR	TEAM/LEVEL	G	AB	R	H	2B	3B	HR	RBI	BB	SB	AVG	OBP	SLG
1992	Toledo AAA	79	271	29	76	20	0	10	39	16	4	.280	.323	.465
1992	MLE	79	263	26	68	17	0	9	35	14	3	.259	.296	.426
1992	Detroit	23	54	3	22	4	0	1	5	6	1	.407	.467	.537

WILL CLARK
San Francisco Giants
First Baseman
$75

Has about an 11 percent chance to get 3000 career hits . . . McGriff has passed him as the top-rated first baseman in the National League, perhaps because of Will's nagging injuries. Clark would still be second. His 73 RBI in '92 were (essentially) a career low. If he was fast he'd be a perfect player. He hits for average, for power, good K/W judgment, good defense, good baserunner.

YEAR	TEAM/LEVEL	G	AB	R	H	2B	3B	HR	RBI	BB	SB	AVG	OBP	SLG
1991	San Francisco	148	565	84	170	32	7	29	116	51	4	.301	.359	.536
1992	San Francisco	144	513	69	154	40	1	16	73	73	12	.300	.384	.476
1993	Projected	150	561	84	169	33	5	23	97	65	8	.301	.374	.501
		140	461	54	138	48	0	3	30	95	20	.289	.419	.414

ROYCE CLAYTON
San Francisco Giants
Shortstop
$20

His .224 average as a rookie doesn't represent his offensive potential, but he's never going to put a huge number of runs on the board. I think he'll hit .250, but without walks, power, or stolen bases, that doesn't have a lot of impact. Played well defensively, still appears to have control of the Giants shortstop job, and at 23 has room to grow.

YEAR	TEAM/LEVEL	G	AB	R	H	2B	3B	HR	RBI	BB	SB	AVG	OBP	SLG
1992	Phoenix	48	192	30	46	6	2	3	18	17	0	.240	.300	.339
1992	San Francisco	98	321	31	72	7	4	4	24	26	8	.224	.281	.308
1993	Projected	112	367	44	86	13	4	4	35	29	15	.234	.290	.324

DAVE COCHRANE
Seattle Mariners
Utilityman
$10

Was used by the Mariners as a catcher, first baseman, third baseman, shortstop, left fielder, right fielder, DH, and pinch hitter before he went on the DL July 31 with something requiring foot surgery. He played all right, well enough that he can expect to be back in the majors this year. At 30 he is beyond time of becoming a regular.

YEAR	TEAM/LEVEL	G	AB	R	H	2B	3B	HR	RBI	BB	SB	AVG	OBP	SLG
1991	Seattle	65	178	16	44	13	0	2	22	9	0	.247	.286	.354
1992	Seattle	65	152	10	38	5	0	2	12	12	1	.250	.309	.322
1993	Projected	89	255	24	63	13	1	5	28	14	1	.247	.286	.365

(handwritten) 65 126 4 32 0 0 2 2 15 2 .284 .333 .32

CRAIG COLBERT
San Francisco Giants
Catcher
$5

Nobody could quite figure out what he was doing in the majors, other than that Rosen and Craig were determined that Decker should spend a full season in Triple-A. Colbert is 27 and has no obvious assets as a major league player. His .230 batting average as a rookie is probably about as good as it's going to get for him.

YEAR	TEAM/LEVEL	G	AB	R	H	2B	3B	HR	RBI	BB	SB	AVG	OBP	SLG
1991	Phoenix AAA	42	142	9	35	6	2	2	13	11	0	.246	.299	.359
1992	Phoenix AAA	36	140	16	45	8	1	1	12	3	0	.321	.336	.414
1992	San Francisco	49	126	10	29	5	2	1	16	9	1	.230	.277	.325

GREG COLBRUNN
Montreal Expos
Catcher/First Baseman
$23

Appears to be the genuine article. Drafted as a catcher (1987), Colbrunn missed the entire 1991 season following a tendon transplant and ligament reconstruction in his elbow. The injury moves him to first base at least for now, but he appears to be a good enough hitter to have a helluva career even if he can't catch. Plate discipline needs work, limited speed, some power.

YEAR	TEAM/LEVEL	G	AB	R	H	2B	3B	HR	RBI	BB	SB	AVG	OBP	SLG
1992	Indianapolis AAA	57	216	32	66	19	1	11	48	7	1	.306	.333	.556
1992	MLE	57	204	23	54	16	0	7	35	5	0	.265	.282	.446
1992	Montreal	52	168	12	45	8	0	2	18	6	3	.268	.294	.351

ALEX COLE
Pittsburgh Pirates
Right Fielder
$16

Career snapped back after he was traded to Pittsburgh July 3. Cole has only two skills—speed and the ability to get on base—but those are two skills that you *want* to go together, since they both are adaptable to the same task. If a manager can't take those two skills and find a way to use a player, he's in the wrong line of work.

YEAR	TEAM/LEVEL	G	AB	R	H	2B	3B	HR	RBI	BB	SB	AVG	OBP	SLG
1991	Cleveland	122	387	58	114	17	3	0	21	58	16	.295	.386	.354
1992	Two Teams	105	302	44	77	4	7	0	15	28	16	.255	.318	.315
1993	Projected	105	334	48	87	7	3	1	20	40	28	.260	.340	.308

(handwritten) 88 217 30 40 0 11 0 9 0 16 .184 .184 .28

VINCE COLEMAN
New York Mets
Left Fielder
$26

Adding together his two years with the Mets makes just about one full season—and it isn't a good one. He's played 143 games, batted 507 times, and scored just 82 runs. Scoring runs is his job. His stolen base percentage, 83 percent with St. Louis, has dropped to 73 percent, which removes most of the value of the steals. If he doesn't come back this year, the end is near.

YEAR	TEAM/LEVEL	G	AB	R	H	2B	3B	HR	RBI	BB	SB	AVG	OBP	SLG
1991	New York	72	278	45	71	7	5	1	17	39	37	.255	.347	.327
1992	New York	71	229	37	63	11	1	2	21	27	24	.275	.355	.358
1993	Projected	98	356	51	92	12	4	3	25	37	48	.258	.328	.340
		70	170	27	55	15	0	3	25	15	11	.324	.378	.465

DARNELL COLES
Cincinnati Reds
First/Third Baseman
$13

Coming off his best season since he drove in 86 runs in '86. Piniella got him regular work with the platoon edge in 70 percent of his at bats, and the recipe worked at least for one year. His season was ended by a severely sprained ankle, August 25. As I've written several times, he has always reminded me of Bill Robinson, who had his best years in his thirties.

YEAR	TEAM/LEVEL	G	AB	R	H	2B	3B	HR	RBI	BB	SB	AVG	OBP	SLG
1991	Phoenix AAA	83	328	43	95	23	2	6	65	27	0	.290	.352	.433
1992	Cincinnati	55	141	16	44	11	2	3	18	3	1	.312	.322	.482
1993	Projected	68	151	18	36	10	1	4	17	9	1	.238	.281	.397

CRIS COLON
Texas Rangers
Shortstop
$14

A 24-year-old Venezuelan shortstop, tagged himself as a hot prospect by hitting .392 in 26 games at Tulsa in '91. Tall, rangy, has excellent shortstop's arm but bad defensive habits, poor footwork, screws up routine plays, and is afraid of contact on the double play. Immature; has poor work habits. At the plate will swing at anything. Raw ability makes him a Grade C prospect.

YEAR	TEAM/LEVEL	G	AB	R	H	2B	3B	HR	RBI	BB	SB	AVG	OBP	SLG
1992	Tulsa AA	120	415	35	109	16	3	1	44	16	7	.263	.287	.323
1992	MLE	120	409	32	103	14	3	0	41	12	5	.252	.273	.301
1992	Texas	14	36	5	6	0	0	0	1	1	0	.167	.189	.167

JEFF CONINE
Kansas City Royals
Outfielder/First Baseman
$23

He's a power hitter in a very poor home run park, and since the Royals re-signed Joyner he'll have to play the outfield. He doesn't have an outfielder's speed and doesn't know what he's doing out there, although he can dive for a ball and get back on his feet faster than anybody you ever saw. Apart from those things, I like him a lot.

YEAR	TEAM/LEVEL	G	AB	R	H	2B	3B	HR	RBI	BB	SB	AVG	OBP	SLG
1992	Omaha AAA	110	397	69	120	24	5	20	72	54	4	.302	.383	.539
1992	MLE	110	382	55	105	22	4	13	58	43	2	.275	.348	.455
1992	Kansas City	28	91	10	23	5	2	0	9	8	0	.253	.313	.352

GARY COOPER
Houston Astros

Third Baseman

$3

Expansion prospect, has hit .300 two years in a row at Tucson, but isn't going to budge Caminiti. A 28-year-old graduate of Brigham Young University, has some secondary offensive skills and can play credible third base. No long-term future as a regular (would hit .250 to .260 with 8–10 homers a year), but could hold the job a year or two for one of the new teams.

YEAR	TEAM/LEVEL	G	AB	R	H	2B	3B	HR	RBI	BB	SB	AVG	OBP	SLG
1991	Tucson AAA	120	406	86	124	25	6	14	75	66	7	.305	.402	.500
1992	Tucson AAA	127	464	66	139	31	3	9	73	47	8	.300	.363	.438
1992	MLE	127	434	42	109	24	1	5	47	30	5	.251	.300	.346
		134	522	46	134	37	0	4	71	28	9	.285	.31	.389

SCOTT COOPER
Boston Red Sox

First/Third Baseman

$23

I don't know what it means, but Cooper played better last year than Wade Boggs did. He's a fine third baseman, or at least has been when I've seen him play, a .270 hitter with some power, and his strikeout/walk ratio is better than even. He's 25, and he's waited several years for a shot. Nineteen ninety-three should be a breakthrough year for him.

YEAR	TEAM/LEVEL	G	AB	R	H	2B	3B	HR	RBI	BB	SB	AVG	OBP	SLG
1991	Boston	14	35	6	16	4	2	0	7	2	0	.457	.486	.686
1992	Boston	123	337	34	93	21	0	5	33	37	1	.276	.346	.383
1993	Projected	125	419	41	112	21	1	8	43	37	1	.267	.327	.379

JOEY CORA
Chicago White Sox

Utilityman

$16

One of the better backup infielders in the American League. He's a switch hitter, hits around .250, doesn't waste a lot of outs by swinging at bad pitches. He's a good baserunner, a quick and reliable second baseman although he doesn't throw well enough to be used much at third or short. Every team can use a guy like Joey Cora.

YEAR	TEAM/LEVEL	G	AB	R	H	2B	3B	HR	RBI	BB	SB	AVG	OBP	SLG
1991	Chicago	100	228	37	55	2	3	0	18	20	11	.241	.313	.276
1992	Chicago	68	122	27	30	7	1	0	9	22	10	.246	.371	.320
1993	Projected	100	231	37	59	10	2	1	18	25	13	.255	.328	.329
		36	16	17	5	12	0	0	6	44	9	.315	.725	1.063

WILFREDO CORDERO
Montreal Expos

Shortstop

$38

His one notable weakness is that he strikes out a lot. There is no apparent reason that Cordero would not be a star. He's 21 years old and in the majors, playing a key defensive position; that alone puts him into a group of rare and valuable players. He also can hit, and the defensive reports are good. **Grade A prospect.**

YEAR	TEAM/LEVEL	G	AB	R	H	2B	3B	HR	RBI	BB	SB	AVG	OBP	SLG
1992	Indianapolis AAA	52	204	32	64	11	1	6	27	24	6	.314	.384	.466
1992	Montreal	45	126	17	38	4	1	2	8	9	0	.302	.353	.397
1993	Projected	151	516	61	135	20	2	9	50	40	8	.262	.315	.360

TIM COSTO
Cincinnati Reds
First Baseman
$7

A big right-handed hitter, was a first-round draft pick of the Indians and came to the Reds in the wake of the Reggie Jefferson paperwork foulup. He hit for power for the first time in his career last year, but his strikeout rate and consequent batting average will limit his playing time. The Reds think he may be ready to play, but I doubt it. Grade C prospect.
YEAR

YEAR	TEAM/LEVEL	G	AB	R	H	2B	3B	HR	RBI	BB	SB	AVG	OBP	SLG
1992	Chattanooga AA	121	424	63	102	18	2	28	71	48	4	.241	.332	.491
1992	MLE	121	417	52	95	16	1	28	58	35	2	.228	.288	.472
1992	Cincinnati	12	36	3	8	2	0	0	2	5	0	.222	.310	.278

HENRY COTTO
Seattle Mariners
Left Fielder
$16

A good bench player, fifth outfielder, shouldn't play as much as he did in 1992. A strong defensive outfielder and an amazing percentage base stealer, but doesn't get on base enough and has very limited power. Had dramatic platoon split in '92 (.321 against left-handers, .175 against right-handers), but that's just a small-sample fluke. Since 1988 is 97–15 as a base stealer.

YEAR	TEAM/LEVEL	G	AB	R	H	2B	3B	HR	RBI	BB	SB	AVG	OBP	SLG
1991	Seattle	66	177	35	54	6	2	6	23	10	16	.305	.347	.463
1992	Seattle	108	294	42	76	11	1	5	27	14	23	.259	.294	.354
1993	Projected	91	235	31	61	9	1	4	22	13	16	.260	.298	.357
		150	411	49	98	16	0	4	31	18	30	.238	.272	.307

CHRIS CRON
Chicago White Sox
First Baseman
$2

A 29-year-old veteran of more than a thousand minor league games. His walk frequency almost doubled last year, the raw total jumping from 47 to 94 in just a few more at bats. It must have been something he was working on. As a major leaguer he's a .250-range hitter with a little power, not enough to keep a first baseman in the league. Grade D prospect.

YEAR	TEAM/LEVEL	G	AB	R	H	2B	3B	HR	RBI	BB	SB	AVG	OBP	SLG
1991	Edmonton AAA	123	461	74	134	21	1	22	91	47	6	.291	.361	.484
1992	Vancouver AAA	141	500	76	139	29	0	16	81	94	12	.278	.407	.432
1992	MLE	141	482	60	121	24	0	13	64	75	8	.251	.352	.382

CHAD CURTIS
California Angels
Right Fielder
$35

He could develop into a very good player. He's young (24), and has diverse skills reflected in his secondary average, as a rookie, of .328. He's a good outfielder and a good baserunner, but then, so was Dante Bichette; that only goes so far. Curtis will either regress this year, like Milt Cuyler (below) and Brian McRae, or become a quality player. I'm betting on the latter.

YEAR	TEAM/LEVEL	G	AB	R	H	2B	3B	HR	RBI	BB	SB	AVG	OBP	SLG
1991	MLE	115	405	58	110	21	3	7	44	36	26	.272	.331	.390
1992	California	139	441	59	114	16	2	10	46	51	43	.259	.341	.372
1993	Projected	154	543	71	142	22	2	11	57	55	45	.262	.329	.370

MILT CUYLER
Detroit Tigers

Center Fielder

$22

If you look up "sophomore slump" in the dictionary, there's a picture . . . Cuyler went on the disabled list July 25 with tendinitis in his right knee, ending a miserable season. His stolen base total went from 41 to 8, and maybe the knee is responsible for that, but his strikeout/walk ratio went from 92/52 to 62/10, and that doesn't fit. He should bounce back.

YEAR	TEAM/LEVEL	G	AB	R	H	2B	3B	HR	RBI	BB	SB	AVG	OBP	SLG
1991	Detroit	154	475	77	122	15	7	3	33	52	41	.257	.335	.337
1992	Detroit	89	291	39	70	11	1	3	28	10	8	.241	.275	.316
1993	Projected	127	426	67	107	12	2	5	39	43	32	.251	.320	.338
		24	107	1	18	7	0	3	23	0	0	.168	.168	.290

KAL DANIELS
Chicago Cubs (Released)

Left Fielder

$7

He reminds me of Rico Carty about 1973, when Rico's ability seemed to have been drained by knee problems. Daniels's career is undergoing an extremely difficult transition, but I suspect that there is still considerable hitting ability buried beneath the muck and injuries. As a rule, if you can hit you can hit. Daniels isn't hitting, but I suspect that he still can.

YEAR	TEAM/LEVEL	G	AB	R	H	2B	3B	HR	RBI	BB	SB	AVG	OBP	SLG
1991	Los Angeles	137	461	54	115	15	1	17	73	63	6	.249	.337	.397
1992	Two Teams	83	212	21	51	11	0	6	25	22	0	.241	.315	.377
1993	Projected	82	249	36	66	14	1	10	42	36	2	.265	.358	.450

DOUG DASCENZO
Chicago Cubs

Center Fielder

$13

See "Henry Cotto". A likeable reserve outfielder, but he has no power and doesn't get on base enough or steal bases effectively enough to help the team as a leadoff man . . . had an excellent year as a pinch hitter, 9-for-20, but when you have to send a Doug Dascenzo to the plate 400 times in a year, you're going to lose a lot of runs.

YEAR	TEAM/LEVEL	G	AB	R	H	2B	3B	HR	RBI	BB	SB	AVG	OBP	SLG
1991	Chicago	118	239	40	61	11	0	1	18	24	14	.255	.327	.314
1992	Chicago	139	376	37	96	13	4	0	20	27	6	.255	.304	.311
1993	Projected	123	281	34	69	13	2	2	23	25	11	.246	.307	.327
		160	513	34	131	15	8	6	22	30	0	.255	.297	.316

JACK DAUGHERTY
Texas Rangers

Alleged Outfielder

$2

It takes a long time for stats to even out, a dozen times longer than people think it does. Daugherty hit .300 in '89 and '90, has hit around .200 the last two years. He's been a .260 hitter all along . . . so he's a .260-hitting first baseman with no power, no speed, a brutal outfielder. Who the hell needs a guy like that?

YEAR	TEAM/LEVEL	G	AB	R	H	2B	3B	HR	RBI	BB	SB	AVG	OBP	SLG
1990	Texas	125	310	36	93	20	2	6	47	22	0	.300	.347	.435
1991	Texas	58	144	8	28	3	2	1	11	16	1	.194	.270	.264
1992	Texas	59	127	13	26	9	0	0	9	16	2	.205	.295	.276

DARREN DAULTON
Philadelphia Phillies
Catcher
$55

I think we'd be hard-pressed to find any historical precedent for Daulton's amazing season (Stan Lopata?), even more hard-pressed than we would be for Pendleton's emergence a year earlier. Weight training gets a lot of bad press in baseball, but I think weight training primarily has made possible these late-in-life developments . . . I would not *expect* him to be an MVP candidate again in 1993.

YEAR	TEAM/LEVEL	G	AB	R	H	2B	3B	HR	RBI	BB	SB	AVG	OBP	SLG
1991	Philadelphia	89	285	36	56	12	0	12	42	41	5	.196	.297	.365
1992	Philadelphia	145	485	80	131	32	5	27	109	88	11	.270	.385	.524
1993	Projected	142	473	62	111	21	1	17	70	78	8	.235	.343	.391

ALVIN DAVIS
Kintetsu Buffaloes
First Baseman
No Value

My belief is that a young player who has old player's skills has little room to develop. Alvin Davis came to the majors with an old player's skills, drawing lots of walks and hitting for power, but slow as the devil and with no defensive value. You can't *develop* those things, so he never got any better than his rookie season. He was 33 when he was 23.

YEAR	TEAM/LEVEL	G	AB	R	H	2B	3B	HR	RBI	BB	SB	AVG	OBP	SLG
1990	Seattle	140	494	63	140	21	0	17	68	85	0	.283	.387	.429
1991	Seattle	145	462	39	102	15	1	12	69	56	0	.221	.299	.335
1992	California	40	104	5	26	8	0	0	16	13	0	.250	.331	.327

CHILI DAVIS
Minnesota Twins(Free Agent)
Designated Hitter
$30

His home runs dropped from 29 to 12, but he remained one of the better DHs in the league. His .386 on-base percentage (1992) makes him valuable despite his weaknesses . . . has been essentially a line drive/ground ball hitter most of his career. For some reason he was able to get the ball in the air consistently in '91, but returned to form last year.

YEAR	TEAM/LEVEL	G	AB	R	H	2B	3B	HR	RBI	BB	SB	AVG	OBP	SLG
1991	Minnesota	153	534	84	148	34	1	29	93	95	1	.277	.385	.507
1992	Minnesota	138	444	63	128	27	2	12	66	73	4	.288	.386	.439
1993	Projected	136	464	63	118	23	2	15	65	78	4	.254	.362	.409
		123	354	42	108	20	3	0	39	51	7	.305	.373	.378

DOUG DAVIS
Texas Rangers
Catcher
No Value

Basically a minor league Jamie Quirk, has been in the minors for many years, never playing regularly and never hitting much even in the minor leagues. He got into six games with the Angels a few years ago and one with Texas last year, but I would be surprised if he were ever to see a major league roster again, except maybe as a coach.

YEAR	TEAM/LEVEL	G	AB	R	H	2B	3B	HR	RBI	BB	SB	AVG	OBP	SLG
1992	Tulsa AA	14	39	3	8	2	0	0	1	3	0	.205	.262	.256
1992	Oklahoma City AAA	61	194	20	36	10	0	4	25	22	0	.186	.276	.299
1992	Texas	1	1	0	1	0	0	0	0	0	0	1000	1000	1000

ERIC DAVIS
Los Angeles Dodgers

Left Fielder

$25

He'll be 31 in May, and it's hard to imagine his health record *improving* in his thirties. His 1991 collection of injuries included a herniated disc in his neck, a strained left shoulder, a sore wrist after being hit by a pitch, and a season-ending portfolio of wrist, shoulder, and hand surgery. Still a tremendous base stealer when healthy; still has as many strikeouts as hits.

YEAR	TEAM/LEVEL	G	AB	R	H	2B	3B	HR	RBI	BB	SB	AVG	OBP	SLG
1991	Cincinnati	89	285	39	67	10	0	11	33	48	14	.235	.353	.386
1992	Los Angeles	76	267	21	61	8	1	5	32	36	19	.228	.325	.322
1993	Projected	90	294	42	74	12	1	13	47	43	15	.252	.347	.432
		63	249	3	55	6	2	0	31	24	24	.221	.289	.261

GLENN DAVIS
Baltimore Orioles

First Baseman/Designated Hitter

$26

A hot streak in July gave him respectable stats, but then he hit .232 with two homers in 26 games in August, only 2 homers in 24 games in September, so he was about back where he started. At 32 it is certainly not impossible for him to launch a strong comeback, but I doubt that the odds in favor of it are greater than 30 percent.

YEAR	TEAM/LEVEL	G	AB	R	H	2B	3B	HR	RBI	BB	SB	AVG	OBP	SLG
1991	Baltimore	49	176	29	40	9	1	10	28	16	4	.227	.307	.460
1992	Baltimore	106	398	46	110	15	2	13	48	37	1	.276	.338	.422
1993	Projected	95	328	41	82	16	1	14	49	35	4	.250	.322	.433

RUSS DAVIS
New York Yankees

Third Baseman

$4

A low-round draft pick in 1988, struggled at plate until last year but kept himself in baseball with glove work and occasional flashes of power. Last year he made a great leap forward in his second year at Double-A, increasing his batting average 68 points and almost tripling his home runs. A Rookie of the Year candidate in 1994, not 1993, if he gets a shot.

YEAR	TEAM/LEVEL	G	AB	R	H	2B	3B	HR	RBI	BB	SB	AVG	OBP	SLG
1991	Albany AA	135	473	57	103	23	3	8	58	50	3	.218	.296	.330
1992	Albany AA	132	492	77	140	23	4	22	71	49	3	.285	.354	.482
1992	MLE	132	473	63	122	20	2	17	58	34	2	.258	.308	.416

ANDRE DAWSON
Chicago Cubs

Right Fielder

$33

If he is playing in another park his batting average will probably drop about 20 points, more or less depending on which park. Has multi-year record of hitting his best in the cooler months (April, May, and September); has not hit well in the heat of the summer in at least four years, making me wonder how well he might play in Florida if he does sign there.

YEAR	TEAM/LEVEL	G	AB	R	H	2B	3B	HR	RBI	BB	SB	AVG	OBP	SLG
1991	Chicago	149	563	69	153	21	4	31	104	22	4	.272	.302	.488
1992	Chicago	143	542	60	150	27	2	22	90	30	6	.277	.316	.456
1993	Projected	131	484	53	130	23	3	18	78	28	7	.269	.309	.440
		137	521	57	147	33	0	13	76	38	8	.282	.331	.420

STEVE DECKER
San Francisco Giants
Catcher
$8

Spent the summer at Phoenix, trying to overcome the career crisis precipitated by his struggles in 1991, when I and Roger Craig both predicted he would be NL Rookie of the Year. He was unimpressive at Phoenix, hitting .282 (but that's the PCL; anything below .300 is poor), hitting only 8 home runs. Will have good years, but future is hazy after two straight off years.

YEAR	TEAM/LEVEL	G	AB	R	H	2B	3B	HR	RBI	BB	SB	AVG	OBP	SLG
1991	San Francisco	79	233	16	48	7	1	5	24	16	0	.206	.262	.309
1992	Phoenix AAA	125	450	50	127	22	2	8	74	47	2	.282	.348	.393
1992	MLE	125	422	32	99	17	1	5	48	29	1	.235	.284	.315

ROB DEER
Detroit Tigers
Right Fielder
$30

Fifth player to hit 30 homers with less than 400 at bats, the others being Mantle, Aaron, Schmidt, and Rudy York . . . tied the record for fewest RBI by a player with 30 or more homers, 64, by Felix Mantilla . . . first player to have 30 homers with less than 100 runs produced (Runs + RBI - Home Runs) . . . in his career has struck out 32 percent more frequently than Dave Kingman.

YEAR	TEAM/LEVEL	G	AB	R	H	2B	3B	HR	RBI	BB	SB	AVG	OBP	SLG
1991	Detroit	134	448	64	80	14	2	25	64	89	1	.179	.314	.386
1992	Detroit	110	393	66	97	20	1	32	64	51	4	.247	.337	.547
1993	Projected	131	439	62	94	17	1	25	64	71	3	.214	.324	.428
		86	338	68	114	26	0	39	64	18	7	.337	.371	.760

REX DELANUEZ
Minnesota Twins
Outfielder
$2

Is listed here because I like to look for young players with good secondary skills. Delanuez is a 25-year-old outfielder who played Double-A last year and isn't regarded as a real prospect by anyone, but he has had secondary averages over .350 at every minor league stop. Has some power, walks a lot, and has stolen bases. Grade D prospect.

YEAR	TEAM/LEVEL	G	AB	R	H	2B	3B	HR	RBI	BB	SB	AVG	OBP	SLG
1991	Visalia A	111	406	78	125	23	2	11	65	84	39	.308	.433	.456
1992	Orlando AA	132	437	71	117	34	2	12	59	69	13	.268	.375	.437
1992	MLE	132	432	62	112	35	2	10	51	52	9	.259	.339	.419
		132	427	53	107	36	2	8	43	35	5	.251	.307	.400

JUAN DE LA ROSA
Toronto Blue Jays
Outfielder
$8

Highly touted. A graceful center fielder, outstanding arm, had never looked like a major league hitter until '92, when he hit .329 with power at Knoxville. Knoxville's a tough park, and you don't usually hit at Knoxville unless you can hit, but otherwise I'm skeptical of him. His multi-year hitting record is terrible, and his strikeout/walk ratio was terrible last year. He's 25 years old; Grade C prospect.

YEAR	TEAM/LEVEL	G	AB	R	H	2B	3B	HR	RBI	BB	SB	AVG	OBP	SLG
1991	Knoxville AA	122	382	37	82	11	1	4	33	17	17	.215	.252	.280
1992	Knoxville AA	136	508	68	167	32	12	12	53	15	16	.329	.353	.510
1992	MLE	136	499	61	158	30	9	11	47	11	12	.317	.331	.479
		136	490	54	149	28	6	10	41	7	8	.304	.314	.447

CARLOS DELGADO
Toronto Blue Jays
Catcher
$39

The best hitting prospect in the minor leagues, spent all year at Dunedin. He hit 30 home runs in the Florida State League, which is roughly equivalent to 108 at High Desert. Twenty years old, has already played more minor league games (364) than most of the outstanding catchers in baseball history . . . unlimited offensive potential; has major league arm but overall defense is a question mark. **Grade A prospect.**

YEAR	TEAM/LEVEL	G	AB	R	H	2B	3B	HR	RBI	BB	SB	AVG	OBP	SLG
1990	St. Catharines A	67	226	29	64	13	0	6	39	35	2	.283	.385	.420
1991	Myrtle Beach A	132	441	72	126	18	2	18	71	74	9	.286	.395	.458
1992	Dunedin A	133	485	83	157	30	2	30	100	59	2	.324	.402	.579
		134	529	94	188	42	2	42	129	44	0	.355	.405	.680

RICK DEMPSEY
Baltimore Orioles
Catcher
No Value

The last man cut by the Orioles in spring training, was kept as a coach and activated to back up Tackett while Hoiles was out with an injury. Among the top characters in the game in the last generation, has entertained fans and teammates with staged antics for 20 years. In another time, he'd have become the new Nick Altrock or Al Schacht.

YEAR	TEAM/LEVEL	G	AB	R	H	2B	3B	HR	RBI	BB	SB	AVG	OBP	SLG
1990	Los Angeles	62	128	13	25	5	0	2	15	23	1	.195	.318	.281
1991	Milwaukee	60	147	15	34	5	0	4	21	23	0	.231	.329	.347
1992	Baltimore	8	9	2	1	1	0	0	0	2	0	.111	.273	.111

DELINO DeSHIELDS
Montreal Expos
Second Baseman
$66

One of four young second basemen today who has Hall of Fame ability, DeShields has avoided major injuries so far and made steady progress as a hitter. Exceptional athlete and said to be extremely intelligent. His 1992 ratio of double plays to errors (71–15) was substantial improvement from 1991. Still very young (24 in January), and like many young players he loses a step late in the season.

YEAR	TEAM/LEVEL	G	AB	R	H	2B	3B	HR	RBI	BB	SB	AVG	OBP	SLG
1991	Montreal	151	563	83	134	15	4	10	51	95	56	.238	.347	.332
1992	Montreal	135	530	82	155	19	8	7	56	54	46	.292	.359	.398
1993	Projected	146	557	84	154	21	6	8	56	79	54	.276	.366	.379
		189	497	81	176	23	12	4	61	11	36	.354	.368	.47

MIKE DEVEREAUX
Baltimore Orioles
Center Fielder
$53

The Andy Van Slyke of the American League. He's been a sort of "sustained surprise" in the major leagues, playing vastly better defense than he was expected to, surprising some people by establishing himself as a major league hitter, then playing at a better level in 1991 and a better one yet in 1992 . . . with bases loaded went 13-for-24 with 38 RBI, 1.000 slugging percentage.

YEAR	TEAM/LEVEL	G	AB	R	H	2B	3B	HR	RBI	BB	SB	AVG	OBP	SLG
1991	Baltimore	149	608	82	158	27	10	19	59	47	13	.260	.313	.431
1992	Baltimore	156	653	76	180	29	11	24	107	44	10	.276	.321	.464
1993	Projected	156	614	76	158	25	5	18	76	47	8	.257	.310	.402

ALEX DIAZ
Milwaukee Brewers
Pinch Runner
$1

Minor league center fielder, called up by the Brewers in mid-summer to pinch run and save an occasional inning on Robin's legs. Not a major league hitter; only 25 but has been in the Mets and Expos systems. Switch hitter; he might get some playing time if it turns out he can hit a little from one side or the other. No prospect.

YEAR	TEAM/LEVEL	G	AB	R	H	2B	3B	HR	RBI	BB	SB	AVG	OBP	SLG
1992	Denver AAA	106	455	67	122	17	4	1	41	24	42	.268	.309	.330
1992	MLE	106	433	49	100	14	2	0	30	17	31	.231	.260	.273
1992	Milwaukee	22	9	5	1	0	0	0	1	0	3	.111	.111	.111

MARIO DIAZ
Texas Rangers
Shortstop
$1

Thirty-one-year-old veteran, spent most of the year at Oklahoma City. A somewhat unusual player. He's a shortstop, and a better hitter than your typical reserve infielder. He is not error-prone at shortstop, but plays short with a stiff back, which a lot of people think affects his range. The Rangers were desperate and they still wouldn't use him. Almost never walks.

YEAR	TEAM/LEVEL	G	AB	R	H	2B	3B	HR	RBI	BB	SB	AVG	OBP	SLG
1991	Two Teams AAA	61	219	32	70	15	0	3	31	2	2	.320	.326	.429
1992	MLE	61	208	23	59	12	0	2	22	1	0	.284	.287	.370
1992	Texas	19	31	2	7	1	0	0	1	1	0	.226	.250	.258

GARY DISARCINA
California Angels
Shortstop
$22

He had the kind of year which enables you to keep your job to see if maybe you'll play better. I suspect he might; his 1991 season at Edmonton was better than this level, although his 1990 season was worse. He wasn't obviously overmatched at the end of the '92 season. Played more innings at shortstop than anyone in the league except Ripken, defense was good.

YEAR	TEAM/LEVEL	G	AB	R	H	2B	3B	HR	RBI	BB	SB	AVG	OBP	SLG
1991	California	18	57	5	12	2	0	0	3	3	0	.211	.274	.246
1992	California	157	518	48	128	19	0	3	42	20	9	.247	.283	.301
1993	Projected	142	478	47	118	15	1	3	39	22	8	.247	.280	.301

BENNY DISTEFANO
Houston Astros
Outfielder/Pinch Hitter
$8

A one-time prospect in the Pirates system, went through the minors quickly (1982–1984) but career stalled after he hit .167 in 45 games in '84. He's been up and down ever since, also spent one year in Japan, where he hit .215 for the Chunichi Dragons. He's now 31, and not the worst player in the National League. Ratio of power to strikeouts is good.

YEAR	TEAM/LEVEL	G	AB	R	H	2B	3B	HR	RBI	BB	SB	AVG	OBP	SLG
1991	Rochester AAA	124	427	52	114	23	2	18	83	41	5	.267	.335	.457
1991	MLE	124	412	40	99	20	1	14	64	31	3	.240	.293	.396
1992	Houston	52	60	4	14	0	2	0	7	5	0	.233	.303	.300

CHRIS DONNELS
New York Mets
Third Baseman
$9

Eddie Yost–type player; I've always liked him. He got a chance to play in August, when the Mets were preoccupied with their autopsy, and didn't play well. He isn't the kind of player who gets many chances, but I suspect that the Mets would do well to put him at third base and give him time to get his feet on the ground. No star potential.

YEAR	TEAM/LEVEL	G	AB	R	H	2B	3B	HR	RBI	BB	SB	AVG	OBP	SLG
1992	Tidewater AAA	81	279	35	84	15	3	5	32	58	12	.301	.419	.430
1992	MLE	81	267	27	72	12	2	3	24	45	8	.270	.375	.363
1992	New York	45	121	8	21	4	0	0	6	17	1	.174	.275	.207

BILLY DORAN
Cincinnati Reds
Second Baseman
$16

He's in a battle to save his career after hitting .235 at age 34, although his .289 secondary average remains very good. Back problems have reduced his range in the field and his arm never was notable, but a second baseman needs to make good decisions in the middle of the field, and he does. Outstanding strikeout/walk ratio. Probably will not have a regular job by this August.

YEAR	TEAM/LEVEL	G	AB	R	H	2B	3B	HR	RBI	BB	SB	AVG	OBP	SLG
1991	Cincinnati	111	361	51	101	12	2	6	35	46	5	.280	.359	.374
1992	Cincinnati	132	387	48	91	16	2	8	47	64	7	.235	.342	.349
1993	Projected	123	376	49	96	18	2	6	36	63	11	.255	.362	.362
		153	413	45	81	20	2	10	59	82	9	.196	.329	.327

BRIAN DOWNING
Texas Rangers (Retired)
Designated Hitter
No Value

He called it quits in early October, bringing one of the more remarkable careers of our time to a conclusion. You've heard of the worm who went into his cocoon and emerged as a hornet? That's Brian. What he became not only is not what he started out as, it's also not *a natural outgrowth* of what he started out as. He surprised us all, and I'll miss him.

YEAR	TEAM/LEVEL	G	AB	R	H	2B	3B	HR	RBI	BB	SB	AVG	OBP	SLG
1990	California	96	330	47	90	18	2	14	51	50	0	.283	.354	.414
1991	Texas	123	407	76	113	17	2	17	49	58	1	.278	.377	.455
1992	Texas	107	320	53	89	18	0	10	39	62	1	.278	.407	.428
		91	233	30	65	19	0	3	29	66	1	.279	.438	.399

D. J. DOZIER
San Diego Padres
Outfielder
$4

He's 27 years old, could have been a good major league player if he had turned his attention to it about seven years earlier. It's hard to evaluate him now, since he has unusual athletic ability and little enough playing time that he may have more growth ahead than a typical player at the same age. Posted .234 batting average but .396 secondary average at Tidewater. Grade C prospect.

YEAR	TEAM/LEVEL	G	AB	R	H	2B	3B	HR	RBI	BB	SB	AVG	OBP	SLG
1991	Tidewater AAA	43	171	19	46	7	5	1	22	13	8	.269	.332	.386
1992	Tidewater AAA	64	197	32	46	8	3	7	25	37	6	.234	.357	.411
1992	New York	25	47	4	9	2	0	0	2	4	4	.191	.264	.234

ROB DUCEY
California Angels
Outfielder
$9

At one time I liked him a lot, but five years of trying to find a major league job have certainly taken the luster off of his future. Strikes out much more now than he did several years ago, while hitting for less power. Runs "well", but not well enough to steal 40 bases or anything. Nineteen ninety-three may be his last chance.

YEAR	TEAM/LEVEL	G	AB	R	H	2B	3B	HR	RBI	BB	SB	AVG	OBP	SLG
1990	Toronto	19	53	7	53	5	0	0	7	7	1	.302	.387	.396
1991	Toronto	39	68	8	16	2	2	1	4	6	2	.235	.297	.368
1992	Two Teams	54	80	7	15	4	0	0	2	5	2	.188	.233	.238
		69	*92*	*6*	*14*	*6*	*0*	*0*	*0*	*4*	*2*	*.152*	*.188*	*.217*

MARIANO DUNCAN
Philadelphia Phillies
Left Fielder/Second Baseman/Shortstop
$24

He had 40 doubles last year and 17 walks, about as strange a combination of those two as you will ever see. Duncan's ability to play several positions, his ability to smash a left-handed pitcher and his exceptional base stealing would make him one of the most valuable bench players in baseball. As a regular, his inconsistency and low on-base percentage are major detriments.

YEAR	TEAM/LEVEL	G	AB	R	H	2B	3B	HR	RBI	BB	SB	AVG	OBP	SLG
1991	Cincinnati	100	333	46	86	7	4	12	40	12	5	.258	.288	.411
1992	Philadelphia	142	574	74	153	40	3	8	50	17	23	.267	.292	.389
1993	Projected	123	444	56	115	18	4	9	44	18	14	.259	.288	.378

SHAWON DUNSTON
Chicago Cubs
Shortstop
$27

Season was ended May 5 by a herniated disc in his back; had surgery and is expected back in '93. No one took strong advantage of the opportunity created by his absence, so the job is still waiting for him, and I would expect him back at full speed. His throwing arm, power, speed, and .265 batting average make him above-average regular despite offensive and defensive inconsistency.

YEAR	TEAM/LEVEL	G	AB	R	H	2B	3B	HR	RBI	BB	SB	AVG	OBP	SLG
1991	Chicago	142	492	59	128	22	7	12	50	23	21	.260	.292	.407
1992	Chicago	18	73	8	23	3	1	0	2	3	2	.315	.342	.384
1993	Projected	148	522	65	136	25	5	12	56	20	22	.261	.288	.397

LENNY DYKSTRA
Philadelphia Phillies
Center Fielder
$36

He'd be a perennial All-Star if he could stay healthy, but then you could say the same thing about a hundred other guys. The Pete Reiser of our era, he plays with reckless abandon and has the scars to prove it; missed time in '92 with a hairline fracture of his right wrist, a strained hamstring, and a broken left hand. He turns 30 in February.

YEAR	TEAM/LEVEL	G	AB	R	H	2B	3B	HR	RBI	BB	SB	AVG	OBP	SLG
1991	Philadelphia	63	246	48	73	13	5	3	12	37	24	.297	.391	.427
1992	Philadelphia	85	345	53	104	18	0	6	39	40	30	.301	.375	.406
1993	Projected	99	385	65	112	20	3	6	36	57	28	.291	.382	.405
		107	*444*	*58*	*137*	*23*	*0*	*9*	*66*	*43*	*36*	*.309*	*.370*	*.421*

DAMION EASLEY
California Angels
Third Baseman
$7

An Angel "prospect" in the tradition of Lee Stevens, John Orton, and Dante Bichette. He played shortstop in the minors, but was pushed to third by the emergence of DiSarcina and the submergence of Gaetti. I frankly don't believe that he will hit enough to help the team as a third baseman, but then, neither does Gaetti, and Easley at least is young enough to surprise.

YEAR	TEAM/LEVEL	G	AB	R	H	2B	3B	HR	RBI	BB	SB	AVG	OBP	SLG
1992	Edmonton AAA	108	429	61	124	18	3	3	44	31	26	.289	.340	.366
1992	MLE	108	396	36	91	12	1	1	26	18	13	.230	.263	.273
1992	California	47	151	14	39	5	0	1	12	8	9	.258	.307	.311

JIM EISENREICH
Kansas City Royals
Utility Outfielder
$11

There's probably one guy like this in every town, who is adopted by the call-in shows as someone who should be a regular. Any time he gets two hits in a week the talk shows are bombarded by questions about why he doesn't play regularly . . . singles hitter, good defensive player within the limits of his ability, which includes average speed and poor arm.

YEAR	TEAM/LEVEL	G	AB	R	H	2B	3B	HR	RBI	BB	SB	AVG	OBP	SLG
1991	Kansas City	135	375	47	113	22	3	2	47	20	5	.301	.333	.392
1992	Kansas City	113	353	31	95	13	3	2	28	24	11	.269	.313	.340
1993	Projected	106	322	35	88	18	2	3	32	23	7	.273	.322	.370
		91	331	15	77	4	3	2	9	28	17	.232	.292	.281

KEVIN ELSTER
New York Mets
Shortstop
$6

Lost his season to surgery on right shoulder, April 15. Sometimes now a player will come back from injury stronger than he was, because of his rehabilitation program. Unless that happens, Elster's career may end quickly. He's a .225 hitter without speed and without *real* power. A player like that tends to play only until it is clear that he isn't going to improve.

YEAR	TEAM/LEVEL	G	AB	R	H	2B	3B	HR	RBI	BB	SB	AVG	OBP	SLG
1991	New York	115	348	84	84	16	2	6	36	40	2	.244	.318	.351
1992	New York	6	18	4	4	0	0	0	0	0	0	.222	.222	.222
1993	Projected	88	210	22	47	12	1	5	24	23	1	.224	.300	.362

ALVARO ESPINOZA
Cleveland Indians
Shortstop
$3

After three seasons as the Yankees' regular shortstop, during which he scored as many as 51 runs, he spent the season at Colorado Springs (Triple-A affiliate), where he had his best minor league numbers ever. His talents were always stretched to be a regular, but at 30 and with expansion coming, he should have several more seasons as a major league backup infielder.

YEAR	TEAM/LEVEL	G	AB	R	H	2B	3B	HR	RBI	BB	SB	AVG	OBP	SLG
1991	New York	148	480	51	123	23	2	5	33	16	4	.256	.282	.344
1992	Colorado Sp AA	122	483	64	145	36	6	9	79	21	2	.300	.333	.455
1992	MLE	122	457	41	119	30	3	6	51	13	1	.260	.281	.379
		122	421	18	93	24	0	3	23	5	0	.221	.239	.285

CECIL ESPY
Pittsburgh Pirates
Right Fielder
$9

A quasi-regular for the Rangers in '88 and '89, was playing quite a bit for the Pirates until they acquired Alex Cole. Hit the pines then, but continued to work as pinch hitter, pinch runner, defensive sub in the outfield. That's the right role for him . . . originally drafted by White Sox in 1980, played for Dodgers in 1983, and has played more than a thousand minor league games.

YEAR	TEAM/LEVEL	G	AB	R	H	2B	3B	HR	RBI	BB	SB	AVG	OBP	SLG
1991	Pittsburgh	43	82	7	20	4	0	1	11	5	4	.244	.281	.329
1992	Pittsburgh	112	194	21	50	7	3	1	20	15	6	.258	.310	.340
1993	Projected	87	176	22	43	9	3	1	17	15	8	.244	.304	.347

PAUL FARIES
San Diego Padres
Infielder
$8

Right-handed leadoff type, has good on-base percentage and SB totals in the minors. Has played second, third, and short; best chance to play in San Diego is second, but sprained his ankle in '91 when he had a chance, spent '92 back at Vegas waiting for Stillwell to keel over. I think he could be a pretty decent regular second baseman, but I like Gardner better.

YEAR	TEAM/LEVEL	G	AB	R	H	2B	3B	HR	RBI	BB	SB	AVG	OBP	SLG
1991	San Diego	27	130	13	23	3	1	0	7	14		.177	.262	.215
1992	Las Vegas AAA	125	457	77	134	15	6	1	40	40		.293	.353	.359
1992	MLE	125	424	47	101	11	2	0	24	24		.238	.279	.274
		125	*391*	*17*	*68*	*7*	*0*	*0*	*8*	*8*		*.174*	*.190*	*.192*

MONTY FARISS
Texas Rangers
Outfielder/Infielder
$9

Trying to find a spot. Was a middle infielder in the minors, hits very well for a middle infielder but couldn't handle the defensive responsibilities. He's trying to crash the party now as an outfielder, but will have to hit significantly more to do that. I like him as a left fielder, but the Rangers have several people who could play left, including Juan Gonzalez. Grade C prospect.

YEAR	TEAM/LEVEL	G	AB	R	H	2B	3B	HR	RBI	BB	SB	AVG	OBP	SLG
1991	Oklahoma City AAA	137	494	84	134	31	9	13	73	91	4	.271	.383	.449
1992	Oklahoma City AAA	49	187	28	56	13	3	9	38	31	5	.299	.397	.449
1992	Texas	67	166	13	36	7	1	3	21	17	0	.217	.297	.325
		85	*145*	*0*	*16*	*1*	*0*	*6*	*4*	*3*	*0*	*.110*	*.128*	*.117*

MIKE FELDER
San Francisco Giants
Outfielder
$16

Did a fine job as the Giants' fourth outfielder, hitting .286 with 14 stolen bases. Better yet, since the experiment with making him a regular has already failed several times, they may even keep him in his role this time . . . a switch hitter who actually hits about the same each way. Has always hit poorly in Candlestick. Should continue to play at the same level.

YEAR	TEAM/LEVEL	G	AB	R	H	2B	3B	HR	RBI	BB	SB	AVG	OBP	SLG
1991	San Francisco	132	348	51	92	10	6	0	18	30	21	.264	.325	.328
1992	San Francisco	145	322	44	92	13	3	4	23	21	14	.286	.330	.382
1993	Projected	136	331	47	85	9	4	3	26	28	20	.257	.315	.335
		158	*296*	*37*	*92*	*16*	*0*	*8*	*38*	*12*	*7*	*.31*	*.338*	*.446*

JUNIOR FELIX
California Angels
Center Fielder
$21

Started brilliantly, but at season's end he was giving hits back to the league. Regarded two years ago as a potential superstar, is within two months of playing himself out of a regular job. He has enough skills to be valuable coming off the bench, but don't know if he would accept the job . . . strikeout rate has gone up 20 percent in past two years, while power has dropped.

YEAR	TEAM/LEVEL	G	AB	R	H	2B	3B	HR	RBI	BB	SB	AVG	OBP	SLG
1991	California	66	230	32	65	10	2	2	26	11	7	.283	.321	.370
1992	California	139	509	63	125	22	5	9	72	33	8	.246	.289	.361
1993	Projected	119	425	60	112	18	5	9	56	33	11	.264	.317	.393

FELIX FERMIN
Cleveland Indians
Shortstop
$9

The prototype of the singles-hitting shortstop with no secondary offense who can make the routine plays at short. Alvaro Espinoza, Mario Diaz, Rafael Bournigal, and Alex Arias are all very similar players. There are more just like them in the minors . . . career on-base and slugging averages are very close to .300 . . . reportedly was the Indians' highest-paid player in '92.

YEAR	TEAM/LEVEL	G	AB	R	H	2B	3B	HR	RBI	BB	SB	AVG	OBP	SLG
1990	Cleveland	148	414	47	106	13	2	1	40	26	3	.256	.297	.304
1991	Cleveland	129	424	30	111	13	2	0	31	26	5	.262	.307	.302
1992	Cleveland	79	58	27	58	7	2	0	13	18	0	.270	.326	.321

TONY FERNANDEZ
New York Mets
Shortstop
$50

When two teams that have had him decide that he's not worth the trouble, we probably should pay attention to that, but on the other hand he does play 150 games a year, hit better than a typical shortstop, and make some outstanding plays at short. Like Coleman, Bonilla, Murray, etc., probably won't hit as well with the Mets as he has with other teams.

YEAR	TEAM/LEVEL	G	AB	R	H	2B	3B	HR	RBI	BB	SB	AVG	OBP	SLG
1991	San Diego	145	558	81	152	27	5	4	38	55	23	.272	.337	.360
1992	San Diego	155	622	84	171	32	4	4	37	56	20	.275	.337	.359
1993	Projected	153	600	80	161	29	6	5	46	61	23	.268	.336	.362

CECIL FIELDER
Detroit Tigers
First Baseman
$66

In '90–'91 he made his numbers off of left-handed pitchers, hitting .335 against them with a .733 slugging percentage (.243/.489 against right-handers). Last year the Tigers didn't see very many left-handers, and Fielder didn't hit them at a comparable level . . . his 1992 ratio of RBI to hits (124 RBI on 145 hits) is among the 30 best of all time.

YEAR	TEAM/LEVEL	G	AB	R	H	2B	3B	HR	RBI	BB	SB	AVG	OBP	SLG
1991	Detroit	162	624	102	163	25	0	44	133	78	0	.261	.347	.513
1992	Detroit	155	594	80	145	22	0	35	124	73	0	.244	.325	.458
1993	Projected	159	596	94	152	21	1	41	121	84	0	.255	.347	.500

(handwritten:) 148 594 58 127 19 0 26 115 68 0 .215 .359 .401

BIEN FIGUEROA
St. Louis Cardinals
Infielder
$1

A 29-year-old shortstop, has been at Louisville since 1989, hitting .217, .240, and .204 until last year, when he hit .285 in 94 games. Was called up as a backup infielder when the major league team was killing second baseman, and was recalled in September, giving him the chance to hit a three-run double against the Cubs. No prospect, but could make an expansion roster.

YEAR	TEAM/LEVEL	G	AB	R	H	2B	3B	HR	RBI	BB	SB	AVG	OBP	SLG
1991	Louisville AAA	96	269	18	55	8	2	0	14	20	1	.204	.265	.249
1992	Louisville AAA	94	319	44	91	11	1	1	23	33	2	.285	.353	.335
1992	MLE	94	305	33	77	9	0	0	17	25	1	.252	.309	.282
		94	291	22	63	7	0	0	11	17	0	.216	.260	.24

STEVE FINLEY
Houston Astros
Center Fielder
$55

Has had two nearly identical seasons, which clearly establishes his level of ability. In that he's 28 and a couple of years away from free agency, I would expect him to stay at that level for the next few years. Made subtle improvements last year, improving his strikeout/walk ratio and his stolen base percentage. Played every game for the Astros. He's a quality player.

YEAR	TEAM/LEVEL	G	AB	R	H	2B	3B	HR	RBI	BB	SB	AVG	OBP	SLG
1991	Houston	159	596	84	170	28	10	8	54	42	34	.285	.331	.406
1992	Houston	162	607	84	177	29	13	5	55	58	44	.292	.355	.407
1993	Projected	161	580	73	160	23	7	6	51	48	37	.276	.331	.371

JOHN FINN
Milwaukee Brewers
Second Baseman/Utilityman
$1

Has been discussed as a prospect after hitting .276 at El Paso, but he's long odds. He's 25 years old, which is old for Double-A, and .276 at El Paso is like .230 in the majors. No power, a little speed. Was a 10th-round draft pick; will reach Triple-A but will start to look like a hundred other guys. Grade D prospect.

YEAR	TEAM/LEVEL	G	AB	R	H	2B	3B	HR	RBI	BB	SB	AVG	OBP	SLG
1991	A and AA	128	453	93	126	24	3	2	49	60	27	.278	.365	.358
1992	El Paso AA	124	439	83	121	12	6	1	47	71	30	.276	.380	.337
1992	MLE	124	412	55	94	9	3	0	31	40	19	.228	.296	.265
		124	385	27	67	6	0	0	15	9	8	.174	.197	.190

CARLTON FISK
Chicago White Sox
Catcher
$8

Missed the first two months of the season with an inflamed tendon and a bone spur in his right foot, shared playing time with Karkovice about 50/50 after returning on June 5. He didn't play badly and Karkovice didn't play tremendously well, so his status appears unchanged. He hasn't announced his retirement as of this writing . . . clearly now has Hall of Fame credentials.

YEAR	TEAM/LEVEL	G	AB	R	H	2B	3B	HR	RBI	BB	SB	AVG	OBP	SLG
1991	Chicago	134	460	42	111	25	0	18	74	32	1	.285	.378	.451
1992	Chicago	62	188	12	43	4	1	3	21	23	3	.229	.313	.309
1993	Projected	69	208	20	49	10	1	6	27	22	2	.236	.309	.380

MIKE FITZGERALD
California Angels
Catcher
$5

Lost playing time as the season progressed, but got some hits late to push his batting average off the interstate. He probably hits left-handers well enough to be a useful platoon player, but wasn't used that way by Wathan and Rodgers, who have a bunch of right-handed-hitting catchers, but no left-hander except Myers, who was hurt. Career is about over.

YEAR	TEAM/LEVEL	G	AB	R	H	2B	3B	HR	RBI	BB	SB	AVG	OBP	SLG
1990	Montreal	111	313	36	76	18	1	9	41	60	8	.243	.365	.393
1991	Montreal	71	198	17	40	5	2	4	28	22	4	.202	.278	.308
1992	California	95	189	19	40	2	0	6	17	22	2	.212	.294	.317
		119	180	21	40	0	0	8	16	22	2	.222	.307	.306

JOHN FLAHERTY
Boston Red Sox
Catcher
$4

He's 25 years old, has far less potential as a hitter than Eric Wedge. (The Red Sox media guide says that he once had a six-game hitting streak at New Britain.) Very slow, singles hitter, has reputation as good defensive catcher. If his defensive reputation holds up he will have a career as a backup catcher and get occasional shots at playing time. Grade D prospect.

YEAR	TEAM/LEVEL	G	AB	R	H	2B	3B	HR	RBI	BB	SB	AVG	OBP	SLG
1991	Pawtucket AAA	45	156	18	29	7	0	3	13	15	0	.186	.257	.288
1992	Pawtucket AAA	31	104	11	26	3	0	0	7	5	0	.250	.291	.279
1992	Boston	35	66	3	13	2	0	0	2	3	0	.197	.229	.227
		39	28	0	0	1	0	0	0	1	0	.000	.034	.000

DARRIN FLETCHER
Montreal Expos
Catcher
$14

The retirement of Carter and injury to Colbrunn give him a chance to be the number-one catcher. To this point his career average is .237, and while I don't think that represents his ability, it is certainly enough to make one question whether he can hold a regular job. His competition is Tim Laker, who needs at least a year of Triple-A, and Bob Natal.

YEAR	TEAM/LEVEL	G	AB	R	H	2B	3B	HR	RBI	BB	SB	AVG	OBP	SLG
1990	Two Teams	11	23	3	3	1	0	0	1	1	0	.130	.167	.174
1991	Philadelphia	46	136	5	31	8	0	1	12	5	0	.228	.255	.309
1992	Montreal	83	222	13	54	10	2	2	26	14	0	.243	.289	.333
		120	308	21	77	12	4	3	40	23	0	.250	.302	.344

SCOTT FLETCHER
Milwaukee Brewers
(Released)
Second Baseman
$17

He's 34 years old, came to the Milwaukee camp as a non-roster invitee and had his best season in years. He can still run, he's a fine second baseman, but looking ahead you have to anticipate that his performance will drop to his true level of ability, which isn't .275. Brewers didn't pick up his option, but he should be able to find a team after the expansion draft.

YEAR	TEAM/LEVEL	G	AB	R	H	2B	3B	HR	RBI	BB	SB	AVG	OBP	SLG
1991	Chicago	90	248	14	51	10	1	1	28	17	0	.206	.262	.266
1992	Milwaukee	123	386	53	106	18	3	3	51	30	17	.275	.335	.360
1993	Projected	124	384	40	95	17	2	3	46	32	6	.247	.305	.326
		156	524	92	161	26	5	5	74	43	34	.307	.360	.405

TOM FOLEY
Montreal Expos
(Released)
Utilityman
$6

Had been a reserve infielder in Montreal for six and a half years, which is very unusual. (How many guys can you name who stayed in one place six years as a backup?) His career there is apparently over due to the emergence of young infielders (Cordero, Barberie, Berry). He'll be looking for a job, I suppose, but he doesn't have a lot to sell.

YEAR	TEAM/LEVEL	G	AB	R	H	2B	3B	HR	RBI	BB	SB	AVG	OBP	SLG
1990	Montreal	73	164	11	35	2	1	0	12	12	0	.213	.266	.238
1991	Montreal	86	168	12	35	11	1	0	15	14	2	.208	.269	.286
1992	Montreal	72	115	7	20	3	1	0	5	8	3	.174	.230	.217
		58	*62*	*2*	*5*	*0*	*1*	*0*	*0*	*2*	*4*	*.081*	*.109*	*.113*

BROOK FORDYCE
New York Mets
Catcher
$9

Probably will be a late callup in 1993, and if all goes well may challenge Hundley for playing time in 1994. He was rated by *Baseball America* as the number-10 prospect in the Eastern League, and I suspect that he may be better than that. Only 22, has more offensive potential than Hundley and despite rep as suspect defensively threw out 39 percent of base stealers in the Eastern League.

YEAR	TEAM/LEVEL	G	AB	R	H	2B	3B	HR	RBI	BB	SB	AVG	OBP	SLG
1991	St. Lucie A	115	406	42	97	19	3	7	55	37	4	.239	.305	.352
1992	Binghamton AA	116	418	59	117	28	0	11	60	37	1	.280	.340	.426
1992	MLE	116	412	49	105	26	0	8	51	26	0	.255	.299	.376
		116	*406*	*39*	*93*	*24*	*0*	*5*	*42*	*15*	*2*	*.229*	*.257*	*.328*

ERIC (Flash) FOX
Oakland Athletics
Outfielder
$3

A 29-year-old switch hitter, had an unexpected opportunity due to a rash of injuries and played very well for a month. No prospect; probably has no future in the majors. Good baserunner (despite costly mistake in the ALCS) and good defensive outfielder, has stolen as many as 49 bases in the minors (Huntsville, 1989) but in the long run wouldn't hit enough to keep his playing time.

YEAR	TEAM/LEVEL	G	AB	R	H	2B	3B	HR	RBI	BB	SB	AVG	OBP	SLG
1992	AA and AAA	96	361	58	89	19	3	6	21	43	21	.247	.325	.366
1992	MLE	96	346	47	74	14	1	3	16	31	15	.214	.279	.286
1992	Oakland	51	143	24	34	5	2	3	13	13	3	.238	.299	.364

JULIO FRANCO
Texas Rangers
Second Baseman/Left Fielder
$28

On and off the DL because of bruised knee, finally had surgery in September. Because of his work habits I suspect that he will regain most of his ability, but Frye is a better defensive second baseman than Franco, and appears to have the second base job. That leaves left field as Franco's most natural position, and the Rangers have a phone book full of left fielders.

YEAR	TEAM/LEVEL	G	AB	R	H	2B	3B	HR	RBI	BB	SB	AVG	OBP	SLG
1991	Texas	146	589	108	201	27	3	15	78	65	36	.342	.408	.474
1992	Texas	35	107	19	25	7	0	2	8	15	1	.234	.328	.355
1993	Projected	120	470	76	136	21	2	8	52	61	24	.289	.371	.394

JEFF FRYE
Texas Rangers
Second Baseman
$30

Was called up after the All-Star break, and by season's end appeared to have the second base job firmly under control. I like him a lot. He's a Marty Barrett type, .260 to .280 hitter with no power, runs pretty well, has control of the strike zone, is smart, and works hard on defense. Should be a regular for five to six years and should help the team.

YEAR	TEAM/LEVEL	G	AB	R	H	2B	3B	HR	RBI	BB	SB	AVG	OBP	SLG
1992	Oklahoma City AAA	87	337	64	101	26	2	2	28	51	11	.300	.409	.407
1992	MLE	87	323	50	87	22	1	1	22	39	7	.269	.348	.353
1992	Texas	67	199	24	51	9	1	1	12	16	1	.256	.320	.327
		47	75	0	15	0	1	1	2	4	0	.200	.200	.267

TRAVIS FRYMAN
Detroit Tigers
Shortstop/Third Baseman
$71

He will be difficult to move off of shortstop, no matter what Trammell does. Trammell is 35. Fryman is 24, and a quality shortstop—so how can you move Fryman to accommodate Trammell? Two years of steady production clearly establish a level of ability, and at his age it could get a lot better . . . unquestionably has MVP-type ability . . . has always hit very poorly in Tiger Stadium.

YEAR	TEAM/LEVEL	G	AB	R	H	2B	3B	HR	RBI	BB	SB	AVG	OBP	SLG
1991	Detroit	149	557	65	144	36	3	21	91	40	12	.259	.309	.447
1992	Detroit	161	659	87	175	31	4	20	96	45	8	.266	.316	.416
1993	Projected	158	603	76	160	35	2	23	93	42	9	.265	.313	.444

GARY GAETTI
California Angels
Third/First Baseman/Ballast
$12

The Angels seem to be having some trouble grasping the fact that the man can't hit anymore. It's been four years now, and the situation is going from bad to pathetic. Last year he had a .267 on-base percentage, and 13 doubles in 456 at bats. This is weak production from a third baseman, and now he's at first. He's 34.

YEAR	TEAM/LEVEL	G	AB	R	H	2B	3B	HR	RBI	BB	SB	AVG	OBP	SLG
1991	California	152	586	58	144	22	1	18	66	33	5	.246	.293	.379
1992	California	130	456	41	103	13	2	12	48	21	3	.226	.267	.342
1993	Projected	113	409	41	97	19	1	12	52	23	3	.237	.278	.377
		108	326	24	62	4	3	6	30	9	1	.190	.212	.282

GREG GAGNE
Minnesota Twins
Shortstop
$27

Odd collection of abilities, and therefore difficult to project. Outstanding defensive shortstop, and has a little pop as a hitter, but chases the first pitch and when he gets behind in the count the at bat is pretty much over. Not fast but good baserunner until a year or two ago. At 31, my guess is he will lose his job within two years.

YEAR	TEAM/LEVEL	G	AB	R	H	2B	3B	HR	RBI	BB	SB	AVG	OBP	SLG
1991	Minnesota	139	408	52	108	23	3	8	42	26	11	.265	.310	.395
1992	Minnesota	146	439	53	108	23	0	7	39	19	6	.246	.280	.346
1993	Projected	138	400	45	98	22	3	7	39	23	9	.245	.286	.368
		153	470	54	108	23	0	6	36	12	1	.230	.269	.37

ANDRES GALARRAGA
St. Louis Cardinals
(Released)
First Baseman
$16

The basic problem is that he was never as good a hitter as his 1987–88 stats made people believe he was, and is forced now to adjust to and be happy with a different level of production . . . strikeout/walk ratio is ugly and degenerating, although he might (or might not) still capable of busting out with a 25-homer, 90-RBI season. Fine defensive first baseman.

YEAR	TEAM/LEVEL	G	AB	R	H	2B	3B	HR	RBI	BB	SB	AVG	OBP	SLG
1991	Montreal	107	375	34	82	13	2	9	33	23	5	.219	.268	.336
1992	St. Louis	95	325	38	79	14	2	10	39	11	5	.243	.282	.391
1993	Projected	87	292	32	73	16	1	9	38	17	4	.250	.291	.404
		83	205	42	76	15	2	11	45	0	5	.376	.376	.418

DAVE GALLAGHER
New York Mets
Utility Outfielder
$9

A player of common skills, a singles hitter and a good defensive outfielder who runs fairly well, but not *well*. A good "fundamental" player, as a consequence of spending several eons in the minor leagues. Now 32, his true level of ability is halfway between the .293 average of 1991 and the .240 mark of '92. Major league career will probably end within two years.

YEAR	TEAM/LEVEL	G	AB	R	H	2B	3B	HR	RBI	BB	SB	AVG	OBP	SLG
1991	California	90	270	32	79	17	0	1	30	24	2	.293	.355	.367
1992	New York	98	175	20	42	11	1	1	21	19	4	.240	.307	.331
1993	Projected	56	101	11	27	7	0	1	11	9	2	.267	.327	.366
		106	80	8	7	5	2	1	12	14	6	.088	.263	.238

MIKE GALLEGO
New York Yankees
Second Baseman/Shortstop
$13

Very much like Dave Gallagher, except that he's an infielder. Missed most of the season with a bruised heel and a fractured wrist, played well when he was in the lineup. His combination of defense and secondary offensive skills makes him valuable if he hits .240, but that's not automatic, and he's got to stay in the lineup. He's 32 (41 days younger than Gallagher).

YEAR	TEAM/LEVEL	G	AB	R	H	2B	3B	HR	RBI	BB	SB	AVG	OBP	SLG
1991	Oakland	159	482	67	119	15	4	12	49	67	6	.247	.343	.369
1992	New York	53	173	24	44	7	1	3	14	20	0	.254	.343	.358
1993	Projected	110	314	36	72	10	1	5	27	37	4	.229	.311	.315

RON GANT
Atlanta Braves
Left Fielder
$63

He had an off year only with respect to his own expectations; certainly nobody loses a job by hitting .259 with 17 homers, 80 RBI, and 32 stolen bases. He got messed up for a month in mid-summer, perhaps hiding an injury, and didn't get any hits for a while. He's only 28; he's going to have a lot more outstanding seasons before he stops hitting for good . . .

YEAR	TEAM/LEVEL	G	AB	R	H	2B	3B	HR	RBI	BB	SB	AVG	OBP	SLG
1991	Atlanta	154	561	101	141	35	3	32	105	67	34	.251	.338	.496
1992	Atlanta	153	544	74	141	22	6	17	80	45	32	.259	.321	.415
1993	Projected	156	568	94	150	29	5	26	87	59	35	.264	.333	.470
		152	527	47	141	9	9	2	55	31	30	.268	.308	.33

JIM GANTNER
Milwaukee Brewers
Second/Third Baseman
No Value

At this writing is expected to retire. He didn't really have a job at season's end. Of course, he's lost his job several times before and gotten it back, but he's 39, and as a rule, only superstars make it to age 39 . . . played his entire career with one team, which contrary to what you hear is actually more common now than it has ever been.

YEAR	TEAM/LEVEL	G	AB	R	H	2B	3B	HR	RBI	BB	SB	AVG	OBP	SLG
1990	Milwaukee	88	323	36	85	8	5	0	25	29	18	.263	.328	.319
1991	Milwaukee	140	526	63	149	27	4	2	47	27	4	.283	.320	.361
1992	Milwaukee	101	256	22	63	12	1	1	18	12	6	.246	.278	.313

CARLOS GARCIA
Pittsburgh Pirates
Shortstop/Second Baseman
$23

Probably the best shortstop in baseball who doesn't have a job, may replace Lind at second base. He has a shortstop's range and a good arm, hit .303 at Buffalo with 13 homers, 70 RBI (MLE: .270 with 9, 54), has speed to steal bases. Work habits are good. Has just turned 25, so he has time . . . only negative is a common one, chases bad pitches. Grade B prospect.

YEAR	TEAM/LEVEL	G	AB	R	H	2B	3B	HR	RBI	BB	SB	AVG	OBP	SLG
1992	Buffalo AAA	113	426	73	129	28	9	13	70	24	21	.303	.342	.502
1992	MLE	113	407	56	110	24	6	9	54	18	14	.270	.301	.425
1993	Pittsburgh	22	39	4	8	1	0	0	4	0	0	.205	.195	.231

JEFF GARDNER
San Diego Padres
Second Base
$12

He's 29, but it's unbelievable that this guy can't get a major league job. He's Wally Backman with good defense. He could hit .260 to .300 in the majors with some walks—.340 on-base percentage, maybe better—and Joe McIlvaine says that he turns the double play as well as Bill Mazeroski. He's wasted half his career in the minor leagues. Can play regularly if he gets a break.

YEAR	TEAM/LEVEL	G	AB	R	H	2B	3B	HR	RBI	BB	SB	AVG	OBP	SLG
1991	Tidewater AAA	136	504	73	147	23	4	1	56	73	6	.292	.393	.359
1992	Las Vegas AAA	120	439	82	147	30	5	1	51	67	7	.355	.424	.433
1992	MLE	120	402	50	110	22	2	0	31	40	4	.274	.339	.338
		120	365	18	73	14	0	0	11	13	1	.200	.228	.233

RICH GEDMAN
St. Louis Cardinals
Backup Catcher
$2

Over the last four years has hit below .200 against right-handers and left-handers, below .200 at home and on the road, and .159 with runners in scoring position. . . did hit better over the second half of '92, but that's only 54 at bats . . . his value isn't offensive or defensive, and he's not a baserunner. If the Cardinals are serious about contending they need a real backup catcher.

YEAR	TEAM/LEVEL	G	AB	R	H	2B	3B	HR	RBI	BB	SB	AVG	OBP	SLG
1991	St. Louis	46	94	7	10	1	0	3	8	4	0	.106	.140	.213
1992	St. Louis	41	105	5	23	4	0	1	8	11	0	.219	.291	.286
1993	Projected	40	101	7	22	6	0	2	11	11	0	.218	.295	.337
		36	116	3	36	7	0	0	8	18	0	.310	.403	.371

STEVE GIBRALTER
Cincinnati Reds
Outfielder
$4

Had a big year in the Midwest League at the age of 20. A Texas native, sixth-round draft pick in 1990; lacks outstanding speed, so will have to make it with his bat if he makes it. I can't translate stats from A Ball into major league equivalents, but the Midwest League is a good league and Cedar Rapids is not an easy place to hit. Grade B prospect.

YEAR	TEAM/LEVEL	G	AB	R	H	2B	3B	HR	RBI	BB	SB	AVG	OBP	SLG
1990	Reds R	52	174	26	45	11	3	4	27	23	8	.259	.353	.425
1991	Charleston A	140	544	72	145	36	7	6	71	31	11	.267	.309	.392
1992	Cedar Rapids A	137	529	92	162	32	3	19	99	51	12	.306	.378	.486
		134	514	112	179	28	0	32	127	71	13	.348	.407	.569

KIRK GIBSON
Retired
Left Fielder
No Value

Unhappy with his projected role as a bench player, he forced the Royals to trade him during spring training by mouthing off and acting erratically, then was released by the Pirates on May 6. Had he accepted the role, he would have been an extremely valuable reserve, with his power, baserunning, and ability to hit a right-handed pitcher. He didn't want to do it.

YEAR	TEAM/LEVEL	G	AB	R	H	2B	3B	HR	RBI	BB	SB	AVG	OBP	SLG
1990	Los Angeles	89	315	59	82	20	0	8	38	39	26	.260	.345	.400
1991	Kansas City	130	462	81	109	17	6	16	55	69	18	.236	.341	.403
1992	Pittsburgh	16	56	6	11	0	0	2	5	3	3	.196	.237	.304

BERNARD GILKEY
St. Louis Cardinals
Left Fielder
$20

Split his playing time between hitting leadoff and hitting somewhere else. When leading off, he hit .233 (45/193); when not leading off he hit .372 (71/191) . . . fast, but ineffective base stealer. I think players in that class normally make limited improvement as base stealers, but I can't prove that . . . I like Gilkey. I wasn't surprised he hit .300, and I expect he will have more good years.

YEAR	TEAM/LEVEL	G	AB	R	H	2B	3B	HR	RBI	BB	SB	AVG	OBP	SLG
1991	St. Louis	81	268	28	58	7	2	5	20	39	14	.216	.316	.313
1992	St. Louis	131	384	56	116	19	4	7	43	39	18	.302	.364	.427
1993	Projected	126	413	55	109	19	4	6	37	52	25	.264	.346	.373

JOE GIRARDI
Chicago Cubs
Catcher
$18

The .270 batting average masks a large number of weaknesses. Only 5 of his 73 hits went for extra bases, about the lowest percentage in the majors, plus he doesn't walk, so his secondary average was .100, among the lowest in the majors. . . . Doesn't throw well, grounds into too many double plays because he hits the ball on the ground.

YEAR	TEAM/LEVEL	G	AB	R	H	2B	3B	HR	RBI	BB	SB	AVG	OBP	SLG
1991	Chicago	21	47	3	9	2	0	0	6	6	0	.191	.283	.234
1992	Chicago	91	270	19	73	3	1	1	12	19	3	.270	.320	.300
1993	Projected	91	265	21	69	11	1	2	23	16	3	.260	.302	.332
		161	493	35	137	4	2	2	18	32	6	.278	.322	.306

DAN GLADDEN
Detroit Tigers

Left Fielder

$17

On the Tigers, he qualifies as a young guy. Went on the DL May 13 with a broken thumb, missed a month. He was red-hot for a month after that, right before the All-Star game, but then fell into a slump, hitting .239 the second half. . . a marginal regular if he hits .280, and far below the margin if he hits .254. Career should be nearly over.

YEAR	TEAM/LEVEL	G	AB	R	H	2B	3B	HR	RBI	BB	SB	AVG	OBP	SLG
1991	Minnesota	126	461	65	114	14	9	6	52	36	15	.247	.306	.356
1992	Detroit	113	417	57	106	20	1	7	42	30	4	.254	.304	.357
1993	Projected	96	346	44	89	15	2	4	32	23	11	.257	.304	.347
		100	*369*	*49*	*98*	*26*	*0*	*8*	*32*	*24*	*0*	*.266*	*.310*	*.401*

JERRY GOFF
Montreal Expos

Catcher/Third Baseman

$1

A 29-year-old backstop, has all but disappeared behind Fletcher, Laker, Natal, and Colbrunn, but played 94 games for the Triple-A affiliate. He was in the majors in '90 and wasn't bad, but is lifetime .237 hitter in the minors, so it isn't too likely he would hit for a sustained period of time. No prospect, trying to find a niche somewhere as a third catcher.

YEAR	TEAM/LEVEL	G	AB	R	H	2B	3B	HR	RBI	BB	SB	AVG	OBP	SLG
1990	Montreal	52	119	14	27	1	0	3	7	21	0	.227	.343	.311
1991	Indianapolis AAA	57	191	32	48	10	2	9	37	22	2	.251	.338	.466
1992	Indianapolis AAA	94	314	37	75	17	1	14	39	32	0	.239	.311	.433
		131	*437*	*42*	*102*	*24*	*0*	*19*	*41*	*42*	*0*	*.333*	*.301*	*.419*

LEO GOMEZ
Baltimore Orioles

Third Baseman

$51

Ron Santo/Sal Bando type. Slow but has a good arm, works hard on his defense but makes mistakes, excellent hitter. He will play 12 years as a regular, and he'll have some outstanding ones. Right-handed batter but to this point has not hit left-handers well; that will come. Also to this point has been very ineffective when he swings at the first pitch.

YEAR	TEAM/LEVEL	G	AB	R	H	2B	3B	HR	RBI	BB	SB	AVG	OBP	SLG
1991	Baltimore	118	391	40	91	17	2	16	45	40	1	.233	.302	.409
1992	Baltimore	137	468	62	124	24	0	17	64	63	2	.265	.356	.425
1993	Projected	151	548	76	139	23	2	22	77	79	2	.254	.348	.423
		156	*545*	*84*	*157*	*31*	*0*	*18*	*83*	*86*	*3*	*.288*	*.365*	*.444*

RENE GONZALES
California Angels

Infielder

$17

Was having a dream season until awakened by a pitch from Jaime Navarro on August 11. The pitch broke his arm, and ended his season. He had played so little in the previous five years with Baltimore and Toronto that his hitting skills are hard to pin down exactly, but if I was a betting man I'd bet that 1992 was a fluke, and he won't approach it again.

YEAR	TEAM/LEVEL	G	AB	R	H	2B	3B	HR	RBI	BB	SB	AVG	OBP	SLG
1991	Toronto	71	118	16	23	3	0	1	6	12	0	.195	.289	.246
1992	California	104	329	47	91	17	1	7	38	41	7	.277	.363	.398
1993	Projected	99	293	37	69	11	1	2	23	16	3	.235	.317	.300
		137	*540*	*78*	*159*	*31*	*2*	*13*	*70*	*70*	*14*	*.294*	*.325*	*.431*

JOSE GONZALEZ
Philadelphia Phillies
Outfielder
$1

A fine athlete and a fine defensive outfielder, played several years with the Dodgers but didn't hit enough to claim a job. He's now 28, played with the Angels early last year but was released by them July 30, and signed with the Phillies. They sent him to Scranton, where he played a few games and then disappeared. He could start the '93 season anywhere; no prospect.

YEAR	TEAM/LEVEL	G	AB	R	H	2B	3B	HR	RBI	BB	SB	AVG	OBP	SLG
1990	Los Angeles	106	99	15	23	5	3	2	8	6	3	.232	.280	.404
1991	Three Teams	91	117	15	13	2	1	2	7	13	8	.111	.205	.197
1992	California	33	55	4	10	2	0	0	2	7	0	.182	.270	.218

JUAN GONZALEZ
Texas Rangers
Center Fielder (should be in left)
$77

There are three players in baseball history who have hit 600 home runs: Aaron, Ruth, and Willie Mays. Juan Gonzalez will be the fourth. He's only 23 and doesn't really know what he's doing. He'll swing at bad pitches and doesn't concede anything with two strikes, so the third strike is almost a gimme, but he's unbelievably strong, and a good athlete in other ways.

YEAR	TEAM/LEVEL	G	AB	R	H	2B	3B	HR	RBI	BB	SB	AVG	OBP	SLG
1991	Texas	142	545	78	144	34	1	27	102	42	4	.264	.321	.479
1992	Texas	155	584	77	152	24	2	43	109	35	0	.260	.304	.529
1993	Projected	154	578	80	152	32	3	33	104	37	2	.263	.307	.500

LUIS GONZALEZ
Houston Astros
Left Fielder
$25

A good player to have in '93. He rallied after a horrible start and trip to Tucson to finish the season with numbers comparable to his rookie season. In my opinion he is never likely to hit much more than .250, and will have to make his mark by developing his power. The Astrodome will work against him, but his '92 season doesn't represent what he could do.

YEAR	TEAM/LEVEL	G	AB	R	H	2B	3B	HR	RBI	BB	SB	AVG	OBP	SLG
1991	Houston	137	473	51	120	28	9	13	69	40	10	.254	.320	.433
1992	Houston	122	387	40	94	19	3	10	55	24	7	.243	.289	.385
1993	Projected	121	396	49	101	23	5	12	58	32	12	.255	.311	.429

(handwritten) 107 301 29 68 10 0 7 41 8 4 .226 .276 .329

TOM GOODWIN
Los Angeles Dodgers
Outfielder
$3

Pinch ran and served as defensive sub for the Dodgers during their pennant chase (chuckle) . . . Grade D prospect, on the border of being no prospect but could fool us if he spends enough time with Brett Butler. He has great speed but no power, and his batting averages at Albuquerque (.273, .301) don't suggest that he will hit over .250 in the majors.

YEAR	TEAM/LEVEL	G	AB	R	H	2B	3B	HR	RBI	BB	SB	AVG	OBP	SLG
1992	Albuquerque AAA	82	319	48	96	10	4	2	28	37	27	.301	.372	.376
1992	Los Angeles	73	80	15	17	1	1	0	3	6	8	.233	.291	.274
1993	Projected	96	198	25	47	8	1	1	13	15	14	.237	.291	.303

MARK GRACE
Chicago Cubs
First Baseman
$55

The most important skill in baseball is the ability to get on base, and Grace, with a .380 on-base percentage last year (.373 lifetime), scores well in that category. Excellent defensive player, good baserunner, rarely strikes out; only thing he lacks is power, but with 37 doubles even that isn't really a negative . . . has consistently hit better when hitting 4–5 than when hitting 2–3.

YEAR	TEAM/LEVEL	G	AB	R	H	2B	3B	HR	RBI	BB	SB	AVG	OBP	SLG
1991	Chicago	160	619	87	169	28	5	8	58	70	3	.273	.346	.373
1992	Chicago	158	603	72	185	37	5	9	79	72	6	.307	.380	.430
1993	Projected	160	608	78	177	32	3	10	74	71	8	.291	.365	.403
		154	587	55	201	46	5	10	100	74	9	.342	.416	.489

CRAIG GREBECK
Chicago White Sox
Shortstop/Second Baseman
$21

Got the White Sox shortstop job after Guillen's injury, and held it until he himself broke his foot in the first week of August. In 630 major league at bats he has hit 40 doubles and 10 homers, driven in 75 runs and drawn 76 walks, so you can see there is considerable offensive ability there. He'll play regularly somewhere.

YEAR	TEAM/LEVEL	G	AB	R	H	2B	3B	HR	RBI	BB	SB	AVG	OBP	SLG
1991	Chicago	107	224	37	63	16	3	6	31	38	1	.281	.386	.460
1992	Chicago	88	287	24	77	21	2	3	35	30	0	.268	.341	.387
1993	Projected	136	389	43	100	21	2	6	44	45	2	.257	.340	.368
		69	352	9	91	26	1	0	39	22	0	.259	.302	.338

GARY GREEN
Cincinnati Reds
Shortstop
No Value

Your traditional good field/no hit shortstop, now 31 years old and still has his major league average over the Mendoza line, which is an upset in view of the fact that he hit .193 for Nashville last year and .218 for Oklahoma City the year before. No future in the majors, even with expansion. Doesn't run well enough to be utility infielder/pinch runner.

YEAR	TEAM/LEVEL	G	AB	R	H	2B	3B	HR	RBI	BB	SB	AVG	OBP	SLG
1990	Texas	62	88	10	19	3	0	0	8	6	1	.216	.263	.250
1991	Oklahoma City AAA	100	308	36	67	4	2	2	30	35	1	.218	.299	.263
1992	Nashville AAA	101	316	23	61	12	1	3	27	22	0	.193	.249	.266
		102	324	10	55	20	0	4	24	9	0	.170	.192	.287

WILLIE GREENE
Cincinnati Reds
Third Baseman
$38

Was traded twice in the low minors. Don't know what to make of that . . . sucker can hit. A number-one draft pick out of high school, 21 years old, above-average fielder, average speed, well liked. Has a history of lower back pain, but wasn't bothered by it last year . . . was called up late because Sabo was hurt, and wasn't overmatched. May move to left. **Grade A prospect.**

YEAR	TEAM/LEVEL	G	AB	R	H	2B	3B	HR	RBI	BB	SB	AVG	OBP	SLG
1992	Chattanooga AA	96	349	47	97	19	2	15	66	46	8	.278	.362	.473
1992	MLE	96	340	38	88	17	1	15	54	34	5	.259	.326	.447
1992	Cincinnati	29	93	10	25	5	2	2	13	10	0	.269	.337	.430

MIKE GREENWELL
Boston Red Sox

Left Fielder

$27

Slugging percentages since 1987: .570, .531, .443, .434, .419, .278. He had surgery in July on his knee and elbow, hoping to reverse this. He's an odd talent, in that he runs fairly well, or used to, but is a poor outfielder. Still, a .300 hitter is a .300 hitter; there aren't an awful lot of them, and hitting ability is often astonishingly resilient.

YEAR	TEAM/LEVEL	G	AB	R	H	2B	3B	HR	RBI	BB	SB	AVG	OBP	SLG
1991	Boston	147	544	76	163	26	6	9	83	43	15	.300	.350	.419
1992	Boston	49	180	16	42	2	0	2	18	18	2	.233	.307	.278
1993	Projected	146	543	71	162	30	4	13	77	54	10	.298	.362	.440

TOMMY GREGG
Atlanta Braves

Pinch Hitter

$2

Missed most of the year with a broken bone in his right hand. He hit .295 in a 38-game rehabilitation at Richmond, then got a few at bats in September . . . at 29, he's emerging as a good candidate for the Japanese league . . . line drive hitter, doesn't make contact consistently enough to be a .300 hitter. Can fill in at first, left or right.

YEAR	TEAM/LEVEL	G	AB	R	H	2B	3B	HR	RBI	BB	SB	AVG	OBP	SLG
1990	Atlanta	124	239	18	63	13	1	5	32	20	4	.264	.322	.389
1991	Atlanta	72	107	13	20	8	1	1	4	12	2	.187	.275	.308
1992	Atlanta	18	19	1	5	0	0	1	1	1	1	.263	.300	.421

KEN GRIFFEY, JR.
Seattle Mariners

Center Fielder

$94

Has made progress as a hitter each year since he came up, and now is among the three or four best hitters in the American League. He's losing speed at the same rate he increases power, but then . . . 25 percent chance to get 3000 career hits, 2 percent for 4000, 9 percent chance of 500 career homers . . . more than two years younger than Pat Listach, Kenny Lofton, or Eric Karros.

YEAR	TEAM/LEVEL	G	AB	R	H	2B	3B	HR	RBI	BB	SB	AVG	OBP	SLG
1991	Seattle	154	548	76	179	42	1	22	100	71	18	.327	.399	.527
1992	Seattle	142	565	83	174	39	4	27	103	44	10	.308	.361	.535
1993	Projected	157	567	85	178	36	3	26	96	62	15	.314	.382	.526

ALFREDO GRIFFIN
Toronto Blue Jays

Shortstop

$2

Still in top shape at 36, hasn't lost anything except a little bat speed. He didn't have it to spare. His game is, as it has always been, a combination of spectacular plays and terminal over-reaching. If Alfredo Griffin was a burglar, he'd steal the crown jewels but get caught on the way out trying to pick up a candy bar.

YEAR	TEAM/LEVEL	G	AB	R	H	2B	3B	HR	RBI	BB	SB	AVG	OBP	SLG
1991	Los Angeles	109	350	27	85	6	2	0	27	22	5	.243	.286	.271
1992	Toronto	63	150	21	35	7	0	0	10	9	3	.233	.273	.280
1993	Projected	64	175	16	38	7	2	1	14	11	2	.217	.263	.297
		65	200	11	41	7	4	2	18	13	1	.205	.252	.310

MARQUIS GRISSOM
Montreal Expos
Center Fielder
$59

Spiked his game with 59 extra base hits and 78 steals, including twice as many thefts of third (24) as any other major leaguer. With his on-base percentage he's not exactly Rickey Henderson. His talents are about the same as Juan Samuel's were, but he has two advantages. 1) He's a good center fielder rather than a bad second baseman. 2) He doesn't strike out as much.

YEAR	TEAM/LEVEL	G	AB	R	H	2B	3B	HR	RBI	BB	SB	AVG	OBP	SLG
1991	Montreal	148	558	73	149	23	9	6	39	34	76	.267	.310	.373
1992	Montreal	159	653	99	180	39	6	14	66	42	78	.276	.322	.418
1993	Projected	157	581	84	158	28	6	10	55	41	71	.272	.320	.392
		155	509	69	136	17	6	6	44	40	69	.267	.321	.369

JEFF GROTEWOLD
Philadelphia Phillies
Pinch Hitter
$5

Left-handed hitter, minor league first baseman and catcher. The Phillies, in their mystical and borderline divine way, decided that he was a hitter and made him their top pinch hitter. He attracted some attention by hitting three pinch-hit home runs in a week, but his credentials to even hold the job are pretty difficult to see. Very strong, slow; I don't expect much from him.

YEAR	TEAM/LEVEL	G	AB	R	H	2B	3B	HR	RBI	BB	SB	AVG	OBP	SLG
1990	Reading AA	127	412	56	111	33	1	15	72	62	2	.269	.363	.464
1991	Scranton AAA	87	276	33	71	13	5	5	38	25	0	.257	.321	.395
1992	Philadelphia	72	65	7	13	2	0	3	5	9	0	.200	.307	.369

KELLY GRUBER
Toronto Blue Jays
Third Baseman
$32

In a way, he's like Andres Galarraga. He had a year that was really out of his range of ability, and has found the experience disorienting. Encountering pressure and criticism for just being what he is, he's tried to compensate and adjust, and his career has skidded out of control. Good defensive player, good effort, has lost most of his speed at 31.

YEAR	TEAM/LEVEL	G	AB	R	H	2B	3B	HR	RBI	BB	SB	AVG	OBP	SLG
1991	Toronto	113	429	58	108	18	2	20	65	31	12	.252	.308	.443
1992	Toronto	120	446	42	102	16	3	11	43	26	7	.229	.275	.352
1993	Projected	110	410	50	102	17	2	15	59	30	10	.249	.300	.410
		100	384	58	102	18	1	19	75	34	13	.273	.333	.506

JUAN GUERRERO
Houston Astros
Shortstop/Third Baseman
$11

Raw prospect taken from the Giants in the Rule 5 Draft. Difficult to evaluate because he hit like Al Simmons one year at Shreveport, but otherwise hasn't impressed at bat. We are wary of stats in the second year at Double-A, but at his worst he should hit enough to hold a shortstop's job, and with luck he might hit enough to play third. Grade C prospect.

YEAR	TEAM/LEVEL	G	AB	R	H	2B	3B	HR	RBI	BB	SB	AVG	OBP	SLG
1990	Shreveport AA	118	390	55	94	21	1	16	47	26	4	.241	.296	.423
1991	Shreveport AA	128	479	78	160	40	2	19	94	46	14	.334	.395	.545
1992	Houston	79	125	8	25	4	2	1	14	10	1	.200	.261	.288

PEDRO GUERRERO
St. Louis Cardinals
First Baseman
$10

He has lost his speed, and he never did have any defensive value. He was never in demand as a clubhouse leader. That leaves hitting, and in his day he was the best hitter in baseball, him or Jack Clark. Last year he hit .219. I'm not saying that he *won't* come back and hit enough this year to carry the whole package, but he is 36.

YEAR	TEAM/LEVEL	G	AB	R	H	2B	3B	HR	RBI	BB	SB	AVG	OBP	SLG
1991	St. Louis	115	427	41	116	12	1	8	70	37	4	.272	.326	.361
1992	St. Louis	43	146	10	32	6	1	1	16	11	2	.219	.270	.295
1993	Projected	86	231	21	66	14	1	6	40	20	1	.286	.343	.433
		129	316	32	100	22	1	11	64	0	0	.316	.316	.497

OZZIE GUILLEN
Chicago White Sox
Shortstop
$33

His season ended April 21, when he collided with Tim Raines chasing a bloop single and ripped two tendons in his knee. The injury may prevent him from attempting to steal bases, which would help the White Sox although it would hurt his value in rotisserie. He never did put any runs on the scoreboard. Was working out with the team in September, is expected back.

YEAR	TEAM/LEVEL	G	AB	R	H	2B	3B	HR	RBI	BB	SB	AVG	OBP	SLG
1990	Chicago	160	516	61	144	21	4	1	58	26	13	.279	.312	.341
1991	Chicago	154	524	52	143	20	3	3	49	11	21	.273	.284	.340
1992	Chicago	12	40	5	8	4	0	0	7	1	1	.200	.214	.300

RICKY GUTIERREZ
San Diego Padres
Shortstop/Second Baseman
$5

A product of the Baltimore system, had been bumped by Manny Alexander as the Orioles' shortstop-of-the-future-if-we-ever-need-one, and came to San Diego in the Craig Lefferts trade. It appears unlikely that he will hit enough to be a significant player, but since he is only 22 it is too early to write that in ink. He has hit at times.

YEAR	TEAM/LEVEL	G	AB	R	H	2B	3B	HR	RBI	BB	SB	AVG	OBP	SLG
1991	AA and AAA	133	446	77	117	11	7	0	45	81	15	.262	.376	.318
1992	Rochester AAA	125	431	54	109	9	3	0	41	53	14	.253	.331	.288
1992	MLE	125	417	41	91	7	1	0	31	41	9	.218	.288	.239
		125	403	28	73	5	0	0	21	29	4	.181	.236	.194

CHRIS GWYNN
Kansas City Royals
Right Fielder
$14

Now 28, he has developed into a pretty fair hitter, which was a surprise to me. Was limited to 84 at bats in '92 by a strained calf muscle and a dislocated shoulder. Built quite a bit like his brother, average arm, average speed, more power than Tony. He's only 28, so the possibility exists that he could stumble into a regular job although that's not in anyone's plans.

YEAR	TEAM/LEVEL	G	AB	R	H	2B	3B	HR	RBI	BB	SB	AVG	OBP	SLG
1991	Los Angeles	94	139	18	35	5	1	5	22	10	1	.252	.301	.410
1992	Kansas City	34	84	10	24	3	2	1	7	3	0	.286	.303	.405
1993	Projected	82	207	26	54	7	2	4	26	12	1	.261	.301	.372
		130	330	42	84	11	2	7	45	21	2	.255	.29	.364

TONY GWYNN
San Diego Padres
Right Fielder
$58

Season ended September 8 due to a sprained ligament in his left knee. He may be the only major league player who actually hits for a better average when behind in the count. Over the last four years has hit .301 when the first pitch was a ball, but .324 (with much less power) when starting out behind in the count. A Hall of Famer.

YEAR	TEAM/LEVEL	G	AB	R	H	2B	3B	HR	RBI	BB	SB	AVG	OBP	SLG
1991	San Diego	134	530	69	168	27	11	4	62	34	8	.317	.355	.432
1992	San Diego	128	520	77	165	27	3	6	41	46	3	.317	.371	.415
1993	Projected	136	542	72	171	25	5	5	57	42	10	.315	.365	.408
		144	564	65	177	23	7	4	73	38	17	.314	.357	.401

CHIP HALE
Minnesota Twins
Second Baseman
$2

His career has gone into an eclipse behind Knoblauch, and at 29 he is no prospect, but his credentials are pretty good. Left-handed batter, could hit .260 in the majors with as many walks as strikeouts or a few more, runs well, rarely makes an error at second, and can turn the double play. There are several major league teams that could use him.

YEAR	TEAM/LEVEL	G	AB	R	H	2B	3B	HR	RBI	BB	SB	AVG	OBP	SLG
1991	Portland AAA	110	352	45	85	16	3	1	37	47	3	.241	.327	.313
1992	Portland AAA	132	474	77	135	24	8	1	53	73	3	.285	.376	.376
1992	MLE	132	463	61	124	23	7	0	42	59	2	.268	.351	.348
		132	452	43	113	22	6	0	31	45	1	.250	.325	.318

MEL HALL
New York Yankees (Free Agent)
Left/Right Fielder
$25

Escaped the platoon role in his 12th major league season, but still did not hit enough either against left-handers or overall to justify his everyday status (.346 slugging percentage against lefties). Hot weather hitter, normally fades in September. Average speed, defense not an asset, .280 average with .206 secondary average is just not enough offense for a regular left fielder.

YEAR	TEAM/LEVEL	G	AB	R	H	2B	3B	HR	RBI	BB	SB	AVG	OBP	SLG
1991	New York	141	492	67	140	23	2	19	80	26	0	.285	.321	.455
1992	New York	152	583	67	163	36	3	15	81	29	4	.280	.310	.429
1993	Projected	137	480	56	132	25	2	15	57	42	1	.275	.305	.429
		122	377	45	101	14	1	15	33	55	6	.268	.361	.430

BOB HAMELIN
Kansas City Royals
First Baseman
$4

A 25-year-old Kent Hrbek type, he was a hot prospect in 1989, but had been almost forgotten after two years because he's overweight, has back problems, and wasn't hitting. Despite everything I honestly believe that he may be as good a hitter as Hrbek, and he started hitting again last year. Royals have a truckload of DHs and first baseman. Grade C prospect.

YEAR	TEAM/LEVEL	G	AB	R	H	2B	3B	HR	RBI	BB	SB	AVG	OBP	SLG
1992	Baseball City A	11	44	7	12	0	1	1	6	2	0	.273	.304	.386
1992	Memphis AA	35	120	23	40	8	0	6	22	26	0	.333	.452	.550
1992	Omaha AAA	27	95	9	19	3	1	5	15	14	0	.200	.295	.411
		19	70	0	0	0	2	4	8	2	6	.000	.027	.118

DARYL HAMILTON
Milwaukee Brewers
Utility Outfielder
$29

A manager's dream, a good player who can be used in a dozen different ways. Major league batting average is .292 after more than a thousand at bats, so it is time to stop wondering if his bat is for real. A classic number-two hitter, left-handed singles hitter, excellent speed, doesn't walk much but strikes out even less. Can bat leadoff, play any outfield spot.

YEAR	TEAM/LEVEL	G	AB	R	H	2B	3B	HR	RBI	BB	SB	AVG	OBP	SLG
1991	Milwaukee	122	405	64	126	16	6	1	57	33	16	.311	.361	.385
1992	Milwaukee	128	470	67	140	19	7	5	62	45	41	.298	.356	.400
1993	Projected	145	487	72	140	18	4	3	59	43	32	.287	.345	.359
	(handwritten)	134	535	70	154	22	8	9	67	57	66	.288	.360	.409

JEFF HAMILTON
Los Angeles Dodgers
(Released)
Third Baseman
$1

Still trying to come back from a 1990 rotator cuff injury. He hit .302 in 55 games at Albuquerque, where he hit .360 before coming to the majors in 1987. The injury he suffered was to his central skill, since throwing was what he did best. Only 29 years old, but a long-odds recovery project. Has no speed, a little bit of power.

YEAR	TEAM/LEVEL	G	AB	R	H	2B	3B	HR	RBI	BB	SB	AVG	OBP	SLG
1989	Los Angeles	151	548	45	134	35	1	12	56	20	0	.245	.272	.378
1991	Los Angeles	41	94	4	21	4	0	1	14	4	0	.223	.255	.298
1992	Albuquerque AAA	55	159	21	48	12	0	5	30	13	0	.302	.350	.472
	(handwritten)	69	224	38	75	20	0	9	46	22	0	.335	.394	.545

TODD HANEY
Montreal Expos
Infielder
$8

Diminutive second baseman/singles hitter, originally in the Seattle system . . . hobbies include hang gliding, bull riding, and mountain climbing . . . has a little speed and probably could hit .280 in a good year, but no power, hitting record inconsistent . . . Grade C prospect. Has no chance to take a job from DeShields, but with Foley and Owen gone, could take over as a backup infielder.

YEAR	TEAM/LEVEL	G	AB	R	H	2B	3B	HR	RBI	BB	SB	AVG	OBP	SLG
1991	Indianapolis AAA	132	510	68	159	32	3	2	39	47	11	.312	.377	.398
1991	MLE	132	489	54	138	28	2	1	31	37	8	.282	.333	.354
1992	Indianapolis AAA	57	200	30	53	14	0	6	33	37	1	.265	.379	.425

DAVE HANSEN
Los Angeles Dodgers
Third Baseman
$11

A fine prospect a year ago, has developed a lower back problem which hinders his swing. If he can get rid of that, which is a big If, and get another shot, which is far from certain, should hit over .250 with a fair number of doubles and 70+ walks as a regular. Decent defensive third baseman, could become a good one.

YEAR	TEAM/LEVEL	G	AB	R	H	2B	3B	HR	RBI	BB	SB	AVG	OBP	SLG
1991	Los Angeles	53	56	3	15	4	0	1	5	2	1	.268	.293	.393
1992	Los Angeles	132	341	30	73	11	0	6	22	34	0	.214	.286	.299
1993	Projected	135	381	41	94	14	1	5	39	45	3	.247	.326	.328

SHAWN HARE
Detroit Tigers
Right Fielder
$7

Filled in while Deer and Gladden were hurt. His 4-for-45 start as a major league hitter will make it hard for him to get his lifetime average up, but he is probably capable of hitting .265 to .275 in the majors with double-digit home run totals. That's not enough to elbow anybody aside, but there are worse hitters who have jobs.

YEAR	TEAM/LEVEL	G	AB	R	H	2B	3B	HR	RBI	BB	SB	AVG	OBP	SLG
1991	AA and AAA	111	377	64	112	30	2	13	70	42	3	.297	.368	.491
1992	Toledo AAA	57	203	31	67	12	2	5	34	31	6	.330	.412	.483
1992	Detroit	15	26	0	3	1	0	0	5	2	0	.115	.172	.154

BRIAN HARPER
Minnesota Twins
Catcher
$50

Outstanding line-drive hitter, slow, not much of an arm. He's 33 and has been the Twins' everyday catcher for four years, but a great deal of what causes aging is psychological release, fatigue; the older player no longer wants it as much as his younger rival. Harper waited 10 years for his chance, so I'd bet on him to hang on to his job as long as possible.

YEAR	TEAM/LEVEL	G	AB	R	H	2B	3B	HR	RBI	BB	SB	AVG	OBP	SLG
1991	Minnesota	123	441	54	137	28	1	10	69	14	1	.311	.336	.447
1992	Minnesota	140	502	58	154	25	0	9	73	26	0	.307	.343	.410
1993	Projected	134	476	53	139	24	1	9	61	20	2	.292	.321	.403

(handwritten) 128 450 48 124 23 2 9 77 14 4 .276 .292 .396

DONALD HARRIS
Texas Rangers
Center Fielder
$1

Until now his attention has been divided by attempts to play pro football. His football career is over at 25, and he may progress because of that. Fine defensive center fielder, very flashy, good arm, and strong enough to hit home runs, but can't read a breaking pitch and will swing at anything, swings two feet over a curve because he doesn't know it will break. Grade D prospect.

YEAR	TEAM/LEVEL	G	AB	R	H	2B	3B	HR	RBI	BB	SB	AVG	OBP	SLG
1992	Tulsa AA	83	303	39	77	15	2	11	39	9	4	.254	.291	.426
1992	MLE	83	298	36	72	14	1	10	36	6	3	.242	.257	.396
1992	Texas	24	33	3	6	1	0	0	1	0	1	.182	.182	.212

LENNY HARRIS
Los Angeles Dodgers
Utilityman
$19

What's this tell you about the Dodgers: Harris played 135 games, *normally batting second*, but scored only 28 runs all year . . . platoon player, hasn't hit left-handers and has no power, but one of the better bench players in the National League. Good singles hitter, good baserunner, can play second base or third for a week, short or any outfield spot for a day.

YEAR	TEAM/LEVEL	G	AB	R	H	2B	3B	HR	RBI	BB	SB	AVG	OBP	SLG
1991	Los Angeles	145	429	59	123	16	1	3	38	37	12	.287	.349	.350
1992	Los Angeles	135	347	28	94	11	0	0	30	24	19	.271	.318	.303
1993	Projected	142	407	49	113	16	1	2	34	32	15	.278	.330	.337

(handwritten) 149 467 70 132 21 2 4 38 40 11 .283 .339 .362

VINCE HARRIS
San Diego Padres
Outfielder
$5

The fastest player in the Texas League last year, stole 38 bases in 79 games for Wichita. He's a switch hitter, a slap hitter, has hit only one home run in 551 minor league games. Draws some walks, 25 years old. Comparable to Dave Gallagher except faster than Gallagher; comparable to Lance Johnson except Johnson's batting average will be 30 points higher and Harris will walk more often.

YEAR	TEAM/LEVEL	G	AB	R	H	2B	3B	HR	RBI	BB	SB	AVG	OBP	SLG
1991	Wichita AA	112	381	78	109	12	1	0	39	63	48	.286	.387	.323
1992	Wichita AA	80	242	36	68	12	1	1	20	35	38	.281	.374	.351
1992	MLE	80	227	23	53	8	0	0	13	19	22	.233	.293	.269
		80	212	10	38	4	0	0	6	3	6	.179	.191	.198

BILL HASELMAN
Seattle Mariners
Catcher
$3

Power-hitting catcher, a minor league veteran but only 26 years old. He was in the Texas system, but the Rangers were cool to him anyway, and completely lost interest when Rodriguez came along. His defensive reputation is not good and his average would probably be under .240, but his arm is OK and he could hit a home run every 30 or 40 at bats.

YEAR	TEAM/LEVEL	G	AB	R	H	2B	3B	HR	RBI	BB	SB	AVG	OBP	SLG
1991	Oklahoma City AAA	126	442	57	113	22	2	9	59	61	10	.256	.344	.376
1992	Two Teams AAA	105	360	57	91	19	2	20	62	54	4	.253	.350	.483
1992	MLE	105	340	36	71	15	1	12	40	35	1	.209	.283	.365
		105	320	15	51	11	0	4	18	16	0	.159	.209	.231

BILLY HATCHER
Boston Red Sox(Released)
Outfielder
$1

Don Zimmer's comment about him was "He's not the greatest player in the world, but he always gives 100 percent, and on this team that really sticks out." Provides no offense—a .260 hitter with no power, rarely walks and is a poor percentage base stealer. Has a left fielder's arm. In my opinion his skills are overtaxed even as a reserve.

YEAR	TEAM/LEVEL	G	AB	R	H	2B	3B	HR	RBI	BB	SB	AVG	OBP	SLG
1991	Cincinnati	138	442	45	116	25	3	4	41	26	11	.262	.312	.360
1992	Two Teams	118	409	47	102	19	2	3	33	22	9	.249	.290	.328
1993	Projected	96	314	35	80	16	2	3	22	19	10	.255	.297	.347
		78	249	23	58	13	2	3	11	16	11	.265	.318	.384

CHARLIE HAYES
New York Yankees
Third Baseman
$27

His position is secure for the first time in his career after he had two hot streaks, one early and one late, to finish at .257 with 18 homers. His overall offense is not impressive (no speed and very poor K/W ratio), but his defense *is* impressive, so that reduces the pressure on him to hit. Doubt that he will hit at quite the same level this year.

YEAR	TEAM/LEVEL	G	AB	R	H	2B	3B	HR	RBI	BB	SB	AVG	OBP	SLG
1991	Philadelphia	142	460	34	106	23	1	12	53	16	3	.230	.257	.363
1992	New York	142	509	52	131	19	2	18	66	28	3	.257	.297	.409
1993	Projected	147	514	49	129	23	1	13	60	25	4	.251	.286	.375
		152	519	46	127	27	0	8	54	22	5	.245	.28	.313

VON HAYES
California Angels
(Released)
Right Fielder
$4

At age 34 it can't be assumed that he has any ability left. If he catches a job somewhere he'll probably be a role player, fourth outfielder. I wouldn't mind having him in that role. He still runs well enough, takes a walk when it's offered. If he hits a little those things are bonuses, but if he doesn't hit they won't keep him in the league.

YEAR	TEAM/LEVEL	G	AB	R	H	2B	3B	HR	RBI	BB	SB	AVG	OBP	SLG
1991	Philadelphia	77	284	43	64	15	1	0	21	31	9	.225	.303	.285
1992	California	94	307	35	69	17	1	4	29	37	11	.225	.305	.326
1993	Projected	76	247	35	60	13	1	5	30	37	8	.243	.342	.364
		111	187	35	51	9	1	6	31	37	5	.273	.393	.428

BERT HEFFERNAN
Seattle Mariners
Catcher
No Value

No prospect, played eight games with Seattle, which appear likely to compose most of his major league career. He was originally property of the Brewers, traded to the Dodgers for Darren Holmes, taken by Seattle under Rule 5. The Mariners picked up Heffernan and Haselman (they probably couldn't tell them apart) because their own catching was terrible. Haselman can play a little; Heffernan hit OK last year but usually hasn't.

YEAR	TEAM/LEVEL	G	AB	R	H	2B	3B	HR	RBI	BB	SB	AVG	OBP	SLG
1992	Jacksonville AA	58	196	16	56	9	0	2	23	29	1	.286	.380	.362
1992	Calgary AAA	15	46	8	14	2	0	1	4	7	4	.304	.396	.413
1992	MLE	73	233	19	61	9	0	1	22	26	2	.262	.336	.313
		131	420	30	108	16	0	1	40	45	0	.257	.329	.300

SCOTT HEMOND
Oakland Athletics
Catcher/Utilityman
$4

At 27 he has reached the end of his prospect status, without emerging as a potential regular. He begins now his search for a niche, a spot. There are worse players in the majors. He runs well for a catcher (stole 45 bases at Huntsville in '89), walks occasionally, and will hit doubles, but has no real power and won't hit .250 . . . will never play regularly.

YEAR	TEAM/LEVEL	G	AB	R	H	2B	3B	HR	RBI	BB	SB	AVG	OBP	SLG
1991	Tacoma AAA	92	327	50	89	19	5	3	31	39	11	.272	.361	.388
1991	MLE	92	310	37	72	13	1	2	33	35	8	.232	.298	.313
1992	Two Teams	22	32	7	7	2	0	0	2	3	1	.219	.278	.281

DAVE HENDERSON
Oakland Athletics
Center Fielder
$6

Lost almost the entire season to strained hamstrings. LaRussa has a great faith in older players, and will probably give him every chance to re-establish himself in 1993 . . . not really fast enough to play center field anymore. In my opinion the odds are that his 1993 season will be disappointing, but it's too early to write him off. He's been written off before.

YEAR	TEAM/LEVEL	G	AB	R	H	2B	3B	HR	RBI	BB	SB	AVG	OBP	SLG
1991	Oakland	150	572	86	158	33	0	25	85	58	6	.276	.346	.465
1992	Oakland	20	63	1	9	1	0	0	2	2	0	.143	.169	.159
1993	Projected	105	325	42	80	19	1	11	41	30	3	.246	.310	.412

RICKEY HENDERSON
Oakland Athletics
Left Fielder
$64

He remains the best leadoff man in baseball, by far. The hamstring pulls which have interrupted his last two seasons are not going to magically go away, but he may be able to adjust his training to reduce them—or, if he wants, he could stop stealing bases and remain an exceptionally valuable player. Remains essentially on target to challenge Ty Cobb's career record for runs scored.

YEAR	TEAM/LEVEL	G	AB	R	H	2B	3B	HR	RBI	BB	SB	AVG	OBP	SLG
1991	Oakland	134	470	105	126	17	1	18	57	98	58	.268	.400	.423
1992	Oakland	117	396	77	112	18	3	15	46	95	48	.283	.426	.457
1993	Projected	130	451	94	123	22	2	14	48	99	56	.273	.404	.424
		143	506	111	134	26	1	13	50	103	64	.265	.389	.377

CARLOS HERNANDEZ
Los Angeles Dodgers
Catcher
$14

Has been passed by Piazza as the Dodgers' future of the catcher, which is a damn shame. Hernandez could be a fine starting catcher for somebody. Active defensive catcher, excellent arm, can hit .260 to .290 with some power. He's not going to put *a lot* of runs on the board, but then how many catchers do? . . . Second Venezuelan to catch in the major leagues.

YEAR	TEAM/LEVEL	G	AB	R	H	2B	3B	HR	RBI	BB	SB	AVG	OBP	SLG
1990	Albuquerque	52	143	11	45	8	1	0	16	8	2	.315	.348	.385
1991	Albuquerque	95	345	60	119	24	2	8	44	24	5	.345	.387	.496
1992	Los Angeles	69	173	11	45	4	0	3	17	11	0	.260	.316	.335
		43	1	0	0	0	0	0	0	0	0			

CESAR HERNANDEZ
Cincinnati Reds
Outfielder
$4

Was recalled when Reggie Sanders was out and wound up with some of Billy Hatcher's work when Hatcher was traded. It's an old story, but here's one more young player whose inability to grasp the strike zone is going to prevent him from having much of a career. Hernandez runs and throws well, good outfielder, in some ways reminiscent of Cesar Geronimo. He'll never hit.

YEAR	TEAM/LEVEL	G	AB	R	H	2B	3B	HR	RBI	BB	SB	AVG	OBP	SLG
1992	Chattanooga AA	93	328	50	91	23	4	2	27	19	12	.277	.325	.399
1992	MLE	94	318	41	81	21	2	3	22	14	8	.255	.286	.362
1992	Cincinnati	34	51	6	14	4	0	0	4	0	6	.275	.375	.353
		0	0	0	0	0	0	0	0	0	4			

JOSE HERNANDEZ
Cleveland Indians
Shortstop
$4

Was cut by the Rangers and acquired by Cleveland to play shortstop for them at Double-A. He is not beyond time of developing (23 years old) and is not a hopeless hitter. As badly as the Rangers need a shortstop, one would think they would not have cut him if there were any chance, but certainly teams do make mistakes like that. Grade D prospect.

YEAR	TEAM/LEVEL	G	AB	R	H	2B	3B	HR	RBI	BB	SB	AVG	OBP	SLG
1991	Texas	45	98	8	18	2	1	0	4	3	0	.184	.208	.224
1992	Canton AA	130	404	56	103	16	4	3	46	37	7	.255	.315	.337
1992	MLE	130	397	47	96	15	2	2	38	26	4	.242	.288	.305
		130	390	38	89	14	0	1	30	15	7	.228	.257	.272

PHIL HIATT
Kansas City Royals
Third Baseman/Right Fielder
$3

Good athlete, has outstanding power and a throwing arm. He has a huge, sweeping swing that would work better in slow-pitch softball, and he wouldn't hit .200 in the majors at this point. Third base doesn't seem to be working out due to sluggish footwork; probably will be moved to right field. He's young enough (23) to improve, but has miles to go. Grade D prospect.

YEAR	TEAM/LEVEL	G	AB	R	H	2B	3B	HR	RBI	BB	SB	AVG	OBP	SLG
1991	A and AA	137	521	70	141	28	7	11	66	31	34	.271	.319	.415
1992	AA and AAA	134	501	74	122	20	5	29	87	27	6	.244	.289	.477
1992	MLE	134	485	60	106	19	4	19	71	18	3	.219	.247	.392
		134	469	46	'90	18	3	9	55	T	0	.192	.208	.30¹

DONNIE HILL
Minnesota Twins
(Released)
Infielder
No Value

Was released by the Twins on July 17 although he was hitting .294 at the time. He's been released before, and then went to the minors to re-establish himself, but at 32 that may be more difficult this time . . . has played for four major league teams, but all in one division, the American League West . . . hit 26 career home runs, 22 of them on the road.

YEAR	TEAM/LEVEL	G	AB	R	H	2B	3B	HR	RBI	BB	SB	AVG	OBP	SLG
1990	California	103	352	36	93	18	2	3	32	29	1	.264	.319	.352
1991	California	77	209	36	50	8	1	1	20	30	1	.239	.335	.301
1992	Minnesota	25	51	7	15	3	0	0	2	5	0	.294	.368	.353

GLENALLEN HILL
Cleveland Indians
Left Fielder
$19

I would stay away from him in '93. Hill is the ultimate perennial prospect. The scouts have been raving about his tools since he was 19, but he never did anything with them until last year. He was 27 years old last year, the age of peak accomplishment, and although he did hit 18 homers his strikeout/walk ratio was awful, his on-base percentage only .287.

YEAR	TEAM/LEVEL	G	AB	R	H	2B	3B	HR	RBI	BB	SB	AVG	OBP	SLG
1991	Two Teams	72	221	29	57	8	2	8	25	23	6	.258	.324	.421
1992	Cleveland	102	369	38	89	16	1	18	49	20	9	.241	.287	.436
1993	Projected	95	303	42	77	14	2	12	39	23	9	.254	.307	.432
		88	237	46	65	12	3	6	29	26	9	.274	.346	.426

CHRIS HOILES
Baltimore Orioles
Catcher
$45

He hit .327 with a .667 slugging percentage when the bases were empty, .209 with a .309 slugging percentage when there were men on base. I doubt that it means anything, but if he does that again he's going to get a reputation . . . threw out only 20 percent of opposition baserunners, the lowest in the American League. He's a fine hitter, and he needs to be.

YEAR	TEAM/LEVEL	G	AB	R	H	2B	3B	HR	RBI	BB	SB	AVG	OBP	SLG
1991	Baltimore	107	341	36	83	15	0	11	31	29	0	.243	.304	.384
1992	Baltimore	96	310	49	85	10	1	20	40	55	0	.274	.384	.506
1993	Projected	129	418	57	106	19	1	17	51	56	2	.254	.342	.426
		162	526	65	127	28	2	14	62	57	4	.241	.316	.382

DAVE HOLLINS
Philadelphia Phillies
Third Baseman
$52

All of sudden there are three to five third basemen in the National League who can win an MVP award anytime. Power and walks gave him secondary average of .345 . . . in my opinion his '92 season could not likely have been a fluke. It's just too solid. . . . The word "intense," which is often sportswriter code for "jerk," is used in every story about him.

YEAR	TEAM/LEVEL	G	AB	R	H	2B	3B	HR	RBI	BB	SB	AVG	OBP	SLG
1991	Philadelphia	56	151	18	45	10	2	6	21	17	1	.298	.378	.510
1992	Philadelphia	156	586	104	158	28	4	27	93	76	9	.270	.369	.469
1993	Projected	157	574	87	149	23	3	21	79	76	7	.260	.346	.420
		158	362	70	140	18	2	15	65	72	3	.214	.339	.368

SAM HORN
Baltimore Orioles
Designated Hitter
$15

He hit a triple last year, the first of his major league career. Still looking for a stolen base . . . he is a .235 hitter and he is the slowest man in the major leagues, but he is also one of the strongest. In his career he has 35 homers, 103 RBI per 600 at bats . . . slowed, so to speak, by a strained muscle in his side.

YEAR	TEAM/LEVEL	G	AB	R	H	2B	3B	HR	RBI	BB	SB	AVG	OBP	SLG
1991	Baltimore	121	317	45	74	16	0	23	61	41	0	.233	.326	.502
1992	Baltimore	63	152	13	38	10	1	5	19	21	0	.235	.326	.401
1993	Projected	86	233	28	55	11	0	13	37	32	0	.236	.328	.451
		109	314	43	72	12	0	21	58	43	0	.229	.322	.468

STEVE HOSEY
San Francisco Giants
Outfielder
$6

Impressive athlete, a big guy (6-3, 215) who can run . . . a first-round draft pick in 1989, does not appear to me to be ready to help the Giants win. He'd probably hit around .250 in the majors. His power and speed are not in the Barry Bonds category, and his strikeout/walk ratio will be very poor. He is young enough (24) to show significant development.

YEAR	TEAM/LEVEL	G	AB	R	H	2B	3B	HR	RBI	BB	SB	AVG	OBP	SLG
1992	Phoenix AAA	125	462	64	132	28	7	10	65	39	15	.286	.346	.442
1992	MLE	125	433	42	103	22	3	6	42	24	9	.238	.278	.344
1992	San Francisco	21	56	6	14	1	0	1	6	0	1	.250	.241	.321

DAVID HOWARD
Kansas City Royals
Shortstop
$14

He played far better last year than he had in '91. He improved his average to .224, and his defense was better than his offense. None of this should be considered praise. I thought a year ago he should have been playing Double-A. Last year he moved up to Triple-A. He's 26. He doesn't have the strength or skills to be a good major league shortstop.

YEAR	TEAM/LEVEL	G	AB	R	H	2B	3B	HR	RBI	BB	SB	AVG	OBP	SLG
1991	Kansas City	94	236	20	51	7	0	1	17	16	3	.216	.267	.258
1992	Kansas City	74	219	19	49	6	2	1	18	15	3	.224	.271	.283
1993	Projected	116	344	29	75	8	2	2	29	25	6	.218	.274	.270
		158	468	39	101	10	2	3	40	35	9	.215	.269	.267

THOMAS HOWARD
Cleveland Indians
Left Fielder/Center Fielder
$11

He hit .277 last year, in spite of which I would not want him on my team in '93. 1) I don't think he is really a .277 hitter. 2) His secondary average was .159. 3) He was 27 last year, the age of fluke years. If he hits .275+ every year, which is certainly possible, he will have a Dave Gallagher–type career. No star potential.

YEAR	TEAM/LEVEL	G	AB	R	H	2B	3B	HR	RBI	BB	SB	AVG	OBP	SLG
1991	San Diego	106	281	30	70	12	3	4	22	24	10	.349	.309	.356
1992	Two Teams	122	361	37	100	15	2	2	32	17	15	.277	.308	.346
1993	Projected	110	326	37	86	18	2	3	30	24	14	.264	.314	.359
		98	281	37	72	21	2	4	28	31	13	.256	.300	.364

PAT HOWELL
New York Mets
Center Fielder
$1

Very fast, was called up in July when the Mets were quite concerned about their outfield defense. Essentially he's no prospect—24 years old, a singles hitter with a low average and poor strikeout/walk ratio. In the majors he could pinch run and play late-inning defense, but that's not enough because there's always somebody who can do those things and hit a little bit, too.

YEAR	TEAM/LEVEL	G	AB	R	H	2B	3B	HR	RBI	BB	SB	AVG	OBP	SLG
1992	Tidewater AAA	104	405	46	99	8	3	1	22	22	21	.244	.290	.286
1992	MLE	104	391	35	85	6	2	0	17	17	16	.217	.250	.243
1992	New York	31	75	9	14	1	0	0	1	2	4	.187	.218	.200

DANN HOWITT
Seattle Mariners
Outfielder
$1

Tall and strong, built like a Division II power forward. Good athlete, good arm, could hit home runs if he could make contact. Originally in the A's system, had an outstanding year at Huntsville in 1989, but hasn't built on it since. Now 29 years old, no prospect. I don't understand why he can't hit better, but the fact is that he doesn't.

YEAR	TEAM/LEVEL	G	AB	R	H	2B	3B	HR	RBI	BB	SB	AVG	OBP	SLG
1992	Two Teams AAA	93	318	54	95	22	6	7	60	35	9	.299	.367	.472
1992	MLE	93	299	36	76	18	3	4	41	24	5	.254	.310	.375
1992	Two Teams	35	85	7	16	4	1	2	10	8	1	.188	.250	.329

KENT HRBEK
Minnesota Twins
First Baseman
$23

His season was ruined by problems with his shoulders, for which he scheduled shoulder surgery after the season. He hit very well through June (.301 with good power), but nothing after July 1 (.189 with very little power). He'll be 33 in May, so it's 95 percent certain that his best years are behind him. He may come back a long way, but I'd be wary of him.

YEAR	TEAM/LEVEL	G	AB	R	H	2B	3B	HR	RBI	BB	SB	AVG	OBP	SLG
1991	Minnesota	132	462	72	131	20	1	20	89	67	4	.284	.373	.461
1992	Minnesota	112	394	52	96	20	0	15	58	71	5	.244	.357	.409
1993	Projected	127	435	60	120	23	1	18	74	68	4	.276	.374	.457
		142	476	68	144	26	2	21	80	65	3	.303	.390	.498

REX HUDLER
St. Louis Cardinals
Utilityman
$11

A very valuable role player, tore a knee ligament and missed most of May and June. The Cardinals, who are deep in infielders, had a rash of injuries at that time, and this left Hudler unavailable during the part of the season when he would have been most valuable. Now 32, a .250 hitter with unusual power for a utility infielder, can run and can also play outfield.

YEAR	TEAM/LEVEL	G	AB	R	H	2B	3B	HR	RBI	BB	SB	AVG	OBP	SLG
1991	St. Louis	101	207	21	47	10	2	1	15	10	12	.227	.260	.309
1992	St. Louis	61	98	17	24	4	0	3	5	2	2	.245	.265	.378
1993	Projected	55	102	13	25	5	1	2	8	5	6	.245	.280	.373
		47	106	9	26	6	2	1	11	8	10	.245	.298	.368

MIKE HUFF
Chicago White Sox
Right Fielder
$7

Capable of hitting .270 in the major leagues, has endangered his career by not doing it. Modest talent, right-handed hitter with no power, just a little speed, now 29 years old. One of the key things the White Sox need to improve in '93 is their offense in right field. Just letting Warren Newson play would be too simple, I guess.

YEAR	TEAM/LEVEL	G	AB	R	H	2B	3B	HR	RBI	BB	SB	AVG	OBP	SLG
1991	Two Teams	102	243	42	61	10	2	3	25	37	14	.251	.361	.346
1992	Chicago	60	115	13	24	5	0	0	8	10	1	.209	.273	.252
1993	Projected	56	136	22	36	7	2	2	16	19	5	.265	.355	.390
		52	147	31	48	9	4	4	24	28	9	.327	.434	.524

TIM HULETT
Baltimore Orioles
Utilityman
$12

Backup second baseman/third baseman, hits very well for a player in that role. Uppercuts, hits the ball in the air, doesn't run well . . . missed some time last summer after his son was struck and killed by a car . . . no possibility of moving up to regular status, but his role in the majors is absolutely secure for one more year.

YEAR	TEAM/LEVEL	G	AB	R	H	2B	3B	HR	RBI	BB	SB	AVG	OBP	SLG
1991	Baltimore	79	206	29	42	9	0	7	18	13	0	.204	.255	.350
1992	Baltimore	57	142	11	41	7	2	2	21	10	0	.289	.340	.408
1993	Projected	69	162	18	40	9	1	3	16	14	1	.247	.307	.370
		81	182	25	39	11	0	4	11	18	2	.214	.313	.341

DAVID HULSE
Texas Rangers
Center Fielder
$14

Probably nailed down a major league job by hitting .304 after being recalled August 10. Will start the year as the Rangers' center fielder, but in my opinion is unlikely to hold the job. Very fast, but not a good arm and didn't play center in the minors. Undisciplined hitter, overswings, and is not strong enough to drive the ball. Has had several minor league injuries. Grade C prospect.

YEAR	TEAM/LEVEL	G	AB	R	H	2B	3B	HR	RBI	BB	SB	AVG	OBP	SLG
1992	Tulsa AA	88	354	40	101	14	3	3	20	20	17	.285	.329	.367
1992	MLE	96	377	42	101	13	2	2	20	15	14	.268	.296	.329
1992	Texas	32	92	14	28	4	0	0	2	3	3	.304	.326	.348

MIKE HUMPHREYS
New York Yankees
Outfielder
$8

Acquired from the Padres for Oscar Azocar, he is actually a little bit better player than Azocar. He would hit for about the same average (.250), but walks a lot, can steal some bases, and has shown occasional power in minors (19 homers at Double-A and Triple-A in 1990). Can fill in at third base. Turns 26 in April, could be OK player off the bench.

YEAR	TEAM/LEVEL	G	AB	R	H	2B	3B	HR	RBI	BB	SB	AVG	OBP	SLG
1991	Columbus AAA	117	413	71	117	23	5	9	53	63	34	.283	.377	.429
1992	Columbus AAA	114	408	83	115	18	6	6	46	59	37	.282	.370	.400
1992	MLE	114	391	66	98	16	3	4	36	46	26	.251	.330	.338
		114	374	49	87	14	0	0	26	33	15	.233	.280	.254

TODD HUNDLEY
New York Mets
Catcher
$24

Isn't it ironic that the Mets came up with Todd Hundley in the very same year that they inducted Jerry Grote into their Hall of Fame. . .Hundley is not a good hitter, but he isn't really a .209 hitter, either; the batting average will improve over time. He hit .186 before the All-Star break, .232 after. He should hit near .250.

YEAR	TEAM/LEVEL	G	AB	R	H	2B	3B	HR	RBI	BB	SB	AVG	OBP	SLG
1991	Tidewater AAA	125	454	62	124	24	4	14	66	51	1	.273	.344	.436
1992	New York	123	358	32	75	17	0	7	32	19	3	.209	.256	.316
1993	Projected	119	347	35	80	17	1	6	36	28	2	.231	.288	.337
		115	336	38	85	17	2	5	40	37	1	.253	.327	.360

BRIAN HUNTER
Atlanta Braves
First Baseman
$20

His average dropped but he had an impressive season. Most of his hits were for extra bases and he averaged more than two bases per hit, things only done by guys like Killebrew and McGwire. He had a mid-season slump when the pitchers figured out that he would chase an outside breaking pitch, but he adjusted and finished hot. **Has an outside chance to be a star.**

YEAR	TEAM/LEVEL	G	AB	R	H	2B	3B	HR	RBI	BB	SB	AVG	OBP	SLG
1991	Atlanta	97	271	32	68	16	1	12	50	17	0	.251	.296	.450
1992	Atlanta	102	238	34	57	13	2	14	41	21	1	.239	.292	.487
1993	Projected	136	442	53	104	18	1	20	65	36	3	.235	.293	.416

JEFF HUSON
Texas Rangers
Infielder/Shortstop
$18

He hit well enough to keep a shortstop in work, .261 with a secondary average of .286, best among AL shortstops. He can't any more play shortstop than he can fly. He doesn't have a shortstop's arm or feet, which combined with Reimer and lesser problems to create an awful mess on the left side of the Ranger defense. Would be OK second baseman; the Rangers need a shortstop.

YEAR	TEAM/LEVEL	G	AB	R	H	2B	3B	HR	RBI	BB	SB	AVG	OBP	SLG
1991	Texas	119	268	36	57	8	3	2	26	39	8	.213	.312	.287
1992	Texas	123	318	49	83	14	3	4	24	41	18	.261	.342	.362
1993	Projected	132	331	49	79	14	2	2	28	44	13	.239	.328	.311
		141	344	49	75	14	1	0	32	47	8	.218	.312	.23

PETE INCAVIGLIA
Houston Astros
Right Fielder
$17

Lost weight a year ago and came to camp as a non-roster player, continued to strike out as often as before and didn't have a good power year, but his average went up and he could run out a double. Only 29, so a return to full-time status can't be ruled out. I am of the general opinion that a leopard doesn't change his spots.

YEAR	TEAM/LEVEL	G	AB	R	H	2B	3B	HR	RBI	BB	SB	AVG	OBP	SLG
1991	Detroit	97	337	38	72	12	1	11	38	36	1	.124	.290	.353
1992	Houston	113	349	31	93	22	1	11	44	25	2	.266	.319	.430
1993	Projected	97	300	34	75	16	1	13	44	27	2	.250	.312	.440
		81	251	37	57	10	1	15	44	29	2	.227	.307	.474

DARRIN JACKSON
San Diego Padres
Center Fielder
$33

Must be considered a proven, quality regular after two solid seasons. The two most important offensive statistics are on-base percentage and slugging percentage, and Jackson's OBP is poor (.283) and his slugging percentage is unimpressive (.392). Still, he's a surprisingly good center fielder, he has some power and some speed, and that should be enough to keep him in his job for several years.

YEAR	TEAM/LEVEL	G	AB	R	H	2B	3B	HR	RBI	BB	SB	AVG	OBP	SLG
1991	San Diego	122	359	51	94	12	1	21	49	27	5	.262	.315	.476
1992	San Diego	155	587	72	146	23	5	17	70	26	14	.249	.283	.392
1993	Projected	153	508	61	124	17	2	18	58	29	10	.244	.285	.392
		157	429	50	102	11	0	19	46	32	6	.238	.291	.396

BROOK JACOBY
Cleveland Indians
Milwaukee *Third Baseman*
$14

Returned to Cleveland and inherited playing time when Thome was hurt early in the year. Over the last four years has hit 27 homers before the All-Star break, only 8 after. Grounded into 13 double plays, a scary number for 291 at bats. His career is about over at 33, but he could last two more years as a pinch hitter/defensive sub at first and third.

YEAR	TEAM/LEVEL	G	AB	R	H	2B	3B	HR	RBI	BB	SB	AVG	OBP	SLG
1991	Two Teams	122	419	28	94	21	1	4	44	27	2	.224	.274	.308
1992	Cleveland	120	291	30	76	7	0	4	36	28	0	.261	.324	.326
1993	Projected	118	367	40	98	18	1	8	48	35	1	.267	.331	.387
		116	443	50	120	29	2	12	60	42	2	.271	.334	.427

JOHN JAHA
Brewers
First Baseman
$21

A favorite of minor league watchers after big numbers at El Paso and Denver. Those are great places to hit, plus Jaha is 26 years old and a first baseman, so he's not Hank Greenberg. He is, however, not a big oaf; he is a good first baseman and runs well. Lost job in September, could hit .285 and slug .500 in a good year. Grade C prospect.

YEAR	TEAM/LEVEL	G	AB	R	H	2B	3B	HR	RBI	BB	SB	AVG	OBP	SLG
1992	Denver AAA	79	274	61	88	18	2	18	69	50	6	.321	.434	.599
1992	MLE	79	259	45	73	15	1	13	51	36	4	.282	.369	.498
1992	Milwaukee	47	133	17	30	3	1	2	10	12	10	.226	.291	.308
		15	7	0	0	0	1	0	0	0	14	.000	.000	.128

CHRIS JAMES
San Francisco Giants
Left Fielder
$6

I can't really explain why he is in the major leagues. He doesn't hit for average or much power (.402 career slugging percentage), doesn't run well, and has an awful strikeout/walk ratio. It isn't defense. He can hit left-handers well enough to be marginally useful in a platoon role, but that isn't the way he is actually used.

YEAR	TEAM/LEVEL	G	AB	R	H	2B	3B	HR	RBI	BB	SB	AVG	OBP	SLG
1991	Cleveland	115	437	31	104	16	2	5	41	18	3	.238	.273	.318
1992	San Francisco	111	248	25	60	10	4	5	32	14	2	.242	.285	.375
1993	Projected	72	213	21	55	11	2	5	25	12	2	.258	.298	.399
		33	178	17	50	12	0	5	18	10	2	.281	.319	.433

DION JAMES
New York Yankees
Right Fielder
$13

Had a good year as a reserve, and could be consistently valuable in that role. Missed 1991 with injuries. His .359 on-base percentage and average/above average speed make him a useful 1 or 2 hitter. As a left-handed line-drive hitter, fits the traditional mold of a pinch hitter, and is a lifetime .282 hitter. Has very little power and isn't a good baserunner.

YEAR	TEAM/LEVEL	G	AB	R	H	2B	3B	HR	RBI	BB	SB	AVG	OBP	SLG
1989	Two Teams	134	415	41	119	18	0	5	40	49	2	.287	.363	.366
1990	Cleveland	87	248	28	68	15	2	1	22	27	5	.274	.347	.363
1992	New York	67	145	24	38	8	0	3	17	22	1	.262	.359	.379
		47	42	20	8	1	0	5	12	17	0	.190	.424	.571

STAN JAVIER
Philadelphia Phillies
Utility Outfielder
$16

Traded to Philadelphia in mid-season for Steve Searcy. Fine reserve outfielder, comparable to Henry Cotto. Good outfielder, has the speed to cover center, arm could be stronger. Exceptional percentage base stealer, will take a walk. Would be more useful to a pennant contender than a team like the Phillies, who are always tempted to push him into the lineup.

YEAR	TEAM/LEVEL	G	AB	R	H	2B	3B	HR	RBI	BB	SB	AVG	OBP	SLG
1991	Los Angeles	121	176	21	36	5	3	1	11	16	7	.205	.376	.395
1992	Two Teams	130	334	42	83	17	1	1	29	37	18	.249	.327	.314
1993	Projected	131	284	42	70	12	3	2	24	34	13	.246	.327	.331
		132	234	42	57	7	5	3	19	31	8	.244	.332	.355

GREGG JEFFERIES
Kansas City Royals
Third Baseman
$46

Very strong, quick bat; has some unusual positives. Runs well and is aggressive on the bases, almost never strikes out. He probably will win a batting title, and could hit 50 or more doubles. Made progress in the field last year, but is still below average defensive third baseman. The Royals call him "Pugsley" and play the theme from *The Addams Family* when he comes to the plate.

YEAR	TEAM/LEVEL	G	AB	R	H	2B	3B	HR	RBI	BB	SB	AVG	OBP	SLG
1991	New York	136	486	59	132	19	2	9	62	47	26	.272	.336	.374
1992	Kansas City	152	604	66	172	36	3	10	75	43	19	.285	.329	.404
1993	Projected	151	577	77	164	33	3	14	73	49	19	.284	.340	.425
		150	550	88	156	30	3	18	71	55	19	.284	.341	.477

REGGIE JEFFERSON
Cleveland Indians
First Baseman
$8

According to *Baseball America*, Jefferson's "offensive potential is scary." He is big (6-4, 210), a switch hitter, and can hit the ball a long way. He hit .337 in a callup, but I think his offensive potential has some limits. He's about the same age as Frank Thomas, has battled injuries for two years, and will strike out 25 percent to 27 percent of his at bats in the majors.

YEAR	TEAM/LEVEL	G	AB	R	H	2B	3B	HR	RBI	BB	SB	AVG	OBP	SLG
1992	Colorado Sp AAA	57	218	49	68	11	4	11	44	29	1	.312	.390	.550
1992	MLE	57	206	31	56	9	2	8	28	18	0	.272	.330	.451
1992	Cleveland	24	89	8	30	6	2	1	6	1	0	.337	.352	.483
		0	0	0	4	3	2	0	0	0	0	—	—	

DOUG JENNINGS
Baltimore Orioles
Outfielder
$7

At 28 he is running out of time, but he had a good year at Rochester and the Orioles have put him on their 40-man roster, so he may get another shot in '93. He's a little guy, listed at 5-10 but looks smaller, whose career was disrupted when the A's took him from California under Rule 5. Hits OK for fourth or fifth outfielder.

YEAR	TEAM/LEVEL	G	AB	R	H	2B	3B	HR	RBI	BB	SB	AVG	OBP	SLG
1991	Tacoma AAA	95	332	43	89	17	2	3	44	47	5	.268	.368	.358
1992	Rochester AAA	119	396	70	109	23	5	14	76	68	11	.275	.390	.465
1992	MLE	119	381	54	94	18	3	13	58	52	7	.247	.337	.412
		119	366	38	79	13	1	12	40	36	3	.216	.286	.355

SHAWN JETER
Chicago White Sox
Outfielder
$2

A 26-year-old left-handed hitter, was called up for a month while Dan Pasqua was on the DL and was recalled in September. He's been in the minors since 1985, originally in the Toronto system. He's very fast, a line-drive hitter but not a good hitter and no power. Could take Mike Huff's job in '93, or get a shot with an expansion team. Grade D prospect.

YEAR	TEAM/LEVEL	G	AB	R	H	2B	3B	HR	RBI	BB	SB	AVG	OBP	SLG
1992	Vancouver AAA	96	379	61	114	18	5	2	34	38	26	.301	.367	.391
1992	MLE	96	364	48	99	15	3	1	27	30	18	.272	.327	.338
1992	Chicago	13	18	1	2	0	0	0	0	0	0	.111	.111	.111
		0	0	0	0	0	0	0	0	0	0	—		

HOWARD JOHNSON
New York Mets
Center Fielder/Third Baseman
$33

His season was put out of its misery on August 2 by a hairline fracture in his right wrist; he later had surgery on the wrist, his left shoulder, and both knees. (He's lucky he didn't have Trevor Wilson's doctor, or he'd have wound up as a balloon.) He's 32 and will have to adapt, but I expect another big year or two.

YEAR	TEAM/LEVEL	G	AB	R	H	2B	3B	HR	RBI	BB	SB	AVG	OBP	SLG
1991	New York	156	564	108	146	34	4	38	117	78	30	.259	.342	.535
1992	New York	100	350	48	78	19	0	7	43	55	22	.223	.329	.337
1993	Projected	133	483	75	118	23	1	21	76	66	30	.244	.335	.427
		166	646	102	158	27	2	35	109	77	38	.256	.339	.477

LANCE JOHNSON
Chicago White Sox

Center Fielder
$29

An acceptable player but not a championship-quality regular, doesn't push the team toward the title. Very fine center fielder, one of six Gold Glove quality center fielders in the American League. A .280 hitter and a base stealer, but doesn't get on base enough (.318 OBP last year) to score very many runs, and doesn't have power to drive in many.

YEAR	TEAM/LEVEL	G	AB	R	H	2B	3B	HR	RBI	BB	SB	AVG	OBP	SLG
1991	Chicago	160	588	72	161	14	13	0	49	26	26	.274	.304	.342
1992	Chicago	157	567	67	158	15	12	3	47	34	41	.279	.318	.363
1993	Projected	159	576	72	158	16	8	2	50	33	36	.274	.314	.340
		161	585	77	158	17	9	1	53	32	37	.270	.308	.318

CHIPPER JONES
Atlanta Braves

Shortstop
$40

It is contrary to my philosophy to project a minor league player as a major league star, but one would be hard-pressed to invent a specific reason why Jones would not be one. He reached Double-A last year, age 20, and was immediately the best player in the Southern League. Some people doubt his ability to play shortstop. **The absolute definition of a Grade A prospect.**

YEAR	TEAM/LEVEL	G	AB	R	H	2B	3B	HR	RBI	BB	SB	AVG	OBP	SLG
1992	Durham A	59	223	38	61	17	1	3	28	29	10	.274	.355	.399
1992	Greenville AA	67	266	43	92	17	11	9	42	11	14	.346	.367	.594
1992	MLE	67	258	35	84	15	5	9	35	7	9	.326	.343	.527
		67	260	27	76	13	0	9	28	3	4	.304	.312	.456

CHRIS JONES
Houston Astros

Outfielder
$1

A 27-year-old from the Cincinnati Reds organization, started the year with Houston as a defensive sub in the outfield and sometime pinch hitter, sent to Tucson in June and came back in August. Nothing about him resembles a major league player. He couldn't hit .250, not much power, not much speed, prone to strikeouts. No prospect.

YEAR	TEAM/LEVEL	G	AB	R	H	2B	3B	HR	RBI	BB	SB	AVG	OBP	SLG
1991	Cincinnati	52	89	14	26	1	2	2	6	2	2	.292	.304	.416
1992	Houston	54	63	7	12	2	1	1	4	7	3	.190	.271	.302
1992	Tucson AAA	45	170	25	55	9	8	3	28	18	7	.324	.384	.524
		36	277	43	98	16	15	5	52	29	11	.354	.418	.54

TIM JONES
St. Louis Cardinals

Shortstop/Second Baseman
$8

Pulled a rib cage muscle in May, when he could have played for the Cardinals. Thirty years old, has been up and down since 1988. Not real fast, no power, sub-.250 hitter but can do the job at shortstop or second. The Cardinals need to shake out their infield, but with expansion and the possibility of Ozzie leaving, this probably isn't the moment when Jones' career will end.

YEAR	TEAM/LEVEL	G	AB	R	H	2B	3B	HR	RBI	BB	SB	AVG	OBP	SLG
1990	St. Louis	67	128	9	28	7	1	1	12	12	3	.219	.291	.313
1991	MLE	86	295	27	68	8	0	4	23	31	14	.231	.304	.298
1992	St. Louis	67	145	9	29	4	0	0	3	11	5	.200	.256	.228
		48	0	0	0	0	0	0	0	0	0	—	—	—

BRIAN JORDAN
St. Louis Cardinals
Outfielder or Football Player
$1

Made himself a lot of money by playing well for a short time while Felix Jose was out, and is certainly an impressive athlete. In my opinion he will never be a good baseball player. At 26 his skills should be nearly mature. We can make a certain allowance for his lack of experience, but the fact is that he is nowhere near ready. Grade D prospect.

YEAR	TEAM/LEVEL	G	AB	R	H	2B	3B	HR	RBI	BB	SB	AVG	OBP	SLG
1991	Louisville AAA	61	212	35	56	11	4	4	24	17	10	.264	.342	.410
1992	Louisville AAA	43	155	23	45	3	1	4	16	8	13	.290	.337	.400
1992	St. Louis	55	193	17	40	9	4	5	22	10	7	.207	.250	.373
		67	231	11	35	15	7	6	28	12	1	.152	.193	.355

RICKY JORDAN
Philadelphia Phillies
First Baseman
$22

Missed the first month with a broken jaw, no impact on future. Despite OK batting average he doesn't create enough runs to play regularly as a first baseman. Appears to have larger-than-normal platoon differential, hit .371 against lefties last year and has hit them well throughout his career. Ability to hit a left-hander makes him worth keeping around as a reserve.

YEAR	TEAM/LEVEL	G	AB	R	H	2B	3B	HR	RBI	BB	SB	AVG	OBP	SLG
1991	Philadelphia	101	301	38	82	21	3	9	49	14	0	.272	.304	.452
1992	Philadelphia	94	276	33	84	19	0	4	34	5	3	.304	.313	.417
1993	Projected	112	354	39	96	22	1	7	48	13	2	.271	.297	.398
		130	432	45	108	25	2	10	62	21	1	.250	.285	.387

TERRY JORGENSEN
Minnesota Twins
First/Third Baseman
$13

Jorgensen was a hot prospect for the Twins several years ago, but his career stalled after he played poorly in a 1989 callup. Not that he's old; he's only 26. In any case, he has re-emerged as a prospect after his third and best season at Portland, and with the Twins needing help at third base *and* first base, is well positioned to move up. Grade C prospect.

YEAR	TEAM/LEVEL	G	AB	R	H	2B	3B	HR	RBI	BB	SB	AVG	OBP	SLG
1992	Portland AAA	135	505	78	149	32	2	14	71	54	2	.295	.364	.450
1992	MLE	135	491	61	135	31	1	10	56	43	1	.275	.333	.403
1992	Minnesota	22	58	5	18	1	0	0	5	3	1	.310	.349	.328
		0	0	0	0	0	0	0	0	0	1	—	—	—

FELIX JOSE
St. Louis Cardinals
Right Fielder
$41

He seems to get a little bit better every year, and has pushed his clearly established level of skills to such a point that he can expect a long major league career. He missed the first month of '92 with a strained right hamstring, but played awfully well the rest of the year. Defense is *much* better than it was when he came up.

YEAR	TEAM/LEVEL	G	AB	R	H	2B	3B	HR	RBI	BB	SB	AVG	OBP	SLG
1991	St. Louis	154	568	69	173	40	6	8	77	50	20	.305	.360	.438
1992	St. Louis	131	509	62	150	22	3	14	75	40	28	.295	.347	.432
1993	Projected	145	526	63	145	27	2	13	71	42	21	.276	.329	.409
		159	545	61	140	32	1	12	67	44	14	.257	.312	.385

WALLY JOYNER
Kansas City Royals
First Baseman
$33

Run-of-the-mill first baseman, good defense, but not the run producer you would like at that position. The Royals made a mistake in signing him to a long-term contract. 1) He's not a championship quality player; 2) he obstructs the development of Conine or Hamelin, one of whom could be a better player; 3) he (further) clogs the left end of the defensive spectrum.

YEAR	TEAM/LEVEL	G	AB	R	H	2B	3B	HR	RBI	BB	SB	AVG	OBP	SLG
1991	California	143	551	79	166	34	3	21	96	52	2	.301	.360	.488
1992	Kansas City	149	572	66	154	36	2	9	66	55	11	.269	.336	.386
1993	Projected	159	601	73	166	33	1	18	84	63	6	.276	.345	.424
		169	630	80	178	30	0	27	102	71	1	.283	.355	.459

DAVE JUSTICE
Atlanta Braves
Right Fielder
$51

Has yet to match the 28 homers he hit as a rookie in 1990, and people are beginning to realize that he doesn't really have Hall of Fame ability. His power and walks make him a more valuable hitter than his .256 average of 1992 would suggest, and he is almost certain to have better seasons—30 homer, 100 RBI, 100 run seasons. A valuable player.

YEAR	TEAM/LEVEL	G	AB	R	H	2B	3B	HR	RBI	BB	SB	AVG	OBP	SLG
1991	Atlanta	109	396	67	109	25	1	21	87	65	8	.275	.377	.503
1992	Atlanta	144	484	78	124	19	5	21	72	79	2	.256	.359	.446
1993	Projected	140	483	79	128	25	2	23	80	79	8	.265	.368	.468
		136	482	80	132	31	0	25	88	79	14	.274	.376	.474

RON KARKOVICE
Chicago White Sox
Catcher
$29

Has as good an arm as anybody in baseball, although he doesn't get rid of the ball like Rodriguez, and is strong enough to hit 25 homers in a year although he hasn't yet. The White Sox need to find somebody who has two *left*-handed catchers and work out a deal. Karkovice is not destined for stardom, but will have better seasons than 1992.

YEAR	TEAM/LEVEL	G	AB	R	H	2B	3B	HR	RBI	BB	SB	AVG	OBP	SLG
1991	Chicago	75	167	25	41	13	0	5	22	15	0	.246	.310	.413
1992	Chicago	123	342	39	81	12	1	13	50	30	10	.237	.302	.392
1993	Projected	121	309	42	74	15	1	10	39	29	5	.239	.305	.392
		119	276	45	67	18	1	7	28	28	0	.243	.313	.391

ERIC KARROS
Los Angeles Dodgers
First Baseman
$41

Didn't play as well as Reggie Sanders, but won the rookie award because Sanders missed time. Good defense, capable now of hitting 20–30 points higher than .257, young enough to improve. Will have to show exceptional consistency to be a star. He won't hit .320 or hit 40 home runs, so he'll have to do what he could do—hit .280 with 30 home runs—every year.

YEAR	TEAM/LEVEL	G	AB	R	H	2B	3B	HR	RBI	BB	SB	AVG	OBP	SLG
1991	Albuquerque AAA	132	488	88	154	33	8	22	101	58	3	.316	.391	.551
1992	Los Angeles	149	545	63	140	30	1	20	88	37	2	.257	.304	.426
1993	Projected	151	551	68	152	31	1	18	78	42	4	.276	.327	.434
		153	557	73	164	32	1	16	68	47	6	.294	.349	.442

MIKE KELLY
Atlanta Braves
Outfielder
$2

Arizona State star who was the second player taken in the 1991 draft. He's regarded as a good center fielder, played at Greenville in '92 and hit .225 with 160 strikeouts, but was cited by *Baseball America* as the fourth best prospect in the league anyway. My guess is that the strikeouts will plague him for the rest of his career; Grade C prospect.

YEAR	TEAM/LEVEL	G	AB	R	H	2B	3B	HR	RBI	BB	SB	AVG	OBP	SLG
1991	Durham A	35	124	29	31	6	1	6	17	19	6	.250	.356	.460
1992	Greenville AA	133	471	82	106	18	4	24	70	65	22	.225	.325	.433
1992	MLE	133	464	69	101	16	2	23	59	43	14	.218	.284	.409
		133	457	56	96	14	0	22	48	21	6	.210	.245	.385

PAT KELLY
New York Yankees
Second Baseman
$21

Came into his own after the All-Star break last year, hitting .254 the second half with .414 slugging, 6-for-7 as a base stealer. Limited potential, should never have been projected as a star but could hit 35 doubles, 15 homers in a good year, which would make him very valuable at second. Uppercuts, hits fly balls and strikes out.

YEAR	TEAM/LEVEL	G	AB	R	H	2B	3B	HR	RBI	BB	SB	AVG	OBP	SLG
1991	New York	96	298	35	72	12	4	3	23	15	12	.242	.288	.339
1992	New York	106	318	38	72	22	2	7	27	25	8	.226	.301	.374
1993	Projected	112	347	47	87	18	3	6	34	23	15	.251	.297	.372
		118	376	56	102	14	4	5	41	21	22	.271	.310	.376

ROBERTO KELLY
Cincinnati Reds
Outfielder
$51

It is my opinion that Kelly will be a better player than O'Neill, and that the Reds will win the trade by a substantial margin if they can keep Kelly. O'Neill has better hitting stats then Kelly in the past and O'Neill has a right fielder's arm, which Kelly doesn't, but Kelly has speed, and the better hitting stats are probably attributable more to the park than the player.

YEAR	TEAM/LEVEL	G	AB	R	H	2B	3B	HR	RBI	BB	SB	AVG	OBP	SLG
1991	New York	126	486	68	130	22	2	20	69	45	32	.267	.333	.444
1992	New York	152	580	81	158	31	2	10	66	41	28	.272	.322	.384
1993	Projected	158	580	80	161	27	2	15	67	42	37	.278	.326	.409
		164	580	79	164	23	2	20	68	43	46	.283	.332	.433

JEFF KENT
New York Mets
Second Base
$27

When you *have* to trade a star player you can't break even, but Kent is real quality. He can play second base or third, and could be a Bobby Grich type, one of the few middle infielders who hits 20 home runs and plays good defense, also could walk 70 times. That's if you're lucky, of course; his strikeouts could swallow his offense. He's a good prospect.

YEAR	TEAM/LEVEL	G	AB	R	H	2B	3B	HR	RBI	BB	SB	AVG	OBP	SLG
1991	Knoxville AA	139	445	68	114	34	1	12	61	80	25	.256	.379	.418
1992	Two Teams	102	305	52	73	21	2	11	50	27	2	.239	.312	.430
1993	Projected	126	431	64	105	27	1	12	58	51	13	.244	.324	.394
		150	557	76	137	33	0	13	66	75	24	.249	.335	.38

JEFF KING
Pittsburgh Pirates
Infielder
$23

Value has shot up, despite his .231 average. Two things have happened. First, he demonstrated an unexpected ability to play second base (while Lind was out), and later was used at first and short. Second, after hitting .187 before the All-Star break he hit .268 the second half with 45 RBI. He's near his peak and has become arbitration-eligible; **recommend you consider drafting him in '93.**

YEAR	TEAM/LEVEL	G	AB	R	H	2B	3B	HR	RBI	BB	SB	AVG	OBP	SLG
1991	Pittsburgh	33	109	16	26	1	1	14	18	14	3	.239	.328	.376
1992	Pittsburgh	130	480	56	111	21	2	14	65	27	4	.231	.272	.371
1993	Projected	142	511	63	121	20	2	16	67	36	6	.237	.287	.378
		154	542	70	131	19	2	18	67	45	8	.312	.300	.384

MIKE KINGERY
Oakland Athletics
Outfielder
No Value

Was sent to Tacoma April 30, hit .306 there. Good outfielder, right fielder's arm, runs well, outstanding hustle, just doesn't hit enough to stay in the majors. I'm not sure why he wasn't called up when the A's had all the outfield injuries . . . 32 years old now . . . managerial type, has a degree from Willmar Community College in Minnesota. Was born on Cy Young's birthday.

YEAR	TEAM/LEVEL	G	AB	R	H	2B	3B	HR	RBI	BB	SB	AVG	OBP	SLG
1990	San Francisco	105	207	24	61	7	1	0	24	12	6	.295	.335	.338
1991	San Francisco	91	110	13	20	2	2	0	8	15	1	.182	.280	.236
1992	Oakland	12	28	3	3	0	0	0	1	1	0	.107	.138	.107
		0	0	0	0	0	0	0	0	0	0	–	–	–

WAYNE KIRBY
Cleveland Indians
Pinch Runner
$6

Outfielder, has been in the Dodger system since the Eisenhower administration. He was slow to start hitting, spent four years at A Ball, eventually broke free of the Dodgers, signed with Cleveland, and had a super year at Colorado Springs. Left-handed hitter, 29 years old, not going to take a job away from Belle, Lofton, Hill, or Whiten, but a good fifth outfielder.

YEAR	TEAM/LEVEL	G	AB	R	H	2B	3B	HR	RBI	BB	SB	AVG	OBP	SLG
1992	Colorado Sp AAA	123	470	101	162	18	16	11	74	36	51	.345	.392	.521
1992	MLE	123	441	65	133	15	8	7	48	23	31	.302	.336	.420
1992	Cleveland	21	18	9	3	1	0	1	1	3	0	.167	.286	.389
		0	0	0	0	0	0	0	0	0	0	–	–	–

RYAN KLESKO
Atlanta Braves
First Baseman
$16

A 6-3, 220-pound first baseman who hit .368 at Sumter in 1990. He started slowly at Richmond due to a hyperextended elbow, but hit well toward the end of the season, and he *will* be a good major league hitter. Takes a vicious cut at the ball, but doesn't strike out a lot. Only 21, has a temper, doesn't work on his defense. Grade B prospect, star potential.

YEAR	TEAM/LEVEL	G	AB	R	H	2B	3B	HR	RBI	BB	SB	AVG	OBP	SLG
1991	Greenville AA	126	419	64	122	22	3	14	67	75	14	.291	.404	.458
1992	Richmond AAA	123	418	63	105	22	2	17	59	41	3	.251	.323	.435
1992	MLE	123	409	50	96	19	1	15	47	31	2	.235	.289	.396
		123	400	37	87	16	0	13	35	21	1	.218	.257	.385

CHUCK KNOBLAUCH
Minnesota Twins
Second Baseman
$68

Super young player, at other times might have ranked as the best second baseman in the league, but Baerga and Alomar are even more exciting. Most young second basemen are unable to stay healthy—but if he does, I think Knoblauch will be a Hall of Famer. He's a .300 hitter who walks and steals bases, and a Gold Glove quality defensive player. Great self-confidence.

YEAR	TEAM/LEVEL	G	AB	R	H	2B	3B	HR	RBI	BB	SB	AVG	OBP	SLG
1991	Minnesota	151	565	78	159	24	6	1	50	59	25	.281	.351	.350
1992	Minnesota	155	600	104	178	19	6	2	56	88	34	.297	.384	.358
1993	Projected	156	584	94	171	26	7	3	59	75	29	.293	.373	.377
		151	568	84	164	33	8	4	62	62	24	.289	.359	.396

RANDY KNORR
Toronto Blue Jays
Catcher
$12

In another organization he might be the prize prospect. Very slow, hitting record inconsistent, but he might develop into a fine hitter. Syracuse is a tough place to hit; there normally isn't a lot of difference between what a hitter does there and what he will do in Toronto. Called up July 30, disabled August 20 with sprained ligament in his thumb. Grade B prospect.

YEAR	TEAM/LEVEL	G	AB	R	H	2B	3B	HR	RBI	BB	SB	AVG	OBP	SLG
1991	AA and AAA	115	416	36	102	20	0	5	48	33	3	.245	.303	.329
1992	Syracuse AAA	61	228	27	62	13	1	11	27	17	1	.272	.319	.482
1992	MLE	61	219	20	53	11	0	8	20	12	0	.242	.281	.402
		61	210	13	44	9	0	5	13	7	0	.210	.236	.324

KEVIN KOSLOFSKI
Kansas City Royals
Outfielder
$11

Has been in the minors for nine years, career was going nowhere until he unexpectedly started to hit in 1991. He will probably inherit Eisenreich's job as the Royals' fourth outfielder. He runs well but is poor percentage base stealer, excellent outfielder with a fair arm. Doubt that he can hold a regular job, but should hit .270 or better, and it's not *all* singles. Grade C prospect.

YEAR	TEAM/LEVEL	G	AB	R	H	2B	3B	HR	RBI	BB	SB	AVG	OBP	SLG
1992	Omaha AAA	78	280	29	87	12	5	4	32	21	8	.311	.362	.432
1992	MLE	78	270	23	77	11	4	2	25	16	5	.285	.325	.378
1992	Kansas City	55	133	20	33	0	2	3	13	12	2	.248	.313	.346
		32	0	17	0	0	0	4	1	8	0	—	.200	.031

CHAD KREUTER
Detroit Tigers
Catcher
$6

A switch hitter from the Texas system, had never hit a lick before last year, when he hit .253 overall and hit over .300 the last two months. He may have actually learned to hit. If true, this would be the fourth time in baseball history this had happened, for somebody to learn to hit at age 27. He'll go back to .220 . . .

YEAR	TEAM/LEVEL	G	AB	R	H	2B	3B	HR	RBI	BB	SB	AVG	OBP	SLG
1991	Texas	3	4	0	0	0	0	0	0	0	0	.000	.000	.000
1992	Detroit	67	190	22	48	9	0	2	16	20	0	.253	.321	.332
1993	Projected	75	196	26	42	9	1	3	19	32	1	.214	.325	.316
		82	202	30	36	9	2	4	22	44	2	.178	.325	.302

JOHN KRUK
Philadelphia Phillies
First Baseman/Right Fielder
$53

Has consistently hit much better when playing first base than when playing in the outfield. Does he look like an outfielder to you? One of the identifying marks of a bad organization is that they ask players to do things they're not good at . . . Kruk is like Smoky Burgess, will still be in the league as a pinch hitter when he's 40 years old and weighs 250 . . .

YEAR	TEAM/LEVEL	G	AB	R	H	2B	3B	HR	RBI	BB	SB	AVG	OBP	SLG
1991	Philadelphia	152	538	84	158	27	6	21	92	67	7	.294	.367	.483
1992	Philadelphia	144	507	86	164	30	4	10	70	92	3	.323	.423	.458
1993	Projected	146	492	69	144	22	3	12	70	77	7	.293	.388	.423
		148	477	52	124	14	2	14	70	62	11	.260	.315	.415

JEFF KUNKEL
Released
Infielder
$1

Released by the Cubs on September 19. A first-round draft pick, he was a highly regarded prospect with an outstanding throwing arm. His career was undermined by his inability to learn the strike zone, and at the end of his career he had made almost no progress on that issue. At Denver last year he hit .288, but with 29 strikeouts and 6 walks.

YEAR	TEAM/LEVEL	G	AB	R	H	2B	3B	HR	RBI	BB	SB	AVG	OBP	SLG
1992	Two Teams AAA	75	291	44	80	13	4	9	51	12	5	.275	.302	.440
1992	MLE	75	278	29	67	10	2	7	37	7	2	.241	.260	.367
1992	Chicago	20	29	0	4	2	0	0	1	0	0	.138	.138	.207
		0	0	0	0	0	0	0	0	0	0	—	—	—

STEVE LAKE
Philadelphia Phillies
Backup Catcher
$2

YearMissed all of August and most of September with a knee problem. Lake has a terrific throwing arm and hits as well your typical backup catcher, but he's not much use if he's not there . . . had just 2 RBI last year because he hit .050 with men on base (1 for 20) . . . goes on an All-Star team with Mickey Rivers, John Wetteland . . .

YEAR	TEAM/LEVEL	G	AB	R	H	2B	3B	HR	RBI	BB	SB	AVG	OBP	SLG
1990	Philadelphia	28	80	4	20	2	0	0	6	3	0	.250	.286	.275
1991	Philadelphia	58	158	12	36	4	1	1	11	2	0	.228	.238	.285
1992	Philadelphia	20	53	3	13	2	0	1	2	1	0	.245	.255	.340
		0	0	0	0	0	0	1	0	0	0	—	—	—

TIM LAKER
Montreal Expos
Catcher
$3

Called up by the Expos in August, and penciled in as a candidate for the starting job. This is what is known as optimism. Laker is said to have an extraordinary throwing arm, and had an OK year with the bat at Harrisburg, but he's only 23, and had never hit before 1992. Grade C prospect; I frankly don't believe he will hold the job this year.

YEAR	TEAM/LEVEL	G	AB	R	H	2B	3B	HR	RBI	BB	SB	AVG	OBP	SLG
1992	Harrsburg AA	117	409	55	99	19	3	15	68	39	3	.242	.312	.413
1992	MLE	117	394	43	84	17	2	10	53	25	2	.213	.260	.343
1992	Montreal	28	46	8	10	3	0	0	4	2	1	.217	.250	.283
		0	0	0	0	0	0	0	0	0	0	—	—	—

TOM LAMPKIN
San Diego Padres
Catcher
$4

Another perennial catching hopeful, now 29. Runs better than most catchers, doesn't throw well, singles hitter who would hit around .250 in the majors. Has had trials with Cleveland and San Diego and will have more; has improved his plate coverage in the last two years and might be able to stick as backup catcher . . . anybody remember that teams used to carry three catchers?

YEAR	TEAM/LEVEL	G	AB	R	H	2B	3B	HR	RBI	BB	SB	AVG	OBP	SLG
1991	San Diego	38	58	4	11	3	1	0	3	3	0	.190	.230	.276
1992	Las Vegas AAA	108	340	45	104	17	4	3	48	53	15	.306	.405	.406
1992	MLE	108	314	27	78	12	1	2	29	32	9	.248	.318	.312
		108	288	9	52	7	0	1	10	11	3	.181	.211	.215

RAY LANKFORD
St. Louis Cardinals
Center Fielder
$72

As a rookie he hit the ball on the ground 58 percent of the time. Last year he hit the ball in the air 53 percent of the time . . . was having a good year base stealing until he was caught nine times in September, giving him the league lead. In my opinion should continue to perform at or near the magnificent level of 1992, and probably will have even better seasons.

YEAR	TEAM/LEVEL	G	AB	R	H	2B	3B	HR	RBI	BB	SB	AVG	OBP	SLG
1991	St. Louis	151	568	83	142	23	15	9	69	41	44	.251	.301	.392
1992	St. Louis	153	598	87	175	40	6	20	86	72	42	.293	.371	.480
1993	Projected	155	567	76	152	31	9	16	77	62	40	.268	.340	.439
		157	546	65	129	22	12	12	68	52	38	.236	.303	.386

CARNEY LANSFORD
Oakland Athletics
(retired)
Third Baseman
No Value

He retired after driving in 75 runs, the most he had driven in in five years, and actually just five away from his career high. He spent 10 years as Oakland's third baseman, and while he perhaps failed to move Sal Bando off the franchise All-Star team, he gave them 10 years that were the best he could give. Retired with more than 2000 career hits.

YEAR	TEAM/LEVEL	G	AB	R	H	2B	3B	HR	RBI	BB	SB	AVG	OBP	SLG
1990	Oakland	134	507	58	136	15	1	3	50	45	16	.268	.333	.320
1991	Oakland	5	16	0	1	0	0	0	1	0	0	.063	.063	.063
1992	Oakland	135	496	65	130	30	1	7	75	43	7	.262	.325	.369
		165	976	130	259	60	2	14	149	86	14	.265	.325	.374

MIKE LANSING
Montreal Expos
Shortstop
$3

A base-stealing shortstop, in a year or two will be seriously blocked behind Wilfredo Cordero. He'll never beat out Cordero, but evaluated on his own merits he looks fairly decent. He could hit .250 to .260 in the majors with a reasonable strikeout/walk ratio, steal some bases, and is reported to be an adequate shortstop although he has made some errors. Grade B prospect.

YEAR	TEAM/LEVEL	G	AB	R	H	2B	3B	HR	RBI	BB	SB	AVG	OBP	SLG
1991	Miami A	103	384	54	110	20	7	6	55	40	29	.286	.355	.422
1992	Harrisburg AA	128	483	66	135	19	6	6	52	52	45	.280	.353	.381
1992	MLE	128	464	51	116	17	4	4	42	34	34	.250	.301	.330
		128	445	36	97	15	2	2	32	16	23	.218	.245	.274

BARRY LARKIN
Cincinnati Reds

Shortstop
$76

Can win an MVP Award anytime. He was healthier than usual last year, missing only a few weeks with a sprained knee, and hit, fielded, and ran the bases with his usual ferocity. Lifetime .296 hitter; the last shortstops to hit near .300 for a career average were Appling, Cronin, Arky Vaughn, Lou Boudreau, Johnny Pesky, and Cecil Travis, all of whom retired about 1950.

YEAR	TEAM/LEVEL	G	AB	R	H	2B	3B	HR	RBI	BB	SB	AVG	OBP	SLG
1991	Cincinnati	123	464	88	140	27	4	20	69	55	24	.302	.378	.506
1992	Cincinnati	140	533	76	162	32	6	12	78	63	15	.304	.377	.454
1993	Projected	141	538	81	157	26	5	12	68	59	23	.292	.362	.426
		142	543	86	152	20	4	12	58	55	31	.280	.346	.398

GENE LARKIN
Minnesota Twins

Right Fielder/First Baseman
$10

He's a puzzle; I can't really tell you why he continues to play although his offense never rises above replacement level even in a good year. Last year he was awful, hitting just .246 without power, but his playing time grew steadily as the season wore on; he played almost regularly in September. There are 50 guys in the minors who play the same positions and can hit better.

YEAR	TEAM/LEVEL	G	AB	R	H	2B	3B	HR	RBI	BB	SB	AVG	OBP	SLG
1991	Minnesota	98	255	34	73	14	1	2	19	30	2	.286	.361	.373
1992	Minnesota	115	337	38	83	18	1	6	42	28	7	.246	.308	.359
1993	Projected	94	272	32	71	16	1	4	29	29	4	.261	.332	.371
		73	217	26	59	14	1	2	16	30	1	.272	.360	.327

MIKE LAVALLIERE
Pittsburgh Pirates

Catcher
$27

Can't anticipate that his role or production will change over the next two to three years. Left-handed platoon catcher, singles hitter who walks quite a bit and hardly ever strikes out, bats eighth (he drew 14 intentional walks last year) and plays good defense. Has no power and is one of the slowest players in baseball. Drives in and scores about 30 runs a year.

YEAR	TEAM/LEVEL	G	AB	R	H	2B	3B	HR	RBI	BB	SB	AVG	OBP	SLG
1991	Pittsburgh	108	336	25	97	11	2	3	41	33	2	.289	.351	.360
1992	Pittsburgh	95	293	22	75	13	1	2	29	44	0	.256	.350	.328
1993	Projected	112	329	26	87	14	1	3	36	45	2	.264	.353	.340
		129	365	30	99	15	1	4	43	46	4	.271	.353	.35

MANUEL LEE
Toronto Blue Jays

Shortstop
$26

Until he missed most of September with a sore knee, he was having his best year. He cut his strikeouts from 107 to 73, increased his walks from 24 to 50, and hiked his average 29 points. I would take these changes to be the result of a deliberate effort which was successful, and therefore something that will continue. He played well at shortstop.

YEAR	TEAM/LEVEL	G	AB	R	H	2B	3B	HR	RBI	BB	SB	AVG	OBP	SLG
1991	Toronto	138	445	41	104	18	3	0	29	24	7	.234	.274	.288
1992	Toronto	128	396	49	104	10	1	3	39	50	6	.263	.343	.316
1993	Projected	139	444	49	110	13	3	4	40	38	6	.248	.307	.318
		150	492	49	116	16	5	5	41	26	6	.236	.274	.319

SCOTT LEIUS
Minnesota Twins
Third Baseman
$25

One of the Twins regulars who collapsed in August, pulling the Twins out of the race. Seems to have a huge platoon differential, career average of .307 against left-handed pitchers, .228 against right-handers. His defense is good, but he's not going to hit enough if he plays every day to hold a regular job. He'll slip back into the platoon role.

YEAR	TEAM/LEVEL	G	AB	R	H	2B	3B	HR	RBI	BB	SB	AVG	OBP	SLG
1991	Minnesota	109	199	35	57	7	2	5	20	30	5	.286	.378	.417
1992	Minnesota	129	409	50	102	18	2	2	35	34	6	.249	.309	.318
1993	Projected	118	319	41	82	16	2	3	29	32	5	.257	.325	.348
		107	229	32	62	14	2	4	23	30	4	.271	.355	.412

MARK LEMKE
Atlanta Braves
Second Baseman
$25

Like Leius, a good enough hitter against left-handers and a good enough defensive player to be valuable platoon player, but stretched to play every day. At one time I thought he would hit a little better, but after 1048 major league at bats you figure a .226 hitter is a .226 hitter . . . in his career is 1-for-10 as a base stealer. Is 27 years old.

YEAR	TEAM/LEVEL	G	AB	R	H	2B	3B	HR	RBI	BB	SB	AVG	OBP	SLG
1991	Atlanta	136	269	36	63	11	2	2	23	29	1	.234	.305	.312
1992	Atlanta	155	427	38	97	7	4	6	26	50	0	.227	.307	.304
1993	Projected	149	439	48	106	18	2	6	39	49	2	.241	.318	.333
		143	457	58	115	29	0	6	52	48	4	.255	.327	.359

PATRICK LENNON
Colorado Rockies
Outfielder/Designated Hitter
$10

A big DH from the Seattle system. He was out most of the '92 season with tendinitis in his wrist, signed with the Rockies as a six-year free agent. He can hit—he can hit .275 in the majors, with some power—but with Seattle he had to play the outfield in the minors so that Tino Martinez could play first, and he is *really* a bad outfielder.

YEAR	TEAM/LEVEL	G	AB	R	H	2B	3B	HR	RBI	BB	SB	AVG	OBP	SLG
1990	A and AA	93	330	53	96	12	6	13	52	25	16	.291	.341	.482
1991	Calgary AAA	112	416	75	137	29	5	15	74	46	12	.329	.400	.531
1991	MLE	112	386	49	107	24	3	9	55	24	7	.277	.329	.425
		112	356	23	77	19	1	3	36	2	2	.216	.221	.302

MARK LEONARD
San Francisco Giants
Left Fielder
$14

I've been arguing for him to get a chance for two or three years. He had good numbers until September, when he played lots and hit little. On balance he wasn't great but wasn't awful, posting a .273 secondary average. They are beginning to realize he can hit. Not a good outfielder, at the plate looks more like George Brett than anyone I've ever seen. Grade C prospect.

YEAR	TEAM/LEVEL	G	AB	R	H	2B	3B	HR	RBI	BB	SB	AVG	OBP	SLG
1991	San Francisco	64	129	14	31	7	1	2	14	12	0	.240	.306	.357
1992	San Francisco	55	128	13	30	7	0	4	16	16	0	.234	.331	.383
1993	Projected	121	438	52	114	16	1	13	55	54	2	.260	.341	.390
		187	748	91	198	25	2	22	84	92	4	.265	.348	.392

JESSE LEVIS
Cleveland Indians
Catcher
$16

A 24-year-old left-handed singles-hitting catcher. The release of Junior Ortiz probably means that his time has come. Only 5-9, will hit about like Mike LaValliere, possibly better. Doesn't have a strong arm, defense not a positive. With his ability to pinch hit would be more valuable to a National League team, but Alomar's injuries will get him work. Grade B prospect.

YEAR	TEAM/LEVEL	G	AB	R	H	2B	3B	HR	RBI	BB	SB	AVG	OBP	SLG
1992	Colorado Sp AAA	87	253	39	92	20	1	6	44	37	1	.364	.444	.522
1992	MLE	87	237	25	76	16	0	4	28	24	0	.321	.383	.439
1992	Cleveland	28	43	2	12	4	0	1	3	0	0	.279	.279	.442
		0	0	0	0	0	0	0	03	0	6	10	—	—	—

DARREN LEWIS
San Francisco Giants
Center Fielder
$17

A real good player to acquire. He had a disappointing season, in many different ways. Had walked a lot in '91, but didn't in '92. He has an absolutely awful batting record in Candlestick Park (.192 career mark, .274 on the road), so he may be helped if the team moves. Even if they don't, he's a young player who is better than his 1992 numbers.

YEAR	TEAM/LEVEL	G	AB	R	H	2B	3B	HR	RBI	BB	SB	AVG	OBP	SLG
1991	San Francisco	72	222	41	55	5	3	1	15	36	13	.248	.358	.311
1992	San Francisco	100	320	38	74	8	1	1	18	29	28	.231	.295	.272
1993	Projected	79	256	34	65	7	2	1	19	24	16	.254	.318	.309
		58	192	30	56	6	3	1	20	09	4	.292	.355	.370

MARK LEWIS
Cleveland Indians
Shortstop
$30

Offensively, he's not really any better than Felix Fermin, at least not yet. He probably will be; he's 23, and should improve significantly at bat. In the field, he led the American League in errors, with 25, but 16 of them were in the first two months, so that's a little misleading. A fair summary is that he's not helping anybody win yet. He's young, and probably will develop.

YEAR	TEAM/LEVEL	G	AB	R	H	2B	3B	HR	RBI	BB	SB	AVG	OBP	SLG
1991	Cleveland	84	314	29	83	15	1	0	30	15	2	.264	.293	.318
1992	Cleveland	122	413	44	109	21	0	5	30	25	4	.264	.308	.351
1993	Projected	123	436	47	116	22	1	6	47	24	5	.266	.304	.362
		124	459	50	123	23	2	7	64	23	6	.268	.303	.373

JIM LEYRITZ
New York Yankees
Utilityman
$14

His home run rate last year—7 in 144 at bats—would certainly keep him in work if he could do it consistently, but since this easily exceeds his best ratio in a long minor league career, that seems unlikely. Sometimes players do learn to pull the ball late in life . . . was used primarily as a DH and catcher, also bit parts at first, third, and right field.

YEAR	TEAM/LEVEL	G	AB	R	H	2B	3B	HR	RBI	BB	SB	AVG	OBP	SLG
1991	New York	32	77	8	14	3	0	0	4	13	0	.182	.300	.221
1992	New York	63	144	17	37	6	0	7	26	14	0	.257	.341	.444
1993	Projected	77	221	17	54	11	0	5	26	27	1	.244	.327	.362
		91	298	17	71	16	0	3	26	40	2	.238	.328	.322

MARK LIEBERTHAL
Philadelphia Phillies
Catcher
$18

A 21-year-old right-handed-hitting catcher, the Phillies' number-one draft pick in the 1990 draft. When he signed he was skinny, but has filled out. Reportedly handles pitchers well, throws well—and hit .286 at Double-A at age 20. Hasn't yet hit for power, but he's ten years younger than Darren Daulton. **Grade A prospect.**

YEAR	TEAM/LEVEL	G	AB	R	H	2B	3B	HR	RBI	BB	SB	AVG	OBP	SLG
1991	Two Teams A	88	295	41	89	19	0	0	38	26	1	.302	.360	.366
1992	AA and AAA	102	353	34	97	17	1	2	41	21	4	.275	.318	.346
1992	MLE	102	341	26	84	14	0	1	31	13	2	.246	.274	.296
		102	329	18	71	11	0	0	21	5	0	.216	.228	.249

JOSE LIND
Pittsburgh Pirates
Second Baseman
$26

Probably the best defensive second baseman in baseball, is able to stay in the lineup of one of baseball's best teams without contributing offensively. The rumor mill says he will be traded; I guess you'll know by the time you read this . . . has exceptional range, doesn't turn a lot of double plays because he doesn't cheat toward the bag in DP situations.

YEAR	TEAM/LEVEL	G	AB	R	H	2B	3B	HR	RBI	BB	SB	AVG	OBP	SLG
1991	Pittsburgh	150	502	53	133	16	6	3	54	30	7	.265	.306	.339
1992	Pittsburgh	135	468	38	110	14	1	0	39	26	3	.235	.275	.269
1993	Projected	124	418	39	105	18	3	2	40	27	5	.251	.297	.323
		113	368	40	100	22	5	4	41	28	7	.272	.323	.391

JIM LINDEMAN
Philadelphia Phillies
Outfielder/Pinch Hitter
$6

Had back trouble last year, went on the DL May 13 with a sore back and later had minor surgery on the back . . . he's 31, and he doesn't hit enough to help a team as a first baseman. He's got 514 major league at bats—about one season's worth—with a .232 average, 14 homers. No speed, not a bad athlete.

YEAR	TEAM/LEVEL	G	AB	R	H	2B	3B	HR	RBI	BB	SB	AVG	OBP	SLG
1990	Detroit	12	32	5	7	1	0	2	8	2	0	.219	.265	.438
1991	Philadelphia	65	95	13	32	5	0	0	12	13	0	.337	.413	.389
1992	Philadelphia	29	39	6	10	1	0	1	6	3	0	.256	.310	.359
		0	0	0	0	0	0	2	0	0	0	—	—	—

PAT LISTACH
Milwaukee Brewers
Shortstop
$42

He is the relatively rare case where a player's minor league hitting stats really don't represent his ability, because he has only been switch hitting for a couple of years, and his skills are still progressing rapidly. He also takes the widest turns around the bases in the league . . . has been known to go from third to home by way of downtown Chicago.

YEAR	TEAM/LEVEL	G	AB	R	H	2B	3B	HR	RBI	BB	SB	AVG	OBP	SLG
1991	MLE	138	448	64	95	12	3	0	30	46	23	.212	.285	.252
1992	Milwaukee	149	579	93	168	19	6	1	47	55	54	.290	.352	.349
1993	Projected	157	567	90	151	16	5	2	48	59	46	.266	.335	.323
		165	555	87	134	13	4	3	49	63	38	.241	.319	.295

GREG LITTON
San Francisco Giants
Utilityman
$4

He still has more major league hits than strikeouts, but it's close (141–132) and the strikeouts are gaining. Has a little power (very little), no speed . . . played mostly second base last year while Thompson was out. Has no future to speak of. The Giants have better young shortstops, and Litton doesn't hit enough to be useful anywhere else.

YEAR	TEAM/LEVEL	G	AB	R	H	2B	3B	HR	RBI	BB	SB	AVG	OBP	SLG
1991	San Francisco	59	127	13	23	7	1	1	15	11	0	.181	.250	.276
1992	San Francisco	68	140	9	32	5	0	4	15	11	0	.229	.285	.350
1993	Projected	88	193	19	45	12	1	4	25	15	1	.233	.288	.368
		108	*246*	*29*	*62*	*19*	*2*	*4*	*35*	*19*	*2*	*.252*	*.306*	*.394*

SCOTT LIVINGSTONE
Detroit Tigers
Third Baseman
$23

Is probably entering the pivotal season of his career, which will decide whether he is a long-term regular or a good bench player. I would guess the latter. Three reasons. First, although he has hit .285 so far, I suspect he might be more like a .270 hitter. Second, his secondary average was .162. Third, if Trammell returns strong there will be a squeeze for playing time.

YEAR	TEAM/LEVEL	G	AB	R	H	2B	3B	HR	RBI	BB	SB	AVG	OBP	SLG
1991	Detroit	44	127	19	37	5	0	2	11	10	2	.291	.341	.378
1992	Detroit	117	354	43	100	21	0	4	46	21	1	.282	.319	.376
1993	Projected	110	345	44	94	16	0	6	43	27	2	.272	.325	.371
		103	*386*	*45*	*88*	*11*	*0*	*8*	*40*	*33*	*3*	*.262*	*.308*	*.366*

KENNY LOFTON
Cleveland Indians
Center Fielder
$43

Like Listach, he hit much better than I thought he would, and had tremendous rookie season. A left-handed hitter, he annihilated left-handed pitchers, hitting .369 against them with a .466 on-base percentage . . . a better player than Vince Coleman was, because he walks instead of striking out and can play center field. Was 63 percent base stealer in the PCL in '91, 85 percent in majors in '92.

YEAR	TEAM/LEVEL	G	AB	R	H	2B	3B	HR	RBI	BB	SB	AVG	OBP	SLG
1991	Houston	20	74	9	15	1	0	0	0	5	2	.203	.253	.216
1992	Cleveland	148	576	96	164	15	8	5	42	68	66	.285	.362	.365
1993	Projected	110	345	44	94	16	0	6	43	27	2	.272	.325	.371
		92	*114*	*0*	*24*	*17*	*0*	*7*	*44*	*0*	*0*	*.21*	*.211*	*.544*

JAVIER LOPEZ
Atlanta Braves
Catcher
$38

Trim, athletic catcher, looks very strong. One of the four super prospects at Greenville last year, improved his batting tremendously and also received good reports for his defense. Average arm, just 22 years old. The Braves don't exactly have Johnny Bench in his prime, so the way is clear for him. Two years younger than Piazza, and in my opinion a better player. **Grade A prospect.**

YEAR	TEAM/LEVEL	G	AB	R	H	2B	3B	HR	RBI	BB	SB	AVG	OBP	SLG
1991	Durham A	113	384	43	94	14	2	11	51	25	10	.245	.294	.378
1992	Greenville AA	115	442	64	142	28	3	16	60	24	7	.321	.362	.507
1992	MLE	115	432	53	132	25	1	15	50	16	4	.306	.330	.472
		115	*422*	*43*	*122*	*22*	*0*	*14*	*40*	*8*	*1*	*.289*	*.302*	*.441*

TOREY LOVULLO
New York Yankees
Utilityman
$3

He seems to have been around forever, but he's only 27, and he did have a fine year at Columbus (average .295, secondary average .370). Even balance of skills. He's come a long way since he was brought prematurely to the majors by the Tigers five years ago, deserves another chance to play, and may get it with expansion coming.

YEAR	TEAM/LEVEL	G	AB	R	H	2B	3B	HR	RBI	BB	SB	AVG	OBP	SLG
1991	Columbus AAA	106	395	74	107	24	5	10	75	59	4	.271	.361	.433
1992	Columbus AAA	131	468	69	138	33	5	19	89	64	9	.295	.379	.509
1992	MLE	131	449	54	119	29	2	16	70	50	6	.265	.339	.445
		131	430	35	100	25	0	13	51	36	3	.233	.292	.381

SCOTT LYDY
Oakland Athletics
Outfielder
$7

A second-round draft pick in 1989, made slow progress until last year, when he hit .306 at Double-A, and may emerge by mid-season as a candidate for the A's outfield. He is reported to be a highly motivated young man with unusually good work habits, also runs well and drew 92 walks last year, far more than he had before. Grade C prospect.

YEAR	TEAM/LEVEL	G	AB	R	H	2B	3B	HR	RBI	BB	SB	AVG	OBP	SLG
1992	Reno A	33	124	29	49	13	2	2	27	26	9	.395	.500	.581
1992	Huntsville AA	109	387	64	118	20	3	9	65	67	16	.305	.409	.442
1992	MLE	109	370	54	101	16	1	6	55	48	12	.273	.356	.370
		109	353	46	84	12	0	3	45	29	8	.238	.296	.297

STEVE LYONS
Boston Red Sox
Utilityman
$3

Purchased by the Red Sox in June, was used once or twice a month as an outfielder or first baseman, occasionally as a pinch runner or pinch hitter. I think he's a useful player—a left-hander on the bench, can play infield or outfield, good baserunner, not the worst hitter you could find. His skills would support more playing time than he had in '92.

YEAR	TEAM/LEVEL	G	AB	R	H	2B	3B	HR	RBI	BB	SB	AVG	OBP	SLG
1990	Chicag	94	146	22	28	6	1	1	11	10	1	.192	.245	.267
1991	Boston	87	212	15	51	10	1	4	17	11	10	.241	.277	.354
1992	Three Teams	48	55	5	11	0	2	0	4	3	1	.200	.241	.273
		9	0	0	0	0	3	0	0	0	0	—	—	—

KEVIN MAAS
New York Yankees
Designated Hitter/First Baseman
$22

Playing time has been taken away from him indirectly by the signing of Tartabull. Maas has real power, but does have an extremely poor record of hitting in RBI situations, lifetime .185 batting average with men in scoring position. Will have more 20-homer seasons and will score some runs because he walks, but is slow, low-average hitter without a good defensive position.

YEAR	TEAM/LEVEL	G	AB	R	H	2B	3B	HR	RBI	BB	SB	AVG	OBP	SLG
1991	New York	148	500	69	110	14	1	23	63	83	5	.220	.333	.390
1992	New York	98	286	35	71	12	0	11	35	25	3	.248	.305	.406
1993	Projected	111	352	51	85	16	1	17	48	54	3	.241	.342	.438
		124	428	67	99	20	2	23	61	83	3	.231	.356	.449

MIKE MACFARLANE
Kansas City Royals
Catcher
$42

Had a frustrating season, power MIA until August. He hit .171 in April, contributing to the Royals' dismal start, but saved his season somewhat by murdering the ball over the last two months (.574 slugging percentage). Over half of his season's hits were for extra bases, set a franchise record for times hit with the pitch (15). Slow for a catcher, average defense, capable of 90-RBI season.

YEAR	TEAM/LEVEL	G	AB	R	H	2B	3B	HR	RBI	BB	SB	AVG	OBP	SLG
1991	Kansas City	84	267	34	74	18	2	13	41	17	1	.277	.330	.506
1992	Kansas City	127	402	51	94	28	3	17	48	30	1	.234	.310	.445
1993	Projected	146	475	52	116	29	3	18	67	34	2	.244	.295	.432
		165	518	53	138	30	3	19	86	38	3	.252	.300	.421

SHANE MACK
Minnesota Twins
Left Fielder
$67

The most underrated player in baseball, has hit .300 three times in a row, scored 100 runs, hits for power, steals bases. Let's see, what else is there a player can do . . . he takes walks, and tied Macfarlane for the league lead in HBP . . . he plays hard and likes to bust up a DP. His throwing arm isn't very good, but he's a good left fielder.

YEAR	TEAM/LEVEL	G	AB	R	H	2B	3B	HR	RBI	BB	SB	AVG	OBP	SLG
1991	Minnesota	143	442	79	137	27	8	18	74	34	13	.310	.363	.529
1992	Minnesota	156	600	101	189	31	6	16	75	64	26	.315	.394	.467
1993	Projected	154	588	93	176	21	4	17	76	58	24	.299	.362	.435
		152	576	85	163	11	2	18	77	52	22	.283	.342	.403

DAVE MAGADAN
New York Mets
(Free Agent)
Third Baseman
$20

Moved back to third and had the same season as '89, when he was trying to establish himself. Had a .390 on-base percentage, but I don't think 33 runs scored was exactly what the Mets were dreaming of . . . season was ended August 9 by fractured wrist. He is expected to leave New York as a free agent. Has the skills of a damn fine pinch hitter.

YEAR	TEAM/LEVEL	G	AB	R	H	2B	3B	HR	RBI	BB	SB	AVG	OBP	SLG
1991	New York	124	418	58	108	23	0	4	51	83	1	.258	.378	.342
1992	New York	99	321	33	91	9	1	3	28	56	1	.283	.390	.346
1993	Projected	121	387	53	110	19	2	4	47	73	1	.284	.398	.375
		143	453	73	129	29	3	5	66	90	1	.285	.403	.385

MIKE MAKSUDIAN
Minnesota Twins
Catcher/First Baseman
$11

Was claimed on waivers from Toronto, a smart move because he is good enough to help the Twins. In Toronto he was buried amidst the columns of young catchers, but his abilities should be enough to get him a major league job. Left-handed hitter with square body, can give Harper an occasional day off, help fill the void at first if Hrbek isn't able to play.

YEAR	TEAM/LEVEL	G	AB	R	H	2B	3B	HR	RBI	BB	SB	AVG	OBP	SLG
1991	MLE	102	321	39	84	16	4	5	41	36	1	.262	.336	.383
1992	Syracuse	101	339	38	95	17	1	13	58	32	4	.280	.343	.451
1992	MLE	101	326	28	82	14	0	10	43	23	2	.252	.301	.387
		101	313	18	69	11	0	7	28	14	0	.220	.284	.322

CANDY MALDONADO
Toronto Blue Jays
Left Fielder
$27

May have had his best all-around season in 1992. He's been playing for his job for two years, was a free agent after a fine year in '90, didn't draw any interest, signed in Toronto but the front office still doesn't think he should play every day. Marginal regular unless he plays his best, but has enough specialized skills to play for several more years.

YEAR	TEAM/LEVEL	G	AB	R	H	2B	3B	HR	RBI	BB	SB	AVG	OBP	SLG
1991	Two Teams	86	288	37	72	15	0	12	48	36	4	.250	.342	.427
1992	Toronto	137	489	64	133	25	4	20	66	59	2	.272	.357	.462
1993	Projected	131	468	55	114	22	1	15	63	50	3	.244	.317	.391
		125	437	46	95	19	0	10	60	41	4	.217	.285	.336

JEFF MANTO
Atlanta Braves
Third Baseman
$8

Had an opportunity with Cleveland a couple of years ago, probably due for another one. He's a product of the Angels system, where everybody compiles good minor league numbers if you don't put them in context. He's a good enough hitter that if he could *really* play third he'd have a job, and a good enough first baseman that he'd have a job if he could *really* hit.

YEAR	TEAM/LEVEL	G	AB	R	H	2B	3B	HR	RBI	BB	SB	AVG	OBP	SLG
1991	Cleveland	47	128	15	27	7	0	2	13	14	2	.211	.306	.313
1992	Richmond AAA	127	450	65	131	24	1	13	68	57	1	.291	.374	.436
1992	MLE	127	439	52	120	21	0	11	54	43	0	.273	.338	.396
		127	428	39	109	18	0	9	40	29	0	.255	.302	.360

KIRT MANWARING
San Francisco Giants
Catcher
$16

Unexpectedly took control of the Giants' catching job after several other people failed. His defense was outstanding, as he threw out 51 percent of opposition baserunners (best in the league), and he hit .270 for the first three months, stopped hitting just before the All-Star break. Doubt that he can hold everyday job. Very few teams win pennants with defense-only catchers.

YEAR	TEAM/LEVEL	G	AB	R	H	2B	3B	HR	RBI	BB	SB	AVG	OBP	SLG
1991	San Francisco	67	178	16	40	9	0	0	19	9	1	.225	.271	.275
1992	San Francisco	109	349	24	85	10	5	4	26	29	2	.244	.311	.335
1993	Projected	112	331	23	75	11	2	3	27	24	2	.227	.279	.299
		115	313	22	65	12	0	2	28	19	2	.208	.253	.265

TOM MARSH
Philadelphia Phillies
Left Fielder
$1

Another Phillies conundrum: what *exactly* do they see in these guys? Marsh is a minor league outfielder, 27 years old, not much speed, humorous strikeout/walk ratio, a lifetime .246 hitter in the minor leagues. Oh—power; he doesn't have a lot of power, either. Spent a couple of months in the majors while Wes Chamberlain was unavailable. No prospect.

YEAR	TEAM/LEVEL	G	AB	R	H	2B	3B	HR	RBI	BB	SB	AVG	OBP	SLG
1991	Reading AA	67	236	27	62	12	5	7	35	11	8	.263	.295	.445
1992	Scranton AAA	45	158	26	38	7	2	8	25	10	5	.241	.294	.462
1992	Philadelphia	42	125	7	25	3	2	2	16	2	0	.200	.215	.304
		39	92	0	12	0	2	0	7	0	0	.130	.130	.130

AL MARTIN
Pittsburgh Pirates
Outfielder
$11

Originally in the Braves system, big left-handed batter (6-2, 220 pounds) who can run, but slow to develop as a hitter. The Braves ran out of time, and he signed as a minor league free agent with Pittsburgh, went to Buffalo and had a marvelous season in a *pitcher's* park. Comparable to Glenallen Hill; Grade C prospect but with impressive upper boundary.

YEAR	TEAM/LEVEL	G	AB	R	H	2B	3B	HR	RBI	BB	SB	AVG	OBP	SLG
1991	MLE	130	441	46	104	20	1	10	44	25	19	.236	.277	.354
1992	Buffalo AAA	125	420	85	128	16	15	20	59	35	20	.305	.363	.557
1992	MLE	125	400	66	108	14	10	14	45	26	13	.270	.315	.460
		125	380	47	88	12	5	8	31	17	6	.232	.265	.353

CARLOS MARTINEZ
Cleveland Indians
First Baseman
$13

Singles-hitting first baseman who never walks, has pipe cleaners for legs. His overall offense is not what is expected of a major league first baseman or DH and he is hardly Mark Grace with the glove, but he will keep getting chances because he could hit .300. Will never hold a regular job for long, even if he does hit .300.

YEAR	TEAM/LEVEL	G	AB	R	H	2B	3B	HR	RBI	BB	SB	AVG	OBP	SLG
1991	Cleveland	72	257	22	73	14	0	5	30	10	3	.284	.310	.397
1992	Cleveland	69	228	23	60	9	1	5	35	7	1	.263	.283	.377
1993	Projected	63	197	20	55	10	1	4	28	8	2	.279	.307	.401
		57	166	17	50	11	1	3	21	9	3	.301	.337	.439

CHITO MARTINEZ
Baltimore Orioles
Right Fielder
$18

Experienced a predictable relapse after posting remarkable major league and minor league numbers in 1991, but still, he wasn't bad, and his career totals through 414 major league at bats are rather impressive (.268 with 18 homers). A good bench player used almost exclusively in right field, may be able to get past Joe Orsulak to earn more playing time.

YEAR	TEAM/LEVEL	G	AB	R	H	2B	3B	HR	RBI	BB	SB	AVG	OBP	SLG
1991	Baltimore	67	216	32	58	12	1	13	33	11	1	.269	.303	.514
1992	Baltimore	83	198	26	53	10	1	5	25	31	0	.268	.366	.404
1993	Projected	127	432	59	109	15	2	24	62	50	4	.252	.330	.463
		168	666	92	165	20	3	43	99	69	8	.248	.318	.480

DAVE MARTINEZ
Cincinnati Reds
Center Fielder
$20

Piniella used him as a platoon player because he had always hit right-handers well, but then he didn't. Good defensive outfielder and a natural number-two hitter, but needs to come back in order to hold his playing time. In that he is still young (28) and had hit well in four of five previous years, I think he will bounce back in '93.

YEAR	TEAM/LEVEL	G	AB	R	H	2B	3B	HR	RBI	BB	SB	AVG	OBP	SLG
1991	Montreal	124	396	47	117	18	5	7	42	20	16	.295	.332	.419
1992	Cincinnati	135	393	47	100	20	5	7	31	42	12	.254	.323	.354
1993	Projected	121	393	51	109	14	5	7	39	30	15	.277	.329	.392
		107	393	55	118	8	5	7	47	18	18	.300	.331	.399

DOMINGO MARTINEZ
Toronto Blue Jays
First Baseman
$13

Buried in the Blue Jays' list of prospects and has played almost a thousand minor league games, but can hit a little. He's been in the Toronto system since 1985, spending two years or more at every level but steadily improving his numbers. Has never had a significant injury in his seven minor league seasons; 1991 season was quite a bit better than 1992. Grade C prospect.

YEAR	TEAM/LEVEL	G	AB	R	H	2B	3B	HR	RBI	BB	SB	AVG	OBP	SLG
1991	Syracuse AAA	126	467	61	146	16	2	17	83	41	6	.313	.371	.465
1992	Syracuse AAA	116	438	55	120	22	0	21	62	33	6	.274	.333	.468
1992	MLE	116	421	40	103	19	0	17	46	24	4	.245	.285	.411
		116	404	25	86	16	0	13	30	15	2	.123	.211	.346

EDGAR MARTINEZ
Seattle Mariners
Third Baseman
$74

He's not the best defensive third baseman in the world, and his batting record with men in scoring position is not everything you might expect. Still, there's a real shortage of .340 hitters, an even bigger shortage of .340 hitters with 46 doubles and 18 homers. His numbers look like something out of the California League . . . had surgery for bone spur September 12; will hit .310 again next year.

YEAR	TEAM/LEVEL	G	AB	R	H	2B	3B	HR	RBI	BB	SB	AVG	OBP	SLG
1991	Seattle	150	544	98	167	35	1	14	52	84	0	.307	.405	.452
1992	Seattle	135	528	100	181	46	3	18	73	54	14	.343	.404	.544
1993	Projected	146	527	89	163	33	2	14	58	75	5	.309	.395	.459
		157	526	78	145	20	1	10	43	96	0	.276	.387	.375

RAY MARTINEZ
California Angels
Second Baseman
$2

Who is the only second baseman of any quality ever developed by the Angels organization? I believe Jerry Remy is the only one. Their other noteworthy second basemen—Bobby Knoop, Sandy Alomar, Bobby Grich—were all lifted from other organizations . . . Martinez seems to be in the tradition of Mark McLemore, a .250 hitter with no secondary offense. Grade D prospect.

YEAR	TEAM/LEVEL	G	AB	R	H	2B	3B	HR	RBI	BB	SB	AVG	OBP	SLG
1991	Palm Springs A	106	371	58	100	13	5	2	41	66	10	.270	.388	.348
1992	AA and AAA	118	396	58	111	24	5	6	49	33	7	.280	.345	.386
1992	MLE	118	366	34	81	16	1	2	28	17	3	.221	.256	.287
		118	336	6	57	8	0	0	7	1	0	.152	.154	.176

TINO MARTINEZ
Seattle Mariners
First Baseman
$32

In my opinion what Martinez hit as a rookie fairly represents his ability, and therefore is not likely to move upward or downward sharply. He's 25 now, young enough to improve a little, so let's say he hits .275 with 20 homers a year; that will keep him in the league. It is my opinion, as it has been for years, that he has little if any star potential.

YEAR	TEAM/LEVEL	G	AB	R	H	2B	3B	HR	RBI	BB	SB	AVG	OBP	SLG
1991	Seattle	36	112	11	23	2	0	4	9	11	0	.205	.272	.330
1992	Seattle	136	460	53	118	19	2	16	66	42	2	.257	.316	.411
1993	Projected	156	560	69	145	28	2	17	73	65	3	.259	.336	.407
		176	660	85	172	37	2	18	80	88	4	.261	.348	.408

JOHN MARZANO
Boston Red Sox
Catcher
$1

Has dropped hopelessly behind Wedge and Flaherty in the Sox battery list, and his career in Boston is probably over. He started the season on the disabled list after surgery to repair a slight tear in his rotator cuff, was activated in July and hit .080. He'll get a look somewhere else, but there's very little demand for .080-hitting catchers with rotator cuff injuries.

YEAR	TEAM/LEVEL	G	AB	R	H	2B	3B	HR	RBI	BB	SB	AVG	OBP	SLG
1990	Boston	32	83	8	20	4	0	0	6	5	0	.241	.281	.289
1991	Boston	49	114	10	30	8	0	0	9	1	0	.263	.271	.333
1992	Boston	19	50	1	4	2	1	0	1	2	0	.080	.132	.160
		0	0	0	0	2	0	0	3	0	—	1.000	—	

DON MATTINGLY
New York Yankees
First Baseman
$34

He continues his laborious comeback; last year was his best since 1989. With 184 hits he did re-establish himself as a 3000-hit candidate (23 percent chance of 3000 hits; at one time it was 34 percent). He made 472 batting outs last year, which would be no big deal if he had also driven in and scored 100 runs. Just an average first baseman.

YEAR	TEAM/LEVEL	G	AB	R	H	2B	3B	HR	RBI	BB	SB	AVG	OBP	SLG
1991	New York	152	587	64	169	35	0	9	68	46	2	.288	.339	.394
1992	New York	157	640	89	184	40	0	14	86	39	3	.288	.327	.416
1993	Projected	136	532	67	155	34	1	14	73	38	1	.291	.339	.438
		125	424	45	126	28	2	14	60	37	6	.297	.354	.472

ROB MAURER
Texas Rangers
First Baseman
$12

Played at Oklahoma City again last year and didn't have a good year, but then there wasn't any challenge. Maurer is a good major league hitter, Rance Mulliniks type with a little more power, blocked behind Palmeiro. His defense is a plus, but not Gold Glove quality; has had problem in the past with his temper, but was more under control last year. Should make an expansion team.

YEAR	TEAM/LEVEL	G	AB	R	H	2B	3B	HR	RBI	BB	SB	AVG	OBP	SLG
1991	Oklahoma City AAA	132	459	76	138	41	3	20	77	96	2	.301	.420	.534
1992	Oklahoma City AAA	135	493	76	142	34	2	10	82	75	1	.288	.382	.426
1992	MLE	135	474	60	123	29	1	7	64	58	0	.259	.340	.369
		135	455	44	104	24	0	4	46	41	0	.229	.292	.308

DERRICK MAY
Chicago Cubs
Left Fielder
$18

His year was a personal breakthrough, and with Walton apparently dead and Andre Dawson probably gone, the Cubs will need him in the lineup. His secondary average was .154, so you couldn't honestly say that he has proven anything. In my opinion he will improve *slightly* as a hitter, moving perhaps into the Mel Hall class; I don't believe he will be a 100-run or 100-RBI guy.

YEAR	TEAM/LEVEL	G	AB	R	H	2B	3B	HR	RBI	BB	SB	AVG	OBP	SLG
1991	MLE	82	297	34	79	15	2	2	35	13	4	.266	.297	.350
1992	Chicago	124	351	33	96	11	0	8	45	14	5	.274	.306	.373
1993	Projected	131	418	44	115	22	1	8	37	29	3	.275	.305	.390
		138	485	55	134	33	2	8	29	44	1	.276	.336	.402

BRENT MAYNE
Kansas City Royals
Catcher
$16

A weak hitter so far, but you have to love him. Good athlete, exceptional mobility for a catcher, and a real take-charge guy on the field. He barks directions to veterans as if somebody had elected him. Good arm, better overall defense than Macfarlane. Intelligent player, can also play third and looks very much like Bob Boone on the field. May never hit enough to hold a job.

YEAR	TEAM/LEVEL	G	AB	R	H	2B	3B	HR	RBI	BB	SB	AVG	OBP	SLG
1991	Kansas City	85	231	22	58	8	0	3	31	23	2	.251	.315	.325
1992	Kansas City	82	213	16	48	10	0	0	18	11	0	.225	.260	.272
1993	Projected	105	324	31	81	12	1	2	37	29	3	.250	.312	.312
		128	435	46	114	14	2	4	56	47	6	.262	.334	1.331

DAVE McCARTY
Minnesota Twins
Outfielder
$3

A 6-5 slugger, the third player taken in the 1991 draft, played at Orlando in '92 and had a fine year. His manager, Phil Roof, said he could be a 25-home-run type, and that may be conservative; with luck, he may be the Twins' cleanup hitter after Hrbek. Expected to spend the summer at Triple-A, but the Twins have been known to skip that.

YEAR	TEAM/LEVEL	G	AB	R	H	2B	3B	HR	RBI	BB	SB	AVG	OBP	SLG
1991	A and AA	43	138	34	42	7	0	6	19	23	3	.304	.422	.486
1992	AA and AAA	137	483	82	137	18	2	19	87	60	7	.284	.369	.447
1992	MLE	137	475	70	129	17	2	15	75	45	4	.272	.335	.411
		137	467	58	121	16	2	11	63	30	1	.259	.304	.368

LLOYD McCLENDON
Pittsburgh Pirates
Right Fielder
$13

One of several players Leyland uses as a first baseman/right fielder, also is emergency catcher although he didn't catch an inning in '92. He's 33, built like Gates Brown, often bats cleanup when he is in the lineup. Obviously has no chance of playing regularly, but could last two to three more years as a pinch hitter/reserve outfielder. Fun to watch.

YEAR	TEAM/LEVEL	G	AB	R	H	2B	3B	HR	RBI	BB	SB	AVG	OBP	SLG
1991	Pittsburgh	85	163	24	47	7	0	7	24	18	2	.288	.366	.460
1992	Pittsburgh	84	190	26	48	8	1	3	20	28	1	.253	.350	.353
1993	Projected	70	135	17	33	6	0	3	16	16	1	.244	.325	.356
		56	80	8	18	4	0	3	12	4	1	.225	.262	.350

RODNEY McCRAY
New York Mets
Outfielder
No Value

Light hitter, has been used almost exclusively as a pinch runner and to give the guy running the video board one more chance to show that shot of him running through the fence . . . he was sent to Tidewater on May 18 and played only eight games there, so apparently he may have been released, or hurt, or something. No future either way.

YEAR	TEAM/LEVEL	G	AB	R	H	2B	3B	HR	RBI	BB	SB	AVG	OBP	SLG
1991	Vancouver AAA	83	222	37	51	9	5	0	13	26	14	.230	.329	.315
1991	Chicago	17	7	2	2	0	0	0	0	0	1	.286	.286	.286
1992	New York	18	1	1	0	0	0	0	0	0	2	.000	.000	.000
		19	0	0	0	0	0	0	0	0	3	—	—	—

WILLIE McGEE
San Francisco Giants
Right/Center Fielder
$20

He can still hit singles, and he can still run when the wheels are working. His stats last year were not very different from his stats as a rookie, ten years ago. I've never been a Willie McGee fan, and I'm not sure that he has much value, but apart from periodic injuries his skills have not undergone any clear change—and may not for several years.

YEAR	TEAM/LEVEL	G	AB	R	H	2B	3B	HR	RBI	BB	SB	AVG	OBP	SLG
1991	San Francisco	131	497	67	155	30	3	4	43	34	17	.312	.357	.408
1992	San Francisco	138	474	56	141	20	2	1	36	29	13	.297	.339	.354
1993	Projected	130	478	62	135	22	5	4	44	34	17	.282	.330	.374
		122	482	68	129	24	8	7	52	39	21	.268	.322	.371

RUSS McGINNIS
Texas Rangers
Catcher
$1

Minor league veteran who was called up while Ivan Rodriguez was out. McGinnis is 29, got his first major league look last year but has been with the Brewers, A's and Cubs . . . Gene Tenace/Mickey Tettleton type skills, drew 79 walks last year in 99 minor league games, also hit 18 homers. Not a good catcher, can also play third but not well. No prospect.

YEAR	TEAM/LEVEL	G	AB	R	H	2B	3B	HR	RBI	BB	SB	AVG	OBP	SLG
1992	Oklahoma City AAA	99	330	63	87	19	1	18	51	79	0	.264	.414	.491
1992	MLE	99	318	49	75	16	0	14	40	61	0	.236	.359	.418
1992	Texas	14	33	2	8	4	0	0	7	3	0	.242	.306	.364
		0	0	0	0	0	0	0	0	0	0	—	—	—

FRED McGRIFF
San Diego Padres
First Baseman
$86

He had probably his best season, although one of his years is so much like another that this is a bit like distinguishing the best episode of *Gilligan's Island*. There have been players who were equally consistent, but I'm not sure there has ever been a hitter of the same quality who was *more* consistent than McGriff . . . probably the best first baseman in baseball.

YEAR	TEAM/LEVEL	G	AB	R	H	2B	3B	HR	RBI	BB	SB	AVG	OBP	SLG
1991	San Diego	153	528	84	147	19	1	31	106	105	4	.278	.396	.494
1992	San Diego	152	531	79	152	30	4	35	104	96	8	.286	.394	.494
1993	Projected	155	550	88	156	26	2	34	100	105	6	.284	.398	.524
		158	569	97	160	22	0	33	96	114	4	.281	.401	.494

MARK McGWIRE
Oakland Athletics
First Baseman
$69

Of his career hits, 28.5 percent are home runs, the highest percentage of all time. Only other guys over 25 percent are Rob Deer (27.5), Killebrew (27.5), Gorman Thomas (25.5) and Ralph Kiner (25.4) . . . his slugging percentage against left-handed pitchers last year was .804. The A's only face the best left-handers . . . hits the ball in the air more consistently than any other player.

YEAR	TEAM/LEVEL	G	AB	R	H	2B	3B	HR	RBI	BB	SB	AVG	OBP	SLG
1991	Oakland	154	483	62	97	22	0	22	75	93	2	.201	.330	.383
1992	Oakland	139	467	87	125	22	0	42	104	90	0	.268	.385	.585
1993	Projected	149	486	80	116	21	1	32	92	101	1	.239	.370	.484
		159	505	73	107	20	2	22	80	112	2	.212	.355	.390

TIM McINTOSH
Milwaukee Brewers
Catcher
$6

A catcher who can't really catch, was in the majors all year but had limited playing time and didn't do anything with it. In minors was very consistent hitter, probably would hit .240 to .260 in majors with 10 to 12 homers, OK offense for a catcher but not enough to earn playing time at his other positions (first base, left field). Will have better years, no star potential.

YEAR	TEAM/LEVEL	G	AB	R	H	2B	3B	HR	RBI	BB	SB	AVG	OBP	SLG
1991	MLE	122	437	50	110	16	5	12	66	26	1	.252	.294	.394
1992	Milwaukee	35	77	7	14	3	0	0	6	3	1	.182	.229	.221
1993	Projected	83	197	26	50	12	1	6	28	11	2	.254	.293	.416
		131	317	45	86	21	2	12	30	19	3	.271	.313	.464

JEFF McKNIGHT
New York Mets
Utilityman
$3

Came up in mid-August after hitting .307 at Tidewater, filled in at all four infield spots and helped his career. He's 30 years old now, had a trial with Baltimore as a six-year free agent, but didn't impress there and wound up back with the Mets. Has no chance of being a regular, but could wind up with Bill Pecota's job if the Mets move Pecota.

YEAR	TEAM/LEVEL	G	AB	R	H	2B	3B	HR	RBI	BB	SB	AVG	OBP	SLG
1992	Tidewater AAA	102	352	43	108	21	1	4	43	51	3	.307	.395	.406
1992	MLE	102	336	33	92	17	0	2	33	39	2	.274	.349	.342
1992	New York	31	85	10	23	3	1	2	13	2	0	.271	.287	.400
		0	0	0	0	0	2	2	0	0	0	–	–	–

MARK McLEMORE
Baltimore Orioles
Second Baseman
$11

By the standards of backup infielders he had a pretty good year with the bat, hit .246 and scored 40 runs in limited playing time. He is often used as a pinch runner, sometimes pinch hitter, but isn't a good second baseman and can't be used at third or short, so in that way his job is more like that of the traditional reserve *outfielder* than reserve infielder.

YEAR	TEAM/LEVEL	G	AB	R	H	2B	3B	HR	RBI	BB	SB	AVG	OBP	SLG
1991	Houston	21	61	6	9	1	0	0	2	6	0	.148	.221	.164
1992	Baltimore	101	228	40	56	7	2	0	27	21	11	.246	.308	.294
1993	Projected	87	239	33	53	8	1	1	22	24	8	.222	.293	.276
		73	250	26	50	9	0	2	17	27	5	.200	.278	.260

JIM McNAMARA
San Francisco Giants
(Free Agent)
Catcher
No Value

Longtime minor league catcher, no prospect, no future, was probably surprised to find himself in the major leagues to begin with. His career minor league average is .228, and he's basically been a backup in the minors for several years . . . started the year playing quite a bit, which is one more sign that Roger Craig has in fact lost his grip.

YEAR	TEAM/LEVEL	G	AB	R	H	2B	3B	HR	RBI	BB	SB	AVG	OBP	SLG
1991	Shreveport AA	39	109	13	30	8	2	2	20	21	2	.275	.389	.440
1992	Phoenix AAA	23	67	5	14	3	0	0	3	14	0	.209	.346	.254
1992	San Francisco	30	74	6	16	1	0	1	9	6	0	.216	.275	.270
		37	81	7	18	0	0	2	15	0	0	.222	.222	.296

BRIAN McRAE
Kansas City Royals
Center Fielder
$20

Gold Glove quality outfielder, but isn't going to have a job if he doesn't hit better than he did in '92. He seemed to be concentrating on being more disciplined at the plate, which was needed, and he drew 42 walks after taking only 24 in '91. Unfortunately his hits were down more than his walks were up, giving him the lowest batting average of any major league regular.

YEAR	TEAM/LEVEL	G	AB	R	H	2B	3B	HR	RBI	BB	SB	AVG	OBP	SLG
1991	Kansas City	152	629	86	164	28	9	8	64	24	20	.261	.288	.372
1992	Kansas City	149	533	63	119	23	5	4	52	42	18	.223	.285	.385
1993	Projected	135	518	67	128	22	7	6	55	32	17	.247	.291	.351
		121	503	71	137	21	9	8	58	22	16	.272	.303	.377

KEVIN McREYNOLDS
Kansas City Royals
Left Fielder
$19

Didn't play much the second half because of dislocated shoulder, bruised and sprained ankle. He hit .169 in April, when the Royals' season was lost, plus he hit .224 with men in scoring position and .195 when leading off an inning . . . exceptional outfielder and baserunner for a big slow guy . . . I doubt that he has any good years left.

YEAR	TEAM/LEVEL	G	AB	R	H	2B	3B	HR	RBI	BB	SB	AVG	OBP	SLG
1991	New York	143	522	65	135	32	1	16	74	49	6	.259	.322	.416
1992	Kansas City	109	373	45	92	25	0	13	49	67	7	.247	.357	.418
1993	Projected	135	474	60	122	25	2	17	68	64	7	.257	.346	.426
		161	575	75	152	25	4	21	87	61	7	.264	.335	.431

SCOTT MEADOWS
Baltimore Orioles
Outfielder
$1

Could become a hot prospect if there is a sudden surge of demand for slow leadoff men . . . singles hitter who will take a walk, which is a good start, but just average speed. Has played second and third, now seems to be mostly in the outfield. Could have a career as a pinch hitter . . . was a college teammate of Dave Burba. No relation to Audrey Meadows.

YEAR	TEAM/LEVEL	G	AB	R	H	2B	3B	HR	RBI	BB	SB	AVG	OBP	SLG
1991	MLE	107	353	50	102	20	0	3	41	56	2	.289	.386	.371
1992	AA and AAA	110	380	48	108	10	2	3	23	55	8	.284	.380	.345
1993	MLE	110	364	37	92	7	1	1	17	40	5	.253	.327	.286
		110	348	26	76	4	0	2	11	25	2	.218	.271	.247

BOB MELVIN
Kansas City Royals
Catcher
$3

Almost never played with the Royals despite .318 average, most of it against Randy Johnson. For some reason he can hit Randy . . . does the worst job of framing pitches I've ever seen. He'll lunge at a ball two inches out of the strike zone, time after time, makes every pitch look tough. It's one of those things you can't believe nobody has told him to *stop that*.

YEAR	TEAM/LEVEL	G	AB	R	H	2B	3B	HR	RBI	BB	SB	AVG	OBP	SLG
1990	Baltimore	93	301	30	73	14	1	5	37	11	0	.243	.267	.346
1991	Baltimore	79	228	11	57	10	5	1	23	11	0	.250	.279	.307
1992	Kansas City	32	70	5	22	5	0	0	6	5	0	.314	.351	.386
		0	0	0	0	0	0	0	0	0	0	—	—	—

ORLANDO MERCED
Pittsburgh Pirates
First Baseman
$17

Returned to his true level of ability last year after playing over his head as a rookie. Appears to have unnaturally large platoon differential, so far has hit .193 (28/145) with zero home runs against left-handers, so offense may improve if he is kept more strictly within the platoon role. Limited speed, limited power, better first baseman than right fielder. No star potential.

YEAR	TEAM/LEVEL	G	AB	R	H	2B	3B	HR	RBI	BB	SB	AVG	OBP	SLG
1991	Pittsburgh	120	411	83	113	17	2	10	50	64	8	.275	.373	.399
1992	Pittsburgh	134	405	50	100	28	5	6	60	52	5	.247	.332	.385
1993	Projected	127	398	59	101	19	4	7	50	52	8	.254	.340	.374
		120	391	68	102	10	3	8	40	52	11	.261	.348	.363

HENRY MERCEDES
Oakland Athletics
Catcher
No Value

The A's answer to Jim McNamara, a .228 career hitter in the minor leagues who was called up in September to take a few defensive innings between plate appearances. He must be a good defensive player, or he wouldn't be in baseball, but no power and no threat to the Mendoza line . . . goes on an All-Star team with Dan Ford, Richard Dotson, Oscar Azocar.

YEAR	TEAM/LEVEL	G	AB	R	H	2B	3B	HR	RBI	BB	SB	AVG	OBP	SLG
1991	Modesto A	116	388	55	100	17	3	4	61	68	5	.258	.369	.348
1992	Tacoma AAA	85	246	36	57	9	2	0	20	26	1	.232	.305	.285
1992	MLE	85	236	27	47	7	1	0	15	20	0	.199	.262	.237
		85	226	18	37	5	0	0	10	14	0	.164	.213	.186

LUIS MERCEDES
Baltimore Orioles
Left Fielder
$12

I had him listed as a Rookie of the Year longshot a year ago, but he started the season cold and spent the warm months at Rochester. Luis Polonia–type player, fast, could hit close to .300 in the majors with reasonable number of walks, but no power and bad defense. The emergence of Brady Anderson means that the Orioles don't need him.

YEAR	TEAM/LEVEL	G	AB	R	H	2B	3B	HR	RBI	BB	SB	AVG	OBP	SLG
1991	MLE	102	357	53	108	12	3	1	28	50	16	.303	.388	.361
1992	Rochester AAA	102	407	62	128	15	1	3	29	44	35	.314	.380	.378
1992	MLE	102	388	48	107	12	0	2	22	34	24	.276	.334	.322
		102	369	34	86	9	0	1	15	24	13	.233	.280	.266

MATT MERULLO
Chicago White Sox
Catcher
$2

Line-drive hitter, was in the majors early in the year while Fisk was not available, didn't do anything to help himself or the team. He skipped Triple-A, which was probably a mistake. His defense isn't good, his bat isn't good, he doesn't run or hit with power. Seems unlikely to get beyond the status of fringe player, and career may be over.

YEAR	TEAM/LEVEL	G	AB	R	H	2B	3B	HR	RBI	BB	SB	AVG	OBP	SLG
1990	Birmingham AA	102	378	57	110	26	1	8	50	34	2	.291	.353	.429
1991	Chicago	80	140	8	32	1	0	5	21	9	18	.229	.268	.343
1992	Chicago	24	50	3	9	1	1	0	3	1	8	.180	.208	.240
		0	0	0	0	1	2	0	0	0	0	—	—	—

HENSLEY MEULENS
New York Yankees
Third Baseman
$12

Established himself as a prospect in 1987, so seems much older than he is (25). After bombing in '91 he went back to Columbus and re-certified himself, duplicating his 1990 season offensively and showing great improvement at third base. He will receive another major league trial in '93; will strike out but capable of hitting .250 with 20 homers. Grade C prospect.

YEAR	TEAM/LEVEL	G	AB	R	H	2B	3B	HR	RBI	BB	SB	AVG	OBP	SLG
1991	New York	96	288	37	64	8	1	6	29	18	3	.222	.276	.319
1992	Columbus AAA	141	534	96	147	28	2	26	100	60	15	.275	.352	.481
1992	MLE	141	513	76	126	24	1	19	79	47	10	.246	.309	.407
		141	482	56	105	20	0	12	58	34	5	.218	.261	.320

KEITH MILLER
Kansas City Royals
Second Baseman
$28

Scrappy singles hitter, a better player for the Royals than I had expected. Runs hard, great effort in the field, but very poor fundamentals due to not playing there consistently, often throws before setting his feet. Gets on base one way or another, good baserunner, seems absolutely fearless. Missed a month with fracture of left leg or would have had his best major league season.

YEAR	TEAM/LEVEL	G	AB	R	H	2B	3B	HR	RBI	BB	SB	AVG	OBP	SLG
1991	New York	98	275	41	77	22	1	4	23	23	14	.280	.345	.411
1992	Kansas City	106	416	57	118	24	5	1	23	11	16	.250	.279	.307
1993	Projected	128	471	67	125	20	2	4	38	41	24	.265	.324	.342
		150	526	77	132	16	0	7	53	71	32	.256	.340	.321

JOE MILLETTE
Philadelphia Phillies
Shortstop
$1

If Tom Marsh was an infielder, he'd be Joe Millette. Undrafted free agent, a career .233 hitter in the minors, didn't get out of A Ball until he was almost 25 and then came to the majors a year later because the Phillies started with Kim Batiste and headed down. No prospect, but if he played every day he could lead the league in grounding into double plays.

YEAR	TEAM/LEVEL	G	AB	R	H	2B	3B	HR	RBI	BB	SB	AVG	OBP	SLG
1991	Reading AA	115	353	52	87	9	4	3	28	36	6	.246	.326	.320
1992	Scranton AAA	53	181	14	49	8	0	1	15	12	1	.271	.327	.331
1992	Philadelphia	30	71	4	14	0	0	0	2	4	1	.197	.260	.197
		7	0	0	0	0	0	0	0	0	1	—	—	—

RANDY MILLIGAN
Baltimore Orioles
First Baseman
$25

May have been thinking home run too much in Camden Yards. A .288 hitter on the road, he hit just .193 in Baltimore, the only major league regular to hit under .200 in his home park. Had almost as many walks (106) as hits (111) . . . career in Baltimore is probably almost over. He's 31, a replaceable talent, but has enough seniority to earn some real money.

YEAR	TEAM/LEVEL	G	AB	R	H	2B	3B	HR	RBI	BB	SB	AVG	OBP	SLG
1991	Baltimore	141	483	57	127	17	2	16	70	84	0	.263	.373	.406
1992	Baltimore	137	462	71	111	21	1	11	53	106	0	.240	.383	.361
1993	Projected	126	419	60	106	20	2	13	57	91	3	.253	.386	.403
		115	376	49	101	19	3	15	61	76	6	.269	.392	.455

KEITH MITCHELL
Atlanta Braves
Outfielder
$4

After hitting .318 for Atlanta in '91, was returned to Richmond and appeared to be, um . . . less than highly motivated. He's only 23 and can hit, also runs well and walks a lot, so you have to think that ability may surface sometime. He is accumulating a thick file of negative information—a late-night DWI incident, his performance in '92, plus he's related to Kevin Mitchell.

YEAR	TEAM/LEVEL	G	AB	R	H	2B	3B	HR	RBI	BB	SB	AVG	OBP	SLG
1991	Atlanta	48	66	11	21	0	0	2	5	8	3	.318	.392	.409
1992	Richmond AAA	121	403	45	91	19	1	4	50	66	14	.226	.338	.308
1992	MLE	121	395	36	83	17	0	3	40	50	9	.210	.299	.276
		121	387	27	75	15	0	2	30	34	4	.194	.255	.248

KEVIN MITCHELL
Seattle Mariners
Left Fielder
$33

His season was ended September 1 when doctors discovered a "stress factor of the sesamoid bone in his left foot." Of course we all know there isn't any such bone; he was just fat. Actually, he was red hot when he went out (31 RBI in his last 23 games) and has determined to lose weight and work out this winter, so may come back strong.

YEAR	TEAM/LEVEL	G	AB	R	H	2B	3B	HR	RBI	BB	SB	AVG	OBP	SLG
1991	San Francisco	113	371	52	95	13	1	27	69	58	2	.256	.338	.515
1992	Seattle	99	360	48	103	24	0	9	67	35	0	.286	.351	.428
1993	Projected	126	443	65	122	22	2	23	79	49	3	.275	.348	.490
		153	526	82	141	20	4	37	91	63	6	.268	.346	.532

PAUL MOLITOR
Milwaukee Brewers
Designated Hitter/First Baseman
$80

Has had 190 or more hits in four of the last five years, and now has a 29 percent chance of getting 3000 career hits. He batted third for the Brewers most of the year, not his natural role, but did a good job. He stole 31 bases at the age of 35, one of the best totals ever at that age. A great player.

YEAR	TEAM/LEVEL	G	AB	R	H	2B	3B	HR	RBI	BB	SB	AVG	OBP	SLG
1991	Milwaukee	158	665	133	216	32	13	17	75	77	19	.325	.399	.489
1992	Milwaukee	158	609	89	195	36	7	12	89	73	31	.320	.389	.461
1993	Projected	149	601	90	174	32	4	12	66	68	22	.290	.362	.416
		140	592	91	153	28	1	12	43	63	13	.258	.330	.376

RAUL MONDESI
Los Angeles Dodgers
Outfielder
$25

The best prospect in the Texas League; a manager told us he was the best he had seen at that level since Griffey. He's thin (5-11, 150) but fast, strong, and has an amazing throwing arm. Strikes out five times for each walk, which will slow his development at bat; was demoted by Dodgers from Triple-A to Double-A to punish him for attitude. Grade B prospect.

YEAR	TEAM/LEVEL	G	AB	R	H	2B	3B	HR	RBI	BB	SB	AVG	OBP	SLG
1990	Great Bend A	44	175	35	53	10	4	8	31	11	30	.303	.349	.543
1991	Three Levels	83	328	58	91	17	8	8	39	13	17	.277	.318	.451
1992	AA and AAA	52	204	31	60	6	9	6	28	10	5	.294	.327	.500
		21	80	4	29	0	10	4	17	7	0	.363	.414	.763

MICKEY MORANDINI
Philadelphia Phillies
Second Baseman
$28

Apparently is unpopular with the biker contingent of the Phillie roster, too gentle to be well liked. As a ballplayer I like him quite a lot. He doesn't hit left-handers (.189 career mark) and his strikeout/walk ratio is poor, but he's fast, a good baserunner and a fine second baseman. I think he will play almost regularly, and have good years.

YEAR	TEAM/LEVEL	G	AB	R	H	2B	3B	HR	RBI	BB	SB	AVG	OBP	SLG
1991	Philadelphia	98	325	38	81	11	4	1	20	29	13	.249	.313	.317
1992	Philadelphia	127	422	47	112	8	8	3	30	25	8	.265	.305	.344
1993	Projected	129	432	54	111	17	5	3	31	37	12	.257	.316	.340
		131	442	61	110	26	2	3	32	49	16	.249	.324	.337

RUSS MORMAN
Cincinnati Reds
First Baseman
$1

A 30-year-old veteran, has been bouncing between Triple-A and the majors since 1985. He's really not a bad player, excellent defensive first baseman and a pretty good line drive hitter. He had his best minor league season at Nashville last year (.510 slugging percentage) . . . needs to find a job backing up a left-handed hitter with no glove, like Mo Vaughn or Paul Sorrento.

YEAR	TEAM/LEVEL	G	AB	R	H	2B	3B	HR	RBI	BB	SB	AVG	OBP	SLG
1991	Omaha AAA	88	316	46	83	15	3	7	50	43	10	.263	.349	.396
1992	Nashville AAA	101	384	53	119	31	2	14	63	36	5	.310	.369	.510
1992	MLE	101	371	42	106	28	1	13	50	30	3	.286	.339	.472
		101	358	31	93	25	0	12	37	24	1	.260	.306	.430

HAL MORRIS
Cincinnati Reds
First Baseman
$38

A consistent .300 hitter until last year, he had his poorest year due to a broken right hand in April (hit by a pitch by Charlie Leibrandt) and a pulled hamstring in August. Since he is in his prime (28) and well-motivated due to becoming arbitration eligible, he should be a good bet to have a strong comeback in '92. Capable of winning a batting title.

YEAR	TEAM/LEVEL	G	AB	R	H	2B	3B	HR	RBI	BB	SB	AVG	OBP	SLG
1991	Cincinnati	136	478	72	152	33	1	14	59	46	10	.318	.374	.479
1992	Philadelphia	115	395	41	107	21	3	6	53	45	6	.271	.347	.385
1993	Projected	145	489	64	144	27	2	11	58	48	11	.294	.358	.425
		175	583	87	181	33	1	16	63	57	16	.310	.366	.453

JOHN MORRIS
California Angels
(Released)
Outfielder
No Value

At one time the top prospect in the Royals system, he never got where he was going because of back trouble and other problems. Last year he was on the DL with viral gastritis, and was released August 7. He's a clever guy, funny and well-educated, and could get a job as a broadcaster, or will earn a good living some other way.

YEAR	TEAM/LEVEL	G	AB	R	H	2B	3B	HR	RBI	BB	SB	AVG	OBP	SLG
1990	St. Louis	18	18	0	2	0	0	0	0	3	0	.111	.238	.111
1991	Philadelphia	85	127	15	28	2	1	1	6	12	2	.220	.293	.276
1992	California	43	57	4	11	1	0	1	3	4	1	.193	.258	.263
		1	0	0	0	0	0	1	0	0	0			

JOHN MOSES
Seattle Mariners
(Released)
Outfielder
No Value

Recalled from Calgary August 9, was able to get three hits in less than two months. He's 35 and his average over the last three years is just .200, so I would guess that even expansion isn't going to extend his career. Hell, he can't even hit at Calgary anymore . . . was a good defensive outfielder, no longer fast enough to fill in in center.

YEAR	TEAM/LEVEL	G	AB	R	H	2B	3B	HR	RBI	BB	SB	AVG	OBP	SLG
1990	Minnesota	115	172	26	38	3	1	1	14	19	2	.221	.303	.267
1991	Colorado Sp AAA	74	298	58	88	18	3	3	31	36	11	.295	.371	.406
1992	Seattle	21	22	3	3	1	0	0	1	5	0	.136	.296	.182
		0	0	0	0	0	0	0	0	0	0			

RANCE MULLINIKS
Toronto Blue Jays
Designated Hitter
NoValue

Missed almost all of 1992 with a disc problem in his back, and career is probably over. He hit well in the minors and the Angels thought he was a coming star. Then they realized he couldn't play shortstop, so they decided he was a bum. Bobby Cox saved his career by making him a platoon player, and his walks and doubles made him valuable in that role.

YEAR	TEAM/LEVEL	G	AB	R	H	2B	3B	HR	RBI	BB	SB	AVG	OBP	SLG
1990	Toronto	57	97	11	28	4	0	2	16	22	2	.289	.417	.392
1991	Toronto	97	240	27	60	12	1	2	24	44	0	.250	.364	.333
1992	Toronto	3	2	1	1	0	0	0	0	1	0	.500	.667	.500
		0	0	0	0	0	0	0	0	0	0	—	—	—

PEDRO MUNOZ
Minnesota Twins
Right Fielder
$29

One of the puzzles of the season. He was playing almost every day through mid-July, driving in a lot of runs and the Twins were winning, when for some reason Kelly began giving some of his playing time to turkeys. He got his time back in September, but had lost his power stroke. Has excellent arm, stole a few bases in the minors. Big, strong guy.

YEAR	TEAM/LEVEL	G	AB	R	H	2B	3B	HR	RBI	BB	SB	AVG	OBP	SLG
1991	Minnesota	51	138	15	39	7	1	7	26	9	3	.283	.327	.500
1992	Minnesota	127	418	44	113	16	3	12	71	17	4	.270	.298	.409
1993	Projected	138	458	54	132	24	3	14	69	28	12	.288	.329	.445
		149	498	64	157	32	3	16	67	39	20	.303	.354	.476

DALE MURPHY
Philadelphia Phillies
Right Fielder
$4

On the DL April 15 with infection in left knee, back May 7, out for season May 12 after arthroscopic knee surgery. The good news is that nobody took control of his job. The bad news is that there is scant evidence he can still play. He hasn't hit higher than .252 since 1987, can't run, and doesn't connect often enough for his power to justify his overall game.

YEAR	TEAM/LEVEL	G	AB	R	H	2B	3B	HR	RBI	BB	SB	AVG	OBP	SLG
1991	Philadelphia	153	544	66	137	33	1	18	81	48	1	.252	.309	.415
1992	Philadelphia	18	62	5	10	1	0	2	7	1	0	.161	.175	.274
1993	Projected	119	371	40	92	19	1	14	55	36	3	.248	.314	.418
		217	680	75	174	37	2	26	103	71	6	.256	.326	.431

EDDIE MURRAY
New York Mets

First Baseman
$27

A run-of-the-mill first baseman now, still has all of his old characteristics, but in faded colors. Still an RBI man, but hasn't actually driven in 100 runs in seven years. Still gets hot every September, but not as 'hot. Used to be a good baserunner for a guy with average speed; now he's a good baserunner for a guy who is actually slow.

YEAR	TEAM/LEVEL	G	AB	R	H	2B	3B	HR	RBI	BB	SB	AVG	OBP	SLG
1991	Los Angeles	153	576	69	150	23	1	19	96	55	10	.260	.321	.403
1992	New York	156	551	64	144	37	2	16	93	66	4	.261	.336	.423
1993	Projected	151	520	66	141	28	1	18	85	64	6	.271	.351	.433
		146	489	68	138	19	0	20	77	62	8	.282	.363	.444

GREG MYERS
California Angels

Catcher
$12

After backing up Borders until July 30, he was traded to California, and went on the disabled list in August with a chip fracture in his right hand. He's not star material, but in my opinion he is the best catcher the Angels have, and could get some playing time if they realize this. A .240 hitter with some power, erratic arm. **Could be a good pickup.**

YEAR	TEAM/LEVEL	G	AB	R	H	2B	3B	HR	RBI	BB	SB	AVG	OBP	SLG
1991	Toronto	107	309	25	81	22	0	8	36	21	0	.262	.306	.411
1992	Two Teams	30	78	4	18	7	0	1	13	5	0	.231	.271	.359
1993	Projected	121	384	37	96	20	0	9	44	30	0	.250	.304	.372
		212	690	70	174	33	0	17	75	55	0	.252	.307	.374

TIM NAEHRING
Boston Red Sox

Shortstop/Second Baseman
$12

After struggling with the bat, and his back, for a year and a half, he finally began hitting late in the year, 17-for-50 after September 1. I think he is a far better hitter than he has yet shown, but with Reed in place and Valentin in control of the shortstop job, Naehring will have to try to build up from utilityman. I like him.

YEAR	TEAM/LEVEL	G	AB	R	H	2B	3B	HR	RBI	BB	SB	AVG	OBP	SLG
1991	Boston	20	55	1	6	1	0	0	3	6	0	.109	.197	.127
1992	Boston	72	186	12	43	8	0	3	14	18	0	.231	.308	.323
1993	Projected	108	317	32	76	17	0	8	35	33	0	.240	.311	.369
		144	448	52	109	26	0	13	56	48	0	.243	.317	.384

BOB NATAL
Montreal Expos

Catcher
$11

A 27-year-old minor league catcher, was late bloomer and regarded as very marginal prospect until last year, when he battled (unsuccessfully) for the American Association batting title. Defense is good, not outstanding skills but quick release, fundamentally solid. Will battle Laker, Fletcher for Expos' job; is better hitter than Laker. Grade C prospect; possibility is there for a big surprise season.

YEAR	TEAM/LEVEL	G	AB	R	H	2B	3B	HR	RBI	BB	SB	AVG	OBP	SLG
1991	AA and AAA	116	377	49	99	20	3	13	62	55	2	.263	.363	.435
1992	Indianapolis AAA	96	344	50	104	19	3	12	50	28	3	.302	.359	.480
1992	MLE	96	325	36	85	16	1	7	36	20	2	.262	.304	.382
		96	306	22	66	13	0	2	22	12	1	.216	.241	.278

TROY NEEL
Oakland Athletics
Outfielder
$10

A late bloomer, has established some value. As a pre-rookie in '92 he had almost the same batting and slugging average as Albert Belle, and while he isn't quite *that* good a hitter, he is a major league hitter. He's 27, so won't develop further, and was a minor league first baseman, forced to play outfield. Grade C prospect.

YEAR	TEAM/LEVEL	G	AB	R	H	2B	3B	HR	RBI	BB	SB	AVG	OBP	SLG
1992	MLE	112	370	47	113	29	1	11	57	46	1	.305	.382	.478
1992	Oakland	24	53	8	14	3	0	3	9	5	0	.264	.339	.491
1993	Projected	96	252	34	67	16	0	8	38	35	2	.266	.355	.425
		168	457	60	120	29	0	13	67	65	4	.266	.359	.417

AL NEWMAN
Texas Rangers
Utilityman
$12

A .225 hitter and has less power than any other major league player, but his walks, speed, and defense at second and third make him a useful utility infielder anyway. Has multi-year record of hitting 40 points better in the late innings of a game than he does overall. Best defensive position is second base, where he can use his intelligence in the middle of the field.

YEAR	TEAM/LEVEL	G	AB	R	H	2B	3B	HR	RBI	BB	SB	AVG	OBP	SLG
1991	Minnesota	118	246	25	47	5	0	0	19	23	4	.191	.260	.211
1992	Texas	116	246	25	54	5	0	0	12	34	9	.220	.317	.240
1993	Projected	103	227	24	50	8	1	0	17	24	6	.220	.295	.364
		90	208	23	46	11	2	0	22	14	3	.221	.270	.298

WARREN NEWSON
Chicago White Sox
Right Fielder
$13

A combination of Walt (No-Neck) Williams and Gary Redus, has Williams's body and Redus's job and secondary offensive skills. He hit only .221 but had more walks (37) than hits (30), so his on-base percentage (.387) was the second-best on the White Sox, behind Big Frank. His secondary average was .338. If he got enough playing time, it would be better than that . . .

YEAR	TEAM/LEVEL	G	AB	R	H	2B	3B	HR	RBI	BB	SB	AVG	OBP	SLG
1991	Chicago	71	132	20	39	5	0	4	25	28	5	.295	.419	.424
1992	Chicago	63	136	19	30	3	0	1	11	37	3	.221	.387	.265
1993	Projected	66	162	24	44	7	1	4	20	33	4	.272	.395	.401
		69	188	29	58	11	2	7	29	29	5	.305	.401	.500

MELVIN NIEVES
Atlanta Braves
Outfielder
$30

A 21-year-old power-hitting outfielder, hit 26 homers and drove in 108 runs at Durham/Greenville in '92. A switch hitter, hits for power both ways, can also run and play defense. Has been compared to Ruben Sierra. He strikes out enough to cause himself some problems, but wouldn't lead the league in Ks even now, and definitely won't in three years. **Grade A prospect.**

YEAR	TEAM/LEVEL	G	AB	R	H	2B	3B	HR	RBI	BB	SB	AVG	OBP	SLG
1992	Durham	31	106	18	32	9	1	8	32	17	4	.302	.395	.632
1992	Greenville AA	100	350	61	99	23	5	18	76	52	6	.283	.381	.531
1992	MLE	100	343	50	92	21	2	18	63	33	3	.268	.332	.499
		100	336	39	85	19	0	18	50	14	0	.283	.283	.478

DAVE NILSSON
Milwaukee Brewers

Catcher
$23

Famous for hitting .418 at El Paso in '91 (65 games), also hit .394 at Helena in '87, but overall minor league batting average .294. Bounced up and down in '92, appeared to have about 50 percent of the catcher's job at season's end. Won't strike out much, should hit .260+ and at 23 has the potential to develop some power. Defense is adequate, maybe better. Looks good.

YEAR	TEAM/LEVEL	G	AB	R	H	2B	3B	HR	RBI	BB	SB	AVG	OBP	SLG
1992	Denver AAA	66	240	38	76	16	7	3	39	23	10	.317	.369	.479
1992	Milwaukee	51	164	15	38	8	0	4	25	17	2	.232	.304	.354
1993	Projected	96	323	40	92	22	2	5	46	29	5	.285	.344	.412
		141	482	65	156	36	4	6	67	41	8	.303	.358	.432

OTIS NIXON
Atlanta Braves

Center Fielder
$27

Slumped in September, and thus wound up with numbers distinctly down from his superb 1991 season. Stolen base percentage dropped sharply, on-base percentage down 23 points. He's 34, but that doesn't mean much for a player with great speed and a slow bat. Great bunter. I don't anticipate a sudden relapse, but then I also didn't anticipate that he would be this good.

YEAR	TEAM/LEVEL	G	AB	R	H	2B	3B	HR	RBI	BB	SB	AVG	OBP	SLG
1991	Atlanta	124	401	81	119	10	1	0	26	47	72	.297	.371	.327
1992	Atlanta	120	456	79	134	14	2	2	22	39	41	.294	.348	.346
1993	Projected	124	366	63	100	7	1	1	21	39	52	.273	.343	.306
		128	276	47	86	0	0	0	20	39	63	.239	.333	.239

JUNIOR NOBOA
New York Mets (Released)

Second Baseman
$1

He was waived by the Mets in late July, accepted assignment to Tidewater but played only six games there before disappearing. We don't know where he is. I used to think he was a pretty good hitter for a middle infielder, but he didn't have much defense, and didn't take advantage of his opportunities. Only 28, but his career may be over.

YEAR	TEAM/LEVEL	G	AB	R	H	2B	3B	HR	RBI	BB	SB	AVG	OBP	SLG
1990	Montreal	81	158	15	42	7	2	0	14	7	4	.266	.294	.335
1991	Montreal	67	95	5	23	3	0	1	2	1	2	.242	.250	.305
1992	New York	46	47	7	7	0	0	0	3	3	0	.149	.212	.149
		25	0	9	0	0	0	0	4	5	0	-	1.000	-

MATT NOKES
New York Yankees

Catcher
$20

Has established a sort of level, hitting 20 homers twice in a row for the first time after bouncing up and down from 1987 to 1990. No defensive catcher, doesn't create huge number of runs. Playing time appears reasonably secure unless there's a free agent; Yankee Double-A and Triple-A catchers (Kiki Hernandez and Brad Ausmus) both have some potential but are not ready.

YEAR	TEAM/LEVEL	G	AB	R	H	2B	3B	HR	RBI	BB	SB	AVG	OBP	SLG
1991	New York	135	456	52	122	20	0	24	77	25	3	.268	.308	.469
1992	New York	121	384	42	86	9	1	22	59	37	0	.224	.293	.424
1993	Projected	135	406	44	102	15	1	19	60	31	2	.251	.304	.433
		149	428	46	118	21	1	16	61	25	4	.276	.316	.457

CHARLIE O'BRIEN
New York Mets
Catcher
$8

A good defensive catcher, can catch for anybody as long as they don't really intend to win or anything. Had one of his best seasons with the bat last year, lifting his career batting average to .205 and posting his best batting and slugging percentages in three years. Mets had 4.15 ERA with O'Brien in the lineup, 3.31 with the rookie.

YEAR	TEAM/LEVEL	G	AB	R	H	2B	3B	HR	RBI	BB	SB	AVG	OBP	SLG
1991	New York	69	168	16	31	6	0	2	14	17	0	.185	.272	.256
1992	New York	68	156	15	33	12	0	2	13	16	0	.212	.289	.327
1993	Projected	54	111	10	22	6	0	1	11	11	0	.198	.270	.279
		40	66	3	11	0	0	0	9	6	0	.167	.236	.167

PETE O'BRIEN
Seattle Mariners
First Baseman/Designated Hitter
$12

He's the same age as Gary Gaetti (born 1958), and continues to shadow Gaetti's batting stats. In '91 Gaetti hit .246 with 18 homers, 66 RBI; O;Brien hit .248 with 17 and 88. In '92 Gaetti hit .226 with 12 homers, 48 RBI; O'Brien hit .222 with 14 and 52. All 14 homers were before the All-Star break. I'm sure he'll be better at 35.

YEAR	TEAM/LEVEL	G	AB	R	H	2B	3B	HR	RBI	BB	SB	AVG	OBP	SLG
1991	Seattle	152	560	58	139	29	3	17	88	44	0	.248	.300	.402
1992	Seattle	134	396	40	88	15	1	14	52	40	2	.222	.289	.371
1993	Projected	93	295	30	73	15	1	8	39	29	1	.247	.315	.386
		52	194	20	58	15	1	2	26	18	0	.298	.358	.418

TROY O'LEARY
Milwaukee Brewers
Outfielder
$12

A 23-year-old left-handed leadoff-type hitter, has been in the Brewer system since '87. Good athlete, was a 13th-round draft pick because he didn't play baseball in high school (football player). *Baseball America* listed him the ninth-best prospect in the Milwaukee system two years ago, dropped off the list after poor '91 season but will recover after fine '92. Grade B prospect.

YEAR	TEAM/LEVEL	G	AB	R	H	2B	3B	HR	RBI	BB	SB	AVG	OBP	SLG
1991	Stockton A	126	418	63	110	20	4	5	46	73	4	.263	.377	.366
1992	El Paso AA	135	506	92	169	27	8	5	79	59	28	.334	.399	.449
1992	MLE	135	469	61	132	22	4	3	52	33	18	.281	.329	.365
		135	432	30	95	17	0	1	25	7	8	.220	.232	.266

PAUL O'NEILL
New York Yankees
Right Fielder
$31

O'Neill is a good player, and could come back with one or two strong seasons. The trade is a classic Yankee blunder—failing to realize that 1) O'Neill is 30, and won't be the player in his thirties that he was in his twenties, and 2) almost two-thirds of O'Neill's career home runs were hit in Cincinnati, and he won't hit with the same power in New York.

YEAR	TEAM/LEVEL	G	AB	R	H	2B	3B	HR	RBI	BB	SB	AVG	OBP	SLG
1991	Cincinnati	152	532	71	136	36	0	28	91	73	12	.256	.346	.481
1992	Cincinnati	148	496	59	122	19	1	14	66	77	6	.246	.346	.373
1993	Projected	151	517	63	129	28	1	18	75	72	11	.250	.341	.412
		154	538	67	136	37	1	22	84	67	16	.253	.336	.448

KEN OBERKFELL
California Angels

Utilityman
No Value

Was purchased from Edmonton July 9 in a vain effort to make Gary Gaetti feel young (Ken Reitz apparently could not be located). He hit .264 but with a secondary average below .100, didn't drive in or score any runs. He played some second base and DH'd, a unique combination . . . everybody needs a 36-year-old, 210-pound singles hitter to DH for them.

YEAR	TEAM/LEVEL	G	AB	R	H	2B	3B	HR	RBI	BB	SB	AVG	OBP	SLG
1990	Houston	77	150	10	31	6	1	1	12	15	1	.207	.281	.280
1991	Houston	53	70	7	16	4	0	0	14	14	0	.229	.357	.286
1992	California	41	91	6	24	1	0	0	10	8	0	.264	.317	.275
		29	112	3	32	0	0	0	6	2	0	.286	.298	.286

JOSE OFFERMAN
Los Angeles Dodgers

Shortstop
$34

He was expected to make 35 errors, but overachieved. With a .260 average and 23 stolen bases he could be said to have established himself in '92—and simultaneously to have endangered his career with 42 errors, 16 caught stealing, and 98 strikeouts. There hasn't been a shortstop in a long time who could play regularly with a .935 fielding percentage. Dodgers will be looking.

YEAR	TEAM/LEVEL	G	AB	R	H	2B	3B	HR	RBI	BB	SB	AVG	OBP	SLG
1991	Los Angeles	52	113	10	22	2	0	0	3	25	3	.195	.345	.212
1992	Los Angeles	149	534	67	139	20	8	1	30	57	23	.260	.331	.333
1993	Projected	155	550	74	142	13	4	2	40	67	36	.258	.339	.307
		161	566	81	145	6	0	3	50	77	49	.256	.345	.283

JOHN OLERUD
Toronto Blue Jays

First Baseman
$39

He continues to hit poorly with runners in scoring position (.217 last year), but continues to make steady all-around progress as a hitter. Set career highs in batting, slugging, on-base percentage in '92. He's only 24, so he could still improve by several steps, or could take the league by storm. I still see him as a young Rusty Staub, and I recommend him highly.

YEAR	TEAM/LEVEL	G	AB	R	H	2B	3B	HR	RBI	BB	SB	AVG	OBP	SLG
1991	Toronto	139	454	64	116	30	1	17	68	68	0	.256	.353	.438
1992	Toronto	138	458	68	130	28	0	16	66	70	1	.284	.375	.450
1993	Projected	149	531	75	147	29	1	21	78	86	1	.277	.378	.454
		150	604	82	164	30	2	26	90	102	1	.272	.377	.457

JOSE OLIVA
Texas Rangers

Third Base Prospect
$8

Only 22 years old, had a good year in Double-A at 21 and has real potential as a hitter. Physically he looks a little like a young Orlando Cepeda, very strong and with quick hands; defensively has outstanding arm but slow feet and doesn't work on his defense. Power now is to dead center; needs to pull the ball or go with the pitch. Grade B prospect.

YEAR	TEAM/LEVEL	G	AB	R	H	2B	3B	HR	RBI	BB	SB	AVG	OBP	SLG
1991	Charlotte A	108	384	55	92	17	4	14	59	44	9	.240	.321	.414
1992	Tulsa AA	124	445	57	120	28	6	16	75	40	3	.270	.328	.467
1992	MLE	124	439	53	114	26	5	14	69	31	2	.260	.309	.437
		122	433	49	108	24	4	12	63	22	1	.249		

102 Oberkfell–Orsulak

JOE OLIVER
Cincinnati Reds
Catcher
$33

After struggling until late June, got red-hot and hit extremely well the rest of the year. Nothing in his previous record suggested that he would hit this way, so I suppose he made some adjustments. When a hitter has a three-month hot streak like this, most of the time he will relapse somewhat the following year. I would anticipate a .240 season.

YEAR	TEAM/LEVEL	G	AB	R	H	2B	3B	HR	RBI	BB	SB	AVG	OBP	SLG
1991	Cincinnati	94	269	21	58	11	0	11	41	18	0	.216	.265	.379
1992	Cincinnati	143	485	42	131	25	1	10	57	35	2	.270	.316	.388
1993	Projected	136	420	36	104	21	0	11	54	35	2	.248	.305	.376
		129	355	30	77	17	0	12	51	35	2	.217	.287	.366

GREG OLSON
Atlanta Braves
Catcher
$4

His season was ended September 19, as you probably remember, by a broken leg. He hopes to be ready to start the '93 season, but the injuries are serious. Hits well first half of season (career .272 with 12 homers), but fades second half (.222 with 4 homers). Javy Lopez will take his job in '94 if not '93; defense will give him long career as a backup.

YEAR	TEAM/LEVEL	G	AB	R	H	2B	3B	HR	RBI	BB	SB	AVG	OBP	SLG
1990	Atlanta	121	364	34	84	23	0	8	52	37	1	.231	.304	.360
1991	Atlanta	133	411	46	99	25	0	6	44	44	1	.241	.316	.345
1992	Atlanta	95	302	27	72	14	2	3	27	34	2	.238	.316	.328
		57	193	8	55	3	4	0	10	24	3	.233	.318	.290

JOSE OQUENDO
St. Louis Cardinals
Second Baseman
$23

Dislocated his shoulder diving for a ball opening day, was out six weeks, came back to play a few games, then lost most of the season to a bone spur in his heel. Peña or Alicea will probably play second for St. Louis, but Oquendo is too good a player to be out of a job; may get a crack at short if Ozzie leaves.

YEAR	TEAM/LEVEL	G	AB	R	H	2B	3B	HR	RBI	BB	SB	AVG	OBP	SLG
1991	St. Louis	127	366	37	88	11	4	1	26	67	1	.240	.357	.301
1992	St. Louis	14	35	3	9	3	1	0	3	5	0	.257	.350	.400
1993	Projected	98	271	26	70	9	2	1	22	47	1	.258	.368	.317
		182	507	49	131	15	3	2	41	89	2	.258	.369	.312

JOE ORSULAK
Baltimore Orioles
Right Fielder
$16

He'll turn 31 in May, and to be frank he's about outlived his usefulness. He's a .280 hitter, actually led the Orioles in hitting in '92, has a fine throwing arm, and when he came up he was very fast. He isn't fast anymore, doesn't have any power, and the combination doesn't put a lot of runs on the board (about 4.8 per 27 outs).

YEAR	TEAM/LEVEL	G	AB	R	H	2B	3B	HR	RBI	BB	SB	AVG	OBP	SLG
1991	Baltimore	143	486	57	135	22	1	5	43	28	6	.278	.321	.358
1992	Baltimore	117	391	45	113	18	3	4	39	28	5	.289	.342	.381
1993	Projected	133	442	50	119	19	3	6	46	36	6	.269	.324	.367
		149	493	55	125	20	3	8	53	44	7	.253	.315	.355

JUNIOR ORTIZ
Cleveland Indians
(Released)
Catcher
$6

Longtime backup, he played regularly during Alomar's injuries, which is the next best thing to playing regularly. His defense is average or below, and with a secondary average of .082 he's not going to drive in or score runs. He is not terribly slow, but probably the worst baserunner in the majors, aggressive but without speed or judgment. There are other backup catchers I'd rather have.

YEAR	TEAM/LEVEL	G	AB	R	H	2B	3B	HR	RBI	BB	SB	AVG	OBP	SLG
1991	Minnesota	61	134	9	28	5	1	0	11	15	0	.209	.293	.261
1992	Cleveland	86	244	20	61	7	0	0	24	12	1	.250	.296	.279
1993	Projected	75	169	14	43	6	0	1	16	12	1	.248	.305	.376
		64	94	8	25	5	0	2	8	12	1	.266	.369	.383

JOHN ORTON
California Angels
Catcher
$3

His career average is .203, but I doubt that he's really a .203 hitter. I suspect he's more like a .185 hitter. His defense is excellent, he is 27 years old, and the Angels have a mammoth need for a catcher, so if you envision the best-case scenario, he could get hot, hit .270 for a couple of months and hold the job all year. Still . . .

YEAR	TEAM/LEVEL	G	AB	R	H	2B	3B	HR	RBI	BB	SB	AVG	OBP	SLG
1992	Edmonton AAA	49	149	28	38	9	3	3	25	28	0	.255	.379	.416
1992	California	43	114	11	25	3	0	2	12	7	1	.219	.276	.298
1993	Projected	53	140	15	28	6	0	2	13	12	1	.200	.263	.286
		63	166	19	31	9	0	2	14	17	1	.187	.263	.277

SPIKE OWEN
Montreal Expos
(Free Agent)
Shortstop
$20

He seems certain to leave Montreal due to the development of Wilfredo Cordero, but is a quality player in his own right. He's an average defensive shortstop at 32, but his walks, baserunning, and occasional power are a solid combination for a middle infielder. A better hitter right-handed than left-handed. May have made a mistake in becoming a switch hitter, which is common.

YEAR	TEAM/LEVEL	G	AB	R	H	2B	3B	HR	RBI	BB	SB	AVG	OBP	SLG
1991	Montreal	139	424	39	108	22	8	3	26	42	2	.255	.321	.366
1992	Montreal	122	386	52	104	16	3	7	40	50	9	.269	.348	.381
1993	Projected	139	424	45	99	19	4	4	31	56	7	.233	.323	.325
		156	462	38	94	22	5	1	22	62	5	.203	.297	.258

MIKE PAGLIARULO
Minnesota Twins
(Released)
Third Baseman
$4

Had surgery to repair a perforated eardrum, March 28, later broke his wrist, also requiring surgery. This forced Kelly to increase playing time for Leius, which hurt the team, and then Pagliarulo came back and went through spring training in August, which was worse. Injuries have taken away his power, his speed, and his durability. I will be surprised if he ever plays well again.

YEAR	TEAM/LEVEL	G	AB	R	H	2B	3B	HR	RBI	BB	SB	AVG	OBP	SLG
1991	Minnesota	121	365	38	102	20	0	6	36	21	1	.279	.322	.384
1992	Minnesota	42	105	10	21	4	0	0	9	1	1	.200	.213	.238
1993	Projected	106	299	26	72	16	1	8	30	21	1	.241	.291	.381
		170	493	42	123	28	2	16	57	41	1	.249	.307	.412

TOM PAGNOZZI
St. Louis Cardinals
Catcher
$30

Had an outstanding first half (.282 average through June) but slumped the second half under one of the heaviest workloads in baseball. Generic catcher, throws OK but not great, had some speed a couple of years ago but has lost it, .250 hitter with limited power who could probably hit a little better and run a lot better if he played about 40 fewer games.

YEAR	TEAM/LEVEL	G	AB	R	H	2B	3B	HR	RBI	BB	SB	AVG	OBP	SLG
1991	St. Louis	140	459	38	121	24	5	2	57	36	9	.264	.319	.351
1992	St. Louis	139	485	33	121	26	3	7	44	28	2	.249	.290	.359
1993	Projected	145	483	36	123	22	2	5	49	34	6	.255	.304	.340
		151	481	39	125	18	1	3	54	40	10	.260	.311	.320

RAFAEL PALMEIRO
Texas Rangers
First Baseman
$60

Didn't match his MVP-candidate season of '91, but there are players who wouldn't complain about 22 homers and 85 RBI. Has an estimated 16 percent chance to get 3000 hits, which may be too optimistic, but he should clear 2000 and hit 200 home runs. A product of the same Miami Cuban community as Jose Canseco; the Rangers may be hoping he will be a good influence.

YEAR	TEAM/LEVEL	G	AB	R	H	2B	3B	HR	RBI	BB	SB	AVG	OBP	SLG
1991	Texas	159	631	115	203	49	3	26	88	68	4	.322	.389	.532
1992	Texas	159	608	84	163	27	4	22	85	72	2	.268	.352	.434
1993	Projected	160	621	90	183	36	4	20	86	64	3	.295	.361	.462
		161	634	96	203	45	4	18	87	56	4	.320	.35	.489

DEAN PALMER
Texas Rangers
Third Baseman
$34

One of the "new Mike Schmidts," like Matt Williams; actually it might be better to think of him as the new Matt Williams. Not much of a third baseman, good arm but slow reactions and was error prone early in the year. Has quick swing but chases bad pitches. He's only 24, so will improve; doubt that he can push average over .260 but could hit 40 home runs.

YEAR	TEAM/LEVEL	G	AB	R	H	2B	3B	HR	RBI	BB	SB	AVG	OBP	SLG
1991	Texas	81	268	38	50	9	2	15	37	32	0	.187	.281	.403
1992	Texas	152	541	74	124	25	0	26	72	62	10	.229	.311	.420
1993	Projected	155	550	75	127	26	3	29	81	54	6	.231	.300	.447
		158	559	76	130	27	6	32	90	46	2	.233	.291	.474

MARK PARENT
Baltimore Orioles
Catcher
$1

Lance Parrish's poor cousin, a huge, slow catcher. Now 31 years old, has a little power (18 major league homers in 522 at bats) and a good arm, but no other major league skills. Got a chance to play in San Diego during Santiago's injuries, has bounced around since, surfacing in Baltimore during Hoiles's stay on the DL. No future.

YEAR	TEAM/LEVEL	G	AB	R	H	2B	3B	HR	RBI	BB	SB	AVG	OBP	SLG
1992	Rochester AAA	101	356	52	102	24	0	17	69	35	4	.287	.348	.497
1992	MLE	101	339	40	85	19	0	13	53	27	2	.251	.306	.422
1992	Baltimore	17	34	4	8	1	0	2	4	3	0	.235	.316	.441
		0	0	0	0	0	0	0	0	0	0	-	-	-

DEREK PARKS
Minnesota Twins
Catcher
$3

Former first-round draft pick, a right-handed hitting catcher with a home run swing, has .227 career average in the minor leagues (587 games) but is only 24 and appears to be making some progress. He had more hits than strikeouts last year, for the first time since 1988, and got a seven-game look by the parent team. Grade D prospect.

YEAR	TEAM/LEVEL	G	AB	R	H	2B	3B	HR	RBI	BB	SB	AVG	OBP	SLG
1991	Orlando AA	92	256	31	55	14	0	6	31	31	0	.215	.325	.340
1992	Portland AAA	79	249	33	61	12	0	12	49	25	0	.245	.317	.438
1992	MLE	79	243	26	55	11	0	9	38	20	0	.226	.285	.383
		79	237	19	49	10	0	6	27	15	0	.207	.254	.325

LANCE PARRISH
Seattle Mariners
Catcher
$21

Released by the Angels in June, signed by the Mariners a few days later and played at pretty much his normal level the rest of the year. His skills have been fading inch by inch for years, and one presumes that he can't come back. I won't argue with that, but Parrish loves to train. If he adjusts his training routine, he might have a surprise left.

YEAR	TEAM/LEVEL	G	AB	R	H	2B	3B	HR	RBI	BB	SB	AVG	OBP	SLG
1991	California	119	402	38	87	12	0	19	51	35	0	.216	.285	.388
1992	Two Teams	93	275	26	64	13	1	12	32	24	1	.233	.294	.418
1993	Projected	94	342	32	75	14	1	12	40	32	1	.219	.286	.371
		95	409	38	86	15	1	12	48	40	1	.210	.281	.340

DAN PASQUA
Chicago White Sox
Right Fielder
$15

The answer to the old riddle, of course, is that if a tree falls in the forest and nobody hears it, nobody gives a shit whether it makes any noise or not. The same can be said of a power hitter who doesn't hit homers. Hamstring pulls have reduced his playing time to where we are uncertain whether he does or does not still have power, and—

YEAR	TEAM/LEVEL	G	AB	R	H	2B	3B	HR	RBI	BB	SB	AVG	OBP	SLG
1991	Chicago	134	417	71	108	22	5	18	66	62	0	.259	.358	.465
1992	Chicago	93	265	26	56	16	1	6	33	36	0	.211	.305	.347
1993	Projected	94	262	34	65	13	1	10	39	36	1	.248	.339	.420
		95	259	42	74	10	1	14	45	36	2	.286	.373	.491

JOHN PATTERSON
San Francisco Giants
Second Baseman/Center Fielder
$2

Started the season with the Giants, playing second while Robby Thompson was hurt, but broke his finger on May 6, went to Phoenix off the DL. Was voted the best defensive second baseman in the Texas League in 1991. *Baseball America* cited him as eighth-best prospect overall, but after 1992 season was learned to have re-injured his rotator cuff. Grade D prospect.

YEAR	TEAM/LEVEL	G	AB	R	H	2B	3B	HR	RBI	BB	SB	AVG	OBP	SLG
1992	Phoenix AAA	94	362	52	109	20	6	2	37	33	22	.301	.366	.406
1992	MLE	94	338	34	85	15	3	1	24	20	13	.251	.293	.322
1992	San Francisco	32	103	10	19	1	1	0	4	5	5	.184	.229	.214
		0	0	0	0	0	0	0	0	0	0			

BILL PECOTA
New York Mets
Utilityman
$16

Played second, third, and short for the Mets, batting in all nine spots in the batting order. He's as good a fundamental player as I've ever seen, does everything well except that he just isn't much of a hitter. Best defensive position is second base, but is average defensive shortstop or third baseman. Will never be projected as a regular again, but career should continue.

YEAR	TEAM/LEVEL	G	AB	R	H	2B	3B	HR	RBI	BB	SB	AVG	OBP	SLG
1991	Kansas City	125	398	53	114	23	2	6	45	41	16	.286	.356	.399
1992	New York	117	269	28	61	13	0	2	26	25	9	.227	.293	.297
1993	Projected	89	238	32	58	10	1	3	22	26	9	.244	.318	.332
		51	207	36	55	7	2	4	18	27	9	.266	.350	.377

JORGE PEDRE
Chicago Cubs
Catcher
$1

A product of the Kansas City system, cut from their 40-man roster and picked up by Iowa. In the majors I would expect him to hit around .220 with very little power, no speed, poor strikeout/walk ratio. Looks very strong, like a weight lifter; wouldn't want to try to move him off the plate. Arm is just average. Looking for spot as backup, no real prospect.

YEAR	TEAM/LEVEL	G	AB	R	H	2B	3B	HR	RBI	BB	SB	AVG	OBP	SLG
1991	MLE	131	465	44	103	29	0	6	51	19	1	.222	.252	.323
1992	Iowa AAA	98	296	31	75	17	1	6	34	26	2	.253	.315	.378
1992	MLE	98	285	22	64	14	0	4	24	17	1	.225	.268	.316
		98	274	13	53	11	0	2	14	8	0	.193	.216	.255

JULIO PEGUERO
Los Angeles Dodgers
Center Fielder
$2

Played with the Phillies the first two months, filling in a little in center field, and was traded to the Dodgers as a player to be named. Partial payment for Stan Javier; earlier in his career he was one of three players exchanged for Carmelo Martinez. He is 24 years old, very fast, and considered an excellent defensive outfielder. Grade D prospect.

YEAR	TEAM/LEVEL	G	AB	R	H	2B	3B	HR	RBI	BB	SB	AVG	OBP	SLG
1991	Scranton AAA	133	506	71	138	20	9	2	39	40	21	.273	.326	.360
1992	Two Teams AAA	104	365	54	94	18	2	2	29	37	15	.258	.329	.334
1992	MLE	104	350	39	79	12	0	0	20	28	10	.226	.283	.260
		104	335	24	64	6	0	0	11	19	5	.191	.234	.200

DAN PELTIER
Texas Rangers
Outfielder
$7

There are some things to like here. He's big and slow, but has a right fielder's arm and a good, level, left-handed swing, the basic description of a pinch hitter. Usually looks at a couple of pitches before he swings. With Canseco in right field rather than Sierra, will get some playing time during injuries. Grade C prospect; would have to develop power to be regular.

YEAR	TEAM/LEVEL	G	AB	R	H	2B	3B	HR	RBI	BB	SB	AVG	OBP	SLG
1991	Oklahoma City AAA	94	345	38	79	16	4	3	31	43	6	.229	.313	.325
1992	Oklahoma City AAA	125	450	65	133	30	7	7	53	60	1	.296	.381	.440
1992	MLE	125	433	51	116	26	5	5	41	46	0	.268	.338	.386
		125	416	37	99	22	3	3	29	32	0	.238	.292	.327

GERONIMO PEÑA
St. Louis Cardinals
Second Baseman
$35

Development had been slowed by injuries and illness. He's bigger (195 pounds) and stronger than he used to be, but not as fast. This has led to criticism of his defense, which may give Luis Alicea the first shot at the second base job. Pe:a is a better hitter than Alicea, maybe good enough to play third base, plus he still runs well. He should play somewhere.

YEAR	TEAM/LEVEL	G	AB	R	H	2B	3B	HR	RBI	BB	SB	AVG	OBP	SLG
1990	Louisville	118	390	65	97	24	6	6	35	69	24	.249	.383	.387
1991	St. Louis	104	185	38	45	8	3	5	17	18	15	.243	.322	.400
1992	St. Louis	62	203	31	62	12	1	7	31	24	13	.305	.386	.478
		20	221	24	79	16	0	9	45	32	11	.357	.439	.561

TONY PEÑA
Boston Red Sox
Catcher
$17

The Red Sox continue to insist that his defense justifies his offense, but then, the Red Sox finished last, too. When he was young he could hit, ran well, and had a great arm, but his reputation was that he wasn't a good handler of pitchers and didn't call a good game. So he's now exactly the opposite of what he originally was.

YEAR	TEAM/LEVEL	G	AB	R	H	2B	3B	HR	RBI	BB	SB	AVG	OBP	SLG
1991	Boston	141	464	45	107	23	2	5	48	37	8	.231	.291	.321
1992	Boston	133	410	39	99	21	1	1	38	24	3	.241	.284	.305
1993	Projected	121	387	40	95	18	1	5	42	30	5	.245	.300	.338
		109	364	41	91	15	1	9	46	36	7	.250	.318	.371

TERRY PENDLETON
Atlanta Braves
Third Baseman
$69

The historical precedent for Terry's dramatic leap forward is Bob Elliott, 1940s third baseman who vaulted from defensive player/limited bat to MVP/perennial star after being traded from the Pirates to the Braves in 1947. One of four players to follow up an MVP season with a better year and not win a repeat MVP. The others were Frank Robinson (1962), Yogi Berra (1956), and Joe DiMaggio (1948).

YEAR	TEAM/LEVEL	G	AB	R	H	2B	3B	HR	RBI	BB	SB	AVG	OBP	SLG
1991	Atlanta	153	586	94	187	34	8	22	86	43	10	.319	.363	.517
1992	Atlanta	160	640	98	199	39	1	21	105	37	5	.311	.345	.473
1993	Projected	155	595	76	166	28	3	13	78	40	7	.279	.324	.402
		150	550	54	133	17	5	5	51	43	9	.242	.297	.318

WILLIAM PENNYFEATHER
Pittsburgh Pirates
Outfielder
$5

Exceptional athlete, was a wide receiver for Syracuse before signing with the Pirates from a tryout camp. Is 24 years old, was called up to serve as a defensive sub in the outfield and occasionally pinch run. That appears to be his future. Although he hit .337 in 51 games at Carolina, his record, as a whole, would suggest that he is not likely to hit. Grade D prospect.

YEAR	TEAM/LEVEL	G	AB	R	H	2B	3B	HR	RBI	BB	SB	AVG	OBP	SLG
1991	Carolina AA	42	149	13	41	5	0	0	9	7	3	.275	.310	.309
1992	AA and AAA	106	359	47	105	19	3	7	37	11	10	.292	.314	.421
1992	MLE	106	347	39	93	17	1	5	31	7	7	.268	.282	.366
		106	335	31	81	15	0	3	25	3	4	.242	.249	.313

TONY PEREZCHICA
Cleveland Indians
Second Baseman
$1

Only 27 (in April), or so at least he says, he was a prospect dog's years ago in the Giant system, hit very well from 1984 to 1988 but stopped hitting in 1989, when he separated his shoulder diving for a ball, and has never been the same since. Born in Mexico, but played high school ball in Palm Springs, California, and lives in Arizona.

YEAR	TEAM/LEVEL	G	AB	R	H	2B	3B	HR	RBI	BB	SB	AVG	OBP	SLG
1991	Phoenix AAA	51	191	41	56	10	4	8	34	18	1	.293	.367	.513
1992	Colorado Sp AAA	20	70	8	12	1	0	2	9	4	1	.171	.227	.271
1992	Cleveland	18	20	2	2	1	0	0	1	2	0	.100	.182	.150
		16	0	0	0	1	0	0	0	0	8	—	—	—

GERALD PERRY
St. Louis Cardinals
First Baseman
$2

Expansion will keep his career sputtering along for one more year. Left-handed line-drive hitter, pinch hit 54 times last year, among the most in the league. A .240 hitter with limited power, not much speed, not much help on defense. Will bat a hundred times, and anybody might have a good year in 100 at bats, so his career could last into '94.

YEAR	TEAM/LEVEL	G	AB	R	H	2B	3B	HR	RBI	BB	SB	AVG	OBP	SLG
1991	St. Louis	109	242	29	58	8	4	6	36	22	15	.240	.300	.380
1992	St. Louis	87	143	13	34	8	0	1	18	15	3	.238	.311	.315
1993	Projected	54	114	13	28	7	0	2	15	10	5	.246	.306	.360
		21	85	13	22	6	0	3	12	5	7	.259	.293	.435

GENO PETRALLI
Texas Rangers
Catcher
$9

He had his first off year with the bat after hitting .255 or better seven straight times, but on the other hand he threw out 48 percent of opposing base stealers (20 of 42), helping to reduce his bad-glove reputation. With Ivan Rodriguez around he's not going to catch much in Texas, but has done enough that his career will continue somewhere. Bat should bounce back.

YEAR	TEAM/LEVEL	G	AB	R	H	2B	3B	HR	RBI	BB	SB	AVG	OBP	SLG
1991	Texas	87	199	21	54	8	1	2	20	21	2	.271	.339	.352
1992	Texas	94	192	11	38	12	0	1	18	20	0	.198	.274	.276
1993	Projected	73	146	12	36	7	1	1	13	19	1	.247	.333	.329
		52	98	13	34	2	2	1	8	18	2	.347	.448	.439

GARY PETTIS
Detroit Tigers
Center Fielder
$8

Filled in for Milt Cuyler late in the year, played better than his .201 average would suggest. He had almost as many walks as hits, stole 14 bases in limited playing time, and can still play center field about as well as anybody. He'll never be a regular again, but could still be useful on the bench as pinch runner/defensive sub/sixth outfielder.

YEAR	TEAM/LEVEL	G	AB	R	H	2B	3B	HR	RBI	BB	SB	AVG	OBP	SLG
1991	Texas	137	282	37	61	7	5	0	19	54	29	.216	.341	.277
1992	Two Teams	78	159	27	32	5	3	1	12	29	14	.201	.323	.289
1993	Projected	58	121	18	26	5	1	1	8	20	11	.215	.326	.298
		32	83	9	20	5	0	1	4	11	8			

TONY PHILLIPS
Detoit Tigers

Utilityman
$70

Has completed a remarkable rise from spare part to star, leading the American League in runs scored at the age of 33. I think it's almost impossible to overstate his value; he does everything better than Cecil Fielder except hit home runs . . . Basketball has had many "sixth man" stars, but baseball has had only a few comparable players—Jimmy Dykes, Frankie Frisch. Will continue to play well.

YEAR	TEAM/LEVEL	G	AB	R	H	2B	3B	HR	RBI	BB	SB	AVG	OBP	SLG
1991	Detroit	146	564	87	160	28	4	17	72	79	10	.284	.371	.438
1992	Detroit	159	606	114	167	32	3	10	64	114	12	.276	.387	.388
1993	Projected	147	559	88	142	21	3	9	55	96	13	.254	.363	.351
		135	572	62	127	10	3	8	46	78	14	.248	347	.326

MIKE PIAZZA
Los Angeles Dodgers

Catcher
$35

Has tremendously strong hands, which are invaluable to a catcher and a hitter. So much has been said and written about him that his expectations may be unrealistic. I like him, and he does have a chance to be a star, but there are other young players that I like more, like Willie Greene, Melvin Nieves, and Chipper Jones. **Grade A prospect**, should hit .265 to .280 with power.

YEAR	TEAM/LEVEL	G	AB	R	H	2B	3B	HR	RBI	BB	SB	AVG	OBP	SLG
1992	AA and AAA	125	472	72	165	33	5	23	89	50	1	.350	.414	.587
1992	MLE	125	431	45	124	23	2	13	55	30	0	.288	.334	.441
1992	Los Angeles	21	69	5	16	3	0	1	7	4	0	.232	.284	.319
		0	0	0	0	0	0	0	0	0	0	—	—	

PHIL PLANTIER
Boston Red Sox

Right Fielder
$36

His 1991 season matched Willie McCovey in '59; last year matched McCovey in '60. This is Butch Hobson in a nutshell: Plantier hit .239 in April, .176 in May, .250 in June, .322 in July—and was sent to the minors in early August. His future remains very bright. I believe he will overcome his current problems and be one of the best hitters of the 1990s.

YEAR	TEAM/LEVEL	G	AB	R	H	2B	3B	HR	RBI	BB	SB	AVG	OBP	SLG
1991	Boston	53	148	27	49	7	1	11	35	23	1	.331	.420	.615
1992	Boston	108	349	46	86	19	0	7	30	44	2	.246	.332	.361
1993	Projected	108	337	54	93	19	1	16	51	48	2	.276	.366	.481
		108	325	62	100	19	2	25	72	52	2	.308	.403	.609

LUIS POLONIA
California Angels

Left Fielder
$31

His stolen base percentage is killed by playing in Anaheim. On the road he is a 75 percent base stealer (last year 79 percent), but in California barely over 60 percent. It's not just him; the Angels' team stolen base percentage is always ten to fifteen points lower at home than on the road. He slumped late in '92, his first significant slump since he came to the majors.

YEAR	TEAM/LEVEL	G	AB	R	H	2B	3B	HR	RBI	BB	SB	AVG	OBP	SLG
1991	California	150	604	92	179	28	8	2	50	52	48	.296	.352	.379
1992	California	149	577	83	165	17	4	0	35	45	51	.286	.337	.329
1993	Projected	140	528	76	158	18	7	3	43	43	41	.299	.352	.377
		131	479	69	151	19	10	6	57	41	31	.315	.369	.434

TODD PRATT
Philadelphia Phillies
Catcher
$9

In the Red Sox system from 1985 to 1991, never looked like a hitter until 1991, when he began to work out seriously in the off-season, then hit .292 with power at Pawtucket. Acquired by the Phillies in the winter draft, he continued to hit in Double-A, Triple-A, and the majors in 1992. I like him; could be a big surprise if he gets playing time.

YEAR	TEAM/LEVEL	G	AB	R	H	2B	3B	HR	RBI	BB	SB	AVG	OBP	SLG
1992	AA and AAA	82	257	40	84	15	2	13	54	54	3	.327	.441	.553
1992	MLE	82	248	32	75	13	0	10	45	43	1	.302	.405	.476
1992	Philadelphia	16	46	6	13	1	0	2	10	4	0	.283	.340	.435

TOM PRINCE
Pittsburgh Pirates
Backup Catcher
$3

Pirates' number-three catcher, strictly defense. He's better than a .177 hitter, but not much. Is 28 years old, spent five years at Buffalo, was usually the backup there. At one time it was common to carry a third catcher, but it isn't now; suspect Leyland does it so he can pinch hit, use both of his catchers in one game, and still have a catcher on the bench.

YEAR	TEAM/LEVEL	G	AB	R	H	2B	3B	HR	RBI	BB	SB	AVG	OBP	SLG
1990	Buffalo	94	284	38	64	13	0	7	37	39	4	.225	.326	.345
1991	Pittsburgh	26	34	4	9	3	0	1	2	7	0	.265	.405	.441
1992	Pittsburgh	27	44	1	4	2	0	0	5	6	1	.091	.192	.136
28		*54*	*0*	*0*	*0*	*0*	*0*	*0*	*8*	*5*	*2*	*.000*	*.085*	*.019*

KIRBY PUCKETT
Minnesota Twins (Free Agent)
Center Fielder
$82

The heart and soul of the Twins, in the free agent market at this writing. Has surged to 1812 hits in record time, and has an estimated 41 percent chance to get 3000. He started later than Brett or Yount, but has more hits than Brett at the same age (1783), 400 fewer than Yount. He has had more 200-hit seasons than Brett and Yount combined.

YEAR	TEAM/LEVEL	G	AB	R	H	2B	3B	HR	RBI	BB	SB	AVG	OBP	SLG
1991	Minnesota	152	611	92	195	29	6	15	89	31	11	.319	.352	.460
1992	Minnesota	160	639	104	210	38	4	19	110	44	17	.329	.374	.490
1993	Projected	150	590	87	181	33	4	15	88	44	11	.307	.355	.453
		140	*521*	*70*	*152*	*28*	*4*	*11*	*66*	*44*	*5*	*.292*	*.349*	*.420*

HARVEY PULLIAM
Kansas City Royals
Outfielder
$4

Powerfully built outfielder, spent his third year at Omaha after hitting well in 18-game trial in '91. Little or no star potential, but will be in the majors somewhere in '93. Should hit around .250, some power but not Power, not much speed. Compact swing, won't strike out much, and looks like a better hitter than his records show. Grade D prospect.

YEAR	TEAM/LEVEL	G	AB	R	H	2B	3B	HR	RBI	BB	SB	AVG	OBP	SLG
1991	Omaha AAA	104	346	35	89	18	2	6	39	31	2	.257	.318	.373
1992	Omaha AAA	100	359	55	97	12	2	16	60	32	4	.270	.338	.448
1992	MLE	100	346	44	84	11	1	10	48	25	2	.243	.294	.367
		100	*333*	*33*	*71*	*10*	*0*	*4*	*36*	*18*	*0*	*.213*	*.254*	*.27?*

TOM QUINLAN
Toronto Blue Jays

Third Baseman

$1

Doesn't appear to be a prospect. Was called up to back up third while Gruber was missing, so the Blue Jays must be comfortable with his defense at third, but he's a lifetime .229 hitter through 749 minor league games. Was named team MVP at Knoxville in '90 without great numbers . . . was outstanding amateur hockey player, drafted in the fourth round by the Calgary Flames.

YEAR	TEAM/LEVEL	G	AB	R	H	2B	3B	HR	RBI	BB	SB	AVG	OBP	SLG
1992	Syracuse AAA	107	349	43	75	17	1	6	36	43	1	.215	.317	.321
1992	MLE	107	338	31	64	14	0	4	26	31	0	.189	.257	.266
1992	Toronto	13	15	2	1	1	0	0	2	2	1	.067	.176	.133
		0	0	0	0	0	0	0	0	40	2	—	—	—

LUIS QUINONES
Minnesota Twins

Infielder

$2

Returned to the minors last year after three years as a backup infielder in Cincinnati. He's now 31 (in late April), but his skills would appear to be within the range of players who are *almost* good enough to have a job in the majors, and thus expansion might enable him to get back on somebody's bench. Has more power than the typical backup infielder, less speed.

YEAR	TEAM/LEVEL	G	AB	R	H	2B	3B	HR	RBI	BB	SB	AVG	OBP	SLG
1990	Cincinnati	83	145	10	35	7	0	2	17	13	1	.241	.301	.331
1991	Cincinnati	97	212	15	47	4	3	4	20	21	1	.222	.297	.325
1992	Portland AAA	88	276	45	67	7	4	12	49	41	1	.243	.338	.428
		79	340	75	87	10	5	20	78	61	1	.256	.369	.491

CARLOS QUINTANA
Boston Red Sox

First Baseman

$3

Missed the 1992 season after being hurt in a car accident. Suffered nerve damage in his left hand, broken left arm, broken bone in his right foot. At this writing no one will offer an opinion about whether he will be in uniform in 1993. I doubt that he can return, but Mo Vaughn and Phil Plantier have failed so far to take effective control of his job.

YEAR	TEAM/LEVEL	G	AB	R	H	2B	3B	HR	RBI	BB	SB	AVG	OBP	SLG
1989	Boston	34	77	6	16	5	0	0	6	7	0	.208	.274	.273
1990	Boston	149	512	56	147	28	0	7	67	52	1	.287	.354	.383
1991	Boston	149	478	69	141	21	1	11	71	61	1	.295	.375	.412
		149	444	82	135	14	2	15	75	70	1	.304	.379	.416

JAMIE QUIRK
Oakland Athletics

Catcher

$9

One of the most reliable rules in baseball is that career length is a function of quality. The players who last to age 40, normally, are only the best players. Yet Quirk, who was a minor league teammate and close friend of George Brett, seems likely, incredibly enough, to make his career last longer than George's . . . no hitter; defensive skills have become pretty good.

YEAR	TEAM/LEVEL	G	AB	R	H	2B	3B	HR	RBI	BB	SB	AVG	OBP	SLG
1991	Oakland	76	203	16	53	4	0	1	17	16	0	.261	.321	.296
1992	Oakland	78	177	16	39	7	1	2	11	16	0	.220	.294	.305
1993	Projected	82	183	14	41	7	0	2	19	17	0	.224	.290	.295
		86	189	12	43	7	0	2	27	78	0	.228	.255	.295

TIM RAINES
Chicago White Sox
Left Fielder
$54

Scored 102 runs for the second straight year as the Sox leadoff man, also played better in the field than he had in '91. Now 33 years old, he remains a viable, if marginal, candidate for the Hall of Fame, on the basis of a 22 percent chance to get 3000 hits. Is now sixth on the all-time stolen base list, will vault to fourth by early June.

YEAR	TEAM/LEVEL	G	AB	R	H	2B	3B	HR	RBI	BB	SB	AVG	OBP	SLG
1991	Chicago	155	609	102	163	20	6	5	50	83	51	.268	.359	.345
1992	Chicago	144	551	102	162	22	9	7	54	81	45	.294	.380	.405
1993	Projected	142	532	90	150	26	5	8	57	79	46	.282	.375	.395
		140	513	78	138	30	1	9	60	77	47	.269	.364	.384

RAFAEL RAMIREZ
Houston Astros (Free Agent)
Shortstop
$7

Has been in Houston for five years, and has gradually lost playing time to Cedeno and Guerrero, among others. Also missed time last summer with a partially torn muscle in his chest. He must be a hell of a good guy to stay in the majors as long as he has with his talents. Has good arm, doesn't make as many errors as he used to.

YEAR	TEAM/LEVEL	G	AB	R	H	2B	3B	HR	RBI	BB	SB	AVG	OBP	SLG
1991	Houston	101	233	17	55	10	0	1	20	13	3	.236	.274	.292
1992	Houston	73	176	17	44	6	0	1	13	7	0	.250	.283	.301
1993	Projected	87	226	21	55	12	1	2	19	12	3	.243	.282	.332
		101	276	25	66	18	2	3	25	17	6	.239	.283	.357

KEN RAMOS
Cleveland Indians
Outfielder
$8

Minor league leadoff hitter, .339 average at Canton was the highest in the Eastern League in five years. His 82 walks gave him a .442 on-base percentage. He played at the University of Nebraska, signed with Cleveland as an undrafted free agent in 1989, works very hard, and is fundamentally sound, an outstanding bunter. Grade C prospect, but I'd love to have him.

YEAR	TEAM/LEVEL	G	AB	R	H	2B	3B	HR	RBI	BB	SB	AVG	OBP	SLG
1991	Canton AA	74	257	41	62	6	3	2	13	28	8	.241	.317	.311
1992	Canton AA	125	442	93	150	23	5	5	42	82	14	.339	.442	.448
1992	MLE	125	432	78	140	22	3	4	35	58	9	.324	.404	.417
		125	422	63	130	21	1	3	28	34	4	.308	.360	.384

FERNANDO RAMSEY
Chicago Cubs
Center Fielder
$4

A 27-year-old Panamanian outfielder, has played 687 minor league games (a real prospect will normally go through the minors in 400 or less). Has outstanding speed and is regarded as a good center fielder, but career .256 hitter in the minors with very poor K/W ratio, no power . . . competed for Panama in the 1984 Summer Olympics (track) . . . Grade D prospect.

YEAR	TEAM/LEVEL	G	AB	R	H	2B	3B	HR	RBI	BB	SB	AVG	OBP	SLG
1992	Iowa AAA	133	480	62	129	9	5	1	38	23	39	.269	.305	.315
1992	MLE	133	461	44	110	7	2	0	27	15	23	.239	.263	.262
1992	Chicago	18	25	0	3	0	0	0	2	0	0	.120	.120	.120
		0	0	0	0	0	0	0	0	0	0	-	-	-

WILLIE RANDOLPH
New York Mets
Second Baseman
$18

Was hit by a pitch by Bob Walk, August 14, and missed most of the last two months with broken wrist. He's now 38, and has played more games at second base than anyone except Eddie Collins, Joe Morgan, Nellie Fox, and Charlie Gehringer. Lou Whitaker is less than a half-season behind . . . not a championship quality player anymore, but also not the worst in the league.

YEAR	TEAM/LEVEL	G	AB	R	H	2B	3B	HR	RBI	BB	SB	AVG	OBP	SLG
1991	Milwaukee	124	431	60	141	14	3	0	54	75	4	.327	.424	.374
1992	New York	90	286	29	72	11	1	2	15	29	1	.252	.352	.318
1993	Projected	79	252	29	64	10	1	1	21	37	2	.254	.349	.313
		66	218	29	56	9	1	0	27	45	3	.257	.384	.307

RANDY READY
Oakland Athletics
Utilityman
$14

A secondary average guy, so his .200 average doesn't reflect his value. He had as many walks as hits, played six defensive positions, pinch hit, pinch ran, and batted in all nine spots of the order. Appears to have larger-than-normal platoon split; will have to fight for his job in the spring of '93 but should catch on.

YEAR	TEAM/LEVEL	G	AB	R	H	2B	3B	HR	RBI	BB	SB	AVG	OBP	SLG
1991	Philadelphia	76	205	32	51	10	1	1	20	47	2	.249	.385	.322
1992	Oakland	61	125	17	25	2	0	3	17	25	1	.200	.329	.288
1993	Projected	53	116	17	28	7	1	2	15	22	1	.241	.362	.371
		45	107	17	31	12	2	1	13	19	1	.290	.397	.467

JEFF REBOULET
Minnesota Twins
Shortstop
$12

Very impressive as a shortstop, has quick feet and a shortstop's arm. I like him better than Gagne as a defensive player. He had a .414 on-base percentage at Portland (.286 with 35 walks in 48 games), but he'll be 29 in April, and his batting record as a whole says forget it. Will have four- to five-year career as backup infielder.

YEAR	TEAM/LEVEL	G	AB	R	H	2B	3B	HR	RBI	BB	SB	AVG	OBP	SLG
1991	Portland AAA	134	391	50	97	27	3	3	46	57	5	.248	.345	.355
1992	Portland AAA	48	161	21	46	11	1	2	21	35	3	.286	.414	.404
1992	Minnesota	73	137	15	26	7	1	1	16	23	3	.190	.311	.277
		98	113	9	6	3	1	0	11	11	3	.053	.137	.09

GARY REDUS
Pittsburgh Pirates
First Baseman/Outfielder
$13

He does everything Rickey Henderson does, but just not quite as well. Does, or did; he's now 36, and unmistakably not the player he was four years ago, when Jim Leyland rescued his career from unwarranted obscurity. His decreased playing time last year resulted from a strained hamstring, and does not indicate that Leyland has reduced his role. Has been a superb platoon player.

YEAR	TEAM/LEVEL	G	AB	R	H	2B	3B	HR	RBI	BB	SB	AVG	OBP	SLG
1991	Pittsburgh	98	252	45	62	12	2	7	24	28	17	.246	.324	.393
1992	Pittsburgh	76	176	26	45	7	3	3	12	17	11	.256	.321	.381
1993	Projected	64	132	20	32	9	2	3	12	16	7	.242	.324	.409
		52	88	14	19	12	1	3	12	15	3	.216	.330	.477

DARREN REED
Minnesota Twins
Outfielder
$3

A 27-year-old right-handed hitter. He was an amateur catcher, signed with the Yankees in '84. The Yankees made him an outfielder, and until 1987 he was a hot prospect, but was included in a trade to the Mets. The Mets tried to make him back into a catcher, which was a disaster, and he's had a series of injuries since then. Grade D prospect.

YEAR	TEAM/LEVEL	G	AB	R	H	2B	3B	HR	RBI	BB	SB	AVG	OBP	SLG
1990	Tidewater AAA	104	359	58	95	21	6	17	74	51	15	.265	.362	.499
1992	Two Teams	56	114	12	20	4	0	5	14	8	0	.175	.232	.342
1993	Projected	70	188	19	32	8	0	8	23	13	0	.170	.224	.340
		81	262	26	44	12	0	11	32	18	0	.168	.221	.340

JEFF REED
Cincinnati Reds (Free Agent)
Catcher
$1

Had surgery to remove a bone spur in his elbow in May and didn't play much. The Dan Wilson of his day, got to be a hot prospect in the mid-1980s for no obvious reason, then was stuck with the label of a disappointment because people were reluctant to admit that they had been deluding themselves. His career may end at any moment.

YEAR	TEAM/LEVEL	G	AB	R	H	2B	3B	HR	RBI	BB	SB	AVG	OBP	SLG
1990	Cincinnati	72	175	12	44	8	1	3	16	24	0	.251	.340	.360
1991	Cincinnati	91	270	20	72	15	2	3	31	23	0	.267	.321	.370
1992	Cincinnati	15	25	2	4	0	0	0	2	1	0	.160	.192	.160
		0	0	0	0	0	0	0	0	0	0	-	-	-

JODY REED
Boston Red Sox
Second Baseman
$24

His numbers took a left turn about June 1; he had to have been playing with an injury of some sort. He hit .302 with 15 doubles in April and May, .219 with 12 doubles the rest of the year, and didn't play as well as he has in the field. With the emergence of Valentin, faces a challenge from Naehring. A good player if healthy.

YEAR	TEAM/LEVEL	G	AB	R	H	2B	3B	HR	RBI	BB	SB	AVG	OBP	SLG
1991	Boston	153	618	87	175	42	2	5	60	60	6	.283	.349	.382
1992	Boston	143	550	64	136	27	1	3	40	62	7	.247	.321	.316
1993	Projected	144	561	71	152	36	1	5	51	66	6	.271	.348	.365
		145	572	78	168	45	1	7	62	70	5	.294	.371	.413

KEVIN REIMER
Texas Rangers
Left Fielder
$31

Good left-handed hitter, very strong, but the worst defensive outfielder in the major leagues, and among the worst I have ever seen. Lost playing time late in the year so the Rangers could play Hulse in center field, Gonzalez in left, although Hulse isn't really a center fielder. Needs to learn to play first or get with a team that will DH him every day.

YEAR	TEAM/LEVEL	G	AB	R	H	2B	3B	HR	RBI	BB	SB	AVG	OBP	SLG
1991	Texas	139	394	46	106	22	0	20	69	33	0	.269	.332	.477
1992	Texas	148	494	56	132	32	2	16	58	42	2	.267	.336	.437
1993	Projected	155	550	58	144	31	4	18	76	48	3	.262	.321	.431
		162	616	60	156	30	6	20	94	54	4	.253	.313	.419

HAROLD REYNOLDS
Seattle Mariners

Second Baseman
$17

Has been bumped out of his job in Seattle by Bret Boone. His career will continue if he will accept a reserve role, or he may sign with some team like California that doesn't know what the hell they're doing. There is never a shortage of second basemen, and there are 10 better second basemen trapped in Triple-A. Could pinch run and play late-inning defense.

YEAR	TEAM/LEVEL	G	AB	R	H	2B	3B	HR	RBI	BB	SB	AVG	OBP	SLG
1991	Seattle	161	631	95	160	34	6	3	57	72	28	.254	.332	.341
1992	Seattle	140	458	55	113	23	3	3	33	45	15	.247	.316	.330
1993	Projected	142	529	73	132	24	4	3	43	62	24	.250	.328	.327
		144	600	91	151	25	5	3	53	79	33	.252	.339	.325

KARL RHODES
Houston Astros

Outfielder
$5

Sixth-outfielder, Dave Gallagher–type, hasn't been able to land a major league job but may be able to with expansion and the team running out of options. Left-handed hitter, .250 to .260 hitter in majors with no power but good number of walks and some speed. Has been at Triple-A for years but is only 24. No star potential but could develop into regular. Grade D prospect.

YEAR	TEAM/LEVEL	G	AB	R	H	2B	3B	HR	RBI	BB	SB	AVG	OBP	SLG
1991	Houston	44	136	7	29	3	1	1	12	14	2	.213	.289	.272
1992	Tucson AAA	94	332	62	96	16	10	2	54	55	8	.289	.386	.416
1993	MLE	94	312	40	76	12	5	1	34	35	5	.244	.320	.324
		94	292	18	56	8	0	0	14	15	2	.192	.231	.219

ERNEST RILES
Houston Astros (Free Agent)

Utilityman
$8

Hit .307 for Tucson and was recalled by Astros in late July. He played all four infield positions for the Astros and pinch hit, avoiding left-handed pitchers. He's 32 now; in his day he was Pat Listach, so to speak, hit .286 as a rookie in 1985 and finished third in the American League Rookie of the Year voting, but was unable to follow up on it.

YEAR	TEAM/LEVEL	G	AB	R	H	2B	3B	HR	RBI	BB	SB	AVG	OBP	SLG
1991	Oakland	108	281	30	60	8	4	5	32	31	3	.214	.290	.324
1992	Tucson AAA	60	202	37	62	17	3	1	35	30	2	.307	.390	.436
1992	Houston	39	61	5	16	1	0	1	4	2	1	.262	.281	.328
		15	0	0	0	0	0	1	0	0	0	—	—	—

BILLY RIPKEN
Baltimore Orioles

Second Baseman
$13

If he wasn't Cal Ripken's brother his career would have ended several years ago. He is a real good defensive second baseman, but a nightmare at the plate, bunts any time he has a chance but still manages to ground into a great number of double plays. A .240 hitter with no power, no walks, no speed. On his own, his glove wouldn't keep him in the majors.

YEAR	TEAM/LEVEL	G	AB	R	H	2B	3B	HR	RBI	BB	SB	AVG	OBP	SLG
1991	Baltimore	104	287	24	62	11	1	0	14	15	0	.216	.253	.261
1992	Baltimore	111	330	35	76	15	0	4	36	18	2	.230	.275	.312
1993	Projected	106	310	32	77	15	1	2	27	19	2	.248	.292	.323
		101	290	29	78	15	2	0	28	20	2	.269	.316	.331

CAL RIPKEN
Baltimore Orioles

Shortstop
$62

Probably had an injury of some sort in June but played through it. He hit under .200 with no home runs through July and August, ruining his season's stats; 1992 season was the poorest of a career which has mostly been a sustained decline. Now within 400 games of Gehrig's record, which seems like nothing but who *else* do you know who will play the next 400 games?

YEAR	TEAM/LEVEL	G	AB	R	H	2B	3B	HR	RBI	BB	SB	AVG	OBP	SLG
1991	Baltimore	162	650	99	210	46	5	34	114	53	6	.323	.374	.566
1992	Baltimore	162	637	73	160	29	1	14	72	64	4	.251	.323	.366
1993	Projected	162	610	79	166	33	2	23	86	66	4	.272	.343	.446
		162	583	85	172	37	3	32	100	68	4	.295	.369	.533

LUIS RIVERA
Boston Red Sox

Shortstop
$9

Eased out of the regular shortstop job at the All-Star break hit .167 over the second half. He doesn't have the skills of a regular shortstop—.230 hitter with no speed or power, error-prone. Speaking for myself, I wouldn't want him as a backup, because there is no one thing he does well enough that you would put him in the game to do it.

YEAR	TEAM/LEVEL	G	AB	R	H	2B	3B	HR	RBI	BB	SB	AVG	OBP	SLG
1991	Boston	129	414	64	107	22	3	8	40	35	4	.258	.318	.384
1992	Boston	102	288	17	62	11	1	0	29	26	4	.215	.287	.260
1993	Projected	83	259	29	59	13	1	3	27	22	3	.228	.288	.320
		64	230	41	56	15	1	6	25	18	2	.243	.298	.376

DOUG ROBBINS
Baltimore Orioles

Catcher
$3

A tenth-round selection in 1988, now 26 years old. He also plays first base, from which you might infer, correctly, that he doesn't throw like Ivan Rodriguez. He also doesn't hit for power, but his ability to get on base might make him useful to a major league team as a third catcher/first baseman/pinch hitter. Grade D prospect.

YEAR	TEAM/LEVEL	G	AB	R	H	2B	3B	HR	RBI	BB	SB	AVG	OBP	SLG
1991	Hagerstown AA	92	286	45	87	12	1	0	28	71	4	.304	.444	.353
1992	Rochester AAA	93	288	45	89	19	1	6	46	43	8	.309	.402	.444
1992	MLE	93	273	34	74	15	0	4	35	33	5	.271	.350	.370
		93	258	23	59	11	0	2	24	23	2	.229	.292	.295

BIP ROBERTS
Cincinnati Reds

Utilityman
$70

Enormously valuable player. Plays second, third, left, and center, has lifetime batting average of .299, to which he adds walks, speed, and doubles. Career got a late start when the Padres looked at him in 1986. He was OK, hit .253 in 101 games, but they sent him back down anyway, just as they did with Shane Mack, and he wasted two years at Las Vegas.

YEAR	TEAM/LEVEL	G	AB	R	H	2B	3B	HR	RBI	BB	SB	AVG	OBP	SLG
1991	San Diego	117	424	66	119	13	3	3	32	37	26	.281	.342	.347
1992	Cincinnati	147	532	92	172	34	6	4	45	62	44	.323	.393	.432
1993	Projected	155	550	93	163	25	5	6	46	59	44	.296	.365	.393
		163	568	94	154	16	4	8	47	56	44	.271	.370	.356

HENRY RODRIGUEZ
Los Angeles Dodgers
Outfielder
$10

Emerged as a prospect when he hit 28 homers, drove in 109 for San Antonio in 1990, wasted 1991, hit well last year and got some playing time while Strawberry was out. Will battle Tom Goodwin, Billy Ashley, Raul Mondesi for a spot in the Dodgers' outfield after the big-money free agent outfield runs out of trials. Grade C prospect.

YEAR	TEAM/LEVEL	G	AB	R	H	2B	3B	HR	RBI	BB	SB	AVG	OBP	SLG
1992	Albuquerque AAA	94	365	59	111	21	5	14	72	31	1	.304	.351	.504
1992	MLE	94	337	36	83	14	2	8	44	19	0	.246	.287	.371
1992	Los Angeles	53	146	11	32	7	0	3	14	8	0	.219	.258	.329
		12	0	0	0	0	0	0	0	0	0	—		—

IVAN RODRIGUEZ
Texas Rangers
Catcher
$66

I think the Rangers ought to appoint Rodriguez the team captain. It's a way of saying, "Yeah, we know he's only 21 years old, but he is the only guy here who knows how to play this game." Excellent bunter, baserunner, superb arm (you probably know he threw out 52 percent of opposing base stealers, best in the major leagues). Will hit 20+ homers in a few years.

YEAR	TEAM/LEVEL	G	AB	R	H	2B	3B	HR	RBI	BB	SB	AVG	OBP	SLG
1991	Texas	88	280	24	74	16	0	3	27	5	0	.264	.276	.354
1992	Texas	123	420	39	109	16	1	8	37	24	0	.260	.300	.360
1993	Projected	139	474	43	127	21	1	13	58	19	1	.268	.296	.399
		155	528	47	143	26	1	18	79	14	2	.271	.290	.426

DAVE ROHDE
Houston Astros
Second Baseman
$5

A traditional expansion-type player, although in this particular expansion he may be bypassed for younger players (he'll be 29 in May). In four years of Triple-A ball he's hit .318 with many walks, stolen bases. In the majors he would hit around .260, on-base percentage around the league average, no power, OK defense at second. Grade D prospect, but deserves a job.

YEAR	TEAM/LEVEL	G	AB	R	H	2B	3B	HR	RBI	BB	SB	AVG	OBP	SLG
1991	Tucson AAA	73	253	36	94	10	4	1	40	52	15	.372	.479	.455
1992	Colorado Sp AAA	121	448	85	132	17	14	4	55	57	13	.295	.378	.422
1992	MLE	121	424	55	108	14	7	2	35	37	7	.255	.315	.335
		121	400	25	84	11	0	0	15	17	1	.210	.242	.28

BOBBY ROSE
Yokohama Taiyo Whales
Infielder
No Value

Opened the season as the California second baseman, but didn't play real well (a low batting average and too many errors, although other elements of his game were OK). He was injured in the crash of the Angels team bus, went on the disabled list May 22 with a sprained ankle, and Sojo took the second base job in his absence. Was sold to Yokohama on October 16.

YEAR	TEAM/LEVEL	G	AB	R	H	2B	3B	HR	RBI	BB	SB	AVG	OBP	SLG
1991	California	22	65	5	18	5	1	1	8	3	0	.277	.304	.431
1992	California	30	84	10	18	5	0	2	10	8	1	.214	.295	.345
1992	Edmonton AAA	20	74	11	20	1	3	2	11	6	1	.270	.325	.446
		10	64	12	22	0	6	2	12	4	1	.344	.382	.58

118 Rodriguez–Russell

RICO (Tabula) ROSSY
Kansas City Royals
Shortstop
$1

Played quite a bit of shortstop for the Royals and wasn't bad in the field, but wasn't strong at the plate and was sent down for missing a sign during a period when the Royals weren't executing and McRae was frustrated. He played well with Omaha, and could resurface somewhere in '93 . . . takes too many walks to be a Royal, anyway. No prospect.

YEAR	TEAM/LEVEL	G	AB	R	H	2B	3B	HR	RBI	BB	SB	AVG	OBP	SLG
1991	Richmond AAA	139	482	58	124	25	1	2	48	67	4	.257	.352	.326
1992	Kansas City	59	149	21	32	8	1	1	12	20	0	.215	.310	.302
1992	Omaha AAA	48	174	29	55	10	1	4	17	34	3	.316	.422	.454
		37	299	37	78	12	1	7	22	48	6	.392	.510	.568

RICH ROWLAND
Detroit Tigers
Catcher
$12

Realizing what goes with the Tigers, he made an effort to hit for more power last year, hit twice as many homers as before, but more strikeouts and a lower average. He's 26, isn't going to take Tettleton's job but appears to be as good as some catchers who do have jobs—Joe Oliver, Greg Olson, etc. Threw out 48 percent of opposing base stealers. Grade C prospect.

YEAR	TEAM/LEVEL	G	AB	R	H	2B	3B	HR	RBI	BB	SB	AVG	OBP	SLG
1991	Toledo AAA	109	383	56	104	25	0	13	68	60	4	.272	.374	.439
1992	Toledo AAA	136	473	75	111	19	1	25	82	56	9	.235	.317	.438
1992	MLE	136	464	68	102	16	0	24	75	51	7	.220	.297	.409
		136	455	61	93	15	0	23	68	46	5	.204	.277	.385

STAN ROYER
St. Louis Cardinals
First/Third Baseman
$6

Louisville, where Royer compiled the stats below, is a relatively tough place to hit. Royer came to the Cardinals from the Oakland system in the Felix Jose/Willie McGee trade, is an impressive athlete but blocked at third by Zeile, and (despite the good numbers in his September trial) probably wouldn't hit enough to hold a first baseman's job. Grade D prospect.

YEAR	TEAM/LEVEL	G	AB	R	H	2B	3B	HR	RBI	BB	SB	AVG	OBP	SLG
1992	Louisville AAA	124	444	55	125	31	2	11	77	32	0	.282	.333	.435
1992	MLE	124	425	41	106	26	1	8	58	24	0	.249	.290	.372
1992	St. Louis	13	31	6	10	2	0	2	9	1	0	.323	.333	.581
		0	0	0	0	0	0	0	0	0	0	—	—	—

JOHN RUSSELL
Texas Rangers
Catcher
No Value

An outfielder who tried to convert to catcher, started the year at Tulsa, hit 10 homers in 46 games and was called up while Rodriguez was hurt. He tore a ligament in his thumb and went on the DL June 25. He has two outstanding weaknesses—he can't throw well (for a catcher) and strikes out like Rob Deer without hitting like Deer—and those have swallowed his career.

YEAR	TEAM/LEVEL	G	AB	R	H	2B	3B	HR	RBI	BB	SB	AVG	OBP	SLG
1990	Texas	68	128	16	35	4	0	2	8	11	1	.273	.331	.352
1991	Texas	22	27	3	3	0	0	0	1	1	0	.111	.138	.111
1992	Tulsa AA	46	163	26	42	11	0	10	27	17	0	.258	.344	.509
		70	301	49	81	22	0	20	53	33	6	.269	.341	.542

CHRIS SABO
Cincinnati Reds
Third Baseman
$27

Went on the disabled list April 8 with a jammed right ankle, came back in two weeks but was slowed by the ankle all year, playing only 30 games with a .214 average after the break. Willie Greene, a fine prospect, played well in September, and will challenge for the third base job. If he is traded he will probably not hit for comparable power in another park.

YEAR	TEAM/LEVEL	G	AB	R	H	2B	3B	HR	RBI	BB	SB	AVG	OBP	SLG
1991	Cincinnati	153	582	91	175	35	3	26	88	44	19	.301	.354	.505
1992	Cincinnati	96	344	42	84	19	3	12	43	30	4	.244	.302	.422
1993	Projected	135	502	73	133	33	2	18	64	46	16	.265	.327	.446

(handwritten: 174 650 104 182 47 1 24 85 62 28 .276 .338 .459)

LUIS SALAZAR
Chicago Cubs
Utilityman
$6

The most important stat for a position player is on-base percentage, because how many runners you have on base essentially determines how many runs you score. Salazar is a good athlete with some power, but his on-base percentages have always been low, and in his mid-thirties have reached the point of being absurdly low. Hits left-handers well.

YEAR	TEAM/LEVEL	G	AB	R	H	2B	3B	HR	RBI	BB	SB	AVG	OBP	SLG
1991	Chicago	103	333	34	86	14	1	14	38	15	0	.258	.292	.432
1992	Chicago	98	255	20	53	7	2	5	25	11	1	.208	.237	.310
1993	Projected	73	209	19	51	8	1	5	22	10	1	.244	.279	.364

(handwritten: 48 163 18 49 9 0 5 19 9 1 .301 .337 .448)

TIM SALMON
California Angels
Right Fielder
$32

Cited by *Baseball America* as the best prospect in the Pacific Coast League. It is difficult to make an accurate projection for him as a major league hitter because his '92 performance is dramatically better than what he has done before, his average up 100 points. He had fought injuries until last year. If '92 represents a real level of ability, he'll be a star. **Grade A prospect.**

YEAR	TEAM/LEVEL	G	AB	R	H	2B	3B	HR	RBI	BB	SB	AVG	OBP	SLG
1992	Edmonton AAA	118	409	101	142	38	4	29	105	91	9	.347	.469	.672
1992	MLE	118	372	60	105	27	1	18	62	53	4	.282	.372	.505
1992	California	23	79	8	14	1	0	2	6	11	1	.177	.283	.266

(handwritten: 0 0 0 0 0 0 0 0 0 — —)

JUAN SAMUEL
Kansas City Royals
(Released)
Second Baseman/Right Fielder
$18

Joined the Royals about the same time as Sampen and quickly confirmed that he is, in fact, an awful outfielder. Was supposed to be a star; at 32 must decide whether he wants to be a role player, and then try to find the right team and the right role. He *can't* really play the outfield, but can still run and hits well enough to pinch hit.

YEAR	TEAM/LEVEL	G	AB	R	H	2B	3B	HR	RBI	BB	SB	AVG	OBP	SLG
1991	Los Angeles	153	594	74	161	22	6	12	58	49	23	.271	.328	.389
1992	Two Teams	76	224	22	61	8	4	0	23	14	8	.272	.318	.344
1993	Projected	129	448	54	112	24	6	9	47	40	22	.250	.311	.391

(handwritten: 182 672 86 163 40 8 18 71 66 36 .243 .310 .402)

REY SANCHEZ
Chicago Cubs
Shortstop
$20

Another Felix Fermin/Alvaro Espinoza type, got substantial playing time during the absence of Dunston and Vizcaino and played well enough to earn additional looks. He missed time with chicken pox and, more seriously, stiffness in his back, which took September away from him after he had hit .311 (as a regular) in August. Is 25 years old, will get another trial as an everyday shortstop.

YEAR	TEAM/LEVEL	G	AB	R	H	2B	3B	HR	RBI	BB	SB	AVG	OBP	SLG
1991	Iowa AAA	126	417	60	121	16	5	2	46	37	13	.290	.356	.367
1991	MLE	126	400	43	104	13	2	1	33	25	7	.260	.304	.310
1992	Chicago	74	255	24	64	14	3	1	19	10	2	.251	.285	.341
		22	110	5	24	15	4	1	5	0	0	.218	.218	.455

RYNE SANDBERG
Chicago Cubs
Second Baseman
$92

Jerry Coleman said during the AL playoffs that Roberto Alomar was the best all-around second baseman in baseball. Alomar is great, but there's no way he's better than Sandberg. Sandberg will score as many runs, drive in more, and play a better second base . . . the four greatest players in Cubs history have been Banks, Anson, Williams, and Santo. I think Sandberg is better than any of them.

YEAR	TEAM/LEVEL	G	AB	R	H	2B	3B	HR	RBI	BB	SB	AVG	OBP	SLG
1991	Chicago	158	585	104	170	32	2	26	100	87	22	.291	.379	.485
1992	Chicago	158	612	100	186	32	8	26	87	68	17	.304	.371	.510
1993	Projected	152	583	94	163	28	4	22	81	67	20	.280	.354	.455
		146	554	88	140	24	0	18	75	66	23	.253	.332	.394

DEION SANDERS
Atlanta Braves/Falcons
Center Fielder/Cornerback
$20

I am writing this in October, waiting for the other shoe to drop. I am guessing that the Braves will release Sanders after the season, on the grounds that they don't need a player they can't count on, and he will sign with somebody else, somebody who doesn't have as many good young outfielders. I have no idea what to expect of him in the rest of his career.

YEAR	TEAM/LEVEL	G	AB	R	H	2B	3B	HR	RBI	BB	SB	AVG	OBP	SLG
1991	Atlanta	54	110	16	21	1	2	4	13	12	11	.191	.270	.345
1992	Atlanta	97	303	54	92	6	14	8	28	18	26	.304	.346	.495
1993	Projected	103	272	48	70	8	6	6	27	25	23	.257	.320	.397
		109	241	42	48	10	0	4	26	32	26	.199	.293	.311

REGGIE SANDERS
Cincinnati Reds
Outfielder
$41

I had him pegged as the top Rookie of the Year candidate, and he actually played a little better than I had expected. He missed the award, but proved himself a true Cincinnati Red, by making two trips to the DL. If he's healthy, he's going to be one of the top 10 outfielders in the National League—a 20/20 man with other skills to back it up.

YEAR	TEAM/LEVEL	G	AB	R	H	2B	3B	HR	RBI	BB	SB	AVG	OBP	SLG
1991	Chattanooga AA	86	302	50	95	15	8	8	49	41	15	.315	.394	.497
1992	Cincinnati	116	385	62	104	26	6	12	36	48	16	.270	.356	.462
1993	Projected	139	521	81	148	27	7	16	62	60	21	.284	.358	.455
		162	657	100	192	28	8	20	88	72	26	.292	.312	.451

TRACY SANDERS
Cleveland Indians
Outfielder
$8

A 23-year-old power hitter, listed by *Baseball America* as the fourth-best prospect in the Eastern League. A 58th-round draft pick, has had three solid seasons to become a prospect. He walks a lot, strikes out a lot but not a prohibitive amount, is a bad defensive outfielder, and batted .241 at Canton last year, but hit 17 homers over the second half. Grade C prospect.

YEAR	TEAM/LEVEL	G	AB	R	H	2B	3B	HR	RBI	BB	SB	AVG	OBP	SLG
1991	Kinston A	118	421	80	112	20	8	18	63	83	8	.266	.393	.480
1992	Canton AA	114	381	66	92	11	3	21	87	77	3	.241	.371	.451
1992	MLE	114	375	55	86	10	2	18	73	55	1	.229	.328	.411
		14	369	44	80	9	1	15	59	33	0	.217	.281	.369

BENITO SANTIAGO
San Diego Padres
Catcher
$38

Will probably play somewhere else. His hitting record in San Diego is normal, just a little better than on the road . . . it is obvious to any sophisticated fan that Santiago is tremendously overrated. He is injury prone, doesn't get on base much, and makes too many errors. Those are big negatives. He is still better than an average catcher, but not much.

YEAR	TEAM/LEVEL	G	AB	R	H	2B	3B	HR	RBI	BB	SB	AVG	OBP	SLG
1991	San Diego	152	580	60	155	22	3	17	87	23	8	.267	.296	.403
1992	San Diego	106	386	37	97	21	0	10	42	21	2	.251	.287	.383
1993	Projected	132	475	52	126	21	2	14	66	27	6	.265	.305	.406
		158	564	67	155	21	4	18	90	33	10	.275	.315	.422

NELSON SANTOVENIA
Chicago White Sox
Catcher
$1

Played a couple of games with the White Sox in July, returned to Vancouver and hit .263 on the year, 6 homers in 91 games. The White Sox have no real use for a third right-handed-hitting catcher, so he'll be somewhere else if he is in the majors. He's 31, third-catcher type, hurt by the fact that teams don't carry three catchers anymore.

YEAR	TEAM/LEVEL	G	AB	R	H	2B	3B	HR	RBI	BB	SB	AVG	OBP	SLG
1991	Montreal	41	96	7	24	5	0	2	14	2	0	.250	.255	.365
1992	Vancouver AAA	91	281	24	74	13	0	6	42	37	0	.263	.346	.384
1992	MLE	91	271	19	64	13	0	4	33	29	0	.236	.310	.328
		91	261	14	54	13	0	2	24	21	0	.207	.266	.280

MACKEY SASSER
New York Mets
Catcher
$11

He's what Mike LaValliere would be if Mike LaValliere couldn't really catch. The scouts call a good field/no hit catcher a "Catch and Throw Guy." Sasser is a "Lunge and Lob Guy." The right role for him is left-handed pinch hitter/third catcher, in the AL he could DH once a week. The attempts to make him a catcher are just messing up his career.

YEAR	TEAM/LEVEL	G	AB	R	H	2B	3B	HR	RBI	BB	SB	AVG	OBP	SLG
1991	New York	96	228	18	62	14	2	5	35	9	0	.272	.298	.417
1992	New York	92	141	7	34	6	0	2	18	3	0	.241	.248	.326
1993	Projected	102	219	19	61	13	1	4	31	10	0	.279	.310	.402
		112	295	31	88	20	2	6	44	17	0	.298	.357	.411

STEVE SAX
Chicago White Sox
Second Baseman
$26

He has three years left on his contract, which at the moment looks like a big item. If Guillen returns strong Grebeck will be looking for playing time, which will probably mean that Sax, for the first time in his career, could be less than a full-time regular. Not a particularly good second baseman now; needs bat to snap back if he's going to have value.

YEAR	TEAM/LEVEL	G	AB	R	H	2B	3B	HR	RBI	BB	SB	AVG	OBP	SLG
1991	New York	158	652	85	198	38	2	10	56	41	31	.304	.345	.414
1992	Chicago	143	567	74	134	26	4	4	47	43	30	.236	.290	.317
1993	Projected	142	560	68	151	22	3	5	43	41	33	.270	.319	.346
		141	553	62	168	18	2	6	39	39	36	.304	.350	.376

STEVE SCARSONE
Baltimore Orioles
Second Baseman
$7

Played a couple of weeks with the Phillies early in the year, didn't show much and went back to Scranton, then was traded to Baltimore in August. He's been in the minors for seven years (731 games) with a .251 batting average, but does have some speed, appears to have added a little power, and has hit better in recent seasons. Horrible strikeout/walk ratio. Grade D prospect.

YEAR	TEAM/LEVEL	G	AB	R	H	2B	3B	HR	RBI	BB	SB	AVG	OBP	SLG
1992	Two Teams AAA	112	407	56	110	26	4	12	60	30	13	.270	.324	.442
1992	MLE	112	395	50	98	22	3	10	54	26	9	.248	.295	.395
1992	Philadelphia	18	30	3	5	0	0	0	0	2	0	.167	.219	.167
		0	0	0	0	0	0	0	0	0	0	—	—	—

JEFF SCHAEFER
Seattle Mariners (Free Agent)
Backup Shortstop
$5

Glove man; playing time was virtually eliminated by the development of Omar Vizquel as a hitter, which made it unnecessary to pinch hit for Vizquel, which made it unnecessary for Schaefer to play late-inning defense. May or may not land the same job with some other team. As Garagiola used to say, you can shake a tree and a dozen gloves will fall out.

YEAR	TEAM/LEVEL	G	AB	R	H	2B	3B	HR	RBI	BB	SB	AVG	OBP	SLG
1990	Seattle	55	107	11	22	3	0	0	6	3	4	.206	.239	.234
1991	Seattle	84	164	19	41	7	1	1	11	5	3	.250	.272	.323
1992	Seattle	65	70	5	8	2	0	1	3	2	0	.114	.139	.186
		46	0	0	0	0	0	1	0	0	0	—	—	—

DICK SCHOFIELD
New York Mets
Shortstop
$17

I'm not a big fan of one-way players, whether they are hitters or glove men, but Schofield is a better player than most of the group. He bunts well and will take a walk, so he doesn't waste as many outs at the bottom of the order as, let's say, Lance Parrish. Not fast but a good baserunner, not spectacular at short but doesn't make many mistakes.

YEAR	TEAM/LEVEL	G	AB	R	H	2B	3B	HR	RBI	BB	SB	AVG	OBP	SLG
1991	California	134	427	44	96	9	3	0	31	50	8	.225	.310	.260
1992	Two Teams	143	423	52	87	18	2	4	36	61	11	.206	.311	.286
1993	Projected	137	420	51	92	14	3	4	34	62	8	.219	.320	.295
		131	417	50	97	10	4	4	32	63	5	.233	.333	.305

MIKE SCIOSCIA
Los Angeles Dodgers
Catcher
$15

Career is endangered by .221 batting average and simultaneous development of Piazza. As a manager ages he sometimes tends to exaggerate the skills of veteran players, which has happened to Lasorda as it has to Sparky. Scioscia has had a good career, but despite expansion it seems unlikely that he can still play every day. Would be valuable for late-inning defense; might hit better in limited role.

YEAR	TEAM/LEVEL	G	AB	R	H	2B	3B	HR	RBI	BB	SB	AVG	OBP	SLG
1991	Los Angeles	119	345	39	91	16	2	8	40	47	4	.264	.353	.391
1992	Los Angeles	117	348	19	77	6	3	3	24	32	3	.221	.286	.282
1993	Projected	61	163	14	40	8	0	3	18	20	2	.245	.328	.350
		5	0	9	0	10	0	3	12	8	1	—	1000	0

GARY SCOTT
Chicago Cubs
Third Baseman/Utility Infielder
$9

Is still trying to recover from an abortive attempt to jump him from A Ball to the majors in '91. He's only 24, played much better at Iowa last year than the year before, hitting .263 but with .271 secondary average, played some short as well as third. He still needs work, but it's too early to give up on him. Grade C prospect.

YEAR	TEAM/LEVEL	G	AB	R	H	2B	3B	HR	RBI	BB	SB	AVG	OBP	SLG
1992	Chicago	36	96	8	11	2	0	2	11	5	0	.156	.198	.240
1992	Iowa AAA	95	354	48	93	26	0	10	48	37	3	.263	.338	.421
1992	MLE	95	341	34	80	22	0	8	34	25	1	.235	.287	.370
		95	328	20	67	18	0	6	20	13	0	.204	.255	.314

DAVID SEGUI
Baltimore Orioles
First Baseman
$17

Dave Bergman, Mike Squires–type player, a glove man at first base. Switch hitter, and better than is reflected in his .233 average. Should hit over .260 and could hit .300, lack of power will probably keep him from being regular first baseman. Hits ball on the ground and isn't fast, so double plays are a concern; lack of speed/power are a problem for him as an outfielder.

YEAR	TEAM/LEVEL	G	AB	R	H	2B	3B	HR	RBI	BB	SB	AVG	OBP	SLG
1991	Baltimore	86	212	15	59	7	0	2	22	12	1	.278	.316	.340
1992	Baltimore	115	189	21	44	9	0	1	17	20	1	.233	.306	.296
1993	Projected	96	250	28	68	13	0	2	29	26	2	.272	.341	.348
		77	311	35	92	17	0	3	44	32	5	.296	.362	.374

KEVIN SEITZER
Kansas City Royals
Third Baseman
$29

McRae's sudden benching of Seitzer and Stillwell in mid-1991 was peevish and irrational, and was the one largest factor in the Royals' miserable 1992 season. In essence, McRae took two regulars out behind the barn and shot them because the team wasn't playing well. The Royals don't have enough talent to do that. Seitzer is a middle-of-the-pack third baseman, does some things well.

YEAR	TEAM/LEVEL	G	AB	R	H	2B	3B	HR	RBI	BB	SB	AVG	OBP	SLG
1991	Kansas City	85	234	28	62	11	3	1	25	29	4	.265	.350	.350
1992	Milwaukee	148	540	74	146	35	1	5	71	57	13	.270	.337	.367
1993	Projected	154	544	75	153	27	3	6	54	61	10	.281	.354	.375
		160	546	76	160	19	5	7	37	65	7	.292	.367	.383

SCOTT SERVAIS
Houston Astros
Catcher
$15

Hit .400 in September to push average from .194 to .239, but with a secondary average of .098, I wouldn't say he was any threat to the memory of Mickey Cochrane. The right-handed half of a platoon, with Taubensee, who was a little better but not much . . . threw out only 24 percent of opposing baserunners, but the ERA with him catching was good (3.38).

YEAR	TEAM/LEVEL	G	AB	R	H	2B	3B	HR	RBI	BB	SB	AVG	OBP	SLG
1991	Tucson AAA	60	219	34	71	12	0	2	27	13	0	.324	.377	.406
1992	Houston	77	205	12	49	9	0	0	15	11	0	.239	.294	.283
1993	Projected	73	212	17	49	8	0	1	18	10	1	.231	.266	.283
		69	219	22	49	7	0	2	21	9	2	.224	.254	.282

MIKE SHARPERSON
Los Angeles Dodgers
Second/Third Baseman
$26

Excellent platoon player, value is in his ability to get on base. He has had a wider-than-normal platoon gap over the last four years, hitting .317 against left-handed pitchers, but .250 against right-handers. Line drive hitter, normally used by Lasorda as number-two hitter. A natural second baseman, got to play some there after Samuel was released. As a third baseman, just survives.

YEAR	TEAM/LEVEL	G	AB	R	H	2B	3B	HR	RBI	BB	SB	AVG	OBP	SLG
1991	Los Angeles	105	216	24	60	11	2	2	20	25	1	.278	.355	.375
1992	Los Angeles	128	317	48	95	21	0	3	36	47	2	.300	.387	.394
1993	Projected	128	310	37	87	14	1	2	30	42	6	.281	.366	.352
		128	303	26	79	7	2	1	24	37	10	.261	.34	.307

JON SHAVE
Texas Rangers
Second Baseman
$9

No relation to Razor Shines. Appears to be comparable to Jeff Frye, the young second baseman who has just reached the major league Rangers. A knee injury in '91 forced his shift from short to second, and limits his range at second. Has trouble going to his left. Excellent work habits, very intelligent, hits in .280s by dumping the ball over the infield. Grade C prospect.

YEAR	TEAM/LEVEL	G	AB	R	H	2B	3B	HR	RBI	BB	SB	AVG	OBP	SLG
1991	Gastonia A	55	213	29	62	11	0	2	24	20	11	.291	.355	.371
1992	Tulsa AA	118	453	57	130	23	5	2	36	37	6	.287	.343	.373
1992	MLE	118	446	53	123	21	4	1	33	28	4	.276	.319	.348
		118	439	49	116	19	3	0	30	19	2	.264	.28	.321

GARY SHEFFIELD
San Diego Padres
Third Baseman
$79

Had among the most remarkable seasons in memory, jumping his average 136 points. He had about the same season that Stan Musial had in 1955 or Don Mattingly in 1987, but they had laid a foundation for it. In view of his youth (he turned 24 after the season) it is virtually certain that he will have more seasons like the one he has just had.

YEAR	TEAM/LEVEL	G	AB	R	H	2B	3B	HR	RBI	BB	SB	AVG	OBP	SLG
1991	Milwaukee	50	175	25	34	12	2	2	22	19	5	.194	.277	.320
1992	San Diego	146	557	87	184	34	3	33	100	48	5	.330	.385	.580
1993	Projected	157	568	83	167	31	2	22	86	54	17	.294	.355	.472
		168	579	79	150	28	1	11	72	60	25	.259	.328	.368

DARRELL SHERMAN
San Diego Padres
Outfielder
$18

Tiny outfielder, Brett Butler–type player. He was probably the best player in the Texas League the first half of the season, moved up to Las Vegas the second half. Very fast; an opposing manager told me "he's a Punch-and-Judy hitter but he knows it." This was a compliment, meaning he stays within himself. Fair arm, has hit .298 through 471 minor league games. Grade C prospect.

YEAR	TEAM/LEVEL	G	AB	R	H	2B	3B	HR	RBI	BB	SB	AVG	OBP	SLG
1991	Wichita AA	131	502	93	148	17	3	3	48	74	43	.295	.391	.359
1992	AA and AAA	135	489	108	150	19	3	9	47	82	52	.307	.406	.413
1992	MLE	135	454	68	115	13	0	6	29	47	30	.253	.323	.322
		135	*419*	*28*	*80*	*7*	*0*	*3*	*11*	*12*	*8*	*.191*	*.213*	*.224*

TOMMY SHIELDS
Baltimore Orioles
Infielder
$2

Spent a week in the majors during Hulett's absence. A 28-year-old minor leaguer, played at Notre Dame and signed with the Pirates, was traded to Baltimore in 1991 and had his best season last year. Has played all nine positions in a game. He probably could hit .250 to .260 in the majors in a good year, but strikeout/walk ratio poor, limited power. Grade D prospect.

YEAR	TEAM/LEVEL	G	AB	R	H	2B	3B	HR	RBI	BB	SB	AVG	OBP	SLG
1991	Rochester AAA	116	412	69	119	18	3	6	52	32	16	.289	.354	.391
1992	Rochester AAA	121	431	58	130	23	3	10	59	30	13	.302	.352	.439
1992	MLE	121	410	44	109	18	1	7	45	23	8	.266	.305	.366
		121	*389*	*30*	*88*	*13*	*0*	*4*	*31*	*16*	*3*	*.226*	*.257*	*.290*

CRAIG SHIPLEY
San Diego Padres
Utility Infielder
$1

The new Rob Picciolo, he now has six walks, one of them intentional, in 265 major league at bats. Riddoch had him leading off several times last year (oh, right, we *need* that .262 on-base percentage leading off). A minor league shortstop, plays second-third-short in the majors, apparently pretty well. Now 30 years old, no player/no prospect.

YEAR	TEAM/LEVEL	G	AB	R	H	2B	3B	HR	RBI	BB	SB	AVG	OBP	SLG
1991	San Diego	37	91	6	25	3	0	1	6	2	0	.275	.298	.341
1992	San Diego	52	105	7	26	6	0	0	7	2	1	.248	.262	.305
1993	Projected	64	154	10	36	5	0	2	13	4	1	.234	.253	.305
		76	*203*	*13*	*46*	*4*	*0*	*0*	*19*	*6*	*1*	*.227*	*.249*	*.305*

TERRY SHUMPERT
Kansas City Royals
Second Baseman
$6

He was playing shortstop at Omaha, but that appears to have been just an experiment. What I like about him is his decision making on defense; he plays second with a lot of self-confidence. Very strong, quick, but lunges at pitches and has no control of the strike zone. Hits everything in the air. These are difficult things to overcome.

YEAR	TEAM/LEVEL	G	AB	R	H	2B	3B	HR	RBI	BB	SB	AVG	OBP	SLG
1991	Kansas City	144	369	45	80	16	4	5	34	30	17	.217	.283	.322
1992	Kansas City	36	94	6	14	5	1	1	11	3	2	.149	.175	.255
1993	Projected	67	142	17	31	11	2	1	14	9	5	.218	.265	.345
		98	*190*	*28*	*48*	*17*	*3*	*1*	*17*	*15*	*8*	*.253*	*.301*	*.309*

RUBEN SIERRA
Oakland Athletics
Right Fielder
$73

Has already surpassed his idol, Clemente, in career stolen bases and 100-RBI seasons, has 65 percent of Clemente's career home runs and more than 50 percent of his doubles. Has about a 28 percent chance to get 3000 career hits. Hits for average and power. Very durable, and one of the best RBI men in the game. Much better right-handed hitter than left-handed. Excellent baserunner, inconsistent outfielder.

YEAR	TEAM/LEVEL	G	AB	R	H	2B	3B	HR	RBI	BB	SB	AVG	OBP	SLG
1991	Texas	161	661	110	203	44	5	25	116	56	16	.307	.357	.502
1992	Two Teams	151	601	83	167	34	7	17	87	45	14	.278	.323	.443
1993	Projected	156	620	89	179	35	6	23	102	52	13	.289	.344	.476
		161	639	95	191	31	5	29	117	59	12	.299	.358	.507

DAVE SILVESTRI
New York Yankees
Shortstop
$10

A member of the 1988 Olympic team, was a second-round draft pick of the Astros, traded to the Yankees in 1990. He had two short stays in the majors last year, spent most of the year at Columbus. Has more power than most shortstops, 32 homers over the last two minor league seasons, and also has some speed. Walks and strikes out quite a bit. Grade C prospect.

YEAR	TEAM/LEVEL	G	AB	R	H	2B	3B	HR	RBI	BB	SB	AVG	OBP	SLG
1991	Albany AA	140	512	97	134	31	8	19	83	83	20	.262	.366	.465
1992	Columbus AAA	118	420	83	117	25	5	13	73	58	19	.279	.373	.455
1992	MLE	118	403	66	100	22	2	9	58	46	13	.248	.325	.380
		118	366	49	83	19	0	5	43	34	7	.215	.272	.309

MIKE SIMMS
Houston Astros
Right Fielder/First Baseman
$2

Was projected to replace Glenn Davis when Davis was traded, but lost out to Bagwell. A 26-year-old power hitter, has played 765 minor league games. He hit 39 homers at Asheville in '87, but has done nothing much in his major league trials or at Tucson over the last three years. Strikes out more than 100 times a year, lacks speed. No prospect.

YEAR	TEAM/LEVEL	G	AB	R	H	2B	3B	HR	RBI	BB	SB	AVG	OBP	SLG
1991	Houston	49	123	18	25	5	0	3	16	18	1	.203	.301	.317
1992	Tucson AAA	116	404	73	114	22	6	11	75	61	7	.282	.379	.448
1992	MLE	116	379	47	89	17	3	6	48	39	4	.235	.306	.343
		116	354	21	64	12	0	1	21	17	1	.181	.218	.28

MATT SINATRO
Seattle Mariners
(Released)
Catcher
$1

His career chugs improbably along. He spent some of the '92 season at Calgary, and some of it on the DL with a pinched nerve in his neck. He now has 10 major league seasons, with a grand total of 252 at bats—25 per season. I wonder if this is a record? I would think . . . 3-for-28 performance in '92 drops his career batting average below .200.

YEAR	TEAM/LEVEL	G	AB	R	H	2B	3B	HR	RBI	BB	SB	AVG	OBP	SLG
1990	Seattle	30	50	2	15	1	0	0	4	4	1	.300	.352	.320
1991	Seattle	5	8	1	2	0	0	0	1	1	0	.250	.333	.250
1992	Seattle	18	28	0	3	0	0	0	0	0	0	.107	.107	.107
		31	48	0	4	0	0	0	0	0	0	.083	.083	.083

DON SLAUGHT
Pittsburgh Pirates
Catcher
$28

You probably heard that his batting average was the highest by a catcher with more than 250 at bats since Elston Howard, 1961. The wonders of sliced data; if you used a 300-at-bat cutoff he wouldn't qualify, if you used 200 AB somebody else would be there . . . excellent hitter, OK fielder; Slaught/LaValliere combination may well be the strongest platoon ever at catcher.

YEAR	TEAM/LEVEL	G	AB	R	H	2B	3B	HR	RBI	BB	SB	AVG	OBP	SLG
1991	Pittsburgh	77	220	19	65	17	1	1	29	21	1	.295	.363	.395
1992	Pittsburgh	87	255	26	88	17	3	4	37	17	2	.345	.384	.482
1993	Projected	97	262	24	74	18	2	4	24	19	1	.282	.345	.412
		107	269	22	60	18	1	4	9	21	0	.223	.278	.346

DWIGHT SMITH
Chicago Cubs
Outfielder
$14

Hit .298 from June 1 on, providing hope that his two-year slump is over. A disciplined hitter in the minors, but when he went into a slump the Cubs reduced his playing time, and then he began pressing, trying to hit everything. A natural DH; I will never understand why an American League team wouldn't trade for him and say "You're our DH. Have a good career."

YEAR	TEAM/LEVEL	G	AB	R	H	2B	3B	HR	RBI	BB	SB	AVG	OBP	SLG
1991	Chicago	90	167	16	38	7	2	3	21	11	2	.228	.279	.347
1992	Chicago	109	217	28	60	10	3	3	24	13	9	.276	.318	.392
1993	Projected	117	244	30	64	16	2	4	29	20	8	.262	.318	.393
		125	271	32	68	22	1	5	34	27	7	.251	.319	.38

LONNIE SMITH
Atlanta Braves (Free Agent)
Left Fielder
$12

There's got to be a book in this guy. There are so many stories about his career, so many fine teams that he's been a part of, the '80 Phillies, '82 Cardinals, '85 Royals, '90 and '91 Braves. Despite his .247 average last year, he's still a dangerous hitter. In left field, where his speed once compensated for his multitudinous mistakes, it no longer does.

YEAR	TEAM/LEVEL	G	AB	R	H	2B	3B	HR	RBI	BB	SB	AVG	OBP	SLG
1991	Atlanta	122	353	58	97	19	1	7	44	50	9	.275	.377	.394
1992	Atlanta	84	158	23	39	8	2	6	33	17	4	.247	.324	.437
1993	Projected	83	219	31	58	14	2	4	25	29	5	.265	.351	.402
		82	280	39	77	20	2	2	17	41	6	.275	.368	.372

MARK SMITH
Baltimore Orioles
Outfielder
$6

The Orioles' number-one pick in 1991, he played well at Double-A last year, hitting .288 with 15 stolen bases, .351 on-base percentage. Needs to develop power, but is young enough (22) and big enough (195 pounds) that it might come. He led the Eastern League with 32 doubles; sometimes doubles will become homers as a player matures . . . his father is a cancer surgeon. Grade C prospect.

YEAR	TEAM/LEVEL	G	AB	R	H	2B	3B	HR	RBI	BB	SB	AVG	OBP	SLG
1991	Frederick A	38	148	20	37	5	1	4	29	9	1	.250	.296	.378
1992	Hagerstown AA	128	472	51	136	32	6	4	62	45	15	.288	.351	.407
1992	MLE	128	452	41	116	26	4	3	50	31	10	.257	.304	.352
		128	432	31	96	20	2	2	38	17	5	.222	.262	.292

128   Slaught–Sojo

OZZIE SMITH
St. Louis Cardinals
Shortstop
$56

In his prime as a hitter at the age of 38. They say his defense has slipped, but you can't prove it by me, and he now hits well enough to be very valuable as a second baseman. Hell, he hits enough now to play the outfield if he has to. They don't let me vote, but if it was my Hall of Fame, he'd walk right in.

YEAR	TEAM/LEVEL	G	AB	R	H	2B	3B	HR	RBI	BB	SB	AVG	OBP	SLG
1991	St. Louis	150	550	96	157	30	3	3	50	83	35	.285	.380	.367
1992	St. Louis	132	518	73	153	20	2	0	31	59	43	.295	.367	.342
1993	Projected	134	492	63	132	19	2	1	37	64	30	.268	.353	.321
		136	466	53	111	18	2	2	43	69	17	.238	.33	.28

J. T. SNOW
New York Yankees
First Baseman
$20

A 25-year-old switch hitter, best known for his defense, but hit .313 with 15 homers, 70 walks at Columbus, and is now taken seriously as a prospect. Should be comparable to Pete O'Brien, when Pete O'Brien was good, could hit .280 or so. His father, Jack Snow, was a receiver in the NFL, and J.T. was recruited by Notre Dame as a quarterback. Grade B prospect.

YEAR	TEAM/LEVEL	G	AB	R	H	2B	3B	HR	RBI	BB	SB	AVG	OBP	SLG
1991	Albany AA	132	477	78	133	33	3	13	76	67	5	.279	.364	.442
1992	Columbus AAA	135	492	81	154	26	4	15	78	70	3	.313	.395	.474
1992	MLE	135	470	64	132	23	2	12	62	55	2	.281	.356	.415
		135	448	47	110	20	0	9	46	40	1	.246	.307	.350

CORY SNYDER
San Francisco Giants
Utility Outfielder
$10

Had a hot streak in June, fell into his old habits then and hit .243 after the All-Star break. Played first and third for the Giants, all three outfield spots. He's now 30, has two skills (power and a throwing arm). Tries to hit every pitch out of the park. Strikeout/walk ratio still among the worst in baseball. Strongly recommend that you not draft him.

YEAR	TEAM/LEVEL	G	AB	R	H	2B	3B	HR	RBI	BB	SB	AVG	OBP	SLG
1991	Two Teams	71	166	14	29	4	1	3	17	9	0	.175	.216	.265
1992	San Francisco	124	390	48	105	22	2	14	57	23	4	.269	.311	.444
1993	Projected	120	374	41	88	19	1	14	49	20	2	.235	.274	.404
		116	358	34	71	16	0	14	41	17	0	.198	.237	.360

LUIS SOJO
California Angels
Second Baseman
$26

Started the season in Edmonton, but was called up in May and very quietly had a good year. He's a contact hitter, rarely walks or strikes out, and so bats second for the Angels although his on-base percentage is low. The .272 batting average in '92 is a reasonable estimate of his ability, and combined with his defense should keep him in the majors for several years.

YEAR	TEAM/LEVEL	G	AB	R	H	2B	3B	HR	RBI	BB	SB	AVG	OBP	SLG
1991	California	113	364	38	94	14	1	3	20	14	4	.258	.295	.327
1992	California	106	368	37	100	12	3	7	43	14	7	.272	.299	.378
1993	Projected	115	381	40	97	14	1	5	33	15	6	.255	.283	.336
		124	394	43	94	16	0	3	23	16	5	.239	.268	.302

PAUL SORRENTO
Cleveland Indians

First Baseman

$31

Finally got a chance to play, did what we had projected him to do. Strictly platooned, has never hit lefties but has only 55 lifetime at bats against them. Capable of hitting 20 home runs a year, even as a part-time player. Clumsy first baseman, normally has his glove or his feet in the wrong position, or both. No speed, but a legitimate hitter.

YEAR	TEAM/LEVEL	G	AB	R	H	2B	3B	HR	RBI	BB	SB	AVG	OBP	SLG
1991	Minnesota	26	47	6	12	2	0	4	13	4	0	.255	.314	.553
1992	Cleveland	140	458	52	123	24	1	18	60	51	0	.269	.341	.443
1993	Projected	142	474	56	127	29	1	19	70	59	1	.268	.349	.454

(handwritten) 144 490 60 131 34 1 20 80 67 2 .267 .355 .463

SAMMY SOSA
Chicago Cubs

Center Fielder

$27

Hand was broken on July 12 by a Dennis Martinez pitch. Returned July 27, fouled a ball off his ankle August 7 and was out for the season. In between injuries he hit .260, which doesn't make him a good leadoff man, but if he played regularly and hit .260 he'd be a 20/20 man or even a 20/40 man. Played well in center field.

YEAR	TEAM/LEVEL	G	AB	R	H	2B	3B	HR	RBI	BB	SB	AVG	OBP	SLG
1991	Chicago	116	316	39	64	10	1	10	33	14	13	.203	.240	.335
1992	Chicago	67	262	41	68	7	2	8	25	19	15	.260	.317	.393
1993	Projected	138	503	70	121	20	4	14	58	33	30	.241	.287	.380

(handwritten) 209 744 99 178 33 6 20 89 51 45 .234 .283 .378

TIM SPEHR
Kansas City Royals

Catcher

$9

Had some playing time in 1991 when Macfarlane was out, but spent '92 in Omaha. Hits out of Charlie Lau stance, but pulls the ball and had good power year, 15 homers in 336 at bats. Threw out 52 percent of base stealers in his major league trial in '91. If the Royals lose one of their catchers to expansion, he'll be in KC as the backup.

YEAR	TEAM/LEVEL	G	AB	R	H	2B	3B	HR	RBI	BB	SB	AVG	OBP	SLG
1991	Kansas City	37	74	7	14	5	0	3	14	9	1	.189	.282	.378
1992	Omaha AAA	109	336	48	85	22	0	15	42	61	4	.253	.384	.452
1992	MLE	109	324	38	73	20	0	10	33	49	2	.225	.327	.380

(handwritten) 109 312 28 61 18 0 5 24 37 0 .196 .289 .301

BILL SPIERS
Milwaukee Brewers

Shortstop

$13

Brewers' first-round pick in 1987, paid off with a fine 1991 season (.283 batting average, .401 slugging), but then had back surgery in November *and* December, missed almost all of 1992. Listach has taken over the shortstop job, which will push Spiers if he's healthy into a battle for the second base job . . . good bunter, good baserunner. Worth more than $13 if he's healthy.

YEAR	TEAM/LEVEL	G	AB	R	H	2B	3B	HR	RBI	BB	SB	AVG	OBP	SLG
1990	Milwaukee	112	363	44	88	15	3	2	36	16	11	.242	.274	.317
1991	Milwaukee	133	414	71	117	13	6	8	54	34	14	.283	.337	.401
1992	Milwaukee	12	16	2	5	2	0	0	2	1	1	.313	.353	.438

(handwritten) 0 0 0 0 0 0 0 0 0 0 0

ED SPRAGUE
Toronto Blue Jays
Catcher/Third Baseman/World Series Hero
$17

Recalled July 30, when Myers was traded. A third baseman at Stanford, was converted to catcher, but he and Borders are both right-handed, so there's no platoon edge. He struggled at the plate his first two years as a pro, but has hit for good power at Syracuse the last two seasons. OK young player, but will probably get buried behind Randy Knorr, Carlos Delgado, etc.

YEAR	TEAM/LEVEL	G	AB	R	H	2B	3B	HR	RBI	BB	SB	AVG	OBP	SLG
1991	Toronto	61	160	17	44	7	0	4	20	19	0	.275	.361	.394
1992	Syracuse AAA	100	369	49	102	18	2	16	50	44	0	.276	.358	.466
1992	Toronto	22	47	6	11	2	0	1	7	3	0	.234	.280	.340
		0	0	0	0	0	0	0	0	0	0	—	—	

STEVE SPRINGER
New York Mets
Third Baseman
$1

Career minor leaguer, now 32 years old, has been a regular third basemen at the Triple-A level since 1985, and got five at bats for the Mets in August. He's hit a few homers the last two years (17, then 16), which might have done him some good if he had done it five years earlier. Doesn't figure to get a chance to play, even with expansion.

YEAR	TEAM/LEVEL	G	AB	R	H	2B	3B	HR	RBI	BB	SB	AVG	OBP	SLG
1991	Calgary AA	109	412	62	106	25	2	17	70	28	8	.257	.303	.451
1992	Tidewater AAA	117	427	57	124	16	0	16	70	22	9	.290	.323	.440
1992	MLE	117	409	44	106	13	0	12	54	17	6	.259	.289	.379
		117	391	31	88	10	0	8	38	12	3	.25	.28	.312

MATT STAIRS
Montreal Expos
Left Fielder
$16

Listed as a top prospect for '92 after a big year at Harrisburg. He started last year at Indianapolis and was yanked up and down at least twice, couldn't get into a rhythm and didn't hit at either level. He's still young, 24, but his value is down because of the off year, and also because the Expos have abandoned hope for him as an infielder. Grade C prospect.

YEAR	TEAM/LEVEL	G	AB	R	H	2B	3B	HR	RBI	BB	SB	AVG	OBP	SLG
1991	Harrisburg AA	129	505	87	168	30	10	13	78	66	23	.333	.411	.509
1992	Indianapolis AAA	110	401	57	107	23	4	11	56	49	11	.267	.351	.426
1992	Montreal	13	30	2	5	2	0	0	5	7	0	.167	.316	.233
		0	0	0	0	0	0	0	0	0	0	—	—	

ANDY STANKIEWICZ
New York Yankees
Utility Infielder
$24

Inherited a job when Sax was traded, Gallego got hurt, and Kelly didn't play well. As befits someone nicknamed "Stanky," he's a scrappy middle infielder, hustles. He was 27 last year, and I frankly don't believe that his '92 stats represent his ability. He's a good defensive player, which will keep him in the league for years, but I don't believe he will hit much again.

YEAR	TEAM/LEVEL	G	AB	R	H	2B	3B	HR	RBI	BB	SB	AVG	OBP	SLG
1991	Columbus AAA	125	372	47	101	12	4	1	42	29	29	.272	.333	.333
1991	MLE	125	359	38	88	10	2	0	33	23	21	.245	.291	.284
1992	New York	116	400	52	107	22	2	2	25	38	9	.268	.338	.348
		107	441	66	126	34	2	4	17	53	0	.286	.362	.38

MIKE STANLEY
New York Yankees

Catcher

$17

Refused demotion by the Rangers and signed minor league contract with the Yankees, which worked out well. He was billed as a coming star five years ago and obviously hasn't become one, but his lifetime on-base percentage is .352, which is excellent for a catcher. Has never done anything against right-handers, which is why he's never been a regular. Nokes/Stanley platoon was effective. Below average arm.

YEAR	TEAM/LEVEL	G	AB	R	H	2B	3B	HR	RBI	BB	SB	AVG	OBP	SLG
1991	Texas	95	181	25	45	13	1	3	25	34	0	.249	.372	.381
1992	New York	68	173	24	43	7	0	8	27	33	0	.249	.372	.428
1993	Projected	98	193	25	48	9	1	4	23	36	0	.249	.367	.368
		128	213	26	53	11	2	0	19	34	0	.249	.365	.319

DAVE STATON
San Diego Padres

Left Fielder

$9

Power-hitting outfielder, turns 25 in April. His lifetime minor league slugging percentage is .528, but most of that has been done in good hitter's parks; I don't really think he's a major league hitter. He was regarded as a poor defensive outfielder anyway, and tore his rotator cuff in August, which may force a move to first base. Grade D prospect.

YEAR	TEAM/LEVEL	G	AB	R	H	2B	3B	HR	RBI	BB	SB	AVG	OBP	SLG
1991	Las Vegas AAA	107	375	61	100	19	1	22	74	44	1	.267	.346	.499
1992	Las Vegas AAA	96	335	47	94	20	0	19	76	34	0	.281	.353	.510
1992	MLE	96	314	28	73	14	0	13	46	20	0	.232	.278	.401
		96	293	9	52	8	0	7	16	6	0	.177	.194	.276

TERRY STEINBACH
Oakland Athletics

Catcher

$41

Had his best season at the plate since 1987, the year of the fluke stats. He hit .340 with runners in scoring position, so the post-season announcers dubbed him best clutch hitter on the team. Also played well *behind* the plate; threw out 44 percent of base stealers, fourth best in the majors. May leave Oakland as free agent; should be good wherever he is.

	TEAM/LEVEL	G	AB	R	H	2B	3B	HR	RBI	BB	SB	AVG	OBP	SLG
1991	Oakland	129	456	50	125	31	1	6	67	22	2	.274	.312	.386
1992	Oakland	128	438	48	122	20	1	12	53	45	2	.279	.345	.411
1993	Projected	131	443	43	117	20	1	10	60	31	2	.264	.312	.381
		134	448	38	112	20	1	8	67	17	2	.250	.277	.353

RAY STEPHENS
Texas Rangers

Backup Catcher

No Value

A career minor leaguer who got a few at bats with the Rangers in August. He spent several years at Louisville, finally left the Cardinal system as a six-year free agent and signed with Philadelphia, which traded him to Texas for a player to be named if anybody remembers. He's 30, a career .236 hitter in the minors without much power. No prospect.

YEAR	TEAM/LEVEL	G	AB	R	H	2B	3B	HR	RBI	BB	SB	AVG	OBP	SLG
1991	Oklahoma City AAA	60	165	16	46	7	0	7	28	24	0	.279	.383	.448
1992	Two Teams AAA	71	235	26	67	9	0	7	34	18	0	.285	.333	.413
1992	MLE	71	226	21	58	6	0	5	27	13	0	.257	.297	.350
		71	217	16	49	3	0	3	20	8	0	.226	.253	.281

PHIL STEPHENSON
San Diego Padres
Pinch Hitter
$1

Now has 298 major league at bats, .201 batting average. He's a better hitter than that, but may be out of chances to prove it at 32. He had some good minor league seasons—drew 129 walks at Pittsfield, hit .293 with 22 homers at Iowa, hit .332 at Vegas. His older brother Gene is head coach at Wichita State, won the NCAA championship a couple of years ago.

YEAR	TEAM/LEVEL	G	AB	R	H	2B	3B	HR	RBI	BB	SB	AVG	OBP	SLG
1990	San Diego	103	182	26	38	9	1	4	19	30	2	.209	.319	.335
1991	San Diego	11	7	0	2	0	0	0	0	2	0	.286	.444	.286
1992	San Diego	53	71	5	11	2	1	0	8	10	0	.155	.259	.211
		95	135	10	20	4	2	0	16	12	0	.148	.218	.207

LEE STEVENS
California Angels
First Baseman
$16

Former number-one draft pick, inherited the first base job in May when Alvin Davis didn't hit. His batting average at the end of June was .200, so his playing time dropped accordingly. His minor league numbers are superficially impressive, but his major league totals of .225 with 14 homers in 618 at bats aren't really out of line with what we should expect. Can do somewhat better.

YEAR	TEAM/LEVEL	G	AB	R	H	2B	3B	HR	RBI	BB	SB	AVG	OBP	SLG
1991	California	18	58	8	17	7	0	0	9	6	1	.293	.354	.414
1992	California	106	312	25	69	19	0	7	37	29	1	.221	.288	.349
1993	Projected	128	449	46	108	23	1	13	58	38	3	.241	.300	.383
		150	586	67	147	27	2	19	79	47	5	.251	.306	.401

KURT STILLWELL
San Diego Padres
Second Baseman
$19

Padres filled one infield hole with Sheffield, the other with Stillwell. He started out hot, but wound up the season among the worst-hitting regulars in the league, and doesn't field well enough to get by with that. Missed a few weeks late in the year with a sore back, which may have been hurting him all season. May return to short in '93.

YEAR	TEAM/LEVEL	G	AB	R	H	2B	3B	HR	RBI	BB	SB	AVG	OBP	SLG
1991	Kansas City	122	385	44	102	17	1	6	51	33	3	.265	.322	.361
1992	San Diego	114	379	35	86	15	3	2	24	26	4	.227	.274	.298
1993	Projected	99	328	37	82	16	3	4	34	27	2	.250	.307	.354
		84	277	39	78	17	3	6	44	28	0	.282	.348	.430

KEVIN STOCKER
Philadelphia Phillies
Shortstop
$5

The Phillies' Double-A shortstop, their second pick in 1991 (behind Tyler Green). He's probably not a major league hitter at this point, but he's just turned 23, and could improve substantially, also was bothered last year by petty injuries. Doesn't strike out a lot. Switch hitter, can steal some bases. They say his defense is good, and I suspect it will need to be. Grade C prospect.

YEAR	TEAM/LEVEL	G	AB	R	H	2B	3B	HR	RBI	BB	SB	AVG	OBP	SLG
1992	Clearwater A	63	244	43	69	13	4	1	33	27	15	.283	.360	.381
1992	Reading AA	62	240	31	60	9	2	1	13	22	17	.250	.318	.317
1992	MLE	62	232	24	52	8	1	0	10	14	11	.224	.268	.267
		62	224	17	44	7	0	0	7	6	5	.196	.227	.228

DOUG STRANGE
Chicago Cubs

Third Baseman

$11

Started the season at Iowa, was called up and got a shot at playing regularly in May, which was Strange. A 29-year-old originally from the Tigers system, has good field/no hit reputation, but has hit .293 to .307 the last three years in Triple-A, although failing to follow up in the majors. No prospect, will continue to get time filling in for injured players.

YEAR	TEAM/LEVEL	G	AB	R	H	2B	3B	HR	RBI	BB	SB	AVG	OBP	SLG
1992	Iowa AAA	55	212	32	65	16	1	4	26	9	3	.307	.332	.448
1992	MLE	55	202	22	55	13	0	3	18	6	1	.272	.293	.381
1992	Chicago	52	94	7	15	1	0	1	5	10	1	.160	.240	.202
		49	0	0	0	0	0	0	0	14	1	—	1.000	—

DARRYL STRAWBERRY
Los Angeles Dodgers

Right Fielder

$34

The back problem (herniated disc) that cost him a month of the 1991 season cost him almost all of 1992. He is past 30 now, and back problems are inherently serious, so it's time to fundamentally re-evaluate him and expect less, not that he can't still have a good year. He says he'll be back for spring training, but the Dodgers aren't counting on him until June.

YEAR	TEAM/LEVEL	G	AB	R	H	2B	3B	HR	RBI	BB	SB	AVG	OBP	SLG
1991	Los Angeles	139	505	86	134	22	4	28	99	75	10	.265	.361	.491
1992	Los Angeles	43	156	20	37	8	0	5	25	19	3	.237	.322	.385
1993	Projected	83	282	46	74	14	1	16	54	39	6	.262	.352	.489
		123	408	72	111	20	2	27	83	59	9	.272	.364	.524

FRANKLIN STUBBS
Milwaukee Brewers

First Baseman

$8

Demanded a trade when Jaha was called up to play some first base, so the Brewers tried to trade him. A lot of front offices got a good laugh out of that. Jaha didn't hit, so Stubbs continued to play once in a while, but he's not just a guy who hit .229. He's a .229 hitter. He will never play regularly again.

YEAR	TEAM/LEVEL	G	AB	R	H	2B	3B	HR	RBI	BB	SB	AVG	OBP	SLG
1991	Milwaukee	103	362	48	77	16	2	11	38	35	13	.213	.282	.359
1992	Milwaukee	92	288	37	66	11	1	9	42	27	11	.229	.297	.368
1993	Projected	65	193	24	44	7	1	7	25	20	8	.228	.300	.383
		38	98	19	22	3	1	5	8	13	5	.224	.305	.429

WILLIAM SUERO
Milwaukee Brewers

Second Baseman

$2

Was a top prospect in the Toronto system for three or four years, but had a bad attitude rep and was traded to the Brewers in '91 as the player to be named in the Candy Maldonado deal. Regarded as average defensively, has some speed, and is a good enough hitter to play second, but plays brilliantly for a month and then doesn't. He's 26 now, Grade D prospect.

YEAR	TEAM/LEVEL	G	AB	R	H	2B	3B	HR	RBI	BB	SB	AVG	OBP	SLG
1992	Denver AAA	75	276	42	71	10	9	1	25	31	16	.257	.332	.370
1992	MLE	75	263	31	58	8	5	0	18	22	11	.221	.281	.289
1992	Milwaukee	18	16	4	3	1	0	0	0	2	1	.188	.316	.250
		0	0	0	0	0	0	0	0	0	0	—	—	—

134 Strange–Tackett

B. J. SURHOFF
Milwaukee Brewers
Catcher
$30

There has been talk for years of moving him from behind the plate, and in '92 he did start 23 games at other positions (first base, DH, third base, left, and center). He had probably his best season defensively, throwing out base stealers 41 percent of the time. If he is going to play anywhere else, particularly first or the outfield, he'll have to hit more than he usually has.

YEAR	TEAM/LEVEL	G	AB	R	H	2B	3B	HR	RBI	BB	SB	AVG	OBP	SLG
1991	Milwaukee	143	505	57	146	19	4	5	68	26	5	.289	.319	.372
1992	Milwaukee	139	480	63	121	19	1	4	62	46	14	.252	.314	.321
1993	Projected	146	508	61	137	22	3	6	65	41	13	.270	.324	.360
		153	536	59	153	25	5	8	68	36	12	.285	.380	.396

DALE SVEUM
Chicago White Sox
Shortstop
$11

Had trials as a shortstop for two teams which were desperate for a shortstop (Philadelphia and the White Sox) and quickly convinced both teams that he was not a solution to the problem, not even for a little while. They could have asked me; I'd have told them the same thing. He isn't a natural shortstop and hasn't hit .250 since 1987.

YEAR	TEAM/LEVEL	G	AB	R	H	2B	3B	HR	RBI	BB	SB	AVG	OBP	SLG
1991	Milwaukee	90	266	33	64	19	1	4	43	32	2	.241	.320	.365
1992	Two Teams	94	249	28	49	13	0	4	28	28	1	.197	.273	.297
1993	Projected	65	193	24	44	7	1	7	25	20	8	.228	.300	.383
		36	137	20	39	1	2	10	22	12	15	.285	.342	.340

PAT TABLER
Toronto Blue Jays
Designated Hitter/First Baseman
$1

I don't honestly understand why he is still in the majors. He's a one-dimensional player, a singles hitter—who no longer hits singles. Why the Blue Jays have continued to hold on to him and continued to give him at bats that could have been given to John Olerud or Ed Sprague is just impossible for me to grasp. He is a very nice man.

YEAR	TEAM/LEVEL	G	AB	R	H	2B	3B	HR	RBI	BB	SB	AVG	OBP	SLG
1990	Two Teams	92	238	18	65	15	1	2	29	23	0	.273	.338	.370
1991	Toronto	82	185	20	40	5	1	1	21	29	0	.216	.318	.270
1992	Toronto	49	135	11	34	5	0	0	16	11	0	.252	.306	.289
		16	85	2	28	5	0	0	11	0	0	.329	.329	.388

JEFF TACKETT
Baltimore Orioles
Catcher
$15

Beat out Rick Dempsey (by an eyelash) for the 25th roster spot, then got playing time while Hoiles was hurt. He hit better than I would have expected, .240 with as many secondary bases as singles. With his defense, which is real good, there are worse catchers around. I would expect his playing time to go down, rather than up, over a period of years.

YEAR	TEAM/LEVEL	G	AB	R	H	2B	3B	HR	RBI	BB	SB	AVG	OBP	SLG
1991	Baltimore	6	8	1	1	0	0	0	0	2	0	.125	.300	.125
1992	Baltimore	65	179	21	43	8	1	5	24	17	0	.240	.307	.380
1993	Projected	75	209	23	43	6	0	3	19	23	2	.206	.284	.278
		85	239	25	43	4	0	4	14	29	4	.180	.269	.209

DANNY TARTABULL
New York Yankees
Right Fielder/Designated Hitter
$39

His signing by the Yankees was strange given New York's young outfield talent, but then who said this was a logical universe. As usual, DT was one of the best hitters in baseball when he was in the lineup. As usual, he missed 30-odd games with various minor injuries and played the outfield with the aplomb of a pregnant camel in a forest fire.

YEAR	TEAM/LEVEL	G	AB	R	H	2B	3B	HR	RBI	BB	SB	AVG	OBP	SLG
1991	Kansas City	132	484	78	153	35	3	31	100	65	6	.316	.397	.593
1992	New York	123	421	72	112	19	0	25	85	103	2	.266	.409	.489
1993	Projected	135	476	74	132	27	2	25	88	84	4	.277	.386	.500
		147	531	76	152	35	4	25	91	65	6	.286	.409	.508

JIM TATUM
Milwaukee Brewers
Third Base Prospect
$24

A third-round draft pick in 1985, was released by San Diego, sat out a year after a messy divorce, played 30 games, and was released by Cleveland, finally hooked on with Brewers. He's a major league hitter, a good hitter, and only 25; his MLE from 1991 is almost as good as '92. Grade B prospect; I expect him to have a solid major league career.

YEAR	TEAM/LEVEL	G	AB	R	H	2B	3B	HR	RBI	BB	SB	AVG	OBP	SLG
1991	El Paso AA	130	493	99	158	27	8	18	128	63	5	.320	.399	.517
1992	Denver AAA	130	492	74	162	36	3	19	101	40	8	.329	.382	.530
1992	MLE	130	464	54	134	30	1	13	74	29	5	.289	.331	.442
		130	436	34	106	24	0	7	47	18	2	.243	.276	.346

EDDIE TAUBENSEE
Houston Astros
Catcher
$17

Traded to Cleveland for Lofton and started the season platooning with Scott Servais, but hit .213 in April, .150 in May, and .087 in June before being sent to Tucson on June 12. Hit .338 in 20 games there, then was recalled and hit .262 with a .409 slugging percentage the rest of the season. Major league hitter, and throws better than Servais. Reasonable draft choice.

YEAR	TEAM/LEVEL	G	AB	R	H	2B	3B	HR	RBI	BB	SB	AVG	OBP	SLG
1991	Cleveland	26	66	5	16	2	1	0	8	5	0	.242	.288	.303
1992	Houston	104	297	23	66	15	0	5	28	31	2	.222	.299	.323
1993	Projected	99	278	27	68	15	1	5	28	25	1	.245	.307	.360
		94	259	31	70	15	2	5	28	19	0	.270	.320	.402

MICKEY TETTLETON
Detroit Tigers
Catcher
$60

There are 26 seasons in history in which a catcher has hit 30 home runs. Nine of those 26, more than a third, played for Sparky. Bench did it four times (for Sparky), Lance Parrish twice, Matt Nokes once, and Mickey Tettleton twice . . . the last two years Tettleton has been better than the league average at throwing out runners. Tied for the league lead in walks.

YEAR	TEAM/LEVEL	G	AB	R	H	2B	3B	HR	RBI	BB	SB	AVG	OBP	SLG
1991	Detroit	154	501	85	132	17	2	31	89	101	3	.263	.387	.491
1992	Detroit	157	525	82	125	25	0	32	83	122	0	.238	.379	.469
1993	Projected	147	484	74	113	19	1	22	67	111	3	.233	.376	.413
		137	453	66	101	13	2	12	57	100	6	.228	.376	.348

TIM TEUFEL
San Diego Padres
Infielder
$14

He's one of the comparatively few players who was billed as a coming star, failed to do that, failed to hold on to a regular job, but grabbed hold of a spot on the bench and has kept it now for several years. He's a better hitter than your typical utility infielder, despite the .224 average last year. He has a little power and can hit a left-hander.

YEAR	TEAM/LEVEL	G	AB	R	H	2B	3B	HR	RBI	BB	SB	AVG	OBP	SLG
1991	Two Teams	117	341	41	74	16	0	12	44	51	9	.217	.319	.370
1992	San Diego	101	246	23	55	10	0	6	25	31	2	.224	.312	.337
1993	Projected	99	241	30	55	17	1	6	29	31	3	.228	.316	.382
		97	236	37	55	24	2	6	33	31	4	.233	.32	.408

FRANK THOMAS
Chicago White Sox
First Basemen
$98

A legend in search of an appropriate nickname. He's the closest thing to Ted Williams that we're ever likely to see. He's right-handed, and nobody is ever going to compare him to a splinter, but as a hitter . . . well, he's pretty much Ted Williams. I predict that he will never steal 70 bases. This is about the only limit I would want to put on him.

YEAR	TEAM/LEVEL	G	AB	R	H	2B	3B	HR	RBI	BB	SB	AVG	OBP	SLG
1991	Chicago	158	559	104	178	31	2	32	109	138	1	.318	.453	.553
1992	Chicago	160	573	115	185	46	2	24	115	122	6	.323	.439	.536
1993	Projected	160	562	116	186	38	3	30	112	139	5	.331	.464	.569
		160	551	117	187	30	4	36	109	156	4	.339	.485	.604

JIM THOME
Cleveland Indians
Third Baseman
$23

A year ago he was a Rookie of the Year candidate. Instead, he opened the season on the DL with strained wrist ligaments, came back, hurt his shoulder, finished the season in Colorado Springs, and wasn't a September call up. He's only 22, and in 155 minor league at bats he hit .329. He is still a **Grade A prospect** in my book.

YEAR	TEAM/LEVEL	G	AB	R	H	2B	3B	HR	RBI	BB	SB	AVG	OBP	SLG
1991	Cleveland	27	98	7	25	4	2	1	9	5	1	.255	.298	.367
1992	AA and AAA	42	155	27	51	13	3	3	28	30	0	.329	.444	.510
1992	Cleveland	40	117	8	86	38	3	2	12	10	2	.228	.285	.330
		38	89	0	121	63	3	1	0	20	4	1.532	1.42	2.392

MILT THOMPSON
St. Louis Cardinals
(Released)
Left Fielder
$18

With the emergence of Gilkey and the outstanding play of Jose and Lankford, was reduced to pinch hitting and some spot starts. He's a good hitter, lacks the range to play center every day or the arm to play right, but can fill in at any of the three outfield spots. Left-handed hitter, and quite possibly the best fourth outfielder in baseball.

YEAR	TEAM/LEVEL	G	AB	R	H	2B	3B	HR	RBI	BB	SB	AVG	OBP	SLG
1991	St. Louis	115	326	55	100	16	5	6	34	32	16	.307	.368	.442
1992	St. Louis	109	208	31	61	9	1	4	17	16	18	.293	.350	.404
1993	Projected	124	320	43	86	15	3	4	27	30	20	.269	.331	.372
		139	432	55	111	21	5	4	37	44	22	.257	.326	.356

Tartabull–Thompson 137

ROBBY THOMPSON
San Francisco Giants
Second Baseman
$35

The question which becomes prominent here, as Thompson reaches 32 (in May) and continues to have back problems every year, is whether Robby hits well enough to move to a less demanding defensive position and hold a job. He has more power than some first basemen, and you'd have to think his range at first would be a real asset. Probably doesn't throw well enough to move to third.

YEAR	TEAM/LEVEL	G	AB	R	H	2B	3B	HR	RBI	BB	SB	AVG	OBP	SLG
1991	San Francisco	144	492	74	129	24	5	19	48	63	14	.262	.352	.447
1992	San Francisco	128	443	54	115	25	1	14	49	43	5	.260	.333	.415
1993	Projected	142	485	64	124	25	3	13	50	48	12	.256	.323	.400
		156	527	74	133	25	5	12	51	53	19	.282	.321	.387

RYAN THOMPSON
New York Mets
Center Fielder
$9

Went to the Mets, along with Jeff Kent, in the Cone trade. A 13th-round pick in 1987, now 25 years old, his career was slowed by injuries until last season. Was listed by *Baseball America* as the number-eight prospect in the International League after hitting .282 with 41 extra-base hits, went straight into the Mets lineup after the trade and didn't embarrass himself. Grade C prospect.

YEAR	TEAM/LEVEL	G	AB	R	H	2B	3B	HR	RBI	BB	SB	AVG	OBP	SLG
1992	Syracuse AAA	112	429	74	121	20	7	14	46	43	10	.282	.351	.459
1992	MLE	112	405	50	97	16	4	9	31	29	6	.240	.290	.365
1992	New York	30	108	15	24	7	1	3	10	8	2	.222	.274	.389
		0	0	0	0	0	0	0	0	0				

DICKIE THON
Texas Rangers (Released)
Shortstop
$15

There *are* players whose careers end in an expansion year. There are many players close to the margin, so if your ability level drops significantly, an expansion won't necessarily save you. Thon doesn't hit enough to make up for lack of range, and at 34 that's not going to change for the better. Didn't play much the last two months of the season because of a sore shoulder.

YEAR	TEAM/LEVEL	G	AB	R	H	2B	3B	HR	RBI	BB	SB	AVG	OBP	SLG
1991	Philadelpia	146	539	44	136	18	4	9	44	25	11	.252	.283	.351
1992	Texas	95	275	30	68	15	3	4	37	20	12	.247	.293	.367
1993	Projected	80	274	25	68	11	2	4	25	17	7	.248	.292	.347
		65	273	20	68	7	1	4	13	14	2	.249	.286	.326

GARY THURMAN
Kansas City Royals
Utility Outfielder
$16

A Gary Pettis/Milt Cuyler/Brian McRae type player, could have played regularly but came up when KC was in the grip of Bo Mania, and the Royals gave his chance to Bo. Fine, fine outfielder, one of the fastest men in the league, and has a better arm than McRae, but a .250 hitter without power or walks. Only 28, will be around for several years.

YEAR	TEAM/LEVEL	G	AB	R	H	2B	3B	HR	RBI	BB	SB	AVG	OBP	SLG
1991	Kansas City	80	184	24	51	9	0	2	13	11	15	.277	.320	.359
1992	Kansas City	88	200	25	49	6	3	0	20	9	9	.245	.281	.305
1993	Projected	68	180	22	48	6	2	1	14	11	12	.267	.309	.339
		48	160	19	47	6	1	2	8	13	15	.294	.347	.381

RON TINGLEY
California Angels
Catcher
$12

He hit .197, which improved his career average, and impressed defensively, throwing out 46 percent of base stealers. He began the season on the roster because Orton was hurt, then got to stay when Parrish was released. He'll be 34 in May, so he's just trying to survive, but the Angels need a lot of help behind the plate, and he's probably a better player than Orton.

YEAR	TEAM/LEVEL	G	AB	R	H	2B	3B	HR	RBI	BB	SB	AVG	OBP	SLG
1991	California	45	115	11	23	7	0	1	13	8	1	.200	.258	.287
1992	California	71	127	15	25	2	1	3	8	13	2	.197	.282	.299
1993	Projected	68	132	14	27	5	0	2	12	11	1	.205	.266	.288
		65	87	13	29	8	0	1	16	9	0	.212	.260	.292

ALAN TRAMMELL
Detroit Tigers
Shortstop (Maybe)
$15

Broke his ankle running out an infield hit on May 15, was expected to miss six weeks but never came back. In his absence, Fryman established himself as one of the top shortstops in baseball, and there is talk of Trammell shifting to third or even left field this season. Given his ankle problems of the last two years and the possible position switch, I don't recommend drafting him.

YEAR	TEAM/LEVEL	G	AB	R	H	2B	3B	HR	RBI	BB	SB	AVG	OBP	SLG
1991	Detroit	101	375	57	93	20	0	9	55	37	11	.248	.320	.373
1992	Detroit	29	102	11	28	7	1	1	11	15	2	.275	.370	.392
1993	Projected	105	390	49	105	18	2	8	54	46	9	.269	.346	.387
		183	678	87	182	25	3	15	97	77	16	.268	.343	.386

BRIAN TRAXLER
Los Angeles Dodgers
First Baseman
$4

A 25-year-old first baseman with a Hack Wilson body, even more so than Kirby. He looks very strong and looks like a hitter, but his record is unimpressive. He's kind of a Bill Buckner–type hitter, doesn't strike out and can drive the ball, but doesn't build enough onto that to make himself really valuable. A 15th-round draft pick, can't run. Grade D prospect.

YEAR	TEAM/LEVEL	G	AB	R	H	2B	3B	HR	RBI	BB	SB	AVG	OBP	SLG
1991	San Antonio AA	103	379	50	97	24	0	7	61	53	1	.256	.348	.375
1992	Albuqueque AAA	127	393	58	119	26	4	11	58	36	1	.303	.359	.473
1992	MLE	127	363	35	89	18	1	6	35	22	0	.245	.288	.350
		127	333	12	59	10	0	1	12	8	0	.177	.196	.216

JEFF TREADWAY
Atlanta Braves
Second Baseman
$12

Missed the first three months of the season with hand surgery, then didn't hit when he came back. When you're on the roster as the offensive second baseman, and the defensive second baseman outhits you, you're in trouble. He is 30, not a good fielder, not a good baserunner, so his bat will have to come back if he's going to keep his job.

YEAR	TEAM/LEVEL	G	AB	R	H	2B	3B	HR	RBI	BB	SB	AVG	OBP	SLG
1991	Atlanta	106	306	41	96	17	2	3	32	23	2	.320	.368	.418
1992	Atlanta	61	126	5	28	6	1	0	5	9	1	.222	.274	.286
1993	Projected	80	235	26	65	12	1	4	25	16	2	.277	.323	.387
		99	344	47	102	18	1	8	45	23	3	.297	.341	.424

SCOOTER TUCKER
Houston Astros

Catcher
$8

Former Giant farmhand, the Astros picked him off the waiver wire after a 1991 season in which he hit .284 in the Texas League. He was called up from Tucson when Taubensee went down, but went 6-for-50 with the bat and went back down. I kind of like him. I see him as a .250- to .260-hitting catcher with pretty decent arm. Grade D prospect.

YEAR	TEAM/LEVEL	G	AB	R	H	2B	3B	HR	RBI	BB	SB	AVG	OBP	SLG
1992	Tucson AAA	83	288	36	87	15	1	1	29	28	5	.302	.368	.372
1992	MLE	83	270	23	69	12	0	0	18	18	3	.256	.302	.300
1992	Houston	20	50	5	6	1	0	0	3	3	1	.120	.200	.140

6 0 0 0 0 0 0 0 0 0 — = — (handwritten)

SHANE TURNER
Seattle Mariners

Infielder
$1

Thirty-year-old veteran originally in the Yankee system, played briefly for Philadelphia (1988) and Baltimore (1990). A left-handed batter, has very little power, used to have some speed but has lost most of that. Consistent .280 hitter in the minors; it's hard to tell how much of that average he would lose if he came to the majors. No prospect.

YEAR	TEAM/LEVEL	G	AB	R	H	2B	3B	HR	RBI	BB	SB	AVG	OBP	SLG
1992	Calgary AAA	76	242	31	68	17	3	0	26	35	10	.281	.377	.376
1992	MLE	76	227	20	53	14	1	0	16	22	6	.233	.301	.304
1992	Seattle	34	74	8	20	5	0	0	5	9	2	.270	.341	.338

0 0 0 0 0 0 0 0 0 — — — (handwritten)

JOSE URIBE
San Francisco Giants
(Free Agent)

Shortstop
$13

Started season backing up Royce Clayton, got part of his job back when Clayton didn't hit and took advantage, hitting .364 in May. Played off and on in June and July, then hardly at all after it became apparent the Giants weren't going anywhere. One of the worst hitters in baseball, any value he has is defensive, and his defense is not as highly regarded as it once was.

YEAR	TEAM/LEVEL	G	AB	R	H	2B	3B	HR	RBI	BB	SB	AVG	OBP	SLG
1991	San Francisco	90	231	23	51	8	4	1	12	20	3	.221	.283	.303
1992	San Francisco	66	162	24	39	9	1	2	13	14	2	.241	.299	.346
1993	Projected	82	208	21	49	7	2	1	12	16	3	.236	.290	.303

98 254 18 59 5 3 0 11 18 4 .232 .283 .226 (handwritten)

JOHN VALENTIN
Boston Red Sox

Shortstop
$23

A fifth-round pick out of Seton Hall in 1988, he didn't start to hit until 1991, when he reached Pawtucket. His .276 average of last year gives him firm control of the shortstop job, but is an optimistic estimate of what he will hit. The reports on his defense are good, and his secondary offensive skills are good. Grade B prospect.

YEAR	TEAM/LEVEL	G	AB	R	H	2B	3B	HR	RBI	BB	SB	AVG	OBP	SLG
1992	Pawtucket AAA	97	331	47	86	18	1	9	29	48	1	.260	.358	.402
1992	MLE	97	320	35	75	17	0	7	21	35	0	.234	.310	.353
1992	Boston	58	185	21	51	13	0	5	25	20	1	.276	.351	.427

27 50 7 27 9 0 3 29 5 2 .540 .582 .900 (handwritten)

JOSE VALENTIN
Milwaukee Brewers
Shortstop Prospect
$2

A 23-year-old switch-hitting middle infielder. A year ago, *Baseball America* ranked him as the number-five prospect in the San Diego organization, mainly on the strength of his 1991 season, when he hit 17 home runs for Wichita. Went to Milwaukee in the Sheffield trade and had a poor year for Denver, which combines with the emergence of Listach to deprive him of any obvious future.

YEAR	TEAM/LEVEL	G	AB	R	H	2B	3B	HR	RBI	BB	SB	AVG	OBP	SLG
1991	Wichita AA	129	447	73	112	22	5	17	68	55	8	.251	.335	.436
1992	Denver AAA	139	492	78	118	19	11	3	45	53	9	.240	.317	.341
1992	MLE	139	471	57	97	16	5	2	33	39	6	.206	.267	.274
		135	450	36	78	13	0	1	21	25	3	.173	.217	.209

DAVE VALLE
Seattle Mariners
Catcher
$17

After a miserable 1991, bounced back to set career highs in playing time, matching his career on-base percentage and slugging average. The other catchers in Seattle are Lance Parrish and Bill Haselman, with nobody in the minors, so Valle isn't exactly being pushed for his job. Is regarded as a good defensive catcher, but given the state of Seattle's pitching, it might be time for a change.

YEAR	TEAM/LEVEL	G	AB	R	H	2B	3B	HR	RBI	BB	SB	AVG	OBP	SLG
1991	Seattle	132	324	38	63	8	1	8	32	34	0	.194	.286	.299
1992	Seattle	124	367	39	88	16	1	9	30	27	0	.240	.305	.362
1993	Projected	93	310	35	68	11	1	7	29	34	1	.219	.297	.329
		62	253	31	48	6	1	5	28	41	2	.190	.303	.281

ANDY VAN SLYKE
Pittsburgh Pirates
Center Fielder
$71

Nobody made a big deal about it, but he had an MVP season, too, the finest season of a distinguished career. He led the National League in hits and doubles. He'd had back trouble in recent years, and switched to a lighter bat and a shorter stroke to try to reduce the strain on his back. The result was more singles and doubles, fewer homers but a good trade.

YEAR	TEAM/LEVEL	G	AB	R	H	2B	3B	HR	RBI	BB	SB	AVG	OBP	SLG
1991	Pittsburgh	138	491	87	130	24	7	17	83	71	10	.265	.355	.446
1992	Pittsburgh	154	614	103	199	45	12	14	89	58	12	.324	.381	.505
1993	Projected	143	532	78	146	26	6	15	75	66	12	.274	.355	.430
		132	450	53	93	7	0	16	61	74	12	.207	.319	.329

JOHN VANDERWAL
Montreal Expos
Left Fielder
$19

I believe in this guy; I think he's a good line-drive hitter, could hit 35 doubles. He got some playing time last year with the injury to Calderon and didn't hit as well as he should have, but he is capable of having better years. He and Moises Alou would be a good platoon combination, Vanderwal being a little better player in the long run.

YEAR	TEAM/LEVEL	G	AB	R	H	2B	3B	HR	RBI	BB	SB	AVG	OBP	SLG
1991	Indianapolis AAA	133	478	84	140	36	8	15	71	79	8	.293	.393	.496
1991	Montreal	21	61	4	13	4	1	1	8	1	0	.213	.222	.361
1992	Montreal	105	213	21	51	8	2	4	20	24	3	.239	.316	.352
		189	365	38	89	12	3	7	32	47	6	.244	.306	.357

GARY VARSHO
Pittsburgh Pirates
Utility Outfielder/Pinch Hitter
$14

Left-handed line-drive-hitting outfielder, your basic pinch hitter. He's part of Leyland's everybody-gets-to-play system, played right field and some left when Bonds was out. Fairly fast, good baserunner, has 24 career stolen bases with only four caught stealing. Right fielder's arm, but sometimes has trouble judging fly balls. Now 31, probably will stay in his 1991 role despite off year.

YEAR	TEAM/LEVEL	G	AB	R	H	2B	3B	HR	RBI	BB	SB	AVG	OBP	SLG
1991	Pittsburgh	99	187	23	51	11	2	4	23	19	9	.273	.344	.417
1992	Pittsburgh	103	162	22	36	6	3	4	22	10	5	.222	.266	.370
1993	Projected	100	151	19	36	9	1	2	17	12	6	.238	.294	.351
		97	142	16	36	12	0	0	12	14	7	.254	.34	.38

JIM VATCHER
San Diego Padres
Outfielder
$3

Originally in the Phillies system, went to Atlanta in the Dale Murphy deal and to the Padres after the Braves released him. Gets a cup of coffee with the Padres once a year, not that he's any worse player than Gerald Clark, and I suppose is hoping to expand his time with expansion. He'll be 27 in May and isn't really a prospect, but could fill in if needed.

YEAR	TEAM/LEVEL	G	AB	R	H	2B	3B	HR	RBI	BB	SB	AVG	OBP	SLG
1991	Las Vegas AAA	117	395	67	105	28	6	17	67	53	4	.266	.355	.496
1992	Las Vegas AAA	111	280	41	77	15	3	8	35	39	2	.275	.367	.436
1993	MLE	111	262	25	59	11	1	5	21	23	1	.225	.288	.332
		111	244	9	41	7	0	2	7	7	0	.168	.190	.224

GREG VAUGHN
Milwaukee Brewers
Left Fielder
$30

His career average after three-plus years is .234, and three-plus years are normally enough to show what you can do. With his power and speed and a few walks, .234 will keep him in the lineup, and he's capable of compiling Albert Belle–type numbers in a good year. He had 15 steals in 30 attempts, which isn't any help, and is average or above left fielder.

YEAR	TEAM/LEVEL	G	AB	R	H	2B	3B	HR	RBI	BB	SB	AVG	OBP	SLG
1991	Milwaukee	145	542	81	132	24	5	27	98	62	2	.244	.319	.456
1992	Milwaukee	141	501	77	114	18	2	23	78	60	15	.228	.313	.409
1993	Projected	147	512	77	122	25	2	24	84	58	10	.238	.316	.436
		153	523	77	130	32	2	25	92	56	5	.249	.321	.461

MO VAUGHN
Boston Red Sox (Boomer Jooner)
First Baseman
$26

Standing at first he reminds you of George Scott, but when he makes a play it's more like Dick Stuart. Hit .204 in April and .125 in May, which earned him a demotion to Pawtucket to get his bat started, and he did hit much better after his recall. He can hit. He's going to be a 25-to-30-home-run guy when he gets his land legs.

YEAR	TEAM/LEVEL	G	AB	R	H	2B	3B	HR	RBI	BB	SB	AVG	OBP	SLG
1991	Boston	74	219	21	57	12	0	4	32	26	2	.260	.339	.370
1992	Boston	113	355	42	83	16	2	13	57	47	3	.234	.326	.400
1993	Projected	128	410	47	109	22	1	14	62	53	2	.266	.350	.427
		143	466	52	135	28	0	15	67	59	1	.290	.370	.417

RANDY VELARDE
New York Yankees

Infielder
$23

He had by far his best season at 29 (he's now 30), and in that case one would ordinarily assume he was over his head. In Velarde's case there are indications that this may be his true level of ability, and he was just slow to get there. When he came up I thought he was going to be good, and he has played well before for brief periods.

YEAR	TEAM/LEVEL	G	AB	R	H	2B	3B	HR	RBI	BB	SB	AVG	OBP	SLG
1990	New York	95	229	21	48	6	2	5	19	20	0	.210	.275	.319
1991	New York	80	184	19	45	11	1	1	15	18	3	.245	.322	.332
1992	New York	121	412	57	112	24	1	7	46	38	7	.272	.333	.386
		162	*640*	*95*	*179*	*37*	*2*	*13*	*77*	*58*	*11*	*.280*	*.340*	*.402*

GUILLERMO VELASQUEZ
San Diego Padres

First Base Prospect
$11

The reincarnation of Willie Montanez. He's 25 years old, was signed out of Mexico in 1987, and has become an "RBI man" (if you bat him fourth in a hitter's park he'll drive in runs). In the past has increased his power in his second year at each level. Good defense, isn't going to take McGriff's job, but at worst will have a career as a pinch hitter.

YEAR	TEAM/LEVEL	G	AB	R	H	2B	3B	HR	RBI	BB	SB	AVG	OBP	SLG
1992	Las Vegas	136	512	68	158	44	4	7	99	44	4	.309	.359	.451
1992	MLE	136	473	41	119	32	1	4	60	26	3	.252	.291	.349
1992	San Diego	15	23	1	7	0	0	1	5	1	0	.304	.333	.435
		0	*0*	*0*	*0*	*0*	*0*	*0*	*0*	*0*	*0*	*—*	*—*	*—*

ROBIN VENTURA
Chicago White Sox

Third Baseman
$66

Does everything well except run, ranks with Edgar Martinez as the top third basemen in the league, and is a better fielder than Edgar. He dropped seven homers, but picked up t13 doubles, so that's not a bad deal. At 25 he is young enough to improve, but even if he doesn't he is probably going to be the best third baseman the White Sox have ever had.

YEAR	TEAM/LEVEL	G	AB	R	H	2B	3B	HR	RBI	BB	SB	AVG	OBP	SLG
1991	Chicago	157	606	92	172	25	1	23	100	80	2	.284	.367	.442
1992	Chicago	157	592	85	167	38	1	16	93	93	2	.282	.375	.431
1993	Projected	158	576	78	159	28	1	14	82	82	3	.276	.366	.401
		159	*560*	*71*	*157*	*18*	*1*	*12*	*71*	*71*	*4*	*.270*	*.352*	*.370*

HECTOR VILLANUEVA
Chicago Cubs (Released)

Catcher
$9

He has considerable hitting ability, but he has grown to the size of a small island, and at the start of last year couldn't get the bat around his gut. After he hit in the ones for three months the Cubs sent him to Iowa, where he did better. Not much of a catcher, but if he were to hit the way he can, they'd forgive him for that.

YEAR	TEAM/LEVEL	G	AB	R	H	2B	3B	HR	RBI	BB	SB	AVG	OBP	SLG
1991	Chicago	71	192	23	53	10	1	13	32	21	0	.276	.346	.542
1992	Chicago	51	112	9	17	6	0	2	13	11	0	.152	.228	.259
1993	Projected	101	298	29	71	14	1	11	42	25	0	.238	.297	.403
		131	*474*	*49*	*125*	*22*	*2*	*20*	*71*	*39*	*0*	*.269*	*.320*	*.445*

JOSE VIZCAINO
Chicago Cubs

Utility Infielder

$16

Got the chance he had been looking for when Dunston went out, but didn't have the season he wanted, or even the season he is capable of having. The season, in all likelihood, was the turning point in his career; it is unlikely now that he will be a regular. Missed the last month of the season after surgery to repair torn muscles in his left (non-throwing) hand.

YEAR	TEAM/LEVEL	G	AB	R	H	2B	3B	HR	RBI	BB	SB	AVG	OBP	SLG
1991	Chicago	93	145	7	38	5	0	0	10	5	2	.262	.283	.297
1992	Chicago	86	285	25	64	10	4	1	17	14	3	.225	.260	.298
1993	Projected	97	234	21	58	7	2	1	19	14	4	.248	.290	.308
		108	183	17	52	4	0	0	21	14	5	.284	.335	.36

OMAR VIZQUEL
Seattle Mariners

Shortstop

$32

Hit 64 points better than his career average and also got the best defensive reviews of his career as he made only seven errors. I would be surprised if he hit .300 this year, but there's always been something about him that I liked, plus he's only 26 (in April), so you can't say that he's not just getting better. I'd like to have him.

YEAR	TEAM/LEVEL	G	AB	R	H	2B	3B	HR	RBI	BB	SB	AVG	OBP	SLG
1991	Seattle	142	426	42	98	16	4	1	41	45	7	.230	.302	.293
1992	Seattle	136	483	49	142	20	4	0	21	32	15	.294	.340	.352
1993	Projected	144	460	42	120	15	3	2	33	38	10	.261	.317	.320
		152	437	35	98	10	2	4	45	44	5	.224	.285	.293

JACK VOIGT
Baltimore Orioles

Outfielder

$3

The Moonlight Graham of the '90s, was called up August 1, pinch ran for Randy Milligan, was doubled off on a line drive and was replaced in the field by David Segui. Didn't get in another game and was sent down August 5. Good baserunner, outfielder, can also play third. Even balance of offensive skills. Good secondary average. Is 26 years old, coming off best season; Grade D prospect.

YEAR	TEAM/LEVEL	G	AB	R	H	2B	3B	HR	RBI	BB	SB	AVG	OBP	SLG
1991	Rochester AAA	83	267	46	72	11	4	6	35	40	9	.270	.365	.408
1992	Rochester AAA	129	443	74	126	23	4	16	64	58	9	.284	.372	.463
1992	MLE	129	422	57	105	18	2	12	49	44	6	.249	.320	.386
		129	401	40	84	13	0	8	34	30	3	.209	.265	.302

CHICO WALKER
New York Mets

Utilityman

$14

Has spent two full seasons in the majors after playing 1646 minor league games, which must be more than anybody in the majors today. Switch hitter, plays all over the field, like Tony Phillips, and is still outstanding baserunner at 34. He'd have about 1500 hits by now if he'd come up with the Red Sox about 1980, but they didn't think he could play.

YEAR	TEAM/LEVEL	G	AB	R	H	2B	3B	HR	RBI	BB	SB	AVG	OBP	SLG
1991	Chicago	124	374	51	96	10	1	6	34	33	13	.257	.315	.337
1992	Two Teams	126	253	26	73	12	1	4	38	27	15	.289	.351	.391
1993	Projected	77	177	21	42	7	1	3	18	19	6	.237	.311	.339
		28	101	16	11	2	1	2	0	11	0	.109	.191	.23

LARRY WALKER
Montreal Expos
Right Fielder
$65

With Canseco and Sierra having off years in '92, the two best right fielders in baseball were both playing in Canada, Carter and Walker. As an offensive player Walker does some of everything you can, plus he led National League right fielders with 16 assists, including two 9-3 groundouts . . . career batting stats are much better on the road than in Montreal. Capable of having an MVP season.

YEAR	TEAM/LEVEL	G	AB	R	H	2B	3B	HR	RBI	BB	SB	AVG	OBP	SLG
1991	Montreal	137	487	59	141	30	2	16	64	42	14	.290	.349	.458
1992	Montreal	143	528	85	159	31	4	23	93	41	18	.301	.353	.506
1993	Projected	146	506	72	142	26	3	20	72	49	20	.281	.344	.462
		149	484	59	125	21	2	17	51	57	22	.258	.340	.45

TIM WALLACH
Montreal Expos
Third/First Baseman
$13

After two straight seasons in the .220s it is time for him to consider another role, like broadcaster. Wallach is an RVL, a Respected Veteran Leader, and the problem with RVLs is that they hang around after they can't play anymore. Two years ago I was comparing him to Brooks Robinson, and it still fits. Brooks didn't know when to quit, either.

YEAR	TEAM/LEVEL	G	AB	R	H	2B	3B	HR	RBI	BB	SB	AVG	OBP	SLG
1991	Montreal	151	577	60	130	22	1	13	73	50	2	.225	.292	.334
1992	Montreal	150	537	53	120	29	1	9	59	50	2	.223	.296	.331
1993	Projected	120	443	45	108	24	1	11	58	37	3	.244	.302	.377
		90	349	37	96	19	1	13	57	24	4	.275	.322	.481

DAN WALTERS
San Diego Padres
Catcher
$22

Called up in June when Santiago got hurt, was hitting .394 at Las Vegas at the time. Is 26 years old, didn't hit much his first five years as a pro, but has hit .310 over his last three minor league seasons, albeit in good hitter's parks. Threw out 28 percent of base stealers, slightly below NL average. Santiago is not expected back, apparently leaving Walters with the job.

YEAR	TEAM/LEVEL	G	AB	R	H	2B	3B	HR	RBI	BB	SB	AVG	OBP	SLG
1992	Las Vegas AAA	35	127	16	50	9	0	2	25	10	0	.394	.440	.512
1992	San Diego	57	179	14	45	11	1	4	22	10	1	.251	.295	.391
1993	Projected	122	404	31	101	17	0	7	44	22	0	.250	.289	.344
		181	629	48	157	23	6	10	66	34	0	.250	.288	.337

JEROME WALTON
Chicago Cubs
Center Fielder
$8

Was sent to Triple-A Iowa on June 12 with a .127 batting average. A week later he went out for the season with a bulging disc. After three years of progressive degeneration, anyone would conclude that there must be some underlying problem here. It is certainly possible for him to snap back, but I really don't know any reason to urge you to bet on it.

YEAR	TEAM/LEVEL	G	AB	R	H	2B	3B	HR	RBI	BB	SB	AVG	OBP	SLG
1990	Chicago	101	392	63	103	16	2	2	21	50	14	.263	.350	.329
1991	Chicago	123	270	42	59	13	1	5	17	19	7	.219	.275	.330
1992	Chicago	30	55	7	7	0	1	0	1	9	1	.127	.273	.164
		0	0	0	0	0	1	0	0	0	0			

KEVIN WARD
San Diego Padres
Left Fielder
$2

Finally made it to the majors in 1991 after seven-plus years in the minors. He was a quarterback and wide receiver at the University of Arizona. Not a great hitter, but not as bad as he showed last year, might hit left-handers well enough to be useful as a platoon player, but at 31 probably won't hang around long enough for anybody to find out. No prospect.

YEAR	TEAM/LEVEL	G	AB	R	H	2B	3B	HR	RBI	BB	SB	AVG	OBP	SLG
1991	San Diego	44	107	13	26	7	2	2	8	9	1	.243	.308	.402
1991	Las Vegas AAA	83	276	51	89	17	6	6	43	58	10	.322	.445	.493
1992	San Diego	81	147	12	29	5	0	3	12	14	2	.197	.274	.293
		79	18	0	0	0	0	0	0	0	0	.000	.000	.000

TURNER WARD
Toronto Blue Jays
Utility Outfielder
$13

Switch hitter who failed as a regular with Cleveland, trying to find the right role on somebody's bench. Has pretty good speed, can play every outfield position adequately, so fits well in Toronto, where neither Maldonado nor Carter are good outfielders. Career major league batting average is .282, slugging average .388, but he isn't that good a hitter. Could have six- to eight-year career as extra outfielder.

YEAR	TEAM/LEVEL	G	AB	R	H	2B	3B	HR	RBI	BB	SB	AVG	OBP	SLG
1990	Cleveland	14	46	10	16	2	1	1	10	3	3	.348	.388	.500
1991	Two Teams	48	113	12	27	7	0	0	7	11	0	.239	.306	.301
1992	Toronto	18	29	7	10	3	0	1	3	4	0	.345	.424	.552
		0	0	2	0	0	0	2	0	0	0	–	–	–

LENNY WEBSTER
Minnesota Twins
Backup Catcher
$14

Still seems like a kid, but he'll be 28 this season. Serviceable second-string catcher, has .287 average through 87 major league games but nobody thinks he's that good a hitter. Has had a reputation for a strong arm, but threw out only 24 percent of runners stealing last year. Won't take job away from Harper, but catchers do get hurt, and Harper isn't young.

YEAR	TEAM/LEVEL	G	AB	R	H	2B	3B	HR	RBI	BB	SB	AVG	OBP	SLG
1991	Minnesota	18	34	7	10	1	0	3	8	6	0	.294	.390	.588
1992	Minnesota	53	118	10	33	10	1	1	13	9	0	.280	.331	.407
1993	Projected	72	220	27	55	13	0	3	25	22	1	.250	.318	.350
		91	322	44	77	16	0	5	37	35	2	.239	.319	.335

MITCH WEBSTER
Los Angeles Dodgers
Utility Outfielder
$18

Was a regular outfielder with Montreal, 1986–88, and in his mid-thirties must be counted among the better fourth outfielders around. He's a switch hitter, can play any outfield position, will take a walk, is a good percentage base stealer, has a little bit of power, hits in the .260s. Established a Dodger franchise record with 17 pinch hits.

YEAR	TEAM/LEVEL	G	AB	R	H	2B	3B	HR	RBI	BB	SB	AVG	OBP	SLG
1991	Three Teams	107	203	23	42	8	5	2	19	21	2	.207	.281	.325
1992	Los Angeles	135	262	33	70	12	5	6	35	27	11	.267	.334	.420
1993	Projected	126	249	32	61	16	4	5	31	19	9	.245	.299	.402
		117	236	31	52	20	3	4	27	11	7	.220	.285	.381

146 Ward–Whitaker

ERIC WEDGE
Boston Red Sox
Catcher?
$14

Scheduled for elbow surgery at this writing. Wedge has potential as a hitter and was regarded as a good defensive catcher when he was in college (Wichita State) and in the low minors. Knee and elbow problems cast doubt on his future as a catcher, and as a DH, well, he's just another damned DH. Grade C prospect, will rate higher if he can catch.

YEAR	TEAM/LEVEL	G	AB	R	H	2B	3B	HR	RBI	BB	SB	AVG	OBP	SLG
1992	Pawtucket AAA	65	211	28	63	9	0	11	40	32	0	.299	.389	.498
1992	MLE	65	203	20	55	8	0	8	29	23	0	.271	.345	.429
1992	Boston	27	68	11	17	2	0	5	11	13	0	.250	.370	.500

JOHN WEHNER
Pittsburgh Pirates
Third Baseman
$8

Came up in the middle of the 1991 season and hit way over his head for 37 games before back problem sent him to the DL. Still trying to get back to where he was. There has been some talk of turning him into a utility infielder. He'll do battle this spring with Jeff King and Kevin Young, the winner getting the third base job.

YEAR	TEAM/LEVEL	G	AB	R	H	2B	3B	HR	RBI	BB	SB	AVG	OBP	SLG
1992	Buffalo AAA	60	223	37	60	13	2	7	27	29	10	.269	.354	.439
1992	MLE	60	214	28	51	11	1	5	21	22	6	.238	.309	.369
1992	Pittsburgh	55	123	11	22	6	0	0	4	12	3	.179	.252	.228

WALT WEISS
Oakland Athletics
Shortstop
$17

Missed the first two months of the season with bruised ribs, but was in the lineup the second half of the season and kept popping up on those "great plays of the week" shows. He drew 43 walks, which keeps him from being the worst hitter in the league, but with his defense and the lack of competition, he'll probably continue to play regularly when healthy.

YEAR	TEAM/LEVEL	G	AB	R	H	2B	3B	HR	RBI	BB	SB	AVG	OBP	SLG
1991	Oakland	40	133	15	30	6	1	0	13	12	6	.226	.286	.286
1992	Oakland	103	316	36	67	5	2	0	21	43	6	.212	.305	.241
1993	Projected	86	263	31	63	9	1	1	22	31	6	.240	.320	.293

LOU WHITAKER
Detroit Tigers
Second Baseman
$33

Sparky platooned him all season to keep his 35-year-old knees strong. It worked out; when he was in the lineup he was very, very good. Even playing two-thirds of the time, he had more production than 75 percent of the other second basemen. He led the American League in batting with runners in scoring position, .369. Will platoon again this year.

YEAR	TEAM/LEVEL	G	AB	R	H	2B	3B	HR	RBI	BB	SB	AVG	OBP	SLG
1991	Detroit	138	470	94	131	26	2	23	78	90	4	.279	.391	.489
1992	Detroit	130	453	77	126	26	0	19	71	81	6	.278	.386	.461
1993	Projected	131	451	73	116	21	2	13	60	81	6	.257	.370	.399

DEVON WHITE
Toronto Blue Jays
Center Fielder
$46

He's miscast as a leadoff man, with his power and low on-base percentage, but as anybody who has really studied the issue will tell you, it doesn't make a hell of a lot of difference. With his defense—he is the best defensive outfielder in the majors—he would be in the lineup if he didn't hit anything, and he does have power and speed.

YEAR	TEAM/LEVEL	G	AB	R	H	2B	3B	HR	RBI	BB	SB	AVG	OBP	SLG
1991	Toronto	156	642	110	181	40	10	17	60	55	33	.282	.342	.455
1992	Toronto	153	641	98	159	26	7	17	60	47	37	.248	.303	.390
1993	Projected	156	618	91	152	27	6	15	58	55	33	.246	.308	.382

MARK WHITEN
Cleveland Indians
Right Fielder
$27

His 72 walks were a surprise, and if he can do that every year *and* add 5 or 10 homers, he'll be one of the better right fielders in the league. Finished second in the league with 14 assists, and with Barfield out, maybe for good, he *does* have the most feared throwing arm in the league. Just turned 26 in November, so there's still time for him to develop.

YEAR	TEAM/LEVEL	G	AB	R	H	2B	3B	HR	RBI	BB	SB	AVG	OBP	SLG
1991	Two Teams	116	407	46	99	18	7	9	45	30	4	.243	.297	.388
1992	Cleveland	148	508	73	129	19	4	9	43	72	16	.254	.347	.360
1993	Projected	143	516	69	140	18	5	13	52	53	12	.271	.339	.401

CURTIS WILKERSON
Kansas City Royals
Utilityman
$16

A 32-year-old veteran, was the regular shortstop in Texas in 1984 and a utilityman there from 1985 to 1988. He signed with the Royals as a free agent and played well. He can play second, third, or short without embarrassing himself, which in Kansas City means he can play almost every day, since Miller is injury prone, Howard can't hit, and Jefferies can't field.

YEAR	TEAM/LEVEL	G	AB	R	H	2B	3B	HR	RBI	BB	SB	AVG	OBP	SLG
1991	Pittsburgh	85	191	20	36	9	1	2	18	15	2	.188	.243	.277
1992	Kansas City	111	296	27	74	10	1	2	29	18	18	.250	.292	.311
1993	Projected	99	231	23	53	8	2	1	22	14	8	.229	.273	.294

RICK WILKINS
Chicago Cubs
Catcher
$26

If he can hit every year the way he did last year, he's going to have a heck of a career. I think that's optimistic—I doubt that he's really a .270 hitter—but he is probably capable of hitting 15 to 20 homers a year, plus his average will be respectable and his arm is good (threw out 37 percent of base stealers last year). Looks pretty good.

YEAR	TEAM/LEVEL	G	AB	R	H	2B	3B	HR	RBI	BB	SB	AVG	OBP	SLG
1991	Chicago	86	203	21	45	9	0	6	22	19	3	.222	.307	.355
1992	Chicago	83	244	20	66	9	1	8	22	28	0	.270	.344	.414
1993	Projected	104	303	28	74	12	1	11	36	27	2	.244	.306	.399

JERRY WILLARD
Released
Pinch Hitter
$2

Weight problem and years of rust have reduced him from poor defensive catcher to emergency catcher, but he's still one of the few left-handed catchers around who could hit well enough to justify a roster spot as a bat on the bench. If he played regularly he could hit 25 homers, but it would probably have to be as a DH. Cut by Montreal; trying to hook on.

YEAR	TEAM/LEVEL	G	AB	R	H	2B	3B	HR	RBI	BB	SB	AVG	OBP	SLG
1990	MLE	121	373	55	99	19	0	20	64	73	2	.265	.386	.477
1991	MLE	91	270	34	76	21	0	7	32	35	0	.281	.364	.437
1992	Two Teams	47	48	2	11	1	0	2	8	2	0	.229	.260	.375

BERNIE WILLIAMS
New York Yankees
Center Fielder
$28

We've been hearing about him for three years now, but this time he's here to stay, and he's going to be a good one. Still only 24, he's a fine center fielder with range and a strong arm. Career minor league on-base percentage of .392, plus he's fast. If they put him in the leadoff spot he might score 100 runs.

YEAR	TEAM/LEVEL	G	AB	R	H	2B	3B	HR	RBI	BB	SB	AVG	OBP	SLG
1992	Columbus AAA	95	363	68	111	23	9	8	50	52	20	.306	.389	.485
1992	MLE	95	347	54	95	20	4	6	39	41	14	.274	.351	.406
1992	New York	62	261	39	73	14	2	5	26	29	7	.280	.354	.406

GERALD WILLIAMS
New York Yankees
Right Fielder
$12

Another Yankee outfield prospect, 14th-round pick out of Grambling in 1987. Has needed an adjustment year at every level, which is why he's just making it to the majors at 26. Devon White–type player, might hit as well as Devon, with luck. Fine athlete—runs well, has best arm among Yankee outfielders other than Barfield. Because of age, he's only a Grade C prospect.

YEAR	TEAM/LEVEL	G	AB	R	H	2B	3B	HR	RBI	BB	SB	AVG	OBP	SLG
1992	Columbus AAA	142	547	92	156	31	6	16	86	38	36	.285	.334	.452
1992	MLE	142	525	73	134	27	3	12	68	30	26	.255	.351	.406
1992	New York	15	27	7	8	2	0	3	6	0	2	.296	.296	.704

MATT WILLIAMS
San Francisco Giants
Third Baseman
$46

His season wasn't pretty, but it wasn't a total disaster. Williams hit .227 with 66 RBI and had a terrible year; Jeff King hit .231 and drove in 65 and they thought it was a great year. He drew 39 walks, 6 more than his previous high. Defensively, he's one of the best in the league. He'll be 27 this season, and I expect him to come back strong.

YEAR	TEAM/LEVEL	G	AB	R	H	2B	3B	HR	RBI	BB	SB	AVG	OBP	SLG
1991	San Francisco	157	589	72	158	24	5	34	98	33	5	.268	.310	.499
1992	San Francisco	146	529	58	120	13	5	20	66	39	7	.227	.286	.384
1993	Projected	142	530	66	133	22	3	27	85	34	6	.251	.296	.457

REGGIE WILLIAMS
California Angels
Outfielder
$2

Signed by the Angels in 1988 as an undrafted free agent, was a September callup after hitting .272 and stealing 44 bases for Triple-A Edmonton. No power, but he is patient, drew 88 walks last year. A good minor league leadoff man, but in view of his strikeouts it seems unlikely that he will hit enough to hold a major league job.

YEAR	TEAM/LEVEL	G	AB	R	H	2B	3B	HR	RBI	BB	SB	AVG	OBP	SLG
1992	Edmonton AAA	139	519	96	141	26	9	3	64	88	44	.272	.375	.374
1992	MLE	139	481	57	103	17	3	1	38	50	19	.214	.288	.268
1992	California	14	26	5	6	1	1	0	2	1	0	.231	.259	.346

CRAIG WILSON
St. Louis Cardinals
Third Baseman
$13

He backed up Zeile for four months and hit .300, but when Zeile was sent down they sent Wilson down with him. He's not really a .300 hitter, of course, but is a good third baseman and can play second in a pinch, so an occasional .300 batting average could keep him in the majors indefinitely. Square body but no power.

YEAR	TEAM/LEVEL	G	AB	R	H	2B	3B	HR	RBI	BB	SB	AVG	OBP	SLG
1990	St. Louis	55	121	13	30	2	0	0	7	8	0	.248	.290	.264
1991	St. Louis	60	82	5	14	2	0	0	13	6	0	.171	.222	.195
1992	St. Louis	61	106	6	33	6	0	0	13	10	1	.311	.368	.368

DAN WILSON
Cincinnati Reds
Catcher
$12

The new Jeff Reed. He was the Reds' number-one pick in the 1989 June draft (seventh overall), and has moved up a rung each year since then. He's very intelligent, and scouts rave about his defense, but he'll hit below .250 with no power. A guy like that can hold a job, but there's no reason to think he'll be a star. Was a September callup.

YEAR	TEAM/LEVEL	G	AB	R	H	2B	3B	HR	RBI	BB	SB	AVG	OBP	SLG
1992	Nashville	106	366	27	92	16	1	4	34	31	1	.251	.310	.333
1992	MLE	106	354	21	80	14	0	3	27	26	0	.226	.279	.291
1992	Cincinnati	12	25	2	9	1	0	0	3	10	0	.360	.429	.400

NIGEL WILSON
Toronto Blue Jays
Outfield Prospect
$12

Yet another power hitter from the Blue Jays' outfielder factory, can run and throw and everything. A horrible strikeout/walk ratio will hinder his progress as a hitter, and that makes him a Grade B prospect, but he's only 23, and might hit now better than Maldonado. Will battle with Derek Bell and Juan Delarosa for playing time in the Blue Jays outfield of the future.

YEAR	TEAM/LEVEL	G	AB	R	H	2B	3B	HR	RBI	BB	SB	AVG	OBP	SLG
1991	Dunedin A	119	455	64	137	18	13	12	55	29	26	.301	.350	.477
1992	Knoxville AA	137	521	85	143	34	7	26	69	33	13	.274	.325	.516
1992	MLE	137	514	76	136	32	5	25	61	25	9	.265	.299	.492

WILLIE WILSON
Oakland Athletics
Center Fielder
$16

Essentially the same player that he was five or six years ago, except that he walks more and isn't such a pain in the ass. Still extremely fast, no arm. Had problems when asked to be a role player in Kansas City, but has apparently adapted well in Oakland . . . career was irreparably damaged by a hitting coach who tried to convert him from Pete Rose to Mickey Mantle.

YEAR	TEAM/LEVEL	G	AB	R	H	2B	3B	HR	RBI	BB	SB	AVG	OBP	SLG
1991	Oakland	113	294	38	70	14	4	0	28	18	20	.238	.290	.313
1992	Oakland	132	396	38	107	15	5	0	37	35	28	.270	.329	.333
1993	Projected	109	290	35	75	14	5	1	32	25	18	.259	.317	.352

DAVE WINFIELD
Toronto Blue Jays
Designated Hitter
$39

The best DH in the league, and one of the best hitters in the league, at age 40. As long as a player is in good shape *and is not in a decline phase*, I wouldn't be unduly concerned about what year he was born. The *chance* of a sudden drop in performance is certainly greater at 41 than it is at 31, but he might drive in 120.

YEAR	TEAM/LEVEL	G	AB	R	H	2B	3B	HR	RBI	BB	SB	AVG	OBP	SLG
1991	California	150	568	75	149	27	4	28	86	56	7	.262	.326	.472
1992	Toronto	156	583	92	169	33	3	26	108	82	2	.290	.377	.491
1993	Projected	145	544	69	137	24	3	18	78	65	3	.252	.332	.406

HERM WINNINGHAM
Boston Red Sox
Outfielder
$3

He was a good reserve outfielder in Cincinnati, but was just terrible last year, and even with expansion may have trouble finding a job. He may fool us, but from what you can tell he appears to have genuinely lost what little offensive ability he did have, as opposed to having merely suffered an off year. Not a good outfielder, no longer a successful base stealer.

YEAR	TEAM/LEVEL	G	AB	R	H	2B	3B	HR	RBI	BB	SB	AVG	OBP	SLG
1991	Cincinnati	98	169	17	38	6	1	1	4	11	4	.225	.272	.290
1992	Boston	105	234	27	55	8	1	1	14	10	6	.235	.266	.291
1993	Projected	70	116	13	27	5	1	1	7	7	7	.233	.276	.319

TED WOOD
San Francisco Giants
Outfielder
$7

Looks like the new Pat Sheridan. Left-handed hitting outfielder, gap hitter, so a move to Florida could help him some. Has OK strike zone judgment and is regarded as a fine outfielder, good range and a strong arm. Was a second-round draft pick in 1988, and a member of the Olympic team that summer. Grade C prospect, probably won't hit enough to be a regular.

YEAR	TEAM/LEVEL	G	AB	R	H	2B	3B	HR	RBI	BB	SB	AVG	OBP	SLG
1992	Phoenix AAA	110	418	70	127	24	7	7	63	48	9	.304	.377	.445
1992	MLE	110	390	46	99	19	3	4	41	30	5	.254	.307	.349
1992	San Francisco	24	58	5	12	2	0	1	3	6	0	.207	.292	.293

TRACY WOODSON
St. Louis Cardinals
Third Baseman
$13

Thirty-year-old minor league veteran, was having a good year at Louisville and got called up when Zeile was sent down. He continued to hit the ball in the major leagues, which may give him a corner on a career. Was the Dodgers' third-base prospect at one time, showed OK bat but nothing special, and dropped out of the picture after failing major league trials.

YEAR	TEAM/LEVEL	G	AB	R	H	2B	3B	HR	RBI	BB	SB	AVG	OBP	SLG
1992	Louisville AAA	109	412	62	122	23	2	12	59	24	4	.296	.335	.449
1992	MLE	109	393	46	103	19	1	9	44	18	2	.262	.294	.384
1992	St. Louis	31	114	9	35	8	0	1	22	3	0	.307	.331	.404

CRAIG WORTHINGTON
Cleveland Indians
Third Baseman
$2

A Rookie of the Year candidate in 1989, but put on weight, didn't hustle, and fumbled the job away. He had an indifferent year for Colorado Springs in '92, played nine games with the Indians in May but didn't hold the job then, either. His defense was good in '89, even outstanding, but he's very slow, almost too slow to play third. Only 28; can't be entirely written off.

YEAR	TEAM/LEVEL	G	AB	R	H	2B	3B	HR	RBI	BB	SB	AVG	OBP	SLG
1990	Baltimore	133	425	46	96	17	0	8	44	63	1	.226	.328	.322
1991	Baltimore	31	102	11	23	3	0	4	12	12	0	.225	.313	.373
1992	Colorado Sp AAA	90	319	47	94	25	0	6	57	33	0	.295	.365	.429

RICK WRONA
Cincinnati Reds
Catcher
$1

A 29-year-old catcher, got some playing time with the Cubs in 1989 due to Berryhill's injury but failed to hold a job and has bounced around since. Undisciplined hitter without power, lifetime .232 hitter in the minor leagues. Doesn't throw well; has injury history, has been released a couple of times. Help me out here; I'm looking for the good parts . . .

YEAR	TEAM/LEVEL	G	AB	R	H	2B	3B	HR	RBI	BB	SB	AVG	OBP	SLG
1991	Tulsa AA	27	82	4	13	0	1	3	7	5	0	.159	.207	.293
1992	Nashville AAA	40	118	16	29	8	2	2	10	5	1	.246	.282	.398
1992	Cincinnati	11	23	0	4	0	0	0	0	0	0	.174	.174	.174

ERIC YELDING
Chicago White Sox
Outfielder
$1

An outfielder/shortstop, originally a first-round draft pick of the Toronto Blue Jays, best remembered for his years with the Houston Astros. As a shortstop, he's pretty much Jose Offerman, while as a hitter, he isn't. Doesn't hit well enough to play in the outfield and can't really play short. Was traded from Houston to White Sox in July and spent remainder of season in Vancouver.

YEAR	TEAM/LEVEL	G	AB	R	H	2B	3B	HR	RBI	BB	SB	AVG	OBP	SLG
1991	Houston	78	276	19	67	11	1	1	20	13	11	.243	.276	.301
1992	Vancouver AAA	93	338	47	89	11	5	0	29	26	32	.263	.313	.325
1992	Cincinnati	93	323	34	74	8	2	0	20	19	21	.229	.272	.266

DMITRI YOUNG
St. Louis Cardinals
Third Baseman (Not)
$37

The fourth player taken in the 1991 draft, had impressive year in the Midwest League at age 18 and is probably the second-best hitting prospect in the minors (behind Delgado). Powerfully built, along the lines of Pedro Guerrero, Don Baylor, or Kevin Mitchell; weight could be a problem. Made 42 errors at third; showed incredible ability to screw up a rundown. Will have to move. **Grade A prospect.**

YEAR	TEAM/LEVEL	G	AB	R	H	2B	3B	HR	RBI	BB	SB	AVG	OBP	SLG
1990	(Rio Mesa High School, Oxnard, California)													
1991	Johnson City R	37	129	22	33	10	2	2	22	21	2	.256	.364	.380
1992	Springfield A	135	493	74	153	36	6	14	72	51	14	.310	.378	.493

ERIC YOUNG
Los Angeles Dodgers
Second Base Prospect

A very fast second baseman, turned 26 last November. Got called up in late July after hitting .340 in Albuquerque, took over as the starter in August, and has a good chance of opening the season as the regular second baseman. Young's minor league batting record looks like a right-handed Brett Butler, although not quite as good. Good range at second but makes a lot of errors.

$19

YEAR	TEAM/LEVEL	G	AB	R	H	2B	3B	HR	RBI	BB	SB	AVG	OBP	SLG
1992	Albuquerque AAA	94	350	61	118	16	5	3	49	33	28	.337	.393	.437
1992	MLE	94	321	37	89	11	2	1	29	20	17	.277	.320	.333
1992	Los Angeles	49	132	9	34	1	0	1	11	8	6	.258	.300	.288

GERALD YOUNG
Colorado Rockies
Outfielder
$3

Continues to get chances by hitting over .300 when he gets demoted to Tucson. He hit .321 in 1987 (274 at bats), then stole 65 bases in 1988, but it's been all downhill from there. His major league batting average since then is .218. Young draws some walks and is a brilliant center fielder, so if he could just keep his average around .250 he would have a job.

YEAR	TEAM/LEVEL	G	AB	R	H	2B	3B	HR	RBI	BB	SB	AVG	OBP	SLG
1990	Houston	57	154	15	27	4	1	1	4	20	6	.175	.269	.234
1991	Houston	108	142	26	31	3	1	1	11	24	16	.218	.327	.275
1992	Houston	74	76	14	14	1	1	0	4	10	6	.184	.279	.224

KEVIN YOUNG
Pittsburgh Pirates
Third Base Prospect
$19

Young is still young, 23. At three minor league levels over the last two seasons he has hit .322 with a good number of doubles. His defense at third is a question. The trade of Buechele opened up third base, while the expected loss of Bonds may open up a spot in the outfield. He is a major league hitter and will play somewhere. Grade B prospect.

YEAR	TEAM/LEVEL	G	AB	R	H	2B	3B	HR	RBI	BB	SB	AVG	OBP	SLG
1991	Carolina AA	75	263	36	90	19	6	3	33	15	9	.342	.394	.494
1992	Buffalo AAA	137	490	91	154	29	6	8	65	67	18	.314	.406	.447
1992	MLE	137	467	70	131	25	4	5	50	51	12	.281	.351	.383

ROBIN YOUNT
Milwaukee Brewers
Center Fielder
$24

Yount still has more hits than Pete Rose had at the same age. Yount got to 3000 just before his 37th birthday; Rose, just after . . . of the 18 3000-hit men, the only two younger than Yount were Cobb (34) and Aaron . . . eight of the 18 hit .300 or better in the year of their 3000th hit, the best being .389 by both Cobb and Speaker.

YEAR	TEAM/LEVEL	G	AB	R	H	2B	3B	HR	RBI	BB	SB	AVG	OBP	SLG
1991	Milwaukee	130	503	66	131	20	4	10	77	54	6	.260	.332	.376
1992	Milwaukee	150	557	71	147	40	3	8	77	53	15	.264	.325	.390
1993	Projected	135	504	69	127	27	4	9	70	58	10	.252	.329	.375

EDDIE ZAMBRANO
Pittsburgh Pirates
Outfielder
$3

Zambrano is a 27-year-old outfielder from Venezuela, never hit until signing with the Pirates in 1991 as a six-year free agent. Since then, in what amounts to a full season at Buffalo (538 at bats) he has hit .300 with 19 homers and 114 RBI. You'd think that would catch somebody's eye, but he didn't get a September callup from the Pirates. Grade D prospect.

YEAR	TEAM/LEVEL	G	AB	R	H	2B	3B	HR	RBI	BB	SB	AVG	OBP	SLG
1991	Minor AA/AAA	131	413	47	117	25	8	6	74	39	5	.283	.349	.426
1992	Buffalo AAA	126	394	47	112	22	4	16	79	51	3	.284	.368	.482
1992	MLE	126	377	36	95	19	2	11	61	39	2	.252	.322	.401

TODD ZEILE
St. Louis Cardinals
Third Baseman
$29

Demotion on August 10 came despite having hit .291 in June and .297 in July. His power and RBI numbers were much less than expected, and hitting coach Don Baylor was upset that Zeile didn't take extra BP. Anyway, he went to Louisville with a good attitude, hit the hell out of the ball, and returned in September with his power stroke back. Still looks good.

YEAR	TEAM/LEVEL	G	AB	R	H	2B	3B	HR	RBI	BB	SB	AVG	OBP	SLG
1991	St. Louis	155	565	76	158	36	3	11	81	62	17	.280	.353	.412
1992	St. Louis	126	439	52	113	18	4	7	48	68	7	.257	.352	.364
1993	Projected	142	498	64	130	27	2	13	63	68	9	.261	.350	.402

EDDIE ZOSKY
Toronto Blue Jays
Shortstop
$10

Dick Schofield, Spike Owen–type player. Last spring it was assumed that the shortstop job was Zosky's to lose, and he lost it. A .231 average for Syracuse followed, and his stock is way down. Manny Lee played surprisingly well, and that doesn't help him. Zosky is supposed to be a good defensive player, so the Blue Jays will find someone who is willing to give him a look.

YEAR	TEAM/LEVEL	G	AB	R	H	2B	3B	HR	RBI	BB	SB	AVG	OBP	SLG
1991	Syracuse AAA	119	511	69	135	18	4	6	39	35	9	.264	.315	.350
1992	Syracuse AAA	96	342	31	79	11	6	4	38	19	3	.231	.270	.333
1992	MLE	96	330	23	67	9	3	3	28	14	2	.203	.235	.276

BOB ZUPCIC
Boston Red Sox
Outfielder
$16

Hit .328 with three home runs before the break, .247 with no homers after. He's got a little more power than he has shown, but the .247 average is much closer to his ability than the .328. Forced into the lineup by the losses of Greenwell and Burks and the poor play of Vaughn and Plantier, he is better defensively than you would expect from a guy named Zupcic.

YEAR	TEAM/LEVEL	G	AB	R	H	2B	3B	HR	RBI	BB	SB	AVG	OBP	SLG
1991	Pawtucket AAA	129	429	70	103	27	1	18	70	55	10	.240	.323	.434
1992	Boston	124	392	46	108	19	1	3	43	25	2	.276	.322	.352
1993	Projected	107	335	36	83	18	0	5	35	26	4	.248	.302	.346

Pitchers

JIM ABBOTT
California Angels
Starting Pitcher
$62

I like him more than ever now, and despite his 1992 won–lost mark he's closer than ever to breaking into the superstar class. The two best things that can happen for a pitcher are a strikeout and a ground ball, and Abbott is one of the few pitchers who gets both, plus he has learned to pitch up in the strike zone on artificial turf.

YEAR	TEAM/LEVEL	G	IP	W–L	PCT.	HITS	SO	BB	ERA
1990	California	33	212	10–14	.417	246	105	72	4.51
1991	California	34	243	18–11	.621	222	158	73	2.89
1992	California	29	211	7–15	.318	208	130	68	2.77

KYLE ABBOTT
Philadelphia Phillies
Starting Pitcher
$16

The two unluckiest starting pitchers in the majors last year were probably both named Abbott, Jim and Kyle. Kyle is a decent pitcher, but when your luck runs bad long enough you inevitably start trying to be perfect, and that's death for a pitcher. It will be a challenge for him to get his 0–11 start in '92 out of his head.

YEAR	TEAM/LEVEL	G	IP	W–L	PCT.	HITS	SO	BB	ERA
1991	Edmonton AAA	27	180	14–10	.583	173	120	46	3.99
1991	California	5	20	1–2	.333	22	12	13	4.58
1992	Philadelphia	31	133	1–14	.067	147	88	45	5.13

PAUL ABBOTT
Minnesota Twins
Pitching Prospect
$3

Right-hander, has major league stuff highlighted by exceptional changeup. In the last two years he has walked 56 men in 83 innings at Portland, plus he injured himself horsing around in spring training last year, so it's hard to find real evidence of his maturity. I think he may very well be a good pitcher eventually, but "eventually" may be several years away.

YEAR	TEAM/LEVEL	G	IP	W–L	SAVES	HITS	SO	BB	ERA
1991	Minnesota	15	47	3–1	0	38	43	36	4.75
1992	Portland AAA	7	46	4–1	0	30	46	31	2.33
1992	Minnesota	6	11	0–0	0	12	13	5	3.27

JIM ACKER
Seattle Mariners
Relief Pitcher
$1

Cut by Seattle after two bad years, but his career may not be over. He throws a hard sinker, a pitch that's not fundamentally different from a soft sinker, and might be able to adjust, like Bob Locker did with the same pitch, to regain his effectiveness. He couldn't get the innings he needed to stay sharp; expansion might get him another opportunity.

YEAR	TEAM/LEVEL	G	IP	W–L	SAVES	HITS	SO	BB	ERA
1990	Toronto	59	92	4–4	1	103	54	30	3.83
1991	Toronto	54	88	3–5	1	77	44	36	5.20
1992	Seattle	17	31	0–0	0	45	11	12	5.28

JUAN AGOSTO
Seattle Mariners
(Released)
Left-Handed Spot Reliever
$1

One of the hardest-working relievers in the game for several years, he slid out of the majors last summer after allowing a batting average around .350 to left-handed hitters, the men he is expected to get out. The batting average against him with men in scoring position was .397, which will tend to shorten your career. Don't see anything about him to like.

YEAR	TEAM/LEVEL	G	IP	W–L	SAVES	HITS	SO	BB	ERA
1990	Houston	82	92	9–8	4	91	50	39	4.29
1991	St. Louis	72	86	5–3	2	92	34	39	4.81
1992	Two Teams	39	50	2–4	0	66	25	12	6.12

RICK AGUILERA
Minnesota Twins
Closer
$55

Started poorly but finished strong, putting his numbers in their usual range. In the next five years the policy of designating a closer and giving him all the save situations may break up, but as long as Aguilera is designated a closer his numbers will have the appearance of great value, and his grip on the closer's role is very strong. He's a fine pitcher.

YEAR	TEAM/LEVEL	G	IP	W–L	SAVES	HITS	SO	BB	ERA
1990	Minnesota	56	65	5–3	32	55	61	19	2.76
1991	Minnesota	63	69	4–5	42	44	61	30	2.35
1992	Minnesota	64	67	2–6	41	60	52	17	2.84

SCOTT ALDRED
Detroit Tigers
Pitching Suspect
$2

A 16th-round selection in the 1987 draft, Aldred pitched fairly well in the low minors, after which the Tigers inexplicably decided that he was an outstanding prospect. They've been trying to force him to be a major league pitcher ever since, but in the last three years he's gone 18–29 for Toledo and has shown absolutely nothing in 137 innings at the major league level.

YEAR	TEAM/LEVEL	G	IP	W–L	PCT.	HITS	SO	BB	ERA
1991	Detroit	11	57	2–4	.333	58	35	30	5.18
1992	Toledo AAA	16	86	4–6	.400	92	81	47	5.13
1992	Detroit	16	65	3–8	.273	80	34	33	6.78

GERALD ALEXANDER
Texas Rangers
Relief Pitcher
$4

No fastball, changes speeds well and throws strikes, looks like he deceives hitters by changing his arm angle on the curve. Received some ink after going 19–3 at two minor league levels in 1990. He will have several major league trials over the next few years and will pitch well at times, but probably will never break into the top echelons.

YEAR	TEAM/LEVEL	G	IP	W–L	SAVES	HITS	SO	BB	ERA
1991	Texas	30	89	5–3	0	14	50	48	5.24
1991	Oklhoma City AAA	38	106	7–5	2	100	93	36	4.50
1992	Texas	3	2	1–0	0	5	1	1	27.00

DANA ALLISON
Oakland Athletics
Relief Pitcher
$4

Didn't pitch in the majors last year after bombing in 11 games in '91. A 26-year-old left-hander, has pitched brilliantly at the Double-A level and below, including '92, but has yet to pitch *well* at Triple-A or passably in the majors. I expect him to get another shot this year, and wouldn't be shocked if his performance improved. Grade D prospect.

YEAR	TEAM/LEVEL	G	IP	W–L	SAVES	HITS	SO	BB	ERA
1991	Oakland	11	11	1–1	0	16	4	5	7.36
1992	Huntsville AA	22	61	4–1	1	51	40	5	2.93
1992	Tacoma AAA	19	45	2–3	0	63	17	17	4.84

TAVO ALVAREZ
Montreal Expos
Starting Pitcher
$21

A Mexican Bret Saberhagen, born knowing how to pitch. Is 21 years old, has exceptional control, 90–92 MPH fastball, changes speeds well, and learns quickly. Has minor league record of 34–17 with 2.49 ERA in 61 starts. Has pitched too many innings at a very young age, and so must be considered a candidate for arm trouble, but otherwise looks fantastic. **Grade A prospect.**

YEAR	TEAM/LEVEL	G	IP	W–L	PCT.	HITS	SO	BB	ERA
1991	Sumter A	25	153	12–10	.545	152	158	58	3.24
1992	West Palm Beach A	19	139	13–4	.765	124	83	24	1.49
1992	Harrisburg AA	7	47	4–1	.800	48	42	9	2.85

WILSON ALVAREZ
Chicago White Sox
Pitcher
$16

Still has tremendous ability; 1992 was a lost season for him when he opened the year in the bullpen, lost his control in May, and never was able to regain it. My experience is that when a young pitcher's control deserts him, as happened to Melido Perez a few years ago, it can take several years for him to get it back.

YEAR	TEAM/LEVEL	G	IP	W–L	PCT.	HITS	SO	BB	ERA
1991	Birmingham AA	23	152	10–6	.625	109	165	74	1.83
1991	Chicago	10	56	3–2	.600	47	32	29	3.51
1992	Chicago	34	100	5–3	.625	103	66	65	5.20

LARRY ANDERSEN
San Diego (Free Agent)
Relief Pitcher
$19

Opened the 1992 season trying to pitch with a sore right shoulder, couldn't get anybody out and went back on the DL in early May. His ERA after the All-Star break was 2.20 with 16 Ks and only 7 hits allowed, so despite his age (40 in May) I suspect he can still pitch . . . since 1989 has 0.43 ERA in September.

YEAR	TEAM/LEVEL	G	IP	W–L	SAVES	HITS	SO	BB	ERA
1990	Two Teams	65	96	5–2	7	79	93	27	1.79
1991	San Diego	38	47	3–4	13	39	40	13	2.30
1992	San Diego	34	35	1–1	2	26	35	8	3.34

KEVIN APPIER
Kansas City Royals
Starting Pitcher
$63

Was having Cy Young season until stopped by an inflammation of the rotator cuff. Injury isn't believed serious . . . I have never seen a player change so dramatically in appearance and delivery in a short period of time. When he came up he was almost skinny, kind of flopped around on the mound. Now he looks exactly like Goose Gossage in Gossage's prime. Hell of a pitcher.

YEAR	TEAM/LEVEL	G	IP	W–L	PCT.	HITS	SO	BB	ERA
1990	Kansas City	32	186	12–8	.600	179	127	54	2.76
1991	Kansas City	34	208	13–10	.565	205	158	61	3.42
1992	Kansas City	30	208	15–8	.652	167	150	68	2.46

TONY AQUINO
Kansas City Royals
Starting Pitcher
$18

Has lost weight and changed his name (he used to be called Luis) . . . throws strikes, gets hurt every summer. Some of his injuries are probably attributable to his managers' leaving him in the game when he was tired, but others seem random. Not a bad pitcher, not a good pitcher. No star potential, but a useful utility pitcher/ninth man on the staff.

YEAR	TEAM/LEVEL	G	IP	W–L	PCT.	HITS	SO	BB	ERA
1990	Kansas City	20	68	4–1	.800	59	28	27	3.16
1991	Kansas City	38	157	8–4	.667	152	80	47	3.44
1992	Kansas City	15	68	3–6	.333	81	11	20	4.52

JACK ARMSTRONG
Cleveland Indians
Starting Pitcher
$4

He's almost out of chances after pitching miserable ball for two and a half years . . . he may have a problem with his stretch move. He pitches extremely well with the bases empty but gets hammered with men on. Over four years the batting average against him is .237 with the bases empty, but .307 when there is a man on . . . will probably have to solve this problem in the minors.

YEAR	TEAM/LEVEL	G	IP	W–L	PCT.	HITS	SO	BB	ERA
1990	Cincinnati	29	166	12–9	.571	151	110	59	3.42
1991	Cincinnati	27	140	7–13	.350	158	93	54	5.48
1992	Cleveland	35	167	6–15	.286	176	114	67	4.64

BRAD ARNSBERG
Chicago Cubs
Relief Pitcher
No Value

A one-time prospect in the Yankee system, he pitched well for Texas in 1990 (6–1, 2.15 ERA) but couldn't get anybody out with Texas in '91 or Cleveland in '92, then posted 0–8 record, 6.51 ERA for the Iowa Cubs. Stuff was never good; if he shows up in the majors next year you should just assume somebody is desperate for pitching.

YEAR	TEAM/LEVEL	G	IP	W–L	SAVES	HITS	SO	BB	ERA
1991	Texas	9	10	0–1	0	10	8	5	8.38
1992	Cleveland	8	11	0–0	0	13	5	11	11.81
1992	Iowa AAA	20	75	0–8	1	95	33	27	6.51

RENE AROCHA
St. Louis Cardinals
Starting Pitcher
$31

One of the leading candidates for NL Rookie of the Year in 1993. A 26-year-old right-hander, he defected from the Cuban national team when they were playing in the States in the summer of 1991 and pitched impressively for Louisville last summer. He has outstanding ability, polished by more experience than the typical rookie. Rated by *Baseball America* the third best prospect in the American Association.

YEAR	TEAM/LEVEL	G	IP	W–L	PCT.	HITS	SO	BB	ERA
1990	(Not in Organized Baseball)								
1991	(Not in Organized Baseball)								
1992	Louisville AAA	25	167	12–7	.632	145	128	67	2.70

ANDY ASHBY
Philadelphia Phillies
Starting Pitcher
$5

A Phillies' prospect in the noble tradition of Jason Grimsley and Bruce Ruffin. He's a big guy with good movement on his fastball, but he's been in the minors for parts of seven seasons with a lifetime won–lost mark of 39–51. The record hasn't shown any dramatic improvement in recent years. I'm sure he'd pitch better with a better team behind him.

YEAR	TEAM/LEVEL	G	IP	W–L	PCT.	HITS	SO	BB	ERA
1991	Philadelphia	8	42	1–5	.167	41	26	19	6.00
1992	Scranton AAA	7	33	0–3	.000	23	18	14	3.00
1992	Philadelphia	10	37	1–3	.250	42	24	21	7.54

PAUL ASSENMACHER
Chicago Cubs
Relief Pitcher
$25

I've always regarded him as one of the Rodney Dangerfields of baseball, a good pitcher who never got a key job and the respect that goes with it. However, he did not pitch well the second half of the '92 season, and I would be a little concerned about him in '93 . . . will be in the majors at least as a role player for several more years.

YEAR	TEAM/LEVEL	G	IP	W–L	SAVES	HITS	SO	BB	ERA
1990	Chicago	74	103	7–2	10	90	95	36	2.80
1991	Chicago	75	103	7–8	15	85	117	31	3.24
1992	Chicago	70	68	4–4	8	72	67	26	4.10

PEDRO ASTACIO
Los Angeles Dodgers
Starting Pitcher
$32

Right-hander, was an emergency callup in July and pitched far better in the majors than he ever had in the minors. Excellent sinker and good control, but started last year with a dead arm, pitching long relief for Albuquerque. Runs to the mound, pumps the air after strikeouts; ML success was attributed to feeding off the excitement of major league crowds.

YEAR	TEAM/LEVEL	G	IP	W–L	PCT.	HITS	SO	BB	ERA
1991	San Antonio AA	19	113	4–11	.267	142	62	39	4.78
1992	Albuquerque AAA	24	99	6–6	.500	115	66	44	5.47
1992	Los Angeles	11	82	5–5	.500	80	43	20	1.98

JIM AUSTIN
Milwaukee Brewers

Relief Pitcher

$22

Is 29 years old, made the Show after outstanding seasons at El Paso and Denver . . . pitches up in the strike zone, throws all fly balls, and jams the hitters. I doubt that he'll ever have a 1.85 ERA again and I don't expect to see him as a closer, but don't see any reason he wouldn't remain effective as a middle-inning reliever.

YEAR	TEAM/LEVEL	G	IP	W–L	PCT.	HITS	SO	BB	ERA
1991	Denver AAA	20	44	6–3	3	35	37	24	2.45
1991	Milwaukee	5	9	0–0	0	8	3	11	8.31
1992	Milwaukee	47	58	5–2	0	38	30	32	1.85

STEVE AVERY
Atlanta Braves

Starting Pitcher

$63

Pitched brilliantly in '92, but the Braves didn't score many runs for him and stuck him with 11–11 won–lost log . . . ground ball pitcher, like many such has consistent record of pitching badly on artificial turf (4.98 career ERA) . . . needs a lot of work on holding runners . . . didn't pitch well in August/September last year, but I doubt that there is a problem.

YEAR	TEAM/LEVEL	G	IP	W–L	PCT.	HITS	SO	BB	ERA
1990	Atlanta	21	99	3–11	.214	121	75	45	5.64
1991	Atlanta	35	210	18–8	.692	189	137	65	3.38
1992	Atlanta	35	234	11–11	.500	216	129	71	3.20

BOBBY AYALA
Cincinnati Reds

Pitcher

$11

Right-handed pitcher, was signed as an undrafted free agent in 1988 and established himself as a prospect by pitching brilliantly in the low minors in 1990. Wasted 1991, but had fine season at Chattanooga (Double-A) in '92. Good fastball, good size, pretty good control. Good strikeout/walk ratio. Grade B prospect; will probably start the season in the minor leagues.

YEAR	TEAM/LEVEL	G	IP	W–L	PCT.	HITS	SO	BB	ERA
1991	Chattanooga AA	39	91	3–1	.750	79	92	58	4.67
1992	Chattanooga AA	27	170	12–6	.667	152	154	58	3.54
1992	Cincinnati	5	29	2–1	.667	33	23	13	4.34

BOB AYRAULT
Philadelphia Phillies

Right-Handed Relief Pitcher

$14

Anonymous 27-year-old middle reliever, never a hot prospect. He was drafted by the Reds, Padres, and Pirates but didn't sign, signed with an independant team and was purchased by Phillies. Minor league strikeout rates very good, about one per inning, with decent control . . . limited right-handed batters to .162 batting average. No star potential but expect him to hang in the league for several years.

YEAR	TEAM/LEVEL	G	IP	W–L	SAVES	HITS	SO	BB	ERA
1991	Scranton AAA	68	99	8–5	3	91	103	47	4.83
1992	Scranton AAA	20	25	5–1	6	19	30	15	4.97
1992	Philadelphia	30	43	2–2	0	32	27	17	3.12

BRETT BACKLUND
Pittsburgh Pirates
Right–Handed Starting Pitcher
$21

Fifth-round 1992 draft pick, held out before signing and then vaulted to Triple-A in five weeks by dominating lower levels. University of Iowa product, regarded as intelligent, self-confident, and can throw four pitches for strikes. **Grade A prospect**; will battle with Neagle and others for space in the Pirate rotation, but Leyland probably won't rush him.

YEAR	TEAM/LEVEL	G	IP	W–L	PCT.	HITS	SO	BB	ERA
1992	Augusta A	5	25	3–0	1.000	10	31	4	0.36
1992	Carolina AA	3	19	1–1	.500	11	17	3	1.89
1992	Buffalo AAA	4	25	3–0	1.000	15	9	11	2.16

SCOTT BAILES
California Angels
(Released)
Relief Pitcher
$1

I frankly don't understand what the hell he is doing in the majors. The batting average against him was .351 overall, .375 with men in scoring position and .448 facing his first batter. He's never had a good season, never even had a decent season. I don't see any reason he would be in the majors in '93, but I would have said the same thing four years ago.

YEAR	TEAM/LEVEL	G	IP	W–L	SAVES	HITS	SO	BB	ERA
1990	California	27	35	2–0	0	46	16	20	6.37
1991	California	42	52	1–2	0	41	41	22	4.18
1992	California	32	39	3–1	0	59	25	28	7.45

JEFF BALLARD
St. Louis Cardinals
Starting Pitcher
$3

The left-hander, you will remember, who won 18 for the Orioles in '89, then got shelled in '90 and '91. He pitched last year for Louisville and pitched extremely well. He'll probably be back in the majors in '93, and I would not be surprised to see him ring up a solid season. He'll be better off now that people have forgotten about stardom for him.

YEAR	TEAM/LEVEL	G	IP	W–L	PCT.	HITS	SO	BB	ERA
1990	Baltimore	44	133	2–11	.154	152	50	42	4.93
1991	Baltimore	26	124	6–12	.333	153	37	28	5.60
1992	Rochester	24	161	12–8	.600	164	76	34	2.52

JAY BALLER
Philadelphia Phillies
Relief Pitcher
$4

Pitched sensationally for Scranton last summer (1.48 ERA, 66/24 strikeout/walk ratio in 61 innings). This earned him another major league trial, where he continued to pitch like a right-handed Scott Bailes. Now 32 years old; the odds are against his getting another good shot, but his performance at Scranton wasn't luck. If he continues to pitch like that . . .

YEAR	TEAM/LEVEL	G	IP	W–L	SAVES	HITS	SO	BB	ERA
1991	Scranton AAA	61	72	4–4	17	84	79	33	4.98
1992	Scranton AAA	41	61	4–5	20	47	66	24	1.48
1992	Philadelphia	8	11	0–0	0	10	9	10	8.18

SCOTT BANKHEAD
Cincinnati Reds
Relief Pitcher
$23

Small right-hander with a big curve, has always pitched well when healthy. Piniella spotted him a few batters at a time and he made it through the season healthy for the first time since 1989. I expect him to continue to pitch well for several years unless he is overexposed, and as time passes he may be able to carry a heavier load.

YEAR	TEAM/LEVEL	G	IP	W–L	SAVES	HITS	SO	BB	ERA
1990	Seattle	4	13	0–2	0	18	10	7	11.08
1991	Seattle	17	61	3–6	0	73	28	21	4.90
1992	Cincinnati	54	71	10–4	1	57	53	29	2.93

WILLIE BANKS
Minnesota Twins
Starting Pitcher
$6

Perpetual prospect, a number-one draft pick with a great fastball who has thrown some no-hitters in the minor leagues. His control is wobbly, so he's been a sub-.500 pitcher in the minors until last year, when he went 6–1 with a 1.92 ERA at Portland, was called up to help Tom Kelly fulfill his death wish. I regard him as a poor man's Bobby Witt.

YEAR	TEAM/LEVEL	G	IP	W–L	PCT.	HITS	SO	BB	ERA
1991	Portland AAA	25	146	9–8	.529	156	63	76	4.55
1992	Portland AAA	11	75	6–1	.857	62	41	34	1.92
1992	Minnesota	16	71	4–4	.500	80	37	37	5.70

FLOYD BANNISTER
Unemployed
Relief Pitcher
No Value

The very definition of a washed-up veteran, came back from the Land of the Rising Cameras to pitch 36 games for Texas before they realized he wasn't getting any outs. He was released in August, and I wouldn't expect him to get another contract, but you never know. He was a fine pitcher in his day, and people like him.

YEAR	TEAM/LEVEL	G	IP	W–L	SAVES	HITS	SO	BB	ERA
1990	Yakult Japan	9	49	3–2	0	52	31	22	4.04
1991	California	16	25	0–0	0	25	16	10	3.96
1992	Texas	36	37	1–1	0	39	30	21	6.32

BRIAN BARNES
Montreal Expos
Starting Pitcher
$27

Small left-hander, doesn't have good fastball but hides the ball extremely well, changes speeds exceptionally well and has two or three breaking pitches. I love the kid. I think once he gets into a rhythm in the majors he could be a consistent 15- to 17-game winner, strike out 150+ men a year. I'd compare him to Bud Black or Tom Browning.

YEAR	TEAM/LEVEL	G	IP	W–L	PCT.	HITS	SO	BB	ERA
1990	Montreal	4	28	1–1	.500	25	23	7	2.89
1991	Montreal	28	160	5–8	.385	135	117	84	4.22
1992	Montreal	21	100	6–6	.500	77	65	46	2.97

SHAWN BARTON
Seattle Mariners
Relief Pitcher
$1

Neither a pitcher nor a prospect. He's a 29-year-old left-hander, released by the Mets system and invited to camp by the Mariners, pushed into a major league shot despite 4.25 ERA at Calgary because the M's were desperate . . . went to the same high school as Roger Salkeld, although he had moved on before Salkeld got there.

YEAR	TEAM/LEVEL	G	IP	W–L	SAVES	HITS	SO	BB	ERA
1991	Calgary AAA	17	31	2–0	1	25	22	8	2.61
1992	Calgary AAA	30	53	3–5	4	57	31	24	4.25
1992	Seattle	14	12	0–1	0	10	4	7	2.92

MIGUEL BATISTA
Montreal Expos
Starting Pitcher
$1

The Pirates took him last year in the Rule 5 draft, and when they released Bill Landrum used Batista to explain that, saying that they were going to keep Batista and didn't have room for both. He was returned to the Expos on April 23; is said to be smart, likable kid with 90+ fastball, but is probably three years away from being ready to pitch in the majors.

YEAR	TEAM/LEVEL	G	IP	W–L	PCT.	HITS	SO	BB	ERA
1991	Rockford A	23	134	11–5	.688	126	90	57	4.04
1992	Pittsburgh	1	2	0–0	.000	4	1	3	9.00
1992	West Palm Beach A	24	135	7–7	.500	130	92	54	3.79

ROD BECK
San Francisco Giants
Relief Pitcher
$41

If he keeps his weight down and if Roger Craig 1) gets fired, or 2) can resist the temptation to shuttle him back and forth to the starting rotation every couple of months, Beck should be the best relief pitcher in the National League over the next five years. Good fastball, good control, challenges the hitters, and pitches inside, getting popups and weak ground balls.

YEAR	TEAM/LEVEL	G	IP	W–L	SAVES	HITS	SO	BB	ERA
1991	Phoenix AAA	23	71	4–3	6	56	35	13	2.02
1991	San Francisco	31	52	1–1	1	53	38	13	3.78
1992	San Francisco	65	92	3–3	17	62	87	15	1.76

TIM BELCHER
Cincinnati Reds
Starting Pitcher
$38

His ERA jumped because there is a big, big difference between pitching in Dodger Stadium and pitching in Riverfront. His career ERA in Dodger Stadium as a home park was 2.47. He's healthy, a .500 pitcher or slightly better, should have several years left pitching at the current level, and is very capable of having an 18-win season . . . very, very tough for a right-handed batter.

YEAR	TEAM/LEVEL	G	IP	W–L	PCT.	HITS	SO	BB	ERA
1990	Los Angeles	24	153	9–9	.500	136	102	48	4.00
1991	Los Angeles	33	209	10–9	.526	189	156	75	2.62
1992	Cincinnati	35	228	15–14	.517	201	149	80	3.91

STAN BELINDA
Pittsburgh Pirates
Relief Ace, Sort Of
$31

Is racing toward the closer's role at a snail's pace, cutting his ERA a few points a year and picking up a few additional saves. A right-handed pitcher, but has a three-year record of being tougher on left-handed batters than right-handers. Almost two-thirds of the balls hit off him last year were hit in the air.

YEAR	TEAM/LEVEL	G	IP	W–L	SAVES	HITS	SO	BB	ERA
1990	Pittsburgh	55	58	3–4	8	48	55	29	3.55
1991	Pittsburgh	60	78	7–5	16	50	71	35	3.45
1992	Pittsburgh	59	71	6–4	18	58	57	29	3.15

ERIC BELL
Cleveland Indians
Relief Pitcher
$3

Minor league veteran, he went 4–0 with a 0.50 ERA in a 1991 callup, started last year in the majors, was ineffective, went to Colorado Springs and pitched well, posting a 10–7 record with good ERA. Changes speeds, excellent control. He has a .645 career winning pecentage in the minors and could pitch in the majors if he could get over the hump.

YEAR	TEAM/LEVEL	G	IP	W–L	SAVES	HITS	SO	BB	ERA
1991	Cleveland	10	18	4–0	0	5	7	5	0.50
1992	Cleveland	7	15	0–2	0	22	10	9	7.63
1992	Colorado Sp AAA	26	138	10–7	1	161	56	30	3.73

ANDY BENES
San Diego Padres
Starting Pitcher
$56

I still think he's just inches away from breaking through as a front-line star, but the batting average against him jumped last year to .264, and I can't really explain why that happened. Was hit very hard (.326 average) after 75 pitches. He finished the season strong, but that's been his pattern in the past. Frustrating, but basically an excellent pitcher with star potential.

YEAR	TEAM/LEVEL	G	IP	W–L	PCT.	HITS	SO	BB	ERA
1990	San Diego	32	192	10–11	.476	177	140	69	3.60
1991	San Diego	33	223	15–11	.577	194	167	59	3.03
1992	San Diego	34	231	13–14	.481	230	169	61	3.35

JUAN BERENGUER
Kansas City Royals
Relief Pitcher
$4

Berenguer has a huge platoon differential. Last year left-handed batters hit .341 against him, right-handers .188, and over four years the difference is more than a hundred points. This makes him potentially valuable even though age and obesity have destroyed his control. Still has a good fastball; would not be surprised to see him mount a small comeback at 38.

YEAR	TEAM/LEVEL	G	IP	W–L	SAVES	HITS	SO	BB	ERA
1990	Minnesota	51	100	8–5	0	85	77	58	3.41
1991	Atlanta	49	64	0–3	17	43	53	20	2.24
1992	Two Teams	47	78	4–5	1	77	45	36	5.42

MIKE BIELECKI
Atlanta Braves (Free Agent)
Starting Pitcher
$19

Was pitching outstanding ball last summer when stopped by a partially torn ligament in his right elbow. He's expected back at full strength, but he's a free agent, and probably won't re-sign with the Braves, where young pitchers swarm like gnats. At 33 he's a .500 pitcher, but he's a competent professional, a little underrated. Needs to be handled very carefully to avoid injuries.

YEAR	TEAM/LEVEL	G	IP	W–L	PCT.	HITS	SO	BB	ERA
1990	Chicago	36	168	8–11	.421	188	103	70	4.93
1991	Two Teams	41	174	13–11	.542	171	75	56	4.46
1992	Atlanta	19	81	2–4	.333	77	62	27	2.57

MIKE BIRKBECK
New York Mets
Relief Pitcher
$1

Earned a one-game trial with a 4–10 record at Tidewater, but he did have a great strikeout/walk ratio (101/31) . . . 32-year-old control pitcher, was in the majors in '88, when he went 10–8 with Milwaukee. He crashed after that, couldn't get anybody out for a couple of years, but apparently has made some progress getting his game back together. Probably no future.

YEAR	TEAM/LEVEL	G	IP	W–L	PCT.	HITS	SO	BB	ERA
1991	Canton AA	21	39	2–3	.400	39	40	18	3.89
1992	Tidewater AAA	21	117	4–10	.286	108	101	31	4.08
1992	New York	1	7	0–1	.000	12	2	3	9.00

BUD BLACK
San Francisco Giants
Starting Pitcher
$22

A quality starting pitcher and long underrated, but he has reached the fine edge where a control pitcher becomes a poor risk. He struck out 4.17 men per nine innings last year, at which level a pitcher can still be effective. If it drops below 4.00, which it will in a year or two, he will probably not be able to compete. Led NL in home runs allowed.

YEAR	TEAM/LEVEL	G	IP	W–L	PCT.	HITS	SO	BB	ERA
1990	Two Teams	32	207	13–11	.542	181	106	61	3.57
1991	San Francisco	34	214	12–16	.429	201	104	71	3.99
1992	San Francisco	28	177	10–12	.455	178	82	59	3.97

WILLIE BLAIR
Houston Astros
Pitcher
$18

Ended the season in the Astro rotation and pitching well, but still faces a struggle to establish himself as a rotation anchor. He's a control-type pitcher. His career batting average allowed with men on base was .332 before last year—and it went up last year to .342. He just didn't have as many men on last year. He's a gamble.

YEAR	TEAM/LEVEL	G	IP	W–L	PCT.	HITS	SO	BB	ERA
1990	Toronto	27	69	3–5	.375	66	43	28	4.06
1991	Cleveland	11	36	2–3	.400	58	13	10	6.75
1992	Houston	29	79	5–7	.417	74	48	25	4.00

BERT BLYLEVEN
California Angels

Starting Pitcher
$8

Now 42 years old, trying to come back from rotator cuff surgery in 1991, when he was a mere stripling of 40. You have to admire a guy who has rotator cuff surgery at 40 and won't quit, and he could have been worse. He was hit hard (opponents hit .285 against him with 17 homers in 526 at bats) but survived, sort of, because of his control.

YEAR	TEAM/LEVEL	G	IP	W–L	PCT.	HITS	SO	BB	ERA
1989	California	33	241	17–5	.773	225	131	44	2.73
1990	California	23	134	8–7	.533	163	69	25	5.24
1992	California	25	133	8–12	.400	150	70	29	4.74

MIKE BODDICKER
Kansas City Royals

Pitcher
$8

Had a wasted season. Hal McRae, who sometimes will give a pitcher about 107 chances, gave up on Boddicker after one bad start, buried him in the bullpen, and Boddicker could never get straightened out . . . has no fastball, pitches with spectacular changes of speed and arm angles. I'm not *predicting* he'll come back and win 14 again, but I wouldn't be surprised if he does.

YEAR	TEAM/LEVEL	G	IP	W–L	PCT.	HITS	SO	BB	ERA
1990	Boston	34	228	17–8	.680	225	143	69	3.36
1991	Kansas City	30	181	12–12	.500	188	79	59	4.08
1992	Kansas City	29	87	1–4	.200	92	47	37	4.98

JOE BOEVER
Houston Astros

Relief Pitcher
$19

Joined Doug Jones in the Astros' reconstructed bullpen. He tied for the major league lead in game appearances with 81, pitched very well. His stats were about the same as they were with Philadelphia in '91, except that he cut his home runs allowed from 10 to 3 . . . he failed as a closer, but he wasn't *bad* then, and has pitched well for several years in a row.

YEAR	TEAM/LEVEL	G	IP	W–L	SAVES	HITS	SO	BB	ERA
1990	Two Teams	67	88	3–6	14	77	75	51	3.36
1991	Philadelphia	68	98	3–5	0	90	89	54	3.84
1992	Houston	81	111	3–6	2	103	67	45	2.51

BRIAN BOHANON
Texas Rangers

Relief Pitcher
$7

He pitches like Sid Fernandez, except not as well—same peculiar sidearm delivery, similar stuff, same strategies. He just doesn't locate it as well as Sid does, or at least hasn't yet . . . has had constant injuries, highlighted by ulnar nerve transplant in June of '88. Has pitched fairly well in the minor leagues; suspect he would benefit by being in another organization.

YEAR	TEAM/LEVEL	G	IP	W–L	PCT.	HITS	SO	BB	ERA
1991	Texas	11	61	4–3	.571	66	34	23	4.84
1992	Oklahoma City AAA	9	56	4–2	.667	53	24	15	2.73
1992	Texas	18	46	1–1	.500	57	29	25	6.31

ROD BOLTON
Chicago White Sox
Starting Pitcher
$17

A 13th-round draft pick in 1990, has emerged as the top pitching prospect in the White Sox system. Right–hander, best pitch is a sinking fastball, average velocity, also throws a slider and circle change. Challenges the hitters, doesn't give out walks. Has 2.12 career ERA in the minor leagues (475 innings), with strikeout/walk ratio almost 3/1. Grade B prospect.

YEAR	TEAM/LEVEL	G	IP	W–L	PCT.	HITS	SO	BB	ERA
1990	Two Teams A	13	97	10–2	.833	61	95	23	1.23
1991	Minors—Two Levels	27	193	15–10	.600	154	134	44	1.78
1992	Vancouver AAA	27	187	11–9	.550	174	111	59	2.93

TOM BOLTON
Cincinnati Reds
Pitcher
$11

Isn't likely to beat a path to the starting rotation through Belcher, Rijo, and all those guys, but has a chance to re-establish himself as a left-handed spot reliever. Ground ball ratio is one of the highest in all of baseball, with 2.2 ground balls for each fly in '92. His career is basically going nowhere, but there is something about him that I like.

YEAR	TEAM/LEVEL	G	IP	W–L	PCT.	HITS	SO	BB	ERA
1990	Boston	21	120	10–5	.667	111	65	47	3.38
1991	Boston	25	110	8–9	.471	136	64	51	5.24
1992	Two Teams	37	75	4–5	.444	86	50	37	4.54

RICKY BONES
Milwaukee Brewers
Starting Pitcher
$16

Struck out only 3.6 men per nine innings, raising a question of whether he'll stick. Few people can with that kind of a K rate, but strikeouts normally go up for two years at the start of a career. His ERA was over 5.00 in May, June, and July, but somewhat saved his season by pitching better in late season. Gave up 27 homers in 163 innings.

YEAR	TEAM/LEVEL	G	IP	W–L	PCT.	HITS	SO	BB	ERA
1991	Las Vegas AAA	23	136	8–6	.571	155	95	43	4.22
1991	San Diego	11	54	4–6	.400	57	31	18	4.83
1992	Milwaukee	31	163	9–10	.474	169	65	48	4.57

PEDRO BORBON, JR.
Atlanta Braves
Relief Pitcher
$9

Was signed as free agent by the White Sox, pitched brilliantly for the Sarasota White Sox in '88, but was released anyway. He was a starting pitcher then, caught on with Atlanta and continued to kick ass and take names, but the Braves moved him to the bullpen anyway. Atlanta has lots of prospects, but there's nothing here that makes you think this man can't pitch. Grade B prospect.

YEAR	TEAM/LEVEL	G	IP	W–L	SAVES	HITS	SO	BB	ERA
1990	Two Teams A	25	159	15–8	0	146	113	39	3.00
1991	Durham AA	37	91	4–3	5	85	79	35	2.28
1992	Greenville AAA	39	94	8–2	3	73	79	42	3.06

CHRIS BOSIO
Milwaukee Brewers
Starting Pitcher
$42

I've always loved him because he had great strikeout/walk ratios, even when he was getting hit hard, and as you know that ratio is the first thing I look for in a pitcher. On the other hand, he's 30 years old and fat, and I'm wary of that combination. His K rate has dropped from 6.63 per nine innings in 1989 to 4.67 last year.

YEAR	TEAM/LEVEL	G	IP	W–L	PCT.	HITS	SO	BB	ERA
1990	Milwaukee	20	133	4–9	.308	131	76	38	4.00
1991	Milwaukee	32	205	14–10	.583	187	117	58	3.25
1992	Milwaukee	33	231	16–6	.727	223	120	44	3.62

SHAWN BOSKIE
Chicago Cubs
Pitcher
$5

The Cubs obviously see something to like about him, but I'm damned if I know what it is. He's a good athlete with good size and a decent curve, which puts him in a class with Renie Martin or Steve Mura, but his curve isn't a strikeout pitch and his fastball is taterbait. Left-handed batters hit .303 against him last year with a .538 slugging percentage.

YEAR	TEAM/LEVEL	G	IP	W–L	PCT.	HITS	SO	BB	ERA
1990	Chicago	15	98	5–6	.455	99	49	31	3.69
1991	Chicago	28	129	4–9	.308	150	62	52	5.23
1992	Chicago	23	92	5–11	.313	96	39	36	5.01

KENT BOTTENFIELD
Montreal Expos
Starting Pitcher
$4

A 24-year-old right-hander, has pitched more than a thousand innings in the minors, always pitching far better in his second year at each level (combining first years at A Ball, Double-A and Triple-A, he's 20–45 with a 4.58 ERA. His second years he is 34–26, 3.39.) This suggests to me that he's a better bet for '94 than for '93.

YEAR	TEAM/LEVEL	G	IP	W–L	PCT.	HITS	SO	BB	ERA
1990	Jacksonville AA	29	169	12–10	.545	158	121	67	3.41
1991	Indianapolis AAA	29	166	8–15	.348	155	108	61	4.06
1992	Indianapolis AAA	25	152	12–8	.600	139	111	58	3.43

DENIS BOUCHER
Cleveland Indians
Starting Pitcher
$4

Pitched well at Colorado Springs, re-establishing himself as a marginal prospect. He shot prematurely to the majors after going 7–0 with an 0.75 ERA in A Ball in 1990, got beaten up, and has been trying to re-establish momentum ever since. Crafty-type left-hander, no star potential but might be effective if he can ever get a little success to build on.

YEAR	TEAM/LEVEL	G	IP	W–L	PCT.	HITS	SO	BB	ERA
1991	Two Teams	12	58	1–7	.125	74	29	24	6.05
1992	Colorado Sp AAA	20	124	11–4	.733	119	40	30	3.48
1992	Cleveland	8	41	2–2	.500	48	17	20	6.37

RYAN BOWEN
Houston Astros
Starting Pitcher
$8

He made nine starts last year and got the holy hell beat out of him eight times, which may not be a record but it makes quite an average: Opponents hit .333 against him for the season, with a .576 slugging percentage. The scouting reports on him are outstanding. He is supposed to have a 90 MPH fastball and a crackling curve, but something isn't working.

YEAR	TEAM/LEVEL	G	IP	W–L	PCT.	HITS	SO	BB	ERA
1991	Houston	14	72	6–4	.600	73	49	36	5.15
1992	Tucson AAA	21	122	7–6	.538	128	94	64	4.12
1992	Houston	11	34	0–7	.000	48	22	30	10.96

CLIFF BRANTLEY
Philadelphia Phillies
Relief Pitcher
$3

Another in the tradition of Phillie pitching prospects (see Andy Ashby) who have arrived in the majors before achieving any sustained success in the minors. Brantley throws hard and is almost unhittable for a right-handed batter, but he's wilder than Uncle Herman's story about the date with the meter reader, and really doesn't have any business in the major leagues.

YEAR	TEAM/LEVEL	G	IP	W–L	PCT.	HITS	SO	BB	ERA
1991	Philadelphia	6	32	2–2	.500	26	25	19	3.41
1992	Scranton AAA	5	31	3–1	.750	19	26	14	1.76
1992	Philadelphia	28	76	2–6	.250	71	32	58	4.60

JEFF BRANTLEY
San Francisco Giants
Pitcher
$30

He lost the closer's job to Rod Beck and moved to the starting rotation in September. He's a fine, professional pitcher, as witness the fact that in four major league seasons even Roger Craig has been unable to screw him up or hurt his arm. He was a moderately successful starter in the minor leagues, and I suspect he can return successfully to that role.

YEAR	TEAM/LEVEL	G	IP	W–L	SAVES	HITS	SO	BB	ERA
1990	San Francisco	55	87	5–3	19	77	61	33	1.56
1991	San Francisco	67	95	5–2	15	78	81	52	2.45
1992	San Francisco	56	92	7–7	7	67	86	45	2.95

BRAD BRINK
Philadelphia Phillies
Starting Pitcher
$9

The Phillies first pick in 1986, out of USC; his career has been delayed by serious shoulder problems. The Phillies pride themselves on their patience with him, and, patience rewarded, he is now 28, and pitching by far the best ball of his career. Throws hard, throws strikes; looks good but it will be two years before we can assume his shoulder troubles are behind him.

YEAR	TEAM/LEVEL	G	IP	W–L	PCT.	HITS	SO	BB	ERA
1991	Minors—Two Levels	10	63	6–3	.667	53	53	14	2.56
1992	Minors—Two Levels	20	125	9–3	.750	114	104	37	3.46
1992	Philadelphia	8	41	0–4	.000	53	16	13	4.14

JOHN BRISCOE
Oakland Athletics
Starting Pitcher
$1

Ridiculous control record makes him basically no prospect; the A's started him twice in April when their starting rotation was hurt. Third-round draft pick in 1988, has good fastball and has pitched well on occasion, but he skipped Double-A almost entirely, and hasn't yet done anything of note in Triple-A. He wouldn't have been in the majors if the A's had any *real* pitching prospects.

YEAR	TEAM/LEVEL	G	IP	W–L	SAVES	HITS	SO	BB	ERA
1991	Tucson AAA	22	76	3–5	1	73	66	44	3.66
1991	Tucson AAA	33	78	2–5	0	78	66	68	5.88
1992	Oakland	2	7	0–1	0	12	4	9	6.43

DOUG BROCAIL
San Diego Padres
Starting Pitcher
$9

A 6-5, 220-pound right-hander, a former number-one pick who will be 26 years old in May. Has good fastball, change, and breaking pitch, but according to his pitching coach, Mike Roarke, needs to learn when to use them. Posted a 3.97 ERA at Las Vegas in '92, where the ball jumps and anything under 4.00 is good. Grade C prospect.

YEAR	TEAM/LEVEL	G	IP	W–L	PCT.	HITS	SO	BB	ERA
1991	Wichita AA	34	146	10–7	.588	147	108	43	3.87
1992	Las Vegas AAA	29	172	10–10	.500	187	103	63	3.97
1992	San Diego	3	14	0–0	.000	17	15	5	6.43

KEITH BROWN
Cincinnati Reds
Starting Pitcher
$2

Has been a prospect of some stripe since he had a big year at Cedar Rapids in 1987, then moved on to the majors (and pitched well) in late 1988. He had been moved to middle relief and slipped down the totem pole until returning to the rotation last year. He's 29, born on Valentine's Day, and nobody is a prospect at 29, but he deserves a better shot.

YEAR	TEAM/LEVEL	G	IP	W–L	PCT.	HITS	SO	BB	ERA
1990	Nashville AAA	39	94	7–8	.467	83	50	24	2.39
1991	Nashville AAA	47	62	2–5	.286	64	53	32	3.48
1992	Nashville AAA	26	150	12–9	.571	157	102	43	3.61

KEVIN D. BROWN
Seattle Mariners
Relief Pitcher
$1

Once a prospect in the Mets' system, has descended to the level of no prospect. Left-hander, still only 26 years old, but went 6–10 with 4.84 ERA at Calgary, walked more than he struck out. Calgary is a tough place to pitch, and his '92 stats may not be a fair assessment of his ability, but his career is clearly on the fade.

YEAR	TEAM/LEVEL	G	IP	W–L	PCT.	HITS	SO	BB	ERA
1991	Milwaukee	15	64	2–4	.333	66	30	34	5.51
1992	Calgary AAA	32	151	6–10	.375	163	49	64	4.84
1992	Seattle	2	3	0–0	.000	4	2	3	9.00

KEVIN BROWN
Texas Rangers
Starting Pitcher
$62

His strikeout rate shot up dramatically last year, from 4.1 per game to 5.9. This is not common, and it's hard to relate that to his well-publicized visits with a sports psychologist. He now is one of those special pitchers who get both ground balls and strikeouts. He faded in the second half, but since he always has I wouldn't interpret that as revealing anything.

YEAR	TEAM/LEVEL	G	IP	W–L	PCT.	HITS	SO	BB	ERA
1990	Texas	26	180	12–10	.545	175	88	60	3.60
1991	Texas	33	211	9–12	.429	233	96	90	4.40
1992	Texas	35	266	21–11	.656	262	173	76	3.32

TOM BROWNING
Cincinnati Reds
Starting Pitcher
$5

Season was ended June 1 by ruptured ligament in his knee. I've always seen him as a modern Johnny Podres, and Podres's career effectively ended at the same age. I doubt that he can come back, although it is possible. He hasn't pitched *well* for a couple of years. His strikeout rates have been low, and last year reached the unacceptable level of 3.4 per nine innings.

YEAR	TEAM/LEVEL	G	IP	W–L	PCT.	HITS	SO	BB	ERA
1990	Cincinnati	35	228	15–9	.625	235	99	52	3.80
1991	Cincinnati	36	230	14–14	.500	241	115	56	4.18
1992	Cincinnati	16	87	6–5	.545	108	33	28	5.07

JIM BULLINGER
Chicago Cubs
Relief Pitcher
$1

Bullinger was a minor league shortstop from 1986 to 1989, switched to the mound when he was overmatched by Double-A pitching. His fastball is below major league average, and his curve ball wouldn't bend the knees of Gumby. He changes speeds and nibbles, tries to use his defense, which would work sometimes in the minor leagues. Grade D prospect.

YEAR	TEAM/LEVEL	G	IP	W–L	SAVES	HITS	SO	BB	ERA
1991	Minors AA & AAA	28	189	12–13	0	179	158	84	3.99
1992	Iowa AAA	20	22	1–2	14	17	15	12	2.45
1992	Chicago	39	85	2–8	7	72	36	54	4.66

DAVE BURBA
San Francisco Giants
Starter/Reliever
$3

Part of the Seattle trade. He started the year in the Giants' rotation, but on April 27 he pitched six scoreless innings against the Expos, so Roger moved him to the bullpen for a month. Back in the rotation in late May, he was hit hard for a month, was sent to Phoenix, posted a 4.72 ERA there, was recalled and back in the rotation. Grade D prospect.

YEAR	TEAM/LEVEL	G	IP	W–L	SAVES	HITS	SO	BB	ERA
1991	Seattle	22	37	2–2	1	34	16	14	3.68
1991	Phoenix AAA	13	74	5–5	0	86	44	24	4.72
1992	San Francisco	23	71	2–7	0	80	47	31	4.97

TIM BURKE
New York Yankees
Relief Pitcher
$2

Is 34 years old, had worked 66 games per year for seven years before coming to earth last year. His strikeout rates: 6.5 per game from 1985 to 1987, 5.3 from 1988 to 1990, 4.6 over the last two years. When you drop into the 4.0–4.5 range your career normally skids to a halt . . . an evangelical Christian who has occasionally rubbed people the wrong way.

YEAR	TEAM/LEVEL	G	IP	W–L	SAVES	HITS	SO	BB	ERA
1990	Montreal	58	75	3–3	20	71	47	21	2.52
1991	Two Teams	72	102	6–7	6	96	59	26	3.36
1992	Two Teams	38	43	3–4	0	52	15	18	4.15

JOHN BURKETT
San Francisco Giants
Starting Pitcher
$48

One of the better starting pitchers in the National League, throws hard, throws strikes, keeps the ball down, and is able to stay healthy. If he wins 20 games in '93 it's just luck, but if you pitch 200 innings a year and throw strikes you put yourself in the path of good luck . . . a ground ball pitcher, and like many such totally ineffective on artificial turf.

YEAR	TEAM/LEVEL	G	IP	W–L	PCT.	HITS	SO	BB	ERA
1990	San Francisco	33	204	14–7	.667	201	118	61	3.79
1991	San Francisco	36	207	12–11	.522	223	131	60	4.18
1992	San Francisco	32	190	13–9	.591	194	107	45	3.84

TODD BURNS
Texas Rangers
Relief Pitcher
$13

A true junkballer, doesn't throw hard enough to dent bread, but changes speeds as well as anybody in baseball, and always has the hitter off stride. He started 10 times for the Rangers in mid-summer, posting a 3.20 ERA (best on the team), after which they sent him back to rot in the bullpen. This is what happens to junkballers in baseball. Managers like fastballs.

YEAR	TEAM/LEVEL	G	IP	W–L	SAVES	HITS	SO	BB	ERA
1990	Oakland	43	79	3–3	3	78	43	32	2.97
1991	Oakland	9	13	1–0	0	10	3	8	3.38
1992	Texas	35	103	3–5	1	97	55	32	3.84

CHRIS BUSHING
Philadelphia Phillies
Pitching Prospect
$4

A hard-throwing right-hander, originally signed with the Orioles some years ago, went to the Expos system and was taken by the Phillies in the Rule 5 draft. In 397 minor league innings he has struck out 433 men, but his record otherwise is not particularly impressive. My guess would be that the Phillies are hoping he'll develop a breaking pitch.

YEAR	TEAM/LEVEL	G	IP	W–L	SAVES	HITS	SO	BB	ERA
1991	West Palm Beach A	46	65	2–1	9	41	68	41	1.94
1992	Reading AA	22	70	3–6	1	68	72	30	4.35
1992	Nashville AAA	5	10	1–0	0	8	6	6	3.48

MIKE BUTCHER
California Angels

Relief Pitcher
$7

Drafted by the Royals in 1986, was released in '88 and signed with the Angels. He pitched three years at Midland in the Texas League, posting ERAs of 6.55, 6.21, and 5.22. This earned him a promotion to Edmonton, where he walked 18 men in 29 innings, so the Angels brought him to the majors. He does have quite a few strikeouts, decent ERAs in 1992.

YEAR	TEAM/LEVEL	G	IP	W–L	SAVES	HITS	SO	BB	ERA
1991	Midland AA	41	88	9–6	3	93	70	46	5.22
1992	Edmonton AAA	26	29	5–2	4	24	32	18	3.07
1992	California	19	28	2–2	0	29	24	13	3.25

GREG CADARET
New York Yankees

Pitcher
$7

Left-hander, never quite bad enough to bomb out of the league. He's had ERAs between 3.62 and 4.25 for four straight years, but probably hasn't pitched as well as his ERA would suggest. His control record has always been weak, reached a new low last year. He has shuttled constantly between the bullpen and the rotation, which can't have helped.

YEAR	TEAM/LEVEL	G	IP	W–L	SAVES	HITS	SO	BB	ERA
1990	New York	54	121	5–4	3	120	80	64	4.15
1991	New York	68	122	8–6	3	110	105	59	3.62
1992	New York	46	104	4–8	1	104	73	74	4.25

KEVIN CAMPBELL
Oakland Athletics

Relief Pitcher
$2

A 28-year-old right-hander, a product of the Dodger system. He was a starter in the minor leagues for several years, undistinguished record, switched to the bullpen in 1989 and pitched brilliantly for San Antonio (1990) and Tacoma (1991). His control record was awful last year, but that hasn't been typical of him. Suspect his control will improve with major league experience. Grade D prospect.

YEAR	TEAM/LEVEL	G	IP	W–L	SAVES	HITS	SO	BB	ERA
1991	Tacoma AAA	35	75	9–2	2	53	56	35	1.80
1991	Oakland	14	23	1–0	0	13	16	14	2.74
1992	Oakland	32	65	2–3	1	66	38	45	5.12

MIKE CAMPBELL
Texas Rangers

Relief Pitcher
$1

He was a hot prospect in the Seattle system five years ago, a first-round draft pick who went 15–2 for Calgary (Triple-A) in 1987. He was ineffective for Seattle in 1988, apparently without a major injury, and has never pitched well since. He went to the Expos as a part of the Langston trade, was released by the Expos and signed by the Rangers. No prospect.

YEAR	TEAM/LEVEL	G	IP	W–L	SAVES	HITS	SO	BB	ERA
1990	Vancouver AAA	21	66	4–5	0	76	50	30	5.83
1991	Tulsa AA	23	108	5–7	1	104	90	51	5.23
1992	Oklahoma City AAA	9	38	2–3	0	42	22	11	5.68

JOHN CANDELARIA
Los Angeles Dodgers
Relief Pitcher
$13

He pitched 50 games and 25 innings. He and Tony Fossas established a new standard for specialty pitching, I believe the lowest ratios ever of innings/games. Candelaria was effective in the role, but can you really afford to keep a pitcher around to pitch to 100 batters a year? You've got a 10- or 11-man staff, and they have to face about 6100 batters in a season.

YEAR	TEAM/LEVEL	G	IP	W–L	SAVES	HITS	SO	BB	ERA
1990	Two Teams	47	80	7–6	5	87	63	20	3.95
1991	Los Angeles	59	34	1–1	2	31	38	11	3.74
1992	Los Angeles	50	25	2–5	5	20	23	13	2.84

TOM CANDIOTTI
Los Angeles Dodgers
Starting Pitcher
$61

Five pitchers have had 200 innings and an ERA at least a quarter-run below their league average in each of the last five years: Clemens, Maddux, Dennis Martinez, Drabek, and Candiotti. As a 35-year-old knuckleballer, he can look forward to probably eight more years of substantially the same productivity. That may not be long enough for the Dodgers to get things turned around.

YEAR	TEAM/LEVEL	G	IP	W–L	PCT.	HITS	SO	BB	ERA
1990	Cleveland	31	202	15–11	.577	207	128	55	3.65
1991	Two Teams	34	238	13–13	.500	202	167	73	2.65
1992	Los Angeles	32	204	11–15	.423	177	152	63	3.00

MIKE CAPEL
Houston Astros
Relief Pitcher
$5

He could be the new Larry Andersen. A journeyman minor leaguer who's had several cups of coffee, he's now 31, in great shape, and pitching the best ball of his career. In the last two years he's posted ERAs of 2.40 and 2.19 *in the Pacific Coast League.* Larry Andersen made a career for himself in his thirties, and I wouldn't bet that Capel won't.

YEAR	TEAM/LEVEL	G	IP	W–L	SAVES	HITS	SO	BB	ERA
1990	Denver AAA	41	101	4–3	2	98	60	39	4.26
1991	Tucson AAA	30	56	4–2	3	49	44	17	2.40
1992	Tucson AAA	58	82	6–6	18	68	70	36	2.19

DON CARMAN
Texas Rangers
Pitcher
$1

I could never figure out why Carman wasn't a more successful pitcher in the big leagues. According to all reports he worked very hard, was bright, had major league stuff and pretty good control. He would also pitch brilliantly for a month at a time, but then something would always go wrong. He's 33 now and it doesn't matter much, but I never could figure him out.

YEAR	TEAM/LEVEL	G	IP	W–L	PCT.	HITS	SO	BB	ERA
1992	Tulsa AA	12	57	3–3	.500	45	36	12	2.68
1992	Oklahoma City AAA	20	81	4–6	.400	80	43	31	4.02
1992	Texas	2	2	0–0	.000	4	2	0	7.71

CRIS CARPENTER
St. Louis Cardinals
Relief Pitcher
$16

The presence of Lee Smith and Todd Worrell tends to isolate him to obscure moments in the ballgame, plus he's not a left-hander so doesn't fit that slot either. He has an excellent fastball, and his hits/innings and walks/inning ratios have been very good for two straight years. He has given up way too many home runs. Much more valuable in Strat-O-Matic than rotisserie.

YEAR	TEAM/LEVEL	G	IP	W–L	SAVES	HITS	SO	BB	ERA
1990	Louisville AAA	22	143	10–8	0	146	100	21	3.70
1991	St. Louis	59	66	10–4	0	53	47	20	4.23
1992	St. Louis	73	88	5–4	1	69	46	27	2.97

LARRY CARTER
San Francisco Giants
Starting Pitcher
$11

A 6-5 right-hander, cut by the Cardinals system a few years ago. Now 27, he earned a look in September after pitching well at Double-A and Triple-A the last two years. He wasn't terrible in September and must be thought of as a candidate to crack their bullpen-to-starting-rotation shuttle, or even their rotation should they choose to establish one. Grade C prospect.

YEAR	TEAM/LEVEL	G	IP	W–L	PCT.	HITS	SO	BB	ERA
1991	Shreveport AA	24	149	9–8	.529	124	133	51	2.95
1992	Phoenix AAA	28	185	11–6	.647	188	126	62	4.37
1992	San Francisco	6	33	1–5	.167	34	21	18	4.64

LARRY CASIAN
Minnesota Twins
Relief Pitcher
$7

Minor league veteran, started for four years and was converted to the bullpen in 1991. He had an excellent year for Portland (Pacific Coast League) in '92, posting a 2.32 ERA with only 13 walks in 58 games, 62 innings. He's a left-hander, and left-handed relievers are a prized commodity, so he'll probably get several chances to catch a major league job. Grade C prospect.

YEAR	TEAM/LEVEL	G	IP	W–L	SAVES	HITS	SO	BB	ERA
1991	Minnesota	15	18	0–0	0	28	6	7	7.36
1992	Portland AAA	58	62	4–0	11	54	43	13	2.32
1992	Minnesota	6	7	1–0	0	7	2	1	2.70

FRANK CASTILLO
Chicago Cubs
Starting Pitcher
$30

I like everything about Frank Castillo except the fact that he pitches for the Cubs. Castillo is a well-conditioned athlete, mediocre fastball but excellent control, keeps the ball down, changes speeds well, and uses the curve extremely well. He has faded late in the season, but will get over that with experience. It's hard to be a top-flight pitcher in a hitter's park.

YEAR	TEAM/LEVEL	G	IP	W–L	PCT.	HITS	SO	BB	ERA
1990	Charlotte AA	18	111	6–6	.500	113	112	27	3.88
1991	Chicago	18	112	6–7	.462	107	73	37	4.35
1992	Chicago	33	205	10–11	.476	179	135	63	3.46

DARREN CHAPIN
Philadelphia Phillies
Relief Pitcher
$3

A 27-year-old right-hander, a product of the Yankee farm system. He often pitched extremely well in the Yankee system, such as in '91 when he went 10–3 at Columbus with a 1.95 ERA, but could earn only a cursory look by the major league team. Traded to Philadelphia a year ago, he didn't pitch particularly well for Scranton. Grade D prospect.

YEAR	TEAM/LEVEL	G	IP	W–L	SAVES	HITS	SO	BB	ERA
1990	Albany AA	43	53	3–2	21	43	61	21	2.73
1991	Columbus AAA	55	78	10–3	12	54	69	40	1.95
1992	Scranton AAA	40	62	5–4	4	72	67	33	5.11

NORM CHARLTON
Cincinnati Reds
Relief Pitcher
$38

An August slump took the closer role away from him and deprived him of a tremendous season. Intelligent, excellent athlete, throws hard, throws strikes, throws ground balls . . . a lefty, but very effective against right-handers because he has a back-door slider and will pitch inside . . . sinking fastball, so stats are hurt by playing on artificial turf in his home park.

YEAR	TEAM/LEVEL	G	IP	W–L	SAVES	HITS	SO	BB	ERA
1990	Cincinnati	56	154	12–9	2	131	117	70	2.74
1991	Cincinnati	39	108	3–5	1	92	77	34	2.91
1992	Cincinnati	64	81	4–2	26	79	90	26	2.99

SCOTT CHIAMPARINO
Texas Rangers
Starting Pitcher
$8

The key to being a major league pitcher is being able to stay healthy. That's bigger than everything else, because *most* pitchers have enough stuff that they could learn to pitch effectively if they could get a few hundred innings. Chiamparino—he's a fine pitcher. He missed most of the year after reconstructive surgery on his right elbow. He can pitch, but his health is a big gamble.

YEAR	TEAM/LEVEL	G	IP	W–L	PCT.	HITS	SO	BB	ERA
1991	Texas	5	22	1–0	1.000	26	8	12	4.03
1992	Minors—Three Levels	10	62	3–2	.600	52	35	21	2.48
1992	Texas	4	25	0–4	.000	25	13	5	3.55

MIKE CHRISTOPHER
Cleveland Indians
Relief Pitcher
$7

A 29-year-old minor league veteran originally from the Yankee system, moved into the closer role at Albuquerque in 1991, and pitched brilliantly there and also at Colorado Springs last summer. He doesn't have much of a fastball, but I strongly believe that he will be an effective major league pitcher if he can get enough time to settle into a role. The new Dale Mohorcic.

YEAR	TEAM/LEVEL	G	IP	W–L	SAVES	HITS	SO	BB	ERA
1991	Albuquerque AAA	63	77	7–2	16	73	67	30	2.44
1992	Colorado Sp AAA	49	59	4–4	26	59	39	13	2.91
1992	Cleveland	10	18	0–0	0	17	13	10	3.00

MARK CLARK
St. Louis Cardinals
Starting Pitcher
$4

Classic once-around-the-league syndrome. He pitched well against the Mets on June 21, faced them again on June 26 and lasted four innings. The first time he faced Pittsburgh he gave them one run in 8 innings, the second time three runs in 6 ⅔, the third time six in 2 ⅔. He should be back when he regains his confidence.

YEAR	TEAM/LEVEL	G	IP	W–L	PCT.	HITS	SO	BB	ERA
1991	St. Louis	7	22	1–1	.500	17	13	11	4.03
1992	Louisville AAA	9	61	4–4	.500	56	38	15	2.80
1992	St. Louis	20	113	3–10	.231	117	44	36	4.45

ROGER CLEMENS
Boston Red Sox
Starting Pitcher
$96

He is still the best starting pitcher in baseball, and it still is not really a contest. He gets more ground balls than he used to, a 199 ratio of 364/187 as opposed to 349/231 in 1991 . . . crossed the 150-win mark last summer, halfway to 300 . . . by the end of this season he will have more career wins than Sandy Koufax, and fewer losses.

YEAR	TEAM/LEVEL	G	IP	W–L	PCT.	HITS	SO	BB	ERA
1990	Boston	31	228	21–6	.778	193	209	54	1.93
1991	Boston	35	271	18–10	.643	219	241	65	2.62
1992	Boston	32	247	18–11	.621	203	208	62	2.41

PAT CLEMENTS
Baltimore Orioles (Free Agent)
Relief Pitcher
$7

Was sold in mid-summer from the Padres to the Orioles, continued to work as a one-out left-hander . . . . Extraordinarily good ground ball to fly ball ratio (88/36), but career strikeout/walk ratio is less than even, more walks than strikeouts . . . his present value consists largely in having a job, and who knows how long he'll keep that? Won't move up, but could sputter along indefinitely in current role.

YEAR	TEAM/LEVEL	G	IP	W–L	SAVES	HITS	SO	BB	ERA
1990	San Diego	9	13	0–0	0	20	6	7	4.15
1991	San Diego	12	14	1–0	0	13	8	9	3.77
1992	Two Teams	50	48	4–1	0	48	20	23	2.98

VICTOR COLE
Pittsburgh Pirates
Starting Pitcher
$3

He was called up by the Pirates on June 2, when Bob Walk went on the disabled list, to do Walk's job. He did, but not very well, and was sent back down on July 11. Was born in Leningrad, Russia, signed by the Royals in 1988 and traded to the Pirates a couple of years ago for Carmelo Martinez. Grade D prospect.

YEAR	TEAM/LEVEL	G	IP	W–L	PCT.	HITS	SO	BB	ERA
1991	Minors—Three Teams	45	65	2–5	.286	45	67	48	3.03
1992	Buffalo AAA	19	116	11–6	.647	102	69	61	3.11
1992	Pittsburgh	8	23	0–2	.000	23	12	14	5.48

PAT COMBS
Philadelphia Phillies
Starting Pitcher
$2

Needs to get into another organization. He pitched fairly well with the Phillies in 1990, but his career has regressed since then, and the Phillies, whose idea of a hot prospect is Cliff Brantley, obviously don't believe in him. Pitched OK for Scranton last summer (3.79 ERA, strikeout/walk ratio of 71/40 and one hit per inning), and might pitch better for a better team.

YEAR	TEAM/LEVEL	G	IP	W–L	PCT.	HITS	SO	BB	ERA
1991	Philadelphia	14	64	2–6	.250	64	41	43	4.90
1992	Scranton AAA	21	125	5–7	.417	123	77	41	3.61
1992	Philadelphia	4	19	1–1	.500	20	11	12	7.71

DAVID CONE
Toronto Blue Jays
Starting Pitcher
$73

One of the 10 best starting pitchers in baseball, got out of the 14-win rut last year despite walking more people than he had since Little League. Has worked 200 innings for five years in a row with good ERAs all five years, winning records in four of the five . . . needs to get a couple of 20-win years to emerge as a Hall of Fame candidate.

YEAR	TEAM/LEVEL	G	IP	W–L	PCT.	HITS	SO	BB	ERA
1990	New York	31	212	14–10	.583	177	233	65	3.23
1991	New York	34	233	14–14	.500	204	241	73	3.29
1992	Two Teams	35	250	17–10	.630	201	261	111	2.81

JIM CONVERSE
Seattle Mariners
Starting Pitcher
$16

He's short, 5-9, but has 92 MPH fastball and was listed by Baseball America as the number-eight prospect in the Southern League. Since the Mariners are desperate for pitching, they must be credited with some restraint for not calling him up last year—in fact, they probably would have if it wouldn't have made him eligible for the expansion draft. Grade B prospect.

YEAR	TEAM/LEVEL	G	IP	W–L	PCT.	HITS	SO	BB	ERA
1990	Bellingham A	12	67	2–4	.333	50	75	32	3.91
1991	Peninsula A	26	138	6–15	.286	143	137	97	4.97
1992	Jacksonville AA	27	159	12–7	.632	134	157	82	2.66

DENNIS COOK
Cleveland Indians
Starting Pitcher
$17

Returned to the majors last year after unexplained detour in 1991 (has anybody considered the possibility that the Dodgers are trying to lose?) Cook pitches up in the strike zone and gives up bushels of home runs, but his control record is good, and it has long been established that you can survive with that combination. He's 30, but his best years should be ahead of him. Good hitter.

YEAR	TEAM/LEVEL	G	IP	W–L	PCT.	HITS	SO	BB	ERA
1990	Two Teams	47	156	9–4	.692	155	64	56	3.92
1991	Los Angeles	20	18	1–0	1.000	12	8	7	0.51
1992	Cleveland	32	158	5–7	.417	156	96	50	3.82

STEVE COOKE
Pittsburgh Pirates
Left-Handed Pitcher
$7

A starter in the minor leagues, he was called up in July and pitched lunar relief for the Pirates (he got to pitch about once a month). He does not have the credentials of Denny Neagle or Brett Backlund, with whom he will battle for a place in the Pirate rotation when one opens up, but minor league record isn't *bad*, either. Grade C prospect.

YEAR	TEAM/LEVEL	G	IP	W–L	PCT.	HITS	SO	BB	ERA
1991	Minors A & AA	22	129	9–7	.563	103	103	56	2.78
1992	Minors AA & AAA	19	110	8–5	.615	102	90	48	3.51
1992	Pittsburgh	11	23	2–0	1.000	22	10	4	3.52

RHEAL CORMIER
St. Louis Cardinals
Starting Pitcher
$37

He pitched better than is reflected in his 10–10 won–lost record (the Cardinals scored only 3.9 runs per game for him), and must be regarded among the better young starting pitchers in the NL. He almost dropped out of the league in May, when he gave up 26 earned runs in 30 innings, but recovered to pitch superb baseball over the last two months of the season.

YEAR	TEAM/LEVEL	G	IP	W–L	PCT.	HITS	SO	BB	ERA
1991	Louisville AAA	21	128	7–9	.438	140	74	31	4.23
1991	St. Louis	11	68	4–5	.444	74	38	8	4.12
1992	St. Louis	31	186	10–10	.500	194	117	33	3.68

JIM CORSI
Oakland Athletics
Relief Pitcher
$18

He is 31 years old, A's product who went to Houston as a six-year free agent, was released by Astros and returned to Oakland. He looks fat and has limited stuff, but knows how to pitch. Throws 86 MPH fastball, sinker, and slider, challenges hitters. He's not as good as his 1.43 ERA would suggest, and he's not closer material, but a useful pitcher in a support role.

YEAR	TEAM/LEVEL	G	IP	W–L	SAVES	HITS	SO	BB	ERA
1990	Tacoma AAA	5	6	0–0	0	9	3	1	1.50
1991	Houston	47	78	0–5	0	76	53	23	3.71
1992	Oakland	32	44	4–2	0	44	19	18	1.43

DANNY COX
Pittsburgh Pirates
Relief Pitcher
$11

He started the year in the Phillies rotation, was ineffective, went to Pirates on waivers, started eight times for Buffalo with a 1.70 ERA, was called up to Pirates, and pitched quite well over the last two months. I don't expect him to re-emerge as a rotation anchor, but could remain effective for several years if he stays in the bullpen.

YEAR	TEAM/LEVEL	G	IP	W–L	SAVES	HITS	SO	BB	ERA
1990	Louisville AAA	4	11	0–3	0	22	6	10	15.55
1991	Philadelphia	23	102	4–6	0	98	46	39	4.57
1992	Two Teams	25	63	5–3	3	66	48	27	4.60

TIM CREWS
Los Angeles Dodgers
(Released)
Relief Pitcher
$2

The league hit .310 against him last year, and his ERA away from Dodger Stadium was 7.12. Left-handed hitters hit .327. With runners in scoring position the average was .354. His ERA was 4.96 or higher in five out of six months. These are not good numbers. Crews has always had good strikeout/walk ratios, but I've got to suggest that something may be wrong here.

YEAR	TEAM/LEVEL	G	IP	W–L	SAVES	HITS	SO	BB	ERA
1990	Los Angeles	66	107	4–5	5	98	76	24	2.77
1991	Los Angeles	60	76	2–3	6	75	53	19	3.43
1992	Los Angeles	49	78	0–3	0	95	43	20	5.19

CHUCK CRIM
California Angels
Relief Pitcher
$3

The Angels' answer to Tim Crews. Crim has been utterly ineffective for two straight seasons; I'm a little puzzled by why he keeps getting work. His poor stats in 1992 were opposition batting average, home runs allowed, strikeouts, and ERA. His good stats were . . . um, well, his control wasn't too bad. He pitched better than Tim Crews did, I think.

YEAR	TEAM/LEVEL	G	IP	W–L	SAVES	HITS	SO	BB	ERA
1990	Milwaukee	67	86	3–5	11	88	39	23	3.47
1991	Milwaukee	66	91	8–5	3	115	39	25	4.63
1992	California	57	87	7–6	1	100	30	29	5.17

RON DARLING
Oakland Athletics
Starting Pitcher
$29

Can be added to the substantial list of solicitors—Eckersley, Stewart, Honeycutt—whose careers have come back to life on joining the law firm of LaRussa and Duncan. This one you could have seen coming. Darling has always pitched well sometimes, but has lacked consistency. LaRussa and Duncan monitored his workload so that he was able to keep going and get stronger as the year went on.

YEAR	TEAM/LEVEL	G	IP	W–L	PCT.	HITS	SO	BB	ERA
1990	New York	33	126	7–9	.438	135	99	44	4.50
1991	Three Teams	32	194	8–15	.348	185	129	71	4.26
1992	Oakland	33	206	15–10	.600	198	99	72	3.66

DANNY DARWIN
Boston Red Sox
Starting Pitcher
$23

After floundering for a year and a half, first as a starter, then a reliever, he returned to the starting rotation on July 20 and finished the year with a 3.53 ERA as a starter (15 starts). He *could* post a 3.53 ERA all year and go 16–11. He's a .500 pitcher in his late thirties, pitching for a bad team in a hitter's park.

YEAR	TEAM/LEVEL	G	IP	W–L	PCT.	HITS	SO	BB	ERA
1990	Houston	48	163	11–4	.733	136	109	31	2.21
1991	Boston	12	68	3–6	.333	71	42	15	5.16
1992	Boston	51	161	9–9	.500	159	124	53	3.96

MARK DAVIS
Atlanta Braves
Relief Pitcher
$1

Probably the biggest free agent bomb in baseball history. It's not merely that he was 1) extremely expensive, and 2) utterly ineffective. It's much more than that. He was utterly ineffective at key moments of the game, creating negative wins. His salary forced the Royals to waste a roster spot . . . still throws hard and has monster curve, but self-confidence is probably beyond repair.

YEAR	TEAM/LEVEL	G	IP	W–L	SAVES	HITS	SO	BB	ERA
1990	Kansas City	53	69	2–7	6	71	73	52	5.11
1991	Kansas City	29	63	6–3	1	55	47	39	4.45
1992	Two Teams	27	53	2–3	0	64	34	41	7.13

STORM DAVIS
Baltimore Orioles
(Released)
Relief Pitcher
$8

Pitched well last year until August 18, then lost his grip over the last six weeks of the season. He held leadoff hitters to a .197 batting average and walked only eight leadoff men, and this gave him many more good innings than poor ones, but he was still ineffective with men in scoring position. Strikeout rate (53 in 89 innings) was his best since 1988.

YEAR	TEAM/LEVEL	G	IP	W–L	SAVES	HITS	SO	BB	ERA
1990	Kansas City	21	112	7–10	0	129	62	35	4.74
1991	Kansas City	51	114	3–9	2	140	53	46	4.96
1992	Baltimore	48	89	7–3	4	79	53	36	3.43

JOSE DeJESUS
Philadelphia Phillies
Starting Pitcher
$1

Missed all of 1992 and will miss the first half of 1993, at least, with a torn rotator cuff. Before the injury, DeJesus was a wild thrower with one of the major leagues' best fastballs, who could win as many as he lost for that reason. When he comes back he'll be a thrower without the fastball, at least at first. I'd have little interest in owning his rights.

YEAR	TEAM/LEVEL	G	IP	W–L	PCT.	HITS	SO	BB	ERA
1989	Kansas City	3	8	0–0	.000	7	2	8	4.50
1990	Philadelphia	22	130	7–8	.467	97	87	73	3.74
1991	Philadelphia	31	182	10–9	.526	147	118	128	3.42

JOSE DeLEON
Philadelphia Phillies
Starting Pitcher
$10

He has pitched in tough luck for three years, and it has no doubt begun to prey on his mind. He's had some injuries and his fastball is nothing like what it once was, but he still appears to me to have quality stuff—a slider, a split-fingered fastball, an occasional curve. It's hard to maintain confidence in your stuff when you never win.

YEAR	TEAM/LEVEL	G	IP	W–L	PCT.	HITS	SO	BB	ERA
1990	St. Louis	32	183	7–19	.269	168	164	86	4.43
1991	St. Louis	28	163	5–9	.357	144	118	61	2.71
1992	Two Teams	32	117	2–8	.200	111	79	48	4.37

RICH DeLUCIA
Seattle Mariners
Starting Pitcher
$11

Pitches like Mike Boddicker, throws junk and tries to destroy the hitter's timing with arm angles and deception . . . lost his spot in the rotation in mid-July, went on the disabled list August 5 with an inflamed elbow. Can't afford to walk anybody and usually doesn't; will have up and down future, can win 15 games in a good year but probably no star potential.

YEAR	TEAM/LEVEL	G	IP	W–L	PCT.	HITS	SO	BB	ERA
1990	Seattle	5	36	1–2	.333	30	20	9	2.00
1991	Seattle	32	182	12–13	.480	176	98	78	5.09
1992	Seattle	30	84	3–6	.333	100	66	35	5.49

JIM DeSHAIES
San Diego Padres
Left-Handed Starting Pitcher
$17

Started the year with Las Vegas, got back into the rotation just before the All-Star break and pitched fairly well over the second half, but not at the level of his best years in Houston. He pitches up in the strike zone with a mediocre fastball, but somehow he gets by with it . . . over four years has been hit much harder by *left-handed* hitters than right-handers.

YEAR	TEAM/LEVEL	G	IP	W–L	PCT.	HITS	SO	BB	ERA
1990	Houston	34	209	7–12	.368	186	119	84	3.78
1991	Houston	28	161	5–12	.294	156	98	72	4.98
1992	San Diego	15	96	4–7	.364	92	46	33	3.28

JOHN DeSILVA
Detroit Tigers
Starting Pitcher
$13

I regarded him as the Tigers' best pitching prospect a year ago, but this was a minority opinion. He suffered some injuries in an automobile accident, then had an elbow problem and didn't get his season started until July, but finished the schedule dominating Eastern League hitters. I still believe he is the best pitching prospect in the Tigers system. Grade B prospect.

YEAR	TEAM/LEVEL	G	IP	W–L	PCT.	HITS	SO	BB	ERA
1991	AA and AAA	22	132	10–8	.556	113	136	45	3.60
1992	Toledo AAA	7	19	0–3	.000	26	21	8	8.53
1992	London AA	9	52	2–4	.333	51	53	13	4.13

MARK (Huey) DEWEY
New York Mets
Relief Pitcher
$7

Reliever from the Giants system, dumped by the Giants in 1991 despite a 2.78 ERA in 14 games for the big team in 1990. Right-hander with so-so stuff, changes speeds and moves the ball around; the book says that a pitcher like that will need an adjustment period in the majors, but he hasn't. Not regarded as having any star potential, but may surprise.

YEAR	TEAM/LEVEL	G	IP	W–L	SAVES	HITS	SO	BB	ERA
1991	Two Teams AAA	58	76	13–5	13	77	42	43	3.43
1992	Tidewater AAA	43	54	5–7	9	61	55	18	4.31
1992	New York	20	33	1–0	0	37	24	10	4.32

ROB DIBBLE
Cincinnati Reds
Closer
$64

After the All-Star break he posted a 1.59 ERA and struck out 63 batters in 34 innings. That's 16.7 strikeouts per nine innings . . . his strikeout rates, and several other things about him, are historically unique. Many players have been able to excel in baseball by channeling their neurotic aggression. Dibble and Ty Cobb are the only ones who have successfully channeled a psychosis.

YEAR	TEAM/LEVEL	G	IP	W–L	SAVES	HITS	SO	BB	ERA
1990	Cincinnati	68	98	8–3	11	62	136	34	1.74
1991	Cincinnati	67	82	3–5	31	67	124	25	3.17
1992	Cincinnati	63	70	3–5	25	48	110	31	3.07

FRANK DIPINO
St. Louis Cardinals
Relief Pitcher
$3

Missed most of the season after elbow surgery, came back to pitch nine games in September, pitched well. He is 36 years old now, but there are also more spots around for a left-handed reliever than there were a few years ago. He had a trial as a closer in Houston 10 years ago, failed to hold that job but has had long career as early reliever.

YEAR	TEAM/LEVEL	G	IP	W–L	SAVES	HITS	SO	BB	ERA
1990	St. Louis	62	81	5–2	3	92	49	31	4.56
1992	Louisville AAA	18	23	0–3	0	28	10	8	3.97
1992	St. Louis	9	11	0–0	0	9	8	3	1.64

JOHN DOHERTY
Detroit Tigers
Starting Pitcher
$12

Exclusively a reliever in the minors, worked out of the Tigers' bullpen through July, moved into the starting rotation on August 5 and had more good starts than bad ones. He's an extreme finesse-type pitcher, very few walks or strikeouts, and that's a poor-risk category, as there are very few successful major league pitchers like that. Right-hander, 25 years old, has injury history.

YEAR	TEAM/LEVEL	G	IP	W–L	PCT.	HITS	SO	BB	ERA
1990	Lakeland A	30	41	5–1	.833	33	23	5	1.10
1991	London AA	53	65	3–3	.500	62	42	21	2.22
1992	Detroit	47	116	7–4	.636	131	37	25	3.88

JOHN DOPSON
Boston Red Sox
Starting Pitcher
$15

Activated May 15 after elbow problem, pitched very well until August 19, then was beaten up over the last six weeks. ERA was 2.69 in Fenway Park, 6.09 on the road. Ground ball/fly ball ratio is tremendous (2.24 to 1), but gives up quite a few home runs. Weak finish, unimpressive KW ratio and injury history mark him as a pitcher to avoid in '92.

YEAR	TEAM/LEVEL	G	IP	W–L	PCT.	HITS	SO	BB	ERA
1990	Boston	4	18	0–0	.000	13	9	9	2.04
1991	Boston	1	1	0–0	.000	2	0	1	18.00
1992	Boston	25	141	7–11	.389	159	55	38	4.08

KELLY DOWNS
Oakland Athletics
Starting Pitcher
$15

A great candidate to blossom under Duncan. Posted 2.32 ERA in April '92 pitching 5 to 6 innings a start, threw 101 pitches on April 28 and was shelled his next two starts. Didn't throw seven innings again until July 16, threw 98 pitches then and was shelled his next game. Threw 127 pitches August 6, and was plastered his next game. LaRussa and Duncan will find his limits.

YEAR	TEAM/LEVEL	G	IP	W–L	PCT.	HITS	SO	BB	ERA
1990	San Francisco	13	63	3–2	.600	56	31	20	3.43
1991	San Francisco	45	112	10–4	.714	99	62	53	4.19
1992	Two Teams	37	144	6–7	.462	137	71	70	3.37

DOUG DRABEK
Pittsburgh Pirates
Starting Pitcher
$81

Very intelligent, poised. Excellent work habits and careful handling by Leyland have made a perennial All-Star out of a player without spectacular raw skills . . . he pitched the best ball of his career last year, posting 2.77 ERA (2.76 in his Cy Young season) and 177 strikeouts in 257 innings, both figures career highs. Strikeouts per game was also a career high. Always finishes the season strong.

YEAR	TEAM/LEVEL	G	IP	W–L	PCT.	HITS	SO	BB	ERA
1990	Pittsburgh	33	231	22–6	.786	190	131	56	2.76
1991	Pittsburgh	35	235	15–14	.517	245	142	62	3.07
1992	Pittsburgh	34	257	15–11	.577	218	177	54	2.77

BRIAN DRAHMAN
Chicago White Sox
Relief Pitcher
$3

The pitcher the White Sox got from the Brewers for Jerry Reuss a few years ago, has sharp-breaking slider but not much else. Right-hander, 27 years old, saved 30 games for Vancouver with 2.01 ERA last year, but strikeout/walk ratio of 34 to 31 doesn't suggest he had the league overmatched. Grade D prospect; expansion will get him a look.

YEAR	TEAM/LEVEL	G	IP	W–L	SAVES	HITS	SO	BB	ERA
1991	Vancouver AAA	22	24	2–3	12	21	17	13	4.44
1991	Chicago	28	31	3–2	0	21	18	13	3.23
1992	Vancouver AAA	48	58	2–4	30	44	34	31	2.01

MIKE DUNNE
Chicago White Sox
Starting Pitcher
$6

The right-hander who had an outstanding rookie year with the Pirates in 1987 (13–6, 3.03 ERA), dropped out of the league in 1989. Now 30, he pitched his best baseball in several years last season for Vancouver, but the ERA is misleading because he gave up an unusual number of unearned runs (20). Will receive another major league trial this year and could surprise.

YEAR	TEAM/LEVEL	G	IP	W–L	PCT.	HITS	SO	BB	ERA
1991	Vancouver	17	55	2–2	.500	66	21	19	5.40
1992	Vancouver	21	133	10–6	.625	128	78	46	2.78
1992	Chicago	4	13	2–0	1.000	12	6	6	4.26

DENNIS ECKERSLEY
Oakland Athletics
Closer
$88

Well, I'm convinced. The Hall of Fame, I mean. After years as an in-house legend who rarely communicated with the public, Eckersley has begun to appear in TV interviews as a kind of '90s sensitive man, quiet and reflective. As Ryan draws near the end of his career, Eckersley is poised to inherit Ryan's mantle as baseball's mythic elder ass-kicker.

YEAR	TEAM/LEVEL	G	IP	W–L	SAVES	HITS	SO	BB	ERA
1990	Oakland	63	73	4–2	48	41	73	4	0.61
1991	Oakland	67	76	5–4	43	60	87	9	2.96
1992	Oakland	69	80	7–1	51	62	93	11	1.91

TOM EDENS
Minnesota Twins
Relief Pitcher
$19

Posted 1.17 ERA before the All-Star game with five wins, 5.34 afterward with 1–3 record. To give you an idea of where Tom Edens has been, he was traded for Tucker Ashford in 1984. His career was going nowhere until 1990, when the Brewers, out of sheer desperation, called him to the majors despite a 5.40 ERA at Denver. He's still here.

YEAR	TEAM/LEVEL	G	IP	W–L	SAVES	HITS	SO	BB	ERA
1990	Milwaukee	35	89	4–5	2	89	40	33	4.45
1991	Minnesota	8	33	2–2	0	34	19	10	4.09
1992	Minnesota	52	76	6–3	3	65	57	36	2.83

MARK EICHHORN
Toronto Blue Jays
(Released)
Relief Pitcher
$26

Posted 1.98 ERA for California in '91, 2.13 before the All-Star break last year, then faded the second half. Quisenberry type, throws strikes and gets ground balls, is extremely vulnerable to a left-handed line drive hitter. Utterly ineffective if he throws more than 30 pitches in a game . . . as long as he's healthy I'd expect him to be reasonably valuable.

YEAR	TEAM/LEVEL	G	IP	W–L	SAVES	HITS	SO	BB	ERA
1990	California	60	85	2–5	13	98	69	23	3.08
1991	California	70	82	3–3	1	63	49	13	1.98
1992	Two Teams	65	88	4–4	2	86	61	25	3.08

DAVE EILAND
San Diego Padres
Starting Pitcher
$5

The pitcher from the Yankee system who went 31–10 with Columbus from 1989 to 1991. Started the season in the Padres' rotation, made five starts, didn't win, went on the DL with a sore back, made two more starts, went on the DL with a bruised ankle, and went to Las Vegas. Superb control; suspect he can pitch if he can ever get over the hump. Grade D prospect.

YEAR	TEAM/LEVEL	G	IP	W–L	PCT.	HITS	SO	BB	ERA
1991	New York	18	73	2–5	.286	87	18	23	5.33
1991	San Diego	7	27	0–2	.000	33	10	5	5.67
1992	Las Vegas AAA	14	64	4–5	.444	78	31	11	5.23

CAL ELDRED
Milwaukee Brewers
Starting Pitcher
$41

Most pitchers who start out white-hot aren't great pitchers. Jim Nash was 12–1 in the second half of 1966, the most comparable season to Eldred's. Mark Fidrych, Gregg Olson . . . I don't think Eldred is likely to be a *great* pitcher. I do think he will be a good pitcher for a number of years. His control has improved substantially in the last year.

YEAR	TEAM/LEVEL	G	IP	W–L	PCT.	HITS	SO	BB	ERA
1991	Denver AAA	29	185	13–9	.591	161	168	84	3.75
1992	Denver AAA	19	141	10–6	.625	122	99	42	3.00
1992	Milwaukee	14	100	11–2	.846	76	62	23	1.79

DONNIE ELLIOTT
Atlanta Braves
Starting Pitcher
$15

Another Phillies puzzle. A seventh-round pick in 1987, he pitched A Ball from 1988 through 1991 despite marginally phenomenal numbers. Seattle rescued him via the Rule 5 draft, and he wound up at Greenville, where he went 7–2 with a 2.08 ERA, K/W of 100/35 in 104 innings. . . . I haven't seen him pitch, but he looks great in the book.

YEAR	TEAM/LEVEL	G	IP	W–L	PCT.	HITS	SO	BB	ERA
1990	Spartanburg A	20	105	4–8	.333	101	109	46	3.50
1991	Two Teams A	38	158	11–9	.550	120	184	87	3.25
1992	Two Teams AA	25	139	10–5	.667	113	123	46	2.26

ALAN EMBREE
Cleveland Indians
Starting Pitcher
$28

Left-handed pitcher with outstanding fastball, was a fifth-round draft pick out of high school in 1990 and has established himself as one of four top pitching prospects in the Indians' system. Strikeout rates were over one per inning in A Ball, pitched well at Double-A Canton in 1992, may skip Triple-A because of the Indians' need for starting pitchers. **Grade A prospect.**

YEAR	TEAM/LEVEL	G	IP	W–L	PCT.	HITS	SO	BB	ERA
1992	Kinston A	15	101	10–5	.667	89	115	32	3.30
1992	Canton AA	12	79	7–2	.778	61	56	28	2.28
1992	Cleveland	4	18	0–2	.000	19	12	8	7.00

SCOTT ERICKSON
Minnesota Twins
Starting Pitcher
$41

An American original, throws balls that seem to be 20 percent pewter. Found the groove again after the All-Star break, posting 2.69 ERA over the second half. Will be able to win consistently without strikeouts because of unusual groundball/flyball ratio (391/161). 1992 won–lost record (13–12) is more representative of his ability than 20-win season in 1991.

YEAR	TEAM/LEVEL	G	IP	W–L	PCT.	HITS	SO	BB	ERA
1990	Minnesota	19	113	8–4	.667	108	53	51	2.87
1991	Minnesota	32	204	20–8	.714	189	108	71	3.18
1992	Minnesota	32	212	13–12	.520	197	101	83	3.40

HECTOR FAJARDO
Texas Rangers
Starting Pitcher
$8

Big Mexican right-hander, still only 21 years old if his listed birthday is correct, he's hard to evaluate because he's never pitched more than 11 games anywhere before moving on. Came to the Rangers as part of the Buechele trade, and pitched at all four minor league levels in '92. He pitched well, but has bursitis in his shoulder. Grade C prospect because of health record.

YEAR	TEAM/LEVEL	G	IP	W–L	PCT.	HITS	SO	BB	ERA
1991	A, AA, and AAA	30	138	8–8	.500	109	151	52	3.19
1991	Two Teams	6	25	0–2	.000	35	23	11	6.75
1992	R, A, AA, AAA	11	61	5–4	.555	54	53	19	2.51

STEVE FARR
New York Yankees
Closer
$53

Blue-collar pitcher, has had ERAs below 2.20 for three straight years, pitched great for two years before that except for a period in '89 when he tried to pitch with torn cartilage in his knee. Sneaky fast, moves ball up and down, throws right at the batter's fists. . . . As a starter over the last four years is 6–1 with a 1.48 ERA.

YEAR	TEAM/LEVEL	G	IP	W–L	SAVES	HITS	SO	BB	ERA
1990	Kansas City	57	127	13–7	1	99	94	48	1.98
1991	New York	60	70	5–5	23	57	60	20	2.19
1992	New York	50	52	2–2	30	34	37	19	1.56

MIKE FARRELL
Milwaukee Brewers
Starting Pitcher
$16

A horsehide Horatio Alger story, was signed as an undrafted free agent just 18 months ago and has vaulted to hot prospect status by the simple device of getting everybody out. Posted a 2.62 ERA at El Paso, which is roughly equivalent to pitching on the moon. The only other pitcher I ever heard of having an ERA that good at El Paso was Teddy Higuera.

YEAR	TEAM/LEVEL	G	IP	W–L	PCT.	HITS	SO	BB	ERA
1991	R and A	17	90	8–4	.667	75	77	19	2.21
1992	Stockton A	12	84	7–4	.636	75	60	19	2.47
1992	El Paso AA	14	106	7–6	.538	95	66	25	2.62

JEFF FASSERO
Montreal Expos
Lanceur de la gauche
$17

Left-hander, but *not* a one-out reliever like Candelaria or Fossas. 72 percent of the hitters he faced last year were right-handers . . . was dumped by the Cardinals and White Sox as a starting pitcher; the Indians had him in the bullpen and he pitched well, but they cut him anyway. . . . Now 30; I predict he'll have a 10-year major league career with a lot of good moments.

YEAR	TEAM/LEVEL	G	IP	W–L	SAVES	HITS	SO	BB	ERA
1990	Canton AA	61	64	5–4	6	66	61	24	2.80
1991	Montreal	51	55	2–5	8	39	42	17	2.44
1992	Montreal	70	86	8–7	1	81	63	34	2.84

ALEX FERNANDEZ
Chicago White Sox
Starting Pitcher
$25

Career bottomed out with mid-summer return to the minor leagues; he pitched a little better probably after he came back. He's still learning to pitch, and I'm not sure how much White Sox pitching coach Jackie Brown is really helping. It looks to me like he is so afraid of issuing walks that he can't take advantage of the situation when he gets ahead in the count.

YEAR	TEAM/LEVEL	G	IP	W–L	PCT.	HITS	SO	BB	ERA
1990	Chicago	13	88	5–5	.500	89	61	34	3.80
1991	Chicago	34	192	9–13	.409	186	145	88	4.51
1992	Chicago	29	188	8–11	.421	199	95	50	4.27

SID FERNANDEZ
New York Mets
Starting Pitcher
$37

Posted 2.34 ERA after May 1, fairly clearly answering the questions about whether he could still get people out. It was only the third time in his career that he had pitched 200 innings in a season, but he appears to be in better shape than he has been in several years. I'm betting that Fernandez is just entering the best part of his career.

YEAR	TEAM/LEVEL	G	IP	W–L	PCT.	HITS	SO	BB	ERA
1990	New York	30	179	9–14	.391	130	181	67	3.46
1991	New York	8	44	1–3	.250	36	31	9	2.86
1992	New York	32	215	14–11	.560	162	193	67	2.73

MIKE FETTERS
Milwaukee Brewers
Relief Pitcher
$22

One of five Brewer relievers who had a good year, limited hitters to a .185 batting average, with ERA under 2.00 . . . came through the California Angels system as a starting pitcher and was fairly effective, led the Pacific Coast League in strikeouts in 1989. Was traded to Milwaukee for Chuck Crim . . . has a fat face but really isn't fat . . . should remain effective.

YEAR	TEAM/LEVEL	G	IP	W–L	SAVES	HITS	SO	BB	ERA
1990	California	26	68	1–1	1	77	35	20	4.12
1991	California	19	45	2–5	0	53	24	28	4.84
1992	Milwaukee	50	63	5–1	2	38	43	24	1.87

TOM FILER
New York Mets
Starting Pitcher
$1

He's now 37 years old, so I think stardom can be ruled out. Filer's a soft tosser, has had trials with five major league teams, and is best remembered for going 7–0 with Toronto in '85. He tore a ligament in his elbow in the process, missed all of the '86 season, and has been up and down since, although generally pitching well.

YEAR	TEAM/LEVEL	G	IP	W–L	PCT.	HITS	SO	BB	ERA
1991	Iowa AAA	18	113	8–3	.727	126	47	29	4.37
1992	Tidewater AAA	18	100	1–7	.125	106	47	28	2.78
1992	New York	9	22	0–1	.000	18	9	6	2.05

CHUCK FINLEY
California Angels
Starting Pitcher
$40

He was bothered by a hyperextended toe, and didn't begin to pitch well until July 22. Posted a 2.74 ERA over the second half, although his control was still not sharp. He will be back; he's a quality athlete and a quality person, and he was pitching well at the end of the year. Although he struggled, he was better than his 7–12 record suggests.

YEAR	TEAM/LEVEL	G	IP	W–L	PCT.	HITS	SO	BB	ERA
1990	California	32	236	18–9	.667	210	177	81	2.40
1991	California	34	227	18–9	.667	205	171	101	3.80
1992	California	31	204	7–12	.368	212	124	98	3.96

STEVE FIREOVID
Texas Rangers
Starting Pitcher
$1

How many minor leaguers have written books? Rick Wolff, Jerry Kettle, Steve Fireovid are the only ones I can think of . . . made the opening day roster (finally) but was sent down April 21, posted some good stats at Oklahoma City but gave up 130 hits in 105 innings. Now 35 years old, has won 138 games in the minor leagues but only three in the majors.

YEAR	TEAM/LEVEL	G	IP	W–L	PCT.	HITS	SO	BB	ERA
1990	Indianapolis AAA	29	171	10–12	.455	163	84	34	2.63
1991	Buffalo AAA	34	130	9–8	.529	127	72	43	2.90
1992	Oklahoma City AAA	33	105	7–2	.778	130	54	28	3.10

BRIAN FISHER
Seattle Mariners
Starting Pitcher
$9

Fisher came out of the Yankees system years ago, pitched well for the Yankees in 1985 and the Pirates in 1987. He's bounced around like Shelley Winters, was called up by Seattle on July 6 and moved into the starting rotation July 24. He pitched OK as a starter except for his obscene strikeout/walk ratio. Very unlikely to make it through the '93 season in the rotation.

YEAR	TEAM/LEVEL	G	IP	W–L	PCT.	HITS	SO	BB	ERA
1991	Denver AAA	44	98	10–6	.625	98	66	39	4.78
1992	Nashville AAA	24	41	2–1	.667	43	31	12	4.14
1992	Seattle	22	91	4–3	.571	80	26	47	4.53

MIKE FLANAGAN
Baltimore Orioles
Relief Pitcher
No Value

Somehow managed to stay with the Orioles all year despite posting 8.05 ERA . . . the league hit .338 against him, right-handed batters hitting .384 . . . career is obviously over. I was once condemned in *The Sporting News* for writing that Flanagan was "the Orioles' answer to Mike Torrez." Torrez wound up his career 185–160 (.536) with 3.97 ERA, Flanagan 167–143 (.539) with 3.90 ERA.

YEAR	TEAM/LEVEL	G	IP	W–L	SAVES	HITS	SO	BB	ERA
1990	Toronto	5	20	2–2	0	28	5	8	5.31
1991	Baltimore	64	98	2–7	3	84	55	25	2.38
1992	Baltimore	42	35	0–0	0	50	17	23	8.05

DAVE FLEMING
Seattle Mariners
Starting Pitcher
$34

I expect that he will continue to pitch well, although he may not win 17 games again. The most critical thing for Fleming is whether his strikeout rate moves up or down in the next two years. If he pushes it upward, **as most young pitchers do**, then he'll have a long career and win 120 to 150 games. If not, he'll just be effective for a few years.

YEAR	TEAM/LEVEL	G	IP	W–L	PCT.	HITS	SO	BB	ERA
1991	Jacksonville AAA	21	140	10–6	.625	129	109	25	2.70
1991	Seattle	9	18	1–0	1.000	19	11	3	6.62
1992	Seattle	33	228	17–10	.630	225	112	60	3.39

PAUL FLETCHER
Philadelphia Phillies
Starting Pitcher
$12

A 40th-round draft pick in 1988, just scuffled and survived until last year, when he learned to throw a slider, and pitched well at both Double-A and Triple-A. Right-hander, 26 years old, throws the best changeup in the Philadelphia system. Grade C prospect; pitchers who don't learn to pitch until age 25 have a big advantage because their arms aren't abused when they're young.

YEAR	TEAM/LEVEL	G	IP	W–L	PCT.	HITS	SO	BB	ERA
1991	Reading AA	21	121	7–9	.438	111	90	56	3.51
1992	Reading AA	22	127	9–4	.692	103	103	47	2.83
1992	Scranton AAA	4	23	3–0	1.000	17	26	2	2.78

TIM FORTUGNO
California Angels
Pitcher
$18

A 30-year-old rookie, had impressive start after July callup but faded. Didn't enter pro ball until age 24, has belonged to several teams since. The Brewers once bought him from Reno for $2500 and a dozen baseballs . . . *I strongly suspect that he has the ability to surprise, and could have a major league career of surprising quality.* Has bounced around, but enjoyed more success than failure.

YEAR	TEAM/LEVEL	G	IP	W–L	SAVES	HITS	SO	BB	ERA
1991	Denver AAA	26	35	0–1	2	30	39	20	3.57
1992	Edmonton AAA	26	73	6–4	1	69	82	33	3.56
1992	California	14	42	1–1	1	37	31	19	5.18

TONY FOSSAS
Boston Red Sox
Relief Pitcher
$8

Pudgy one-out reliever with no fastball, the league hit .279 against him last year, and he also had poor control record. His platoon differential appears to be immense, leaving him vulnerable to pinch hitters. I don't know if he'll be back this year, but the Red Sox have three middle–aged, mediocre left-handers in the bullpen (Fossas, Hesketh, and Young), and that's too many.

YEAR	TEAM/LEVEL	G	IP	W–L	SAVES	HITS	SO	BB	ERA
1990	Milwaukee	32	29	2–3	0	44	24	10	6.44
1991	Boston	64	57	3–2	1	49	29	28	3.47
1992	Boston	60	30	1–2	2	31	19	14	2.43

STEVE FOSTER
Cincinnati Reds
Relief Pitcher
$13

A 26-year-old right-hander, had a modestly impressive rookie season and figures to move up a slot in the Reds' deep bullpen in '93. He started the season with Cincinnati, was hit hard for a month, went to Nashville, pitched great for a month, was called up, and pitched great the rest of the year except for one start, in which he was battered. Grade C prospect.

YEAR	TEAM/LEVEL	G	IP	W–L	SAVES	HITS	SO	BB	ERA
1991	Cincinnati	11	14	0–0	0	7	11	4	1.93
1992	Nashville AAA	17	50	5–3	1	53	28	22	2.68
1992	Cincinnati	31	50	1–1	2	52	34	13	2.88

JOHN FRANCO
New York Mets
Closer
$34

Discovered the secret of not blowing your ERA in September: Don't pitch in September. Went on the DL in July with an inflamed elbow, returned August 1, back on DL August 20. Since 1989 his ERA in September–October is 5.86 . . . faced only 128 batters in '92, equivalent to Chris Donnels's playing time. I suspect that his injury problems will continue, and progress.

YEAR	TEAM/LEVEL	G	IP	W–L	SAVES	HITS	SO	BB	ERA
1990	New York	55	68	5–3	33	66	56	21	2.53
1991	New York	52	55	5–9	30	61	45	18	2.93
1992	New York	31	33	6–2	15	24	20	11	1.64

MARVIN FREEMAN
Atlanta Braves
Relief Pitcher
$19

Huge right-hander, failed a number of trials as a starting pitcher but finally found a home in the Atlanta bullpen and did a creditable job in a setup role. He had 16 holds, third in the NL . . . fairly good hits/innings, fair control, surprisingly difficult to run on . . . also pitched well in the second half of 1991. I expect him to continue to pitch well.

YEAR	TEAM/LEVEL	G	IP	W–L	SAVES	HITS	SO	BB	ERA
1990	Two Teams	25	48	1–2	1	41	38	17	4.31
1991	Atlanta	34	48	1–0	1	37	34	13	3.00
1992	Atlanta	58	64	7–5	3	61	41	29	3.22

STEVE FREY
California Angels
Relief Pitcher
$11

A left-handed spot reliever, but 1) 69 percent of the hitters he faced last year were right-handed, and 2) left-handed hitters hit five home runs against him in only 53 at bats (!), and have hit him hard throughout his career . . . limited hitters to .127 batting average with men in scoring position . . . can be replaced at any time. There are a lot of guys like him.

YEAR	TEAM/LEVEL	G	IP	W–L	SAVES	HITS	SO	BB	ERA
1990	Montreal	51	56	8–2	9	44	29	29	2.10
1991	Montreal	31	40	0–1	1	43	21	23	4.99
1992	California	51	45	4–2	4	39	24	22	3.57

TODD FROHWIRTH
Baltimore Orioles
Relief Pitcher
$28

Magnificent role player. Like Quisenberry and Eichhorn, vulnerable to a left-handed batter (although it doesn't show in last year's stats) and needs a good infield behind him. There is no question but that the number of pitchers like this is growing, and the acceptance of them as key players is growing. In 40 years, they may well be the rule rather than the exception.

YEAR	TEAM/LEVEL	G	IP	W–L	SAVES	HITS	SO	BB	ERA
1990	Philadelphia	5	1	0–1	0	3	1	6	18.00
1991	Baltimore	51	96	7–3	3	64	77	29	1.87
1992	Baltimore	65	106	4–3	4	97	58	41	2.46

RAMON GARCIA
Chicago White Sox
Starting Pitcher
$2

Started 15 games for the White Sox in 1991 and was back in the minors last year, where he was 9–11 but had respectable 3.71 ERA at Vancouver. Expanson may get him another look . . . doesn't seem to be throwing as hard as he was a couple of years ago, but he's only 23, so his fastball may come back. Has improved control. Grade D prospect.

YEAR	TEAM/LEVEL	G	IP	W–L	PCT.	HITS	SO	BB	ERA
1991	AA and AAA	10	65	6–2	.750	51	55	18	2.20
1991	Chicago	16	78	4–4	.500	79	40	31	5.40
1992	Vancouver AAA	28	170	9–11	.450	165	79	56	3.71

MIKE GARDINER
Boston Red Sox
Starting Pitcher
$9

Not to be confused with Wes Gardner . . . well, OK, go ahead and confuse them. One 4–10 pitcher with a 4.75 ERA is about the same as another. Actually, I suspect Gardiner may have some ability that hasn't surfaced. His K/W rate is OK, and he pitched tremendously well at Williamsport and Pawtucket. May be good major league pitcher if he can get the corner turned.

YEAR	TEAM/LEVEL	G	IP	W–L	PCT.	HITS	SO	BB	ERA
1990	Seattle	5	13	0–2	.000	22	6	5	10.66
1991	Boston	22	130	9–10	.474	140	91	47	4.85
1992	Boston	28	131	4–10	.286	126	79	58	4.75

MARK GARDNER
Montreal Expos
Starting Pitcher
$25

Changes speeds, throws breaking stuff. Hangs his front leg up in the air to destroy the hitter's timing, which is kind of a Montreal team characteristic. He's not as effective as I thought he might become, but as long as he's healthy, which he is, he'll win as many games as he loses, and could surprise us with a 17-win season.

YEAR	TEAM/LEVEL	G	IP	W–L	PCT.	HITS	SO	BB	ERA
1990	Montreal	27	153	7–9	.438	129	135	61	3.42
1991	Montreal	27	168	9–11	.450	139	107	75	3.85
1992	Montreal	33	180	12–10	.545	179	132	60	4.36

SCOTT GARRELTS
San Francisco Giants
Pitcher
$1

You may be wondering what has happened to him. He had major surgery last winter to repair a partially torn tendon in his right elbow, then tried to pitch in the minors. He wasn't ready, and it was decided to call it off rather than risk a re-injury. He'll try again this year; I don't expect him to be an effective pitcher for a couple of years.

YEAR	TEAM/LEVEL	G	IP	W–L	PCT.	HITS	SO	BB	ERA
1989	San Francisco	30	193	14–5	.737	149	119	46	2.28
1990	San Francisco	31	182	12–11	.522	190	80	70	4.15
1991	San Francisco	8	20	1–1	.500	25	8	9	6.41

PAUL GIBSON
New York Mets
Relief Pitcher
$3

A left-hander, but has been consistently more effective against right-handed hitters than left-handers . . . also has consistent record of ineffectiveness against the first batter he faces, and also against the leadoff man in an inning . . . no fastball, is always jerking the hitter's chain, trying to get him to swing at an outside pitch, trying to get him to lunge at a changeup. Very little value.

YEAR	TEAM/LEVEL	G	IP	W–L	SAVES	HITS	SO	BB	ERA
1990	Detroit	61	97	5–4	3	99	56	44	3.05
1991	Detroit	68	96	5–7	8	112	52	48	4.59
1992	New York	43	62	0–1	0	70	49	25	5.23

TOM GLAVINE
Atlanta Braves
Starting Pitcher
$75

My opinion is that Greg Maddux is the *best* starting pitcher in the NL, but that's not a knock at Glavine; there can only be one best. I'd rank Glavine third, as I did a year ago, behind Maddux and Drabek . . . 1992 ratio of strikeouts to wins (129 to 20) would suggest that you might stay away from him in '92. Anything below 7/1 warns of a decline . . .

YEAR	TEAM/LEVEL	G	IP	W–L	PCT.	HITS	SO	BB	ERA
1990	Atlanta	33	214	10–12	.455	232	129	78	4.28
1991	Atlanta	34	246	20–11	.645	201	192	69	2.56
1992	Atlanta	33	225	20–8	.714	197	129	70	2.76

JERRY DON GLEATON
San Francisco Giants
Relief Pitcher
$3

He signed with the Pirates in April and was released by them in July, signed a Triple-A contract with Phoenix on August 4. He will never stop pitching voluntarily and there will always be teams looking for left-handers, so I expect his milk-run career to continue for several more stops. Normally has good control, but couldn't get enough work with the Pirates to stay sharp.

YEAR	TEAM/LEVEL	G	IP	W–L	SAVES	HITS	SO	BB	ERA
1990	Detroit	57	83	1–3	13	62	56	25	2.94
1991	Detroit	47	75	3–2	2	74	47	39	4.06
1992	Pittsburgh	23	32	1–0	0	34	18	19	4.26

GREG GOHR
Detroit Tigers
Starting Pitcher
$6

Right-handed pitching prospect, 25 years old, was the Tigers' number-one draft pick in '89 and is still considered a top prospect despite unimpressive minor league career. He pitched better at Toledo than he had before (8–10 with 3.99 ERA) after he stopped throwing the slider, and worked with three pitches (fastball, curve, change). K/W ratio has improved. Grade C prospect.

YEAR	TEAM/LEVEL	G	IP	W–L	PCT.	HITS	SO	BB	ERA
1990	Lakeland A	25	138	13–5	.722	125	90	50	2.62
1991	AA and AAA	28	159	10–8	.556	134	106	68	4.29
1992	Toledo AAA	22	131	8–10	.444	124	94	46	3.99

DWIGHT GOODEN
New York Mets
Starting Pitcher
$35

Will have more outstanding seasons. It is not unusual for a great pitcher to have a mediocre season in mid-career, particularly coming off an injury. Look at Steve Carlton in 1973 (13–20, 3.90 ERA), Seaver in 1974 (11–11, 3.20), Jim Palmer in 1974 (7–12, 3.27), and Bob Feller in 1949 (15–14, 3.75). They all came back, and Gooden will, too.

YEAR	TEAM/LEVEL	G	IP	W–L	PCT.	HITS	SO	BB	ERA
1990	New York	34	233	19–7	.731	229	223	70	3.82
1991	New York	27	190	13–7	.650	185	150	56	3.60
1992	New York	31	206	10–13	.435	197	145	70	3.67

TOM GORDON
Kansas City Royals
Relief Pitcher
$18

For four straight years he's had a dramatically better ERA as a reliever than as a starter. Even though I don't particularly see any reason for that and don't buy those I've heard, you have to respect that much evidence. Still immature, occasionally seems to forget there's a ballgame in progress; throws fairly hard, best two pitches are two curves. Still has the ability to be a dominant pitcher.

YEAR	TEAM/LEVEL	G	IP	W–L	SAVES	HITS	SO	BB	ERA
1990	Kansas City	32	195	12–11	0	192	175	99	3.73
1991	Kansas City	45	158	9–14	1	129	167	87	3.87
1992	Kansas City	40	118	6–10	0	116	98	55	4.59

GOOSE GOSSAGE
Oakland Athletics
Relief Pitcher
$2

Has been in the major leagues since Robin Yount was in high school . . . power pitchers last forever, and Goose was still pitching well last year until stopped in mid-July with tendinitis in his right bicep. Assuming that he wants to come to back in '93, I would expect him to continue to pitch fairly well and continue to have his innings limited by injuries.

YEAR	TEAM/LEVEL	G	IP	W–L	SAVES	HITS	SO	BB	ERA
1989	Two Teams	42	58	3–1	5	46	30	30	2.95
1991	Texas	44	41	4–2	1	33	28	16	3.57
1992	Oakland	30	38	0–2	0	32	26	19	2.84

JIM GOTT
Los Angeles Dodgers
Relief Pitcher
$29

His ERA was well below 2.00 until he was hit hard in September. He established a career high in games pitched (68) and pitched his most innings since moving to the bullpen in 1987, so perhaps he was simply tired at the end . . . Lasorda has been reluctant to give him a shot as the Dodgers' closer, which is the primary restraint on his value.

YEAR	TEAM/LEVEL	G	IP	W–L	SAVES	HITS	SO	BB	ERA
1990	Los Angeles	50	62	3–5	3	59	44	34	2.90
1991	Los Angeles	55	76	4–3	2	63	73	32	2.96
1992	Los Angeles	68	88	3–3	6	72	75	41	2.45

MAURO GOZZO
Minnesota Twins
Starting Pitcher
$2

Minor league veteran of at least five organizations, has had a cup of coffee or two with Toronto and Cleveland. Right-hander with .585 career winning percentage in the minors, he's only 26 and pitched his best ball in several years with Portland last year, moving between the bullpen and the starting rotation. Grade D prospect; a good bet to be in the majors this year.

YEAR	TEAM/LEVEL	G	IP	W–L	PCT.	HITS	SO	BB	ERA
1990	Syracuse AAA	34	98	3–8	.273	87	62	44	3.58
1991	Colorado Sp AAA	25	130	10–6	.625	143	81	68	5.25
1992	Portland AAA	37	156	10–9	.526	155	108	50	3.35

JOE GRAHE
California Angels
Closer
$26

An ineffective starting pitcher in '91 and early '92, Grahe stepped into the closer's role when Harvey went down and was almost perfect through June (0.68 ERA), July (2.25), and August (0.75), had a couple of bad outings in September . . . throws ground balls, control record has never been outstanding. I would be surprised, but not astonished, if he continued to pitch well.

YEAR	TEAM/LEVEL	G	IP	W–L	SAVES	HITS	SO	BB	ERA
1990	California	8	43	3–4	0	51	25	23	4.98
1991	California	18	73	3–7	0	84	40	33	4.81
1992	California	46	95	5–6	21	85	39	39	3.52

MARK (Research) GRANT
Seattle Mariners
Starter/Reliever
$1

A 29-year-old veteran, started 10 times for the Giants in 1984, went back to the minors, started 25 times in '87, went back to the minors . . . he's never been particularly effective even in the minor leagues. He has developed outstanding control, but left-handed batters hit .336 against him last year. Let's see, if a .260 hitter becomes a .336 hitter, what does Wade Boggs become . . .

YEAR	TEAM/LEVEL	G	IP	W–L	SAVES	HITS	SO	BB	ERA
1989	San Diego	50	116	8–2	2	105	69	32	3.33
1990	Two Teams	59	91	2–3	3	108	69	37	4.73
1992	Seattle	23	81	2–4	0	100	42	22	3.89

MARK GRATER
St. Louis Cardinals
Minor League Closer
$12

Another minor league veteran, has earned only three major league innings with seven years of minor league work, during which his career ERA is 2.30. He doesn't have a fastball to speak of, but has adopted the Eckersley go-right-at-em philosophy with outstanding success in the minors. Grade C prospect; the Cardinals will run out of options on him eventually . . .

YEAR	TEAM/LEVEL	G	IP	W–L	SAVES	HITS	SO	BB	ERA
1990	AA and AAA	53	72	2–2	20	55	61	33	2.99
1991	Louisville AAA	58	80	3–5	12	68	53	33	2.02
1992	Louisville AAA	54	76	7–8	24	74	46	15	2.13

TYLER GREEN
Philadelphia Phillies
Starting Pitcher
$26

The Phillies first pick in 1991, has been dominant when able to pitch, but career has been tentative because of shoulder trouble. Dr. Jobe performed surgery on the shoulder on October 17 and gave a promising diagnosis, saying that the shoulder had "a bunch of debris," which had been removed. Has the best stuff in the Philadelphia system. **Grade A prospect.**

YEAR	TEAM/LEVEL	G	IP	W–L	PCT.	HITS	SO	BB	ERA
1991	Two Teams A	5	28	3–0	1.000	10	39	14	1.29
1992	Reading AA	12	62	6–3	.667	46	67	20	1.88
1992	Scranton AAA	2	10	0–1	.000	7	15	12	6.10

TOMMY GREENE
Philadelphia Phillies
Starting Pitcher
$18

Went on the disabled list May 13 with tendinitis in his shoulder, and stayed there until September. This may be a record. Tendinitis normally clears up in a few weeks if nothing else is irritating the shoulder . . . Greene was terrific in '91, just a hard thrower before that. I like him, but Momma told me never to put my money on a sore-armed pitcher.

YEAR	TEAM/LEVEL	G	IP	W–L	PCT.	HITS	SO	BB	ERA
1990	Two Teams	15	51	3–3	.500	50	21	26	5.08
1991	Philadelphia	36	208	13–7	.650	177	154	66	3.38
1992	Philadelphia	13	64	3–3	.500	75	39	34	5.32

BUDDY GROOM
Detroit Tigers
Starting Pitcher
$16

Seasoned by almost 800 minor league innings, he appears to be ready to pitch and pitch well in the majors. Is 27 years old, has pitched well at every level, although usually not in his first try. Tommy John–type pitcher—left-hander, throws ground balls, has good control, and cuts off the running game. Tommy John–type pitchers usually have their best years in their thirties. I like him.

YEAR	TEAM/LEVEL	G	IP	W–L	PCT.	HITS	SO	BB	ERA
1991	AA and AAA	35	127	9–6	.600	124	88	37	3.98
1992	Toledo AAA	16	109	7–7	.500	102	71	23	2.80
1992	Detroit	12	39	0–5	.000	48	15	22	5.82

KEVIN GROSS
Los Angeles Dodgers
Starting Pitcher
$36

Whether any starter will ever post a winning record with the Dodgers again is doubtful, but I've always defended Gross and I intend to continue. He pitched 205 innings, had a great K/W rate if you don't count Lasorda's intentional walks, and threw a no-hitter. I know he had some bad games, but his won–lost record simply doesn't reflect how well he pitched.

YEAR	TEAM/LEVEL	G	IP	W–L	PCT.	HITS	SO	BB	ERA
1990	Montreal	31	163	9–12	.429	171	111	65	4.57
1991	Los Angeles	46	116	10–11	.476	123	95	50	3.58
1992	Los Angeles	34	205	8–13	.381	182	158	77	3.17

KIP GROSS
Los Angeles Dodgers
Relief Pitcher
$2

The Dodgers' favorite yo-yo, was hit hard in his major league time. He may have a role in the majors as a middle reliever. Ground ball pitcher, had exceptional control record in the minor leagues and could start perhaps if that came back, but he hasn't thrown strikes consistently since 1989. Has had trouble getting out the first hitter. Grade D prospect.

YEAR	TEAM/LEVEL	G	IP	W–L	SAVES	HITS	SO	BB	ERA
1991	Cincinnati	29	86	6–4	0	93	40	40	3.47
1992	Albuquerque AAA	31	108	6–5	8	96	58	36	3.51
1992	Los Angeles	16	24	1–1	0	32	14	10	4.18

MARK GUBICZA
Kansas City Royals
Starting Pitcher
$19

His comeback was coming along splendidly until McRae decided to let him start throwing 120 pitches a start. I'm not down on McRae generally, but any idiot should know enough to put a pitch limit on a pitcher coming back from rotator cuff surgery . . . went on the DL July 11 with stiffness in his shoulder. A fine pitcher, but his future is in doubt.

YEAR	TEAM/LEVEL	G	IP	W–L	PCT.	HITS	SO	BB	ERA
1990	Kansas City	16	94	4–7	.364	101	71	38	4.50
1991	Kansas City	26	133	9–12	.429	168	89	42	5.68
1992	Kansas City	18	111	7–6	.538	110	81	36	3.72

LEE GUETTERMAN
New York Mets
Relief Pitcher
$3

He pitched 58 times last year despite a 7.09 ERA. I wonder if this is some sort of obscure and stupid record, highest total of ERA times games pitched (Lee Guetterman, 1992, 411.22). He posted ERAs over 8.00 in four of the six months. The league hit .335 against him, with a slugging percentage over .500 . . . doubt that he will come back.

YEAR	TEAM/LEVEL	G	IP	W–L	SAVES	HITS	SO	BB	ERA
1990	New York	64	93	11–7	2	80	48	26	3.39
1991	New York	64	88	3–4	6	91	35	25	3.68
1992	Two Teams	58	66	4–5	2	92	20	27	7.09

BILL GULLICKSON
Detroit Tigers
Starting Pitcher
$19

He doesn't walk anybody and the Tigers score 5+ runs a game for him, which is enough to keep his record over .500. You never want to *assume* that what worked last year will work again next year. The Tigers may stop hitting home runs for him, and he could go 5–13. I don't think he's a quality pitcher, and I wouldn't want him on my team.

YEAR	TEAM/LEVEL	G	IP	W–L	PCT.	HITS	SO	BB	ERA
1990	Houston	32	193	10–14	.417	221	73	61	3.82
1991	Detroit	35	226	20–9	.690	256	91	44	3.90
1992	Detroit	34	222	14–13	.519	228	64	50	4.34

ERIC GUNDERSON
Seattle Mariners
Pitcher
$1

Left-handed pitcher from the Giants system, has been getting shelled in Triple-A since 1989. He appears to have learned George Bush's secret of moving forward in your profession through constant failure, as his ERAs at Triple-A (5.04, 8.23, 6.14, and 6.02) have earned him a number of major league trials, with predictable results. No prospect despite good arm.

YEAR	TEAM/LEVEL	G	IP	W–L	SAVES	HITS	SO	BB	ERA
1992	Jacksonville AA	15	23	2–0	2	18	23	7	2.31
1992	Calgary AAA	27	52	0–2	5	57	50	31	6.02
1992	Seattle	9	9	2–1	0	12	2	5	8.68

MARK GUTHRIE
Minnesota Twins
Relief Pitcher
$28

Before '92 he had a 4.60 career ERA as a starter, 2.27 as a reliever (37 games). The Twins moved him to the pen full time, and he pitched awfully well, probably as well as Aguilera. If Aguilera's elbow acts up, as it did for several years, Guthrie is probably the backup plan. He did give up seven homers in 186 at bats to right-handed batters.

YEAR	TEAM/LEVEL	G	IP	W–L	SAVES	HITS	SO	BB	ERA
1990	Minnesota	24	145	7–9	0	154	101	39	3.79
1991	Minnesota	41	98	7–5	2	116	72	41	4.32
1992	Minnesota	54	75	2–3	5	59	76	23	2.88

JOHNNY GUZMAN
Oakland
Starting Pitcher
$4

Has had coffee with the A's the last two years, although he is only 22 and his minor league record is largely unimpressive. Left-hander, has good strikeout/walk ratio and had excellent record at Huntsville. Grade B prospect, but LaRussa isn't likely to give him any serious major league time until 1) he pitches consistently well at Triple-A, or 2) the A's fall out of contention.

YEAR	TEAM/LEVEL	G	IP	W–L	PCT.	HITS	SO	BB	ERA
1991	Tacoma AAA	17	80	2–5	.286	113	40	51	6.78
1992	Huntsville AA	14	90	8–2	.800	87	55	26	3.71
1992	Tacoma AAA	20	69	3–6	.333	70	45	24	5.11

JOSE GUZMAN
Texas Rangers
Starting Pitcher
$40

All indicators about him are positive, except that he does have a history of injury. He has had two consecutive quality seasons, the second one probably better than the first. He has his fastball back, or most of it, he has his confidence back, and he knows how to pitch. Finished the season strong. I expect him to win 15 games or more in '93.

YEAR	TEAM/LEVEL	G	IP	W–L	PCT.	HITS	SO	BB	ERA
1988	Texas	30	207	11–13	.458	180	157	82	3.70
1991	Texas	25	170	13–7	.650	152	125	84	3.08
1992	Texas	33	224	16–11	.593	229	179	73	3.66

JUAN GUZMAN
Toronto Blue Jays
Starting Pitcher
$60

Was having a Cy Young season until he strained a back muscle in late July. Until two years ago his career had been stalled by chronic wildness, but he could always sting the radar guns, and that counts for something, too. I do *not* anticipate greatness; I estimate a 20 percent chance of his wildness recurring, 60 percent chance of career-shortening injury, 20 percent chance of having top-drawer career.

YEAR	TEAM/LEVEL	G	IP	W–L	PCT.	HITS	SO	BB	ERA
1991	Syracuse AAA	12	67	4–5	.444	46	67	42	4.03
1991	Toronto	23	139	10–3	.769	98	123	66	2.99
1992	Toronto	28	181	16–5	.762	135	165	72	2.64

DAVE HAAS
Detroit Tigers
Relief Pitcher
$13

A low-round draft pick, has a repeated pattern of failing at one level, returning the next year and succeeding. In '92 he was 6–3, 3.23 ERA at Toledo, was called up about August 1 and continued to pitch well at the major league level, walking only 16 men in 11 starts. Unimpressive stuff, but I like the record; Grade C prospect.

YEAR	TEAM/LEVEL	G	IP	W–L	PCT.	HITS	SO	BB	ERA
1991	Toledo AAA	28	158	8–10	.444	187	133	77	5.23
1992	Toledo AAA	22	149	9–8	.529	149	112	53	4.18
1992	Detroit	12	62	5–3	.625	68	29	16	3.94

JOHN HABYAN
New York Yankees
Relief Pitcher
$6

After pitching quite well in 1991, he posted an ERA of 1.26 in the first two months of '92, 3.67 in the middle two months, 8.47 after August 1. The league hit .393 against him after the All-Star break. He must have had an injury of some sort, but exactly what isn't known right now. Won't be effective unless he gets it fixed.

YEAR	TEAM/LEVEL	G	IP	W–L	SAVES	HITS	SO	BB	ERA
1990	New York	6	9	0–0	0	10	4	2	2.08
1991	New York	66	90	4–2	2	73	70	20	2.30
1992	New York	56	73	5–6	7	84	44	21	3.84

JOEY HAMILTON
San Diego Padres
Starting Pitcher
$24

A number-one draft pick in 1991, he is regarded as the top prospect in the Padre system. He held out before signing, and then got a late start in '92 because of tendinitis, but pitched impressively at three levels once he finally got his career underway. Expected to start 1993 at Double-A or Triple-A, will get The Call if he pitches well. **Grade A prospect.**

YEAR	TEAM/LEVEL	G	IP	W–L	PCT.	HITS	SO	BB	ERA
1992	Charleston A	7	35	2–2	.500	37	35	4	3.38
1992	High Desert A	8	43	3–3	.500	39	40	16	2.51
1992	Wichita AA	6	35	3–0	1.000	33	26	11	2.86

CHRIS HAMMOND
Cincinnati Reds
Starting Pitcher
$15

Won a three-man battle for the Reds' fifth-starter job, pitched well for two months, then was largely ineffective until September. Has average fastball, curve, and slider, makes his living by changing speeds and moving the ball around. The knock on him is that he is afraid to challenge the hitters with his fastball, but did seem to show more confidence late in the season.

YEAR	TEAM/LEVEL	G	IP	W–L	PCT.	HITS	SO	BB	ERA
1990	Cincinnati	3	11	0–2	.000	13	4	12	6.35
1991	Cincinnati	20	100	7–7	.500	92	50	48	4.06
1992	Cincinnati	28	147	7–10	.412	149	79	55	4.21

CHRIS HANEY
Kansas City Royals
Starting Pitcher
$14

The Royals have been searching for a new Charlie Leibrandt/Bud Black/Larry Gura/Paul Splittorff type, and now have six candidates for that spot on the 40-man roster. Haney is the best of the six, throws a big curve and a soggy fastball, looks good sometimes but as of yet alternates good outings and bad ones. Grade C prospect, no star potential.

YEAR	TEAM/LEVEL	G	IP	W–L	PCT.	HITS	SO	BB	ERA
1991	Montreal	16	85	3–7	.300	94	51	43	4.04
1992	Indianapolis AAA	15	84	5–2	.714	88	61	42	5.14
1992	Two Teams	16	80	4–6	.400	75	54	26	4.61

ERIK HANSON
Seattle Mariners
Starting Pitcher
$26

He who would know the soul of the Seattle Mariners must first get to know Erik Hanson. . . . According to *The Scouting Report: 1992*, "All his pitches (fastball, curve, change-up) are excellent, and he mixes them in a way that keeps hitters guessing." I think his record speaks for itself; it's basically a match for Diego Segui, 1964 . . . career will probably come back, but who knows when?

YEAR	TEAM/LEVEL	G	IP	W–L	PCT.	HITS	SO	BB	ERA
1990	Seattle	33	236	18–9	.667	205	211	68	3.24
1991	Seattle	27	175	8–8	.500	182	143	56	3.81
1992	Seattle	31	187	8–17	.320	209	112	57	4.82

MIKE HARKEY
Chicago Cubs
Starting Pitcher
$5

He missed the first half of the season after 1991 surgery to repair a cartilage tear in his right shoulder. Activated at the break, he started seven times and pitched very well six times, but he was so happy about this that he ruptured the patella tendon in his right knee doing cartwheels. He "faces a long rehabilitation," but is still perceived as extremely valuable.

YEAR	TEAM/LEVEL	G	IP	W–L	PCT.	HITS	SO	BB	ERA
1990	Chicago	27	174	12–6	.667	153	94	59	3.26
1991	Chicago	4	19	0–2	.000	34	15	6	5.30
1992	Chicago	7	38	4–0	1.000	38	21	15	1.89

PETE HARNISCH
Houston Astros
Starting Pitcher
$34

Power pitcher, throws a high fastball and will give up home runs. His 1992 record wasn't everything he had dreamed of, but he made it through the season healthy, and as long as he stays healthy seems certain to have better years. He finished strong, going 4–1 with a 3.13 ERA in his last seven starts. A valuable pitcher, a good investment.

YEAR	TEAM/LEVEL	G	IP	W–L	PCT.	HITS	SO	BB	ERA
1990	Baltimore	31	189	11–11	.500	189	122	86	4.34
1991	Houston	33	217	12–9	.571	169	172	83	2.70
1992	Houston	34	207	9–10	.474	182	164	64	3.70

GENE HARRIS
San Diego Padres
Relief Pitcher
$1

Exactly why he is in the major leagues is not evident from his record. He pitched well for Jacksonville in the Southern League in 1988 and has been ineffective since. He was going to quit baseball last summer and try to play pro football, but relented when traded to San Diego. Throws hard, doesn't have a breaking pitch that he can get over. Grade D prospect.

YEAR	TEAM/LEVEL	G	IP	W–L	SAVES	HITS	SO	BB	ERA
1990	Seattle	25	38	1–2	0	31	43	30	4.74
1991	Calgary AAA	25	35	4–0	4	37	23	11	3.34
1992	Two Teams	22	30	0–2	0	23	25	15	4.15

GREG HARRIS
Boston Red Sox
Relief Pitcher
$23

What I wonder is, how much worse could he be pitching left-handed than the left-handers they have? See, if I was a baseball guy and I had a pitcher who wanted to pitch both ways, I'd figure, "Hey, that'd be great. I could save a roster space." They don't think that way; they figure it's making the game look bad . . . Harris is a very underrated pitcher.

YEAR	TEAM/LEVEL	G	IP	W–L	SAVES	HITS	SO	BB	ERA
1990	Boston	34	184	13–9	0	186	117	77	4.00
1991	Boston	53	173	11–12	2	157	127	69	3.85
1992	Boston	70	108	4–9	4	82	73	60	2.51

GREG W. HARRIS
San Diego Padres
Starting Pitcher
$30

I would recommend very strongly that you draft this man in a rotisserie league or fantasy league. First, his 1992 accomplishments do not represent his ability. He pitched better than his 4–8 record, and better than his ERA. Second, his 1992 injuries (back spasms and a broken finger while bunting) are not arm-related and do not seriously affect his future.

YEAR	TEAM/LEVEL	G	IP	W–L	PCT.	HITS	SO	BB	ERA
1990	San Diego	73	117	8–8	.500	92	97	49	2.30
1991	San Diego	20	133	9–5	.643	116	95	27	2.23
1992	San Diego	20	118	4–8	.333	113	66	35	4.12

MIKE HARTLEY
Philadelphia Phillies
Relief Pitcher
$22

Former prospect from the Los Angeles system, now 31 years old. He set up Mitch Williams last year, and pitched extremely well, certainly better than Williams did. His numbers are likely to expand this year because 1) he should be there from opening day, and 2) the possibility exists that he could move into the closer role. No guarantees but a good risk.

YEAR	TEAM/LEVEL	G	IP	W–L	SAVES	HITS	SO	BB	ERA
1990	Los Angeles	32	79	6–3	1	58	76	30	2.95
1991	Two Teams	58	83	4–1	2	74	63	47	4.21
1992	Philadelphia	46	55	7–6	0	54	53	23	3.44

JEFF HARTSOCK
Chicago Cubs
Pitcher
$1

The Cubs acquired him from the Dodger system a year ago for Steve Wilson, but his record at Triple-A degenerated sharply, as if he was trying to pitch through an injury. In '91 he pitched very well for Albuquerque—3.80 ERA, led the PCL in strikeouts with 123 in 154 innings. Last year he pitched for Des Moines but was completely ineffective. Grade D prospect.

YEAR	TEAM/LEVEL	G	IP	W–L	SAVES	HITS	SO	BB	ERA
1990	Albuquerque	11	46	3–3	0	62	33	30	6.22
1991	Albuquerque	29	154	12–6	0	153	123	78	3.80
1992	Iowa	27	173	5–12	0	177	87	61	4.36

BRYAN HARVEY
California Angels
Closer
$35

After starting the year pitching in his usual overpowering fashion he began to lose his control and get hit. He went on the DL June 7 with an inflamed right elbow and had surgery to shave bone spurs in the elbow on August 14. In general that is not a high-risk surgery. His chances of regaining his former effectiveness are good.

YEAR	TEAM/LEVEL	G	IP	W–L	SAVES	HITS	SO	BB	ERA
1990	California	54	64	4–4	25	45	82	35	3.22
1991	California	67	79	2–4	46	51	101	17	1.60
1992	California	25	29	0–4	13	22	34	11	2.83

HILLY HATHAWAY
California Angels
Left-Handed Starting Pitcher
$16

His real name is "Hillary," but he doesn't advertise the fact. I saw him pitch for Midland; narrow shoulders, whips the ball sidearm, doesn't look strong, best pitch is a slider. He has superb control and is relatively advanced for his age (23). Has gone from 35th-round pick to hot prospect by going 26–11 in the minors. Grade B prospect.

YEAR	TEAM/LEVEL	G	IP	W–L	PCT.	HITS	SO	BB	ERA
1990	Boise A	15	86	8–2	.800	57	113	25	1.46
1991	Quad City A	20	129	9–6	.600	126	110	41	3.35
1992	Midland AA	14	95	7–2	.778	90	69	10	3.21

NEAL HEATON
Milwaukee Brewers
Relief Pitcher
$3

Was released by the Royals after a string of fairly good outings had cut his ERA from 4.85 to 4.07. This makes one wonder if perhaps they didn't want him around for some other reason, but I don't know what it would have been . . . not that he was pitching great. Signed with the Brewers, pitched quite well with Denver and was called up late.

YEAR	TEAM/LEVEL	G	IP	W–L	PCT.	HITS	SO	BB	ERA
1990	Pittsburgh	30	146	12–9	.571	143	68	38	3.45
1991	Pittsburgh	42	69	3–3	.500	72	34	21	4.33
1992	Two Teams	32	42	3–1	.750	43	31	23	4.07

TOM HENKE
Toronto Blue Jays (Free Agent)
Closer
$67

May have been the first closer to average less than one inning per outing. His strikeout rates have dropped and he may not pitch 94 innings in a season again, as he did a few years ago, but he remains as effective as he has ever been when he pitches. Now 35 years old, throws slider, forkball but still lives by the high fastball.

YEAR	TEAM/LEVEL	G	IP	W–L	SAVES	HITS	SO	BB	ERA
1990	Toronto	61	75	2–4	32	58	75	19	2.17
1991	Toronto	49	50	0–2	32	33	53	11	2.32
1992	Toronto	57	56	3–2	34	40	46	22	2.26

MIKE HENNEMAN
Detroit Tigers
Closer
$43

His record was not as good last year as it has been sometimes, but I would not be concerned about him. His opposition batting average was as good as ever, his strikeout rate was *up* and his control record was the best of his career. Eighteen of the 34 runs he allowed were in just five games. I don't think he has lost anything.

YEAR	TEAM/LEVEL	G	IP	W–L	SAVES	HITS	SO	BB	ERA
1990	Detroit	69	94	8–6	22	90	50	33	3.05
1991	Detroit	60	84	10–2	21	81	61	34	2.88
1992	Detroit	60	77	2–6	24	75	58	20	3.96

BUTCH HENRY
Houston Astros
Starting Pitcher
$15

He's an extreme finesse-type pitcher, and there are almost no major league pitchers of that description who are consistently successful. The batting average against him last year was .285, making it hard for him to win without many double plays, and while he does get some ground balls, he doesn't get enough (only 10 ground ball double plays in 1992). He gets too many line drives.

YEAR	TEAM/LEVEL	G	IP	W–L	PCT.	HITS	SO	BB	ERA
1990	Chattanooga AAA	24	143	8–8	.500	151	95	58	4.22
1991	Tucson AA	27	153	10–11	.476	192	97	42	4.80
1992	Houston	28	165	6–9	.400	185	96	41	4.02

DOUG HENRY
Milwaukee Brewers
Closer
$37

Not as good a pitcher as his 1.00 ERA in 1991—but better than his 4.02 last year. Throws 89 MPH fastball, forkball, and hard slider, talks to himself out loud on the mound; you can actually read his lips, talking to himself about what he needs to throw and what he wants to concentrate on . . . I expect him to retain the closer role and improve his ERA in '93.

YEAR	TEAM/LEVEL	G	IP	W–L	SAVES	HITS	SO	BB	ERA
1991	Denver	32	57	3–2	14	47	47	20	2.18
1991	Milwaukee	32	36	2–1	15	16	28	14	1.00
1992	Detroit	60	77	2–6	24	75	58	20	3.96

DWAYNE HENRY
Cincinnati Reds
Relief Pitcher
$17

Now 31 years old, still able to blow away hitters with his fastball but still fighting his control. Piniella tended to use him when the Reds were behind, which gave him limited opportunity for a save, and in that the Reds have Dibble, Charlton, Bankhead, and Foster, it seems extremely unlikely that he will move into a key spot under Perez.

YEAR	TEAM/LEVEL	G	IP	W–L	SAVES	HITS	SO	BB	ERA
1990	Atlanta	34	38	2–2	0	41	34	25	5.63
1991	Houston	52	68	3–2	2	51	51	39	3.19
1992	Cincinnati	60	84	3–3	0	59	72	44	3.33

PAT HENTGEN
Toronto Blue Jays
Relief Pitcher
$13

Season was ended by a strained ligament in his elbow, early August. A hard thrower, no control, no real understanding of what he is doing. His minor league career record is 41–45, and he posted a 4.47 ERA at Syracuse, a pitcher's park. Grade C prospect (because of fastball), but he may be in the rotation because of free agent departures.

YEAR	TEAM/LEVEL	G	IP	W–L	SAVES	HITS	SO	BB	ERA
1990	Knoxville AA	28	153	9–5	0	121	142	68	3.05
1991	Syracuse AAA	31	171	8–9	0	146	155	90	4.47
1992	Toronto	28	50	5–2	0	49	39	32	5.36

GIL HEREDIA
Montreal Expos
Right–Handed Pitcher
$11

Product of the Giants system, came over in a minor league deal because the Expos like to collect pitching prospects and the Giants like to mess with their minds. Heredia is 27 years old, minor league record is outstanding. Superb control, posted ERAs of 2.82 and 2.01 in the Pacific Coast League. Has fragile arm as a result of over-use when he was younger.

YEAR	TEAM/LEVEL	G	IP	W–L	PCT.	HITS	SO	BB	ERA
1991	San Francisco	7	33	0–2	.000	27	13	7	3.82
1992	Phoenix	22	80	5–5	.500	83	37	13	2.01
1992	Two Teams	20	44	2–3	.400	44	22	20	4.23

JEREMY HERNANDEZ
San Diego Padres
Relief Pitcher
$9

Stringbean right-hander, moved up and down last year and was very effective down the stretch (3.24 ERA after the All-Star break). Throws a sinker, control record good, health record good. Early record is like Jeff Montgomery's, in that it doesn't look impressive but if you study it looking for some reason he *won't* be a good pitcher, you don't find it. Grade C prospect.

YEAR	TEAM/LEVEL	G	IP	W–L	SAVES	HITS	SO	BB	ERA
1991	Las Vegas	56	68	4–8	13	76	67	25	4.74
1992	Las Vegas	42	55	2–4	11	53	38	20	2.91
1992	San Diego	26	36	1–4	1	39	25	11	4.17

ROBERTO HERNANDEZ
Chicago White Sox
Relief Pitcher
$38

Moved past Thigpen *and* Radinsky to become the White Sox closer in the final weeks of the season. A first-round draft pick of the Angels in 1986, he was in the California system for four years and never pitched well, began to pitch better immediately on joining the White Sox. Best pitch is split-finger, also throws fastball as out pitch and mixes in slider and change.

YEAR	TEAM/LEVEL	G	IP	W–L	SAVES	HITS	SO	BB	ERA
1990	AA and AAA	28	187	11–10	0	176	111	69	3.31
1991	AA and AAA	11	67	6–2	0	52	65	29	2.81
1992	Chicago	43	71	7–3	12	45	68	20	1.65

XAVIER HERNANDEZ
Houston Astros
Relief Pitcher
$28

One of three Houston relievers who worked 70+ games and 100+ innings last year. Such workloads were at one time fairly common, but then at one time it was widely accepted that relief pitchers were only effective for a year or two. Howe may be the only manager who works his relievers that hard anymore, and I think there is some risk in it . . .

YEAR	TEAM/LEVEL	G	IP	W–L	SAVES	HITS	SO	BB	ERA
1990	Houston	34	62	2–1	0	60	24	24	4.62
1991	Houston	32	63	2–7	3	66	55	32	4.71
1992	Houston	77	111	9–1	7	81	96	42	2.11

OREL HERSHISER
Los Angeles Dodgers
Starting Pitcher
$29

Pitched consistently well except for a sinking spell in July, when he gave up 54 hits in 35 innings and pretty much ruined his stats . . . strikeout rate is 85 percent of what it was in his salad days, which would be normal loss from aging anyway . . . being a ground ball pitcher for the Dodgers is like being a lifeguard for the lemmings.

YEAR	TEAM/LEVEL	G	IP	W–L	PCT.	HITS	SO	BB	ERA
1990	Los Angeles	4	25	1–1	.500	26	16	4	4.26
1991	Los Angeles	21	112	7–2	.778	112	73	32	3.46
1992	Los Angeles	33	211	10–15	.400	209	130	69	3.67

JOE HESKETH
Boston Red Sox
Left-Handed Pitcher
$14

He pitched well as a starting pitcher until June 18, was hit hard from then through August, came back and was pitching well at the end of the season. On balance it was a poor season, but he will have better ones. He gave up 38 doubles in 149 innings, some of which I am sure are attributable to his being a left-hander in Fenway Park.

YEAR	TEAM/LEVEL	G	IP	W–L	SAVES	HITS	SO	BB	ERA
1990	Three Teams	45	60	1–6	5	69	50	25	4.53
1991	Boston	39	153	12–4	0	142	104	53	3.29
1992	Boston	30	149	8–9	1	162	104	58	4.36

GREG HIBBARD
Chicago White Sox
Starting Pitcher
$18

Fifth-starter type, throws a changeup and a sinking fastball as his best pitches, also a curve and slider. Good control, holds runners well, but doesn't have an out pitch he can count on, and gets hurt with his three-four pitches. His 10–7 record may keep him in the rotation for another year, but has little if any potential to have a big season.

YEAR	TEAM/LEVEL	G	IP	W–L	PCT.	HITS	SO	BB	ERA
1990	Chicago	33	211	14–9	.609	202	92	55	3.16
1991	Chicago	32	194	11–11	.500	196	71	57	4.31
1992	Chicago	31	176	10–7	.588	187	69	57	4.40

BRYAN HICKERSON
San Francisco Giants
Relief Pitcher
$19

Left-handed reliever, but not a one–out specialist. Good fastball, no record of consistent success. Coming into the year nothing was expected of him, but he pitched extremely well doing garbage relief, and will be looking for a better job in '93 . . . Minnesota native originally signed by the Twins, came to San Francisco in the Gladden package while he was still in the low minors.

YEAR	TEAM/LEVEL	G	IP	W–L	SAVES	HITS	SO	BB	ERA
1991	Shreveport	23	39	3–4	2	36	41	14	3.00
1991	San Francisco	17	50	2–2	0	53	43	17	3.60
1992	San Francisco	61	87	5–3	0	74	68	21	3.09

KEN HILL
Montreal Expos
Starting Pitcher
$42

Has emerged as one of the better starting pitchers in the National League. He's always had a good fastball, but added a forkball in 1990 and has also steadily improved his control, the combination pushing him into the top rank of NL starters. Excellent athlete; vulnerable to the stolen base. As a ground ball pitcher he is significantly more effective on grass fields than on turf.

YEAR	TEAM/LEVEL	G	IP	W–L	PCT.	HITS	SO	BB	ERA
1990	St. Louis	17	79	5–6	.455	79	58	33	5.49
1991	St. Louis	30	182	11–10	.524	147	121	67	3.57
1992	Montreal	33	218	16–9	.640	187	150	75	2.68

MILT HILL
Cincinnati Reds
Relief Pitcher
$12

A 28th-round draft pick, he demonstrates the principle that if you pitch well long enough the franchise will eventually forgive you for not throwing 90. In six years in the minors Hill has a career ERA of 2.33, with his *worst* being 2.94. After three good years in Triple-A he eventually became the closer there, and will be in the majors in '93.

YEAR	TEAM/LEVEL	G	IP	W–L	SAVES	HITS	SO	BB	ERA
1991	Cincinnati	22	33	1–1	0	36	20	8	3.78
1992	Nashville AAA	53	74	0–5	18	56	70	17	2.66
1992	Cincinnati	14	20	0–0	1	15	10	5	3.15

TYRONE HILL
Milwaukee Brewers
Starting Pitcher
$7

The Brewers' first-round pick in 1991, has pitched well so far and is regarded as one of the bright lights of the organization. His season ended early due to tendinitis in his triceps, and he has walked some people in the low minors, but this may be in part because he turns the hitters into spectators. Grade B prospect, not up this year.

YEAR	TEAM/LEVEL	G	IP	W–L	PCT.	HITS	SO	BB	ERA
1990	(Yucaipa High School, California)								
1991	Helena R	11	60	4–2	.667	43	76	35	3.15
1992	Beloit A	20	114	9–5	.643	76	133	74	3.25

SHAWN HILLEGAS
Oakland Athletics
Starting Pitcher
$1

His one good game of last year was a shutout in Oakland, which earned him a look by the A's after he was cut by the Yankees. His control comes and goes. He doesn't have a breaking pitch and might develop suddenly if he could come up with one, but you're really supposed to take care of those things in the minor leagues.

YEAR	TEAM/LEVEL	G	IP	W–L	PCT.	HITS	SO	BB	ERA
1990	Chicago	7	11	0–0	.000	4	5	5	0.79
1991	Cleveland	51	83	3–4	.429	67	66	46	4.34
1992	Two Teams	26	86	1–8	.111	104	49	37	5.23

ERIC HILLMAN
New York Mets
Left-Handed Pitcher
$4

A left-hander is always in demand, apart from which I see nothing about him to like. The tallest player ever to play for the Mets at 6-10, Hillman doesn't throw exceptionally hard and doesn't have any particular record of minor league success. I think the upper boundary for him is to become the new Lee Guetterman. No prospect.

YEAR	TEAM/LEVEL	G	IP	W–L	PCT.	HITS	SO	BB	ERA
1991	Tidewater AAA	27	161	5–12	.294	184	91	58	4.01
1992	Tidewater AAA	34	91	9–2	.818	93	49	27	3.65
1992	New York	11	52	2–2	.500	67	16	10	5.33

STERLING HITCHCOCK
New York Yankees
Starting Pitcher
$3

Left-hander with 526 strikeouts in 516 minor league innings. *Baseball America* says he did this with "a solid breaking ball, a tricky fastball and a deceptive motion," which sounds to me like they hadn't seen him, either. A "solid" breaking ball, what the hell is that? Grade B prospect, likely to be at Triple-A this year, or for the next five years if Steinbrenner is back.

YEAR	TEAM/LEVEL	G	IP	W–L	PCT.	HITS	SO	BB	ERA
1990	Greensboro A	27	173	12–12	.500	122	171	60	2.91
1991	Prince William A	19	119	7–7	.500	111	101	26	2.64
1992	Albany AA	24	146	6–9	.400	116	155	42	2.58

TREVOR HOFFMAN
Cincinnati Reds
Relief Pitcher
$11

Glenn Hoffman's little brother, was drafted by Cincinnati in 1989 as an infielder, converted to the mound after he hit .212 at Charleston in '90. At two levels in '91 he struck out 75 men in 48 innings, which got his career moving right away. The Reds don't know whether they want him to start or relieve, and they have no shortage of either.

YEAR	TEAM/LEVEL	G	IP	W–L	SAVES	HITS	SO	BB	ERA
1991	A and AA	41	48	1–2	20	32	75	20	1.89
1992	Chattanooga AA	6	30	3–0	0	22	31	11	1.52
1992	Nashville AAA	42	65	4–6	6	57	63	32	4.27

JESSIE HOLLINS
Chicago Cubs
Relief Pitcher
$9

Throws 90, one of the two hardest throwers in the Cub system. A big guy, compared physically to Lee Smith, but his control has periodically exploded, resulting in, for example, 83 walks in 98 innings at Winston-Salem in 1991. At other times his control has been fine. He saved 25 games at Charlotte last summer with a strikeout to walk ratio of 70/32 . . . Grade C prospect.

YEAR	TEAM/LEVEL	G	IP	W–L	SAVES	HITS	SO	BB	ERA
1990	Geneva A	17	97	10–3	0	87	115	49	2.77
1991	Winston–Salem A	41	98	4–8	5	107	74	83	5.67
1992	Charlotte AA	63	70	3–4	25	60	73	32	3.20

BRIAN HOLMAN
Seattle Mariners
Starting Pitcher
$6

Had surgery October 10, 1991, to repair a tear in his rotator cuff. Under pressure, he could have tried to come back in '92, but the Mariners elected to keep his rehabilitation program outside the white lines for a year. This was wise, as what were the chances he was going to pitch well, anyway? His loss was a key to the Mariners' collapse; his return is speculative.

YEAR	TEAM/LEVEL	G	IP	W–L	PCT.	HITS	SO	BB	ERA
1989	Two Teams	33	191	9–12	.429	194	105	77	3.67
1990	Seattle	28	190	11–11	.500	188	121	66	4.03
1991	Seattle	30	195	13–14	.481	199	108	77	3.69

DARREN HOLMES
Milwaukee Brewers
Relief Pitcher
$26

Another pitcher that the Dodgers got rid of to make room for Roger McDowell, Steve Wilson, and Tim Crews. . . . Reminds me of that old country song . . . he's big around the middle and he's broad across the rump/throwing 90 miles an hour and can make his fastball jump. Slightly edited . . . Holmes has closer ability, but can't get to that role behind Henry, Fetters, Austin, Plesac, etc.

YEAR	TEAM/LEVEL	G	IP	W–L	SAVES	HITS	SO	BB	ERA
1990	Los Angeles	14	17	0–1	0	15	19	11	5.19
1991	Milwaukee	40	76	1–4	3	90	59	27	4.72
1992	Milwaukee	41	42	4–4	6	35	31	11	2.55

RICK HONEYCUTT
Oakland Athletics
Left–handed Spot Reliever
$16

Hit hard after the All-Star break, giving up a .306 batting average. LaRussa has been defining his work more and more narrowly, trying to re-define his role to keep him effective. In 1988 he faced 6.0 batters per game, in 1989 4.8, in 1990 4.1, in 1991 3.9, in 1992 3.1. Horsman may take his role completely away from him.

YEAR	TEAM/LEVEL	G	IP	W–L	SAVES	HITS	SO	BB	ERA
1990	Oakland	63	63	2–2	7	46	38	22	2.70
1991	Oakland	43	38	2–4	0	37	26	20	3.58
1992	Oakland	54	39	1–4	3	41	32	10	3.69

VINCE HORSMAN
Oakland Athletics
Relief Pitcher
$19

Worked his way slowly through the Toronto system, not consistently sharp until 1991, replaced the injured Klink. . . . Like Honeycutt, faced only 3.1 men per game on average . . . is this the first time a manager has decided to carry *two* left-handed one-out relievers? . . . Has zero chance of displacing Eckersley for the glory job, and probably wouldn't survive as a closer, anyway.

YEAR	TEAM/LEVEL	G	IP	W–L	SAVES	HITS	SO	BB	ERA
1990	Dunedin A	28	50	4–7	1	53	41	15	3.24
1991	Knoxville AA	42	80	4–1	3	80	80	19	2.34
1992	Oakland	58	43	2–1	1	39	18	21	2.49

CHARLIE HOUGH
Chicago White Sox
Starting Pitcher
$16

I think he is within a year of the end of his career. 1) Knuckleballers usually fade in their mid-forties; Hough is 45. 2) He struck out only 76 men last year. Knuckleballers can't survive without strikeouts. 3) He pitched badly over the second half of the season. 4) The White Sox have good young pitching prospects to compete with him.

YEAR	TEAM/LEVEL	G	IP	W–L	PCT.	HITS	SO	BB	ERA
1990	Texas	32	219	12–12	.500	190	114	119	4.07
1991	Chicago	31	199	9–10	.474	167	107	94	4.02
1992	Chicago	27	176	7–12	.368	160	76	66	3.93

STEVE HOWE
New York Yankees
Relief Pitcher
$16

Next up on Geraldo: Arbitrators who have re-instated seven-time drug violators, and the women who love them. . . . If you want to take the chance that there won't be an eighth relapse, his effectiveness over the last two years would seem to create the possibility that his 1993 accomplishments could greatly exceed his assigned value. It's not like he was an axe murderer, or something.

YEAR	TEAM/LEVEL	G	IP	W–L	SAVES	HITS	SO	BB	ERA
1987	Texas	24	31	3–3	1	33	19	8	4.31
1991	New York	37	48	3–1	3	39	34	7	1.68
1992	New York	20	22	3–0	6	9	12	3	2.45

JAY HOWELL
Los Angeles Dodgers
Relief Pitcher
$22

He started the year on the disabled list, and Lasorda had assigned the closer role to Roger McDowell by the time he returned on May 22. McDowell couldn't hold the job, but that was all right because the Dodgers rarely had the lead, anyway. Howell and Gott both pitched brilliantly as support staff, and I have no idea who will be the closer in '92.

YEAR	TEAM/LEVEL	G	IP	W–L	SAVES	HITS	SO	BB	ERA
1990	Los Angeles	45	66	5–5	16	59	59	20	2.18
1991	Los Angeles	44	51	6–5	16	39	40	11	3.18
1992	Los Angeles	41	47	1–3	4	41	36	18	1.54

PETER HOY
Boston Red Sox
Relief Pitcher
$5

Started the season in the major leagues, was demoted on May 16. I am *certain* there was a good reason Butch Hobson wanted him in the majors, but I haven't any idea what it was. It probably had something to do with pitching well in spring training. A 6-7 left-hander, a member of the 1988 Canadian Olympic team. Good control; bad record.

YEAR	TEAM/LEVEL	G	IP	W–L	SAVES	HITS	SO	BB	ERA
1991	AA and AAA	62	91	5–6	20	65	51	32	1.69
1992	Boston	5	4	0–0	0	8	2	2	7.36
1992	Pawtucket AAA	45	73	3–2	5	83	38	25	4.81

RICH HUISMAN
San Francisco Giants
Starting Pitcher
$21

He was a Grade A prospect until early September, when he had surgery on his bicep. The surgery will keep him out of action until the middle of next summer and casts a pall of uncertain dimensions over the remainder of his life. His minor league numbers couldn't be much better—.681 career winning percentage, 2.09 ERA, 9.9 strikeouts per nine innings. Grade B prospect.

YEAR	TEAM/LEVEL	G	IP	W–L	PCT.	HITS	SO	BB	ERA
1991	San Jose A	26	182	16–4	.800	126	216	73	1.83
1992	Shreveport AA	17	103	7–4	.636	79	100	31	2.35
1992	Phoenix AAA	9	56	3–2	.600	45	44	24	2.41

BRUCE HURST
San Diego Padres
Starting Pitcher
$52

He's more consistent than pitchers are. He now has 10 consecutive seasons in double figures in wins, and seven consecutive winning seasons. In all of baseball history you won't find a lot of pitchers who can match that. He didn't pitch well late in the season, but if there are any indications that his string is about to end, I don't see them.

YEAR	TEAM/LEVEL	G	IP	W–L	PCT.	HITS	SO	BB	ERA
1990	San Diego	33	224	11–9	.550	188	162	63	3.14
1991	San Diego	31	222	15–8	.652	201	141	59	3.29
1992	San Diego	32	217	14–9	.609	223	131	51	3.85

JONATHAN HURST
Montreal Expos
Starting Pitcher
$2

A 26-year-old right-hander, originally signed by the Rangers; he blew away hitters in A Ball but failed several tries at Double-A before turning the corner in 1991. Throws fastball, curve, change, not overpowering but excellent control. Grade D prospect, well down the list of people waiting for a chance to crack the Montreal rotation, but could succeed if the opportunity arose.

YEAR	TEAM/LEVEL	G	IP	W–L	PCT.	HITS	SO	BB	ERA
1991	Two Teams AA	11	67	7–1	.875	44	51	18	1.34
1992	Indianapolis AAA	23	119	4–8	.333	135	70	29	3.77
1992	Montreal	3	16	1–1	.500	18	4	7	5.51

MARK HUTTON
New York Yankees
Starting Pitcher
$13

He will be the first Australian to pitch in the major leagues. His fastball has been clocked at 97 MPH, but who knows, maybe they were confusing miles and kilometers. Throws hard slider, change; probably needs a true breaking pitch to win in the majors. Only 23 years old, 6-6, could develop into something special if he doesn't hurt himself. Grade B prospect.

YEAR	TEAM/LEVEL	G	IP	W–L	PCT.	HITS	SO	BB	ERA
1990	Greensboro A	21	81	1–10	.091	77	72	62	6.31
1991	Ft. Lauderdale A	24	147	5–8	.385	98	117	65	2.45
1992	Albany AA	25	165	13–7	.650	146	128	66	3.59

MIKE IGNASIAK
Milwaukee Brewers
Relief Pitcher
$2

Had been a starting pitcher since signing in 1988, was converted to the bullpen last year, probably as part of Phil Garner's program to improve the Brewer relief corps. His minor league records are not very good, but the Brewers' minor league parks favor the hitter so much that their stats are hard to read. Grade D prospect; nickname is Iggy.

YEAR	TEAM/LEVEL	G	IP	W–L	SAVES	HITS	SO	BB	ERA
1990	El Paso AA	15	83	6–3	0	96	39	34	4.35
1991	Denver AAA	24	138	9–5	1	119	103	57	4.25
1992	Denver AAA	62	92	7–4	10	83	64	33	2.93

JEFF INNIS
New York Mets
Relief Pitcher
$26

Another one like Eichhorn, Olin, Leach, Frohwirth; has all of the same statistical characteristics. Gets ground balls, great DP support, very vulnerable to left-handed hitters. Will throw an overhand curve once in a while and will mix in a knuckleball just for jollies. Did a good job setting up Franco, has always been effective, and in all likelihood will be in the majors until he's pushing 40.

YEAR	TEAM/LEVEL	G	IP	W–L	SAVES	HITS	SO	BB	ERA
1990	New York	18	26	1–3	1	19	12	10	2.39
1991	New York	69	85	0–2	0	66	47	23	2.66
1992	New York	76	88	6–9	1	85	39	36	2.86

DARYL IRVINE
Boston Red Sox
Relief Pitcher
$16

Is 28 years old and with a very poor major league record, but has pitched consistently well in the minors, so can't be written off after 63 major league innings. The Red Sox first-round draft pick in 1985; has been the relief ace at Pawtucket since 1990. He'll be in the majors by the end of 1993 if not by the beginning, and may pitch well. Grade C prospect.

YEAR	TEAM/LEVEL	G	IP	W–L	SAVES	HITS	SO	BB	ERA
1991	Pawtucket AAA	27	33	1–1	17	27	19	13	3.00
1992	Pawtcuket AAA	36	41	4–1	18	32	25	10	1.54
1992	Boston	21	28	3–4	0	31	10	14	6.11

DANNY JACKSON
Pittsburgh Pirates
Starting Pitcher
$27

Pitched 200 innings for the first time since 1988, when he won 23 games for Cincinnati, and pitched fairly well after a rough start (6.39 ERA in April, 3.48 after May 1). His slider doesn't bite quite the way it once did, but he still almost never allows a home run, gets ground balls, and battles his control to a draw.

YEAR	TEAM/LEVEL	G	IP	W–L	PCT.	HITS	SO	BB	ERA
1990	Cincinnati	22	117	6–6	.500	119	76	40	3.61
1991	Chicago	17	71	1–5	.167	89	31	48	6.75
1992	Two Teams	34	201	8–13	.381	211	97	77	3.84

MIKE JACKSON
San Francisco Giants
Relief Pitcher
$22

Don't ask me to explain this, but he's always tended to give up home runs early in the season . . . had ERA under 3.00 in April, May, June, and July, also most of August, but went to the mound 13 times in August, and began to get hit hard on August 28. Assuming that his arm was just tired, he should be his normal self in '93.

YEAR	TEAM/LEVEL	G	IP	W–L	SAVES	HITS	SO	BB	ERA
1990	Seattle	63	77	5–7	3	64	69	44	4.54
1991	Seattle	72	89	7–7	14	64	74	34	3.25
1992	San Francisco	67	82	6–6	2	76	80	33	3.73

MIKE JEFFCOAT
Texas Rangers (Free Agent)
Starting Pitcher
$1

Started the year in the minors and lost most of the season to an inflamed elbow. He is eligible for free agency and the team probably wouldn't agree to arbitration, so he'll be in the job market this winter. Has had three straight poor seasons, is now 33 years old and never did throw hard. He'll have to go to camp somewhere and earn a job.

YEAR	TEAM/LEVEL	G	IP	W–L	SAVES	HITS	SO	BB	ERA
1990	Texas	44	111	5–6	5	122	58	28	4.47
1991	Texas	70	80	5–3	1	104	43	25	4.63
1992	Texas	6	20	0–1	0	28	6	5	7.32

JEFF JOHNSON
New York Yankees
Starting Pitcher
$3

Has made 31 starts for the Yankees over the last two seasons, with discouraging results. According to *The Scouting Report: 1992*, Johnson has a 90 MPH fastball, which, if true, is certainly instructive about the value of a 90 MPH fastball. Has good control but no strikeout pitch, doesn't hold runners well, and of course the Yankee system provides very little support.

YEAR	TEAM/LEVEL	G	IP	W–L	PCT.	HITS	SO	BB	ERA
1991	New York	23	127	6–11	.353	156	62	33	5.88
1992	Columbus AAA	11	58	2–1	.667	41	36	18	2.17
1992	New York	13	53	2–3	.400	71	14	23	6.66

RANDY JOHNSON
Seattle Mariners
Starting Pitcher
$38

Unique talent, nasty left-hander who makes no compromises in his attempt to negotiate the strike zone. The key question is: Will he emerge from this sustained adolescence to become a mature pitcher? I don't know, but 1) he does win some games with a bad team, despite the walks, and 2) to expect a sudden transmogrification *at any particular moment*, like this year, would be optimistic.

YEAR	TEAM/LEVEL	G	IP	W–L	PCT.	HITS	SO	BB	ERA
1991	Seattle	33	201	13–10	.565	151	228	152	3.98
1992	Seattle	31	210	12–14	.462	154	241	144	3.77
1992	Last 11 Starts	11	85	5–2	.714	48	117	47	2.65

JOEL JOHNSTON
Kansas City Royals
Relief Pitcher
$2

He posted a 4.88 ERA with 49 walks in 55 innings in the low minors in '90, so the Royals moved him to Triple-A and gave him a major league shot in '91. He posted a 5.21 ERA at Triple-A, so he started the year in the majors. The Royals do a lot of stuff like this. . . . Good arm, Grade D prospect.

YEAR	TEAM/LEVEL	G	IP	W–L	SAVES	HITS	SO	BB	ERA
1991	Omaha AAA	47	74	4–7	8	60	63	42	5.21
1991	Kansas City	13	22	1–0	0	9	21	9	0.40
1992	Omaha AAA	42	75	5–2	2	80	48	45	6.39

BARRY JONES
New York Mets
Relief Pitcher
$3

One of the best setup men in baseball a couple of years ago, but he apparently lost his self-confidence when Tom Runnells made him the closer in Montreal, and his career has returned to the obscurity from which it sprang. He's big, overweight, throws a fastball and slider. His career has been, and probably will continue to be, a grab bag of good and bad seasons.

YEAR	TEAM/LEVEL	G	IP	W–L	SAVES	HITS	SO	BB	ERA
1990	Chicago	65	74	11–4	1	62	45	33	2.31
1991	Montreal	77	89	4–9	13	76	46	33	3.35
1992	Two Teams	61	70	7–6	1	85	30	35	5.68

BOBBY JONES
New York Mets
Starting Pitcher
$14

Cited by *Baseball America* as the number-one prospect in the Eastern League in 1992. The Mets got him as the compensation pick for losing Darryl Srawberry, which might turn out to be a terrific trade. He's a right-hander who throws a curve and change, not a big fastball, good control. Grade B prospect (because of youth and lack of great fastball).

YEAR	TEAM/LEVEL	G	IP	W–L	PCT.	HITS	SO	BB	ERA
1991	Columbia A	5	24	3–1	.750	20	35	3	1.85
1992	Helena R	1	6	1–0	1.000	4	6	1	0.00
1992	Binghamton AA	23	180	11–4	.733	113	137	42	1.98

CALVIN JONES
Seattle Mariners
Relief Pitcher
$1

A 29-year-old right-hander, has been in the Mariners' system since 1984. He was a starting pitcher for four years, made little progress and got hurt, went back to A Ball to start over as a reliever in 1990. He throws hard but his control record is awful, plus he gets behind and gives up homers. Grade D prospect, being generous.

YEAR	TEAM/LEVEL	G	IP	W–L	SAVES	HITS	SO	BB	ERA
1991	Seattle	27	46	2–2	2	33	42	29	2.53
1992	Calgary AAA	21	33	2–0	3	23	32	22	3.86
1992	Seattle	38	62	3–5	0	50	49	47	5.69

DOUG JONES
Houston Astros
Closer
$60

Strikeout/walk ratio, not counting intentional walks, was 93/12. . . . The Astrodome probably had little to do with his wonderful year. His ERA on the road was 1.12 . . . like Steve Farr, lives by deception and timing. What he did last year was 1) magnificent, and 2) in no sense a fluke. The only thing I would be concerned with is his 1992 workload.

YEAR	TEAM/LEVEL	G	IP	W–L	SAVES	HITS	SO	BB	ERA
1990	Cleveland	66	84	5–5	43	66	55	22	2.56
1991	Cleveland	36	63	4–8	7	87	48	17	5.54
1992	Houston	80	112	11–8	36	96	93	17	1.85

JIMMY JONES
Houston Astros
Starting Pitcher
$12

A starting pitcher with the Padres in 1987–88, has been in the Astros' rotation for almost two years . . . he's just scuffling to survive, with no sense that he is about to take charge. His stuff (two different curves, fastball, and change) is not good, and despite pitching some fine games his record isn't very good, a 4.07 ERA. His value is that he has a job.

YEAR	TEAM/LEVEL	G	IP	W–L	PCT.	HITS	SO	BB	ERA
1990	New York	17	50	1–2	.333	72	25	23	6.30
1991	Houston	26	135	6–8	.429	143	88	51	4.39
1992	Houston	25	139	10–6	.625	135	69	39	4.07

TODD JONES
Houston Astros
Relief Pitcher
$1

The pitcher the Astros got as the compensation pick for losing Nolan Ryan, which *won't* turn out to be a good trade. He's listed here because *Baseball America* ranked him as the number-five prospect in the Texas League. Intimidating pitcher, is credited with good poise (whatever that means), but very wild and has no record of consistent success. No prospect, in my opinion.

YEAR	TEAM/LEVEL	G	IP	W–L	SAVES	HITS	SO	BB	ERA
1991	Osceola A	14	72	4–4	0	68	52	35	4.35
1991	Jackson AA	10	55	4–3	0	51	37	39	4.88
1992	Jackson AA	61	66	3–7	25	53	60	44	3.14

JEFF JUDEN
Houston Astros
Starting Pitcher
$12

A 6-7, 245-pound right-hander, was one of the top pitching prospects in baseball two years ago, but interest in him has cooled due to poor training habits and slow learning curve. He will come back to life. He's only 21 and pitched well for Tucson over the second half of the '92 season (5–3, 2.42 ERA over last 11 starts). Grade B prospect.

YEAR	TEAM/LEVEL	G	IP	W–L	PCT.	HITS	SO	BB	ERA
1991	Jackson AA	16	96	6–3	.667	84	75	44	3.10
1991	Tucson AAA	10	57	3–2	.600	56	51	25	3.18
1992	Tucson AAA	26	147	9–10	.474	149	120	71	4.04

SCOTT KAMIENIECKI
New York Yankees
Starting Pitcher
$12

He pitched very well from August 19 to the end of the season (3.47 ERA in 62 innings), which probably will put him in the rotation to open 1993. He will have stretches where he pitches well and seems to be about to break through, but in my opinion probably never will, and will drop from the rotation in a year or two.

YEAR	TEAM/LEVEL	G	IP	W–L	PCT.	HITS	SO	BB	ERA
1991	Columbus AAA	11	76	6–3	.667	61	58	50	2.36
1991	New York	9	55	4–4	.500	54	34	22	3.90
1992	New York	28	188	6–14	.300	193	88	74	4.36

JIMMY KEY
Toronto Blue Jays (Free Agent)
Starting Pitcher
$48

Pitched extremely well all year except for a sinking spell July 17–August 12, which kept him from leading the league in ERA. Comparable to Bruce Hurst, pitches 200 innings every year without beating himself, and so winds up every year with 12 to 17 wins. He has several years left . . . loses effectiveness after 90 pitches; held left-handed hitters to .176 batting average last year.

YEAR	TEAM/LEVEL	G	IP	W–L	PCT.	HITS	SO	BB	ERA
1990	Toronto	27	155	13–7	.650	169	88	22	4.25
1991	Toronto	33	209	16–12	.571	207	125	44	3.05
1992	Toronto	33	217	13–13	.500	205	117	59	3.53

MARK KIEFER
Milwaukee Brewers
Starting Pitcher
$6

Had poor season at Denver, but he had strep throat and lost 15 pounds in mid-summer, also was distracted by his father's illness and death. Denver is a tough place to pitch, a tough park. Kiefer's best pitch is a sinker . . . his brother, Steve Kiefer, played third base for the Brewers (briefly) a few years ago . . . Grade C prospect.

YEAR	TEAM/LEVEL	G	IP	W–L	PCT.	HITS	SO	BB	ERA
1991	El Paso AA	12	76	7–1	.875	62	72	43	3.33
1991	Denver AAA	17	101	9–5	.643	104	68	41	4.62
1992	Denver AAA	17	163	7–13	.350	168	145	65	4.59

JOHN KIELY
Detroit Tigers
Relief Pitcher
$11

He was signed as an undrafted free agent, and was so highly thought of a few years ago that he was loaned to another organization, but kept pitching well in the minors and eventually pulled through. He had a good control record in the minors, but last year he almost never threw a strike on the first pitch, somehow survived. Grade C prospect.

YEAR	TEAM/LEVEL	G	IP	W–L	SAVES	HITS	SO	BB	ERA
1991	Toledo AAA	42	72	4–2	6	57	60	35	2.13
1991	Toledo AAA	21	32	1–1	9	25	31	7	2.84
1992	Detroit	39	55	4–2	0	44	18	28	2.13

DARRYL KILE
Houston Astros
Starting Pitcher
$16

There's always a story about him, some *reason* he's not pitching well. In about two years we're going to lose interest in what it is . . . went to Tucson after struggling last year, earned return with 3–0 record, but even there his K/W ratio was 34/24 . . . career record is 1–7, 5.40 ERA in day games . . . has star ability and may catch fire some day.

YEAR	TEAM/LEVEL	G	IP	W–L	PCT.	HITS	SO	BB	ERA
1991	Houston	37	154	7–11	.389	144	100	84	3.69
1992	Tucson AAA	9	56	4–1	.800	50	43	32	3.99
1992	Houston	22	125	5–10	.333	124	90	63	3.95

ERIC KING
Detroit Tigers (Free Agent)
Starting Pitcher
$15

He pitched poorly over the first two months of the season, went on the disabled list in late May with an inflamed rotator cuff. When he returned in August he pitched well, 3.07 ERA. That's his history; he gets hot and rolls for a couple of months, and then something happens. Throws hard, throws strikes; a lot of guys his age are just getting their first chance.

YEAR	TEAM/LEVEL	G	IP	W–L	PCT.	HITS	SO	BB	ERA
1990	Chicago	25	151	12–4	.750	135	70	40	3.28
1991	Cleveland	25	151	6–11	.353	166	59	44	4.60
1992	Detroit	17	79	4–6	.400	90	45	28	5.22

BOB KIPPER
Minnesota Twins
Relief Pitcher
$1

Pitched well until June 5 (2.22 ERA in 16 games), then was hit hard for a month, was released by the Twins on July 31, and was not able to catch on anywhere. On the theory that left-handers are always in demand, should be able to get a spring training invitation, and may show up on a roster. He's only 28.

YEAR	TEAM/LEVEL	G	IP	W–L	SAVES	HITS	SO	BB	ERA
1990	Pittsburgh	41	63	5–2	3	44	35	26	3.02
1991	Pittsburgh	52	60	2–2	4	66	28	22	4.65
1992	Minnesota	25	39	3–3	0	40	22	14	4.42

JOE KLINK
Oakland Athletics
Relief Pitcher
$1

Klink missed the season with an elbow problem, and his job has been turned over to Vince Horsman. Klink had a remarkable record of not allowing inherited runners to score, led the American League in that category in both 1990 and 1991. He pitched well, and will probably be able to catch a job somewhere. Will never be a closer.

YEAR	TEAM/LEVEL	G	IP	W–L	SAVES	HITS	SO	BB	ERA
1989	AA and AAA	63	67	4–4	26	48	64	25	2.54
1990	Oakland	40	40	0–0	1	34	19	18	2.04
1991	Oakland	62	62	10–3	2	60	34	21	4.35

KURT KNUDSEN
Detroit Tigers

Relief Pitcher

$6

Your basic Detroit Tigers whoozis prospect. Had been consistently effective in the minors with more than a strikeout per inning, was recalled May 16, pitched 48 times and seemed increasingly confused. His ERA after the All-Star game was 6.55. Pitches up in the strike zone, allowing almost twice as many fly balls as ground balls. Grade C prospect.

YEAR	TEAM/LEVEL	G	IP	W–L	SAVES	HITS	SO	BB	ERA
1991	AA and AAA	46	70	3–5	6	55	84	40	2.96
1991	Toledo AAA	12	18	3–1	1	11	19	6	2.08
1992	Detroit	48	71	2–3	5	70	51	41	4.58

RANDY KRAMER
Seattle Mariners

Starting Pitcher

No Value

A right-hander who pitched 111 innings for the Pirates in 1989 and was given a workout by the Mariners in their pain and desperation. He's 32 years old, has been in the minor leagues since 1982, with a career minor league record of 52–64 and an ERA around 5.00. The league hit almost .400 against him in his 16 innings.

YEAR	TEAM/LEVEL	G	IP	W–L	PCT.	HITS	SO	BB	ERA
1991	Calgary AAA	16	66	4–4	.500	87	24	25	5.86
1992	Calgary AAA	27	64	1–4	.200	87	30	30	6.05
1992	Seattle	4	16	0–1	.000	30	6	7	7.71

BILL KRUEGER
Montreal Expos

Starting Pitcher

$1

Won his first six decisions but was raked over the coals in nine of 11 starts beginning July 6 (45 earned runs in 51 innings), leading the Twins to donate him to Montreal for Darren Reed . . . will be 35 in April, just survives, trying to avoid from moment to moment being knocked out of the league. May launch another comeback from the bullpen.

YEAR	TEAM/LEVEL	G	IP	W–L	PCT.	HITS	SO	BB	ERA
1990	Milwaukee	30	129	6–8	.429	137	64	54	3.98
1991	Seattle	35	175	11–8	.579	194	91	60	3.60
1992	Two Teams	36	179	10–8	.556	189	99	53	4.53

DENNIS LAMP
Released

Relief Pitcher

$4

Was released by the Pirates on June 10, apparently bringing his career to rest after 16 years, 639 games. He hadn't pitched well since 1989. Since 1986 he's had ERAs including 5.05, 5.08, 4.68, 4.70, and 5.14, but kept getting work because he would have a good year every three years or so, and he had a hard-working agent who knew what to do with that.

YEAR	TEAM/LEVEL	G	IP	W–L	SAVES	HITS	SO	BB	ERA
1990	Boston	47	106	3–5	0	114	49	30	4.68
1991	Boston	51	92	6–3	0	100	57	31	4.70
1992	Pittsburgh	21	28	1–1	0	33	15	9	5.14

LES LANCASTER
Detroit Tigers(Released)
Relief Pitcher
$3

I'm not sure who had the worst year of any major league pitcher, but Les certainly would be a candidate. I don't know what the problem was. Lancaster doesn't have one outstanding pitch, but throws a decent fastball, slider, curve, and changeup, couldn't seem to get any of them where he wanted. Has a 50-50 chance for comeback.

YEAR	TEAM/LEVEL	G	IP	W–L	SAVES	HITS	SO	BB	ERA
1990	Chicago	55	109	9–5	6	121	65	40	4.62
1991	Chicago	64	156	9–7	3	150	102	49	3.52
1992	Detroit	41	87	3–4	0	101	35	51	6.33

BILL LANDRUM
Montreal Expos
Relief Pitcher
$9

Was cut by the Pirates, either because he pitched poorly or to save his $1.7 million salary, depending on who you believe. Was ineffective early fighting tendinitis, went to the DL May 16 and wound up in the minors . . . I think he should be back in the majors this year. He had three straight good years before last year and pitched well at Indianapolis.

YEAR	TEAM/LEVEL	G	IP	W–L	SAVES	HITS	SO	BB	ERA
1990	Pittsburgh	54	72	7–3	13	69	39	21	2.13
1991	Pittsburgh	61	76	4–4	17	76	45	19	3.18
1992	Montreal	18	20	1–1	0	27	7	9	7.20

MARK LANGSTON
California Angels
Starting Pitcher
$53

Posted the best control record of his career, only 74 walks in 229 innings, while continuing to be among the league leaders in strikeouts (sixth) and winning more games than you can expect him to win with a bad team. Has .527 career winning percentage for teams which are .456 without him, an impressive +71. His teams have been, on average, far worse than Walter Johnson's.

YEAR	TEAM/LEVEL	G	IP	W–L	PCT.	HITS	SO	BB	ERA
1990	California	33	223	10–17	.370	215	195	104	4.40
1991	California	34	246	19–8	.704	190	183	96	3.00
1992	California	32	229	13–14	.481	206	174	74	3.66

TERRY LEACH
Chicago White Sox
Relief Pitcher
$24

Another submariner, has the same statistical characteristics as Frohwirth, Innis, etc.—good control, no strikeouts, gets lots of ground balls, very tough on right-handers but vulnerable to left-handers, very durable. He's 39 now and has only nine career saves—yet he has pitched well or very well in five of the last six years, and there is no evidence that he is in decline.

YEAR	TEAM/LEVEL	G	IP	W–L	SAVES	HITS	SO	BB	ERA
1990	Minnesota	55	82	2–5	2	84	46	21	3.20
1991	Minnesota	50	67	1–2	0	82	32	14	3.61
1992	Chicago	51	74	6–5	0	57	22	20	1.95

TIM LEARY
Seattle Mariners
Starting Pitcher
$4

He still has a major league arm, but there appears now to be almost no probability of a return to his former status. He has thrown so many wild pitches with the split-fingered fastball that he appears to throw it now like a pitching coach hunting for land mines, and he doesn't throw *anything* with any confidence or sense of purpose.

YEAR	TEAM/LEVEL	G	IP	W–L	PCT.	HITS	SO	BB	ERA
1990	New York	31	208	9–19	.321	202	138	78	4.11
1991	New York	28	121	4–10	.286	150	83	57	6.49
1992	Two Teams	26	141	8–10	.444	131	46	87	5.36

CRAIG LEFFERTS
Baltimore Orioles
(Released)
Starting Pitcher
$31

Converted to starter after nine successful years in the pen, and continued to pitch well. His control is more of an asset to him pitching a lot of innings than it is pitching critical innings. A relief closer needs to come in and *shut things down*; a starter needs to get the percentages working with him and let nature take its course. A hard worker, should continue to win.

YEAR	TEAM/LEVEL	G	IP	W–L	PCT.	HITS	SO	BB	ERA
1990	San Diego	56	79	7–5	.583	68	60	22	2.52
1991	San Diego	54	69	1–6	.143	74	48	14	3.91
1992	Two Teams	32	196	14–12	.538	214	104	41	3.76

CHARLIE LEIBRANDT
Atlanta Braves
Starting Pitcher
$44

This is the guy who should be a pitching coach. If he can win 15 games a year with his stuff, you'd better believe he knows how to pitch . . . he should last two-three more years before his game breaks down again. Now 36, once had a decent fastball but just spots it now, helps himself by picking 10 men a year off first base.

YEAR	TEAM/LEVEL	G	IP	W–L	PCT.	HITS	SO	BB	ERA
1990	Atlanta	24	162	9–11	.450	164	76	35	3.16
1991	Atlanta	36	230	15–13	.536	212	128	56	3.49
1992	Atlanta	32	193	15–7	.682	191	104	42	3.36

AL LEITER
Toronto Blue Jays
Starting Pitcher
$1

He is pitching again, after years of fighting blisters, and who knows, eventually he may even start to pitch well. His career minor league record is 26–46, with an ERA over four, but he did pitch well once, acquired the label of a hot prospect and has never been able to get rid of it. He pitched one inning last year with Toronto.

YEAR	TEAM/LEVEL	G	IP	W–L	PCT.	HITS	SO	BB	ERA
1990	Syracuse AAA	15	78	3–8	.273	59	69	68	4.62
1991	Dunedin A	4	10	0–0	.000	5	5	7	1.86
1992	Syracuse AAA	27	163	8–9	.471	159	108	64	3.86

MARK LEITER
Detroit Tigers
Starter/Reliever
$17

Has posted nearly identical records the last two years in starter/reliever role. He may finally crack the rotation this year. He started last year from May 12 to July 23 and was 5–3, but strained his groin and went on the DL until September, then to the bullpen. A good enough pitcher to win 12–14 games as a starter.

YEAR	TEAM/LEVEL	G	IP	W–L	PCT.	HITS	SO	BB	ERA
1990	New York	8	26	1–1	.500	33	21	9	6.84
1991	Detroit	38	135	9–7	.563	125	103	50	4.21
1992	Detroit	35	112	8–5	.615	116	75	43	4.18

DANILO LEON
Texas Rangers
Relief Pitcher
$3

A 26-year-old right-hander, pitched four years in the Expos chain, was released, and worked his way back by pitching in the Mexican and Italian leagues. Signed by the Rangers, he shot through their system in six weeks, posting a 0.86 ERA in three stops. Was spotty for two months in the majors, season ended early August by strained ligament in right elbow. Grade D prospect.

YEAR	TEAM/LEVEL	G	IP	W–L	SAVES	HITS	SO	BB	ERA
1992	Tulsa AA	12	30	5–0	1	15	34	8	0.60
1991	Oklahoma City AAA	3	5	1–0	0	2	4	3	0.00
1992	Texas	15	18	1–1	0	18	15	10	5.89

RICHIE LEWIS
Baltimore Orioles
Starting Pitcher
$9

Small right-hander. He was drafted by Montreal in 1987, a second-round pick. The Expos started him at Triple-A and let him gradually work his way down the system. He reached West Palm Beach in 1990, and had gotten as far back as Double-A when he was traded to the Orioles. Has had arthroscopic elbow surgery four times, but had a good year at Rochester.

YEAR	TEAM/LEVEL	G	IP	W–L	PCT.	HITS	SO	BB	ERA
1991	Harrisburg AA	34	75	6–5	.545	67	82	40	3.74
1992	Rochester AAA	24	159	10–9	.526	136	154	61	3.28
1992	Baltimore	2	7	1–1	.500	13		4	7 10.80

SCOTT LEWIS
California Angels
Pitcher
$12

A minor league starter, began the year in the majors, started twice and pitched very well both times, but pitched mostly in relief and was hit hard, hence was sent to Edmonton for most of the summer. Throws hard, throws strikes; minor league record is better than it looks because Edmonton is where Gabriel sends pitchers if they don't behave in purgatory. Grade C prospect.

YEAR	TEAM/LEVEL	G	IP	W–L	PCT.	HITS	SO	BB	ERA
1991	California	16	60	3–5	.375	81	37	21	6.27
1992	Edmonton AAA	22	147	10–6	.625	36	88	40	4.17
1992	California	21	38	4–0	1.000	36	18	14	3.99

DEREK LILLIQUIST
Cleveland Indians

Relief Pitcher

$27

The Braves' number one-pick in '87, he shot through the minors in a year and pitched OK for the Braves in '89, but had a slump in '90 and was muscled aside by Tom Glavine and the Peachtree Mafia. Put on waivers by San Diego, had a marvelous year for Cleveland . . . looks fat but is good athlete, like Rick Reuschel. Good hitter . . . should remain effective.

YEAR	TEAM/LEVEL	G	IP	W–L	SAVES	HITS	SO	BB	ERA
1990	Two Teams	28	122	5–11	0	136	63	42	5.31
1991	San Diego	6	14	0–2	0	25	7	4	8.79
1992	Cleveland	71	62	5–3	6	39	47	18	1.75

DOUG LINTON
Toronto Blue Jays

Relief Pitcher

$3

Was called up in August when the wheels were coming off the Blue Jays starting rotation, couldn't get anybody out, and went back down when the Jays got Cone. He has been in the Blue Jays system since 1987, was a sensation his first year (14–2, 1.55 ERA, 155 Ks in 122 innings) but hurt his arm in '88 and has unimpressive record since. Grade D prospect.

YEAR	TEAM/LEVEL	G	IP	W–L	PCT.	HITS	SO	BB	ERA
1991	Syracuse AAA	30	162	10–12	.455	181	93	56	5.01
1992	Syracuse AAA	25	171	12–10	.545	176	126	70	3.69
1992	Toronto	8	24	1–3	.250	31	16	17	8.63

BOB MACDONALD
Toronto Blue Jays

Garbage Man

$8

Picks up loose innings for Gaston, when the Blue Jays are out of the game or have blown somebody out, is called on occasionally to pitch to a left-handed batter, goes to the minor leagues when needed to make room for another pitcher. He may have good stats in that role, and may get a chance to move beyond it due to the free agent losses.

YEAR	TEAM/LEVEL	G	IP	W–L	SAVES	HITS	SO	BB	ERA
1990	Tononto	4	2	0–0	0	0	0	2	0.00
1991	Toronto	45	54	3–3	0	51	24	25	2.85
1992	Toronto	27	47	1–0	0	50	26	16	4.37

GREG MADDUX
Chicago Cubs

Starting Pitcher

$84

In my opinion, the best starting pitcher in the National League. He has won 15 to 20 games every year since 1988, never misses a start, keeps increasing his strikeout totals while improving his control. Not that his control was bad five years ago . . . has about 35 percent of a Hall of Fame career behind him, needs to win 20 two or three more times.

YEAR	TEAM/LEVEL	G	IP	W–L	PCT.	HITS	SO	BB	ERA
1990	Chicago	35	237	15–15	.500	242	144	71	3.46
1991	Chicago	37	263	15–11	.577	232	198	66	3.35
1992	Chicago	35	268	20–11	.645	201	199	70	2.18

MIKE MADDUX
San Diego Padres
Relief Pitcher
$26

Over the last two years Mike Maddux has an ERA of 2.42 in 114 games; Randy Myers has an ERA of 3.83. I am *sure* there is a good reason Greg Riddoch would rather have had Myers on the mound at a key moment of the game, I'm just sure of it . . . has excellent curve, good fastball, and two straight years of quality performance.

YEAR	TEAM/LEVEL	G	IP	W–L	SAVES	HITS	SO	BB	ERA
1990	Los Angeles	11	21	0–1	0	24	11	4	6.53
1991	San Diego	64	99	7–2	5	78	57	27	2.46
1992	San Diego	50	80	2–2	5	71	60	24	2.37

MIKE MAGNANTE
Kansas City Royals
Relief Pitcher
$6

Can throw 70 on a good day . . . has been extremely streaky so far, will pitch brilliantly for two or three weeks, and then seems to lose his mirrors. Listed at 6-1, 180, but looks much smaller on the mound. Deceptive motion, works quickly when on his game. Changes speeds well, will have to develop the confidence to challenge hitters. Limited potential.

YEAR	TEAM/LEVEL	G	IP	W–L	PCT.	HITS	SO	BB	ERA
1991	Omaha AAA	10	66	6–1	.857	53	50	23	3.02
1991	Kansas City	38	55	0–1	.000	55	42	23	2.45
1992	Kansas City	44	89	4–9	.308	115	31	35	4.94

JOE MAGRANE
St. Louis Cardinals
Starting Pitcher
$10

He missed all of 1991 and the first half of 1992 recovering from elbow surgery, got his arm wet in late '92 but didn't pitch well, either in the majors or in the minors. It is anyone's guess what his abilities will be in 1993, but I would tend to be optimistic. He has the basic elements that make a pitcher—knowledge of how to pitch, arm, self-confidence.

YEAR	TEAM/LEVEL	G	IP	W–L	PCT.	HITS	SO	BB	ERA
1989	St. Louis	34	235	18–9	.667	219	127	72	2.91
1990	St. Louis	31	203	10–17	.370	204	100	59	3.59
1992	St. Louis	5	31	1–2	.333	34	20	15	4.02

PAT MAHOMES
Minnesota Twins
Starting Pitcher
$21

Has an outstanding arm, and after pitching well at Orlando and Portland in '91, he began the '92 season in the rotation. He wasn't terrible, but he had only four really good outings in 12 starts, and returned to Portland on June 3. He again pitched well at Portland, with an improved control record, and was back in the rotation in late September. I recommend him.

YEAR	TEAM/LEVEL	G	IP	W–L	PCT.	HITS	SO	BB	ERA
1991	AA and AAA	27	171	11–10	.524	125	177	93	2.32
1992	Portland AAA	17	111	9–5	.643	97	87	43	3.41
1992	Minnesota	14	70	3–4	.429	73	44	37	5.04

ROB MALLICOAT
Houston Astros
Relief Pitcher
$1

Minor league veteran, was a prospect years ago, until he began making regularly scheduled visits to Dr. Jobe's office. In 1985 he went 16–6 with a 1.36 ERA at Osceola. He hadn't really pitched well since 1987 until last year at Tucson, where he started hot and earned a two-month look in mid-summer. It wasn't an encouraging look. No prospect.

YEAR	TEAM/LEVEL	G	IP	W–L	SAVES	HITS	SO	BB	ERA
1991	Houston	24	23	0–2	1	22	18	13	3.86
1991	Tucson AAA	36	48	1–3	3	34	51	20	2.23
1992	Houston	23	24	0–0	0	26	20	19	7.23

BARRY MANUEL
Texas Rangers
Relief Pitcher
$1

The Rangers decided to skip Triple-A with him, kept him on April roster although he had been in the system for five years without pitching Triple-A. It didn't work out . . . has minor league lifetime mark of 18–36 with a 4.39 ERA, 5.14 walks per nine innings. There must be some reason these stats are misleading, but I haven't heard . . . Grade D prospect.

YEAR	TEAM/LEVEL	G	IP	W–L	SAVES	HITS	SO	BB	ERA
1991	Tulsa AA	56	68	2–7	25	63	45	34	3.29
1991	Texas	8	16	1–0	0	7	5	6	1.13
1992	AA and AAA	43	54	3–8	7	60	39	42	4.64

DENNIS MARTINEZ
Montreal Expos
Starting Pitcher
$74

If anybody else had a season like this, he'd probably get noticed. For Martinez, excellence has become so much the norm that people only notice when he loses. By my count he had 25 quality starts in 32 games, but I didn't count 6 innings/3 runs as a quality start; it had to be 7 and 3 or 6 and 2. Consistently wonderful.

YEAR	TEAM/LEVEL	G	IP	W–L	PCT.	HITS	SO	BB	ERA
1990	Montreal	32	226	10–11	.476	191	156	49	2.95
1991	Montreal	31	222	14–11	.560	187	123	62	2.39
1992	Montreal	32	226	16–11	.593	172	147	60	2.47

PEDRO A. MARTINEZ
San Diego Padres
Starting Pitcher
$7

A left-hander with a good arm. After starting out well (26–12 record in A Ball) he seemed to have leveled off at Double-A, posting 17–20 record in two years at Wichita. He added a curve last year, and pitched real well in a hitter's park. If he continues to pitch well at Las Vegas will come to the majors this summer; Grade B prospect.

YEAR	TEAM/LEVEL	G	IP	W–L	PCT.	HITS	SO	BB	ERA
1990	Wichita AA	24	129	6–10	.375	139	88	70	4.80
1991	Wichita AA	26	157	11–10	.524	169	95	57	5.23
1992	Wichita AA	25	166	11–7	.611	153	141	52	3.03

PEDRO J. MARTINEZ
Los Angeles Dodgers
Starting Pitcher
$28

Ramon's brother, didn't have a particulary good year at Albuquerque and has been passed by Astacio. He also didn't have a bad year at Albuquerque, posting respectable 3.81 ERA and striking out 124 in 125 innings. His career minor league record remains extremely impressive, and there is every reason to think he will be a fine pitcher. **Grade A prospect.**

YEAR	TEAM/LEVEL	G	IP	W–L	PCT.	HITS	SO	BB	ERA
1991	Bakersfield A	10	61	8–0	1.000	41	83	19	2.05
1991	AA and AAA	18	116	10–8	.556	85	109	47	2.41
1992	Albuquerque AAA	20	125	7–6	.538	104	124	57	3.81

RAMON MARTINEZ
Los Angeles Dodgers
Starting Pitcher
$22

Until we know what is wrong with his arm, it's hard to evaluate his status. He was out in September with tendinitis in his elbow, a term which is applied to everything from an arm which itches to an arm which is about to fall off. In view of his youth, I suspect the arm will recover. I also suspect that he may not have hit bottom yet.

YEAR	TEAM/LEVEL	G	IP	W–L	PCT.	HITS	SO	BB	ERA
1990	Los Angeles	33	234	20–6	.769	191	223	67	2.92
1991	Los Angeles	33	220	17–13	.567	190	150	69	3.27
1992	Los Angeles	25	151	8–11	.421	141	101	69	4.00

ROGER MASON
Pittsburgh Pirates
Relief Pitcher
$19

A one-time hot prospect whose career has been revived by Jim Leyland, like Slaught, Cole, Bell, Walk, etc. Leyland focuses on the things a player *can* do. Mason is devastating against lefties, and had as many AB facing lefties as facing right-handers, which is unusual even for a pitcher in this role . . . 5.25 ERA over second half, but I believe he will continue to pitch well.

YEAR	TEAM/LEVEL	G	IP	W–L	SAVES	HITS	SO	BB	ERA
1990	Buffalo AAA	29	77	3–5	3	78	45	25	2.10
1991	Pittsburgh	24	30	3–2	3	21	21	6	3.03
1992	Pittsburgh	65	88	5–7	8	80	56	33	4.09

GREG MATHEWS
Philadelphia Phillies
Starting Pitcher
$5

Curve-balling left-hander who won 11 games for the Cardinals as a rookie in 1986, and 11 more in 1987. He had shoulder surgery in 1988, and his career since then resembles the Bataan death march. He's pitched for Louisville, Arkansas, El Paso, Denver, Beloit, Scranton, usually doing more hoping than actual pitching, but returned to the majors after good first half at Scranton. A long-odds project.

YEAR	TEAM/LEVEL	G	IP	W–L	PCT.	HITS	SO	BB	ERA
1991	Denver AAA	13	61	6–3	.667	62	25	27	3.86
1992	Scranton AAA	16	85	3–7	.300	93	63	23	2.96
1992	Philadelphia	14	52	2–3	.400	54	27	24	5.16

TERRY MATHEWS
Texas Rangers
Relief Pitcher
$6

Mathews was the Rangers' first-round draft choice in 1987, and, as first-round picks often will, he reached the major leagues in 1991 although he hadn't really pitched well anywhere above A Ball—in fact, his career record was 7–12 at Double-A, and 7–13 at Triple-A. A minor league starter, converted to relief at the major league level, has good fastball, control record inconsistent.

YEAR	TEAM/LEVEL	G	IP	W–L	SAVES	HITS	SO	BB	ERA
1991	Oklahoma City AAA	18	95	5–6	1	98	63	34	3.49
1991	Texas	34	57	4–0	1	54	51	18	3.61
1992	Texas	40	42	2–4	0	48	26	31	5.95

MATT MAYSEY
Montreal Expos
Relief Pitcher
$1

Right-handed starting pitcher in the minor leagues since 1985, converted to relief last year. His health record is unusually good. When you see the record of a minor league starting pitcher who has been around longer than two years it is virtually always disrupted by injuries, but Maysey's been in there pitching all along. I haven't seen him; record is generally poor. Grade D prospect.

YEAR	TEAM/LEVEL	G	IP	W–L	SAVES	HITS	SO	BB	ERA
1991	Harrisburg AA	15	105	6–5	0	90	86	28	1.89
1991	Indianapolis AAA	12	63	3–6	0	60	45	33	5.14
1992	Indianapolis AAA	35	67	5–3	5	63	38	28	4.30

KIRK McCASKILL
Chicago White Sox
Starting Pitcher
$29

He looks better on the mound than he is. He's a .500 pitcher, 1992 and lifetime (more or less), and over the last three years is 34–43. Throws slider, curve, change, and a toothless fastball; his control isn't good, and he doesn't have a punchout pitch. An exceptional fielder. In my opinion his effectiveness is likely to deteriorate slowly until he is confronted with a career crisis.

YEAR	TEAM/LEVEL	G	IP	W–L	PCT.	HITS	SO	BB	ERA
1990	California	29	174	12–11	.522	161	78	72	3.25
1991	California	30	178	10–19	.345	193	71	66	4.26
1992	Chicago	34	209	12–13	.480	193	109	95	4.18

BOB McCLURE
St. Louis Cardinals
Relief Pitcher
$7

The Zsa Zsa Gabor of baseball, his career seems to go on forever despite no apparent talent. I mean this as a compliment; he is, after all, still getting people out. He's older than George Brett, with whom he was a teammate a couble of decades ago, but pitched more last year than he had since 1987, and pitched well enough to be asked back for '93.

YEAR	TEAM/LEVEL	G	IP	W–L	SAVES	HITS	SO	BB	ERA
1990	California	11	7	2–0	0	7	6	3	6.43
1991	Two Teams	45	33	1–1	0	37	20	13	4.96
1992	St Louis	71	54	1–0	0	52	24	25	3.17

LANCE McCULLERS
Los Angeles
Relief Pitcher
$10

You will remember him, I'm sure, for his years with the San Diego, where he pitched very well (1986–88), and his years with the Yankees, where he didn't. He started last year at Oklahoma City, was called up to the Rangers in May and released in early June, then signed with the Dodgers **and pitched brilliantly at Albuquerque**. He may be poised for a comeback.

YEAR	TEAM/LEVEL	G	IP	W–L	SAVES	HITS	SO	BB	ERA
1992	Oklahoma City AAA	13	25	1–1	1	26	10	11	5.33
1992	Texas	5	5	1–0	0	1	3	8	5.40
1992	Albuquerque AAA	29	44	4–1	12	34	35	10	1.84

BEN McDONALD
Baltimore Orioles
Starting Pitcher
$37

Had difficulty with Camden Yards, gave up 21 homers there in 18 starts, which reversed his 8–5 road record to 5–8 at home. He pitched better late in the season, as always (career ERA of 5.16 before A-Star game, 3.40 after). Still has good fastball and big curve, which unfortunately he hangs twice a game, and has had trouble with runners on base.

YEAR	TEAM/LEVEL	G	IP	W–L	PCT.	HITS	SO	BB	ERA
1990	Baltimore	21	119	8–5	.615	88	65	35	2.43
1991	Baltimore	21	126	6–8	.429	126	85	43	4.84
1992	Baltimore	35	227	13–13	.500	213	158	74	4.24

JACK ♫ McDOWELL
Chicago White Sox
Starting Pitcher
$67

Continues steady progress, 14 wins, 17, 20. In some ways he's a young Jack Morris—durable, tenacious, skillful, doesn't give up a lead. He's tough with men on base (.235 average last year) and men in scoring position (.221); overall league averages go *up* in those situations. Remains effective late in the game. One of the best starting pitchers in baseball.

YEAR	TEAM/LEVEL	G	IP	W–L	PCT.	HITS	SO	BB	ERA
1990	Chicago	33	205	14–9	.609	189	165	77	3.82
1991	Chicago	35	254	17–10	.630	212	191	82	3.41
1992	Chicago	34	261	20–10	.667	247	178	75	3.18

ROGER McDOWELL
Los Angeles Dodgers
Relief Pitcher
$17

Posted 5.66 ERA after the All-Star break, and seems finally to have destroyed the idea that he is a closer. This hasn't been easy. It's taken several years of consistent inconsistency . . . ground ball/fly ball rate more than 3 to 1, very vulnerable to left–handed batters. Over the last four years the batting average against him after he has thrown 30 pitches is .329.

YEAR	TEAM/LEVEL	G	IP	W–L	SAVES	HITS	SO	BB	ERA
1990	Philadelphia	72	86	6–8	22	92	39	35	3.86
1991	Two Teams	71	101	9–9	10	100	50	48	2.93
1992	Los Angeles	65	84	6–10	14	103	50	42	4.09

CHUCK McELROY
Chicago Cubs
Relief Pitcher
$28

One of many pitchers who has failed to claim the job as the Cubs relief ace despite repeated opportunities. Only 25 years old; has time and talent left to establish himself in that role . . . throws 92 MPH fastball, slider, and split-finger fastball. That's too many pitches for a closer; a closer normally has one great pitch, not three good ones. There are exceptions, of course.

YEAR	TEAM/LEVEL	G	IP	W–L	SAVES	HITS	SO	BB	ERA
1990	Philadelphia	16	14	0–1	0	24	16	10	7.71
1991	Chicago	71	101	6–2	3	73	92	57	1.95
1992	Chicago	72	84	4–7	6	73	83	51	3.55

KEVIN McGEHEE
San Francisco Giants
Starting Pitcher
$7

One of several outstanding pitching prospects on the Shreveport team last summer, pitched well enough to move up to Triple-A (at least) this year. He was an 11th-round draft pick and *wasn't* listed by *Baseball America* among the top prospects in the league, but I love that 140/42 K/W ratio all the same. Grade B prospect.

YEAR	TEAM/LEVEL	G	IP	W–L	PCT.	HITS	SO	BB	ERA
1990	Everett A	15	74	4–8	.333	74	86	38	4.76
1991	San Jose A	26	174	13–6	.684	129	171	87	2.33
1992	Shreveport AA	25	158	9–7	.563	146	140	42	2.96

RUSTY MEACHAM
Kansas City Royals
Relief Pitcher
$28

Fun to watch, cocky, bounces around nervously on the mound, pounds the ball impatiently into glove, goes right after the hitter the minute he stands in. Has funny metabolism, eats like a horse but is built like a grasshopper, doesn't look strong but is. Has good fastball, nasty sinker/slider . . . it's unbelievable that the Tigers gave this guy away. He should have many good years.

YEAR	TEAM/LEVEL	G	IP	W–L	SAVES	HITS	SO	BB	ERA
1991	Toledo AAA	26	125	9–7	2	117	70	40	3.09
1991	Detroit	10	28	2–1	0	35	14	11	5.20
1992	Kansas City	64	102	10–4	2	88	64	21	2.74

JOSE MELENDEZ
San Diego Padres
Relief Pitcher
$27

Right–handed pitcher, pitched brilliantly in middle/long relief (1.81 ERA) but was hit hard in three starts. His strikeout/walk ratio, not counting intentional walks, was 82/13. There's probably never been a pitcher in baseball history who had that kind of a ratio and wasn't effective . . . with a new manager and a good track record, should move up a slot in the Padre bullpen.

YEAR	TEAM/LEVEL	G	IP	W–L	SAVES	HITS	SO	BB	ERA
1991	Las Vegas AAA	9	59	7–0	0	54	45	11	3.99
1991	San Diego	31	94	8–5	3	77	60	24	3.27
1992	San Diego	56	89	6–7	0	82	82	20	2.92

TONY MENENDEZ
Cincinnati Reds
Relief Pitcher
$2

A 1.93 ERA wasn't good enough to keep him in the majors last July, but then, he does have more than a thousand minor league innings to say he isn't that good. Is 28 years old, was in the White Sox system for years and then the Rangers, with so–so results, similar to those shown below. Grade D prospect.

YEAR	TEAM/LEVEL	G	IP	W–L	SAVES	HITS	SO	BB	ERA
1991	Oklahoma City AAA	21	116	5–5	0	107	82	62	5.20
1991	Nashville AAA	50	107	3–5	1	98	92	47	4.05
1992	Cincinnati	3	5	1–0	0	1	5	0	1.93

KENT MERCKER
Atlanta Braves
Relief Pitcher
$27

Considered a top prospect as a starting pitcher, he hasn't had a try at that in the majors because the Braves rotation is so strong, and has pitched OK in the bullpen but has missed chances to take the closer role. Left-hander who throws hard and is happy to live and die with the fastball, control record isn't good and isn't improving.

YEAR	TEAM/LEVEL	G	IP	W–L	SAVES	HITS	SO	BB	ERA
1990	Atlanta	36	48	4–7	7	43	39	24	3.17
1991	Atlanta	50	73	5–3	6	56	62	35	2.58
1992	Atlanta	53	68	3–2	6	51	49	35	3.42

JOSE MESA
Cleveland Indians
Starting Pitcher
$8

Has good size, fine arm, four pitches, and is still only 26. At times he will pitch a good game and look like he's ready to break through, but there aren't any good major league pitchers who have more walks than strikeouts, so he's not going to make it unless he develops a pitch that he can use to get out of a situation. Reputation is that concentration lapses.

YEAR	TEAM/LEVEL	G	IP	W–L	PCT.	HITS	SO	BB	ERA
1990	Baltimore	7	47	3–2	.600	37	24	27	3.86
1991	Baltimore	23	124	6–11	.353	151	64	62	5.97
1992	Two Teams	28	161	7–12	.368	169	62	70	4.59

DANNY MICELI
Kansas City Royals
Relief Pitcher
$3

An undrafted free agent signed out of a tryout camp, has established himself as a prospect. He reached Memphis (Double-A) in June and was hit hard at first, but recovered to finish with more than twice as many strikeouts as hits allowed. Has above-average fastball, is developing a slider. Only 22, could be called up this fall if he continues to pitch well. Grade B prospect.

YEAR	TEAM/LEVEL	G	IP	W–L	SAVES	HITS	SO	BB	ERA
1991	Eugene A	25	34	0–1	10	18	43	18	2.14
1992	Appleton A	23	23	1–1	9	12	44	4	1.93
1992	Memphis AA	31	36	3–0	4	19	44	13	2.02

BOB MILACKI
Baltimore Orioles
Starting Pitcher
$9

A big horse with a good fastball, looked ready to bust loose a year ago but went backward instead of forward. He was sent to Rochester on July 15 and pitched fairly well there, although not as well as his 7–1 record would suggest, was recalled in September and pitched OK. Has periodic arm trouble, perhaps as a result of overuse in the minor leagues.

YEAR	TEAM/LEVEL	G	IP	W–L	PCT.	HITS	SO	BB	ERA
1990	Baltimore	27	135	5–8	.385	143	60	61	4.46
1991	Baltimore	31	184	10–9	.526	175	108	53	4.01
1992	Baltimore	23	116	6–8	.429	140	51	44	5.84

SAM MILITELLO
New York Yankees
Starting Pitcher
$36

We were wondering if Militello could have the best minor league record ever in a modern farm system? In 58 minor league games he had a winning percentage of .810 (34–8) and an ERA of 1.76. I don't remember seeing any career numbers like that . . . Selected by *Baseball America* the best prospect in the International League. Doesn't throw hard but throws four pitches. **Grade A prospect.**

YEAR	TEAM/LEVEL	G	IP	W–L	PCT.	HITS	SO	BB	ERA
1991	A and AA	23	149	14–4	.778	105	168	46	1.57
1992	Columbus AAA	22	141	12–2	.857	105	152	46	2.29
1992	New York	9	60	3–3	.500	43	42	32	3.45

KURT MILLER
Texas Rangers
Starting Pitcher
$16

A first-round draft pick who came to Texas in the Buechele trade, will be an outstanding pitcher if the Rangers can avoid hurting his arm over the next four-five years. At 19 (now 20) he was 7–5 in the Texas League. A+ fastball, good velocity with a natural sink, and a good change; needs to get his curve over more consistently. **Grade A prospect.**

YEAR	TEAM/LEVEL	G	IP	W–L	PCT.	HITS	SO	BB	ERA
1991	Augusta A	21	115	6–7	.462	89	103	57	2.50
1992	Charlotte A	12	75	5–4	.556	51	58	29	2.39
1992	Tulsa AA	15	87	7–5	.583	82	72	35	3.72

PAUL MILLER
Pittsburgh Pirates
Pitcher
$6

Went on the DL in mid-July and didn't come back due to stiffness in his shoulder. A low draft pick in 1987, just survived until 1990 and began pitching well. In 1991 he posted a 1.48 ERA in 10 starts at Buffalo, was called up last May, pitched a few times and went back down. Record is very hard to figure; Grade C prospect.

YEAR	TEAM/LEVEL	G	IP	W–L	PCT.	HITS	SO	BB	ERA
1991	AA and AAA	25	156	12–4	.750	110	99	64	2.01
1992	Buffalo AAA	7	27	1–3	.250	32	16	12	4.28
1992	Pittsburgh	6	11	1–0	1.000	11	5	1	2.38

ALAN MILLS
Baltimore Orioles
Relief Pitcher
$21

Moved into Mark Williamson's old role as the first man out of the bullpen, and had the same kind of year Williamson had in '90 . . . in my opinion he will *not* be able to sustain his success once he gets out of that role. His strikeout/walk ratio is poor, and he has no record of consistent success. Could continue to pitch well in long relief.

YEAR	TEAM/LEVEL	G	IP	W–L	SAVES	HITS	SO	BB	ERA
1991	Columbus AAA	38	114	7–5	8	109	77	75	4.43
1991	New York	6	16	1–1	0	16	11	8	4.41
1992	Baltimore	35	103	10–4	2	78	60	54	2.61

BLAS MINOR
Pittsburgh Pirates
Relief Pitcher
$8

His major league career to this point consists of one relief appearance, against the Cubs on July 28 of last year. He pitched the best ball of his career at Buffalo last summer, but that's a pitcher's park. His record before that is vanilla, looks like anybody else's—sixth-round pick, has been hurt, has pitched well sometimes but not consistently. Grade C prospect, based on strong 1992.

YEAR	TEAM/LEVEL	G	IP	W–L	SAVES	HITS	SO	BB	ERA
1991	Buffalo AAA	17	36	2–2	0	46	25	15	5.75
1992	Buffalo AAA	45	96	5–4	18	72	60	26	2.43
1992	Pittsburgh	1	2	0–0	0	3	0	0	4.50

DAVE MLICKI
Cleveland Indians
Starting Pitcher
$7

He was born in Cleveland and now lives in Colorado Springs, so he's a natural for the Indians. He needs a year of Triple-A before he can be taken seriously, even though the Indians need starters. A big guy with excellent strikeout rates, but doesn't have the kind of control he would need to be successful in the majors. Grade C prospect.

YEAR	TEAM/LEVEL	G	IP	W–L	PCT.	HITS	SO	BB	ERA
1991	Columbus A	22	116	8–6	.571	101	136	70	4.20
1992	Canton-Akron AA	27	173	11–9	.550	143	146	80	3.60
1992	Cleveland	4	22	0–2	.000	23	16	16	4.98

DENNIS MOELLER
Kansas City Royals
Starting Pitcher
$3

All pitchers look bad when they lose. This guy doesn't look good even when he's getting people out. He's a left-hander with good size but throws slop, has been quite effective in the minor leagues by changing speeds and not walking people. He's a candidate for the Royals' "new Charlie Leibrandt" strategy, but ranks behind Haney, Magnante, Rasmussen. Grade D prospect.

YEAR	TEAM/LEVEL	G	IP	W–L	PCT.	HITS	SO	BB	ERA
1991	AA and AAA	24	131	11–8	.579	122	105	61	2.95
1992	Omaha AAA	23	121	8–5	.615	121	56	34	2.46
1992	Kansas City	5	18	0–3	.000	24	6	11	7.00

RICH MONTELEONE
New York Yankees
Relief Pitcher
$16

Heavy-set right-hander, had belonged to the Tigers, Mariners and Angels and was losing 60 percent of his decisions as a minor league starting pitcher until somebody thought to try him in the bullpen. Has pitched well for two years, and could conceivably move into a key role although it is unlikely. An All-American football player in high school; lists his hobbies as Tae-Kwon-Do and golf.

YEAR	TEAM/LEVEL	G	IP	W–L	SAVES	HITS	SO	BB	ERA
1991	Columbus AAA	34	47	1–3	17	36	52	7	2.12
1991	New York	26	47	3–1	0	42	34	19	3.64
1992	New York	47	93	7–3	0	82	62	27	3.30

JEFF MONTGOMERY
Kansas City Royals
Closer
$70

Based on 1992 *or* multi-year performance, would rank as the number-two reliever in the American League, behind Eckersley. Challenges the hitter with decent fastball to get ahead in the count, like Eckersley, then carves hitters up with four pitches. He must hide the ball well, because he gets by with a lot of fat pitches. Has now had four straight good seasons, career ERA of 2.57.

YEAR	TEAM/LEVEL	G	IP	W–L	SAVES	HITS	SO	BB	ERA
1990	Kansas City	73	94	6–5	24	81	94	34	2.39
1991	Kansas City	67	90	4–4	33	83	77	28	2.90
1992	Kansas City	65	83	1–6	39	61	69	27	2.18

MIKE MOORE
Oakland Athletics
(Released)
Starting Pitcher
$29

Moore finished 17–12 last year despite very poor peripheral stats. The batting average against him jumped sharply, his strikeouts tumbled, and his home runs allowed nearly doubled. His control was never good to begin with. Although you certainly have to respect a pitcher who can win 17 to 19 games regularly, he really hasn't pitched well in two of the last three years. I'd be wary of him.

YEAR	TEAM/LEVEL	G	IP	W–L	PCT.	HITS	SO	BB	ERA
1990	Oakland	33	199	13–15	.464	204	73	84	4.65
1991	Oakland	33	210	17–8	.680	176	153	105	2.96
1992	Oakland	36	223	17–12	.586	229	117	103	4.12

MIKE MORGAN
Chicago Cubs
Starting Pitcher
$48

Unbelievable record in Wrigley Field (9–2, 1.38 ERA) . . . he's a ground ball pitcher, so one might guess that he would pitch well in a home run park, but I can't believe he can sustain anything like that . . . like most ground ball pitchers, is hit hard on artificial turf . . . two straight quality seasons make him a good bet to have a third one.

YEAR	TEAM/LEVEL	G	IP	W–L	PCT.	HITS	SO	BB	ERA
1990	Los Angeles	33	211	11–15	.423	216	106	60	3.75
1991	Los Angeles	34	236	14–10	.583	197	140	61	2.78
1992	Chicago	34	240	16–8	.667	203	123	79	2.55

JACK MORRIS
Detroit Tigers
Starting Pitcher
$50

The repeated stories about Morris "knowing how to win" are the varnished buffalo turd of the year. Where was this knowledge when he went 6–14 in '89, and lost 18 games in '90? Was that the 19th century? His team scored 5.98 runs a game for him. Score 5.98 runs a game for Jim Abbott or Bill Wegman, and they'll know how to win, too . . .

YEAR	TEAM/LEVEL	G	IP	W–L	PCT.	HITS	SO	BB	ERA
1990	Detroit	36	250	15–18	.455	231	162	97	4.51
1991	Minnesota	35	247	18–12	.600	226	163	92	3.43
1992	Toronto	34	241	21–6	.778	222	132	80	4.04

JAMIE MOYER
Detroit Tigers
Starting Pitcher
$2

Pitched pretty well for Toledo in '92, too well for the Tigers to want him. He had a 2.86 ERA; the Tigers aren't interested in you unless your ERA is at least 4.20 . . . good control, career fell apart in Texas in 1989 due to shoulder trouble, just found himself last year. Needs to get a chance quick, because he won't stay healthy forever.

YEAR	TEAM/LEVEL	G	IP	W–L	PCT.	HITS	SO	BB	ERA
1991	Louisville AAA	20	126	5–10	.333	125	69	43	3.80
1991	St. Louis	8	31	0–5	.000	38	20	16	5.74
1992	Toledo AAA	21	139	10–8	.556	128	80	37	2.86

TERRY MULHOLLAND
Philadelphia Phillies
Starting Pitcher
$51

Extremely fine pitcher, has now pitched well for three straight years. Has extremely good control, not quite Tewksbury-like but the next best thing, and throws harder than BT. Fifteen wins a year could become 18 if the team improves. The Phillies support him with a good offense, but then there is that defense . . . has outstanding record in Philadelphia, poor on the road.

YEAR	TEAM/LEVEL	G	IP	W–L	PCT.	HITS	SO	BB	ERA
1990	Philadelphia	33	181	9–10	.474	172	75	42	3.34
1991	Philadelphia	34	232	16–13	.552	231	142	49	3.61
1992	Philadelphia	32	229	13–11	.542	227	125	46	3.81

MIKE MUNOZ
Detroit Tigers
Relief Pitcher
$21

Sparky spotted him against left-handed hitters; he held the left–handers to a .198 average and wound up with decent overall stats, still not good. There is nothing I see that makes me believe he can move out of that role, or even be terribly successful *in* that role. The only place he ever posted good numbers was San Antonio, 1988.

YEAR	TEAM/LEVEL	G	IP	W–L	SAVES	HITS	SO	BB	ERA
1990	Albuquerque AAA	49	59	4–1	6	65	40	19	4.25
1991	Toledo AAA	38	54	2–3	8	44	38	35	3.83
1992	Detroit	63	47	1–2	2	44	23	24	3.09

ROB MURPHY
Houston Astros

Relief Pitcher

$6

Pitched extremely well in September, giving hope that he may be back. The Mike Flanagan of 1990, he pitched poorly again for most of last year, although in a sheltered role. The rule for a pitcher like this is, don't draft him unless you know something. Pitchers *have* come back after three-year slumps, but I don't want to be depending on it.

YEAR	TEAM/LEVEL	G	IP	W–L	SAVES	HITS	SO	BB	ERA
1990	Boston	68	57	0–6	7	85	54	32	6.32
1991	Seattle	57	48	0–1	4	47	34	19	3.00
1992	Houston	58	55	3–1	0	56	42	21	4.07

JEFF MUSSELMAN
Oakland Athletics

Starting Pitcher

$1

May be back in the majors in '93 after a good year at Tacoma, started 19 times with 3.50 ERA and good control. A graduate of Harvard with a degree in economics, career has been derailed by rotator cuff surgery (1987) and a drinking problem, has now been in the minors for two years. Listed at 6-0, 180; but isn't that big.

YEAR	TEAM/LEVEL	G	IP	W–L	PCT.	HITS	SO	BB	ERA
1990	New York	28	32	0–2	.000	40	14	11	5.63
1991	Tacoma AAA	25	138	5–9	.357	176	81	69	5.79
1992	Tacoma AAA	19	105	7–7	.500	100	75	40	3.50

JOSE MUSSET
California Angels

Reliever

$8

If Dan Quisenberry had had a fastball, he'd have been Jose Musset. A converted infielder, he probably throws 88 but varies arm angle from high sidearm to submarine, and the ball looks like a bullet. I don't normally run A Ball players here, but I saw him last year at Quad City, not having heard anything about him (*Baseball America* hasn't discovered him yet), and was awed.

YEAR	TEAM/LEVEL	G	IP	W–L	SAVES	HITS	SO	BB	ERA
1990	Mesa A	13	63	2–7	0	63	49	41	6.03
1991	Mesa A	10	14	1–1	2	14	10	5	3.21
1992	Quad City A	41	72	8–2	6	41	104	25	2.39

MIKE MUSSINA
Baltimore Orioles

Starting Pitcher

$67

The new Catfish Hunter, a smooth kid with excellent stuff, and was born knowing what to do with it. Pitches above the belt, jams the hitters occasionally, holds baserunners exceptionally well (nine stolen bases against him all year, with Hoiles as the catcher), unusual control for a young pitcher. His strikeout rate went up late in the year, and will continue to ascend.

YEAR	TEAM/LEVEL	G	IP	W–L	PCT.	HITS	SO	BB	ERA
1991	Rochester AAA	19	122	10–4	.714	108	107	31	2.87
1991	Baltimore	12	88	4–5	.444	77	52	21	2.87
1992	Baltimore	32	241	18–5	.783	212	130	48	2.54

RANDY MYERS
San Diego Padres
Manager's Friend
$21

Actually pitched quite well during July and August, while the Padres mounted a mini-push. The rest of the year he stunk like a skunk, but piled up one-inning saves whenever he could get a couple of outs together, and consequently would have value in a rotisserie league. In view of his general ineffectiveness, I would not anticipate that he would retain the closer role.

YEAR	TEAM/LEVEL	G	IP	W–L	SAVES	HITS	SO	BB	ERA
1990	Cincinnati	66	87	4–6	31	59	98	38	2.08
1991	Cincinnati	58	132	6–13	6	116	108	80	3.55
1992	San Diego	65	77	2–6	38	83	61	32	4.46

CHRIS NABHOLZ
Montreal Expos
Starting Pitcher
$32

Pretty much a generic pitcher, mixes a sinking fastball, curve, and changeup, fair control, fair move to first. He is still young (26, and inexperienced for 26) so his strikeouts could move up and his walks down, which could make him substantially more effective. Generally, a young pitcher will improve until he gets hurt, and since Nabholz is healthy his future appears good.

YEAR	TEAM/LEVEL	G	IP	W–L	PCT.	HITS	SO	BB	ERA
1990	Montreal	11	70	6–2	.750	43	53	32	2.83
1991	Montreal	24	154	8–7	.533	134	99	57	3.63
1992	Montreal	32	195	11–12	.478	176	130	74	3.32

CHARLES NAGY
Cleveland Indians
Starting Pitcher
$53

Had one of the more remarkable seasons among major league players, actually pitched better than his 2.96 ERA reflects. Hargrove would leave him in the game to absorb awful punishment at times (August 30 at Oakland, gave up 15 hits in 4 ⅔ innings), which hurt his stats . . . ground ball pitcher/very poor record on turf . . . he will remain effective.

YEAR	TEAM/LEVEL	G	IP	W–L	PCT.	HITS	SO	BB	ERA
1990	Cleveland	9	46	2–4	.333	58	26	21	5.91
1991	Cleveland	33	211	10–15	.400	228	109	66	4.13
1992	Cleveland	33	252	17–10	.630	245	169	57	2.96

JAIME NAVARRO
Milwaukee Brewers
Starting Pitcher
$35

I would be a little bit wary of him in '93; I would look first for a pitcher with a comparable won–lost record, like Nagy or Smiley. His strikeout rate is low and dropping steadily; his control is not exceptional, and he's not a ground ball pitcher. He's a big strong guy and he's been a fine pitcher for two years, but I do *not* anticipate a long career.

YEAR	TEAM/LEVEL	G	IP	W–L	PCT.	HITS	SO	BB	ERA
1990	Milwaukee	32	149	8–7	.533	176	75	41	4.46
1991	Milwaukee	34	234	15–12	.556	237	114	73	3.92
1992	Milwaukee	34	246	17–11	.607	224	100	64	3.33

DENNY NEAGLE
Pittsburgh Pirates

Left-Handed Pitcher
$20

Came to the Pirates as part of the Smiley trade. He was in the rotation early in the year, but wasn't sharp and didn't start after June 6. He was hit hard throughout the season, but I still think he could be outstanding. His minor league record is great (32–10, 2.82 ERA), and although ineffective in the majors he struck out 77 men in 86 innings.

YEAR	TEAM/LEVEL	G	IP	W–L	PCT.	HITS	SO	BB	ERA
1990	A and AA	27	184	20–3	.870	133	186	47	2.10
1991	Portland AAA	19	105	9–4	.692	101	94	32	3.27
1992	Pittsburgh	55	86	4–6	.400	81	77	43	4.48

GENE NELSON
Oakland A's

Reliever
$2

He was waived (bye-bye) on August 11 after the league had hit .335 against him in 52 innings. Actually, he pitched well through June 14, had been unscored upon in eight straight outings, giving up only six hits in 13 innings, then suddenly was unable to get anybody out. This suggests to me that he was just seriously out of sync, and could recover his form.

YEAR	TEAM/LEVEL	G	IP	W–L	SAVES	HITS	SO	BB	ERA
1990	Oakland	51	75	3–3	5	55	38	17	1.57
1991	Oakland	44	49	1–5	0	60	23	23	6.84
1992	Oakland	28	52	3–1	0	68	23	22	6.45

JEFF NELSON
Seattle Mariners
(Released)

Right-Handed Relief Pitcher
$1

Six-foot-eight, was selected by LA in the 1984 draft, and did not win a game in his first three minor league seasons. In the two years after that, however, he went 11–16 with a neat 5.62 ERA, so the Mariners took him in the Rule 5 draft, and in 1992 he fulfilled his early promise, going 1–7 and blowing 8 of 13 save opportunities.

YEAR	TEAM/LEVEL	G	IP	W–L	SAVES	HITS	SO	BB	ERA
1990	Two Teams A	28	103	3–6	6	112	63	43	4.53
1991	AA and AAA	49	61	7–4	33	62	60	24	2.67
1992	Seattle	65	80	1–7	5	71	45	44	3.49

ROD NICHOLS
Cleveland Indians

Reliever/Starter
$8

Started the year with Cleveland, was sent to Colorado Springs in May, posted a 5.67 ERA in nine starts there, was called up July 22 and put in the Indians' rotation. He stayed in the rotation until September 6, wasn't terrible, went back to the bullpen in September while the Indians looked around for starters. Remains a candidate for a starting spot despite thoroughly unimpressive record.

YEAR	TEAM/LEVEL	G	IP	W–L	PCT.	HITS	SO	BB	ERA
1990	Colorado Sp AAA	22	133	12–9	.571	160	74	48	5.13
1991	Cleveland	31	137	2–11	.154	145	76	30	3.54
1992	Cleveland	30	105	4–3	.571	114	56	31	4.53

DAVID NIED
Atlanta Braves
Starting Pitcher
$21

If a spot ever opens up in the Braves' starting rotation, he has a chance to be outstanding. Nied is only 24, but has pitched 748 minor league innings, which is a lot, with generally quality results (57–36 record), and was cited by *Baseball America* as the fifth-best prospect in the International League. Obviously ready to pitch in the major leagues, **Grade A prospect.**

YEAR	TEAM/LEVEL	G	IP	W–L	PCT.	HITS	SO	BB	ERA
1991	A and AA	28	170	15–6	.714	125	101	20	2.01
1992	Richmond AAA	26	168	14–9	.609	144	159	44	2.84
1992	Atlanta	6	23	3–0	1.000	10	19	5	1.17

JERRY NIELSEN
New York Yankees
Relief Pitcher
$18

Left-handed reliever, throws three pitches for strikes (fastball, slider, change), but what draws comment is his makeup, his composure. An 18th-round draft pick in 1988, has pitched brilliantly in relief his entire career, had unsuccessful trial as a starter. The Yankees for some reason gave him four years in A Ball and then decided to skip Triple-A, but good Grade B prospect.

YEAR	TEAM/LEVEL	G	IP	W–L	SAVES	HITS	SO	BB	ERA
1991	Ft. Lauderdale A	42	65	3–3	4	50	66	31	2.78
1992	Albany AA	36	53	3–5	11	38	59	15	1.19
1992	New York	20	20	1–0	0	17	12	18	4.58

RAFAEL NOVOA
Milwaukee Brewers
Starting Pitcher
$4

A hot prospect in the Giants system in 1990, going 14–6 at two levels in the minor leagues and earning a late call to the Giants. He developed tendinitis in his left (pitching) shoulder, and was hit very hard at Phoenix in '91 (5.96 ERA), landed in the Brewers system, at El Paso, where he once again pitched very well in '92. Grade C prospect.

YEAR	TEAM/LEVEL	G	IP	W–L	PCT.	HITS	SO	BB	ERA
1990	A and AA	26	169	14–6	.700	133	179	55	2.50
1991	Phoenix AAA	17	94	6–6	.500	135	46	37	5.96
1992	El Paso AA	22	146	10–7	.588	143	124	48	3.26

EDWIN NUNEZ
Texas Rangers
Relief Pitcher
$4

There aren't very many pitchers who are hit hard with good strikeout/walk ratios, but Nunez is one of the few. After ERAs of 6.04 and 4.85 the last two years, it would seem to me that it might be time for him to go back to the minors and re-establish himself. Still has excellent arm; something of a puzzle.

YEAR	TEAM/LEVEL	G	IP	W–L	SAVES	HITS	SO	BB	ERA
1990	Detroit	42	80	3–1	6	65	66	37	2.24
1991	Milwaukee	23	25	2–1	8	28	24	13	6.04
1992	Two Teams	49	59	1–3	3	63	49	22	4.85

BOBBY OJEDA
Los Angeles Dodgers
Starting Pitcher
$9

He had a generally desultory season, capped by an awful September (0–3 record, 5.47 ERA). He's a 35-year-old pitcher, coming off an off season, pitching for a non-competitive team which is entering a restructuring period with a wealth of young pitchers. A comeback in a new location would not be a shock, but I'm not predicting it.

YEAR	TEAM/LEVEL	G	IP	W–L	PCT.	HITS	SO	BB	ERA
1990	New York	38	118	7–6	.538	123	62	40	3.66
1991	Los Angeles	31	189	12–9	.571	181	120	70	3.18
1992	Los Angeles	29	166	6–9	.400	169	94	81	3.63

STEVE OLIN
Cleveland Indians
Relief Pitcher
$56

Quisenberry-style reliever, saved 29 games. Had 0.21 ERA on the road, but was hurt by home runs in his games in Cleveland. His groundball/flyball ratio is not as extreme as some pitchers in this group, but has the general characteristics of the type, including vulnerability to left-handers. He will continue to be effective, and should save 35 to 45 games this season.

YEAR	TEAM/LEVEL	G	IP	W–L	SAVES	HITS	SO	BB	ERA
1990	Cleveland	50	92	4–4	1	96	64	26	3.41
1991	Cleveland	48	56	3–6	17	61	38	23	3.36
1992	Cleveland	70	84	8–5	29	74	44	25	2.45

OMAR OLIVARES
St. Louis Cardinals
Starting Pitcher
$32

He pitched better last year than he did as a rookie in '91, but his record doesn't show it because the Cardinals moved their fences and the team didn't score at the right times. Throws good fastball, pitch he calls a slider but it breaks more like a curve, slow split-finger that he uses as change. Will continue to be effective and will have better years.

YEAR	TEAM/LEVEL	G	IP	W–L	PCT.	HITS	SO	BB	ERA
1990	St. Louis	9	49	1–1	.500	45	20	17	2.92
1991	St. Louis	28	167	11–7	.611	148	91	61	3.71
1992	St. Louis	32	197	9–9	.500	189	124	63	3.84

FRANCISCO OLIVERAS
San Francisco Giants
(Free Agent)
Pitcher
$6

A 30-year-old veteran, another tribute to Roger Craig's genius with pitchers. He pitched relief (mostly) at Phoenix, was called up in June, relieved four times, pitched good, moved into the rotation, and pitched brilliantly—one game. Then he hurt his back, went on the DL, and struggled the rest of the year. He's not a bad pitcher; might have a good year for a serious manager.

YEAR	TEAM/LEVEL	G	IP	W–L	SAVES	HITS	SO	BB	ERA
1990	San Francisco	33	55	2–2	2	47	41	21	2.77
1991	San Francisco	55	79	6–6	3	69	48	22	3.86
1992	San Francisco	16	45	0–3	0	41	17	10	3.63

GREGG OLSON
Baltimore Orioles
Closer
$60

Odd splits in his record—a horrible career record on artificial turf (3–9, 4.23 ERA) and in day games (1–10, 3.83) as opposed to brilliant records on grass (14–10, 1.93 ERA) and at night (16–9, 1.79). Doesn't pitch as many innings as he did at first, but remains effective . . . with luck will be the first reliever to save 500 games.

YEAR	TEAM/LEVEL	G	IP	W–L	SAVES	HITS	SO	BB	ERA
1990	Baltimore	64	74	6–5	37	57	74	31	2.42
1991	Baltimore	72	74	4–6	31	74	72	29	3.18
1992	Baltimore	60	61	1–5	36	46	58	24	2.05

JESSE OROSCO
Milwaukee Brewers
(Released)
Left-Handed Spot Reliever
$14

Garner spotted him more carefully than McNamara had in Cleveland, and he was one of the most effective pitchers in baseball in his role. Because of pinch hitters, even a left-handed one-out reliever will face a majority of right-handed hitters, so has to be able to get them out, too. Orosco can, and I expect him to remain valuable for two to four years.

YEAR	TEAM/LEVEL	G	IP	W–L	SAVES	HITS	SO	BB	ERA
1990	Cleveland	55	65	5–4	2	58	55	38	3.90
1991	Cleveland	47	46	2–0	0	52	36	15	3.74
1992	Milwaukee	59	39	3–1	1	33	40	13	3.23

DONOVAN OSBORNE
St. Louis Cardinals
Starting Pitcher
$38

He had two hot streaks sandwiched around a mid-summer slump which deprived him of the NL Rookie of the Year award. This is like his game pattern; he's very effective early, tends to get hurt in the middle innings. Throws hard, has two good breaking pitches, exceptional control. If this guy's not going to be a star, you could have fooled me. Should win 200 games.

YEAR	TEAM/LEVEL	G	IP	W–L	PCT.	HITS	SO	BB	ERA
1990	Two Teams A	10	61	2–4	.333	61	42	12	2.93
1991	Arkansas AA	26	166	8–12	.400	177	130	43	3.63
1992	St. Louis	34	179	11–9	.550	193	104	38	3.77

AL OSUNA
Houston Astros
Relief Pitcher
$17

Hasn't developed as quickly as I thought he would. Has started out well both seasons in the majors, but faded down the stretch. Throws a screwball and 88 MPH fastball . . . now 27 years old, a functional part of a deep bullpen, with no indication that he's about to move up or down . . . name is of Mexican origin, but family has lived in California for several generations.

YEAR	TEAM/LEVEL	G	IP	W–L	SAVES	HITS	SO	BB	ERA
1990	Houston	12	11	2–0	0	10	6	6	4.76
1991	Houston	71	69	7–6	12	59	68	46	3.42
1992	Houston	66	62	6–3	0	52	37	38	4.23

DAVE OTTO
Cleveland Indians
Starting Pitcher
$2

Pitched OK the second half of '91 and started '92 in the rotation, but was hit very hard, placing his career in jeopardy. A huge left-hander and a good athlete, has battled knee injuries. Doesn't throw hard, lacks a sharp breaking pitch, and has been advised to keep the ball low so often that he tries to do it, which in my opinion is a mistake.

YEAR	TEAM/LEVEL	G	IP	W–L	PCT.	HITS	SO	BB	ERA
1990	Oakland	2	2	0–0	.000	3	2	3	7.71
1991	Cleveland	18	100	2–8	.200	108	47	27	4.23
1992	Cleveland	18	80	5–9	.357	110	32	33	7.06

LANCE PAINTER
San Diego Padres
Starting Pitcher
$7

Jimmy Key–type left-hander, struck out 201 men at Waterloo in 1991 and followed with a good year for Wichita in '92. He has an OK fastball but throws a lot of off-speed stuff, his best pitch being a slider. Should reach the majors, if he stays healthy, in '94 or late '93. Grade C prospect; will need adjustment period in the majors.

YEAR	TEAM/LEVEL	G	IP	W–L	PCT.	HITS	SO	BB	ERA
1990	Spokane A	23	72	7–3	.700	45	104	16	1.51
1991	Waterloo A	28	200	14–8	.636	162	201	57	2.29
1992	Wichita AA	27	163	10–5	.667	138	137	55	3.53

VINCE PALACIOS
Pittsburgh Pirates
Pitcher
$3

A 29-year-old Mexican right-hander, had been maneuvering for several years for a spot in the Pirates' rotation. He had pitched consistently well in the majors and minors and finally reached the rotation on May 23, but developed tendinitis in his bicep after just two starts, pitched poorly through three more starts and didn't pitch after June 18. His future is hazy.

YEAR	TEAM/LEVEL	G	IP	W–L	SAVES	HITS	SO	BB	ERA
1990	Pittsburgh	7	15	0–0	3	4	8	2	0.00
1991	Pittsburgh	36	82	6–3	3	69	64	38	3.75
1992	Pittsburgh	20	53	3–2	0	56	33	27	4.25

DONN PALL
Chicago White Sox
Relief Pitcher
$7

Picks up odd innings for the Sox, pitching blowouts or when the rest of the staff is tired or when the starter is wasted early. He's been in that role for four-plus years, didn't pitch as well last year as he had the previous three. Throws slider and split-fingered fastball, both look about the same, supposed to get ground balls but didn't last year.

YEAR	TEAM/LEVEL	G	IP	W–L	SAVES	HITS	SO	BB	ERA
1990	Chicago	56	76	3–5	2	63	39	24	3.32
1991	Chicago	51	71	7–2	0	59	40	20	2.41
1992	Chicago	39	73	5–2	1	79	27	27	4.93

CLAY PARKER
Seattle Mariners (Free Agent)
Starting Pitcher
$2

A hot prospect with the Mariners five years ago, after he went 8–1 with a 2.93 ERA at Calgary. He has detoured to the Yankees, Tigers, A's, back to Seattle. The adventure appears to be nearly over, as he pitched the poorest ball of his life last year, went on the DL with tendinitis in his right shoulder and later had shoulder surgery. Has pitched well when healthy.

YEAR	TEAM/LEVEL	G	IP	W–L	PCT.	HITS	SO	BB	ERA
1991	Tacoma AAA	25	132	7–6	.538	123	78	44	3.67
1992	Calgary AAA	3	18	2–1	.667	20	11	3	4.00
1992	Seattle	8	33	0–2	.000	47	20	11	7.56

JEFF PARRETT
Oakland Athletics
Relief Pitcher
$24

Pitched in a key role for the A's, passing leads to Eckersley and pitching in ties and when the A's were behind but close. He had nine wins, 19 holds, only one blown save and only one loss . . . pitched well in '88–'89 but with very heavy workload, collapsed in '90. His performance was not a fluke, but few pitchers are consistently good in his role.

YEAR	TEAM/LEVEL	G	IP	W–L	SAVES	HITS	SO	BB	ERA
1990	Two Teams	67	109	5–10	2	119	86	55	4.64
1991	Atlanta	18	21	1–2	1	31	14	12	6.33
1992	Oakland	66	98	9–1	1	81	78	42	3.02

BOB PATTERSON
Pittsburgh Pirates
Left-Handed Spot Pitcher
$22

Is used a little differently than Candelaria, Orosco, etc.; he will pitch as long as two innings in a game and gets his share of the save opportunities. He'll be 34 in May, lives on a slow curve which is usually hit in the air and nibbles with a little fastball which is almost always outside or low, and which a good hitter normally never swings at.

YEAR	TEAM/LEVEL	G	IP	W–L	SAVES	HITS	SO	BB	ERA
1990	Pittsburgh	55	95	8–5	5	88	70	21	2.95
1991	Pittsburgh	54	66	4–3	2	67	57	15	4.11
1992	Pittsburgh	60	65	6–3	9	59	43	23	2.92

KEN PATTERSON
Chicago Cubs
Left-Handed Spot Reliever
$16

Another example of the Sadowski rule, which is that if two players have similar names they will always play the same position and have about the same stats, so that you can never figure out which is which. Ken Patterson is used more to get one left-hander out than is Bob and has a better fastball, doesn't have good control and is poor fielder.

YEAR	TEAM/LEVEL	G	IP	W–L	SAVES	HITS	SO	BB	ERA
1990	Chicago (AL)	43	66	2–1	2	58	40	34	3.39
1991	Chicago (AL)	43	64	3–0	1	48	32	35	2.83
1992	Chicago (NL)	32	42	2–3	0	41	23	27	3.89

ROGER PAVLIK
Texas Rangers

Starting Pitcher
$18

Big pitcher, looks heavy. He was a second-round pick in '86, had awful control for three years. His control improved a little but he missed most of the '91 season with a ligament problem in his elbow and surprised everybody by coming back in '92 with his best season, earning a major league trial. Good fastball but just fair control, lacks good breaking ball. Grade C prospect.

YEAR	TEAM/LEVEL	G	IP	W–L	PCT.	HITS	SO	BB	ERA
1991	Oklahoma City AAA	8	26	0–5	.000	19	43	26	5.19
1992	Oklahoma City AAA	18	118	7–5	.583	90	104	51	2.98
1992	Texas	13	62	4–4	.500	66	45	34	4.21

ALEJANDRO PEÑA
Atlanta Braves

Relief Pitcher
$16

Missed most of September and the playoffs/World Series with elbow trouble. (The big injury which ate the heart out of his career was to his shoulder, so this isn't the same thing.) I've always liked Pena, but would be reluctant to pick up a pitcher with a sore elbow, particularly when the team has so many options. Doubt that he will regain the closer role.

YEAR	TEAM/LEVEL	G	IP	W–L	SAVES	HITS	SO	BB	ERA
1990	New York	52	76	3–3	5	71	76	22	3.20
1991	Two Teams	59	82	8–1	15	74	62	22	2.40
1992	Atlanta	41	42	1–6	15	40	34	13	4.07

JIM PEÑA
San Francisco Giants

Relief Pitcher
$4

Came up in July and pitched well enough early to hang around. 28 years old, minor league numbers are not good, although not spectacularly bad, had been long reliever last two minor league seasons. I haven't seen him pitch, and pitchers like this do surprise you once in a while, but there is nothing here that makes you think he's going to succeed. Grade D prospect.

YEAR	TEAM/LEVEL	G	IP	W–L	SAVES	HITS	SO	BB	ERA
1991	Shreveport AA	45	83	7–4	2	84	51	41	4.77
1992	Phoenix AAA	33	39	7–3	1	45	27	20	4.15
1992	San Francisco	25	44	1–1	0	49	32	20	3.48

BRAD PENNINGTON
Baltimore Orioles

Relief Pitcher
$11

A young Mitch Williams or Steve Dalkowski, a Wild left-handed reliever with a 96 MPH fastball. He's 6-5, started in '89–'90 and struck out 12 men a game, but walked 10. Converted to relief and has had good ERAs, held International League hitters to a batting average of .101. The Orioles believe he is close to mastering his control, but I'm doubtful. Grade B prospect.

YEAR	TEAM/LEVEL	G	IP	W–L	SAVES	HITS	SO	BB	ERA
1990	Wausau A	32	106	4–9	0	81	142	121	5.18
1991	A and AA	59	67	1–6	17	48	101	69	4.59
1992	A, AA, and AAA	56	76	3–5	14	37	89	54	2.24

MELIDO PEREZ
New York Yankees
Starting Pitcher
$48

And if you want more good news, his control returned in mid-summer. Perez pitched well the first half of last season, and pitched great the second half, posting a 5–9 record but a 2.62 ERA, 109/31 strikeout/walk record in 120 innings. I've always liked him and predict that he will be top-quality pitcher over the next five years.

YEAR	TEAM/LEVEL	G	IP	W–L	PCT.	HITS	SO	BB	ERA
1990	Chicago	35	197	13–14	.481	177	161	86	4.61
1991	Chicago	49	136	8–7	.533	111	128	52	3.12
1992	New York	33	248	13–16	.448	212	218	93	2.87

MIKE PEREZ
St. Louis Cardinals
Relief Pitcher
$25

Posted 6.13 ERA at Louisville in '91, 1.84 in the majors in '92, so you figure it out. Perez held the minor league record for saves, 41 (Springfield, 1987), which was broken last year, and also saved 30+ at Arkansas (1989) and Louisville (1990), but supporting numbers generally weren't great. Started '92 pitching long relief and blowouts, but moved into setup role with Worrell.

YEAR	TEAM/LEVEL	G	IP	W–L	SAVES	HITS	SO	BB	ERA
1991	St. Louis	14	17	0–2	0	19	7	7	5.82
1991	Louisville AAA	37	47	3–5	4	54	39	25	6.13
1992	St. Louis	77	93	9–3	0	70	46	32	1.84

PASCUAL PEREZ
New York Yankees
Starting Pitcher
$10

Is expected to return in '93; I included him here not because I have any idea what to expect from him, but just so you wouldn't forget him if you were making a list and checking it twice. Pascual, despite his reputation and his injury history, is one of those guys like John Tudor who will always pitch well when he is able to pitch.

YEAR	TEAM/LEVEL	G	IP	W–L	PCT.	HITS	SO	BB	ERA
1989	Montreal	33	198	9–13	.409	178	152	45	3.31
1990	New York	3	14	1–2	.333	8	12	3	1.29
1991	New York	14	74	2–4	.333	68	41	24	3.18

HIPOLITO PICHARDO
Kansas City Royals
Starting Pitcher
$29

The best surprise of the Royals' season, entered the rotation after 3–11 record at Double-A in '91 and pitched consistently well. Throws hard, excellent movement on the fastball; when he gets in a groove he just rocks and fires, but when he starts to think he gets in trouble. Looks like Michael Jackson; needs to develop a better breaking pitch. Future is iffy, could regress.

YEAR	TEAM/LEVEL	G	IP	W–L	PCT.	HITS	SO	BB	ERA
1990	Baseball City A	11	45	1–6	.143	47	40	25	3.80
1991	Memphis AA	34	99	3–11	.214	116	75	38	4.27
1992	Kansas City	31	144	9–6	.600	148	59	49	3.95

ED PIERCE
Kansas City Royals

Starting Pitcher

$5

Another of the Royals' many candidates for the new Charlie Leibrandt. A seventh-round pick in 1989, established himself as a prospect by striking out 71 in 39 innings at Eugene, has made gradual progress since. At Memphis in '91 he was 5–11 with a poor K/W rate, but his strikeouts went back up in '92, suggesting that he added a breaking ball. Grade C prospect.

YEAR	TEAM/LEVEL	G	IP	W–L	PCT.	HITS	SO	BB	ERA
1991	Memphis AA	31	136	5–11	.313	136	90	61	3.84
1992	Memphis AA	25	154	10–10	.500	159	131	51	3.81
1992	Kansas City	2	5	0–0	.000	9	3	4	3.38

DAN PLESAC
Milwaukee Brewers (Free Agent)

Relief Pitcher

$27

He may finally have recovered from whatever it was that was bothering him from 1989 through early '92. The Brewers experimented with him as a starter in '91 and early '92, but that didn't go anywhere and he went back to the pen, posting a 2.17 ERA (as a reliever), with ERAs of 1.54 or below in July, August, September, and October.

YEAR	TEAM/LEVEL	G	IP	W–L	SAVES	HITS	SO	BB	ERA
1990	Milwaukee	66	69	3–7	24	67	65	31	4.43
1991	Milwaukee	45	92	2–7	8	92	61	39	4.29
1992	Milwaukee	44	79	5–4	1	64	54	35	2.96

ERIC PLUNK
Cleveland Indians

Middle Relief

$16

Started the year at Canton (Double-A), posted a 1.72 ERA in nine games/16 innings there, was called up in early May and did adequate job in supporting the Indians' big three of Olin, Lilliquist, and Power. He's never been a bad pitcher, was released by the Yankees because he's not a star, and the Yankees figure if you're not a star you're a bum.

YEAR	TEAM/LEVEL	G	IP	W–L	SAVES	HITS	SO	BB	ERA
1990	New York	47	73	6–3	0	58	67	43	2.72
1991	New York	43	112	2–5	0	128	103	62	4.76
1992	Cleveland	58	72	9–6	4	61	50	38	3.64

JIM POOLE
Baltimore Orioles

Relief Pitcher

$7

A left-hander originally signed as a free agent by the Dodgers in 1988. He shot through the Dodger system quickly, pitching 16 games for the big team in 1990. Throws fastball, sinking fastball; pitched well for the Orioles in 1991 after being released by Texas. He isn't making any obvious progress, but I've always liked him. Turns 27 in April; Grade C prospect.

YEAR	TEAM/LEVEL	G	IP	W–L	SAVES	HITS	SO	BB	ERA
1991	Two Teams	29	42	3–2	1	29	38	12	2.36
1992	Rochester AAA	32	42	1–6	10	40	30	18	5.31
1992	Baltimore	6	3	0–0	0	3	3	1	0.00

MARK PORTUGAL
Houston Astros
Starting Pitcher
$11

He was having probably his best season until slowed by a strained shoulder in June, out until July 4, came back to make two starts, pitched well, went back to the DL with bone chips in his right elbow, which were removed July 22. Thirty years old and a free agent, his future is impossible to predict in view of questions about his health and team.

YEAR	TEAM/LEVEL	G	IP	W–L	PCT.	HITS	SO	BB	ERA
1990	Houston	32	197	11–10	.524	187	136	67	3.62
1991	Houston	32	168	10–12	.455	163	120	59	4.49
1992	Houston	18	101	6–3	.667	76	62	41	2.66

DENNIS POWELL
Seattle Mariners
Relief Pitcher
$2

Believe it or not, he is coming off his best major league season, boosting his career winning percentage from .259 (7–20) to .333, and cutting his career ERA from 5.21 to 5.09. He owes his major league career, which has now stretched to seven seasons, to the fact that teams are always looking for a left-hander and to the Seattle Mariners' persistent desperation.

YEAR	TEAM/LEVEL	G	IP	W–L	SAVES	HITS	SO	BB	ERA
1990	Two Teams	11	42	0–4	0	64	23	21	7.02
1991	Calgary	27	174	9–8	0	200	96	59	4.15
1992	Seattle	49	57	4–2	0	49	35	29	4.58

TED POWER
Cleveland Indians
Relief Pitcher
$25

Has pitched 132 games in two years. Now 38 years old, his career will end as soon as he has a bad year or a major injury, but he hasn't had an ERA above 3.71 since 1988. His stuff is comparable to Jeff Reardon's, doesn't have a great fastball but goes right at the hitters with it anyway, likes to jam a power hitter.

YEAR	TEAM/LEVEL	G	IP	W–L	SAVES	HITS	SO	BB	ERA
1990	Pittsburgh	40	52	1–3	7	50	42	17	3.66
1991	Cincinnati	68	87	5–3	3	87	51	31	3.62
1992	Cleveland	64	99	3–3	6	88	51	35	2.54

TIM PUGH
Cincinnati Reds
Starting Pitcher
$21

A 6-6, 220-pound right-hander, was a teammate of Robin Ventura and Monty Fariss at Oklahoma State. Fastball is OK, high 80s, throws a pitch he calls a slip pitch. With the departure of Swindell and his own strong performance in September, Pugh is projected in the rotation. I expect him to be .480 to .500 pitcher, could surprise; Grade C prospect.

YEAR	TEAM/LEVEL	G	IP	W–L	PCT.	HITS	SO	BB	ERA
1991	AA and AAA	28	187	10–12	.455	150	113	67	3.37
1992	Nashville AAA	27	170	12–9	.571	165	117	65	3.55
1992	Cincinnati	7	45	4–2	.667	47	18	13	2.58

ED PUIG
Kansas City Royals

Relief Pitcher

$8

Short, stocky left-handed reliever, spent seven years in the Milwaukee system, initially as a starting pitcher. He made it to Triple-A there, then came to the Royals system as a minor league free agent. The Royals used him as their closer at Memphis (Double-A), and he had his best minor league season. Grade C prospect.

YEAR	TEAM/LEVEL	G	IP	W–L	SAVES	HITS	SO	BB	ERA
1990	AA and AAA	38	50	3–0	8	53	48	20	2.32
1991	Denver AAA	11	14	0–2	0	13	5	3	5.14
1992	Memphis AA	67	75	4–2	25	44	65	21	1.91

PAUL QUANTRILL
Boston Red Sox

Relief Pitcher

$11

A 24-year-old Canadian, was called to the majors July 19 after an undistinguished four-year minor league career, almost entirely as a starting pitcher. He may be better suited to the relief role because he likes to throw every day, and did even when he was starting. Has good control, so-so stuff; doubt that he can handle a key role. Grade D prospect.

YEAR	TEAM/LEVEL	G	IP	W–L	SAVES	HITS	SO	BB	ERA
1991	AA and AAA	30	191	12–8	0	201	93	38	4.01
1992	Pawtucket AAA	19	119	6–8	0	143	56	20	4.46
1992	Boston	27	49	2–3	1	55	24	15	2.19

MIKE RACZKA
Oakland Athletics

Relief Pitcher

No Value

A 30-year-old left-hander, washed out of the Baltimore and San Diego systems and was out of baseball in 1991 before giving it another shot in '92, "earning" a major league look because the A's pitching staff was consuming mass quantities of Miracle Ice. His minor league records are generally awful, although they have improved a little in recent years. No prospect.

YEAR	TEAM/LEVEL	G	IP	W–L	SAVES	HITS	SO	BB	ERA
1990	Two Teams AAA	46	67	7–5	2	59	61	44	4.28
1992	A and AAA	37	58	1–2	1	51	31	27	4.03
1992	Oakland	8	6	0–0	0	8	2	5	8.53

SCOTT RADINSKY
Chicago White Sox

Relief Pitcher

$30

I love this guy. He's pitched well for two and a half years and was considered likely to take Thigpen's job as the closer, but hit an air pocket at exactly the wrong moment, when Thigpen *had* to be replaced, and the job fell to Hernandez. Over-qualified for the job as left-handed one-out reliever. You don't need a heater like his to do that job.

YEAR	TEAM/LEVEL	G	IP	W–L	SAVES	HITS	SO	BB	ERA
1990	Chicago	62	52	6–1	4	47	46	36	4.82
1991	Chicago	67	71	5–5	8	53	49	23	2.02
1992	Chicago	68	59	3–7	15	54	48	34	2.73

PAT RAPP
San Francisco San
Francisco Giants
Pitcher
$9

Is not seen as a top prospect, but has excellent minor league statistics, including last year when he posted a 3.05 ERA at Phoenix. He was a 16th-round draft pick and was used by Phoenix as a swing man, so it's fair to assume that his fastball is not fast, but his control is good and his strikeout/walk ratios are good. Grade C prospect.

YEAR	TEAM/LEVEL	G	IP	W–L	PCT.	HITS	SO	BB	ERA
1991	San Jose A	16	90	7–5	.583	88	73	37	2.50
1991	Shreveport AA	10	60	6–2	.750	52	46	22	2.69
1992	Phoenix AAA	37	121	7–8	.467	115	79	40	3.05

DENNIS RASMUSSEN
Kansas City Royals
Starting Pitcher
$6

I saw him pitch in the minors in August, and never thought he'd be back up. He'd been released by several teams, and it was easy to see why. He ended up the year making six starts for KC, posting a 1.43 ERA during the last five . . . throws 85 percent off-speed stuff, but spots the fastball early in the count. He has a chance.

YEAR	TEAM/LEVEL	G	IP	W–L	PCT.	HITS	SO	BB	ERA
1990	San Diego	32	188	11–15	.423	217	86	62	4.51
1991	San Diego	24	147	6–13	.316	155	75	49	3.74
1992	Two Teams	8	43	4–1	.800	32	12	8	2.53

JEFF REARDON
Atlanta Braves (Released)
Closer
$18

His overall numbers are pretty bad. Opponents hit .291 against him on the year, and he blew 10 saves. In his defense, his period of ineffectiveness in Boston came after he had pitched so little for six weeks that it would have been difficult to stay sharp. I haven't had much faith in him for years, and doubt that he can land another closer job and hold it.

YEAR	TEAM/LEVEL	G	IP	W–L	SAVES	HITS	SO	BB	ERA
1990	Boston	47	51	5–3	21	39	33	19	3.16
1991	Boston	57	59	1–4	40	54	44	16	3.03
1992	Two Teams	60	58	5–2	30	67	39	9	3.41

RICK REED
Kansas City Royals
Starting Pitcher
$15

Minor league veteran, he had a big year for Buffalo in the Pirates system in '91 (14–4, 2.15 ERA), refused assignment to the minor leagues out of spring training and signed with Omaha, then was called up in early June. He pitched well but the Royals didn't score for him and his bullpen blew three or four leads. Outstanding control, no star potential.

YEAR	TEAM/LEVEL	G	IP	W–L	PCT.	HITS	SO	BB	ERA
1990	Pittsburgh	13	54	2–3	.400	62	27	12	4.36
1991	Buffalo AAA	25	168	14–4	.778	151	102	26	2.15
1992	Kansas City	19	100	3–7	.300	105	49	20	3.68

STEVE REED
San Francisco Giants
Relief Pitcher
$20

A 27-year-old submarine-style reliever, established a minor league record with 43 saves in '92, 23 at Shreveport (Double-A) and 20 more at Phoenix (Triple-A). He has pitched 250 minor league games, all of them in relief. **Is never listed as a prospect, but will have a fine major league career.** Has better chance this year if the Giants *don't* move to Tampa.

YEAR	TEAM/LEVEL	G	IP	W–L	SAVES	HITS	SO	BB	ERA
1991	AA and AAA	56	78	4–3	13	79	72	15	3.35
1992	AA and AAA	56	60	1–1	43	45	63	10	2.10
1992	San Francisco	18	16	1–0	0	13	11	3	2.30

TODD REVENIG
Oakland Athletics
Relief Pitcher
$12

Through 115 minor league games, all in relief, he has posted a career ERA of 1.22 (!). This doesn't include two games, two innings for Oakland, where his ERA was zero. A right-hander from Minnesota, he was a 37th-round draft pick from a small college in 1990, but got a major league look in two years. I haven't seen him pitch; the numbers speak for themselves.

YEAR	TEAM/LEVEL	G	IP	W–L	SAVES	HITS	SO	BB	ERA
1991	Madison A	26	29	1–0	13	13	27	10	0.94
1991	Huntsville AA	12	18	1–2	0	11	10	4	0.98
1992	Huntsville AA	53	64	1–1	33	32	49	11	1.70

SHANE REYNOLDS
Houston Astros
Starting Pitcher
$8

A third-round draft pick in 1989, was brought along rapidly despite unimpressive minor league records until last year, when he pitched quite well at Tucson. Made five starts for the major league team, and was hit hard all five times . . . throws mid-80s fastball, split-finger, and curve. Wore number 21 at University of Texas, number worn by Clemens and Swindell. Grade C prospect.

YEAR	TEAM/LEVEL	G	IP	W–L	PCT.	HITS	SO	BB	ERA
1991	Jackson AA	27	151	8–9	.471	165	116	62	4.47
1992	Tucson AAA	25	142	9–8	.529	156	106	34	3.68
1992	Houston	8	25	1–3	.250	42	10	6	7.11

ARMANDO REYNOSO
Atlanta Braves
Starting Pitcher
$9

Was signed out of the Mexican League in late 1990, has pitched at Richmond for two-plus years with good success, three winning records with ERAs of 2.25 to 2.66. Finesse-type pitcher, changes speeds and locations; will need adjustment period in the majors, but could have a good career if he can get past that. Is 26 years old, Grade C prospect.

YEAR	TEAM/LEVEL	G	IP	W–L	PCT.	HITS	SO	BB	ERA
1991	Richmond AAA	22	131	10–6	.625	117	97	39	2.61
1991	Atlanta	6	23	2–1	.667	26	10	10	6.17
1992	Richmond AAA	28	169	12–9	.571	156	108	52	2.66

ARTHUR RHODES
Baltimore Orioles
Starting Pitcher
$42

Among all of the fine rookie pitchers of 1992—Fleming, Eldred, Osborne, Wakefield, Pichardo—Rhodes would be the one I would most like to have. He has all of the characteristics that you look for in a young pitcher who might be outstanding—a power pitcher, consistent success in the minor leagues, a good health record, a fluid motion. There is nothing about him *not* to like.

YEAR	TEAM/LEVEL	G	IP	W–L	PCT.	HITS	SO	BB	ERA
1991	Baltimore	8	36	0–3	.000	47	23	23	8.00
1992	Rochester AAA	17	102	6–6	.500	84	115	46	3.72
1992	Baltimore	15	94	7–5	.583	87	77	38	3.63

DAVE RIGHETTI
San Francisco Giants
Relief Pitcher
$10

His problems are serious, but his contract runs through 1994, so he should get a chance to work them out. The radar gun says he is throwing as hard as ever, but I don't believe it. He's 34, and not able to saw the bat off the way he used to. Could move into left-handed spot reliever role if he gets a manager who understands that stuff.

YEAR	TEAM/LEVEL	G	IP	W–L	SAVES	HITS	SO	BB	ERA
1990	New York	53	53	1–1	36	48	43	26	3.57
1991	San Francisco	61	72	2–7	24	64	51	28	3.39
1992	San Francisco	54	78	2–7	3	79	47	36	5.06

JOSE RIJO
Cincinnati Reds
Starting Pitcher
$72

The fifth-best starting pitcher in the National League, behind Maddux, Drabek, Glavine, and Martinez; would rank higher than that if his health record were better. Has had winning records with ERAs of 2.84 or better for five straight years—in a hitter's park. Strikeout/walk ratio was second-best in the NL, behind Tewksbury's. Needs two 20-win seasons to emerge as Hall of Fame candidate.

YEAR	TEAM/LEVEL	G	IP	W–L	PCT.	HITS	SO	BB	ERA
1990	Cincinnati	29	197	14–8	.636	151	152	78	2.70
1991	Cincinnati	30	204	15–6	.714	165	172	55	2.51
1992	Cincinnati	33	211	15–10	.600	185	171	44	2.56

BILL RISLEY
Montreal Expos
Starting Pitcher
No Value

Not a prospect. He is included in the book because he made one start for Montreal in early July, when the Expos had doubleheaders stacked up due to the Los Angeles riots. A 25-year-old right-hander, originally in the Reds system, has career won–lost mark of 39–47, with poor control (five walks per nine innings). Anything that happens for him would be a surprise.

YEAR	TEAM/LEVEL	G	IP	W–L	PCT.	HITS	SO	BB	ERA
1991	Chattanooga AA	19	108	5–7	.417	81	77	60	3.16
1991	Nashville AAA	8	44	3–5	.375	45	32	26	4.91
1992	Indianapolis AAA	25	96	5–8	.385	105	64	47	6.40

WALLY RITCHIE
Philadelphia Phillies
Left-Handed Relief Pitcher
$3

The new Jerry Don Gleaton, didn't pitch nearly as well as his 3.00 ERA would suggest and was sent down July 29. The league hit .288 against him, his K/W rate was very poor, and he gave up only 13 earned runs but 26 RBI, so he surrendered at least 13 runs that were charged either to the defense or to another pitcher. Will have more trials.

YEAR	TEAM/LEVEL	G	IP	W–L	SAVES	HITS	SO	BB	ERA
1990	Scranton AAA	20	82	4–3	0	75	47	28	4.15
1991	Philadelphia	39	50	1–2	0	44	26	17	2.50
1992	Philadelphia	40	39	2–1	1	44	19	17	3.00

KEVIN RITZ
Detroit Tigers
Starting Pitcher
$1

Goes on an All–Star team with Steve Carlton, Pat Sheridan, and Phil (Red) Roof . . . future is dim after career record of 6–18 with ERA around 6.00. He never pitched particularly well in the minors, his best record being 8–7, with quite a few walks and not many strikeouts. There must be some reason he is in the majors, but I forget what it is right now.

YEAR	TEAM/LEVEL	G	IP	W–L	PCT.	HITS	SO	BB	ERA
1990	Toledo AAA	20	90	3–6	.333	93	57	59	5.22
1991	Toledo AAA	20	126	8–7	.533	116	105	60	3.28
1992	Detroit	23	80	2–5	.286	88	54	44	5.60

BEN RIVERA
Philadelphia Phillies
Starting Pitcher
$30

A 6-6 right-hander, started the year in the Braves' bullpen, was traded to Philadelphia May 28, had a pulled groin, went to Scranton on rehab, junked his two-seam fastball for a four-seam, stopped throwing his slider and split-finger fastball, threw a no-hitter at Scranton, was called up and pitched great his last two months. Probably is *not* ready to be consistent winner.

YEAR	TEAM/LEVEL	G	IP	W–L	PCT.	HITS	SO	BB	ERA
1990	A and AA	29	127	6–7	.462	137	96	59	4.82
1991	Greenville AA	26	159	11–8	.579	155	116	75	3.57
1992	Two Teams	28	117	7–4	.636	99	77	45	3.07

DON ROBINSON
Released
Starting Pitcher
No Value

Career staggered to the line last year when he was released by California in May, Philadelphia in July. He had a brilliant rookie year in 1978, had major shoulder troubles shortly after that, struggled back valiantly to win 15 games in 1982. The shoulder problems returned and brought friends, which attacked his knee and back. He was probably the best hitting pitcher of his era.

YEAR	TEAM/LEVEL	G	IP	W–L	PCT.	HITS	SO	BB	ERA
1990	San Francisco	26	158	10–7	.588	173	78	41	4.57
1991	San Francisco	34	121	5–9	.357	123	78	50	4.38
1992	Two Teams	11	60	2–4	.333	68	26	7	5.10

JEFF ROBINSON
Chicago Cubs
Relief Pitcher
$11

This is the Jeff Robinson who came up with the Giants in 1984, had his best year for the Pirates in '88, has also pitched for the Yankees and Angels. He was signed as a free agent by Iowa, started the year there, was called up May 4 and had his best year since 1988. He will *not* be able to sustain his success or build upon it.

YEAR	TEAM/LEVEL	G	IP	W–L	SAVES	HITS	SO	BB	ERA
1990	New York	54	89	3–6	0	82	43	34	3.45
1991	California	39	57	0–3	3	56	57	29	5.37
1992	Chicago	49	78	4–3	1	76	46	40	3.00

JEFF M. ROBINSON
Texas Rangers
Starter/Reliever
$1

This is the Jeff Robinson who had his best year for the *Tigers* in 1988; I can't keep them straight without notes, either, although I suppose you can if you're a Tigers fan or a Pirates fan. This J.R. has posted ERAs over 5.00 the last three years for Detroit, Baltimore, and Texas. He isn't a major league pitcher, but every GM has to see that for himself.

YEAR	TEAM/LEVEL	G	IP	W–L	PCT.	HITS	SO	BB	ERA
1990	Detroit	27	145	10–9	.526	141	76	88	5.96
1991	Baltimore	21	104	4–9	.308	119	65	51	5.18
1992	Two Teams	24	82	7–5	.583	83	32	36	5.16

RON ROBINSON
Milwaukee Brewers
Starting Pitcher
$1

Easily confused with *Don* Robinson, who is a right-hander of the same size (6-4, 240). Had a fine year as a power pitcher for the Reds in 1986, but had a big workload (70 games, 117 innings) and encountered predictable elbow problems in 1987. Resurfaced as a finesse pitcher and a starter, going 12–5 for Milwaukee in '90, but is still fighting elbow problems.

YEAR	TEAM/LEVEL	G	IP	W–L	PCT.	HITS	SO	BB	ERA
1990	Two Teams	28	180	14–7	.667	194	71	51	3.26
1991	Milwaukee	1	4	0–1	.000	6	0	3	6.23
1992	Milwaukee	8	35	1–4	.200	51	12	14	5.86

RICH RODRIGUEZ
San Diego Padres
Relief Pitcher
$26

Left-hander, probably not as good a pitcher as his fine '92 stats. It's a safe guess that the Padres' bullpen will be re-shuffled, since it makes no sense to use your sixth-best reliever as your closer. The Padres have several left-handers in the bullpen and several candidates for the closer role, so just keep an eye on them coming out of spring training.

YEAR	TEAM/LEVEL	G	IP	W–L	SAVES	HITS	SO	BB	ERA
1990	San Diego	32	48	1–1	1	52	22	16	2.83
1991	San Diego	64	80	3–1	0	66	40	44	3.26
1992	San Diego	61	91	6–3	0	77	64	29	2.37

KENNY ROGERS
Texas Rangers
Relief Pitcher
$18

Left-hander, would make up a perfect bullpen with Mike Jackson and Jerry Reed. Hit hard by right-handers; has been given several shots at the closer's job and has blown them all. Seems well suited to role as left-handed one-out reliever, and could be the first guy to do that job 100 times in a season. Suspect Whiteside will be the closer.

YEAR	TEAM/LEVEL	G	IP	W–L	SAVES	HITS	SO	BB	ERA
1990	Texas	69	98	10–6	15	93	74	42	3.13
1991	Texas	63	110	10–10	5	121	73	61	5.42
1992	Texas	81	79	3–6	6	80	70	26	3.09

KEVIN ROGERS
San Francisco Giants
Starting Pitcher
$28

Switch-hitting left-handed pitcher, started the year at Shreveport, where he had the league over-matched, being cited by *Baseball America* as the second-best prospect in the league. BA says that he has a live arm and outstanding control, which is reflected in his record. He was a low draft pick who moved up steadily by pitching well, made 116 minor league starts. **Grade A prospect.**

YEAR	TEAM/LEVEL	G	IP	W–L	PCT.	HITS	SO	BB	ERA
1991	Shreveport AA	22	118	4–6	.400	124	108	54	3.36
1992	AA and AAA	27	171	11–8	.579	150	172	51	3.16
1992	S Francisco	6	34	0–2	.000	37	26	13	4.24

MEL ROJAS
Montreal Expos
Relief Pitcher
$31

There is very little in Rojas's previous record which predicts his amazing numbers of 1992, including an opponents' batting average of .199. The year is almost identical to the year that Jeff Montgomery had in 1989, when he came out of nowhere to go 7–3, 1.35 ERA, opposition average of .198. Suspect that Rojas will remain effective, although not at the same level.

YEAR	TEAM/LEVEL	G	IP	W–L	SAVES	HITS	SO	BB	ERA
1990	Montreal	23	40	3–1	1	34	26	24	3.60
1991	Montreal	37	48	3–3	6	42	37	13	3.75
1992	Montreal	68	101	7–1	10	71	70	34	1.43

JOHN ROPER
Cincinnati Reds
Starting Pitcher
$20

Right-hander, only 21 years old, has gone 31–20 in the minors with excellent strikeout/walk ratios. Stats below were compiled despite missing six weeks with a back injury from a car accident . . . throws 90+ fastball, late-breaking curve sometimes called a knuckle curve, change. Is described as very poised, mature, doesn't say much but his manager says he learns quickly. **Grade A prospect.**

YEAR	TEAM/LEVEL	G	IP	W–L	PCT.	HITS	SO	BB	ERA
1990	Reds R	13	74	7–2	.778	41	76	31	0.97
1991	Charleston A	27	187	14–9	.609	133	189	67	2.31
1992	Chattanooga AA	20	121	10–9	.526	115	98	36	4.03

WAYNE ROSENTHAL
Texas Rangers

Relief Pitcher

$7

A 6-5, 240-pound Brooklyn native, pitched quite well in the low minors and pitched well at Oklahoma City in 1990, but appears to have lost his confidence and has struggled for the last two years. In 1987 he saved 30 games at Gastonia, striking out 101 in 69 innings. Even in the last two years, his strikeout/walk ratio has remained OK. Grade D prospect.

YEAR	TEAM/LEVEL	G	IP	W–L	SAVES	HITS	SO	BB	ERA
1991	Texas	36	70	1–4	1	72	61	36	5.25
1991	Oklahoma City AAA	57	62	1–6	11	72	54	29	5.69
1992	Texas	6	5	0–0	0	7	1	2	7.71

BRUCE RUFFIN
Milwaukee Brewers

Pitcher

$2

Has had six straight losing records and five straight seasons with winning percentage below .400, which must be some sort of a record. His record over the five years is 23 wins, 46 losses. The league hit .293 against him last year, with a .398 on-base percentage. He was optioned to Denver in late August. I would assume he was about out of chances, but you never know.

YEAR	TEAM/LEVEL	G	IP	W–L	PCT.	HITS	SO	BB	ERA
1990	Philadelphia	32	149	6–13	.316	178	79	62	5.38
1991	Philadelphia	31	119	4–7	.364	125	85	38	3.78
1992	Milwaukee	25	58	1–6	.143	66	45	41	6.67

SCOTT RUSKIN
Cincinnati Reds

Relief Pitcher

$7

Left-handed one-out reliever, was a minor league outfielder/first baseman who converted to the mound in 1989. He came from Montreal to Cincinnati in the Wetteland trade but pitched poorly, which, combined with the quality young arms in the Cincinnati system (Milt Hill, Trevor Hoffman, John Roper, Tim Pugh, etc.), leaves him without a clear hold on a job.

YEAR	TEAM/LEVEL	G	IP	W–L	SAVES	HITS	SO	BB	ERA
1990	Two Teams	67	75	3–2	2	75	57	38	2.75
1991	Montreal	64	64	4–4	6	57	46	30	4.24
1992	Cincinnati	57	54	4–3	0	56	43	20	5.03

JEFF RUSSELL
Oakland Athletics

Relief Pitcher

$38

Pitched magnificently in 1989, but had bone chips and bone spurs on his elbow in 1990, and just got back where he was. Still throws 90 or better, mixes in a slider and a change but sometimes cannot throw slider because of elbow pain. Has had good control since 1988. He will be a free agent, and will probably go to a team which is looking for a closer.

YEAR	TEAM/LEVEL	G	IP	W–L	SAVES	HITS	SO	BB	ERA
1990	Texas	27	25	1–5	10	23	16	16	4.26
1991	Texas	68	79	6–4	30	71	52	26	3.29
1992	Two Teams	59	66	4–3	30	55	48	25	1.63

KEN RYAN
Boston Red Sox

Relief Pitcher

$18

Saved 29 games while posting 1.95 ERA at New Britain, 2.08 at Pawtucket. This puts him in the line of pitchers hoping to ascend to Jeff Reardon's job, now that Reardon is in Atlanta. Ryan was signed as an undrafted free agent in 1986, spent five years as a starter with basically no success, converted to the pen in '91, and has vaulted forward. Grade B prospect.

YEAR	TEAM/LEVEL	G	IP	W–L	SAVES	HITS	SO	BB	ERA
1991	A, AA, and AAA	44	97	3–5	3	78	93	42	2.51
1992	AA and AAA	53	59	3–4	29	50	57	28	1.97
1992	Boston	7	7	0–0	1	4	5	5	6.43

NOLAN RYAN
Texas Rangers

Starting Pitcher

$24

If I were Nolan Ryan, I wouldn't have quit, either. He pitched a lot of good games last year, with just average luck could have finished 10–8 or 11–7, and if his health is better he might win 17 games. He might pitch five or seven more years. Why should he give that up just because people think he is old and should be cast in bronze?

YEAR	TEAM/LEVEL	G	IP	W–L	PCT.	HITS	SO	BB	ERA
1990	Texas	30	204	13–9	.591	137	232	74	3.44
1991	Texas	27	173	12–6	.667	102	203	72	2.91
1992	Texas	27	157	5–9	.357	138	157	69	3.72

BRET SABERHAGEN
New York Mets

Starting Pitcher

$36

Well, this is supposed to be a good year. Saberhagen's numbers in '92 are better than you might think—held opponents to .233 average, struck out 81 in 98 innings with good control. The Mets didn't score for him, and he didn't pitch enough to compile bulk numbers. My view of him last year—that he is a magnificent pitcher for ever-decreasing moments in time—still seems accurate.

YEAR	TEAM/LEVEL	G	IP	W–L	PCT.	HITS	SO	BB	ERA
1990	Kansas City	20	135	5–9	.357	146	87	28	3.27
1991	Kansas City	28	196	13–8	.619	165	136	45	3.07
1992	New York	17	98	3–5	.375	84	81	27	3.50

BILL SAMPEN
Kansas City Royals

Relief Pitcher

$19

Came to Kansas City in the Sean Berry trade. Montreal used him occasionally as a starter, which didn't help his stats. Thirty years old, no star potential, looks good on the mound, but doesn't have a strikeout pitch. He throws about 88, throws a slider but no curve or change to speak of. As long as he's healthy and his control is good, he'll probably have a job.

YEAR	TEAM/LEVEL	G	IP	W–L	SAVES	HITS	SO	BB	ERA
1990	Montreal	59	90	12–7	2	94	69	33	2.99
1991	Montreal	43	92	9–5	0	96	52	46	4.00
1992	Two Teams	52	83	1–6	0	83	37	32	3.25

SCOTT SANDERSON
New York Yankees(Free Agent)
Starting Pitcher
$17

It is difficult to sustain success in anything without organizational support. For a pitcher, that means offense, but it also means pitching coaches and managers who understand what you're trying to do, fielders to make the job easier. If the Yankees can support a pitcher, they hide the fact unusually well. Sanderson, without overpowering stuff, has been regressing toward the mediocrity which engulfed him in the late 1980s.

YEAR	TEAM/LEVEL	G	IP	W–L	PCT.	HITS	SO	BB	ERA
1990	Oakland	34	206	17–11	.607	205	128	66	3.88
1991	New York	34	208	16–10	.615	200	130	29	3.81
1992	New York	33	193	12–11	.522	220	104	64	4.93

MO SANFORD
Cincinnati Reds
Starting Pitcher
$20

A ballyhooed rookie a year ago, but had poor spring training, was sent to Nashville and was inconsistent there. Big guy, excellent athlete in upper body, but fastball is straight, gets Ks with sweeping curve which is normally not a strike. I saw him pitch one of his best games of '92, and wasn't really impressed. Good effort on defense but made several defensive mistakes. Grade B prospect.

YEAR	TEAM/LEVEL	G	IP	W–L	PCT.	HITS	SO	BB	ERA
1991	A and AA	21	129	11–4	.733	88	162	77	2.44
1991	Cincinnati	5	34	1–2	.333	19	31	15	3.86
1992	AA and AAA	29	149	12–8	.600	142	157	71	4.90

RICH SAUVEUR
Kansas City Royals
Relief Pitcher
$1

Left-handed junkballer, was born in Arlington, Virginia, where John F. Kennedy is buried, on the day after JFK was shot. Has been with the Pirates system, the Expos, the Pirates again, the Expos again, the Mets, the Royals . . . will be somewhere else next year. Minor league record isn't terrible; it just isn't *good*. No prospect, but could surprise if he lands a role as one-out specialist.

YEAR	TEAM/LEVEL	G	IP	W–L	SAVES	HITS	SO	BB	ERA
1991	Tidewater AAA	42	45	2–2	6	31	49	23	2.38
1992	Omaha AAA	34	117	7–6	0	93	88	39	3.22
1992	Kansas City	8	14	0–1	0	15	7	8	4.40

BOB SCANLAN
Chicago Cubs
Relief Pitcher
$27

Scanlan lost it so completely late in the year that I would be a little worried about him in '93. It was more than a slump. Carrying a 1.79 ERA into September, he was pasted in almost every outing. Maybe it was a tired arm, but many times what they call a tired arm is an injury awaiting a diagnosis . . . throws hard, has future if healthy.

YEAR	TEAM/LEVEL	G	IP	W–L	SAVES	HITS	SO	BB	ERA
1990	Scranton AAA	23	130	8–11	0	128	74	59	4.85
1991	Chicago	40	111	7–8	1	114	44	40	3.89
1992	Chicago	69	87	3–6	14	76	42	30	2.89

RICK SCHEID
Houston Astros
Relief Pitcher
$2

Hoping to catch a seat on the merry-go-round of left-handed relievers (Pat Clements, Jerry Don Gleaton, Paul Gibson, Frank DiPino, Bob McClure) who have jobs because they have jobs. He's been in Triple-A since 1989; the Astros got him for Eric Yelding, and he pitched the best ball of his career at Tucson (below), working as a starting pitcher.

YEAR	TEAM/LEVEL	G	IP	W–L	SAVES	HITS	SO	BB	ERA
1992	Vancouver AAA	29	35	1–2	0	29	24	28	2.80
1992	Tucson AAA	12	57	2–3	1	49	34	23	2.53
1992	Houston	7	12	0–1	0	14	8	6	6.00

CURT SCHILLING
Philadelphia Phillies
Starting Pitcher
$50

Magnificent young pitcher, arguably the best pitcher in the NL after the All-Star game. There is probably some reason why Baltimore and Houston didn't want him . . . if he keeps pitching eight or nine innings every game, as he did the second half of '92, he will hurt his arm within two years. If that doesn't happen, he's going to have a hell of a career.

YEAR	TEAM/LEVEL	G	IP	W–L	PCT.	HITS	SO	BB	ERA
1990	Baltimore	35	46	1–2	.333	38	32	19	2.54
1991	Houston	56	76	3–5	.375	79	71	39	3.81
1992	Philadelphia	42	226	14–11	.560	165	147	59	2.35

DAVE SCHMIDT
Oakland A's
Relief Pitcher
No Value

36 years old (in April), right-hander with a fragile arm. Schmidt pitched for the Rangers from 1981 to 1985, always pitched well, was traded to the White Sox for Edwin Correa, to Baltimore as a free agent. The Orioles made him a starter in 1989; he hasn't pitched well since. He pitched with Seattle early last year, was released and pitched Triple-A for Oakland. No future.

YEAR	TEAM/LEVEL	G	IP	W–L	SAVES	HITS	SO	BB	ERA
1990	Montreal	34	48	3–3	13	58	22	13	4.31
1991	Montreal	4	4	0–1	0	9	3	2	10.38
1992	Seattle	3	3	0–0	0	7	1	3	18.90

MIKE SCHOOLER
Seattle Mariners
Former Closer
$12

It is important to know what is true, as opposed to what is popular, because you pay a price for anything you believe which is false. Some managers, for example, think that "closer" status is some sort of magic badge which, once bestowed, makes a pitcher able to pitch at key moments. It isn't, and Bill Plummer cost his team a lot of games before he figured this out.

YEAR	TEAM/LEVEL	G	IP	W–L	SAVES	HITS	SO	BB	ERA
1990	Seattle	49	56	1–4	30	47	45	16	2.25
1991	Seattle	34	34	3–3	7	25	31	10	3.67
1992	Seattle	53	52	2–7	13	55	33	24	4.70

PETE SCHOUREK
New York Mets
Pitcher
$21

Recalled from Tidewater May 24, moved immediately into the rotation and stuck, pitching more good games than bad ones. He's a marginal talent, and can be bumped from the rotation if the glamour boys are all healthy, but that's not likely, and the departure of Cone makes his position more secure. He would like to be the new Bob Ojeda or John Tudor; doubt that he will make it.

YEAR	TEAM/LEVEL	G	IP	W–L	PCT.	HITS	SO	BB	ERA
1990	Minors—Three Levels	26	175	16–5	.762	147	136	52	2.57
1991	New York	35	86	5–4	.556	82	67	43	4.27
1992	New York	22	136	6–8	.429	137	60	44	3.64

TIM SCOTT
San Diego Padres
Relief Pitcher
$6

A refugee from the Dodgers' system, says he signed with the Padres because he wanted the chance to beat the Dodgers. He was a starting pitcher and something of a prospect until 1987, when he had the Tommy John surgery. His minor league numbers aren't impressive, but his strikeout/walk ratios have improved dramatically in recent years (28–3 at Las Vegas in '92). Grade D prospect.

YEAR	TEAM/LEVEL	G	IP	W–L	SAVES	HITS	SO	BB	ERA
1991	Las Vegas AAA	41	111	8–8	0	133	74	39	5.19
1992	Las Vegas AAA	24	28	1–2	15	20	28	3	2.25
1992	San Diego	34	38	4–1	0	39	30	21	5.26

SCOTT SCUDDER
Cleveland Indians
Starting Pitcher
$11

Pitched well in the minors from '88 to '90, but after four major league seasons, 70-plus innings each, has never had a winning record or an ERA below 4.35. Tends to throw his curve on first pitch, is tough to hit when he gets ahead but hittable when he has to throw the fastball. Probably out of chances as a starter, will be looking for a role.

YEAR	TEAM/LEVEL	G	IP	W–L	PCT.	HITS	SO	BB	ERA
1990	Cincinnati	21	72	5–5	.500	74	42	30	4.90
1991	Cincinnati	27	101	6–9	.400	91	51	56	4.35
1992	Cleveland	23	109	6–10	.375	134	66	55	5.28

STEVE SEARCY
Los Angeles Dodgers
(Free Agent)
Relief Pitcher
$2

Once a prospect in the Tigers' system, he pitched a few games with the Phillies early in the year, was sent down in June and traded to the Dodgers in July. The Dodgers returned him to a starting role at Albuquerque, where he posted a handsome 6.48 ERA in 12 starts. No prospect, but still has a good arm and some history of minor league success.

YEAR	TEAM/LEVEL	G	IP	W–L	SAVES	HITS	SO	BB	ERA
1990	Detroit	16	75	2–7	0	76	66	51	4.66
1991	Two Teams	34	71	3–3	0	81	53	44	6.59
1992	Philadelphia	10	10	0–0	0	13	5	8	6.10

FRANK SEMINARA
San Diego Padres
Starting Pitcher
$32

Would have been a candidate for Rookie of the Year if he had started sooner. Comes from the Yankee system; the Yankees didn't protect him after he went 16–8 with a 1.90 ERA at Prince William, and the Padres used Rule 5. Has odd sidearm/slingshot delivery which doesn't look fluid, but his health record is excellent—has been in the rotation without injuries since 1989.

YEAR	TEAM/LEVEL	G	IP	W–L	PCT.	HITS	SO	BB	ERA
1991	Wichita AA	27	176	15–10	.600	173	107	68	3.38
1991	Las Vegas AAA	13	81	6–4	.600	92	48	33	4.13
1992	San Diego	19	100	9–4	.692	98	61	46	3.68

SCOTT SERVICE
Cincinnati Reds
Relief Pitcher
$17

A 6-6 right-hander, was signed as an undrafted free agent by the late Tony Luccadello, shot to the majors in two-plus years (1986–88). He was then with the Phillies. His fastball moves and he has a slider, but for some reason the Phillies lost interest in him, and he has bounced around although pitching well, tremendously well last year. Is 25 years old, Grade C prospect.

YEAR	TEAM/LEVEL	G	IP	W–L	SAVES	HITS	SO	BB	ERA
1991	Indianapolis AAA	18	121	6–7	0	83	91	39	2.97
1992	Two Teams AAA	52	95	6–2	6	66	112	44	1.89
1992	Montreal	5	7	0–0	0	15	11	5	14.14

JEFF SHAW
Cleveland Indians
Starting Pitcher
$1

Spent a couple of weeks in the majors and the rest of the year at Colorado Springs, trying to re-establish himself as a prospect or, failing that, at least survive until expansion. He wasn't notably successful, gave up 174 hits in 155 innings. Control pitcher, throws fastball/slider/forkball. Last pitched well at Waterbury in 1987, has 38–40 minor league record since. No prospect.

YEAR	TEAM/LEVEL	G	IP	W–L	PCT.	HITS	SO	BB	ERA
1990	Cleveland	12	49	3–4	.429	73	25	20	6.66
1991	Cleveland	29	72	0–5	.000	72	31	27	3.36
1992	Colorado Sp AAA	25	155	10–5	.667	174	84	45	4.76

KEITH SHEPHERD
Philadelphia Phillies
Relief Pitcher
$19

Originally in the Pirates' system, was released by the Pirates and I believe another organization or two, signed by the White Sox. He flattened out his delivery, was dramatically more effective in the White Sox system, and was traded to the Phillies in August for Dale Sveum. Fregosi said that he didn't do anything impressive except get people out. **Has a chance to be a surprise player.**

YEAR	TEAM/LEVEL	G	IP	W–L	SAVES	HITS	SO	BB	ERA
1991	Two Teams A	49	75	2–3	12	50	62	39	1.68
1992	Two Teams AA	44	94	3–4	7	67	73	24	2.30
1992	Philadelphia	12	22	1–1	2	19	10	6	3.27

STEVE SHIFFLETT
Kansas City Royals
Relief Pitcher
$17

Didn't pitch nearly as well as his 2.60 ERA might suggest, but will have a major league job in '93. A big strong guy, throws sidearm/high sidearm, kind of forces the ball up to the plate. Has a fair fastball, better than the Tekulve types, and good control. Minor league record is consistently good. **Could be a good pickup** for the same reasons as Shepherd.

YEAR	TEAM/LEVEL	G	IP	W–L	SAVES	HITS	SO	BB	ERA
1991	Memphis AA	59	113	11–5	9	105	78	22	2.15
1992	Omaha AAA	32	44	3–2	14	30	19	15	1.65
1992	Kansas City	34	52	1–4	0	55	25	17	2.60

DOUG SIMONS
Montreal Expos
Pitcher
$8

Bob Tewksbury–type left-hander, was taken from the Twins by the Mets under Rule 5, had to spend 1991 in the majors, then was traded to the Expos. He was ineffective with Montreal but pitched very well at Indianapolis. Could work a lot of innings because he works efficiently; will need to catch a break, which took Tewksbury about 10 years. Grade C prospect.

YEAR	TEAM/LEVEL	G	IP	W–L	SAVES	HITS	SO	BB	ERA
1991	New York	42	61	2–3	1	55	38	19	5.19
1992	Indianapolis AAA	32	120	11–4	0	114	66	25	3.08
1992	Montreal	7	5	0–0	0	15	6	2	23.63

HEATHCLIFF SLOCUMB
Chicago Cubs
Relief Pitcher
$11

He'd better start throwing strikes pretty soon, or the league is going to lose one of its best handles. Batters hit .351 against him last year, plus his control was poor; in retrospect that 34/30 strikeout/walk ratio as a rookie should have tipped us off that there were termites in the foundation. Throws hard, minor league record good, outside chance of becoming a quality pitcher.

YEAR	TEAM/LEVEL	G	IP	W–L	SAVES	HITS	SO	BB	ERA
1991	Chicago	52	63	2–1	1	53	34	30	3.45
1992	Iowa AAA	36	42	1–3	7	36	47	16	2.59
1992	Chicago	30	36	0–3	1	52	27	21	6.50

JOE SLUSARSKI
Oakland Athletics
Starting Pitcher
$4

Started the year in the A's rotation due to injuries, but posted 6.97 ERA in May, 6.75 in June. LaRussa likes to work with veteran starting pitchers who know how to pitch, which does not describe Slusarski, but the potential loss of free agents could project him back into the picture. Even if it does, I doubt that he is ready to succeed. Grade D prospect.

YEAR	TEAM/LEVEL	G	IP	W–L	PCT.	HITS	SO	BB	ERA
1991	Oakland	20	109	5–7	.417	121	60	52	5.27
1992	Oakland	15	76	5–5	.500	85	38	27	4.45
1992	Tacoma AAA	11	57	2–4	.333	67	26	18	3.77

JOHN SMILEY
Minnesota Twins
Starting Pitcher
$71

Has been a quality pitcher in four of the last five seasons, and steadily getting better. His 16–9 season in '92 is probably better, in context, than his 20-win season with Pittsburgh in '91. Intense, taciturn sort who seems most comfortable on the mound. I'd compare him to Mickey Lolich, but he has better control than Lolich, or Mike Flanagan, but he throws harder than Flanagan.

YEAR	TEAM/LEVEL	G	IP	W–L	PCT.	HITS	SO	BB	ERA
1990	Pittsburgh	26	149	9–10	.474	161	86	36	4.64
1991	Pittsburgh	33	208	20–8	.714	194	129	44	3.08
1992	Minnesota	34	241	16–9	.640	205	163	65	3.21

BRYN SMITH
St. Louis Cardinals
Starting Pitcher
$10

He went on the disabled list April 9 with a stiff elbow, which later required surgery (they took the stiffness out). After a brief rehab he returned in September, pitching relief, and was OK. Is 37 years old, but knows how to pitch; one more comeback for one more free agent contract isn't impossible. His mother dated Cary Grant, and was introduced to his father by Jane Russell . . .

YEAR	TEAM/LEVEL	G	IP	W–L	PCT.	HITS	SO	BB	ERA
1990	St. Louis	26	141	9–8	.529	160	78	30	4.27
1991	St. Louis	31	199	12–9	.571	188	94	45	3.85
1992	St. Louis	13	21	4–2	.667	20	9	5	4.64

DAN SMITH
Texas Rangers
Left-Handed Starting Pitcher
$21

The Rangers' handling of minor leaguers is erratic. In '91 they tried to vault Smith to Triple-A, which was a disaster as he went 4–17. He returned to Double-A last year, working with Tulsa's outstanding pitching coach Jackson Todd, and was very good. Throws fastball about 87 but good movement, slider, change; intelligent, good athlete with good work habits. Has history of tendinitis. Grade B prospect.

YEAR	TEAM/LEVEL	G	IP	W–L	PCT.	HITS	SO	BB	ERA
1991	Oklahoma City AAA	28	152	4–17	.190	195	85	75	5.52
1992	Tulsa AA	24	146	11–7	.611	110	122	34	2.52
1992	Texas	4	14	0–3	.000	18	5	8	5.02

DAVE SMITH
Chicago Cubs (Released)
Relief Pitcher
$1

Pitched OK in April, didn't pitch from May 10 to May 30, made three appearances then and went on the DL with a strained right elbow, out for the season. He's 38 years old, and there is no reason to anticipate that he will regain his effectiveness, although stranger things have happened (Rush Limbaugh, for example). Has no fastball, and his junk is mostly out of the strike zone.

YEAR	TEAM/LEVEL	G	IP	W–L	SAVES	HITS	SO	BB	ERA
1990	Houston	49	60	6–6	23	45	50	20	2.39
1991	Chicago	35	33	0–6	17	39	16	19	6.00
1992	Chicago	11	14	0–0	0	15	3	4	2.51

LEE SMITH
St. Louis Cardinals
Closer
$57

He's not as effective as he once was, probably. I don't think I'd want to try to hit him . . . there are raps against him. A lot of people don't like him, and he's very easy to run against. As long as he's a dominant pitcher, you say "Who cares?" But if he's not a *dominant* pitcher, everybody will care. So his future is a little dicey.

YEAR	TEAM/LEVEL	G	IP	W–L	SAVES	HITS	SO	BB	ERA
1990	Two Teams	64	83	5–5	31	71	87	29	2.06
1991	St. Louis	67	73	6–3	47	70	67	13	2.34
1992	St. Louis	70	75	4–9	43	62	60	26	3.12

PETE SMITH
Atlanta Braves
Starting Pitcher
$31

The most impossible job in baseball is pitching for a bad team in a hitter's park, because the pitcher's overall record reflects the performance of his team. Smith was in the Atlanta rotation in '88–'89, and was really a decent pitcher then, but had a horrible record because the team and park were impossible. I was glad to see him finally get a chance to succeed.

YEAR	TEAM/LEVEL	G	IP	W–L	PCT.	HITS	SO	BB	ERA
1990	Atlanta	13	77	5–6	.455	77	56	24	4.79
1991	Atlanta	14	48	1–3	.250	48	29	22	5.06
1992	Atlanta	12	79	7–0	1.000	63	43	28	2.05

ZANE SMITH
Pittsburgh Pirates
Starting Pitcher
$43

Went on the DL July 15 with a stiff shoulder, later diagnosed as tendinitis. Returned in August for two starts, but shoulder hurt again and he was out until late September. Gives up a lot of hits but survives with great control and a sinker that often ends up as a 6-4-3 double play. Watch for reports on his shoulder this spring; if he's healthy, he'll win.

YEAR	TEAM/LEVEL	G	IP	W–L	PCT.	HITS	SO	BB	ERA
1990	Two Teams	33	215	12–9	.571	196	130	50	2.55
1991	Pittsburgh	35	228	16–10	.615	234	120	29	3.20
1992	Pittsburgh	23	141	8–8	.500	138	56	19	3.06

JOHN SMOLTZ
Atlanta Braves
Starting Pitcher
$65

Carries himself with great dignity, put the right hat on him and he'd look like an Eastern European count in a Hollywood costume drama. He's got a fastball that tops out at 92, one of the best sliders in the game, and a curve and change for effect. If he gave up fewer homers (17 last year, 16 in '91), he'd be as good as Glavine.

YEAR	TEAM/LEVEL	G	IP	W–L	PCT.	HITS	SO	BB	ERA
1990	Atlanta	34	231	14–11	.560	206	170	90	3.85
1991	Atlanta	36	230	14–13	.519	206	148	77	3.80
1992	Atlanta	35	247	15–12	.556	206	215	80	2.85

JERRY SPRADLIN
Cincinnati Reds

Relief Pitcher
$8

Established a Southern League save record, with 34. He's a big guy (6-7, 220), but a finesse pitcher, manages great control from an indecipherable tangle of arms and legs. Throws fastball, slider, split-finger, and an occasional curve. He'll be 26 in June, still hasn't made it to Triple-A, but there's no specific reason to think he can't pitch. Grade C prospect.

YEAR	TEAM/LEVEL	G	IP	W–L	SAVES	HITS	SO	BB	ERA
1990	Two Teams A	48	86	3–5	17	87	45	22	2.61
1991	Chattanooga AA	48	96	7–3	4	95	73	32	3.09
1992	Chattanooga AA	59	65	3–3	34	52	36	13	1.38

RUSS SPRINGER
New York Yankees

Pitching Prospect
$8

Right-hander, a teammate of Ben McDonald's at LSU, where he was projected as a possible first-round draft pick until brilliant college coaching wiped out his shoulder. The Yankees babied his arm until '91, but he's back now, throwing his fastball close to 90. Rarely listed with all the Yankee pitching prospects, but could be. Grade C prospect, struggled in callup.

YEAR	TEAM/LEVEL	G	IP	W–L	SAVES	HITS	SO	BB	ERA
1991	Ft. Lauderdale A	25	152	5–9	.357	118	138	62	3.49
1992	Columbus AAA	20	124	8–5	.615	89	95	54	2.69
1992	New York	14	1	0–0	.000	18	12	10	6.19

RANDY ST. CLAIRE
Atlanta Braves

Relief Pitcher
$4

Was signed out of a tryout camp in 1978 and is still trying. Had seven saves for Montreal in 1987 with decent peripheral numbers, started out 1988 with seven bad innings, got sent down, and has been searching for a major league niche since then (as if the Braves were looking for pitchers). Son of Ebba St. Claire, major league catcher in the 1950s.

YEAR	TEAM/LEVEL	G	IP	W–L	SAVES	HITS	SO	BB	ERA
1991	Atlanta	19	29	0–0	0	31	30	9	4.08
1992	Richmond AAA	39	72	6–5	4	82	62	21	3.52
1992	Atlanta	10	15	0–0	0	17	7	8	5.87

MIKE STANTON
Atlanta Braves

Relief Pitcher
$23

A candidate for the closer job, along with Wohlers, Mercker, and others. Struggled the first half of the season, but compiled a 2.20 ERA after the All-Star game. His numbers before and after the break were almost identical, except that he allowed six homers the first half, none the second. Throws 90 MPH fastball and has a great slider.

YEAR	TEAM/LEVEL	G	IP	W–L	SAVES	HITS	SO	BB	ERA
1990	Atlanta	7	7	0–3	2	16	7	4	18.00
1991	Atlanta	74	78	5–5	7	62	54	21	2.88
1992	Atlanta	65	64	5–4	8	59	44	20	4.10

DAVE STEWART
Oakland Athletics
Starting Pitcher
$32

His 1991 season was about halfway between 1991, when his control disappeared and his ERA shot over 5.00, and his 20-win level of 1990 and before. Pitched very well over the last two months, 5–5 with a 3.01 ERA, and in the playoffs. Now 36 years old, but probably has at least two-three years left in the rotation.

YEAR	TEAM/LEVEL	G	IP	W–L	PCT.	HITS	SO	BB	ERA
1990	Oakland	36	267	22–11	.667	226	166	83	2.56
1991	Oakland	35	226	11–11	.500	245	144	105	5.18
1992	Oakland	31	199	12–10	.545	175	130	79	3.66

DAVE STIEB
Toronto Blue Jays
(Released)
Starting Pitcher
$7

Started the season late due to herniated disc that plagued him in 1991, went into the rotation on his return but rang up 5.79 ERA in 12 starts and was sent to the bullpen. Pitched better after that, but went on the DL August 9 with a sore elbow and wasn't able to come back. Physical problems of the last two seasons obviously leave his future in doubt.

YEAR	TEAM/LEVEL	G	IP	W–L	PCT.	HITS	SO	BB	ERA
1990	Toronto	33	209	18–6	.750	179	125	64	2.93
1991	Toronto	9	60	4–3	.571	52	29	23	3.17
1992	Toronto	21	96	4–6	.400	98	45	43	5.04

TODD STOTTLEMYRE
Toronto Blue Jays
Starting Pitcher
$22

Returned to his previous standards after a fine 1991 season. He throws a fastball in the low 90s, or at least they claim he does, has a slider and curve, and doesn't walk people, but his career record is .500, 51–51, which isn't very good when you pitch for the best team in baseball, and his career ERA is 4.32. Time may be running out on him.

YEAR	TEAM/LEVEL	G	IP	W–L	PCT.	HITS	SO	BB	ERA
1990	Toronto	33	203	13–17	.433	214	115	69	4.34
1991	Toronto	34	219	15–8	.652	194	116	75	3.78
1992	Toronto	28	174	12–11	.522	175	98	63	4.50

RICK SUTCLIFFE
Baltimore Orioles
Starting Pitcher
$26

The Orioles reportedly signed him because their strength tests showed he was in super shape, which the 237 innings he pitched would tend to confirm. He pitched, at times, much better than the record shows, but had a couple of major slumps. Has free agent option; may be somewhere else in '93. I believe he'd be dramatically more effective at 25 starts/150 innings than the workload of '92.

YEAR	TEAM/LEVEL	G	IP	W–L	PCT.	HITS	SO	BB	ERA
1990	Chicago	5	21	0–2	.000	25	7	12	5.91
1991	Chicago	19	97	6–5	.545	96	52	45	4.10
1992	Baltimore	36	237	16–15	.516	251	109	74	4.47

RUSS SWAN
Seattle Mariners
Relief Pitcher
$11

Swan opened the season in the rotation, but posted 6.14 ERA in nine starts, returned to the bullpen on May 23 and pitched much better, at more or less the same level he had in 1991. Ground ball pitcher; career ERA is two and half runs better on grass fields (2.92, 111 innings) than on artificial turf (5.41, 128 innings), so pitching in Seattle is drawback.

YEAR	TEAM/LEVEL	G	IP	W–L	SAVES	HITS	SO	BB	ERA
1990	Two Teams	13	49	2–4	0	48	16	22	3.65
1991	Seattle	63	79	6–2	2	81	33	28	3.43
1992	Seattle	55	104	3–10	9	104	45	45	4.74

BILL SWIFT
San Francisco Giants
Starter/Reliever
$54

In 1990 Swift started eight times, posting a 2.10 ERA. The Mariners then sent him back to the bullpen, which is what makes the Mariners so special, but in that sense there was a precedent for his dramatic success of 1992. Swift has now posted an ERA of 2.39 or better for three straight years, in spite of which some people *still* don't believe he's good.

YEAR	TEAM/LEVEL	G	IP	W–L	PCT.	HITS	SO	BB	ERA
1990	Seattle	55	128	6–4	.600	135	42	21	2.39
1991	Seattle	71	90	1–2	.333	74	48	26	1.99
1992	San Francisco	30	165	10–4	.714	144	77	43	2.08

GREG SWINDELL
Cincinnati Reds (Free Agent)
Starting Pitcher
$61

Swindell is about as good a pitcher as you can be without an awesome fastball. He has four very good pitches, and throws them all for strikes. His strikeout to walk ratio last year was the fourth-best in the majors; in other years it has been the best. He has averaged 32 starts a year for five years. One of the best.

YEAR	TEAM/LEVEL	G	IP	W–L	PCT.	HITS	SO	BB	ERA
1990	Cleveland	34	215	12–9	.571	245	135	47	4.40
1991	Cleveland	33	238	9–16	.360	241	169	31	3.48
1992	Cinncinnati	31	214	12–8	.600	210	138	41	2.70

FRANK TANANA
Detroit Tigers (Released)
Starting Pitcher
$17

Has now posted three straight winning records in his late thirties, which it wouldn't be fair or logical to attribute entirely to the organization. His chance to have one last big year has probably slipped away, and it becomes more likely that he will reach a sudden end. His strikeout to walk ratio was the poorest in the majors last year (minimum 162 innings), and that *normally* indicates decline.

YEAR	TEAM/LEVEL	G	IP	W–L	PCT.	HITS	SO	BB	ERA
1990	Detroit	34	176	9–8	.529	190	114	66	5.31
1991	Detroit	33	217	13–12	.520	217	107	78	3.69
1992	Detroit	32	187	13–11	.542	188	91	90	4.39

KEVIN TAPANI
Minnesota Twins
Starting Pitcher
$61

The right-handed Greg Swindell. Like Swindell, throws four pitches for strikes, including 90 MPH fastball. Like Swindell, doesn't have a pronounced platoon differential, so loading up the lineup with lefties won't hurt him much. Throws a forkball so gets more grounders than Swindell, who throws curve. Like Swindell, has great K/W ratio—and wins. Needs a 20-win season to emerge as a star.

YEAR	TEAM/LEVEL	G	IP	W–L	PCT.	HITS	SO	BB	ERA
1990	Minnesota	28	159	12–8	.600	164	101	29	4.07
1991	Minnesota	34	244	16–9	.640	225	135	40	2.99
1992	Minnesota	34	220	16–11	.593	226	138	48	3.97

BILLY TAYLOR
Atlanta Braves
Relief Pitcher
$9

A minor league Dennis Eckersley, to overstate his case. Taylor, 31 years old, was in the Rangers system as a starting pitcher, but was cut by them and San Diego after several miserable seasons. Moved to the bullpen, he's adopted a go-right-at-em philosophy with impressive results, including a 1.51 ERA, 22 saves at Greenville in '91. Suspect he can pitch if he gets a chance.

YEAR	TEAM/LEVEL	G	IP	W–L	SAVES	HITS	SO	BB	ERA
1989	Las Vegas AAA	47	79	7–4	1	93	71	27	5.13
1991	Greenville AA	59	78	6–2	22	49	65	15	1.51
1992	Richmond AAA	47	79	2–3	12	72	82	27	2.28

SCOTT TAYLOR
Boston Red Sox
Pitching Prospect
$10

A 25-year-old left-hander, went 9–11 with Pawtucket and got called up in September. Once called "the Bill Lee of the '90s" by Gary Allenson, throws every pitch in the book, including an occasional knuckler. K/W ratio last year in Triple-A, 91/61, was easily worst of his minor league career. Goes into this spring with decent shot at breaking into Sox rotation.

YEAR	TEAM/LEVEL	G	IP	W–L	PCT.	HITS	SO	BB	ERA
1991	AA and AAA	11	48	5–3	.625	52	73	26	2.25
1992	Pawtucket AAA	26	162	9–11	.450	168	91	61	3.67
1992	Boston	4	15	1–1	.500	13	7	4	4.91

DAVE TELGHEDER
New York Mets
Pitching Prospect
$9

Right-handed starter, 26 now, has a minor league career ERA of 3.22, aided by truly outstanding control record. He gets no respect because he doesn't throw hard, features a sinker along with curve and change, all for strikes. It may take a couple more years, but eventually he'll get a shot with someone, and has a chance to be Bob Tewksbury.

YEAR	TEAM/LEVEL	G	IP	W–L	PCT.	HITS	SO	BB	ERA
1990	Two Teams A	28	195	18–7	.720	163	158	24	2.26
1991	Williamsport AA	28	168	13–11	.542	185	90	33	3.60
1992	Tidewater AAA	28	169	6–14	.300	173	118	36	4.21

WALT TERRELL
Detroit Tigers (Released)
Pitcher
$3

His ERA was the highest in the majors of anybody with as many innings, and he bounced into and out of the starting rotation. His ERA when he was "in" was 6.63. This wasn't an aberration; he's pretty much had his head handed to him for the last five years. One might guess that the new Tiger management will cast around for some real pitchers.

YEAR	TEAM/LEVEL	G	IP	W–L	PCT.	HITS	SO	BB	ERA
1990	Two Teams	29	158	8–11	.421	184	64	57	5.24
1991	Detroit	35	219	12–14	.462	257	80	79	4.24
1992	Detroit	36	137	7–10	.412	163	61	48	5.20

BOB TEWKSBURY
St. Louis Cardinals
Starting Pitcher
$61

He's one of the best control pitchers of all time, which is something you couldn't do with a great fastball. Like most pitchers with an 84 MPH fastball, he's been slow to get chances and slow to get respect. I expect him to be a consistent winner in the coming years, and wouldn't want to bet that he won't be just as good next year as he was last.

YEAR	TEAM/LEVEL	G	IP	W–L	PCT.	HITS	SO	BB	ERA
1990	St. Louis	28	145	10–9	.526	151	50	15	3.47
1991	St. Louis	30	191	11–12	.478	206	75	38	3.25
1992	St. Louis	33	233	16–5	.762	217	91	20	2.16

BOBBY THIGPEN
Chicago White Sox
Relief Pitcher
$17

It's an overstatement, but 1990 is really the only time in his career that he has ever pitched well. He saved 34 games in '88 and '89 without pitching particularly well, then had the record-setting year in '90 when he did. He finally booted the closer job in mid-summer, then posted a 7.58 ERA after the All-Star break, putting his career in some jeopardy.

YEAR	TEAM/LEVEL	G	IP	W–L	SAVES	HITS	SO	BB	ERA
1990	Chicago	77	89	4–6	57	60	70	32	1.83
1991	Chicago	67	70	7–5	30	63	47	38	3.49
1992	Chicago	55	55	1–3	22	58	45	33	4.75

MIKE TIMLIN
Toronto Blue Jays
Relief Pitcher
$17

A key member of the Toronto bullpen as a rookie, he missed the first two months of '92 with a sore elbow, came back and pitched long relief and lost causes the second half. He was fair. Best pitch is fastball, but throws a lot of ground balls— career grounder/fly ball ratio is 3.07, as high a ratio as you'll see. His future is very uncertain.

YEAR	TEAM/LEVEL	G	IP	W–L	SAVES	HITS	SO	BB	ERA
1990	Knoxville AA	17	26	1–2	8	20	21	7	1.73
1991	Toronto	63	108	11–6	3	94	85	50	3.16
1992	Toronto	26	44	0–2	1	45	35	20	4.12

RANDY TOMLIN
Pittsburgh Pirates
Starting Pitcher
$33

Throws his fastball roughly 80 miles an hour, so the league hits about .280 against him, but he gets away with it by throwing strikes and avoiding home runs. Best pitch is so-called "Vulcan" change-up, and he throws everything with a crossfire delivery. Motion makes him very tough on lefties, tries to nibble on the outside corner against right-handers.

YEAR	TEAM/LEVEL	G	IP	W–L	PCT.	HITS	SO	BB	ERA
1990	Pittsburgh	12	78	4–4	.500	62	42	12	2.55
1991	Pittsburgh	31	175	8–7	.533	170	104	54	2.98
1992	Pittsburgh	35	209	14–9	.609	226	90	42	3.41

SALOMON TORRES
San Francisco Giants
Pitching Prospect
$6

Established himself as hot prospect by sensational pitching at Clinton in his first professional season, continued to pitch brilliantly at Shreveport through early July, ruined his numbers by being shelled over last two months. Has three quality pitches, plus a leg kick like Marichal's. They say he had a tired arm, but frankly I'd be concerned that they might have ruined him. Grade B prospect, because of health concern.

YEAR	TEAM/LEVEL	G	IP	W–L	PCT.	HITS	SO	BB	ERA
1990	(Not in Organized Baseball)								
1991	Clinton A	28	211	16–5	.762	148	214	47	1.41
1992	Shreveport AA	24	157	6–10	.375	159	147	33	4.23

RICKY TRLICEK
Toronto Blue Jays
Relief Pitcher
$5

Opened the season on the Jays' roster, but was sent down to Syracuse after two outings. Still only 23 years old, he was the Phillies' fourth-round pick in '87 but was released after two seasons of poor control. Toronto signed him, and he turned into a prospect after being converted to relief in 1991, but regressed last year. Throws sinking fastball and hard slider. Grade D prospect.

YEAR	TEAM/LEVEL	G	IP	W–L	SAVES	HITS	SO	BB	ERA
1991	Knoxville AA	41	51	2–5	16	36	55	22	2.45
1992	Toronto	2	2	0–0	0	2	1	2	10.80
1992	Syracuse AAA	35	43	1–1	10	37	35	31	4.36

MIKE TROMBLEY
Minnesota Twins
Starting Pitcher
$25

Right-hander, doesn't throw hard. He was a 14th-round pick in 1989, but pitched well in every minor league stop, chopping his way through the minors like Freddie Krueger going through the freshman dormitory, and continued to pitch well in seven major league starts. Is 26 years old, doesn't look like a pitcher on the mound, but you can't argue with what he's done. Grade B prospect.

YEAR	TEAM/LEVEL	G	IP	W–L	PCT.	HITS	SO	BB	ERA
1991	Orlando AA	27	191	12–7	.632	153	175	57	2.54
1992	Portland AAA	25	165	10–8	.556	149	138	58	3.65
1992	Minnesota	10	46	3–2	.600	43	38	17	3.30

SERGIO VALDEZ
Montreal Expos

Relief Pitcher
$21

His real ability is probably somewhere between his 2.41 ERA of last year and the 5.40 mark which was his previous career ERA. Right-hander, throws fastball, slider, forkball, has good control. Pitched garbage relief in the deep Montreal bullpen, but will move into more key role if he continues to pitch well. Brother Efrain is a Milwaukee farmhand.

YEAR	TEAM/LEVEL	G	IP	W–L	SAVES	HITS	SO	BB	ERA
1990	Two Teams	30	108	6–6	0	115	66	38	4.85
1991	Cleveland	6	16	1–0	0	15	11	5	5.51
1992	Montreal	27	37	0–2	0	25	32	12	2.41

JULIO VALERA
California Angels

Starting Pitcher
$26

Was the opening day pitcher for the Tidewater Mets, traded to California a week later for Dick Schofield. Considered one of the Mets' top prospects, he couldn't get a clean shot at the job among the regular invasions of multi-millionaire free agents, plus he weighed more than they thought he ought. Throws heavy sinking fastball and hard curve; pitched well for the Angels and should continue to.

YEAR	TEAM/LEVEL	G	IP	W–L	PCT.	HITS	SO	BB	ERA
1990	Tidewater AAA	24	158	10–10	.500	146	133	39	3.02
1991	Tidewater AAA	26	176	10–10	.500	152	117	70	3.83
1992	California	30	188	8–11	.421	188	113	64	3.73

TODD VAN POPPEL
Oakland Athletics

Pitching Prospect
$4

Went out in early June with tendinitis in shoulder, was expected back in a month but soreness persisted and he didn't pitch again. Used to have 94 MPH fastball. They say he'll come back strong, and they say he'll develop a breaking pitch, and they say maybe he'll start to throw strikes sometime. With that and $2 you can get a cup of coffee, room service. Grade D prospect.

YEAR	TEAM/LEVEL	G	IP	W–L	PCT.	HITS	SO	BB	ERA
1991	Huntsville AA	24	132	6–13	.316	118	115	90	3.47
1991	Oakland	1	5	0–0	.000	7	6	2	9.64
1992	Tacoma AAA	9	45	4–2	.667	44	29	35	3.97

JOEY VIERRA
Cincinnatti Reds

Relief Pitcher
$5

Little (5-7, 170) lefthander, was a 31st-round pick out of Hawaii in 1987. He's been a middle reliever in the minors, which doesn't indicate a wealth of talent, but his career minor league ERA is 3.03, and he's struck out 345 batters in 386 innings, only 132 walks. He's 27 now, but he'll eventually get a chance to pitch in the major leagues.

YEAR	TEAM/LEVEL	G	IP	W–L	SAVES	HITS	SO	BB	ERA
1990	Nashville AAA	49	58	3–3	1	55	37	25	3.28
1991	Nashville AAA	62	96	5–4	2	81	84	43	4.33
1992	Nashville AAA	52	82	4–1	0	65	62	28	2.98

FRANK VIOLA
Boston Red Sox
Starting Pitcher
$38

He had a couple of difficult stretches, and the Red Sox probably weren't dreaming of a 13–12 record when they signed him, but on the other hand 13–12 isn't a bad record with a last-place team that doesn't hit, and his 3.44 ERA was half a run better than the league norm. His strikeout/walk ratio was his poorest since he learned how to pitch.

YEAR	TEAM/LEVEL	G	IP	W–L	PCT.	HITS	SO	BB	ERA
1990	New York	35	250	20–12	.625	227	182	60	2.67
1991	New York	35	231	13–15	.464	259	132	54	3.97
1992	Boston	35	238	13–12	.520	214	121	89	3.44

JOE VITKO
New York Mets
Pitching Prospect
$8

Big right-hander, 6-8, 210, was listed a year ago as the number-6 prospect in the organization by *Baseball America*. Throws a high-80s fastball, curve, slider, change. In five minor league stops he has five winning records and five good ERAs, but his strikeout/walk ratio at Double-A last year doesn't look like a pitcher who is ready to skip Triple-A. Grade C prospect.

YEAR	TEAM/LEVEL	G	IP	W–L	PCT.	HITS	SO	BB	ERA
1991	St. Lucie A	22	140	11–8	.579	102	105	39	2.24
1992	Binghamton AA	26	165	12–8	.600	163	89	53	3.49
1992	New York	3	5	0–1	.000	12	6	1	13.50

PAUL WAGNER
Pittsburgh Pirates
Pitching Prospect
$11

Right-handed starter, was the Pirates' 13th pick in the '89 draft, out of Illinois State. Sticks mainly with two pitches, 90+ fastball and hard slider, and keeps everything down around the knees or lower. Career minor league numbers are decent—in 478 innings, 443 hits, 183 walks, 366 strikeouts, 3.52 ERA—but they don't knock your socks off. Has a shot at breaking into rotation. Grade C prospect.

YEAR	TEAM/LEVEL	G	IP	W–L	PCT.	HITS	SO	BB	ERA
1992	Carolina AA	19	122	6–6	.500	104	101	47	3.03
1992	Buffalo AAA	8	39	3–3	.500	51	19	14	5.49
1992	Pittsburgh	6	13	2–0	1.000	9	5	5	0.69

TIM WAKEFIELD
Pittsburgh Pirates
Starting Pitcher
$37

He's only 26, which is very young for a successful knuckleballer. Wilhelm didn't come up until he was 28, Hough's first year as a starter was when he was 34, Phil Niekro's first good year was at age 28. Knuckleballers are, as a class, more durable and more consistent than any other group of pitchers . . . has minimized vulnerability to running game with unusual stretch position.

YEAR	TEAM/LEVEL	G	IP	W–L	PCT.	HITS	SO	BB	ERA
1991	Carolina AA	26	183	15–8	.652	155	120	51	2.90
1992	Buffalo AAA	20	135	10–3	.769	122	71	51	3.06
1992	Pittsburgh	13	92	8–1	.889	76	52	35	2.15

BOB WALK
Pittsburgh Pirates
Starter/Reliever
$20

Is 36 now, once again he missed a month or so with groin problems, and once again when he pitched he was effective. Best pitch is a big-breaking curve, but he'll throw anything. Re-signing Walk for two years supposedly helped cost Larry Doughty his job as Pirates GM, but with the loss of Smiley and the injury to Smith it worked out.

YEAR	TEAM/LEVEL	G	IP	W–L	PCT.	HITS	SO	BB	ERA
1990	Pittsburgh	26	130	7–5	.583	136	73	36	3.75
1991	Pittsburgh	25	115	9–2	.818	104	67	35	3.60
1992	Pittsburgh	36	135	10–6	.625	132	60	43	3.20

MIKE WALKER
Seattle Mariners
Pitcher
$1

A 27-year-old right-hander, not to be confused with the other right-handed Mike Walker, who's 26 and started 11 games for the Indians in 1990. *This* Mike Walker was called up to try to stop the bleeding in June, but performed about as well as you would expect from a guy whose lifetime minor league ERA is 4.63. No prospect.

YEAR	TEAM/LEVEL	G	IP	W–L	PCT.	HITS	SO	BB	ERA
1992	Jacksonvill AA	11	62	3–3	.500	63	40	18	4.79
1992	Calgary AAA	12	41	5–1	.833	50	24	19	5.27
1992	Seattle	5	15	0–3	.000	21	5	9	7.36

BRUCE WALTON
Oakland Athletics
Relief Pitcher
$3

Right-hander, has had cups of coffee with the A's the last two seasons. Doesn't have great stuff, but he throws strikes—in eight minor league seasons his K/W ratio is outstanding, 634/208. LaRussa left him in to give up eight runs in three innings on August 19, which is why his ERA was so high. He's 30 now, but still has some chance for a career.

YEAR	TEAM/LEVEL	G	IP	W–L	SAVES	HITS	SO	BB	ERA
1991	Oakland	12	13	1–0	0	11	10	6	6.23
1992	Tacoma AAA	35	81	8–2	8	76	60	21	2.77
1992	Oakland	7	10	0–0	0	17	7	3	9.90

DUANE WARD
Toronto Blue Jays
Reliever
$64

Solidified his position as the top set-up man in the game, and with Henke's occasional ailments he'll pick up 15 or so saves every year. Throws gas, 95 MPH, plus a hard slider, and over the last four seasons has struck out better than a batter an inning. With Henke probably departing as a free agent, Ward will inherit the glory job.

YEAR	TEAM/LEVEL	G	IP	W–L	SAVES	HITS	SO	BB	ERA
1990	Toronto	73	128	2–8	11	101	112	42	3.45
1991	Toronto	81	107	7–6	23	80	132	33	2.77
1992	Toronto	79	101	7–4	12	76	103	39	1.95

ALLEN WATSON
St. Louis Cardinals
Pitching Prospect
$11

Left-hander, was the Cardinals' first pick in the 1991 June draft, straight out of high school. Fastball just major league average, but he changes speeds well, and in 250 minor league innings he's given up 204 hits and 71 walks while striking out 240—getting better, if anything, as he moved up. Will come to St. Louis this year if he continues to pitch well. **Grade A prospect.**

YEAR	TEAM/LEVEL	G	IP	W–L	PCT.	HITS	SO	BB	ERA
1991	Two Teams A	11	53	2–2	.500	38	58	25	2.72
1992	St. Petersburg A	14	90	5–4	.556	81	80	18	1.91
1992	AA and AAA	16	109	9–5	.643	85	102	28	2.06

GARY WAYNE
Minnesota Twins
Relief Pitcher
$17

Left-handed middle reliever, fastball only in the mid-80s but throws a pretty good split-finger pitch. Herky-jerky delivery makes his stuff look better than it is. Only full major league season was 1989, when the Twins had to keep him after taking him from Montreal in the Rule 5 draft. Being a lefty, he could hang around indefinitely with one save a year.

YEAR	TEAM/LEVEL	G	IP	W–L	SAVES	HITS	SO	BB	ERA
1990	Minnesota	38	39	1–1	1	38	28	13	4.19
1991	Minnesota	8	12	1–0	1	11	7	4	5.11
1992	Minnesota	41	48	3–3	0	46	29	19	2.63

DAVE WEATHERS
Toronto Blue Jays
Relief Pitcher
$5

The last pitcher cut by the Blue Jays in the spring of '92, but strained a ligament in his elbow, May 1, and endured a poor season with Syracuse, although the Blue Jays did call him up for three innings and then let him work out and watch the team in September. Third-round pick in 1988, numbers not particularly impressive except for Knoxville in 1991. Grade C prospect.

YEAR	TEAM/LEVEL	G	IP	W–L	SAVES	HITS	SO	BB	ERA
1991	Knoxville AA	24	139	10–7	0	121	114	49	2.45
1991	Toronto	15	14	1–0	0	15	13	17	4.91
1992	Syracuse AAA	12	48	1–4	0	48	30	21	4.66

BILL WEGMAN
Milwaukee Brewers
Starting Pitcher
$31

I thought the Brewers were crazy to sign him to a long-term contract, but he had his second quality season after missing almost two full years with major arm problems . . . actually, the surgery seems to have improved his pitching—ERA before surgery, 4.63; ERA after, 3.07. Throws sliders and fastballs with an occasional change mixed in. Will be 30 this season.

YEAR	TEAM/LEVEL	G	IP	W–L	PCT.	HITS	SO	BB	ERA
1990	Milwaukee	8	30	2–2	.500	37	20	6	4.85
1991	Milwaukee	28	193	15–7	.682	176	89	40	2.84
1992	Milwaukee	35	262	13–14	.481	251	127	55	3.20

BOB WELCH
Oakland Athletics
Starting Pitcher
$19

Nineteen ninety-two was the first time since 1985 he hadn't started at least 33 games. Missed April with multiple injuries and missed several starts in August with a sore elbow. He pitched well when in the rotation, but in view of 1) his age (36), 2) his injuries, and 3) his poor strikeout/walk ratios the last two years, his ability to pitch well if the team declines is questionable.

YEAR	TEAM/LEVEL	G	IP	W–L	PCT.	HITS	SO	BB	ERA
1990	Oakland	35	238	27–6	.818	214	127	77	2.95
1991	Oakland	35	220	12–13	.480	220	101	91	4.58
1992	Oakland	20	124	11–7	.611	114	47	43	3.27

DAVID WELLS
Toronto Blue Jays
Reliever/Starter
$17

On August 20, Gaston left him in to allow 13 earned runs, which saved the rest of the bullpen but ruined Wells's ERA. Except for that game, he didn't pitch significantly worse last year than he had in previous years. He is overweight but is being projected as a possible starter in view of the free agent losses from the Toronto starting corps.

YEAR	TEAM/LEVEL	G	IP	W–L	SAVES	HITS	SO	BB	ERA
1990	Toronto	43	189	11–6	3	165	115	45	3.14
1991	Toronto	40	198	15–10	1	188	106	49	3.72
1992	Toronto	41	120	7–9	2	138	62	36	5.40

DAVID WEST
Minnesota Twins
Starting Pitcher
$7

Perpetual prospect, pitched brilliantly in the Mets system from 1986 to 1989. He's now 27, and 1989 gets further away all the time. People say that he has an attitude problem, which who knows what that means, but he doesn't throw strikes, which is a very specific problem. I suspect he might do better in another organization, and after three-plus years it's certainly time to try.

YEAR	TEAM/LEVEL	G	IP	W–L	PCT.	HITS	SO	BB	ERA
1990	Minnesota	29	146	7–9	.438	142	92	78	5.10
1991	Minnesota	15	71	4–4	.500	66	52	28	4.54
1992	Minnesota	9	28	1–3	.250	32	19	20	6.99

MICKEY WESTON
Philadelphia Phillies
(Free Agent)
Starting Pitcher
$4

Has pitched brilliantly in the minor leagues for years, but has no fastball and so has received only brief looks. Unbelievable control, almost like Tewksbury. In 1988, led Texas League in ERA. In 1989, 8–3 with 2.09 ERA in International League. In 1990, 11–1 with 1.98 ERA, same league. In 1991, led International League in wins with 12, etc., etc., etc. Grade D prospect at 32.

YEAR	TEAM/LEVEL	G	IP	W–L	PCT.	HITS	SO	BB	ERA
1990	Rochester AAA	29	109	11–1	.917	93	58	22	1.98
1991	Syracuse AAA	27	166	12–6	.667	193	60	36	3.74
1992	Scranton AAA	26	171	10–6	.625	166	79	29	3.11

JOHN WETTELAND
Montreal Expos
Closer
$54

His 37 saves were third in the league. Throws low-90s fastballs, with an occasional split-finger fastball, but splitter tends to get away from him. Struggled early, 3.92 ERA before the break, but Alou stuck with him, and after the break it was 1.93. Only relievers with comparable strikeouts/innings ratios were Dibble, Harvey, and Eckersley. Despite brilliant performance of Rojas, he has the closer role.

YEAR	TEAM/LEVEL	G	IP	W–L	SAVES	HITS	SO	BB	ERA
1990	Los Angeles	22	43	2–4	0	44	36	17	4.81
1991	Los Angeles	6	9	1–0	0	5	9	3	0.00
1992	Montreal	67	83	4–4	37	64	99	36	2.92

WALLY WHITEHURST
San Diego Padres
Reliever
$18

The Padres apparently decided to trade Fernandez, and traded him for whatever was offered. Whenever you focus on what you are *giving up* in a trade, you normally blow it. You need to focus on what you are *getting* in a trade. The Padres may start Whitehurst or put him in the bullpen. He has a career ERA as a starter of 4.48, as a reliever of 2.91.

YEAR	TEAM/LEVEL	G	IP	W–L	SAVES	HITS	SO	BB	ERA
1990	New York	38	66	1–0	2	63	46	9	3.29
1991	New York	36	133	7–12	1	142	87	25	4.18
1992	New York	44	97	3–9	0	99	70	33	3.62

MATT WHITESIDE
Texas Rangers
Closer Prospect
$30

The Rangers' closer in late September; with a new manager who knows what his role might be. A 26-year-old right-hander, converted 29 of 30 save opportunities at Tulsa and Oklahoma City last summer, also had 29 saves at Gastonia (A Ball) in 1990. In 45 minor league innings last year, walked only six batters. Best pitch is a sinking fastball, could use a third pitch.

YEAR	TEAM/LEVEL	G	IP	W–L	SAVES	HITS	SO	BB	ERA
1992	Tulsa AA	33	34	0–1	21	31	30	3	2.41
1992	Oklahoma City AAA	12	11	1–0	8	7	13	3	0.79
1992	Texas	20	28	1–1	4	26	13	11	1.93

ED WHITSON
San Diego Padres
Starting Pitcher
No Value

Tore ligaments in his elbow March 8 and missed the season. Every time he tried to throw he had pain in the elbow. He said he couldn't even play golf, and the doctors had warned him that re-injuring the elbow could leave his arm damaged for life. With a winter's rest he may try again, but his career is probably over.

YEAR	TEAM/LEVEL	G	IP	W–L	PCT.	HITS	SO	BB	ERA
1989	San Diego	33	227	16–11	.593	198	117	48	2.66
1991	San Diego	32	229	14–9	.609	215	127	47	2.60
1992	San Diego	13	79	4–6	.400	93	40	17	5.03

KEVIN WICKANDER
Cleveland Indians
Relief Pitcher
$13

The Indians' second pick in the 1986 draft, trying to establish himself in the majors at the age of 28. He spent five months in the majors last year with a good ERA and no losses, but walked 28 men in 41 innings, which will blow up on him sooner or later. Left-hander, has good stuff but control record is generally poor.

YEAR	TEAM/LEVEL	G	IP	W–L	SAVES	HITS	SO	BB	ERA
1991	AA and AAA	32	37	2–2	2	33	31	18	3.41
1992	Colorado Sp AAA	8	11	0–0	2	4	18	6	1.64
1992	Cleveland	44	41	2–0	1	39	38	28	3.07

BOB WICKMAN
New York Yankees
Starting Pitcher
$19

Came to the Yankees with Melido Perez in the Steve Sax deal and had his best minor league season at Columbus. Wickman lost the tip of his right index finger in a farm-machine accident when he was two, and some people think that gives his 90 MPH sinker a little extra action. He's 24, appears to have most of the elements of a quality pitcher. Grade B prospect.

	TEAM/LEVEL	G	IP	W–L	PCT.	HITS	SO	BB	ERA
1991	Birmingham AA	20	131	6–10	.375	127	81	50	3.56
1992	Columbus AAA	23	157	12–5	.706	131	108	55	2.92
1992	New York	8	50	6–1	.857	51	21	20	4.11

BRIAN WILLIAMS
Houston Astros
Starting Pitcher
$24

Originally drafted by the Padres (1987) as a shortstop, didn't sign with them, and became a first-round draft pick of the Astros (1990) as a pitcher. He pitched at all four levels in 1991 despite unimpressive numbers, entered the Astro rotation in June and was OK. Throws fastball with good movement and hard curve, needs to get curve over more often or change speeds to get more strikeouts.

YEAR	TEAM/LEVEL	G	IP	W–L	PCT.	HITS	SO	BB	ERA
1991	Tucson AAA	7	38	0–1	.000	39	29	22	4.93
1992	Tucson AAA	12	70	6–1	.857	78	58	26	4.50
1992	Houston	16	96	7–6	.538	92	54	42	3.92

MIKE WILLIAMS
Philadelphia Phillies
Starting Pitcher
$9

A 24-year-old right-hander, was called up in June to make five starts. A 14th-round pick in 1990, has moved up with a fine change-up, an average fastball, and a slurve. He pitched awfully well last year for Scranton, but was unimpressive in the majors and wasn't called back in September. Will need an adjustment period; 50-50 chance to be a pitcher after that.

YEAR	TEAM/LEVEL	G	IP	W–L	PCT.	HITS	SO	BB	ERA
1991	Reading AA	16	102	7–5	.583	93	51	36	3.69
1992	Scranton AAA	16	93	9–1	.900	84	59	30	2.43
1992	Philadelphia	5	29	1–1	.500	29	5	7	5.34

MITCH WILLIAMS
Philadelphia Phillies
Closer
$33

He has one of the worst control records in major league history, but he's been a closer for five years now, and there is no indication that he is going to lose that job or become seriously ineffective in it. Had a slump last year just after the All-Star break (8.18 ERA in July), but was pitching well and still getting saves at season's end.

YEAR	TEAM/LEVEL	G	IP	W–L	SAVES	HITS	SO	BB	ERA
1990	Chicago	59	66	1–8	16	60	55	50	3.93
1991	Philadelphia	69	88	12–5	30	56	84	62	2.34
1992	Philadelphia	66	81	5–8	29	69	74	64	3.78

MARK WILLIAMSON
Baltimore Orioles
Reliever
$24

Went on the DL April 16 with an inflamed right elbow and didn't return until September. Alan Mills and Frohwirth both did a good job in a similar role, leaving Williamson's future in Baltimore in question. Has decent fastball, which sets up palmball and slider, and was throwing well in September. He'll definitely be pitching for *someone* this season; could be excellent draft pick if people overlook him.

YEAR	TEAM/LEVEL	G	IP	W–L	SAVES	HITS	SO	BB	ERA
1990	Baltimore	49	85	8–2	1	65	60	28	2.21
1991	Baltimore	65	80	5–5	4	87	53	35	4.48
1992	Baltimore	12	19	1–0	1	16	14	10	0.96

CARL WILLIS
Minnesota Twins
Middle Reliever
$28

Proved last year that fine 1991 season was no fluke. Finally established himself at 30 after pitching in seven systems. Most of his minor league duty was pitching long relief in hitter's parks, baseball's equivalent of being a foot soldier at the Russian front. Has a decent fastball but best pitch is a splitter, which some suspect is missing the "L." Will continue to pitch effectively in support role.

YEAR	TEAM/LEVEL	G	IP	W–L	SAVES	HITS	SO	BB	ERA
1990	Colorado Sp AAA	41	99	5–3	2	136	42	32	6.39
1991	Minnesota	40	89	8–3	2	76	53	19	2.63
1992	Minnesota	59	79	7–3	1	73	45	11	2.72

STEVE WILSON
Los Angeles Dodgers
Reliever
$17

Had a pretty good first half but was worked very hard in April and May and was hit hard over the last two months of the season. If he's healthy, he's a decent pitcher, better than a lot of lefties who hang on forever just because they're lefties. Throws fastball with good movement and change-up. He's like Jose DeLeon: He looks good but *something always goes wrong.*

YEAR	TEAM/LEVEL	G	IP	W–L	SAVES	HITS	SO	BB	ERA
1990	Chicago	45	139	4–9	1	140	95	43	4.79
1991	Two Teams	19	21	0–0	2	14	14	9	2.61
1992	Los Angeles	60	67	2–5	0	74	54	29	4.18

TREVOR WILSON
San Francisco Giants
Starting Pitcher
$25

Let's see, if you do unnecessary surgery on a pitcher and cost him a $20-million career, can he sue you for malpractice and collect $20 million? I have a feeling we may be about to find out. Wilson's chance of being a big star has probably evaporated, but he could and should emerge as a successful Bud Black–type starter.

YEAR	TEAM/LEVEL	G	IP	W–L	PCT.	HITS	SO	BB	ERA
1990	San Francisco	27	110	8–7	.533	87	66	49	4.00
1991	San Francisco	44	202	13–11	.542	173	139	77	3.56
1992	San Francisco	26	154	8–14	.364	152	88	64	4.21

BOBBY WITT
Oakland Athletics
Starting Pitcher
$24

It will be interesting to see what Dave Duncan can do with his talent. He teased the Rangers for six years, being always just a month away from greatness. I don't think he throws as hard now as he did three years ago, but he's only 29, and his fastball is still very good. He could make the Canseco trade pay off big even if Sierra walks.

YEAR	TEAM/LEVEL	G	IP	W–L	PCT.	HITS	SO	BB	ERA
1990	Texas	33	222	17–10	.630	197	221	110	3.36
1991	Texas	17	89	3–7	.300	84	82	74	6.09
1992	Two Teams	31	193	10–14	.417	183	125	114	4.29

MARK WOHLERS
Atlanta Braves
Prospective Closer
$22

Was supposed to be the Next Great Closer last spring, but had 8.64 ERA in spring training, so opened the season at Richmond, came back up and pitched well for Atlanta. With his 96 MPH fastball and record of consistent success, there is every reason to be optimistic about his future. You're never sure what to expect of a pitcher until he has to deal with failure.

YEAR	TEAM/LEVEL	G	IP	W–L	SAVES	HITS	SO	BB	ERA
1991	Atlanta	17	20	3–1	2	17	13	13	3.20
1992	Richmond AAA	27	34	0–2	9	32	33	17	3.93
1992	Atlanta	32	35	1–2	4	28	17	14	2.55

KERRY WOODSON
Seattle Mariners
Pitching Prospect
$9

Right-hander, a 29th-round pick in 1988 out of San Jose Community College, where he was a teammate of Scott Erickson. Out pitch is a sinking fastball, also throws a slurve. A year ago, *Baseball America* named him the number-8 prospect in the organization, but he has missed time with elbow problems in each of the last two seasons, so durability is a question. Grade D prospect.

YEAR	TEAM/LEVEL	G	IP	W–L	PCT.	HITS	SO	BB	ERA
1992	Jacksonville AA	11	68	5–4	.556	74	55	36	3.57
1992	Calgary AAA	10	21	1–4	.200	20	9	12	3.43
1992	Seattle	8	14	0–1	.000	12	6	11	3.29

TIM WORRELL
San Diego Padres
Pitching Prospect
$11

Todd Worrell's younger brother, he throws as hard (93 MPH) as his brother did before the injury. He was outstanding in 19 starts at Wichita, then was promoted to Las Vegas, where he had mixed results but threw a no-hitter in his last start. He should be in the majors this year, probably isn't ready to win right away but has bright future. Grade B prospect.

YEAR	TEAM/LEVEL	G	IP	W–L	PCT.	HITS	SO	BB	ERA
1991	Two Teams A	25	150	13–6	.684	135	153	66	3.72
1992	Wichita AA	19	126	8–6	.571	115	109	32	2.86
1992	Las Vegas AAA	10	63	4–2	.667	61	32	19	4.26

TODD WORRELL
St. Louis Cardinals
Relief Pitcher
$32

Made strong comeback last season after missing two years due to elbow and shoulder problems. He won't return to St. Louis in 1993 unless he can be the closer. His ERA after the All-Star break was 0.55, so I would think he can do the job. There's no way to be sure that his elbow won't blow again, but Worrell used to be one of the best.

YEAR	TEAM/LEVEL	G	IP	W–L	SAVES	HITS	SO	BB	ERA
1988	St. Louis	68	90	5–9	32	69	78	34	3.00
1989	St. Louis	47	53	3–5	20	42	41	26	2.96
1992	St. Louis	67	64	5–3	3	45	64	25	2.11

ANTHONY YOUNG
New York Mets
Closer
$18

Began the season as the Mets' fifth starter and threw a complete-game six-hitter in his first start. That was his best outing by far, and after a horrible start on June 25 was sent to the bullpen for good. Assumed the closer role when Franco went out for a month and was brilliant for a while, then again began to struggle. Will have better years; little star potential.

YEAR	TEAM/LEVEL	G	IP	W–L	SAVES	HITS	SO	BB	ERA
1991	Tidewater AAA	25	164	7–9	0	172	93	67	3.73
1991	New York	10	49	2–5	0	48	20	12	3.10
1992	New York	52	121	2–14	15	134	64	31	4.17

CURT YOUNG
New York Yankees
Reliever/Starter
$6

Has three or four good starts every year, just so you can see how good he would have been if he'd been healthy. He isn't and never will be, so his career has become a 100-yard marathon, like one of those dreams you have where somebody is chasing you and you just keep walking and walking and walking. Fits in well with the Yankees.

YEAR	TEAM/LEVEL	G	IP	W–L	PCT.	HITS	SO	BB	ERA
1990	Oakland	26	124	9–6	.600	124	56	53	4.85
1992	Oakland	41	68	4–2	.667	74	27	34	5.00
1992	Two Teams	23	68	4–2	.667	80	20	17	3.99

MATT YOUNG
Boston Red Sox

Pitcher

$3

The Red Sox signed him to a three-year contract after he went 8–18 in 1990, whereupon Young hurt his arm and set his ERA on fire. In April 1992, he threw an eight-inning no-hitter but walked seven and lost. He soon dropped out of the rotation and would appear to have no future, but if his arm comes back you never know.

YEAR	TEAM/LEVEL	G	IP	W–L	SAVES	HITS	SO	BB	ERA
1990	Seattle	34	225	8–18	.308	198	176	107	3.51
1991	Boston	19	89	3–7	.300	92	69	53	5.18
1992	Boston	28	71	0–4	.000	69	57	42	4.58

PETE YOUNG
Montreal Expos

Relief Pitcher

$11

Young is a big (225 pound) right-hander, was a sixth-round pick out of Mississippi State in 1989. Minor league numbers are more consistent than outstanding, and he's been good enough to move up a level a year. A fastball/slider pitcher, has a pretty good shot at holding down a job as a middle reliever this season. Grade C prospect.

YEAR	TEAM/LEVEL	G	IP	W–L	SAVES	HITS	SO	BB	ERA
1991	Harrisburg AA	54	90	7–5	13	82	74	24	2.60
1992	Indianapolis AAA	36	49	6–2	7	53	34	21	3.51
1992	Montreal	13	20	0–0	0	18	11	9	3.98

HIGHEST VALUED PLAYERS BY POSITION

CATCHER

Ivan Rodriguez	$66
Mickey Tettleton	$60
Darren Daulton	$55
Brian Harper	$50
Chris Hoiles	$45
Mike Macfarlane	$42
Terry Steinbach	$41
Benito Santiago	$38
Sandy Alomar, Jr.	$33
Joe Oliver	$33
Tom Pagnozzi	$30
B.J. Surhoff	$30

FIRST BASE

Frank Thomas	$98
Fred McGriff	$86
Paul Molitor	$80
Will Clark	$75
Jeff Bagwell	$70
Mark McGwire	$69
Cecil Fielder	$66
Rafael Palmeiro	$60
Mark Grace	$55
Eric Karros	$41
John Olerud	$39
Hal Morris	$38

SECOND BASE

Ryne Sandberg	$92
Roberto Alomar	$90
Carlos Baerga	$78
Chuck Knoblauch	$68
Delino DeShields	$66
Craig Biggio	$62
Geronimo Peña	$35
Robby Thompson	$35
Lou Whitaker	$33
Jeff Frye	$30
Mickey Morandini	$28
Jeff Kent	$27

THIRD BASE

Gary Sheffield	$79
Edgar Martinez	$74
Terry Pendleton	$69
Robin Ventura	$66
Wade Boggs	$54
Dave Hollins	$52
Leo Gomez	$51
Ken Caminiti	$46
Gregg Jefferies	$46
Matt Williams	$46
Steve Buechele	$45
Dean Palmer	$34

SHORTSTOP

Barry Larkin	$76
Travis Fryman	$71
Jay Bell	$67
Cal Ripken	$62
Ozzie Smith	$56
Tony Fernandez	$50
Pat Listach	$42
Jeff Blauser	$38
Jose Offerman	$34
Ozzie Guillen	$33
Omar Vizquel	$32
Mark Lewis	$30

LEFT FIELD

Barry Bonds	$100
Juan Gonzalez	$77
Shane Mack	$67
Rickey Henderson	$64
Ron Gant	$63
Brady Anderson	$56
Tim Raines	$54
Reggie Sanders	$41
Kevin Mitchell	$33
Luis Polonia	$31
Greg Vaughn	$30
Mike Greenwell	$27

CENTER FIELD

Ken Griffey, Jr.	$94
Kirby Puckett	$82
Ray Lankford	$72
Andy Van Slyke	$71
Brett Butler	$68
Marquis Grissom	$59
Steve Finley	$55
Roberto Kelly	$51
Mike Devereaux	$53
Devon White	$46
Kenny Lofton	$43
Len Dykstra	$36

RIGHT FIELD

Ruben Sierra	$73
Joe Carter	$67
Larry Walker	$65
Jose Canseco	$64
Bobby Bonilla	$59
Tony Gwynn	$58
Jay Buhner	$57
John Kruk	$53
Dave Justice	$51
Felix Jose	$41
Phil Plantier	$36
Chad Curtis	$35

DESIGNATED HITTERS AND UTILITY PLAYERS

Tony Phillips	$70
Bip Roberts	$70
Albert Belle	$53
Danny Tartabull	$39
Dave Winfield	$39

George Bell	$34
Chili Davis	$30
Darryl Hamilton	$29
Kevin Reimer	$29
Kevin Seitzer	$29
Mike Bordick	$28
Julio Franco	$28

RIGHT-HANDED STARTING PITCHER

Roger Clemens	$96
Greg Maddux	$84
Doug Drabek	$81
Dennis Martinez	$74
David Cone	$73
Jose Rijo	$72
Jack McDowell	$67
Mike Mussina	$67
John Smoltz	$65
Kevin Appier	$63
Kevin Brown	$62
Tom Candiotti	$61
Kevin Tapani	$61
Bob Tewksbury	$61
Juan Guzman	$60
Andy Benes	$56
Bill Swift	$54
Charles Nagy	$53
Terry Mulholland	$51
Jack Morris	$50
Curt Schilling	$50
John Burkett	$48
Mike Morgan	$48
Melido Perez	$48
Chris Bosio	$42
Ken Hill	$42
Cal Eldred	$41
Scott Erickson	$41
Jose Guzman	$40
Tim Belcher	$38
Sid Fernandez	$37
Ben McDonald	$37
Tim Wakefield	$37
Kevin Gross	$36
Bret Saberhagen	$36
Dwight Gooden	$35
Jaime Navarro	$35

LEFT-HANDED STARTING PITCHER

Tom Glavine	$75
John Smiley	$71
Steve Avery	$63

Jim Abbott	$62	Matt Whiteside	$30
Greg Swindell	$61	Todd Frohwirth	$28
Mark Langston	$53	Mark Guthrie	$28
Bruce Hurst	$52	Chuck McElroy	$28
Jimmy Key	$48	Rusty Meacham	$28
Charlie Leibrandt	$44	Carl Willis	$28
Zane Smith	$43		
Arthur Rhodes	$42		
Chuck Finley	$40		

RELIEF ACE (CLOSER)

PROSPECTS

Dennis Eckersley	$88	Chipper Jones	$40
Jeff Montgomery	$70	Carlos Delgado	$39
Tom Henke	$67	Wilfredo Cordero	$38
Rob Dibble	$64	Willie Greene	$38
Duane Ward	$64	Javier Lopez	$38
Doug Jones	$60	Dmitri Young	$37
Gregg Olson	$60	Sam Militello	$36
Lee Smith	$57	Mike Piazza	$35
Steve Olin	$56	Jeff Conine	$34
Rick Aguilera	$55	Tim Salmon	$32
John Wetteland	$54	Rene Arocha	$31
Steve Farr	$53	Melvin Nieves	$30
		Alan Embree	$28
		Pedro J. Martinez	$28
		Kevin Rogers	$28

SET-UP MEN

Roberto Hernandez	$38	Tyler Green	$26
Darren Holmes	$34	Raul Mondesi	$25
Todd Worrell	$32	Bret Boone	$24
Mel Rojas	$31	Joey Hamilton	$24
Jeff Brantley	$30	Jim Tatum	$24
Scott Radinsky	$30	Greg Colbrunn	$23
		Carlos Garcia	$23
		Jim Thome	$23
		Tavo Alvarez	$21